Cisco®
A Beginner's Guide

About the Authors

Anthony T. Velte, co-founder of Velte Publishing, Inc., has more than 20 years of experience in the information systems industry in the areas of IT security, audit, networking, systems design, software development, project and program management, and general IT operations and best practices. He is co-author of McGraw-Hill's *Cloud Computing: A Practical Approach, Green IT: Reduce Your Information System's Environmental Impact While Adding to the Bottom Line,* and *Cisco: A Beginners Guide, Fourth Edition,* as well as other publications.

Toby J. Velte, Ph.D., is an international best-selling author of business technology articles and books. He is co-founder of Velte Publishing, Inc., and the co-author of more than a dozen books published by McGraw-Hill. He is co-author of *Green IT: Reduce Your Information System's Environmental Impact While Adding to the Bottom Line* and *Cloud Computing: A Practical Approach.* Dr. Velte is currently part of Microsoft's North Central practice, focused on helping thriving companies with their technology-based initiatives.

About the Technical Reviewer

David Madland, CCIE 2016, has 23 years networking experience, including Cray Research, US West/Qwest, and Cisco Advanced Services. He is a member of the team at US West that became Cisco's first Gold Partner. David is currently an SE with Cisco Systems in Minneapolis, Minnesota, with focus in route switch and data center technologies.

Cisco®
A Beginner's Guide
Fifth Edition

ANTHONY T. **VELTE**
TOBY J. **VELTE**

Mc
Graw
Hill
Education

New York   Chicago   San Francisco   Athens
London   Madrid   Mexico City   Milan
New Delhi   Singapore   Sydney   Toronto

Library of Congress Cataloging-in-Publication Data

Velte, Toby J.
    Cisco : a beginner's guide / Toby J. Velte, Anthony T. Velte. — Fifth edition.
      pages   cm
    ISBN 978-0-07-181231-3 (pbk.)
    1. Computer networks—Design and construction. 2. Cisco Systems, Inc.
3. Internetworking (Telecommunication) 4. TCP/IP (Computer network protocol)
5. Local area networks (Computer networks) I. Velte, Anthony T. II. Title.
    TK5105.5.V43 2013
    004.6—dc23   2013024725

McGraw-Hill Education books are available at special quantity discounts to use as premiums and sales promotions, or for use in corporate training programs. To contact a representative, please visit the Contact Us pages at www.mhprofessional.com.

Cisco®: A Beginner's Guide, Fifth Edition

1234567890 DOC DOC 109876543

ISBN   978-0-07-181231-3
MHID   0-07-181231-8

Sponsoring Editor Amy Jollymore	**Technical Editor** David Madland	**Composition** Cenveo Publisher Services
Editorial Supervisor Jody McKenzie	**Copy Editor** Bart Reed	**Illustration** Lyssa Wald and Cenveo Publisher Services
Project Manager Anupriya Tyagi, Cenveo® Publisher Services	**Proofreader** Claire Splan	**Art Director, Cover** Jeff Weeks
Acquisitions Coordinator Amanda Russell	**Indexer** Karin Arrigoni	**Cover Designer** Jeff Weeks
	Production Supervisor Jean Bodeaux	

For my family and friends—you are awesome.
To my sons, Luke, Jack, and Joey—I am immensely
proud of you.
—ATV

To my children, Connor and Olivia,
for showing me how fun learning can be.
—TJV

At a Glance

Contents

Part I

Cisco Overview

Part II

Cisco Internetworking Tools

Part III

Cisco Business Solutions

Part IV

Designing Cisco Networks

Acknowledgments

We would like to thank Robert Elsenpeter and John Michealson, both of whom contributed heavily to this edition with research and edits. We cannot understate how much we appreciate their exceptional talents and tireless dedication to the project.

We also want to thank our Technical Editor, David Madland—he brought his deep knowledge and experience to the project and did a marvelous job poring over the manuscript to ensure technical accuracy.

Finally, we want to thank Sponsoring Editor Amy Jollymore, Acquisitions Coordinator Amanda Russell, Copy Editor Bart Reed, and Project Manager Anupriya Tyagi. It was a pleasure working with each and every one of them.

Introduction

The volume in your hands is the fifth edition of the worldwide, best-selling introduction to Cisco networking. Since its introduction, each edition of this book has sold tens of thousands of copies worldwide. It is used as courseware in a variety of schools and has been translated into numerous languages, including Spanish, Chinese, Czech, Japanese, Korean, Serbian, Arabic, and German. This level of interest confirms what you already know—Cisco is, and likely will continue to be, a huge player in the communications industry, and people want to better understand how this behemoth works.

Although six years have passed since writing the fourth edition, this book has remained quite popular, and we felt that another refresh was in order. As with the fourth edition, we took the book apart and reexamined it, chapter by chapter. Although we were hard-pressed to find material we thought was no longer pertinent, we certainly found new subjects that just had to be discussed. For instance, Cisco has really kicked up its collaboration efforts with its Cisco Unified Communications solution. With a whole new philosophy and line of products, it's something that needed coverage. In the fourth edition, we really got into the topic of Voice over IP (VoIP). Although this remains pertinent, Cisco has developed the technology into different ways to communicate and collaborate—be it voice, video, or through its own social media offerings. Also, because wireless has become such an indispensable part of networks, that content has been bolstered as well, including configuration details. It's no surprise that security continues to be an important topic, so we also beefed up that content. But at the heart of Cisco's products and technologies are its switches and routers—and we haven't shoved them aside for the new stuff. Of course, all the chapters were updated to cover the latest hardware and software offerings from Cisco.

So what's the reason for all of this work and revision? We continue to think there is an enormous need by networking professionals for a clear, concise introduction to Cisco and its technologies. What is truly needed is a simple understanding of networking and Cisco's role in networking to make sense of many IT issues. So the story begins....

Who Should Read This Book

This book is designed for anybody new to internetworking. It covers what one might refer to as the Internet's technical infrastructure. The software on your desktop or laptop—the web browser, FTP software, or instant messenger—is only the tip of the iceberg. Over the past 30 years, an ever-growing group of dedicated computer scientists, telecommunications engineers, and programmers has been busy designing and building a global infrastructure that is revolutionizing commerce and culture alike. Internetworking has taken on a language all its own—separate even from that used by the computer industry at large.

This book is for aspiring professionals interested in learning about the networking giant, managers in the computing industry whose knowledge of internetworking is weak, computer platform and software pros, and even individuals in the general public with a taste for technology.

This book is for those interested in the Internet and internetworking, not just in Cisco. Technology basics are covered generically before delving into Cisco particulars. Cisco is used for all examples in this book because it has the biggest and most comprehensive product line in the industry and is still the most important player in the field.

For those of you interested in pursuing Cisco certification, read this book to be introduced to industry background, concepts, terms, and technology. Then go on to a test preparation book to nail down your CCNA test.

What This Book Covers

The following is a chapter-by-chapter breakdown of the subject matter covered in this book.

Part I: Cisco Overview

Chapter 1: Cisco and the Internet   The Internet represents the biggest and fastest economic change in history, and sooner or later all our lives will be profoundly affected by it (if they haven't been already). This chapter surveys the Internet as a phenomenon, with a particular eye toward Cisco Systems and how its IOS operating software has vaulted the company to a position among the computer industry elite, alongside Apple, Microsoft, and IBM. The internetworking industry is outlined, and how Cisco's product line matches up to industry niches is explained.

Chapter 2: Networking Primer   Modern internetworking is the culmination of dozens of sophisticated technologies. This chapter explains things from the wire up, starting with electrons passing across cables, up through binary bits and bytes. The major LAN technologies such as Ethernet and Wi-Fi are explained, right down to how they differ and which are rising or fading from use, including high-speed backbone technologies such as ATM, MPLS, and Ethernet. The seven-layer Open Systems Interconnection (OSI) reference model is explained, including the inner workings of the TCP/IP protocol suite—the software used to run the Internet. You'll learn the difference between connection-oriented and connectionless networking, and how domain names are translated to numerical IP addresses. The important networking fundamentals of IP addressing and subnet masks are explained in detail. Broadband technologies such as DSL, cable, and ISDN are covered, as are WAN trunk technologies such as T1 and T3, Frame Relay, and MPLS.

Chapter 3: Cisco Certifications   Like Microsoft and other tech powerhouses, Cisco has a full-fledged certification program for technicians working on their products. This chapter details the subjects and skill levels, and sorts out such details as how Cisco certifications for design differ from the ones already in place for network support, and so forth. Complete explanations are given of exam objectives for each certification. We also highlight a number of ways you can find help preparing for the Cisco exams. This chapter is a must read for anyone interested in pursuing a career in internetworking, or faced with recruiting and managing Cisco certified personnel.

Part II: Cisco Internetworking Tools

Chapter 4: Routing Overview   This chapter focuses on Cisco routing basics. Routing is the bedrock of Cisco's technologies. And we cover basic router hardware components from the printed circuit board up through the CPU, explaining how network administrators can log in to Cisco routing devices to work on them, even rebooting in to ROM to perform such basic tasks as password recovery. The major software components in Cisco routing devices are also surveyed, including the Cisco IOS command interface and feature sets. Cisco's router product line is reviewed here, including some tips on how to select the best routing device to solve a particular internetworking problem.

Chapter 5: Routing Platforms   There are many ways in which Cisco devices transfer network traffic around the Internet, and this chapter takes a close look at those devices, specifically router hardware. This is the chapter in which we look at the router itself, and talk about its components and Cisco's router product line. In addition to the hardware, we'll introduce you to the important software components, including the configuration file and the operating systems—IOS and IOS XR—which are the heart of these devices.

Chapter 6: Configuring Routing   In this chapter we delve deeper into the heart of the router and discuss how, specifically, the device is configured. We'll talk about the different ways you can connect with the router and what you need to say to get the router to do what you want. The chapter will show you how to use the command line, as well as use the Cisco Configuration Professional application for an easy, graphical user interface method of router configuration.

Chapter 7: Switches   The so-called *access layer* is where host devices such as PCs and servers plug in to internetworks. This chapter explains internetwork topology basics, cabling specifications, what bandwidth is, and what distinguishes collision and broadcast domains. High-end LAN backbone switches are also covered, from the perspective of one of the most important subjects in the industry today—whether to design routed or switched networks. The more technical dimensions of switched networking are introduced, including switching protocols, virtual LANs (VLANs), and multilayered switching. Cisco's switch product lines are reviewed.

Chapter 8: Security Overview   Security is a hot topic—certainly one that can (and does) fill books all on its own. In this chapter we'll give you a basic overview of security matters, including traffic-based security (which applies to the traffic from your applications) and user-based security (which is used to set and enforce passwords to access networks and authorizations to use network resources). This chapter first covers the underlying industry standards for security, especially the AAA (Authentication, Authorization, and Accounting) standard. AAA is covered at the command level. Cisco offers several user and device-based security products and allows for implementation of many network security protocols: primarily RADIUS (an industry standard), its proprietary TACACS+, and 802.1X. These are reviewed in detail. Because security is such an important issue—and such a moving target—we'll also talk about best practices to ensure you are meeting your network security needs.

Chapter 9: Access Control   Although it's necessary to keep the bad guys out of your network, it is equally as important to ensure the good guys can get in. To that end, Cisco has developed a number of technologies and techniques to ensure network security, while providing a mechanism through which authorized users can gain access to the network. In this chapter we will talk about such Cisco technologies as SecureX and TrustSec. We'll also talk about the access control list, Cisco's line of Access Control Servers, and its implementation of virtual private networks (VPNs).

Chapter 10: Security Appliances   There was a time when a discussion of Cisco security devices would have been about one topic—firewalls. In this chapter, we talk about Cisco's firewalls, specific models, how they are configured, and how they are managed. Although the firewall is still a huge subject in the world of security devices, it is no longer the only game in town. Cisco has broadened its lineup with Adaptive Security Appliances and Integrated Services Routers. In addition, we'll also discuss what Cisco has to offer for cloud-based security needs as well as specialized modules that can be added to modular switches.

Chapter 11: Cisco Unified Wireless   Until recently, the only way to connect a client to an internetwork was via a thin piece of cable snaking into the back of the PC. As efficient as this has been, it was only a matter of time before someone figured out how to cut the cord and let devices communicate with each other in a wireless medium. And, as it happens—especially in this age of smartphones and tablets— wireless is critical. In this chapter, we cover the fundamentals of wireless networking, and then delve into Cisco's solution. Wireless networking is no longer a "gee-whiz" technology. Today it is mandatory. Wireless networking brings the power of computing and network connectivity to a range of useful applications and is beneficial to fields from healthcare to education and everything in between. Cisco offers solutions for both wireless LANs and wireless WANs with its Aironet and Airespace series. We'll discuss and then show you how to configure them.

Part III: Cisco Business Solutions

Chapter 12: Cisco VoIP   Networks and internetworks are great ways to move data from place to place. However, it isn't just text files and the fourth-quarter earnings statements that can traverse a Cisco-based network infrastructure. Thanks to Voice over IP (VoIP), your organization can use its internetwork as the backbone of your telecommunications system. Additionally, customers who need to get in contact with your organization will benefit from Cisco Unified Communications. It's a new way to deploy VoIP that delivers rich, robust tools in voice, video, and overall intelligence.

Chapter 13: Data Center and Virtualization   With benefits of the Information Age comes a hefty issue—where do we *keep* all that information? In this chapter, we examine storage area networks (SANs), which are akin to LANs but are built with the goal of information storage. We'll talk about SAN designs and construction and then look at the products Cisco offers for its SAN solutions. Another big topic in the world of computing and networking these days has been "the cloud." In this chapter we will talk about Cisco's offerings for private cloud computing systems as well as mechanisms for virtualization.

Chapter 14: Cisco Content Networking and Video Solutions   These days, organizations offer more and richer information on their websites. However, as more people request data from various locations, the need arises to direct the client to the closest, fastest repository of that information. Content delivery networks (CDNs) help resolve congested networks because clients are given the data they need from the best location. This chapter covers CDN basics, along with Cisco's product line for this technology. Additionally, we cover the topic of caching, a way in which service providers and large organizations can maintain frequently accessed web information so that it can be delivered without having to repeatedly go to the Internet to access it.

Part IV: Designing Cisco Networks

Chapter 15: Routing Protocols   Large internetworks, or the Internet, for that matter, wouldn't be possible without routing protocols. This chapter covers fundamental problems confronting any internetwork, as well as how routing protocols are used to adapt to shifting traffic patterns, emerging problems, and topology changes. Basic routing protocol technology is covered here, as are the various major routing protocols in use today—both open standard protocols (RIP, OSPF, BGP) and Cisco-proprietary protocols (IGRP and EIGRP). Cisco's routing protocols are overviewed, down to the command level where routing metrics are set to modify network behavior to meet enterprise requirements.

Chapter 16: Network Management   Network management has become a major issue as internetworks have grown in size and complexity. This chapter covers the standards and technologies that underlie network management systems: the Simple Network Management Protocol (SNMP), remote monitor instrumentation (RMON), and the management information base (MIB). Issues surrounding network management standards are covered, as is Cisco's approach to implementing them. SNMP configuration is introduced at the command level, and Cisco's premiere network management software products—Cisco Prime Infrastructure and Cisco Network Assistant—are also reviewed.

Chapter 17: Network Design Process   There are basics that must be covered when considering any network design decision, whether for a whole new internetwork or a modest expansion of an existing one. The classic three-layer hierarchical design model is reviewed in terms of what to look for in the access, distribution, and backbone layers. Key design subjects such as topology meshing and load balancing are reviewed. How to perform a comprehensive network needs analysis and how to translate it into design solutions using Cisco products is explained, covering such design factors as routing protocols, address design, routing versus switching, WAN services, and traffic load-balancing.

Chapter 18: Troubleshooting Cisco Networks   You've arrived as a network pro when you can troubleshoot an internetwork. This chapter surveys typical internetwork problems and the proper methodology for diagnosing and fixing them. Key Cisco IOS troubleshooting commands are reviewed in terms of how to handle connectivity issues, performance bottlenecks, and other problems. Particular attention is paid to how to track down and isolate configuration problems, how to tune routing protocol metrics, and how to troubleshoot WAN services such as serial line links. Additionally, we cover common wireless network problems, along with how to troubleshoot network performance issues.

How to Read This Book

This book can be picked up and read from the beginning of any chapter. Chapters covering technology start out with the basics and give explanations from the standpoint of the technology's historical background, how it developed, and what the issues and trends surrounding it are. Only then is Cisco specifically covered in terms of IOS commands, Cisco software tools, and Cisco hardware and software products.

This book doesn't try to reinvent the wheel by publishing yet another glossary on internetworking terms and acronyms. Every term introduced in this book is defined and explained in context. But the book should be read with the reader's browser pointed to Cisco's website at www.cisco.com. Although this book stands on its own, it never hurts to browse around to help reinforce newly learned subject matter. Cisco's website contains a wealth of product illustrations, white papers, and other materials. In particular, readers of this book should visit Cisco's excellent online glossary of Cisco Internetworking Terms and Acronyms:

> http://docwiki.cisco.com/w/index.php?title=Category:Internetworking_Terms_
> and_Acronyms_(ITA)

PART I | Cisco Overview

CHAPTER 1 | Cisco and the Internet

The Internet is amazing. There's just no other word to describe a technology that few had even heard of 20 years ago, yet now dominates so much of our collective consciousness. The gold fever surrounding the Internet makes the 1849 California gold rush seem insignificant in comparison. You've no doubt heard the analogies and the clichés—the Internet is the fastest-growing market in history, the fastest-growing technology in history, and the first truly global, real-time marketplace of goods, services, and ideas. The Internet has brought and will continue to bring profound change to all sectors, from business to education to entertainment. The Internet is the information superhighway—that's our road to the future.

Internetworking

The most surprising thing about all the breathless web hype is that most of it is true. Most research houses estimate Internet growth at about 18 percent annually. In fact, we reached the two-billion-user mark sometime in 2010, and this number will continue to rise. There are now 225 million registered Internet domain names, and there are billions of web pages, up from just a million of them a scant 20 years ago. In 2012, advertisers spent an estimated US$39.5 billion on Internet-based ads. No matter how tired we are of hearing this litany of numbers, it is still impressive.

Although most press coverage dotes on visible technologies, such as browsers and cellular Internet phones, the real action is in Internet infrastructure. Billions are invested by serious players who foresee a day when virtually all mass media— radio, telephone, and television—converge onto the Internet. This convergence will use the Internet as a single "pipe" through which virtually all communication will travel. There's disagreement about whether the Internet pipe will run over wireless devices, telephone lines, cable TV wires, or even satellites. In fact, it seems that, for the time being, it's all of the above. However, battle lines are being drawn every day by a multitude of businesses, and a lot of money is being invested. The bets are large, because winning the Internet infrastructure game promises untold riches.

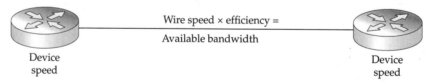

Users connect to servers over this Internet infrastructure, yet few are aware of just how it works. Bandwidth isn't just a matter of telecommunications media running over high-speed, fiber-optic cable. The networking devices sitting at each end of the cables are every bit as important. In many situations, the speed of these devices is as big a factor in the Internet's bandwidth as telecom media.

Voice over IP (VoIP) telephony, streaming media services, videoconferencing, and server-based file storage used to be things associated with a corporate infrastructure. But let's put some names to these services as we know them today: Vonage, Netflix, Skype, and Dropbox.

None of these companies could exist in their present state without Cisco's innovations. Cisco has spent the better part of the last decade acquiring companies that produce technologies of every flavor imaginable—and found ways to integrate them within every layer of Cisco's portfolio. From uber-fast Internet backbone devices, to data-streaming management systems for Internet content providers, to corporate campuses that are wireless mobility enabled, to data centers having switches with direct integration to storage and servers, to home users with USB storage-enabled Wi-Fi routers, Cisco touches every facet of our daily lives.

This book surveys internetworking's infrastructure from the ground up, starting with the underlying technology, up through the product level. If you're a beginner, read this book and you'll know the basics of internetworking. It's written from the perspective of the premier manufacturer of internetworking technology: Cisco Systems. Because the technologies are covered generically, you'll understand the systems and components needed to make any internetwork run, not just one built from Cisco products. But make no mistake: This book is about *infrastructure*—that is, about the devices over which internetworks operate:

- **Routers**   These devices route data between networks, such as local area networks (LANs), wide area networks (WANs), and metro area networks (MANs). Routers put the *inter* in internetworking. Without them, the Internet would not be possible. Routers use Internet Protocol (IP) addresses to figure out how to best route packets through internetworks.

- **Switches**   These devices also forward data on and between LANs, and have replaced the hub as the de facto standard for connecting workstations and servers to the network. Switches are faster than routers, but most don't look high enough in the stack to see or use IP addresses and, therefore, don't have the capability routers do for finding paths through large internetworks. There are, however, switches that incorporate routing. They are commonly referred to as "layer 3 switches," and we'll discuss them in more detail in an upcoming chapter.

- **Firewalls**   Although these can be understood simply as special routers that filter packets to secure data connections between internal and external networks, they are highly evolved security devices that examine communications between devices at many layers and then take specific actions or determine what to allow and what to block.

- **Access servers**   These dedicated devices answer phone calls from remote users and connect them to the internetwork. Most access servers are used by Internet service providers (ISPs) to connect home users and small businesses to the Internet.

Collectively, these devices make up the Internet's infrastructure. The only other major ingredient is telecommunications links to make WAN connections. In this book, we'll cover each device type as it exists within Cisco's product line as well as review WAN technologies. Doing so (from the perspective of Cisco's product line) will give you a more detailed look at the inner workings of internetwork devices.

Cisco's Position in the Computer Industry

We all know that Microsoft Windows is, at this point, the world's most dominant computer operating system. But here's a pop quiz: Can you name the second most important operating system? Choose one:

- **z/OS**   This is IBM's proprietary operating system that runs mainframe computers. This OS's stranglehold on the central corporate and government data centers that handle financial accounting and other sensitive transactions has been released, with estimates as high as 80 percent of mainframes today operating on Linux.

- **Unix/Linux**   There are actually about a dozen proprietary versions of Unix from such computer manufacturers as Apple, Sun, HP, Compaq, Novell, and IBM. Linux is no longer the "new" kid on the block, and due to the flexibility inherent to the OS, it is hot on the heels of good-old UNIX and will soon become the predominant server operating system in enterprise-class client/server applications.

- **IOS**   IOS Stands for Internetwork Operating System, and is Cisco Systems' proprietary operating system for its line of internetworking hardware.

Because this is a Cisco book, this is sort of a loaded question. IOS is the second most important operating system—and by a wide margin. We assert this partly because all Unix flavors and z/OS have lost their edge. Unix, having lost market share to Microsoft Windows, Linux, and MVS, although still a mission-critical technology, has stopped growing altogether. However, the main reason IOS is so important is that Cisco has over a 77 percent share of the Internet router market, and the Internet is the fastest-growing market in history.

 NOTE   Cisco's IOS (Internetwork Operating System) should not be confused with Apple's iOS (formerly iPhone Operating System).

To put that in perspective, Cisco has about the same market share in router technology as Intel enjoys in Windows (or Wintel) hardware platforms. The Wintel regime has been attacked as a monopoly by competitors and the U.S. Department of Justice. Not so with Cisco. IOS is their proprietary operating system architecture, and it runs on their hardware only. This means that Cisco's market leadership garners both hardware and software revenues and gives the company total architectural control over its products.

Cisco's present position has its strengths and weaknesses compared to the Wintel duopoly. On the negative side of the ledger, Cisco products are largely used to run truly open-standard protocols, which reduces the extent to which they can leverage product architecture to assert market control. Cisco doesn't widely freeze any competitor out of design cycles to prepare products that implement emerging technologies, because the technologies implement open standards. On the positive side, Cisco is a single company that makes its own products. This contrasts favorably to Wintel, a pair of companies that rely on hundreds of PC manufacturers to deliver their respective products to a highly fragmented market.

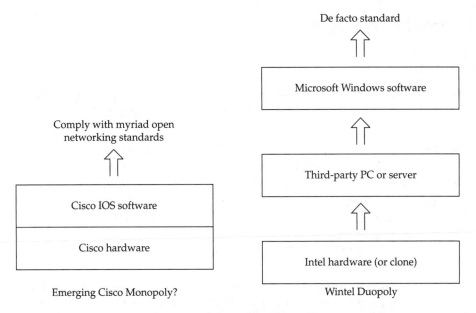

Financially speaking, by the turn of the millennium, Cisco was riding a gravy train with biscuit wheels. Even though most people couldn't tell Cisco from Crisco, chances are some part of their life was touched by a Cisco product. Maybe their computer network at work utilized Cisco gear; maybe the ISP they used for Internet connectivity relied on Cisco gear. But the fact of the matter is that at one point in history, Cisco was the most valuable company on the face of the planet. In March 2000—less than two decades after the company was founded—the company reached a value of half a trillion dollars.

More than a year later, however, all that changed. When the dot-com bubble burst, Cisco fell hard. Many companies no longer needed Cisco's gadgets, and by the spring of 2001, Cisco faced a $2 billion write-off. From its leadership position, with its stock trading at a high of $146 per share in March 2000, Cisco's stock dipped to a low of just over $8 per share in October 2002. Though Cisco fell, it didn't fall as hard as those companies that had to close up shop. Cisco has hung in there and has made a steady climb back to profitability. At the beginning of 2006, Cisco stock was trading at around $20 per share and in mid-2007 was up as high as $33 with revenues of $6.6 billion.

Since the 2008 global recession began, Cisco has again leveled out and has held steadily around $20 a share. The upshot of this lesson in finances? Cisco was down, but they were never out.

This book is not an endorsement of Cisco, however. Like any industry powerhouse, the company has its faults and is duly criticized in these pages when appropriate. But whether you're an individual mulling a career move or a manager weighing your company's Internet strategy, learning how Cisco technology works is your best possible introduction to the world of internetworking.

The Internet Landscape

The Internet isn't a single technology; instead, it's a collection of related technologies that make internetworking possible:

- **Physical media**   From connectors to high-speed, fiber-optic cables, the physical links that connect everything together are the foundation of networking.

- **Network technologies**   LAN protocols run what happens over the wire. The best known is Ethernet, but there are other important ones.

- **TCP/IP**   The Transmission Control Protocol/Internet Protocol is what binds the Internet together. IP handles addressing, and TCP handles messaging. Also included in the Internet Protocol suite is User Datagram Protocol (UDP), which is used to send faster and timelier datagrams in a network. Internet Control Message Protocol (ICMP) is another component that is used to send error messages in a network.

- **Operational technologies**   Internetworks rely on a number of underlying standards and protocols to operate themselves. Without them, internetworking wouldn't be practical.

- **Application protocols**   Network applications define the kinds of useful tasks internetworks can do—from file transfers to web page downloads.

To engineer its products, the networking industry uses a seven-layer architectural guideline called the Open Systems Interconnection (OSI) reference model. It's no coincidence that the preceding list of enabling technologies more or less adheres to the OSI model, from the physical level up.

Before we proceed, a quick word to make sure our terminology is clear: The *Internet* is a global interconnection of individual internetworks. An *internetwork* is any collection of local area networks (LANs) under a single administrative regime (usually an enterprise or an Internet service provider). A private internetwork is mechanically the same as the open Internet. A *host* is a user device, such as a PC, server, mainframe, or printer. A *device* is a piece of networking equipment, such as a router. The generic terms *node* and *station* refer to both hosts and devices. A *LAN segment* is a network medium that hosts a share. An *application protocol* is a software standard that operates web browsers, file transfers, e-mails, and other useful functions. An *intranet* is an internal internetwork operating as a private Web, with enterprise applications software used through web browsers instead of a more traditional graphical user interface (GUI) such as Microsoft Windows.

From a technical standpoint, private internetworks are composed of the same pieces as the Internet itself. The only thing that distinguishes the Internet from a large internetwork is its openness.

Internetworking's Five Major Device Types

A *switch* connects hosts to the internetwork. Switches function much like their predecessor, the network hub; however, they are fundamentally different in that they form a virtual circuit between the sending and receiving hosts. In other words, the switch's bandwidth is reserved for a single switched connection between two hosts as if it were 100 percent dedicated to that virtual circuit. Switches are able to do this by using better electronics than those used by hubs to "slice" bandwidth time into slivers—called *channels*—large enough to service each switch port. Switches have almost all but replaced hubs.

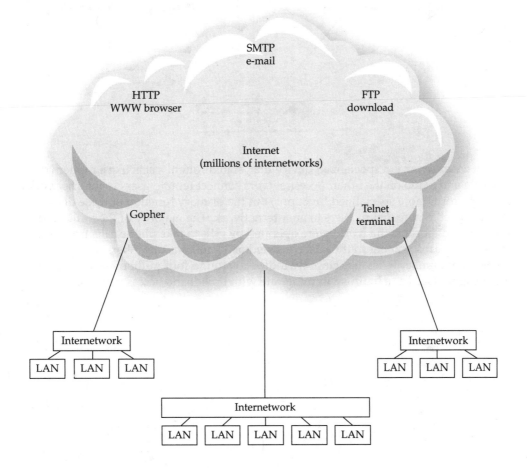

A *router* is an intelligent device that forwards traffic based on the IP address of a message. Whereas switches have ports into which individual hosts plug, routers have interfaces to which LAN segments attach. In simple terms, a router's job is to move *packets* of data between attached LAN segments.

The router is the single most important type of device in internetworking. It provides the flexibility and decision-making power that make it possible to run complicated internetworks. Without the logical capability routers provide, the Internet would be hundreds of times slower and much more expensive. As detailed in the next chapter, internetwork architectures have seven layers: Switches predominantly operate at layer 2, and routers at layer 3. Routers also have the capability to filter traffic based on source and destination addresses, network application, and other parameters.

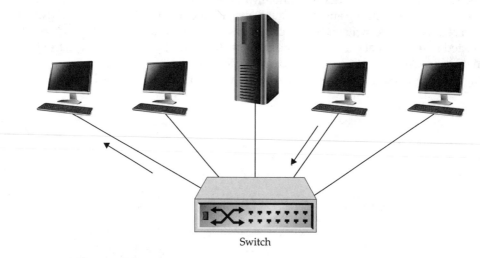

Switch

An *access server* is a specialized device that, stated roughly, acts like a modem on one side and a hub on the other. Access servers connect remote users to internetworks. Some perform more specialized functions, but the primary function of these devices is to connect remote dial-in users to an internetwork. The majority of the millions of access server ports in the world were operated by ISPs to take phone calls from Internet subscribers. This number in the past consisted of 30 million subscribers in the U.S. alone. That number today has since dwindled to around four million. Access servers are being replaced at a brain-swimming rate with broadband access devices.

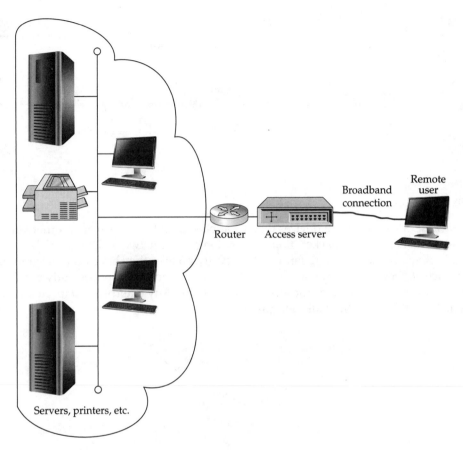

A *broadband access device* allows access to the Internet via a cellular modem, a DOCIS cable modem, or a DSL router. A cellular modem is a radio device that connects a laptop, tablet, smartphone, or router to a cellular carrier's network. This network can be an extension of Internet addressing, as with 3G service (for example, CDMA/ HSPA), or a privately managed internetwork as with 4G (for example, LTE). A cable modem utilizes a municipality's cable TV plant for its medium, and a DSL router utilizes existing copper POTS (Plain Old Telephone Service) cabling.

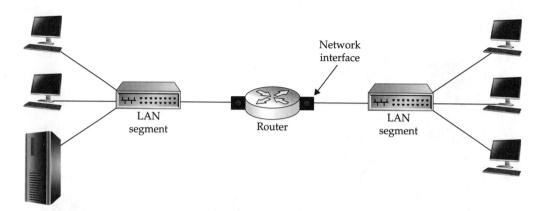

Firewalls are networking devices that act as checkpoints between an internetwork and the outside, filtering packets that don't belong in the network. They work by checking each packet for compliance with security policies they have been programmed to enforce. A firewall forms an intentional traffic choke point and persistently monitors internal/external connections for security compliance. Any enterprise connected to the Internet should have a firewall configured.

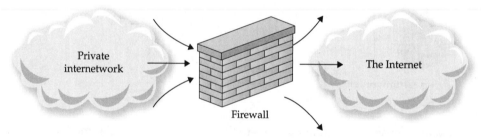

The most powerful firewalls have specialized hardware, but they don't have to. A normal router can be programmed to perform many of the basic duties that a firewall can perform, but a device that only does access lists, network address translation, and port blocking should never be confused with a true firewall. To ensure a much higher level of security, a dedicated firewall device is highly recommended in most instances. Furthermore, firewalls capable of performing stateful inspection, along with intrusion prevention, are generally required to properly safeguard assets from potential threats. Standards such as PCI, NERC, HIPAA, FERC, and Sarbanes–Oxley all require security controls, including those that are commonly performed by firewalls.

Basic Internetwork Topologies

A *topology* is the physical arrangement of nodes within an internetwork. Usually, a topology is expressed as a logical map that graphically represents each node and the media links connecting the nodes. In fact, topology maps are used as the GUI through which most network management software tools operate. Figure 1-1 depicts the basic network elements that are combined in one way or another to make up internetworks.

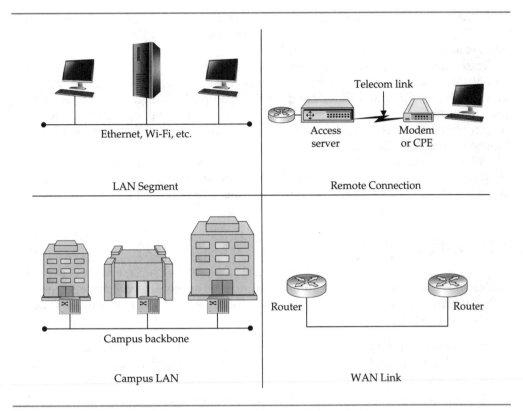

Figure 1-1.   There are four basic elements to internetwork topologies.

The LAN segment is the basic building block of internetworks. Put another way, LAN segments are the network units that internetworks link together. The Internet itself is a collection of millions of LAN segments. The reason we use the formal term LAN *segment* is that local collections of individual segments are commonly referred to as "LANs," even though, strictly speaking, they are actually local internetworks. This may seem like nit-picking, but you'll be happy for the distinction in later chapters.

Remote connections use phone circuits, cable, satellite, and cellular signals to tie physically removed hosts into the LAN segment. The telecom link can be anything from a regular analog voice line to a cellular modem, Digital Subscriber Line (DSL), cable-based broadband, and even satellite broadband.

The current state of the art for long-distance WAN is still OC-768, with a data rate of 40 Gbps (OC stands for optical carrier; Gbps stands for gigabits per second). However, private high-speed MANs and WANs are being built utilizing 100 Gbps Ethernet. Slower WAN links run over technologies you've probably heard of—T1 and T3 (also called DS3), which run at 1.5 Mbps and 45 Mbps, respectively. It should be noted that multitudes of companies are following the lead of carriers by dropping their leased-line WAN links in favor of VPN (virtual private network) links over the public Internet as access costs drop and speed rises.

The *campus LAN* is a double misnomer, but get used to it. Cisco uses it as a generic term to describe local enterprise internetworks. Most exist within a single building, not over an office campus, and all are composed of multiple LAN segments, not a single LAN. But campus LANs are distinguishable by the use of a high-speed backbone segment to interconnect the other local LAN segments. Most "heavy-duty" LAN backbones run over fiber-optic cabling.

WAN (wide area network) links are long-distance telecom links between cities, although some are strung across ocean floors to connect continents. Virtually all new WAN links being installed run over ultra-high-speed fiber-optic links.

Internetwork Players

There is no "Internet network," as such. In other words, there is no separately owned dedicated trunk network operated under the auspices of some central management authority. The Internet is actually a free-for-all collection of individual networks bound together by two things:

- **Shared enabling technologies**   A complex of de facto standards and technologies that not only make the individual internetwork possible, but also enable Internetworks to automatically interact with other internetworks.

- **Internet Protocol (IP)**   A globally accepted communication system that makes it possible to connect and exchange data with otherwise incompatible hosts anywhere on earth. IP unifies communication among virtually all computer systems into a unitary data format and addressing system.

Figure 1-2 lays out approximately how the Internet is formed. The prerequisite is that users need to be on a network of some kind, and nowadays, in an office or plant, this usually means some type of Ethernet LAN. In the past, desktop protocols such as Novell NetWare IPX and AppleTalk used their respective protocols on Ethernet. Today, a vast majority of desktops and the networks they are on use the TCP/IP protocol over Ethernet.

ISPs play a central role in Internet connectivity for enterprises, not just for home users. Peer networking is the arrangement of traffic exchange between ISPs. From the Internet's standpoint, the key juncture is where you connect to the so-called peer network—a group of thousands of high-speed routers that pass IP routes and traffic among one another. Although some very large enterprises (big corporations, government agencies, and universities) have their own direct connections to the peer network, most tap in through ISPs.

Entry to the peer network almost always takes place through a high-speed fiber trunk line, usually controlled by so-called Internet backbone providers (IBPs), such as

The IP addressing scheme makes global connectivity possible.

ISPs connect enterprises to the "peer network."

IP packet format makes interconnection feasible.

Desktop LAN protocols

Network technologies get people connected.

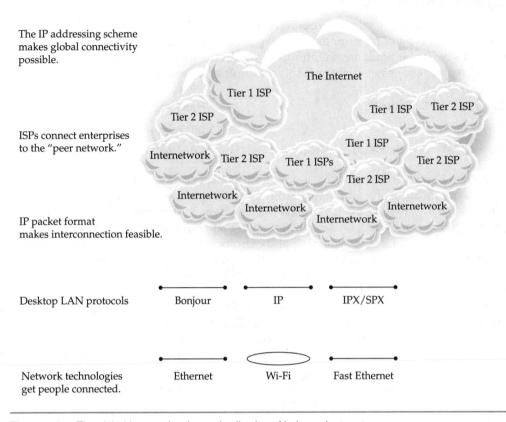

Figure 1-2. The global Internet is a layered collection of independent systems.

AT&T, MCI, and AOL. These IBPs are also called Tier 1 Internet service providers. They connect to each other by "peering" with each other. *Peering* involves a set of agreed-upon connections that Tier 1 ISPs have with each other to exchange network traffic. These are usually ultra-high-speed connections (OC 198 fiber, and so on) that are done at multiple locations around the world known as *peering points.*

NOTE   You may also hear *peering points* referred to as Internet Exchange Points (IXPs).

Tier 2 providers are the next level down. They don't peer directly at the backbone, but instead purchase access "in bulk" from Tier 1 carriers and then resell it to businesses, consumers, and other service providers. Most businesses and general consumers purchase their Internet connectivity through a Tier 2 carrier or a service provider that resells access.

Internetworking Protocols

Protocols are the key to internetworking. A networking *protocol* is an agreed-upon data format and set of rules for message exchange to govern a specific process. The Internet's two most fundamental protocols exist at the lower layers of the OSI model. These are the various network (or LAN) protocols and the IP protocol.

Layer	Protocol	Function
Layer 3	IP	Internetworking
Layer 2	Ethernet, Token Ring, and so on	LAN segment media access

Layers 2 and 3 are the primary focus of this book, because that's where Cisco and its competitors bring physical network infrastructures to life as internetworks. Layer 2 connects the host to its home LAN segment, and layer 3 interconnects LAN segments. (In case you're wondering, layer 1 covers cabling and other physical transport media.)

However, that's just the beginning of the protocol story. There are literally dozens of supplementary protocols, large and small, to do everything, from checking whether a neighboring device is still running to calculating the best path for sending packets to the other side of the world.

For example, consider the Session Initiation Protocol (SIP). SIP is an Internet Engineering Task Force (IETF) standard (RFC 3261) for managing how voice, video, and data can exist on the same network. Most often, you'll see SIP at work as the protocol involved in Voice over IP (VoIP) technologies and devices. Because of this protocol, VoIP can be used on desktop computers, tablets, IP phones, and other devices.

These supplementary protocols can be roughly divided into three groups: maintenance, management, and routing.

Protocol Type	Function	Description
Routing protocols	Best paths	Exchange updates and calculate the best current routes
Management protocols	Health and security	Monitor performance, trip alarms, and reconfigure
Maintenance protocols	Housekeeping	Discover devices, trace routes, and notify neighbors

The maintenance protocols tend to be more proprietary (vendor specific) the closer they are to the network device hardware. For example, the Cisco Discovery Protocol (CDP) keeps track of devices—but only Cisco devices. The management protocols are more generic. However, Cisco is so big that they support the industry-standard protocols in addition to pushing their own proprietary security protocol. A third kind of maintenance protocols called *routing protocols* are what make large, complicated networks possible.

Routing protocols wring much of the labor and complexity out of very large networks by automatically tracking which routes to use between IP addresses. The Border Gateway Protocol (BGP) is the top-level routing protocol that connects everything within cities, between cities, and between continents. On a smaller scale, BGP is also used to connect private networks and autonomous domains. Several other routing protocols are used to track routes within private internetworks. Cisco supports industry-standard routing protocols in addition to pushing a couple of internal routing protocols of their own.

Routing vs. Switching

A few years ago, a technology war was waged between routing and switching. Hubs may have been trampled to death, but neither the switching nor routing camp can declare victory. As devices became less expensive and more powerful, switching emerged as a viable alternative to hubs on the low end and routers on the high end. Because switching is inherently faster, there was a push to replace routed networks with switched networks. The battle took place at both ends of the internetworking landscape. At the low end—called the *access layer*, because this is where hosts gain access to the internetwork—switches have replaced hubs as the device of choice to connect hosts because of switches' higher bandwidth. Switches have also displaced routers as backbones that connect LANs within a building or a campus. Layer 3 switches are able to perform the routing duties that a router would normally perform. Figure 1-3 shows the three different types of switching.

Switching has always been the norm over WAN trunks, such as the fiber-optic links Internet backbone providers operate between cities. In fact, voice telephone systems are switched networks built over permanent physical circuits in the form of the telephone cables running to businesses and homes.

Data switches, of course, don't have dedicated cabling—the switched circuits they create are virtual. That is, they create temporary, logical (not hard-wired) end-to-end circuits that are set up and torn down on an as-needed basis. But nonetheless, data switches are inherently faster than shared networks. The phrase "switch where you can, route where you must" has emerged as the industry motto—the translation being that wherever possible, you should use access switches in place of hubs for host access and LAN switches instead of routers for internetwork connections.

Looking at Figure 1-3, you can see that the two technologies have their respective trade-offs. In a nutshell, routers are slower and more expensive, but are much more intelligent. Indeed, larger internetworks will never be able to entirely do away with routing functionality of some sort. Thus, the industry is seeing the melding of switching's physical layer speed with routing's network layer intelligence. Hybrid devices have been rolled out that incorporate some IP routing intelligence into hardware. These hybrids are variously called layer 3 switches, multilayer switches, and so on.

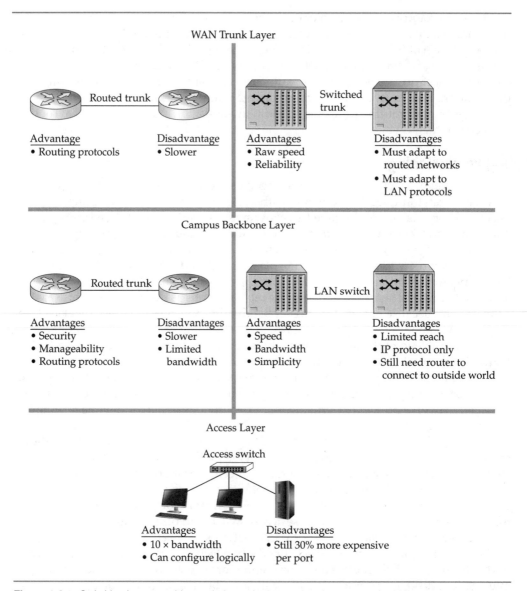

WAN Trunk Layer

Routed trunk

Switched
trunk

Advantage
• Routing protocols

Disadvantage
• Slower

Advantages
• Raw speed
• Reliability

Disadvantages
• Must adapt to
  routed networks
• Must adapt to
  LAN protocols

Campus Backbone Layer

Routed trunk

LAN switch

Advantages
• Security
• Manageability
• Routing protocols

Disadvantages
• Slower
• Limited
  bandwidth

Advantages
• Speed
• Bandwidth
• Simplicity

Disadvantages
• Limited reach
• IP protocol only
• Still need router to
  connect to outside world

Access Layer

Access switch

Advantages
• 10 × bandwidth
• Can configure logically

Disadvantages
• Still 30% more expensive
  per port

Figure 1-3.   Switching is encroaching on hubs at the low end and routers at the high end.

Other Internetworking Trends

Beyond the routing-versus-switching technology war, a number of other trends are afoot in the internetworking industry:

- **Network management**   Several years ago, a big push was undertaken to make large, complicated internetworks more manageable and reliable. To that end, enterprises have adopted network management system (NMS) software products from which their network teams can centrally monitor and troubleshoot internetworks. These NMSs are fed data via several network management protocols. SNMPv3, NetFlow, and IP SLA are all examples.

- **Network security**   Improving network security is on the plate of nearly every internetwork owner. The pervasiveness of the "black hats" has forced the previous decade's practice of expanding a network as quickly and openly as possible to trend toward the implementation of "zones," which are LAN segments in which reside critical applications and databases that are logically "walled off" from the rest of the internetwork. Firewalls, IPS, and DLP, oh my!

- **Virtual private networks (VPNs)**   Traditional leased-line WAN links are quickly being replaced by VPN links. VPNs use encryption to enable enterprises to operate private WANs over the Internet—at a fraction of the cost. Again, encryption used to exact a trade-off in lowered performance, but today's platforms handle this with ease. There are also reliability issues that must sometimes be dealt with.

- **Bye, bye dial-in**   Remote dial-in access technology to the home or small office is being upgraded by replacing POTS circuits with digital circuits. At one time, Integrated Services Digital Network (ISDN) looked like the answer, but now DSL and cable are the services to travel the "last mile" from the local phone company switching office to the small office or home.

- **Faster WAN trunks**   Trunk lines running the Synchronous Optical Network (SONET) standard are advancing at a breakneck pace. The original 52 Mbps OC-1 has been improved over several increments to the present state-of-the-art 40 Gbps OC-768 standard. SONET will be replaced with a new standard, 112 Gbps ITU-T G.709.

- **Backbone technologies**   The campus backbone market had to choose between two high-bandwidth network protocols: Asynchronous Transfer Mode (ATM) and Gigabit Ethernet. ATM lost. The vast majority of campus backbones today are being built with 1 Gbps and 10 Gbps Ethernet. As the name implies, 10 Gigabit Ethernet is the 10,000 Mbps successor to the 1000 Mbps Gigabit Ethernet specification.

- **IP telephony**   For years, conventional telephone lines have been used to facilitate WAN connections, or even the SOHO user, calling an ISP to log into the network. The street runs both ways, however. Thanks to IP telephony, computer networks can be used to transport voice calls. In essence, the calls are converted into the popular Internet Protocol (IP) and the packets sent across the network to their destination, where they are converted back into sound. A primary benefit of IP telephony is a cost savings. With a data network already in place, it's a simple matter to add an IP telephone system. IP telephony is nothing new—it's how telephone companies have sent calls between regional offices for some time now.

■ **Wireless** Conventional computer networks have had a major obstacle: computers having to be tethered to switches and hubs with physical cabling. Obviously, this is not ideal in environments where mobility and computation must meet. The solution is wireless (Wi-Fi) and mobile cellular technology. These allow computers to be connected to the network, without having to be tied down with cabling.

■ **Multimedia** A half-dozen years ago, watching video and streaming music was really only feasible by those with expensive broadband connections. However, as broadband connections have become more affordable and untethered from the limitations of copper-based offerings, such as DSL and cable Internet, and are provided by cellular carriers in our cell phones and thus fit into our pockets, there is far more multimedia content on the Internet than one person can possibly consume. As such, there needs to be an effective, efficient way to give people the content they want.

■ **MPLS** Multiprotocol Label Switching (MPLS) has often been referred to as a key component of the "next-generation IP network." From a network perspective, MPLS is a packet-forwarding and switching technology. MPLS can interconnect to IP, ATM, Frame Relay, and other protocols, making it quite useful for WANs and other networks. MPLS is built for speed and scalability, and supports robust quality of service (QoS). It also allows for many virtual networks to be implemented and logically segmented. This is a common use for MPLS, as ISPs may provide an L2 service to customers over fiber, but encapsulate that traffic within L3 and aggregate it across shared high-speed trunks.

■ **Cloud computing** Cloud computing is perceived as the next "big thing" from many at the executive level. The ability of a company to pay for a service provided by an outside provider, and *not* have to maintain ownership of data centers with all the drudgery of power generation, cooling, heating, floor space, and so on, is very attractive from an operational expense perspective. One thing to note here is that cloud computing from an infrastructure perspective relies heavily on virtualization—not only of applications, but storage, security, and entire platforms. These are some areas where Cisco is trying to make their play. One is in the virtualized switch and firewalls they have that work within the VMware Hypervisor; the second is the Unified Computing System (UCS) server platform that integrates directly with the newer Nexus switch platform, a switching device that can handle hundreds of line-speed 10 Gbps interfaces and share duties passing Fiber Channel over IP, Ethernet over IP, iSCSI, and regular Ethernet traffic simultaneously. Another example is Cisco's participation in a company called VCE (vce.com), where they are partners with EMC and VMware. Their VBlock offering is positioned to be a "cloud in a box" essentially. The EANTC Cloud Mega Test described on vce.com puts a little context to the whole thing.

■ **Mobile Internet** As mentioned previously, cellular broadband access or "mobile Internet connectivity" may have started with e-mail, but has now progressed to full HD video streaming on cellular wireless networks. One can now video chat, stream live events from around the globe into their living room (or anywhere else with a good signal), and keep up to date with work and friends via many, many social networking applications. It is believed that this mobile connectivity has assisted with falling dictators by allowing average, ordinary people to communicate in real time across vast spaces and coordinate peaceful revolution. The mobile Internet has allowed a smarter power grid to begin to be built and has transformed how public safety services such as fire and police departments operate. Whereas the Internet backbone was the fastest growing technology five years ago, mobility has evolved into one of the largest growing networking market segments today.

Cisco's Offerings

Cisco Systems has the broadest and deepest product line in the internetworking business. You'll be surprised the first time you hold their product catalog—so thick and heavy that it's reminiscent of a catalog from a big computer company such as IBM or Hewlett-Packard.

The product line has been in a constant state of flux over the last several years. This is partly due to the industry's relentless introduction of new standards and technologies, causing perpetual product-line turnover. But the flux has as much to do with Cisco's fervid pursuit of technology by acquisition.

The Cisco product line can be broken down into two categories:

■ **Devices** Specific hardware products outlined at the beginning of this chapter

■ **Solutions** The combination of hardware, software, and services to fit certain customer requirements

The industry solutions piece is part hype, but it's a good indication of where and how Cisco sees its individual products put to use. For example, a strategic focus now is on Voice over IP (VoIP). As it stands, Cisco is the predominant IP device maker and key manufacturer of equipment used in telephone company back offices, and even of desktop data phones.

Competition

As mentioned earlier, the salient feature of Cisco's product line is that most devices run the Internetwork Operating System (IOS). Cisco will tell you that this enables customers to do a better job of configuring and managing internetworks. Cisco's competitors will tell you that IOS makes devices more expensive and takes away customer options in making future technology decisions. Both sides are right, of course—everything's a trade-off.

Although Cisco is well entrenched in the internetworking products battle, other companies out there are firing their own salvos, hoping to gain enough ground on the field to make a name for their own companies.

Cisco isn't bulletproof. The company has seen an increase in ambitious organizations trying to eat off its plate. A number of examples show where competitors are gaining ground in the service provider networking race. Challenging the leader are Juniper Networks in high-speed core Internet routers, Brocade in optical storage area networking gear, and Alcatel-Lucent in edge routing.

One of the major reasons Cisco is losing ground in selling to service providers, say analysts, is that service providers are looking for the very best product available. Conversely, in the enterprise market—where Cisco maintains its dominance—a strong brand and a solid distribution channel are normally the deciding factors. Furthermore, service providers also are willing to cobble their networks together using equipment from a range of suppliers. This is not the preferred modus operandi of many corporate network managers—they'd rather use the same supplier across the board.

Customer service is also a factor in Cisco's slippage. Smaller networking companies can more easily give the one-on-one service to individual service providers than Cisco: It's impossible for Cisco to personally manage tens of thousands of enterprise accounts. This can be made up for, on the other hand, by giving a half-dozen carrier customers their undivided attention.

Who Wants to Be a Millionaire?

For many tech companies, the Holy Grail of success isn't discovered just in the development and sale of a great product that people will use every day. Rather, it's having Cisco wave its hand across the company's brow in blessing, then acquiring it. In turn, this transforms the company's executives and employees into instant millionaires—without even having to be the last one voted off the island.

Acquisitions

Cisco is no stranger to acquisitions, building its router, switch security, wireless, and VoIP lines on technology they have acquired.

In 1999 and 2000, Cisco was buying up companies faster than they could get their business names on letterhead. Then the tech bubble burst and Cisco hit the brakes on buying. Slowly but surely, Cisco picked up its buying pace again, and by 2013, the company had acquired nearly 200 companies, assimilating their technologies into Cisco's own.

One of its biggest acquisitions was early in January 2005, with the $450-million acquisition of Airespace, a wireless LAN switch vendor. Although Cisco already had a robust wireless portfolio, Airespace bolstered its product line with easier-to-use, easier-to-configure, easier-to-manage devices. Maybe even more important is the security boost that Airespace provides to Cisco's wireless product catalog.

Cisco doesn't seem to be slowing down its acquisitions, picking up companies that can keep them on the cutting edge of current technology.

Software

Cisco doesn't limit its acquisitions to hardware. About half of 2004's acquisitions were software companies, including Protego and Perfigo, which make security management and enforcement software. Dynamicsoft makes VoIP management software, Jahai Networks makes network management applications, and Twingo develops desktop security applications.

In the future, analysts expect Cisco to acquire software for video-on-demand services, network management software for virtualizing data center resources, and new applications for managing service delivery.

Cisco continues to enhance its software offerings with such technologies as cloud computing and those related to traffic management and security.

While Cisco makes big and small deals with their acquisitions, they seem to have their best luck with some of the smaller ones (less than $1 billion, if you consider that small). For instance, the buyout of Aironet back in 1999 led to extremely popular and profitable wireless equipment, that continues to this day.

Scientific-Atlanta

The acquisition with the longest-reaching implications—at least to the general populace—comes from Cisco's $6.9 billion acquisition of Scientific-Atlanta, the company that makes set-top cable decoders. The acquisition is tied for Cisco's biggest ever (it purchased optical company Cerent in 1999 for the same amount).

The acquisition is somewhat out of character for Cisco. Historically, Cisco's acquisitions have been small companies in Silicon Valley. As Scientific-Atlanta's name belies, this purchase is on the other side of the country and is a large company.

The acquisition was a strategic move for Cisco, as cable companies continue to jockey for position in the IPTV and IP video-on-demand market. Because those operators are already using Cisco gear in their head ends, putting Cisco gear into consumers' homes was a smart move.

Expanding Portfolio

Cisco continues to expand and develop its technology and product offerings by acquiring promising companies with impressive technology or services. Oftentimes, Cisco's acquisitions can make or break a technology. For example, almost a decade ago, when the speculation started as to whether ATM could or should take over as the backbone technology of choice, many observers assumed that Cisco—a company with deep roots in Ethernet—would side with Gigabit Ethernet. Cisco instead went out and acquired StrataCom, the premier ATM technology company, in one of the largest technology mergers ever at that point. And while ATM has since lost the backbone war with Gigabit Ethernet, their acquisition of StrateCom did give ATM more longevity than it likely would have had.

Cisco has also acquired software providers focused on delivering solutions in such areas as network design and management. Cisco has spent years hyping itself as the industry's premier enterprise internetworking solutions vendor, and the company's willingness to adapt to technology trends instead of fighting them has impressed observers.

Since 2006, Cisco has continued its prodigious acquisitions of companies that help further its vision and offerings. Table 1-1 lists Cisco's acquisitions between late 2005 and early 2013 and details how they bolster Cisco's technological positioning.

Acquisition Date	Name	Description
January 29, 2013	Cognitive Security	Applies artificial intelligence to network security
January 23, 2013	Intucell	Self-optimizing network software for the configuration, management, and optimization of cellular networks
December 20, 2012	Meraki	Cloud computing solutions
November 15, 2012	Cloupia	Software automation for data centers
July 16, 2012	Virtuata	Securing virtual machine information
May 3, 2012	Truviso	Data analysis and reporting software
March 28, 2012	ClearAccess	Provisioning and management software for service providers
March 15, 2012	NDS Group	Video software delivery and security for service providers
February 24, 2012	Lightwire	Optical interconnection for high-speed networking
October 20, 2011	BNI Video	Back-office and content delivery network (CDN) services for video
August 29, 2011	Versly	Collaboration services for Microsoft Office
August 21, 2011	AXIOSS Software and Talent	Automated ordering and fulfillment services for networks
March 29, 2011	newScale	Cloud services deployment
February 4, 2011	Inlet Technologies	Adaptive Bit Rate (ABR) digital media processing platforms

Table 1-1.   Cisco's Acquisitions: 2005–2013 (continued)

Acquisition Date	Name	Description
January 26, 2011	Pari Networks	Network configuration and change management (NCCM) for Cisco's smart services
December 1, 2010	LineSider Technologies	Cloud services network management software
September 2, 2010	Arch Rock Corporation	Smart grid technology for the utility industry
August 26, 2010	ExtendMedia	Content Management System (CMS) for video services
May 20, 2010	CoreOptics	Digital Signal Processing (DSP) solutions for service providers
May 18, 2010	MOTO Development Group	Consumer product and product strategy designer
November 2, 2009	Set-Top Box Business of DVN (Holdings)	Cable solutions provider
October 27, 2009	ScanSafe, Inc.	Software-as-a-service (SaaS) web solutions provider
October 13, 2009	Starent Networks, Corp	IP-based mobile infrastructure supplier
October 1, 2009	Tandberg	Video collaboration solutions
April 9, 2009	Tidal Sortware	Data center application management and automation software creator
March 19, 2009	Pure Digital Technologies	Creator of consumer-oriented Flip Video brand
January 27, 2009	Richards-Zeta Building Intelligence	Provides software allowing businesses to integrate building infrastructure with IT applications
September 19, 2008	Jabber	Messaging and presence software provider
August 27, 2008	PostPath	E-mail and calendaring software provider.
July 23, 2008	Pure Networks	Home network management software developer
June 10, 2008	DiviTech A/S	DSM for able service providers
April 8, 2008	Nuova Systems	Data center hardware developer

Table 1-1.   Cisco's Acquisitions: 2005–2013 *(continued)*

Acquisition Date	Name	Description
November 1, 2007	Securent	Policy management software developer
October 23, 2007	Navini Networks	WiMAX 802.16e-2005 broadband wireless developer
September 27, 2007	Ltigent	Web-based business intelligence and analytics reporting
September 18, 2007	Cognio	Spectrum analysis and management for wireless networks
May 21, 2007	BroadWare Technologies	IP-based video surveillance software
March 28, 2007	SpansLogic	Processor manufacturer aimed at improving packet-processing speeds
March 15, 2007	WebEx Communications	Collaboration solutions
March 13, 2007	NeoPath Networks	File storage management
February 21, 2007	Reactivity	Extensible Markup Language (XML) gateway provider
February 8, 2007	Five Across	Customer-oriented social networking for businesses
January 4, 2007	IronPort Systems	Messaging security appliance development
December 15, 2006	Tivella	Digital signage provider
November 13, 2006	Greenfield Networks	Routing and switching manufacturer
October 25, 2006	Orative Corporation	Mobile voice collaboration
August 21, 2006	Arroyo Video Solutions	Video-on-demand
July 6, 2006	Meetinghouse Data Communications	Wireless security software
June 8, 2006	Metreos Corporation	Voice over IP application development
June 8, 2006	Audium Corporation	VoiceXML speech self-service application development and management
November 29, 2005	Intellishield Alert Manager	Web-based security intelligence

Table 1-1.   Cisco's Acquisitions: 2005–2013

Cisco Solutions

Cisco touts itself as the premier "end-to-end enterprise solutions provider" in internetworking. What this means in English is that Cisco has the breadth of product line functionality to fulfill virtually any customer requirement, whether integrated voice/data, optical Ethernet backbones, or integration to VMware environments. In practical terms, Cisco has been able to do this because of its foresight and raw cash. Having over $180 billion in market capitalization at the end of 2003 gave the company the financial muscle between now and then to fill product-line gaps and enter emerging areas by either intensive internal R&D or going out and acquiring the best-of-breed provider. Cisco has acquired well over 70 companies over the past ten years. Each acquisition seems to have been made to assimilate an emerging technology, not to buy the smaller company's installed customer base.

When the company started, Cisco focused on one thing—delivering internetworking capabilities. But over the years, Cisco has stuck its thumb in many pies. Now, while internetworking is its core service, it has expanded on that service to deliver a multitude of other services. Let's take a look at some of Cisco's most interesting, and innovative, services that help keep business and industry productive and dynamic.

Cisco Unified Wireless Networks

It's no secret that smartphones have changed the face of business and regular phone use. To help with that evolution for business, Cisco has introduced its Cisco Unified Wireless Network. This solution (and its accompanying gear) accommodates real-time business-critical application, is secure, and mobile.

The reality is that this technology isn't just "nice" to have—it's necessary. Businesses rely on the amenities afforded by WLANs. They rely on wireless applications, text messaging, voice services, and the like. To achieve this, Cisco Unified Wireless Network combines a solid WLAN infrastructure with high levels of security and wireless services.

 NOTE One of the problems Cisco sought to ameliorate comes in the guise of security. When the organization did not have its own secure WLAN, employees were increasingly deploying their own solutions, which put the whole network at risk.

Cisco Unified Wireless Network delivers scalable, manageable, and secure WLANs to both wired and wireless users. The solution addresses not only the needs of client devices, but also those of its access points and other infrastructure devices. The network is composed of five devices:

- Client devices
- Access points
- Network unification
- Network management
- Mobility services

As the solution grows in size, each element adds capabilities, working with the devices above and below it to create a more utilitarian, secure solution.

TelePresence

In *Star Trek,* Captain Kirk (or Picard or any of the rest of them, for that matter) would talk to Starfleet Command or the captain of a nearby ship on the bridge's giant view screen. This was useful, because it prevented all-out interstellar war with the Klingons because someone forgot to end their e-mail with a smiley face emoticon. Cisco brings us a bit closer to that vision of the future with its TelePresence solution.

 NOTE   TelePresence is a larger animal than just these conference rooms—we'll expand on Cisco's TelePresence line in future chapters. But for this discussion, we're just focusing on the conferencing solution.

Introduced in 2006, Cisco TelePresence allows video conferencing via giant monitors. It gives the productivity and interpersonal communication that comes with a person-to-person meeting, but without having to get on an airplane and travel across the country to accomplish it.

Cisco TelePresence is accomplished in a room made to achieve that lifelike meeting experience (you pay for the time used—but some companies even have their own TelePresence conference rooms). Rooms come in varying sizes, from a small room (CTS-500) with a lone, 37" 1080p television, to a large room (CTS-3200) that can accommodate 18 people with three 65" displays and a high fidelity audio system.

The benefits of using Cisco TelePresence include

- **Streamlined collaboration**   People thousands of miles apart (and often in multiple locations) can connect in a real-time environment.

- **Better communications**   One of the problems with phone calls or e-mails is that the interpersonal cues that we rely on in face-to-face meetings are severely limited or gone altogether. TelePresence maintains those cues and helps eliminate misunderstanding, thus creating a more productive meeting.

- **Stronger relationships**   Co-workers, clients, vendors, and other partners can interact frequently and more interpersonally than via phone calls, e-mails, or even conference calls.

- **Expense**   Time and money in travel are saved by using TelePresence. The solution eliminates the time needed to pack, travel, and deal with jet lag. It also reduces the carbon footprint from all that traveling.

 NOTE   More than 2,000 Cisco TelePresence rooms have already been deployed.

Data Center and Virtualization

Businesses no longer rely on mainframes or even a simple client/server model for their computing needs. Computing is a complex system that depends on intelligent infrastructure that can scale to respond to a company's unique needs. Cisco's solution to the dynamic needs of business computing is its Cisco Unified Data Center architecture.

Server Virtualization The Cisco Unified Computing System (UCS) is optimized for virtualization that unites compute, network, and storage services into a single, unified system. Cisco UCS benefits include

- Merged workloads that reduce operating, capital, space, power, and cooling expenses
- The ability to dynamically move workloads within a virtualized environment
- Optimized performance
- The ability to scale existing applications (or deploy new ones) by creating more virtual machines
- High availability and disaster recovery

Cisco has partnered with Microsoft, Red Hat, and VMware to deliver virtualization services. By using such a solution, businesses can

- Respond quickly to changing IT demand
- Reduce costs
- Simplify operations

Cisco Unified Data Center provides such technologies and goals as:

- Virtualization and server consolidation
- Private cloud computing
- Application-as-a-service (AaaS) and infrastructure-as-a-service (IaaS)

Desktop Virtualization Desktop virtualization is enhanced through Cisco Virtualization Experience Infrastructure (VXI). Using Cisco VXI, IT professionals can deliver

- Simplified desktop operations with fewer servers and simplified cable management
- Secure VM-aware networking and security for virtual desktops
- Scalable performance

Private Clouds Another important component of Cisco's data center and virtualization solution is its ability to create and manage private clouds. These provide strong ways to manage an organization's IT challenges. Private clouds help reduce cost, increase efficiency, and deliver new business models to make the organization more agile and efficient.

Cisco's private cloud solutions include an infrastructure that dynamically allocates resources within a single data center and across multiple centers.

Recent Acquisitions and Their Impact

Cisco's ongoing acquisitions show how it continues to diversify and cover its technological bases. With technology taking off in so many different directions, Cisco is ensuring that it will remain a player no matter where the technology goes.

Let's take a look at some recent acquisitions and talk about how they impact Cisco's overall strategy and offerings.

Nuova Systems One of Cisco's more interesting acquisitions was 2008's purchase of Nuova Systems, a manufacturer of high-performance data center equipment. While the purchase of a networking gear company is somewhat unremarkable and, to be frank, sort of boilerplate stuff at this point, what is more interesting is that the purchase was considered a "spin-in."

When you look at Cisco's portfolio, the Nuova spin-in brought Cisco impressive technology for data centers, and it also brought several experienced networking experts. And it should: Many of them were former Cisco executives. A spin-in is something Cisco has honed over the past 15 years. In this model, a few Cisco employees break off from the company to start their own venture and then rejoin Cisco when the venture is acquired by Cisco.

The Nuova acquisition brought a 10-gigabit Ethernet switch that supports unified fabric and virtualization services. The idea is that it would improve how data center servers communicate and share resources. The switch was developed in collaboration between Cisco and Nuova, relying on Cisco technologies, including Cisco's Nexus operating system (NX-OS).

Cisco initially invested in Nuova Systems in 2006, purchasing about 80 percent of the company. Before the acquisition was complete, Nuova was a majority-owned subsidiary of Cisco.

Nuova was Cisco's 126th acquisition, but Cisco CEO John Chambers noted that this acquisition was different because of the scope and scale of the technology involved.

"Out of the 126 acquisitions we've done, there are probably less than a dozen that signaled a major market transition for Cisco," said Chambers. "Some of these milestones include Crescendo in the switching market, Scientific-Atlanta in the service provider market, and WebEx in the collaboration and Web 2.0 categories. Nuova's product pipeline—which extends well beyond the Nexus 5000—has the potential to be the catalyst to another significant market transition for Cisco."

Acquisition by spin-in was a tack Cisco developed to make innovation more efficient. Chambers explains why they opted to change their methods for this particular acquisition.

"Cisco has literally written the book on technology acquisitions," noted Chambers. "To maintain this strategic advantage, we continually explore new ways to acquire companies and bring new technologies and talent into Cisco. In the case of Nuova Systems, the advantage of a spin-in is that you can jointly develop well-integrated products by closely sharing your technology, expertise, and product roadmaps. The acquired technologies of a spin-in become part of Cisco's technology architecture in a much shorter time than with traditional acquisition methods."

The spin-in strategy was not only used with Nuova. In 2012 the company invested $100 million to create a startup called Insieme that will develop products for software-defined networking (SDN) environments. Insieme was started by three Cisco engineers, and Cisco holds the option to buy the spin-in company for $750 million.

The acquisition model is interesting because it may mark the lack of ability for Cisco to innovate in-house. Because Cisco is such a big company, it may be that, in order to innovate, they have to create a new company to develop the technology and then buy it back.

Tandberg   In 2010, Cisco acquired Oslo, Norway–based video communications developer Tandberg in order to add TelePresence to its portfolio. The acquisition brought the complete line of Tandberg's products to Cisco's TelePresence portfolio.

TelePresence uses large displays to make users feel like they are at a face-to-face meeting, and has been used by such companies as PepsiCo and Bank of America in order to reduce travel expenses and facilitate better collaboration between meeting attendees.

Under the deal, Cisco purchased all outstanding shares of Tandberg for 19 billion kroner, or US$3.3 billion.

"We strongly believe that TelePresence, the next generation of video conferencing, along with Cisco's entire rich collaboration portfolio, powers this new way of working where everyone, everywhere can be more productive through the pervasive use of video and face-to-face collaboration," Marthin De Beer, a Cisco senior vice president, said in a statement.

ScanSafe   Cloud computing is the new "it" thing in the world of computers. Okay, that's not completely accurate. Cloud computing was the "it" thing a few years ago, but it remains an important part of the computing world. To help improve its place in the world of cloud computing, Cisco acquired ScanSafe in 2009.

ScanSafe is the developer of software-as-a-service (SaaS) web security solutions suited for large enterprises down to small businesses.

The acquisition of ScanSafe was seen as a way to build a borderless network security architecture. The ScanSafe acquisition built on a previous acquisition of content security provider IronPort, developer of a web appliance. Adding ScanSafe software to the IronPort appliance expands Cisco's cloud-based security offerings.

Cisco Innovation

Not all of Cisco's solutions technologies were buyouts; some were developed in-house (although many of the major technology additions were through acquisition). The key factor in each is whether Cisco can successfully integrate the new technology into the company's unifying IOS architecture (also known as *fusion*). Despite the wishes of certain competitors, so far, Cisco has done fairly well at that, with some exceptions. Here's an overview of the major solutions areas:

- **IOS feature sets**   IOS can be purchased *a la carte* for many devices, to obtain the functionality needed to deal with the customer's installed environment, whether IBM SNA, Novell NetWare, Bonjour, or vanilla IP.

- **Metro Ethernet**   Cisco has invested heavily in ATM technology, with the StrataCom buyout bringing a full line of ATM WAN switches, multiservice ATM switches, and edge concentrators. Cisco also purchased a company called LightStream to obtain the LightStream 1010 ATM module for connecting to ATM campus LANs.

- **Voice/data integration**   To consolidate its position in the emerging VoIP market, Cisco offers the VCO/4K open programmable voice/data switch, Cisco-to-circuit-switched gateways, and other voice integration products.

- **Network management**   Several disparate management software applications, both homegrown and acquired, are slowly being melded together under the CiscoWorks banner. Right now, things are still a bit of a mess, with three more-or-less standalone products: Resource Manager Essentials for managing routed networks, CWSI Campus for managing switched networks, and NetSys Baseliner for designing network topologies. CWSI and NetSys were acquisitions. Additionally, security management is handled through CS-MARS, which was the result of the acquisition of Protego.

- **ISP connectivity**   Cisco offers "director" products for use by ISPs in managing their high-volume traffic loads. Cisco LocalDirector is a sophisticated server connection management system that manages traffic based on service requested, distribution method, and server availability. Cisco DistributedDirector is similar, but provides dynamic, transparent Internet traffic load distribution management between geographically dispersed servers.

- **Security**   CiscoSecure is the company's integrated client/server security management system. IOS itself incorporates many security commands at the client device level, and CiscoSecure keeps a central database of users, user authorizations, and security event history. Cisco offers the PIX Firewall for traffic-level security and Cisco ASA for traffic and application security. For those accessing a network across the Internet, Cisco offers VPN solutions that are matched with Cisco's products, which are including more and more VPN functionality. Cisco also offers an IOS feature set called IOS Firewall and Secure ACS, which is essentially an expanded set of IOS commands that allows configuration of most midrange and high-end Cisco routers with firewall functionality.

- **Storage area networking (SAN)**   The extent to which a computer network is functional goes beyond whether everyone in an organization has a computer on his or her desktop or whether the network is faster than greased lightning.

The material that courses through the network—namely, the data—must be stored somewhere. For organizations that have a need to store and maintain a great deal of data, storage area networks (SANs) are an increasingly popular option. SANs are communications platforms that interconnect servers and storage devices at gigabit speeds. Products such as the Cisco MDS 9000 Series of multilayer switches help provide an environment in which data can be maintained.

- **Content networking** In order to provide access to specific network content, many organizations are implementing content networking solutions. Content networking provides an intelligent way to route content where it is needed. For example, content networking can help feed e-learning, streaming media, and file distribution. Cisco has developed a number of tools and technologies to help facilitate content networking, including the 7300 Content Engine, which accelerates content delivery, improving scalability and content availability.

- **Wireless** A decade ago, wireless networking technology might have seemed too expensive to be a feasible option for networking. Now, however, wireless is a necessity, especially as smartphones and tablets enter the fray. Cisco is no stranger to the world of wireless, having developed its own enterprise products. However, the company has also extended its reach into the realm of home and small business wireless networking through the acquisition of Linksys in 2003.

- **Voice over IP (VoIP)** Computer networks aren't just useful for transporting data between servers and clients. By utilizing the popular Internet Protocol, telephone conversations can take place across computer networks. Cisco offers a number of devices to help facilitate VoIP, from handsets plugged into switches to wireless IP phones to VoIP-capable routers and switches. VoIP is a popular technology because it allows low-cost telephony within an organization—whether the organization is situated within one building or at branch locations spread across the world.

- **Video distribution** Delivering video across internetworks encompasses multimedia as well as videoconferencing. Anyone who has spent any time watching a movie on their computer or downloading an MP3 file knows how large these files can be. Cisco helps the delivery and management of such files with its Video Portal and Video Portal Manager systems.

These and other Cisco solutions are covered throughout this book. We won't go into them in any detail here; you need to get technical first. That process starts in the next chapter—a primer on internetworking technology basics.

CHAPTER 2 | Networking Primer

Ever wonder how the Internet really works? Most of us, at one time or another, have wondered what happens behind the scenes when surfing web pages, watching videos, sending e-mail, or downloading files. You know instinctively that there must be many devices linking you to the other computer, but how exactly is the connection made? What makes up a message, and how does it find its way through the seemingly chaotic Internet back to your desktop? After all, it wasn't that long ago that incompatibility between various makes and models of computers made exchanging data a headache. Now everybody can connect to the Internet to share data and services without a second thought. How did the computer industry pull it off?

Most laypersons think the answer is technology, and to a point they're right. But the whole answer is that the Internet was brought together by a combination of technology and standards—specifically, *de jure* and *de facto* technical standards. De jure standards are set by trade associations; de facto standards are set by brute economic force. All the routers and switches in the world couldn't form the Internet without standards to make hardware, software, and telecommunications equipment compatible.

The products fueling the Internet were introduced in Chapter 1. Now we'll cover the underlying architectures that made all that technology possible. An understanding of the technologies and standards underpinning an internetwork will give you a clear picture of what happens in the background when you click a link in your browser.

Bits and Bytes

Before going into details on internetworking, it's necessary to cover the basic concepts that explain how computer technology works. We'll do this "from the wire up" to help you understand why systems work the way they do.

The Internet's infrastructure is composed of millions of networking devices—routers, switches, firewalls, and access servers—loosely hooked together through a sophisticated global address system. They're linked mostly by twisted-pair copper cable to the desktop and big trunk lines running over very high-speed fiber-optic cable. However, for the most part, the Internet is a matter of millions of individual hardware devices loosely tied together by a global addressing scheme.

How Computers Understand Data

Networking devices are more or less the same as normal computer platforms, such as your PC. The biggest differences are in configuration: Most types of network equipment have no monitors or disks because they're designed to move data—not store it or present it. However, all network devices are computers in the basic sense that they have CPUs, memory, and operating systems.

Bits Compose Binary Messages

Computing is largely a matter of sending electrical signals between various hardware components. In a standard computer platform, the signals shoot around tiny transistors inside the CPU or memory and travel over ultra-thin wires embedded in printed circuit boards. Once on the outside, electrical signals travel over cables in order to move between devices.

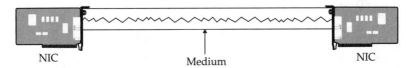

NIC   Medium   NIC

As signals are passed over the cable, network interface cards (NICs) at each end keep track of the electrical pulse waveforms and interpret them as data. The NIC senses each electrical pulse as either an On or Off signal. This is called *binary* transmission—a system in which each On pulse is recorded as the number 1 and each Off signal as the number 0. In machine language, these zeros and ones are *bits*, and a file of bits is a *binary* file.

Whether a signal represents a zero or a one is sensed by fluctuations in the voltage of electrical pulses (or light pulses, over fiber-optic media) during miniscule time intervals. These tiny time intervals are called *cycles per second*, or *Hertz (Hz)* in electrical engineering circles. For example, the CPU in a 100 Mbps NIC can generate 100 million cycles per second. In practical terms, the payoff is that the computer can process 100 million pulses per second and interpret them as either zeros or ones.

How Order Is Maintained Among Bits

All computers use binary transmission at the machine level. Bits are the basic raw material with which they work, usually as a collection of bits in a binary file. Binary files are the stuff that gets put into memory, processed through CPUs, stored on disks, and sent over cables. Both data and software programs are stored as binary files. If you were to look at a data file in any type of computer in binary format, you'd be staring at a page full of zeros and ones. Doing so might make your eyes glaze over, but computers can handle binary format because of *ordinality*—a fancy term for knowing what piece of information is supposed to appear in a certain field position.

The computer doesn't keep track of ordinal positions one by one. It instead keeps track of the bit position at which a field begins and ends. A *field* is a logical piece of information. For example, the computer might know that bit positions 121 through 128 are used to store a person's middle initial, as shown here.

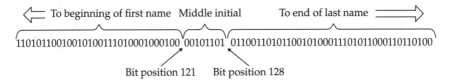

Computers are able to track bit orders with great precision by using clocks that time exactly where a CPU is in a stream of bits. By knowing where fields are, computers can build data from the wire up.

Computer Software Operates on Bytes

For simplicity, however, computers don't operate one bit at a time. There's an interim level one step up from bits called bytes—thus the expression "bits and bytes." A *byte* is a series of eight consecutive bits that are operated upon as a unit.

10110111	00110100	11001100	101110110	11000100
Byte	Byte	Byte	Byte	Byte

3-byte field   2-byte field

From a logical standpoint, the basic unit making up a data field is bytes. This not only makes systems run faster, but also makes them easier to program and debug. You'll never see a programmer declare how many bits long a field should be, but declaring byte lengths is routine. Keeping track of individual bit positions is often left to the computer.

Computer Words

Unlike software, CPUs must deal in bits. At the lowest level, computer hardware deals with On/Off electrical signals pulsing through its circuitry in bits. It would take too long to perform bit-to-byte translations inside a CPU, so computers have what's called a *word size*. The step up from a byte is a *word*, which is the number of bytes a CPU architecture is designed to handle each cycle.

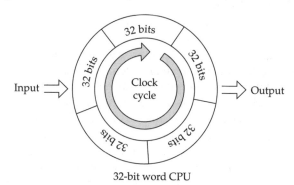

32-bit word CPU

For example, an Intel Xeon-based PC or server is a 32-bit word machine, meaning that it processes 32 bits per clock cycle. But as hardware miniaturization techniques have advanced—and the need to process data faster has grown—the industry has settled on 64-bit word architectures as the way to go. A variety of 64-bit machines is available from HP, IBM, Sun, and manufacturers using Intel's x86_64 and Itanium 2 architecture. Cisco devices use both 32- and 64-bit CPUs.

Compiled Software

The last step up is from bytes to something we humans can understand. As you probably know, software takes the form of source code files written by computer programmers.

The commands that programmers type into source code files are symbols instructing the computer what to do. When a program is written, it's changed into machine language (bits and bytes) by a *compiler,* which is a specialized application that translates software code into machine language files referred to as *executables* or *binaries.* For example, if code is written using the C++ programming language, it is translated through a C++ compiler.

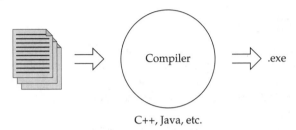

C++, Java, etc.

You may have noticed the .exe and .bin file extensions in your PC's directory. They stand for *executable* and *binary,* respectively. The Cisco IOS (Internetwork Operating System) is executable software. Actually, it's a package containing hundreds of executables that operate device hardware, forward packets, talk to neighboring network devices, and so on.

Computing Architectures

A *computing architecture* is a technical specification of all components that make up a system. Published computing architectures are quite detailed and specific, and most are thousands of pages long. But in certain parts, they are abstract by design, leaving the exact implementation of that portion of the architecture up to the designer.

Function
Functionality
Arrangement
Look and feel
Abstract Interface
Dependencies
Extensions
Products
Implementation

What separates an architecture from a regular product specification is the use of abstract layering. An *abstraction layer* is a fixed interface connecting two system components, and it governs the relationship between each side's function and implementation. If something changes on one side of the interface, by design it should not require changes on the other side. These layers are put in to help guarantee compatibility in two directions:

- Between various components within the system
- Between various products implementing the architecture

Abstraction between components stabilizes system designs, because it allows different development groups to engineer against a stable target. For example, the published interface between the layers in networking software allows hundreds of network interface manufacturers to engineer products compatible with the Fast Ethernet specification.

There are several important computing architectures—some more open than others. The Microsoft Windows/Intel 80x86 Wintel architecture is the stuff of legend.

Other important computing architectures include RAID (redundant array of inexpensive disks), Java, CORBA (Common Object Request Broker Architecture, a vendor-independent architecture and infrastructure that applications use to work together over networks), and dozens more. Yet perhaps the most important computing architecture ever devised is the one that created the Internet: the OSI reference model.

OSI Reference Model

The International Organization for Standardization (ISO), an international engineering organization based in Paris, first published the Open Systems Interconnection (OSI) reference model in 1978. This seven-layer model has become the standard for designing communication methods among network devices, and was the template used to design the Internet Protocol (IP).

The goal of the OSI reference model was to promote interoperability. *Interoperability* means the ability for otherwise incompatible systems to operate together in such a way that they can successfully perform common tasks. A good example of interoperability would be an Ethernet LAN transparently exchanging messages with a SONET ring.

The Seven-Layer Stack

The OSI model divides networks into seven functional layers and therefore is often called the *seven-layer stack*. Each layer defines a function or set of functions performed when data is transferred between applications across the network. Whether the network protocol is IP, Token Ring, or Apple's Bonjour, if it adheres to the OSI model, more or less the same rules are applied at each of the seven layers. The seven layers are outlined in Figure 2-1.

The Layers

As depicted in Figure 2-1, each layer is a protocol for communications between linked devices. Concerning network operations, the key thing to understand is that each layer on each device talks to its counterpart device to manage a particular aspect of the network connection. Concerning interoperability, the key is the fixed interface sitting between each layer. Abstract layering reduces what would otherwise be daunting complexity.

- **Layer 1, the physical layer**   Controls the transport medium by defining the electrical and mechanical characteristics carrying the data signal. Examples include twisted-pair cabling, fiber-optic cabling, coaxial cable, and serial lines. In the case of Wi-Fi, layer 1 is the radio that provides the frequency modulation and signal encoding.

- **Layer 2, the data-link layer**   Controls access to the network and ensures the reliable transfer of frames across the network. The best known data-link specification is Ethernet's Carrier Sense Multiple Access with Collision Detection. 802.11 Wi-Fi utilizes Carrier Sense Multiple Access with Collision Avoidance.

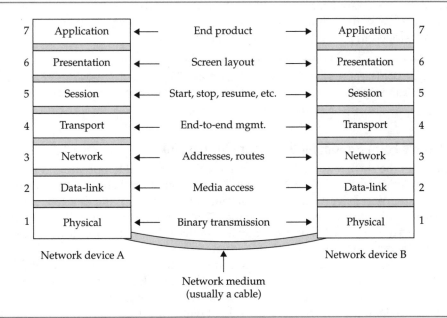

Figure 2-1.   Each OSI layer runs protocols to manage connections between devices.

■ **Layer 3, the network layer**   Manages the movement of data between different networks. Protocols at this layer are responsible for finding the device for which the data is destined. Examples include IPV4, IPV6, IPSec, ICMP, the now defunct Internetwork Packet Exchange (IPX), and Apple's Bonjour.

■ **Layer 4, the transport layer**   Ensures that data reaches its destination intact and in the proper order. The Transmission Control Protocol (TCP) and User Datagram Protocol (UDP) operate at this layer.

■ **Layer 5, the session layer**   Establishes and terminates connections and arranges sessions between two computers. Examples of session layer protocols include Remote Procedure Call (RPC) and the Lightweight Directory Access Protocol (LDAP).

■ **Layer 6, the presentation layer**   Formats data for screen display or printing. Examples of presentation layer protocols include the Lightweight Presentation Protocol (LPP) and NetBIOS.

■ **Layer 7, the application layer**   Contains protocols used to perform useful tasks over a network. Examples of network application protocols include the Simple Mail Transfer Protocol (SMTP) for e-mail, the Hypertext Transfer Protocol (HTTP) for web browsers and servers, Telnet for remote terminal sessions, Remote Desktop Protocol, and hundreds of others.

Layer 7 network applications are the reason the lower six layers exist. Many of these protocols saw their first use in Unix systems, given that the Unix operating system developed in parallel with the Internet.

 NOTE   Don't be misled by the name "application layer." This layer runs network applications, not applications software, such as spreadsheets or inventory. Network applications include e-mail, web browsing (HTTP), FTP, and other useful network tasks.

Peer Layers Form Protocol-Independent Virtual Links

Each layer in the stack relies on the layers above and below it to operate, yet each operates independently of the others, as if it were having an exclusive conversation with its counterpart layer on the other computer. Each layer on the device is said to have established a *virtual link* with the same layer on the other device. With all seven virtual links running, a *network connection* is established, and the two devices are talking as if they were wired directly together.

For example, in Figure 2-2 the sending computer, the Wi-Fi-connected Wintel PC on the left (Host A), processes downward through the stack to send a message, and the Linux mainframe (Host B) receives the message by processing it upward through its stack to understand the data (an FTP download request, in this example). The computers then reverse the process by working through their stacks the other way—this time, for the Linux mainframe to download a file to the Wintel PC through the FTP application.

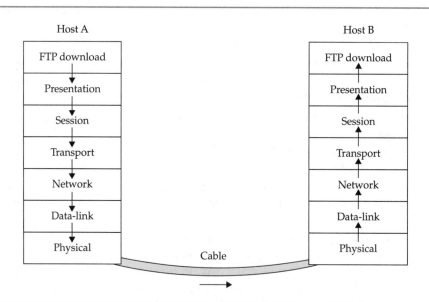

Figure 2-2.   Messages are processed up and down through the seven-layer stack.

In Figure 2-2, you begin to see how the Internet was able to interconnect the world's computers. Because the layers are abstracted and operate independently of one another, the FTP application can successfully run over different implementations of the OSI model—in this example, 4G LTE and Ethernet. You can see that the FTP application doesn't care about the incompatibilities inherent between Windows XP and Linux mainframes, or even those between the 4G LTE and Ethernet network technologies. Its only concern is whether the connected devices are talking FTP in compliance with OSI rules.

OSI Implementation by Layer

Although the seven-layer stack is expressed in vertical terms, looking at things horizontally might help you understand how it works. This is because as a message is processed through the stack, its horizontal length changes.

The first three layers handle the network application being run (application layer), data representation formats (presentation layer), and connection logistics (session layer). These first three layers represent very little of the message. For example, port number 80 identifies which application to run as defined by a port number—the HTTP HTML web page application

---

 NOTE The name "port number" was an unfortunate choice by the IETF (Internet Engineering Task Force) engineers. It takes a while to get used to the fact that an IP port number refers to a software type, not a hardware port. On a related note, the term "socket" is an IP address paired with a port number.

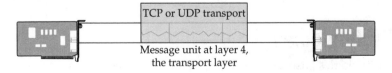

Message unit at the
application, presentation,
and session layers

At the transport layer, the message gets wider. Tasks performed here include making sure the receiver knows the message is coming, ensuring that the receiver won't be overwhelmed with too many packets at a time, making sure that packets sent were indeed received, and retransmitting packets that were dropped. Transport protocols include the Transmission Control Protocol (TCP) and User Datagram Protocol in the TCP/IP suite and the Stream Control Transport Protocol.

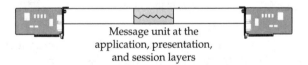

TCP or UDP transport

Message unit at layer 4,
the transport layer

At the network layer, the message gets a bit wider and becomes a *packet* (also called a *datagram*). Each packet's header has a logical (not physical) network address that can be used to route the message through the internetwork. Network layer protocols include the IP portion of the TCP/IP protocol suite and the Internet Group Multicast Protocol, among others.

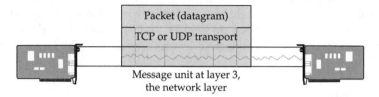

Message unit at layer 3,
the network layer

At the data-link layer, the binary information is read and encased into a format called a *frame*. The precise format for a frame is specified by the network protocol on which the NIC is operating—Ethernet or a WAN technology such as T1, for example. Each frame's header contains so-called media access control (MAC) addresses, which are unique identifiers that act as a kind of serial number for hardware devices.

At the physical level, a message is a series of pulses. The device works to encode or decode the pulses into binary zeros and ones to begin sorting out discrete message units. This signal processing is done in hardware on the network interface card, not in software.

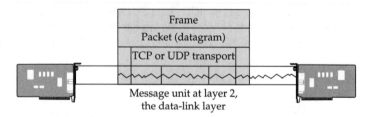

Message unit at layer 2,
the data-link layer

Once all the message-handling protocol information has been stripped away, you're left with payload data. There are many individual message units within a transmission. A network connection is made using a stream of packets, and each individual packet's data cargo contributes to the complete data file the connection needs—a web page download, for example.

Payload data differs by application. For example, a Telnet session will send tiny data files to indicate a keystroke or a carriage return, which may be all contained in a packet or two. At the opposite extreme, an FTP file transfer may send millions of bytes of data spread across thousands of packets.

Network Technologies

Network technologies (also called LAN technologies or network specifications) are used to run the basic unit of all internetworks—the LAN segment. The most widely known network technology is Ethernet, but there are several others, including multiple varieties of wireless (Wi-Fi), cellular Internet, and SONET.

It needs to be stated that Ethernet has displaced the vast majority of its competition. Fiber Distributed Data Interface (FDDI), Copper Distributed Data Interface (CDDI), Asynchronous Transfer Mode (ATM), and Token Ring are all but extinct from campuses and data centers. However, because ATM is still relevant today at a carrier level and its technology is utilized as part of the Synchronous Optical Network (SONET) specification, we will elaborate on it in a section titled "Optical Transport Network," later in this chapter, that's dedicated to carrier-grade networking.

Network technologies are implemented at the data-link layer (layer 2) of the seven-layer OSI reference model. Put another way, network technologies are largely characterized by the physical media they share and how they control access to the shared medium. This makes sense, if you think about it. Networking is connectivity; but to be connected, order must somehow be maintained among those users doing the sharing. For that reason, layer 2 is also called the *media access control layer*, or *MAC layer* for short. The message unit format at this level is the data frame, or just frame.

As such, most network technologies (Ethernet, Token Ring, FDDI, and so on) in and of themselves can only deal with MAC addresses (those serial number–like device identifiers mentioned earlier). A network layer protocol such as IP is needed to route messages through the internetwork. Network technologies alone can only support switched internetwork operation—good only for local areas or simple paths over longer distances, where not much guidance is needed. Network technologies are used at opposite ends of the spectrum:

- **Access LANs (distribution)**   Accept cabling from devices, tie workgroups together, and share resources such as departmental printers and servers
- **Backbone LANs (core)**   Link access LANs and share resources such as database servers, mail servers, and so on

Access LANs, formed by hubs or access switches, give users and devices connectivity to the network at the local level, usually within a floor in an office building. Backbone LANs, formed by routers or LAN switches, tie together access LANs, usually within a building or office campus. Routed internetworks are typically used to distribute traffic between the two.

Ethernet

Xerox Corporation developed version 1 of Ethernet during the early 1970s. Over the subsequent decade, Xerox teamed with Intel and Digital Equipment Corporation to release Version 2 in 1982. Since that time, Ethernet has become the dominant network technology standard. Thanks mostly to economies of scale, the average cost per Ethernet port is now far lower than that of a Token Ring port. Indeed, it has become so much a de facto standard that many manufacturers are integrating Ethernet NICs into computer motherboards in an attempt to do away with the need for separate NIC modules.

Ethernet Architecture

Ethernet operates by contention. Devices sharing an Ethernet LAN segment listen for traffic being carried over the wire and defer transmitting a message until the medium is clear. If two stations send at about the same time and their packets collide, both transmissions are aborted, and the stations back off and wait a random period of time before retransmitting. Ethernet uses the Carrier Sense Multiple Access with Collision Detection (CSMA/CD) algorithm to listen to traffic, sense collisions, and abort transmissions. CSMA/CD is the traffic cop that controls what would otherwise be random traffic. It restricts access to the wire in order to ensure the integrity of transmissions. Figure 2-3 illustrates the CSMA/CD process.

Because the medium is shared, every device on an Ethernet LAN segment receives the message and checks it to see whether the destination address matches its own address. If it does, the message is accepted and processed through the seven-layer stack, and a network connection is made. If the address doesn't match, the packets are dropped.

"All clear?"   Ethernet LAN Segment

"OK, send now"

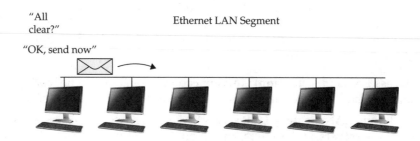

The station senses the "carrier" (the cable) to see if somebody else is transmitting. If the coast is clear, it transmits.

Collision detected; all stations back off, wait random interval, then retransmit.

Figure 2-3.   Ethernet access is controlled by carrier sensing and detecting frame collisions.

NOTE   An algorithm is a structured sequence of rules designed to handle variable processes in an orderly manner automatically. Algorithms are commonplace in computing and networking, because things move so fast there isn't time for a human to intervene.

Ethernet Implementations

Even apart from economies of scale, Ethernet is inherently less expensive, thanks to the random nature of its architecture. In other words, the electronics needed to run Ethernet are easier to manufacture because Ethernet doesn't try to control everything. In a general sense, it only worries about collisions.

Ethernet has several implementation options. The original Ethernet specification ran at 10 Mbps over coaxial cable or 10BaseT twisted-pair cable (T stands for *twisted-pair*—we'll cover cabling specifications in Chapter 6). Fast Ethernet runs at 100 Mbps and runs over 100BaseTX or 100BaseFX fiber-optic cable (F stands for *fiber)*. Gigabit Ethernet runs at 1,000 Mbps (or 1 Gbps) over 1000BaseTX or 1000BaseFX cable. A popular configuration choice right now is Gigabit Ethernet access LANs interconnected through a Gigabit Ethernet backbone LAN, and 10 Gigabit interconnecting data center components. As costs continuously fall, 10 Gbps is being used more and more to interconnect campus LANs. In fact, 40 Gbps links have been deployed widely by carriers, with 100 Gbps being deployed in limited fashion to date.

Gigabit, 10 Gigabit, 40 Gigabit, and 100 Gigabit Ethernet

Gigabit Ethernet is a 1,000 Mbps extension of the Ethernet standard. Gigabit Ethernet is sometimes also referred to as 1000BaseX in reference to the specification for the required copper or fiber-optic cabling. Gigabit Ethernet was promoted by the Gigabit Ethernet Alliance, a nonprofit industry group much like the Ethernet Alliance of today. The push for Gigabit Ethernet is largely motivated by its inherent compatibility with other Ethernet specifications (the original 10 Mbps Ethernet and 100 Mbps Fast Ethernet) and the need for bandwidth-hungry multimedia applications.

Gigabit Ethernet has thoroughly replaced FDDI as the backbone of choice. Its greatest advantage is familiarity, given that Ethernet is the pervasive technology. Originally designed as a LAN technology, at 1,000 Mbps, Gigabit Ethernet can scale to WAN configurations. Ethernet uses variable frame sizing—ranging between a standard 64 bytes and 1,518 bytes per frame up to 9,000 bytes in a "Jumbo" frame—and it does not enjoy the inherent QoS (quality of service) features "built in" to the ATM protocol. However, many network managers are biased in favor of Gigabit Ethernet because it's easy to configure and deploy. Also, it presumably doesn't introduce the added layer of complexity that LANE (LAN emulation) adaptation requires. Like ATM, Gigabit Ethernet backbones operate over a variety of fiber-optic cable types.

As speedy as a Gigabit Ethernet connection is, there is an even faster connection available on much of Cisco's gear, namely 10 Gigabit Ethernet. As the name suggests, 10 Gigabit Ethernet runs ten times faster than Gigabit Ethernet, at 10,000 Mbps. Whereas Gigabit Ethernet was a natural extension of Fast Ethernet, 10 Gigabit Ethernet differs in an important way: namely, the physical medium required to transport its packets. The difference applies in that until recently 10 Gigabit Ethernet did not run across inexpensive twisted-pair cable, as does its Ethernet brethren. Rather, because of the sheer speed of 10 Gigabit Ethernet, single-mode or multimode fiber optics was normally required. In past couple years we have seen the introduction of RJ-45- and 10GBaseT-based line cards available on Cisco's 4900M, 6500, and Catalyst switches and Nexus 2248 and 5500 platforms. We may see wider adaptation of this medium in the years to come as data centers are built using higher standards of copper cabling.

At this time, 10 Gigabit Ethernet is being deployed in WAN, MAN, data center virtualization, and backbone environments—anywhere large amounts of data need to be transported.

The benefit of these modular implementations of Ethernet is that network administrators can leverage their investments in Ethernet networks. In many cases, an organization can upgrade from 10/100 Mbps up to Gigabit or from Gigabit to 10 Gigabit Ethernet without having to reinvest as much in their core infrastructure.

As the section title suggests, there also exists 40 and 100 Gigabit Ethernet. These classes of Ethernet are the progression of the same technology with some additional specifications. They utilize bands or "lanes" of 10 Gb and 25 Gb Ethernet respectively, and include direct support for OTN (Optical Transport Networks), making the 40 and 100 Gbps standards preferable for use by Internet backbone providers.

Wireless

On the LAN front, one of the more exciting and utilitarian technologies of recent years has been the development and growth of wireless networking. At first, clients were able to connect at modest 11 Mbps speeds. However, with recent advances in the technology, clients are able to connect at 300 Mbps, and faster speeds are in development.

There are now a variety of standards for wireless networking, including the ones everybody hears about and many have in their homes: 802.11b, 802.11g, and 802.11n (802.11a is less common).

The first wireless LAN (WLAN) standard was devised in 1997 by the Institute of Electrical and Electronics Engineers (IEEE). It was slow by today's standard, running at a maximum of 2 Mbps. It did not really catch on, of course, so they came up with another standard in 1999 referred to as 802.11b. This commonly deployed standard runs at 11 Mbps.

While working on 802.11b, the IEEE also came up with another specification called 802.11a. This standard runs on the 5 GHz range of the wireless spectrum, whereas 802.11b runs at 2.4 GHz. Because it runs at a higher frequency, 802.11a can support speeds up to 54 Mbps. The downside is that high frequencies tend to be sensitive to obstructions such as furniture, floors, walls, and even trees. So the trade-off is often faster speeds for less range.

In 2003, the 802.11g standard was ratified. In a nutshell, it's like 802.11b, but uses a different algorithm for spreading data across channels—Orthogonal Frequency

Division Multiplexing (OFDM)—similar to 802.11a, so it is faster. It operates on the 2.4 GHz part of the wireless spectrum, just like 802.11b, but provides speeds up to 54 Mbps. Because it's backward compatible, 802.11g also supports 802.11b if the connecting equipment can't run the newer "g" standard.

The 2009 802.11n Wi-Fi standard laid out a multi-antenna, multichannel, multiband, multifrequency radio benchmark. There are single-band (2.4 GHz) 802.11n access points (AP), clients, and bridges capable of 150 Mbps. There is also dual-band (2.4 GHz and 5 GHz) Wi-Fi equipment being sold that supports upward of 300 Mbps. 802.11ac is a current draft specification that pushes connection speeds up to 866 Mbps, with the potential of more than 1 Gbps.

LANs

One of the most prevalent places where wireless is seen is in a LAN environment. Beyond the "hey, cool" factor of wireless (and it is pretty cool), WLANs allow you to connect without having to string Cat 6 cabling all over the place. This is useful in old buildings that might not have suspended ceilings or any place else where stringing cables would be prohibitive.

Connectivity is made possible using a wireless adapter in a client computer and an access point (AP) connected to a LAN switch. Computers then communicate with the network using the wireless card to communicate with the AP.

WANs

Wireless isn't limited just to the LAN world. In fact, wireless WANs are becoming a great option for businesses, especially those with buildings within a few miles of each other.

For example, using a couple of Cisco Aironet 1550 bridges and directional antennas, you can connect two networks with a minimum of fuss. You needn't apply for special licenses for radio broadcasts and, even better, you don't have to pay for a leased T1 or T3 line.

Wireless networking is a rich subject—so rich, in fact, that we've dedicated an entire chapter to it. Flip ahead to Chapter 11 for more information about wireless technologies in general and Cisco's wireless products in particular.

Optical Transport Network

As suggested previously, Optical Transport Network (OTN) refers to carrier-grade, nonstop networking. Many optical transceivers are available for Ethernet and such, but it is important to differentiate between those simple, fiber cable connectors and the Internet backbone systems operated by Internet providers known as OTN.

ATM (Asynchronous Transfer Mode) is no longer a prevalent operational technology within corporate campuses. However, it has been widely adopted at a higher level within the carrier networks because of its connection validation; that is to say it was designed for low-latency voice and video transmission and has been implemented as the modern replacement of our Plain Old Telephone Service (POTS) network backbone. As IP and Multi-Protocol Label Switching (MPLS) become more prevalent, ATM will also be displaced. For example, AT&T implemented a pure IP/ MPLS 40 Gbps network in 2008.

ATM is a data-link network technology that, like Ethernet, Token Ring, and FDDI, is specified at layer 2 of the OSI model. But that's where the similarities end. ATM transmissions send 53-byte cells instead of packets. A *cell* is a fixed-length message unit. Like packets, cells are pieces of a message, but the fixed-length format causes certain characteristics:

- **Virtual circuit orientation**   Cell-based networks run better in point-to-point mode, where the receiving station is ready to actively receive and process the cells.

- **Speed**   The hardware knows exactly where the header ends and data starts in every cell, thereby speeding up processing operations. Currently, ATM networks run at speeds of up to 40 Gbps.

- **Quality of service (QoS)**   Predictable throughput rates and virtual circuits enable cell-based networks to better guarantee service levels to types of priority traffic.

ATM doesn't have a media access control technology, per se. ATM is a switching technology, where a so-called virtual circuit is set up before a transmission starts. This differs sharply from LAN technologies such as Ethernet, which simply transmit a message without prior notification to the receiving host, leaving it up to switches and routers to figure out the best path to take to get there.

ATM cells are much smaller than Ethernet packets. Ethernet packet size can range from 64 bytes to over 1,500 bytes—up to about 25 times larger per message unit. By being so much more granular, ATM becomes that much more controllable. Like token-passing architectures, ATM's deterministic design yields highly effective bandwidth from its raw wire speed. In fact, ATM's effective yield is said to be well above even Token Ring's 75 percent. ATM is designed to run over fiber-optic cable operating the SONET specification.

Synchronous Optical Networking (SONET) is an ANSI standard specifying the physical interfaces that connect to carrier-grade fiber-optic cable at various speeds and utilizes multiple frequencies of light to enable separate control and data channels across a pair of strands of fiber. SONET makes transporting 56K Frame Relay, 1.5 Mbps T1, 45 Mbps T3, dedicated PBX voice traffic, and Gigabit Ethernet across the same physical cable simultaneously possible. SONET specifications are set up for various cable speeds called optical carrier levels, or OC for short. The following is a list of commonly used speeds, past and present:

- OC-1 52 Mbps fiber-optic cable
- OC-3 155 Mbps fiber-optic cable

- OC-12 622 Mbps fiber-optic cable

- OC-24 1.2 Gbps fiber-optic cable

- OC-48 2.5 Gbps fiber-optic cable

- OC-96 4.9 Gbps fiber-optic cable

- OC-192 10 Gbps fiber-optic cable

- OC-256 13.27 Gbps fiber-optic cable

- OC-768 40 Gbps fiber-optic cable

Most intercity links run a minimum of OC-192, although major Internet backbone providers are now wiring OC-768 and higher to meet ever-increasing bandwidth demands. The next standard for increasing speed has begun to emerge, with 100 Gbps G.709 being tested by universities.

WAN Technologies

Wide area networks (WANs) are constantly evolving. A *wide area network* is defined as a computer network spanning distance, from a home office user utilizing a dial-in modem to access their corporate internetwork up to and including the entire Internet. Ten years ago, WAN meant involving a mix of technologies: analog and digital, dial-in and T1. Today the vast majority of WAN topologies involve digital technology, sharing the public Internet and utilizing encryption techniques to keep data private. Most internetworks involve at least some remote users. Enterprises need to connect telecommuters and remote offices, ISPs need to take dial-ins from subscribers, and so on. To that end, there are two basic kinds of wide area networks:

- **Dial-ins**   A dial-in line establishes a point-to-point connection between a central location and one user, or a few at most. In the case of an analog modem, when the dial-in connection is no longer needed, the phone circuit is terminated. Dial-ins also share the stage with broadband technologies.

- **Trunks**   A *trunk* is a high-capacity point-to-point link between offices or distribution stations. Usually, a trunk will connect a number of remote users to a central site. Most trunks run over T1 (1.5 Mbps) or T3 (45 Mbps) telephone lines, although new technologies that allow trunking voice data on IP, such as ATM and Gigabit Ethernet, have been displacing analog connections to corporate PBX systems.

Looked at another way, telephone networks exist on two planes: between telephone switching stations, and between the switching station and the home or office. The zone between the neighborhood switching station and the home or business is often called the *last mile* for its relatively slow telecommunications infrastructure. The term isn't meant literally, of course—the zone between endpoints and the switching station sometimes can be several miles.

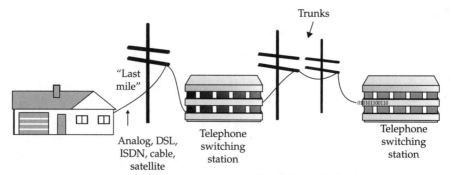

In case you didn't know, telephone switching stations are those small windowless buildings that sit inconspicuously in every neighborhood. Downtown switching stations are much bigger, usually taking up a few floors of the local telephone company building.

The so-called "last mile" has become a key battleground among internetwork vendors. This is because, with the boom in the Internet, the majority of dial-ins are individuals connecting to their ISPs from home. This includes telecommuters accessing their information on the corporate network, not just web surfers. A huge technology battle ensued over the preferred medium for the last mile. The fray has largely been between DSL and cable broadband providers. Satellite companies joined in, bypassing the telephone grid altogether. Broadband cable has taken some of the telephone companies' business away from them with home telephone service operating over broadband connections; the cellular broadband providers have taken a piece of the home user market as well as corporate telecommuters.

Dial-in Technologies

Two technologies have been introduced to bring digital bandwidth into the home and small office: ISDN and DSL. ISDN was introduced in the 1980s, but local telephone carriers were somewhat remiss in making it widely available. While not what one would really think of as dial-in, DSL superseded ISDN by delivering better speeds and wider availability.

Dial-in technologies differ from other WAN media in that connections made using them are temporary. In other words, once the computer user has finished with the session, the circuit is terminated by hanging up the telephone. To this day, most homes are connected through analog phone circuits. Because normal lines are analog, they require modems at each end to operate, and for that reason are referred to by some as *analog/modem* circuits.

The major problem with analog/modem circuits is that they're slow. What slows them down is that the acoustical signals use only a tiny fraction of the raw bandwidth available in copper telephone system cables because they were designed for voice, not data. This is why the state-of-the-art analog home connection is now 56 Kbps—glacially slow compared to the 1000 Mbps Gigabit Ethernet now standard inside office buildings.

ISDN

ISDN, which stands for Integrated Services Digital Network, was proposed as the first digital service to the home. The key improvement over analog/modem lines is that ISDN circuits are digital, and for that reason they use so-called CPEs (customer premise equipment) instead of modems (CPE is an old-time telephony term). ISDN is largely extinct.

ISDN creates multiple channels over a single line. A *channel* is a data path multiplexed over a single communications medium. (To *multiplex* means to combine multiple signals over a single line.) The basic kind of ISDN circuit is a BRI circuit (for Basic Rate Interface) with two so-called *B*, or *bearer*, channels for payload data. Figure 2-4 contrasts an analog/modem circuit with an ISDN BRI circuit.

Each B-channel runs at 64 Kbps, for a total of 128 Kbps payload bandwidth. Having separate B-channels enhances throughput for symmetrical connections—in other words, sessions characterized by the bidirectional simultaneous flow of traffic. A third channel, called the *D* (or *delta*) channel, carries 16 Kbps. The D-channel is dedicated

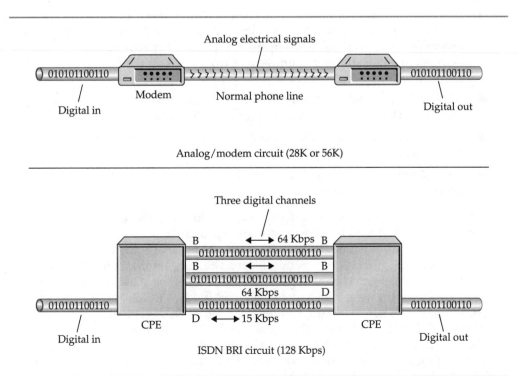

Figure 2-4.   An ISDN BRI circuit brings three digital channels into a home or business.

to network control instead of payload data. Separating control of overhead signals enhances ISDN's performance and reliability.

A second kind of ISDN circuit is a PRI circuit (for Primary Rate Interface). PRI is basically the same as BRI, except that it packages up to 23 B-channels plus one 64 Kbps D-channel, for up to 1.544 Mbps total payload bandwidth. Small businesses used PRI circuits to connect multiple users, competing at the low end of T1's traditional market niche.

DSL

DSL stands for Digital Subscriber Line. As the name implies, DSL also runs digital signals over copper wire. It uses sophisticated algorithms to modulate signals in such a way that much more bandwidth can be squeezed from existing last-mile telephone infrastructure.

DSL is an inherently asymmetric telecommunications technology. What this means is that data can be moved much faster downstream (from the local phone carrier to your home) than upstream. There are more than 10 types of DSL, but only two are important to this discussion (ADSL2+ and VDSL2):

- **ADSL** Asymmetric DSL is a two-way circuit that can handle about 6 Mbps downstream and 640 Kbps upstream.

- **DSL Lite** Also called G. Lite, DSL Lite is a slower, less expensive technology that can carry data at rates between about 1.5 Mbps and 6 Mbps downstream and from 128 Kbps to 384 Kbps upstream. The exact speeds depend on the equipment you install and your distance from the central office. DSL lite was not widely adopted.

- **ADSL2+** ADSL2+ can attain speeds of 24 Mbps downstream, 1.4 Mbps upstream. Double these figures if a pair of wiring called "G.Bond" is used.

- **VDSL Very High Speed DSL** VDSL can attain speeds of 52 Mbps downstream and 16 Mbps upstream.

- **VDSL2 Very High Speed DSL2** VDSL2 can attain speeds of 100 Mbps downstream and 100 Mbps upstream.

DSL's inherent asymmetry fits perfectly with the Internet, where most small office/ home office users download far more data than they upload.

The key fact to know is that DSL requires a special piece of equipment called a DSL modem to operate. Figure 2-5 depicts this. It's the DSL modem that splits signals into upstream and downstream channels. ADSL was the first of the standards to market, whereas ADSL2+ is the most widely deployed worldwide. VDSL2, however, is the fastest, and barring a new standard, will overtake the market eventually. VDSL2 also integrates with FTTH (aka Fiber to the Home), which ISPs are now providing.

Not requiring DSL signal splitting in the home makes DSL much more affordable than ISDN. To use most DSL circuits, you must be located no farther than about four or five miles from the telephone switching station. This distance has shortened as the

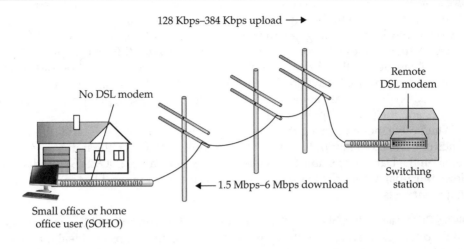

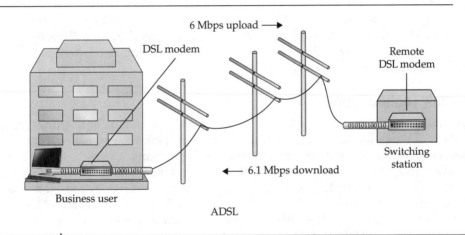

Figure 2-5. DSL modems split traffic into two directional channels to attain high bandwidth

phone companies have deployed fiber to suburbs and placed a required DSL Access Multiplexer (DSLAM) closer to the customers. This piece of equipment used to be located exclusively at a central office.

Cable Modems and Satellite Connections

Two more ways to gain dial-in access are more popularly found running into the back of your television set on a length of coaxial cable. Cable modems and satellite connections are popular ways to access the Internet at high speeds.

Cable Modem   A cable modem connects to an existing cable television feed and to an Ethernet network card in the computer. Though cable modems and dial-up modems provide network access and go by the moniker "modem," the two are very different devices. Although these devices go about their jobs in very different ways, most users will simply recognize this difference primarily in the realm of speed. Top-of-the-line dial-in modems over a Plain Old Telephone Service (POTS) will give up to 56 Kbps. Cable modem downloads range from 384 Kbps to 200 Mbps, depending on the service provider and the package purchased.

When cable modems made their debut, there were no standards, and different brands of cable modems could not talk to each other. However, the industry eventually united on the Data Over Cable Service Interface Specification (DOCSIS) standard. This allows third-party vendors to make compliant cable modems and has resulted in lower equipment costs.

Satellite Connection   If cable and DSL aren't options and you still feel the need for speed, you need look no further than the heavens. Satellite connections are ideal for those who want high-speed network access but are in locations that are not served by cable or DSL service.

Companies such as EchoStar Corp. offer satellite delivery of Internet content. Much like the digital television and movie services provided by 18-inch dishes bolted to the sides and roofs of millions of houses, these services utilize the high-bandwidth broadcasts to deliver high-speed Internet access.

WAN Trunk Technologies

As stated earlier, a trunk is any high-capacity point-to-point data link. Trunks can exist within buildings and office campuses, but they're best known as wide area network links between buildings, cities, regions, and even continents.

WAN technology has evolved markedly over the past decade, and not just with the Internet boom. For example, Frame Relay packet-switching technology proved dramatically less expensive than dedicated leased WAN lines. We'll briefly review the WAN technologies in use today. They all share common characteristics in that they're dedicated circuits (not dial-in and hang-up), with high bandwidth used to connect locations with many users, as opposed to small office/home office sites with one or two users.

Most enterprises are replacing leased-line WAN services with shared infrastructure services. Their primary motive is to save money, but flexibility is also a big benefit.

T1 and T3 Leased Lines

T1 and T3 are the predominant leased-line technologies in use in North America and Japan today. (There are rough equivalents in Europe called E1 and E3.) A leased-line circuit (or part of a circuit) is reserved for use by the enterprise that rents it—and is paid for on a flat monthly rate, regardless of how much it is used.

T1 uses a telecommunications technology called *time-division multiplexing (TDM)* to yield a data rate of about 1.5 Mbps. TDM combines streams of data by assigning each stream a different time slot in a set and repeatedly transmitting a fixed sequence of time slots over a single transmission channel. T1 lines use copper wire, both within and among metropolitan areas. You can purchase a T1 circuit from your local phone carrier or rent a portion of its bandwidth in an arrangement called *fractionalized T1*. Some ISPs are connected to the Internet through T1 circuits.

T3 is a faster option than T1. T3 circuits are dedicated phone connections that carry data at 45 Mbps. T3 lines are used mostly by *Tier 1 ISPs* (ISPs who connect smaller ISPs to the Internet) and by large enterprises. Because of their sheer bandwidth and expense, most T3 lines are leased as fractional T3 lines. T3 lines are also called *DS3* lines.

Frame Relay

Frame Relay switches packets over a shared packet-switching network owned by a carrier such as a regional telephone company, Verizon, or AT&T. As depicted in Figure 2-6 Frame Relay uses local phone circuits to link remote locations. The long-distance hauls are over a telecommunications infrastructure owned by the Frame Relay provider and shared among a number of other customers.

 NOTE   In this context, when we say that Frame Relay switches packets, the switching is a different technology than that of LAN switching.

The primary benefit of Frame Relay is cost efficiency. Frame Relay takes its name from the fact that it puts data into variable-sized message units called frames. It leaves session management and error correction to nodes it operates at various connection points, thereby speeding up network performance. Most Frame Relay customers rent

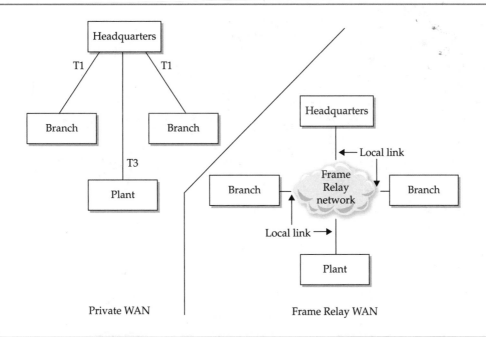

Figure 2-6.   Frame Relay can be an efficient WAN link for intermittent traffic.

permanent virtual circuits, or *PVCs.* A PVC gives the customer a continuous, dedicated connection without having to pay for a leased line, which uses dedicated permanent circuits. Frame Relay customers are charged according to level of usage. They also have the option of selecting between service levels, where QoS is programmed based on what priority the customer's frames are given inside the Frame Relay cloud.

Frame Relay networks themselves sit atop T1 or T3 trunks operated by the Frame Relay network operator. Use of Frame Relay makes economic sense when traffic isn't heavy enough to require a dedicated ATM connection.

VPN

VPNs, which stands for *virtual private networks,* are enterprise internetworks operated over the Internet. Many, many companies are forgoing all of the traditional WAN technologies and implementing some level of VPN connectivity. Site-to-site (S2S) and business-to-business (B2B) VPN internetwork connections are far more cost effective now that the Internet has progressed to the current level of robustness.

VPNs work by using encryption to "tunnel" across a given network path in order to reach remote enterprise locations. *Encryption* is the technique of scrambling data so that only a receiving station with the key to decode it can read it. Other techniques are applied to make sure data integrity is intact (all the contents are still there and unaltered) after a message has traversed a VPN tunnel. Figure 2-7 depicts how an enterprise might use a VPN to interconnect its sites.

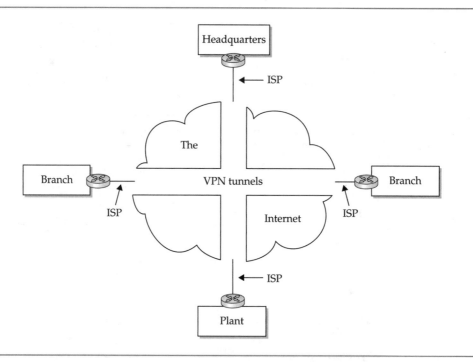

Figure 2-7. VPNs rely on tunneling and encryption to operate over the Internet.

TCP/IP

The Internet runs over TCP/IP, the Transmission Control Protocol/Internet Protocol. TCP/IP is actually a suite of protocols, each performing a particular role to let computers speak the same language. TCP/IP is universally available and is almost certainly running on the computers you use at work and at home. This is true regardless of LAN protocols, because LAN vendors have implemented TCP/IP compatibility in their products. For example, the latest Novell NetWare product can speak TCP/IP.

TCP/IP was designed by the Defense Advanced Research Projects Agency (DARPA) in the 1970s—the design goal being to let dissimilar computers freely communicate, regardless of location. Most early TCP/IP work was done on Unix computers, which contributed to the protocol's popularity as vendors got into the practice of shipping TCP/IP software inside every Unix computer. As a technology, TCP/IP maps to the OSI reference model, as shown in Figure 2-8. Looking at this figure, you can see that TCP/IP focuses on layers 3 and 4 of the OSI reference model. The theory is to leave network technologies to the LAN vendors. TCP/IP's goal is to move messages through virtually any LAN product to set up a connection running virtually any network application.

TCP/IP works because it closely maps to the OSI model at the lowest two levels—the data-link and physical layers. This lets TCP/IP talk to virtually any networking

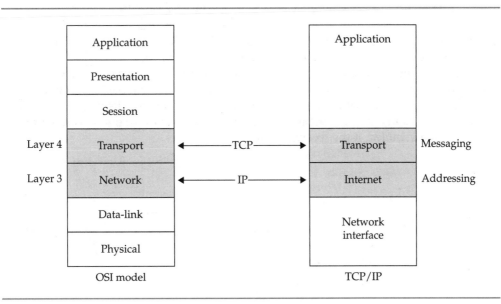

Figure 2-8.   The TCP/IP stack is compliant with the seven-layer reference model.

technology and, indirectly, any type of computer platform. TCP/IP's four abstract layers include

- **Network interface**   This allows TCP/IP to interact with all modern network technologies by complying with the OSI model.

- **Internet**   This defines how IP directs messages through routers over internetworks such as the Internet.

- **Transport**   This defines the mechanics of how messages are exchanged between computers.

- **Application**   This defines network applications to perform tasks such as file transfer, e-mail, and other useful functions.

TCP/IP is the de facto standard that unifies the Internet. A computer that implements an OSI-compliant layer network technology, such as Ethernet or Token Ring, has overcome incompatibilities that would otherwise exist between platforms such as Windows, Unix, Mac, IBM mainframes, and others. We've already covered layers 1 and 2 in our discussion of LAN technologies that connect groups of computers together in a location. Now we'll cover how computers internetwork over the Internet or private internetworks.

TCP/IP Messaging

All data that goes over a network must have a format so that devices know how to handle it. TCP/IP's Internet layer—which maps to the OSI model's network layer—is based on a fixed message format called the *IP datagram*—the bucket that holds the information making up the message. For example, when you download a web page, the stuff you see on the screen was delivered inside datagrams.

Closely related to the datagram is the packet. Whereas a *datagram* is a unit of data, a *packet* is a physical entity consisting of a message unit that passes through the internetwork. People often use the terms interchangeably; the distinction is only important in certain narrow contexts. The key point is that most messages are sent in pieces and reassembled at the receiving end.

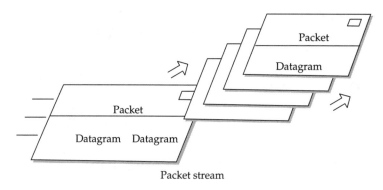

Packet stream

For example, when you send an e-mail to someone, it goes over the wire as a stream of packets. A small e-mail might be only 10 packets; a big one may be split into thousands. At the opposite extreme, a request-for-service message might take only a single packet.

One advantage of this approach is that if a packet is corrupted during transmission, only that packet need be re-sent, not the entire message. Another advantage is that no single host is forced to wait an inordinate length of time for another's transmission to complete before being able to transmit its own message.

TCP vs. UDP as Transport Protocols

An IP message travels using either of two transport protocols: TCP or UDP. TCP stands for Transmission Control Protocol, the first half of the TCP/IP acronym. UDP stands for User Datagram Protocol, used in place of TCP for less-critical messages. Either protocol provides the transport services necessary to shepherd messages through TCP/IP internetworks. TCP is called a *reliable* protocol because it checks with the receiver to make sure the packet was received, sending an ACK (acknowledgement) message when a transmission is complete. UDP is called *unreliable* or *connectionless* because no effort is made to confirm delivery. Both transport technologies operate at layer 4 of the OSI stack.

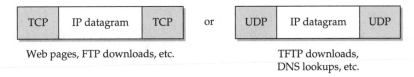

Web pages, FTP downloads, etc.   TFTP downloads,
                                              DNS lookups, etc.

Don't let the name TCP/IP throw you. TCP has no involvement in a UDP message. And while we're at it, don't let the name User Datagram Protocol throw you either. An IP message sent through TCP contains an IP datagram just like a UDP message does.

A key point to know is that only one transport protocol can be used to manage a message. For example, when you download a web page, the packets are handled by TCP with no involvement from UDP. Conversely, a Trivial File Transfer Protocol (TFTP) upload or download is handled entirely by the UDP protocol.

Which transport protocol is used depends on the network application—e-mail, HTTP web page downloads, network management, and so on. As we'll discuss, network software designers will use UDP where possible because it generates less overhead traffic. TCP goes to greater lengths to ensure delivery and sends many more packets than UDP to manage connections. Figure 2-9 shows a sampling of network applications to illustrate the division between the TCP and UDP transports.

The examples in Figure 2-9 highlight a few good points. First, FTP and TFTP do essentially the same thing—handle the transferring of data files. The major difference is that TFTP is mainly used to download and back up network device software, and it uses UDP because failure of such a message is tolerable (TFTP payloads aren't for end users, but for network administrators, who are lower priority). The Domain Name System (DNS), the service that translates from URLs to IP addresses, uses UDP for

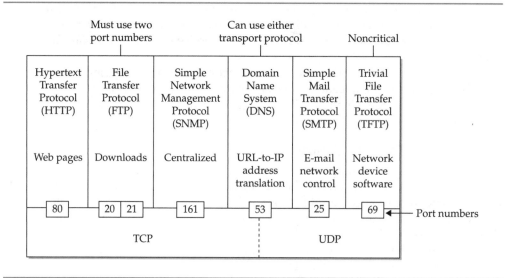

Figure 2-9.   TCP and UDP handle different network applications (port numbers).

client-to-server name lookups and TCP for server-to-server lookups. However, it may use only one of the two for a particular DNS lookup connection.

The IP Datagram Format

The datagram is the basic unit of data inside IP packets. The datagram's format provides fields both for message handling and for the payload data. The datagram layout is depicted in Figure 2-10. Don't be misled by the proportions of the fields in the figure; the data field is by far the largest field in most packets.

Computers connect. The packets making the connection contain your IP address in addition to the destination addresses. They also contain additional information such as an instruction to download a web page. The other 12 packet fields are for handling purposes.

A key fact about IP packets is that they are variable in length. For example, in Ethernet LANs, one packet might be 200 bytes long, another 1,400 bytes. IP packets can grow as large as 4,000 bytes in Token Ring packets.

NOTE   We're talking bytes instead of bits in this context because datagrams contain data, and computers prefer dealing with bytes. On the other hand, when discussing traffic streaming, say, over a cable, the unit of measure is bits—the preferred measure of networking.

A packet has two basic parts: header information and data. The data portion of the packet holds the cargo—the payload that's being sent across the network. The header

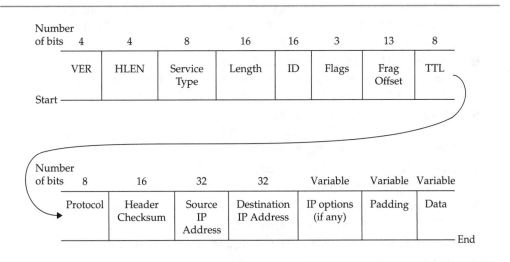

Figure 2-10. The IP datagram format is variable in length.

contains housekeeping information needed by routers and computers to handle the packet and keep it in order with the other packets making up the whole message.

Keep in mind that the CPU handling the packet needs to know where each field starts, down to the exact bit position; otherwise, the entire thing is just a bunch of meaningless zeros and ones. Notice that the three fields that can vary in length are placed toward the right side of the format. If variable-length fields were to the left in the format, it would be impossible for computers to know where the subsequent fields begin. The IP datagram fields are as follows:

- **VER** The version of IP being used by the station that originated the message. The current version is IP version 4. This field lets different versions coexist in an internetwork.

- **HLEN** Stands for *header length*. This tells the receiver how long the header will be so that the CPU knows where the data field begins.

- **Service Type** A code to tell the router how the packet should be handled in terms of level of service (reliability, precedence, delay, and so on).

- . **Length** The total number of bytes in the entire packet, including all header fields and the data field.

- **ID, Flags, and Frags Offset** These fields identify to the router how to packet fragmentation and reassembly, and how to offset for different frame sizes that might be encountered as the packet travels through different LAN segments using different networking technologies (Ethernet, FDDI, and so on).

■ **TTL** Stands for *Time to Live*. A number that is decremented by one each time the packet is forwarded. When the counter reaches zero, the packet is dropped. TTL prevents router loops and lost packets from endlessly wandering internetworks.

■ **Protocol** The transport protocol that should be used to handle the packet. This field almost always identifies TCP as the transport protocol to use, but certain other transports can be used to handle IP packets.

■ **Header Checksum** A *checksum* is a numerical value used to help ensure message integrity. If the checksums in all the message's packets don't add up to the right value, the station knows that the message was garbled.

■ **Source IP Address** The 32-bit address of the host that originated the message (usually a PC or a server).

■ **Destination IP Address** The 32-bit address of the host to which the message is being sent (usually a PC or a server).

■ **IP Options** Used for network testing and other specialized purposes.

■ **Padding** Fills in any unused bit positions so that the CPU can correctly identify the first bit position of the data field.

■ **Data** The payload being sent. For example, a packet's data field might contain some of the text making up an e-mail.

Port Numbers

A port number identifies the network application to the upper layers of the stack. For example, each packet in an e-mail transmission contains the port number 25 in its header to indicate the Simple Mail Transfer Protocol (SMTP). There are hundreds of assigned port numbers. The Internet Assigned Numbers Authority (IANA) coordinates port number assignments according to the following system:

■ **Numbers 1023 and below** "Well-known" ports assigned to public applications (such as SMTP) and to companies to identify network application products

■ **Numbers 1024 to 49151** Reserved for and registered and assigned for use by specific companies

■ **Numbers 49152 to 65535** Assigned dynamically by the end-user application using the network application

Port numbers help the stations keep track of various connections being processed simultaneously. For example, for security reasons, most firewalls are configured to read port numbers in every packet header.

Many beginners are confused as to exactly how port numbers are used. For example, if you're trying to connect to a web server from your PC, you might think that both end-stations would use port 80 (HTTP) to conduct a web page download. In fact, the requesting client uses a random port number in the request packet's source port field and uses assigned HTTP port number 80 only in the destination port field. Figure 2-11 demonstrates how port numbers are used during a transmission.

The client uses a random port number to help keep track of conversations during a connection. A *conversation* is a discrete port-to-port transaction between end-stations. There can be any number of conversations within a single connection.

Looking at Figure 2-11, you can see that the page downloaded in step 2 may have included one of those annoying embedded HTML commands that automatically create a new browser window without your asking for it (a pop-up). The pop-up window requests that a new page be downloaded, thereby creating a whole new stream of HTML code, text, GIFs, and JPEGs to handle—a second conversation, in other words.

At the server end, however, a widely recognized port number, such as 80 for HTTP, must be used—otherwise, the thousands of hosts hitting the web server would have no idea what application to ask for.

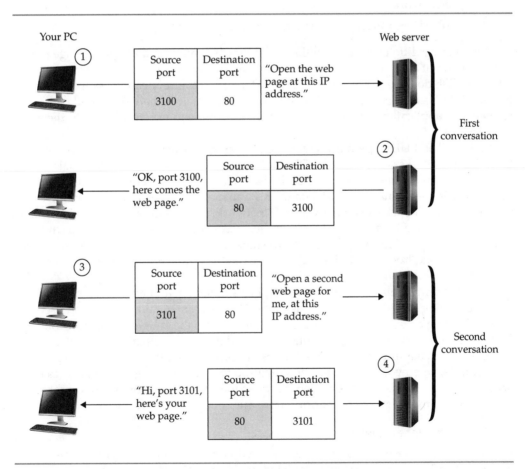

Figure 2-11. Port numbers identify the network application the message is using.

The Transport Layer

The way packets are handled differs according to the type of traffic. There are two techniques for sending packets over a TCP/IP internetwork: connection oriented and connectionless. In the strict sense, of course, a connection is made whenever a packet reaches its destination. *Connection oriented* and *connectionless* refer to the level of effort and control that is applied to handling a message.

Every packet that goes over an internetwork consumes bandwidth, including overhead traffic. Connection assurance mechanisms are not used for certain types of TCP/IP traffic in order to minimize overhead packets where tolerable. Discrimination in packet handling is achieved by the choice of transport protocol:

- **TCP**   The connection-oriented mechanism to transport IP packets through an internetwork
- **UDP**   The connectionless mechanism for transporting packets

The primary difference between the two is that TCP requires an ACK message from the receiver that acknowledges the successful completion of each step of a transmission, whereas UDP does not. That's why UDP is often called the connectionless transport. Because UDP is connectionless, it's faster and more efficient than TCP. UDP is used for network applications, where it is considered tolerable to retransmit should the message fail.

Both TCP and UDP operate at layer 4 of the OSI stack, just above the IP network layer. Internetworks run TCP and UDP traffic simultaneously, but an individual message may be sent using only one of the two. The difference between the two is manifested in the format of the IP datagram's transport wrapper, called a *segment*. When a stream of packets is sent over an IP network, the packets are wrapped in either a TCP segment or a UDP segment and handled according to the rules of that particular transport protocol. These segments hold the data used to transport the packet through the internetwork. Keep in mind that this is not payload data, but information used to manage transportation of the packets.

A packet sent through a TCP connection has a much longer header than one traveling through UDP. The extra fields in the TCP header contain information used for establishing connections and handling errors. TCP is the subsystem responsible for establishing and managing IP connections, and it uses a sophisticated handshake procedure to make sure the two end-stations are properly set up for the transmission. For example, when you click a hyperlink to jump to a new web page, TCP springs into action to "shake hands" with that web server so that the page is downloaded properly. TCP also has procedures for monitoring transmissions and error recovery.

The TCP Segment Format

IP datagrams are placed inside TCP segments when transport is managed by the TCP protocol. The TCP segment format, depicted in Figure 2-12, holds certain pieces of data for establishing TCP connections and managing packet transport.

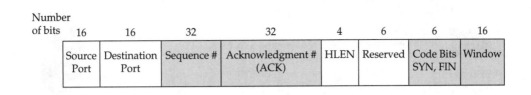

Figure 2-12.   The TCP packet segment holds data used to closely manage packet transport.

The data fields in the TCP segment reflect the protocol's focus on establishing and managing network connections. Each is used to perform a specific function that contributes to ensuring that a connection runs smoothly:

- **Source port**   The application port used by the sending host.

- **Destination port**   The application port used by the receiving host.

- **Sequence number**   Positions the packet's data to fit in the overall packet stream.

- **Acknowledgment number**   Contains the sequence number of the next expected TCP packet, thereby implicitly acknowledging receipt of the prior message.

- **HLEN**   Stands for *header length*. Tells the receiver how long the header will be so that the CPU knows where the data field begins.

- **Reserved**   Bits reserved for future use by the Internet Engineering Task Force (IETF).

- **Code bits**   Contains SYN (synchronize) bits to set up a connection or FIN (finish) bits to terminate one.

- **Window**   Contains the number of bytes the receiving station can buffer or the number of bytes to be sent. This field sets a "capacity window" to ensure that the sender does not overwhelm the receiver with too many packets all at once.

Establishing a TCP Connection

The TCP connection process is often referred to as the "three-way handshake" because the second step involves the receiving station sending two TCP segments at once. The steps in Figure 2-13 show a couple of the TCP segment fields in action. The first TCP segment's sequence number serves as the initial sequence number—the base number used to keep subsequent packets in proper sequence. The Sequence field is used for reassembling out-of-sequence packets into a cogent message at the receiving end.

The example in Figure 2-13 shows a PC connecting to a web server. But any type of end-stations could be talking—a server connecting to another server to perform an e-commerce transaction, two PCs connecting for an IRC (Inter-Regional Connectivity) chat session, or any connection between two end-stations over an IP network.

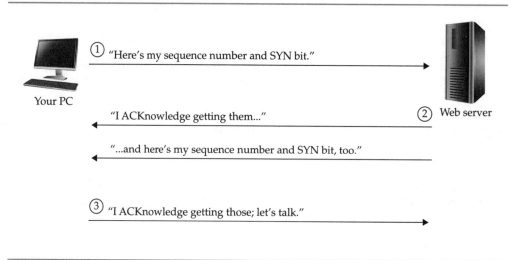

Figure 2-13. The three-way TCP handshake process passes SYN and ACK.

TCP Windowing

It's not enough just to establish the connection; the session must be dynamically managed to make sure things run smoothly. The major task here is to ensure that one station doesn't overwhelm the other by transmitting too much data at once.

This is done using a technique called *windowing,* in which the receiving station updates the other as to how many bytes it's willing to accept. Put another way, the station is saying how much memory buffer it has available to handle received packets. The TCP windowing process is depicted in Figure 2-14, with a too-small window size shown on the left and a proper window size on the right.

Window size is communicated through the ACK messages. As you can see by looking at Figure 2-14, obviously a 1,000-byte window size is no good because it causes a one-to-one ratio between incoming packets and outgoing ACKs—way too much overhead in relation to payload traffic. The right half of Figure 2-14 shows a better window size of 10,000 bytes. As the figure shows, this lets the sending station fire off as many packets as it wants, as long as the cumulative total stays beneath the 10,000-byte window size limit. This permits a more favorable payload-to-overhead message ratio.

The message in the lower-right area is shaded to highlight the fact that window sizes are adjusted dynamically during a session. This is done because of changing conditions within the receiving station. For example, if a web server suddenly picks up connections from other sending hosts, it has less memory buffer available to process your packets, and it adjusts your window size downward.

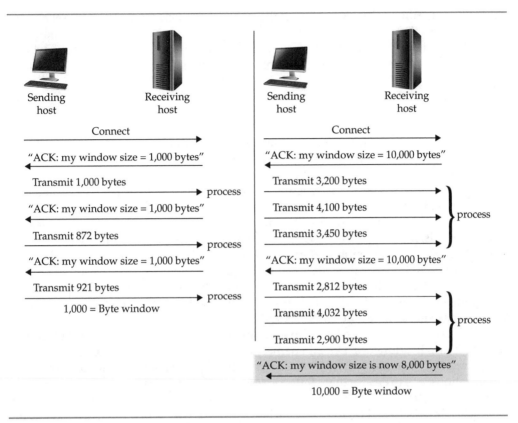

Figure 2-14.   Windowing ensures that the receiving host has the capacity to process incoming packets.

Connectionless IP Packet Handling Through UDP

The User Datagram Protocol (UDP) is connectionless in that it doesn't use acknowledgments or windowing. Compared to TCP, UDP is a "best effort" transport protocol—it simply transmits the message and hopes for the best. The UDP segment format is shown in Figure 2-15. Besides the port numbers to tell which network

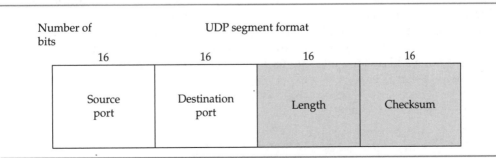

Figure 2-15.   The UDP segment format doesn't have Sequence and Acknowledgement fields.

applications to run, UDP segments basically just declare packet size. The only reliability mechanism in UDP is the checksum, used to verify the integrity of the data in the transmission. The odds that the checksum of a received packet containing altered data will match the checksum of the sent packet are miniscule.

IP Addressing

To go somewhere on the Internet, you must type a Uniform Resource Locator (URL) into the Address field on your browser. A unique domain name combines with its organization category to form a URL, such as http://www.velte.com. Actually, you seldom even have to type a URL; you just click a hyperlink that has the URL stored in the HTML that makes up the web page you're leaving.

URLs only exist to make surfing the Internet easier; they aren't true IP addresses. In other words, if you type the URL **http://www.velte.com** into your browser, a query is sent to a DNS server (configured as the primary DNS server in the PC network configuration) to translate the URL to an IP address, as shown in Figure 2-16.

Translation to IP addresses is necessary because the routers and switches that run the Internet don't recognize domain names. Indeed, an IP address must be used just for your query to get as far as the DNS server.

All Internet addresses are IP addresses. The Internet Assigned Numbers Authority (IANA) issues IP addresses. Domain names used to be issued by an organization called InterNIC (Internet Information Center). The primary responsibility of these organizations was to ensure that all IP addresses and domain names are unique. For example, http://www.velte.com was issued by InterNIC; and its IP address at the time, 209.98.208.34, was issued by the ISP, which, for its part, was issued the IP address from the IANA. The Internet Corporation for Assigned Names and Numbers (ICANN) was started in early 1999 to take over assignment duties. Now, users are still assigned IP addresses by Internet service providers (ISPs). But ISPs now get their IP addresses from a local or regional Internet registry (LIR) or national Internet registry (NIR).

The IP Address Format

Every node on the Internet must have an IP address. This includes hosts as well as networks. There's no getting around this rule because IP addressing is what ties the Internet together. Even stations connected to a LAN with its own addressing system (Bonjour, for example) must translate to IP in order to enter the Internet.

It's somewhat ironic that, despite the requirement that every IP address be unique to the world, at the same time, all IP addresses must be in the same format. IP addresses are 32 bits long and divided into four sections, each 8 bits long, called *octets*.

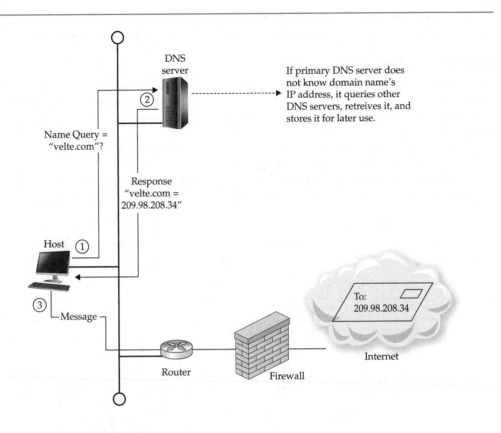

Figure 2-16.   DNS servers find the numerical IP addresses assigned to domain names.

Routers use IP addresses to forward messages through internetworks. Put simply, as the packet hops from router to router, it progresses through various networks until it finally reaches the router to which the destination address is attached.

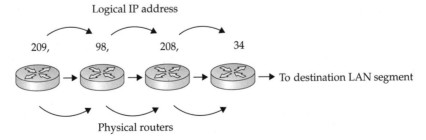

Of course, sometimes a message will go through several router hops before moving closer to its destination. Sometimes, hops are needed to find the next destination.

From Bits to Dotted-Decimal Format

As discussed earlier, computers only understand instructions and data in binary format. This goes for IP addresses, too, but the dotted-decimal format was invented so that people could read binary IP addresses. *Dotted-decimal* takes its name from the fact that it converts bits to decimal numbers for each octet, punctuated with periods. Figure 2-17 shows the conversion of an IP address to dotted-decimal format.

Figure 2-17 also shows the two reserved addresses. Assuming a 24-bit subnet mask, all ones in an octet are for broadcast, where the router automatically forwards a message to all hosts attached to networks addressed thus far in the address. For

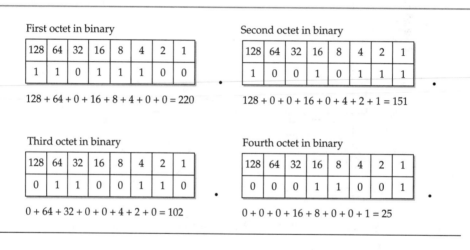

Figure 2-17.   Thirty-two bits define the IP addresses you see in dotted-decimal format.

example, messages addressed to 220.151.102.255 will be forwarded to all interfaces whose first three octets are 220.151.102. The other reserved address—called the "this network" address—is used for technical purposes not discussed here. Just understand that an address like 220.151.102.0 means "this interface" on network 220.151.102. One thing to take note of is that the subnet mask, and the subnet mask alone, defines what the broadcast and network IDs are. For example, 10.255.0.10 with a subnet mask of 255.255.255.0 is a valid IP address, even though the second octet is all ones and the third octet is all zeros. Similarly, 10.1.1.0 with a subnet mask of 255.255.240.0 and all ones in the forth octet is *not* the broadcast address, nor is all zeros the network. Because the mask is a 20-bit mask, *all* of the last 12 bits must be all ones to signify the broadcast and all zeros to signify the network.

IP Address Classes

The Internet Engineering Task Force (IETF) divides IP addresses into three general classes (plus two specialized ones). As mentioned earlier, IP addresses are divided into four dotted-decimal octets. Figure 2-18 shows the first octet number ranges. The shaded octets

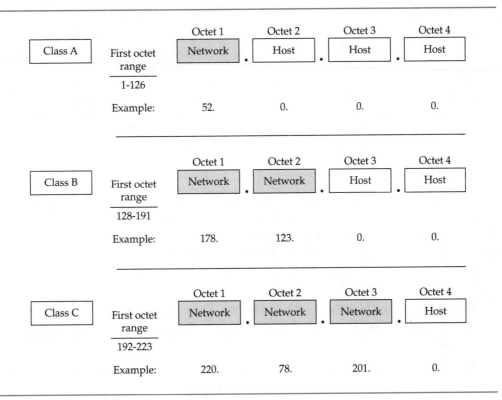

Figure 2-18.   Three IP address classes differ by the octets they use for network addresses.

show how much of the IP address space is reserved for addressing networks. As the shaded portion moves to the right, there are more possible networks, but fewer possible hosts.

This designation of ranges is called the *first octet rule*. Any router in the world can read the first octet of an IP address and know which bits to interpret as part of the network address versus the host address. If routers weren't able to make this distinction, the Internet couldn't work at all.

The majority of networks are numbered using either Class B or Class C IP addresses. The first octet ranges for each class are as follows:

- **0 to 127**   Class A. The range of network numbers is 0.0.0.0 to 127.0.0.0 for 128 networks. However, the network must not consist of only zeros, and 127.0.0.0 is reserved for loopback. What's left is 126 networks (1 to 126). There are 16,777,214 possible host addresses (16,777,216 minus 2).

- **128 to 191**   Class B. The range of network numbers is 128.0.0.0 to 191.255.0.0 for 16,384 networks. There are 65,534 possible host addresses (65,536 minus 2).

- **192 to 223**   Class C. The range of network numbers is 192.0.0.0 to 223.255.255.0 for 2,097,152 networks. There are 254 possible host addresses (256 minus 2).

As you look at the preceding list, you can imagine that only a few very large organizations and service providers have Class A addresses—only 126 of them, in fact.

NOTE   Don't forget that a network, by strict definition, is a LAN segment—an individual, shared-access medium. That's what is meant by the word "network" in the context of IP addressing. A network (or LAN segment) is also identified as a network interface (or interface, for short), because only one network can connect to a router's interface. For example, Ford Motor Company's intranet is probably referred to as a network by its employees, but Ford's network manager must assign unique IP addresses to the tens of thousands of individual networks (LAN segments) connected to the company's router interfaces.

Private Addressing

The IANA reserved three blocks of IP addresses for private addresses. A private IP address is one that is not registered with the IANA and will not be used beyond the bounds of the enterprise's internetwork—in other words, not on the Internet. Privately numbered internetworks are also sometimes called *private internets,* but we term them "internetworks" in this book to avoid confusion. The three blocks of reserved private address space are as follows:

- **10.0.0.0 to 10.255.255.255**   The *10 block* is a single Class A network number.

- **172.16.0.0 to 172.31.255.255**   The *172 block* is 16 contiguous Class B network numbers.

- **192.168.0.0 to 192.168.255.255**   The *192 block* is 256 contiguous Class C network numbers.

Edge devices, such as firewalls and boundary routers, must be assigned public IP addresses to conduct business with the outside. Private addresses are assigned only to hosts that make most or all of their connections within the private internetwork.

That's not to say, however, that a privately addressed host cannot connect to the outside world. Two IP address translation services are used to assign valid public Internet IP numbers temporarily to hosts with permanent private IP addresses. One technique is Network Address Translation (NAT), and the other is Port Address Translation (PAT).

NAT is a one-to-one mapping, whereas PAT is a one-to-many translation. That is, NAT assigns a unique IP address to each host when it connects to the Internet. This address will likely change each time a host reconnects. PAT, on the other hand, assigns the hosts to a single IP address by using different ports. Figure 2-19 depicts how the two work.

Address translation is usually done by a firewall. Keep in mind that these private-to-public translations are temporary. In NAT, when the internal host terminates its connection to the outside, the public IP address is returned to the pool for reuse.

The obvious advantage of private addressing is to have virtually unlimited address space for numbering internal networks and hosts. With a properly configured firewall or edge router to perform NAT or PAT address translation, these privately addressed hosts are still afforded connectivity to the Internet. Moreover, because their actual addresses are "translated" by a temporarily assigned pool number, hackers see no indication of the private internetwork's topology.

Subnetting

Subnetting is the practice of squeezing more network addresses out of a given IP address than are available by default. As discussed, IP address classes define which bits, by default, will address networks versus hosts. What *by default* means here is that upon reading the first octet in an address, a router knows which bits to treat as network address bits. Taking a Class C address as an example, the router will, by default, see the first three octets as network bits, and the final octet as host bits.

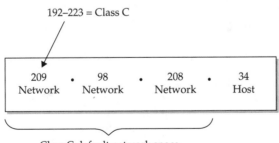

Class C default network space

However, in the real world, most enterprises need more network address space than they are assigned by their ISPs. This creates the need to "cheat" by claiming some of the default host bits for use in addressing networks. This is done by reassigning bits from the host portion of the IP address to the network portion. Figure 2-20 shows two

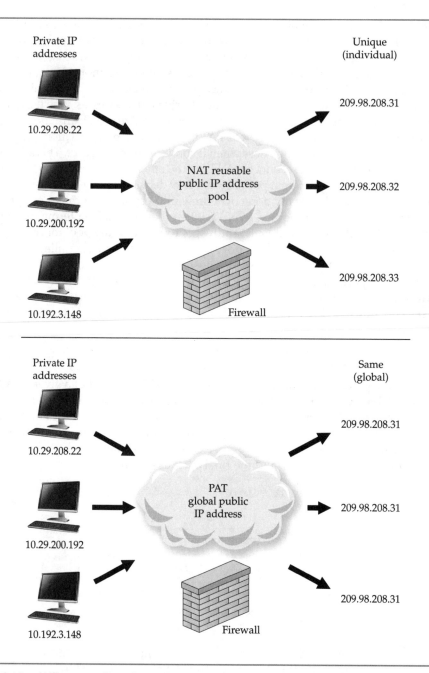

Figure 2-19. NAT temporarily assigns unique, reusable public addresses; PAT assigns a global IP address.

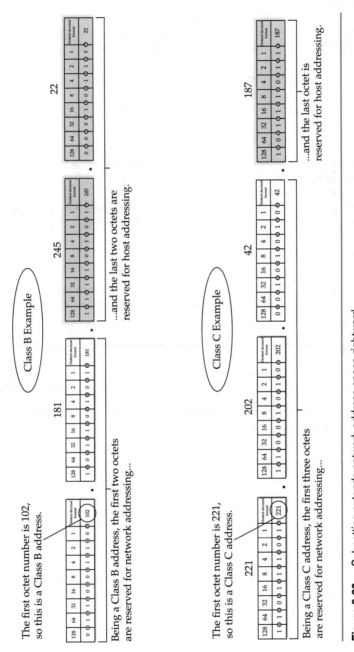

Figure 2-20. Subnetting extends network address space rightward.

IP addresses, one a subnetted Class B and the other a Class C address. They're shown in both dotted-decimal and binary format.

Which class an IP address belongs to is important, because subnets extend to the right, starting from the leftmost bit in the default network address space. In other words, only bit positions in the shaded portions of Figure 2-20 may be encroached for subnet addressing.

Be aware that the majority of enterprises are assigned Class C addresses, meaning that they have, at most, only eight bits with which to work. Indeed, many networks are assigned only a range of host numbers, for example, 221.198.20.32–47.

Whole Octet Subnet Example

Subnetting makes more efficient use of IP addresses without changing them. Take the network in Figure 2-21 as an example. The enterprise was issued the Class B public IP address 151.22.0.0 and subnetted the entire third octet.

Looking at the configuration in Figure 2-21, you can see that there is address space for 254 subnetworks, with space for 254 hosts per subnetwork. The shaded host at the bottom-right area shows a complete subnet address—in this example, host number 1 attached to subnet number 2 within IP address 151.22.0.1. The key feature of this example is that an entire octet—the third octet—is subnetted.

As remote routers work their way through the subnetted addresses in Figure 2-21, the packets will automatically fall through the correct interface in the edge router at the bottom center of the cloud.

What Subnet Masks Look Like and Where They Exist

All subnet masks are 32 bits in length. Take note that masks are not addresses; they are overlays that define how an IP address is to be used. They differ from IP addresses in two key ways:

- **Form**   A subnet mask is represented as a string of ones in binary, or a number (such as 255) in dotted-decimal format.

- **Location**   A subnet mask is applied to a specific host network interface and within the configuration file of the router to which the subnetwork is attached.

The configuration file is managed by the IOS software of the Cisco router. An attached LAN segment is subnetted by entering a statement like this:

```
MyRouter(config-if)#ip address 151.22.1.1 255.255.255.0
```

The MyRouter(config-if)# prompt means, "Configure this network interface on this router," where the command is being entered into a Cisco router named MyRouter. The **ip address** command is used to set the IP address for the network interface in question. The interface's proper IP address is 151.22.1.1 (a Class B address), and the subsequent

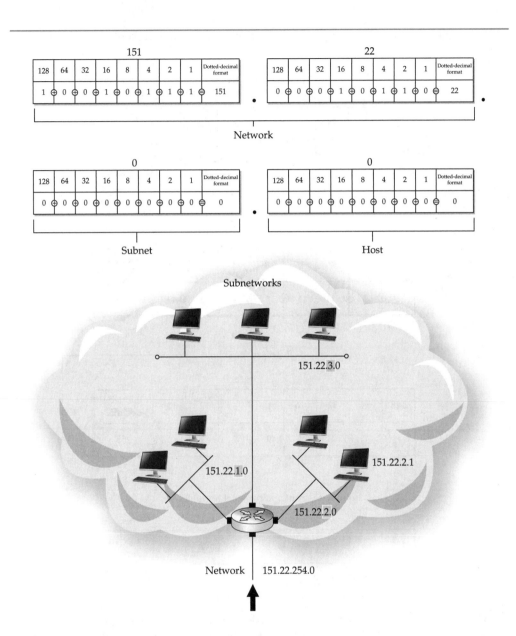

Figure 2-21. Subnetting makes efficient use of address space; this Class B example has room for 254 subnets.

255.255.255.0 tells the router to subnet the entire third octet, represented in bits as follows:

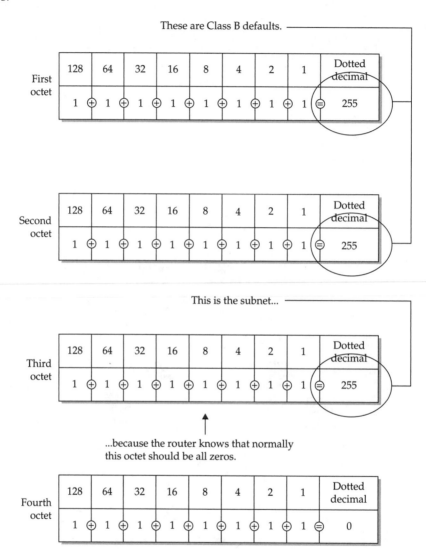

That's not too complicated. A subnet mask is the contiguous string of 1-bits extending from the end of the network address space into the host portion. Where that point is depends on the address class (the preceding example is a Class B). The subnet mask is entered into the router's config file using the **ip address** command to append the subnet mask to the normal IP address and apply it to a specific network interface—and in so doing, a specific LAN segment.

Partial Octet Subnetting

In most cases, however, subnets aren't quite so simple. This is because most enterprises are issued Class C IP addresses, where only the fourth octet is reserved, by default, as host address space. In these cases, the subnet mask extends only partway into the host address space, and is thus represented by a dotted-decimal number less than 255.

The shaded portion in Figure 2-22 represents the host bits claimed for subnetting from the fourth octet. Notice that only half the bits were claimed, and not all eight. This is one of two so-called .240 masks—this one permitting up to 14 subnets. Each subnet in this example has enough address space for 14 hosts—for a total of 196 possible hosts. This example would be input into the router's config file as follows:

```
MyRouter(config-if)#ip address 209.98.208.34 255.255.255.240
```

This command instructs the router that the interface is connected to a subnet with 28 network ID bits and 4 host ID bits. From there, packet delivery into the subnet is automatic.

There are several subnet masks from which to choose, as illustrated with the Class C address examples in Table 2-1. The farther right a mask extends into the host address space, the lower the number of possible hosts per subnet. Which mask to use depends entirely on the needs of the organization. For example, if a network interface on a router is attached to a point-to-point connection with a remote office, only two host addresses are required—one for each end. In this scenario, it would make sense to use the .252 mask, which has only two host addresses.

IP Version 6

While Internet addressing seems to run smoothly and without incident, the shocking truth is that we have run out of IP addresses. Really. It might seem that IPv4, the current 32-bit addressing system, provides more than enough addresses. In fact, using IPv4, there are about four billion addresses available. However, it turns out we need more. The last public IP address was handed out by IANA on February 3, 2011.

Subnet Mask	Network ID Bits	Host ID Bits	Sample Notation	Number of Subnets	Number of Hosts per Subnet
.192	26	6	209.98.208.34/26	2	62
.224	27	5	209.98.208.34/27	6	30
.240	28	4	209.98.208.34/28	14	14
.248	29	3	209.98.208.34/29	30	6
.252	30	2	209.98.208.34/30	62	2

Table 2-1.   Subnet Masks Listed by Number of Network ID Bits

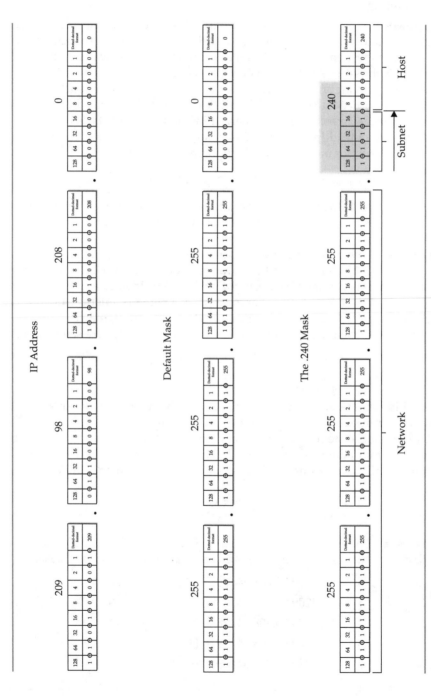

Figure 2-22.   Usually, only part of an octet is subnetted, as in the Class C example.

When the IP addressing scheme was developed in the 1980s, no one had a clue that the Internet would become the behemoth that it has grown into. The sheer pervasiveness of the Internet is gobbling up IP addresses—and it's not just computers, servers, and other network equipment that are using IP addresses. As other devices, such as smartphones and tablets, gain in popularity, more and more IP addresses will be sucked up.

Enter IPv6, also known as IPng ("ng" meaning "next generation"). IPv4 utilizes a 32-bit binary number to identify unique networks and end stations. This allows for around four billion unique addresses. IPv6 is different in that it uses a 128-bit hexadecimal format (numbers range from 0000 to FFFF). This addressing scheme allows for 10^15 unique hosts, or 340,282,366,920,938,463,463,374,607,431,768,211,456 total addresses. Basically, that's one address for every grain of sand on the planet.

In addition to the exponential growth of IP addresses, IPv6 makes some functional improvements over IPv4, including:

- Simplified header format
- Routing efficiency improved with hierarchical network architecture
- Support for popular routing protocols
- Autoconfiguration
- Embedded IPSec
- Greater number of multicast addresses

Format

As noted earlier, IPv6 addresses are 128 bits in size. They are expressed as eight fields of 16-bit, hex notation numbers (0000–FFFF), in this format:

```
x:x:x:x:x:x:x:x
```

Examples of this format are

```
FEDC:BA98:7654:3210:FEDC:BA98:7654:3210
```

and

```
1080:0:0:0:8:800:200C:417A
```

IPv6 addresses can be presented in three ways:

- The most straightforward method is to simply enter the values in each of the eight fields, as follows:

  ```
  1070:200:0:0:900:300C:618A
  ```

  You'll note that it is not necessary to use the leading zeros in an individual field. That is, "200" is the same as "0200."

■ In some cases, IPv6 addresses will contain long strings of zero bits. As such, crafters of the IPv6 addressing scheme have figured out a way to save the 0 key on your keyboard. Rather than enter **0000:0000:0000:0000:0000:0000:00 00:1** or even **0:0:0:0:0:0:0:1**, it is acceptable to indicate two or more groups of zeros using **::**. As such, the aforementioned example can be abbreviated as **::: 1**.

The only hitch to this shorthand is that the :: notation can only be used once in the address. By using the :: notation, IPv6 is able to determine that the "missing" number of values must all be zeros. However, if the :: notation is used more than once, it would be impossible to tell how many sets of zeros are missing from each section.

Table 2-2 shows how different IPv6 addresses can be abbreviated.

■ Finally, given that there will be a fair amount of transition time before IPv6 is completely adopted, there is a format that is used in mixed IPv6/IPv4 environments. That format combines both formats and is represented as:

```
x:x:x:x:x:x:d.d.d.d
```

In this case, the "x" values are the hexadecimal values of the six high-order 16-bit pieces of the address, and the "d" values are the decimal values of the four low-order 8-bit pieces of the address. For example:

```
0:0:0:0:0:FFFF:129.144.40.20
```

To throw a bit of a curveball at you, you are still allowed to utilize the compressed form of the address, even in the mixed format. For instance:

```
::FFF:129:144:40:20
```

IP Prefix

The IPv6 prefix is the portion of the address representing the leftmost, high-order bits. These bits represent the network identifier. The IPv6 prefix is represented using the prefix/prefix length notation. For example, 2001/16 identifies the Internet, whereas 2001: AB18/32 might identify an ISP. And 2001:4637:0:2930/64 identifies a specific network.

Address Type	IPv6 Address	Representation Using ::
Unicast	1070:200:0:0:900:300C:618A	1070:200::900:300C:618A
Multicast	FF01:0:0:0:0:0:0:100	FF01::100
Loopback	0:0:0:0:0:0:0:1	::1
Unspecified Address	0:0:0:0:0:0:0:0	::

Table 2-2.   Abbreviating IPv6 Addresses

Types of Addressing

Three types of addressing are available in IPv6:

- **Unicast**   One host transmits to another on a network. Cisco supports five types of unicast addresses:

    - **Global unicast addresses**, which are comparable to IPv4 global unicast addresses. That is, it is an IPv6 address from the global unicast prefix. Global unicast addresses move upward through organizations, and then to ISPs. Global unicast addresses contain a global routing prefix, a subnet ID, and an interface ID. With the exception of addresses beginning with 000, all global unicast addresses have a 64-bit interface ID. Currently, the global unicast allocation uses a range of addresses starting with the value 001 (2000::/3). Global unicast addresses use one-eighth of the total IPv6 address space and make up the largest block of assigned addresses.

        Figure 2-23 shows the global unicast address format.

    - **Site-local unicast addresses**, which are similar to private addresses (such as 10.0.0.0, 172.16.0.0, and 192.168.0.0) in IPv4.

    - **Link-local unicast addresses**, which are used for neighbor discovery and autoconfiguration. For example, these addresses are used in a network when no router is present.

    - **IPv4-mapped IPv6 addresses**, which are used to represent the address of an IPv4 node as an IPv6 address.

    - **IPv4-compatible IPv6 addresses**, which are used transitionally as IPv6 is used over existing IPv4 networks.

- **Anycast**   One host transmits to the closest destination host. Anycasting is designed to let one host initiate router table updating for a group of hosts. IPv6 can determine which gateway host is closest and sends packets to that host, singly. In turn, that host can anycast to another host in the group, and so

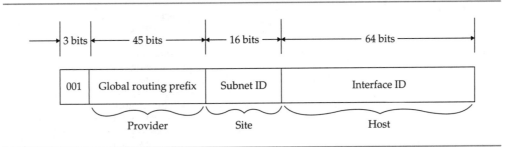

Figure 2-23.   The format of a global unicast IPv6 address.

on, until all routing tables are updated. An anycast address is a global unicast address assigned to a set of interfaces belonging to different nodes.

■ **Multicast**   One host transmits to multiple hosts on a network. The multicast address scheme uses addresses with a prefix of FF00::/8. In total, the multicast address range uses 1/256 of the total IPv6 address space. The second octet following the prefix establishes the lifetime and scope of the multicast address. Permanent multicast addresses have a lifetime parameter set to 0; temporary addresses are set to 1. The next four bits are used to establish the scope of the address.

Figure 2-24 not only shows the multicast address, but also includes the values of these bits. In order to identify specific functions, each block of multicast addresses within the range of FF00:: to FF0F:: is used accordingly:

■ **FF01::1**   All nodes within the interface-local scope.

■ **FF02::1**   All nodes on the local link.

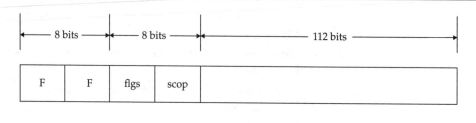

Figure 2-24 shows an IPv6 multicast address divided into sections: 8 bits, 8 bits, and 112 bits. The fields are labeled F, F, flgs, and scop.

flgs: 0 — Permanent
        1 — Transient

scop: 0—reserved
        1—interface-local scope
        2—link-local scope
        3—reserved
        4—admin-local scope
        5—site-local scope
        6—(unassigned)
        7—(unassigned)
        8—organization-local scope
        9—(unassigned)
        A—(unassigned)
        B—(unassigned)
        C—(unassigned)
        D—(unassigned)
        E—(unassigned)
        F—(unassigned)

Figure 2-24.   IPv6 multicast addresses contain specific information about the addresses' lifetime and scope.

- **FF01::2**   All routers within the interface-local scope.
- **FF02::2**   All routers on the link-local scope.
- **FF05::2**   All routers in the site-local scope.
- **FF02::1:FFXX:XXXX**   Solicited-node multicast address. (XX:XXXX represents the last 24 bits of the IPv6 address of node.)

Configuration

Using IPv4, addresses are assigned one of two ways:

- **Statically**   The address must be entered manually.
- **Dynamically**   DHCP/BOOTP automatically assigns IP addresses to a host when they boot onto the network.

IPv6 uses a feature called *stateless autoconfiguration*. This is similar to DHCP in that IP addresses are automatically assigned; however, it differs because a special DHCP application or server is not required. By using DHCP, any router using an IPv6 address becomes a "provider" of IP addresses to the network to which it is attached. To prevent duplicate addresses from being doled out, IPv6 uses a feature called *duplicate address detection (DAD)*.

Address Allocation

Like with IPv4, you can't just decide on an IP address in IPv6 and call it your own—even if there is a seemingly limitless amount. IANA is managing IPv6 addresses much in the way it has managed IPv4 addresses. It has allocated addresses from 2001::/16 to registries from the full address space. Each registry gets a /23 prefix within the 2001::/16 address space. The addresses are allocated as follows:

- **2001:0200::/23 and 2001:0C00::/23**   For use in Asia. These addresses were allocated to Asia Pacific Network Information Centre (APNIC).
- **2001:0400::/23**   For use in the Americas. The addresses were allocated to American Registry for Internet Numbers (ARIN).
- **2001:0600::/23 and 2001:0800::/23**   For use in Europe and the Middle East. These addresses were allocated to Réseaux IP Européens-Network Coordination Centre (RIPE NCC).

Next, the registries allocate a /32 prefix to the IPv6 ISPs, and then the ISPs allocate a /48 prefix to each customer. The /48 prefix of each site could be further allocated to each LAN, using a /64 prefix. Each site could have a maximum of 65,535 LANs.

IPv6 Addresses in a URL

Because the colon (:) is already used to identify a specific port number in a URL (for instance, http://www.thisisjustatest.com:8080), it cannot be used within the address.

As such, it is necessary to find a workaround to use this in web browsers. The chosen way to make IPv6 addresses work as URLs is to enclose them in brackets, like this:

```
http://[2001:0401:3:4F23::AE35]
```

If we wanted to go to a specific port using an IPv6 address, the colon and port number would simply follow the address, like this:

```
http://[2001:0401:3:4F23::AE35]:8080
```

That having been said, using IPv6 as a URL is a giant pain. Best just to use the fully qualified domain name than mess around with the IPv6 address. After all, isn't it easier to remember http://www.thisisjustatest.com than 2001:0401:3:4F23::AE35?

IPv6 isn't going to phase out IPv4 anytime soon. There are plenty of pundits out there who think IPv4 won't run out of address space for more than a decade and that IPv6 doesn't really bring anything new and revolutionary to the IP party. Agree or disagree, this is relevant information to know, because many Cisco devices are ready to go using IPv6 for addressing. At this point in time, however, the vast majority of internetworking is achieved using the 32-bit, four-octet, IPv4.

Putting It All Together

So, what happens behind the scenes when you make a connection across the Internet? Let's take the most common scenario of all, a web page download.

Your PC sends UDP packets to your local DNS server to translate the domain name into an IP address and returns the results. If there's a problem, the DNS lookup will time out, and the browser will complain that the server was not found.

The destination IP address is inserted into the header of your packets, along with your IP address and the port number for HTTP (80). Your request is sent over the TCP transport to the destination host to set up a connection. The route taken to the destination is left up to the routers. They read the IP address and hop the packets from router to router to get to their destination. If the packets can't find the destination host, you will likely see a "destination unreachable" error. Alternatively, if there is a routing loop in the network, the Time-to-Live (TTL) counter will reach zero and the connection attempt will be timed out.

If the routers find the router on which the destination host resides, the packets go through the network interface to enter the host's LAN segment using the destination IP address's subnet mask, if there is one.

The receiving host reads your message and decides whether to respond. To answer your service request, it uses the TCP three-way handshake and windowing techniques, the connection is established, and the requested web page download is executed under the management of TCP windowing.

In simplified terms, that's what happens when a hyperlink is clicked in a browser.

CHAPTER 3 | Cisco Certifications

The ubiquity of internetworking has created a need for more technical talent to install and manage network infrastructure. Industry growth is the biggest factor. The number—and capabilities—of installed routers, switches, and other internetworking devices has grown explosively over the last two decades, and more qualified technicians are needed to take care of them. But industry growth isn't the only factor driving the talent shortage: Another driver of the shortfall is that internetworking technology itself has become a lot more complicated. What used to be a fairly straightforward proposition of hubs and routers has given way to switched networks, virtual LANs, MPLS encapsulated LANs, virtual private networks (VPNs), optical telecommunications media, firewalls, management tools, and more. The onslaught of new and better internetworking technology is coming so fast that it's even hard for established pros to stay current.

If you're considering a career move into a technical area, the advice here is to take a serious look at network engineering. Internetworking professionals—often referred to as *wireheads* or *networkers*—are the people who work with the infrastructure that's largely invisible to network users. This is an entirely different group from the people who code HTML pages or write Java applets. Wireheads are the people who work with routers, switches, firewalls, access servers, and other internetworking devices. Some of them help run office or campus networks, and others work with wide area networks (WANs). A growing number of wireheads work for ISPs and other provider organizations instead of end-user enterprises. In addition, an increasing number of them are with internetwork consulting firms, not as full-time, permanent employees.

Talent shortages are nothing new to the computer business, and they're recognized as a threat. If demand for a vendor's products is hot but customers can't find anybody to install and maintain them, the vendor's growth is curtailed. Another pitfall is having unqualified personnel working on the vendor's equipment. This inevitably leads to technical disasters large and small, and the vendor often ends up taking the brunt of customer dissatisfaction.

The industry response has been vendor certifications. A *certification* is a stamp of approval that a person has a certain level of technical competency with the vendor's products. They're obtained by passing a battery of tests specifically geared to the vendor's product line. These tests sometimes include hands-on lab exercises in addition to written exams. Vendors typically farm out their certification programs to approved training organizations that must adhere to the vendor-designed curriculum. Most vendor certification programs are arranged into a career track with certifications by level (beginner, intermediate, and expert) and sometimes also by area of specialization.

Interestingly, the first well-known certification program came from a network company, not a computer company—the major LAN software vendor, Novell. Novell's theory was that not only are networks quite complicated, but one that malfunctions is highly visible within the customer organization. So, in the 1980s, Novell instituted their Certified Network Administrator (CNA) and Certified Network Engineer (CNE) programs. The idea was a huge success, and soon the want ads were filled with the CNA and CNE acronyms. The certifications became such a standard job requirement that even veteran Novell technicians were forced to qualify.

Other vendors followed Novell's lead with programs of their own, to the point that now online job site ads are an alphabet soup of certification acronyms. Perhaps the best-known certification program is Microsoft's, ranging from the Microsoft Certified Professional (MCP) to the high-end Microsoft Certified Systems Engineer (MCSE)—a hot credential that virtually guarantees high-paying employment.

Certification programs work both ways for the vendor. On one hand, they help keep customers happy; on the other, the vendor's market position is enhanced by having a qualified workforce ready to install and maintain its products. A certification program is a way for vendors to reduce risk, secure market position, and even make some money off their programs. For these reasons, all the major computer companies now have certification programs of one type or another.

However, certifications make just as much sense for the individual. Even the lowest-ranking certification is a virtual pass to a good job with lots of opportunity. For example, a person holding a Cisco Certified Network Associate (CCNA) with little or no real-world experience can get an entry-level job paying $35,000 or more. A CCNA with hands-on Cisco experience can expect to make $50,000 or more depending on the local job market. These figures vary according to region and the type of employer, of course, but that kind of money at the bottom rung speaks to how important certifications have become. Some observe that nowadays the right certification carries more weight than a college degree.

Certifications Overview

Cisco has one of the most extensive certification programs in the computer industry. This may surprise you, but as you read this book, you'll come to understand just how big and complicated the field of internetworking is. Cisco's program certifies five tiers of expertise: Entry, Associate, Professional, Expert, and Architect.

Associate, Professional, and Expert are the main levels, where the majority of certification work is done. Within these tiers, you can be certified in any of several specialties. The overall program is called Cisco Career Certifications, although sometimes the company uses the term "CCIE (Cisco Certified Internetwork Expert) pathway" as a generic reference to the program tiers.

Cisco offers and recommends training courses for its Career Certifications program. Recommended courses are taught by its Cisco Learning Partners, who must use a standardized college-level instruction curriculum designed by Cisco. The training company may not deviate from the approved curriculum. Cisco Learning Partners are authorized on a country-by-country basis, but they may not administer certification exams or issue Cisco certifications. Only one company—Pearson VUE—is retained by Cisco as the exclusive test administrator in the United States. Most tests cost $100 to $300 to take. Because many people don't have access to Cisco equipment to use for practice, the company sponsors a number of practice labs. However, there are a limited number of them, and they cost $500 to $1,000 per day to use.

NOTE Cisco used to have two companies administer the tests, but in 2007 switched to just Pearson VUE.

Career Certifications and Paths

In the past, Cisco offered three distinct certification levels—Associate, Professional, and Expert. However, they have added two additional levels—Entry level and Architect—as bookends to those certifications. The two new levels offer an even more basic level of certification for new Cisco specialists, and a certification showing an even greater level of Cisco knowledge and expertise with the Architect certification.

Cisco offers different levels of certification for specific career paths. *Paths* refers to the specific technologies in which networking professionals can be certified. Cisco's career paths are

- Routing and switching
- Design
- Network security
- Wireless
- Voice
- Data center
- Storage networking
- Service provider
- Service provider operations

Within each career path, there are specific certifications for each level. For instance, the CCDA for network security is different from the CCDA for voice. The following levels are available for Cisco networking professionals.

Entry Level

The starting point for entry-level Cisco certifications begin with either a CCENT, as a first step toward achieving the Associate level, or a Cisco Certified Technician (CCT).

The Cisco Certified Entry Networking Technician (CCENT) certifies that an individual can install, operate, and troubleshoot a small enterprise branch network. The certification validates that the individual can also manage basic network security.

The CCT certification is separate from CCENT. Whereas CCENT demonstrates expertise across all career paths, CCT certifications are specialized. CCTs can diagnose restore, repair, and replace critical Cisco networking and system devices at customer sites. Technicians work closely with the Cisco Technical Assistance Center (TAC) to quickly and efficiently resolve support incidents. There are three current CCT certifications:

- CCT Routing and Switching
- CCT Data Center
- CCT TelePresence

This certification is Cisco's basic level of certification and shows that the individual can perform entry-level network support duties. The curriculum covers networking basics, WAN technologies, basic security and wireless fundamentals, routing and switching basics, and simple network configuration.

In order to proceed to earning a CCNA, the CCENT is the first step.

There is only one exam for CCENT certification, no matter what the desired career path—whether voice, wireless, design, or any of the others. Table 3-1 shows the exam required to earn the CCENT certification.

Associate

The next rung on the Cisco Certifications ladder, after CCENT, is the Associate level. This is a CCNA (for network operations) or a CCDA (for network design). Depending on the specific path that the professional is pursuing, the CCNA or CCDA certification is tailored for a specific specialty, such as network design, routing and switching, or wireless.

The Associate level can be thought of as the apprentice or foundation level of network certification.

Professional

The third level of Cisco certification within each of the certification paths is the Professional level. This level is an advanced level of certification (one can liken it to a Journeyman level) and shows greater skill and knowledge of Cisco technology than the entry and Associate levels. Certifications at this level include CCDP and CCNP.

Expert

The Cisco Certified Internetwork Expert (CCIE) is the most advanced Cisco networking certification. CCIE certification holders represent less than 3 percent of all certified Cisco professionals and less than 1 percent of the networking professionals worldwide.

Required Exam	Recommended Training
640-822 ICND1	Interconnecting Cisco Networking Devices Part 1

Table 3-1. Exam Required For CCENT Certification

The CCIE certification exists for:

- Routing and switching
- Design
- Network security
- Wireless
- Voice
- Data center
- Storage networking
- Service provider
- Service provider operations

Unlike the Associate and Professional levels of certification, there are no prerequisites for taking the exam—that is, no formalized training courses must be taken before the exam. However, in lieu of that training, it is assumed that the candidate will have learned everything that he or she needs to know with a minimum of three years of hands-on experience.

 NOTE In the case of CCDE, Cisco prefers candidates to have at least seven years of experience. For all certification paths, a two-hour written exam is required, followed by an eight-hour, hands-on lab test.

 NOTE Because the requirements for each CCIE career path are identical—a written test and hands-on lab test—we don't list the CCIE requirements individually later in this chapter.

Cisco touts the CCIE as better than other computer industry certification programs. Some wags call it the black belt of network certifications. Cisco claims that "experience is the number-one factor" in earning a CCIE certification. And they have a point, in that the CCIE exam has a grueling hands-on lab exam that is very difficult. The train-cram-test routine so many use to qualify for top-rung technical certifications isn't an option with the CCIE. Much of the exam can only be learned from extensive job experience. Cisco emphasizes that the CCIE certification is "experience based, not training based," as are most other certifications. This shouldn't dissuade the beginner, however, because the CCNA requires only one written exam, and that's a start.

Architect

Cisco Certified Architects (CCAr's) work with more than just the networking technology. They also collect and analyze data from the organization and produce a blueprint for a large-scale, complex, global network. They translate business needs and objectives into the nuts and bolts requirements for a network design.

The Architect level of Cisco's certifications recognizes networking professionals who have demonstrated and can manage the complex networks of large organizations. Earning the CCAr certification is different from the normal route of achieving certifications. There is no recommended syllabus or educational courses to take. Also, there is no testing to achieve said certification. Rather, candidates must meet, in person, a board of Cisco-appointed exam committee members.

Once certified as an Architect, the professional:

- Leads the creation and evolution of Cisco architecture
- Analyzes technology and industry trends
- Selects products and technology
- Identifies organization and resource needs
- Leads the development for network architecture

Specialist

In addition to the aforementioned certifications, Cisco also offers numerous Specialist certifications. These certifications are centered on specific technologies and are targeted at members of the Cisco Partner Program who sell, design, and support Cisco products. Earning these Specialist certifications can help a partner qualify for additional benefits and earn extra plumes for their hats.

Certification Tracks

Conventionally speaking, when one would talk about Cisco certifications, they would mean the Associate, Professional, or Expert levels within the various career paths. The field has been expanded to include the CCENT and CCAr levels of certification.

In this section, we talk about what is required to earn Cisco's various certifications. For each certification path, we examine what is needed for Associate, Professional, and Expert levels (exams differ for each). However, the CCENT exam is the same for each career path.

Routing and Switching

Routing and switching are the most basic elements of Cisco's operations—that's where they started. And earning one of Cisco's Professional-level certifications for routing and switching shows that a network professional knows what's necessary to efficiently and effectively design, build, and maintain a Cisco-based network.

CCNA

The Cisco Certified Network Associate (CCNA) is able to install, configure, operate, and troubleshoot medium-sized routed and switched networks. The CCNA curriculum includes mitigation of basic security threats, introduction of wireless networking concepts, and skills performance.

Required Exam(s)	Description
640-802 CCNA	This test assesses a candidate's knowledge and skills required to install, operate, and troubleshoot a small to medium-size enterprise branch network.
or	
640-822 ICND1	This exam assesses a candidate's knowledge and skills required to successfully install, operate, and troubleshoot a small branch office network.
640-816 ICND2	This exam assesses a candidate's knowledge and skills required to successfully install, operate, and troubleshoot a small to medium-size enterprise branch network.

Table 3-2.   Tests and Training Required for CCNA

This curriculum includes the use of IP, Enhanced Interior Gateway Protocol (EIGRP), Routing Information Protocol Version 2 (RIPv2), VLANs, Ethernet, and access control lists (ACLs). Table 3-2 lists the exams required to earn the CCNA certification.

CCNP

The Cisco Certified Network Professional (CCNP) certification is for individuals with advanced knowledge of networks. CCNP certified individuals can install, configure, and troubleshoot LANs and WANs for organizations with between 100 and 500 nodes.

Topics that must be mastered to achieve this certification include

- Security
- Converged networks
- QoS
- VPNs
- Broadband technologies

The prerequisite for CCNP certification is to have earned a CCNA certification. Table 3-3 lists the tests required to earn CCNP certification.

Design

In order to demonstrate one's mettle in converged network design, Cisco offers Associate and Professional levels of design certification with their Cisco Certified Design Associate (CCDA) and Cisco Certified Design Professional (CCDP). These certifications are used to validate that a networking professional has the knowledge and skills needed to design routed and switched networks.

Required Exams	Recommended Training
642-902 ROUTE	This exam assesses the candidate's knowledge and skills necessary to use advanced IP addressing and routing in implementing scalable and secure Cisco ISR routers connected to LANs and WANs.
642-813 SWITCH	This exam assesses that the candidate has the knowledge and skills necessary to plan, configure, and verify the implementation of complex enterprise switching solutions using Cisco's Campus Enterprise Architecture.
642-832 TSHOOT	This exam assesses that the candidate has the knowledge and skills necessary to (1) plan and perform regular maintenance on complex enterprise routed and switched networks and (2) use technology-based practices and a systematic ITIL-compliant approach to perform network troubleshooting.

Table 3-3.   Tests and Training Required for CCNP

CCDA

Cisco Certified Design Associate (CCDA) is used to demonstrate a professional's ability to design a Cisco converged network. The certification allows the professional to demonstrate the skills required to design routed and switched networks as well as their knowledge of services involving LAN, WAN, and broadband access for organizations.

Table 3-4 describes the required exam.

CCDP

Cisco Certified Design Professional (CCDP) demonstrates advanced knowledge of network design concepts and principles. CCDP-certified professionals can discuss, design, and create advanced addressing and routing, security, network management, data center, and complex IP multicast/multilayered enterprise architectures that include virtual private networking and wireless domains.

Table 3-5 describes the required exams for CCDP certification.

Required Exam	Description
DESGN	This exam indicates a foundation or apprentice knowledge of network design for the Cisco converged networks based on Borderless Network Architecture.

Table 3-4.   CCDA Exam

Required Exams	Description
642-902 ROUTE	This exam certifies that the candidate has the knowledge and skills necessary to use advanced IP addressing and routing in implementing scalable and secure Cisco ISR routers connected to LANs and WANs.
642-813 SWITCH	This exam certifies that the candidate has the knowledge and skills necessary to plan, configure, and verify the implementation of complex enterprise switching solutions using Cisco's Campus Enterprise Architecture. The SWITCH exam also covers secure integration of VLANs, WLANs, voice, and video into campus networks.
ARCH	This exam assesses a candidate's knowledge of the latest development in network design and technologies, including network infrastructure, intelligent network services, and converged network solutions.

Table 3-5.   Exams Required for CCDP Certification

Network Security

Network security is certainly an important and highly valuable skill, and adding the letters behind your name that indicate that you are skilled in Cisco's products is a great achievement, indeed. Being certified in security shows that the network professional is an expert in the basics of IP and IP routing, in addition to having a specialized understanding of security.

CCNA Security

Cisco Certified Network Associate Security (CCNA Security) shows that a professional has Associate-level knowledge and skills required to secure Cisco networks. CCNA Security certification allows the network professional to demonstrate the skills required to develop a security infrastructure, recognize threats and vulnerabilities to networks, and mitigate security threats. The CCNA Security's curriculum is on core security technologies, the installation, troubleshooting and monitoring of network devices to maintain integrity, confidentiality, and availability of data and devices.

Table 3-6 lists the exam required to earn this certification.

CCNP Security

CCNP Security certification program demonstrates the network professional's knowledge and skills as a Cisco Network Security Engineer responsible for security in routers, switches, networking devices and appliances, as well as for choosing, deploying,

Required Exam	Description
640-554 IINS	This exam assesses a candidate's knowledge of securing Cisco routers and switches and their associated networks.

Table 3-6.   Exam Required to Earn CCNA Security

supporting, and troubleshooting firewalls, VPNs, and IDS/IPS solutions for their networking environments.

Table 3-7 lists the exams required to earn the CCNP Security.

Wireless

Cisco offers two certification tracks in wireless LANs. The certifications are used to exhibit the network professional's skill in the design or support of wireless LANs. Wireless LAN specialists must understand radio technologies as they pertain to 802.11 standards, WLAN, bridge topologies, and applications. They must also be able to configure WLAN products, including access points, bridges, and clients, specifically Cisco's Aironet hardware and software.

CCNA Wireless

Cisco Certified Network Associate Wireless (CCNA Wireless) shows Associate-level knowledge and skills to configure, implement, and support of Cisco wireless LANs. With this certification, network professionals can support a basic wireless network on a Cisco WLAN for a small-to-medium business (SMB) or enterprise.

Required Exams	Description
642-637 Secure v1.0	This exam assesses a candidate's knowledge and skills needed to secure Cisco IOS Software router and switch-based networks, and provide security services based on Cisco IOS Software.
642-618 FIREWALL V2.0	This exam assesses a candidate's knowledge and skills needed to implement and maintain Cisco ASA-based perimeter solutions.
642-648 VPN 2.0	This exam tests a candidate's knowledge and skills needed to deploy Cisco ASA-based VPN solutions.
642-627 IPS v7.0	This exam assesses a candidate's knowledge and skills needed to deploy Cisco IPS-based security solutions.

Table 3-7.   Exams Required to Earn CCNP Security

Required Exam	Description
IUWNE (Implementing Cisco Unified Wireless Network Essential)	This exam assesses a candidate's knowledge of installing, configuring, operating, and troubleshooting small-to-medium-size WLANs.

Table 3-8.   Exam Required to Earn CCNA Wireless

The curriculum for this exam includes information and practice activities to prepare the candidate for configuring, monitoring, and troubleshooting basic tasks of a Cisco WLAN in SMB and enterprise networks.

Table 3-8 shows the exam required to earn CCNA Wireless.

CCNP Wireless

CCNP Wireless certification is used to demonstrate the networking professional's skill and knowledge for designing, implementing, and operating Cisco Wireless networks and mobility infrastructures. CCNP Wireless certification emphasizes wireless networking principles and theory. It also recognizes the expertise of wireless professionals who can assess and translate network business requirements into technical specifications that result in successful installations.

Table 3-9 lists the exams required to earn CCNP Wireless certification.

Required Exams	Description
642-732 CUWSS	This exam assesses a candidate's capability to plan and conduct a wireless site survey, to design the RF network, and to conduct a post-installation assessment to ensure compliancy.
642-742 IUWVN V2.0	This exam assesses the candidate's ability to design, implement, and operate Cisco Wireless networks and mobility infrastructures.
642-747 IUWMS 2.0	This exam assesses a candidate's capability to integrate mobility services into the WLAN, to tune and troubleshoot the WLAN, and to implement indoor enterprise mesh networks.
642-737 IAUWS	This exam assesses a candidate's capability to secure the wireless network from security threats via appropriate security policies and best practices, to properly implement security standards, and to properly configure wireless security components.

Table 3-9.   Exams Required to Earn CCNP Wireless Certification

Voice

These certifications show that the network professional is an expert in the field of configuring and maintaining VoIP deployments. Candidates must be knowledgeable about the different Cisco VoIP products and technologies.

CCNA Voice

The Cisco Certified Network Associate Voice (CCNA Voice) certifies Associate-level knowledge and skills required to administer a voice network. The Cisco CCNA Voice certification affirms the skill set for specialized job roles in voice technologies such as voice technologies administrator, voice engineer, and voice manager. It validates skills in VoIP technologies such as IP PBX, IP telephony, handset, call control, and voicemail solutions.

The core of the CCNA Voice certification is the Cisco Unified Communications Manager 8.0 (CUCM 8.0). CUCM 8.0 is typically used by large organizations such as governments, large companies, and colleges. CCNA Voice certification also evaluates the skills and knowledge related to Cisco CallManager Express (CME) and Cisco Unity Express (CUE) solutions, which are typically used by medium and small organizations with less than 2,000 members.

Table 3-10 shows the exam required to earn the CCNA Voice certification.

CCNP Voice

Cisco Certified Network Professional CCNP Voice demonstrates a network professional's advanced knowledge and skills required to integrate into underlying network architectures. Professionals with this certification can implement, operate, configure, and troubleshoot converged IP networks. Network professionals with a CCNP Voice certification can create a collaboration solution that is transparent, scalable, and manageable.

The CCNP Voice focuses on:

- Cisco Unified Communications Manager
- QoS

Required Exam	Description
640-461 ICOMM v8.0	This exam assesses a candidate's knowledge of the architecture, components, functionalities, and features of Cisco Unified Communications solutions.

Table 3-10.   Exam Required to Earn the CCNA Voice Certification

- Gateways
- Gatekeepers
- IP phones
- Voice applications

Table 3-11 lists the exams required to earn the CCNP certification.

Required Exam	Description
642-437 CVOICE v8.0	This exam assesses a candidate's knowledge of implementing and operating gateways, gatekeepers, Cisco Unified Border Element, Cisco Unified Communications Manager Express, and QoS in a voice network architecture.
642-447 CIPT1 v8.0	This exam assesses a candidate's skills in installing and configuring a Cisco Unified Communications Manager solution in a single site and focuses primarily on Cisco Unified Communications Manager Release v8.0, the call routing and signaling component for the Cisco Unified Communications solution.
642-457 CIPT2 v8.0	This exam assesses a candidate's skills in implementing a Cisco Unified Communications Manager solution in a multisite environment, applying a dial plan for a multisite environment, configuring survivability for remote sites during WAN failure, and implementing solutions to reduce bandwidth requirements in the IP WAN.
642-427 TVOICE v8.0	This exam assesses a candidate's knowledge and skills required to troubleshoot Cisco Unified Communications systems and solutions in different deployments.
642-467 CAPPS v8.0	This exam assesses a candidate's knowledge of how to integrate the new Unified Communications Applications, which are part of the new version 8.0 Cisco Voice software.

Table 3-11.   Exams Required to Earn the CCNP Voice Certification

Service Provider

This certification shows that a network professional has expert skills and understanding of technologies relevant to a service provider. Such skills include unicast IP routing, QoS, multicast, MPLS, MPLS VPNs, and multiprotocol BGP. Certification at this level also requires knowledge of a technology area specific to service providers, such as dial-up, DSL, cable, optical, or IP telephony.

CCNA Service Provider

Cisco Certified Network Associate – Service Provider (CCNA SP) focuses on the latest in Service Provider industry core networking technologies and trends, and certifies the network professional's ability to configure and implement Cisco Service Provider Next-Generation networks.

Table 3-12 lists the exams necessary to earn the CCNA SP certification.

CCNP Service Provider

The CCNP Service Provider certification certifies the knowledge and skills that network professionals are required to have in order to deliver a scalable carrier-grade infrastructure capable of rapid expansion to support ongoing introduction of new managed services and other customer requirements.

Table 3-13 lists the exams required to earn the CCNP Service Provider certification.

Service Provider Operations

Service providers are the backbone of Cisco's sales, and the professional with service provider credentials will have no dearth of opportunities. Cisco's service provider certifications show that a networking professional is skilled at troubleshooting, configuration, and making changes for service providers' unique networks.

CCNA Service Provider Operations

Cisco Certified Network Associate in Service Provider Operations (CCNA SP Operations) certifies that the networking professional has the basic knowledge and skills (of a Tier I support engineer) in a troubleshooting environment within carrier-class IP NGN core

Required Exams	Description
640-875 SPNGN1	This exam assesses the basic knowledge and skills necessary to support a service provider network.
640-878 SPNGN2	This exam assesses the knowledge and skills necessary to implement and support a service provider network.

Table 3-12. Exams Required to Earn the CCNA Service Provider Certification

Required Exams	Description
642-883	This exam assesses a candidate's knowledge to configure, verify, and troubleshoot routing protocols using Cisco carrier-grade devices and Cisco IOS, Cisco IOS XE, and Cisco IOS XR software.
642-885	This exam assesses a candidate's knowledge to configure, verify, and troubleshoot IPv4 and IPv6 advanced BGP configuration, IP multicasting, and IPv6 transition mechanisms in implementing and supporting a service provider network.
642-887	This exam assesses a candidate's knowledge of the concepts and implementation of MPLS technology and MPLS-TE services.
642-889	This exam is used to assess the candidate's knowledge of Cisco IOS, IOS XE, and IOS XR operating systems. Candidates can prepare for this exam by taking the Implementing Cisco Service Provider Next-Generation Edge Network Services (SPEDGE) course.

Table 3-13.   Exams Required to Earn the CCNP Service Provider Certification

network infrastructure. CCNA SP Operations curriculum includes incident (event), fault, configuration, change, and performance management procedures, along with NMS tools and protocols.

Table 3-14 describes the exam required to earn this certification.

CCNP Service Provider Operations

The Cisco Certified Network Professional in Service Provider Operations (CCNP SP Operations) certifies that the networking professional has the knowledge and skills required of a Tier II or Tier III support engineer to troubleshoot and maintain service

Required Exams	Description
640-760 SSPO	This exam is designed to introduce entry-level personnel to the SP network operations environment, processes orientation, management tools, and methods, and it enables students to practice their primary job responsibilities and tasks.

Table 3-14.   Exam Required to Earn the CCNA Service Provider Operations Certification

Required Exams	Description
642-770 OFCN	This exam assesses a candidate's knowledge of the SP Network Operations environment, focusing on mid- to upper-level processes management, NMS tools, and troubleshooting skills associated with Tier II and Tier III network operations.
642-775 MSPRP	This exam assesses a candidate's knowledge and use of Interior Gateway Protocols (IGP) such as OSPF and IS-IS as well as an Exterior Gateway Protocol (EGP), BGP, in supporting Service Provider environments. It also assesses the candidate's understanding of advanced routing policies using route maps, with Cisco IOS, and the Routing Policy Language (RPL), with Cisco IOS XR.
642-780 MSPVM	This exam assesses a candidate's knowledge in monitoring and troubleshooting Multi-Protocol Label Switching (MPLS) and associated technologies in service provider networking.
642-785 MSPQS	This exam assesses a candidate's knowledge of QoS mechanisms to support Service Provider networking environments, including how they are monitored, implemented, and troubleshot using both Cisco IOS and IOS XR operating systems.

Table 3-15. Exam Required to Earn the CCNP Service Provider Operations Certification

provider IP NGN core network infrastructures. Networking professionals with a CCNP SP Operations certification can demonstrate knowledge and skills required to isolate network performance problems as well as implement proactive fault measures using operations management processes, frameworks, and network management systems. The CCNP SP Operations curriculum includes maintaining carrier-class routing protocol environments, MPLS VPN and TE deployments, and QoS mechanisms using Cisco IOS and IOS XR.

Table 3-15 lists the exams required to earn this certification.

Technician Certifications

In the summer of 2011, Cisco added the Cisco Certified Technician (CCT) certification to their Career Certification Program. The CCT training and certification programs are designed for technicians who perform onsite support and maintenance of Cisco infrastructure for Routing & Switching, Data Center, and TelePresence solutions.

Required Exam	Description
640-692 RSTECH	This exam assesses a candidate's knowledge and the skills required to perform onsite support and maintenance of Cisco routers, switches, and operating software.

Table 3-16.   Exam Required to Earn the CCT Routing & Switching Certification

The CCT certifications endorse the job skills of field engineers who perform onsite support, maintain Cisco equipment, and work with the Cisco Technical Assistance Center to resolve onsite support issues. The following sections describe the different certifications and which exams are necessary to be granted that certification.

CCT Routing & Switching

Cisco CCT Routing & Switching certification examines the skills required for onsite support and maintenance of Cisco routers, switches, and operating environments. Technicians must be able to identify Cisco router and switch models, accessories, cabling, and interfaces; understand the Cisco IOS Software operating modes and identify commonly found software; and be able to use the Cisco Command Line Interface (CLI) to connect and service products. The CCT Routing & Switching certification is an ideal starting point for supporting other Cisco devices and systems.

Table 3-16 describes the exam required to earn this certification.

CCT Data Center

The CCT Data Center certification examines the skills required for onsite support and maintenance of Cisco Unified Computing Systems and servers. Technicians must be able to identify Cisco Unified Computing System components and servers, accessories, cabling and interfaces; understand the Cisco UCS and NX-OS operating modes and identify commonly found software; and be able to use the Cisco Graphical User Interface to connect and service product components. The prerequisite for this certification is the CCT in Routing & Switching.

Table 3-17 describes the exam required to earn this certification.

Required Exam	Description
640-893 DCTECH	This exam assesses a candidate's knowledge and the skills required to perform onsite support and maintenance of Cisco Data Center System components and operating software.

Table 3-17.   Exam Required to Earn the CCT Data Center Certification

Required Exam	Description
640-792 TPTECH	This exam assesses a candidate's knowledge and the skills required to perform onsite support and maintenance of Cisco TelePresence System components and operating software.

Table 3-18. Exam Required to Earn the CCT TelePresence Certification

CCT TelePresence

Cisco CCT TelePresence certification examines the skills required for onsite support and maintenance of Cisco TelePresence Systems. Technicians must be able to identify Cisco TelePresence models, accessories, cabling, and interfaces; understand the Cisco TelePresence operating modes and identify commonly found software; and be able to use the Cisco Command Line Interface (CLI) to connect and service products and make basic Cisco TelePresence system adjustments. The prerequisite for the CCT TelePresence certification is having first earned the CCT Routing & Switching certification.

Table 3-18 describes the exam required to earn this certification.

Specialist Certifications

The Specialist designation certifies the expertise of experienced technical professionals, and those who have earned Associate- or Professional-level Cisco Career Certifications. By earning specialist certifications, network professionals can enhance their core networking knowledge in technologies such as security, IP communications, and wireless.

These certifications are separate from Cisco's main career path certifications, but can be earned on their own either to supplement an Entry, Associate, or Professional certification, or in lieu of those certifications.

Specialist certifications fall into five categories: collaboration, data center, operating system software, security, and video. A professional who wants to demonstrate skill (or learn that skill) can pursue the Specialist certification.

Collaboration Certifications

The Cisco Collaboration portfolio certifications demonstrate a networking professional's proficiency in designing, implementing, and supporting multiservice voice and multimedia network solutions. These certifications apply mostly to Voice Architects, Voice Networking Engineers, and Voice Analysts.

Required Exams	Description
642-415 UCAD	This exam assesses a candidate's knowledge of technical issues surrounding the design of Voice over Data network and explains a methodology that brings order to approaching the problems faced by planners and designers.
650-251 LCSAUC	This exam assesses the candidate's knowledge and skills needed to support implementing an advanced Unified Communications solution on a network throughout each phase of the lifecycle.
642-642 QoS	This exam assesses the knowledge and skills necessary to configure and troubleshoot Cisco IOS routers running Quality of Service protocols in Service Provider and Enterprise environments.

Table 3-19.   Exams Required to Earn Cisco IP Telephony Design Certification

Cisco IP Telephony Design Specialist

The Cisco IP Telephony Design Specialist certification is for networking professionals who design IP telephony multiservice network solutions. Cisco IP Telephony Design Specialists can design scalable, converged networks using QoS, Cisco Call Manager clustering, H.323, MGCP, or SIP signaling protocols, and assess the scope of work required to integrate legacy TDM PBXs and voicemail systems into an existing data network.

Table 3-19 describes the exams required for this certification.

Cisco Unified Presence Specialist

The Cisco Unified Presence Specialist certification is meant for whose primary responsibility is to design, install, and configure Cisco Unified Presence. The candidate should also possess an understanding of integration with other Cisco Unified Communications products as well as third-party presence solutions, including Microsoft Live Communications Server, Microsoft Office Communications Server, and IBM Lotus Sametime.

Table 3-20 describes the exam required to earn this certification.

Required Exam	Description
642-181 PRSDI	This exam assesses a candidate's knowledge of designing and implementing Cisco Unified Presence solutions.

Table 3-20.   Exam Required to Earn the Cisco Unified Presence Specialist Certification

Required Exam	Description
642-072 CUDN	This exam assesses the candidate's knowledge of the Cisco Unity design process, the infrastructure components affecting Cisco Unity design, and the design of a Cisco Unity solution to meet customer requirements.

Table 3-21. Exam Required to Earn the Cisco Unity Design Specialist Certification

Cisco Unity Design Specialist

The Cisco Unity Design Specialist can install, configure, operate, and maintain a Cisco Unity system in both standalone voicemail and unified messaging environments. The candidate also has the knowledge and expertise necessary to create a variety of sustainable Cisco Unity design solutions tailored to specific customer requirements.

Table 3-21 describes the exam required for this certification.

Cisco Unity Support Specialist

The Unity Support Specialist can install, configure, operate, and maintain a Cisco Unity Connection system in both standalone voicemail and unified messaging environments. Specialists are able to integrate Unity Connection with other collaboration products, implement advanced features, administer Voicemail Class of Service, implement security features, and provision many other new capabilities.

Table 3-22 describes the exam required to earn this certification.

Data Center Certifications

The Cisco Certified Data Center Specialist certification programs are practical, relevant, job-ready certifications geared toward the specific tasks expected of data center network professionals.

The curriculum emphasizes the best practices of data center engineering. Having certified and trained personnel to design, implement, and support modern data centers is critical to the success of business—this is especially true for IT departments that are focusing their data center initiatives on better utilizing their network assets.

Required Exam	Description
642-263 IUC	This exam assesses a candidate's knowledge of Cisco Unity Connection v8.0 installation, networking, and advanced features, options, and configuration settings.

Table 3-22. Exam Required to Earn the Cisco Unity Support Specialist Certification

Required Exam	Description
642-972 DCSAD	This exam assesses a candidate's knowledge of Cisco Data Center Application Services and their ability to design a solution for customers.

Table 3-23.   Exam Required to Earn the Cisco Data Center Application Services Design Certification

Cisco Data Center Application Services Design Specialist

The Cisco Data Center Application Services Design Specialist certification demonstrates a network professional's presales knowledge of selecting and integrating Cisco Data Center Application Services products to design a highly scalable, efficient, and high performance Data Center Application Services solution based on Cisco's Data Center Architecture.

Table 3-23 describes the exam required for this certification.

Cisco Data Center Application Services Support Specialist

The Cisco Data Center Application Services Support Specialist certification demonstrates an individual's post-sales knowledge of implementing, integrating, troubleshooting, and maintaining Cisco Data Center Application Services products in a highly scalable, efficient, and high-performance Data Center Application Services solution based on Cisco's Data Center Architecture.

Table 3-24 describes the exam required to earn this certification.

Cisco Data Center Networking Infrastructure Design Specialist

The Cisco Data Center Networking Infrastructure Design Specialist certification demonstrates an individual's knowledge of selecting and integrating Cisco Data Center products to design a scalable, efficient, and high-performing Data Center Networking solution based on Cisco Data Center Architecture.

Table 3-25 describes the exam required to earn this certification.

Required Exam	Description
642-975 DCASI	This exam assesses a candidate's knowledge and skills in installing and supporting a Cisco Data Center Application Services platform.

Table 3-24.   Exam Required to Earn the Cisco Data Center Application Services Support Certification

Required Exam	Description
642-991 DCUFD	This exam tests a candidate's knowledge of designing Cisco Data Center Unified Fabric solutions.

Table 3-25.   Exam Required to Earn the Cisco Data Center Networking Infrastructure Design Specialist Certification

Cisco Data Center Networking Infrastructure Support Specialist

The Cisco Data Center Networking Infrastructure Support Specialist validates an individual's knowledge of installing, configuring, and troubleshooting Cisco Data Center products to maintain a highly scalable, efficient, and high-performing Data Center Networking environment.

Table 3-26 lists the exams required to earn this certification.

Cisco Data Center Storage Networking Design Specialist

The Cisco Data Center Storage Networking Design Specialist certification demonstrates an individual's ability to select and integrate Cisco storage products in order to design a scalable, efficient storage networking solution based on converged architecture. Cisco Data Center Storage Networking Design Specialist professionals understand how to utilize and employ the features and benefits of the Cisco MDS 9000 Series Multilayer Director and Multilayer Fabric Switches to create a highly available storage network design.

Table 3-27 describes the exam required to earn this certification.

Required Exams	Description
642-973 DCNIS-1	This exam tests a candidate's knowledge of the skills needed by a field engineer to install and support a Cisco Data Center Cat 6K and/or 49xx platform.
642-992 DCUFI	This exam tests a candidate's knowledge of implementing Cisco Data Center Unified Fabric solutions.

Table 3-26.   Exams Required to Earn the Cisco Data Center Networking Infrastructure Support Specialist Certification

Required Exam	Description
642-357 DCSNS	This exam tests a candidate's knowledge of selecting and integrating Cisco storage products to design a scalable, efficient, high-performing storage networking solution based on converged architecture.

Table 3-27.   Exam Required to Earn the Cisco Data Center Storage Networking Design Specialist Certification

Cisco Data Center Storage Networking Support Specialist

The Cisco Data Center Storage Networking Support Specialist certification demonstrates an individual's understanding of how to deploy and optimize the features and benefits of the Cisco MDS 9000 Series Multilayer Director and Multilayer Fabric Switches in order to maintain, implement, and troubleshoot a storage network. In addition, this certification covers the use of Cisco NX-OS and provides a technology overview of Cisco Unified Fabric and Cisco Nexus products.

Table 3-28 describes the exam required to earn this certification.

Cisco Data Center Unified Computing Design Specialist

The Cisco Data Center Unified Computing Design Specialist demonstrates the network professional's ability to design scalable, reliable, and intelligent Data Center Virtualization solutions. Additionally, candidates must demonstrate knowledge of:

- Cisco Unified Computing System B and C Series
- Server virtualization software
- Server operating systems
- Additional Cisco Data Center products

Table 3-29 describes the exam required to earn this certification.

Required Exam	Description
642-359 ICSNS	This exam tests a candidate's ability to install, configure, and troubleshoot Cisco storage products in order to maintain a scalable, efficient storage networking environment.

Table 3-28.   Exam Required to Earn the Cisco Data Center Storage Networking Support Specialist Certification

Required Exam	Description
642-993 DCUCD	This exam tests a candidate's knowledge of designing Cisco Data Center Unified Computing systems.

Table 3-29.   Exam Required to Earn the Cisco Data Center Unified Computing Design Specialist Certification

Cisco Data Center Unified Computing Support Specialist

The Cisco Data Center Unified Computing Support Specialist tests the network professional's knowledge of the fundamentals of the Cisco Unified Computing System and their ability to implement a virtualized data center environment. Cisco Data Center Unified Computing Support Specialist professionals will also be tested on the following components:

- Implementing the Cisco Unified Computing System B and C Series
- Cisco Unified Computing System in an enterprise data center routing and switching infrastructure
- Next-generation Cisco Nexus product family

Table 3-30 describes the exam required to earn this certification.

Operating System Software (Cisco IOS XR Specialist)

The Cisco IOS XR Specialist certification demonstrates the knowledge and skills of a network professional to implement, verification test, and maintain core and edge technologies in a Cisco IOS XR environment. The Cisco IOS XR Specialist course (IMTXR) provides the training, whereas the certification validates and confirms hands-on IOS XR experience for network engineers on Cisco Service Provider carrier-class platforms, such as the CRS, ASR 9000, and XR12000.

Table 3-31 describes the exam required to earn this certification.

Required Exam	Description
642-994 DCUCI	This exam tests a candidate's knowledge of implementing Cisco Data Center Unified Computing systems.

Table 3-30.   Exam Required to Earn the Cisco Data Center Unified Computing Support Specialist Certification

Required Exam	Description
644-906 IMTXR	This exam tests a candidate's knowledge of implementing, verification testing, and maintaining Cisco core and edge technologies using the Cisco IOS XR-based router platforms.

Table 3-31. Exam Required to Earn the Cisco IOS XR Specialist Certification

Security Certifications

The Cisco Certified Security Specialist certifications cover a variety of network security needs, and allow the network professional to demonstrate skill and knowledge in any of these arenas. Although the main career path certifications demonstrate broad knowledge of Cisco security protocols and technology, these specialist certifications home in on specific knowledge and skills.

Cisco ASA Specialist

The Cisco ASA Specialist certification recognizes security professionals who have attained specialized expertise and knowledge of the recommended best practices in designing, implementing, maintaining, and troubleshooting network security solutions, using the Cisco ASA adaptive security appliance. The Cisco ASA Specialist is recognized as the benchmark security product certification for engineers, consultants, and architects who configure advanced Cisco security appliances and VPN solutions, including advanced protocol handling, remote access VPNs, Secure Sockets Layer VPNs, site-to-site VPNs, high-availability VPNs, and failover.

Table 3-32 lists the exams required for this certification.

Cisco Firewall Security Specialist

A Cisco Firewall Security Specialist certification shows a network professional's expertise in the realm of firewall operation and usage. Certification holders are actively involved in developing secure business solutions and designing and delivering multiple levels of secure access to the network.

Table 3-33 lists the exams required to earn this certification.

Required Exams	Description
642-618 FIREWALL V2.0	This exam assesses a candidate's knowledge and skills needed to implement and maintain Cisco ASA-based perimeter solutions.
642-648 VPN 2.0	This exam tests a candidate's knowledge and skills needed to deploy Cisco ASA-based VPN solutions.

Table 3-32. Exams Required to Earn the Cisco ASA Specialist Certification

Require Exams	Description
642-618 FIREWALL V2.0	This exam assesses a candidate's knowledge and skills needed to implement and maintain Cisco ASA-based perimeter solutions.
642-637 SECURE	This exam assesses a candidate's knowledge and skills needed to secure Cisco IOS Software router- and switch-based networks, and provide security services based on Cisco IOS Software.

Table 3-33.   Exams Required to Earn the Cisco Firewall Security Specialist Certification

Cisco IOS Security Specialist

The Cisco IOS Security Specialist certification shows security professionals who demonstrate the knowledge and skills that are required to secure networks, including using Cisco IOS Security features for switch and router security as well as the widely deployed Cisco security appliances. Cisco IOS Security Specialists are able to secure the network environment and provide security services that are based on Cisco IOS Software, such as zone-based policy firewall, Cisco IOS IPS, user-based firewall, secure tunnels using IPSec VPN technology—including PKI, VTI and DVTI, Group Encrypted Transport VPN, and DMVPN—and advanced switch security features.

Table 3-34 describes the exam necessary to earn this certification.

Cisco IPS Specialist

The Cisco IPS Specialist certification recognizes security professionals who can deploy, configure, and troubleshoot the Cisco Intrusion Prevention System (IPS) to work properly in a complete security solution. The Cisco IPS Specialist is the foundation for individuals who can operate and monitor Cisco IOS Software and IPS technologies to prevent, understand, and respond to intrusion attempts.

Table 3-35 describes the exam required to earn this certification.

Require Exams	Description
642-637 SECURE	This exam assesses a candidate's knowledge and skills needed to secure Cisco IOS Software router- and switch-based networks, and provide security services based on Cisco IOS Software.

Table 3-34.   Exam Required to Earn the Cisco IOS Security Specialist Certification

Required Exam	Description
642-627 IPS v7.0	This exam assesses a candidate's knowledge and skills needed to deploy Cisco IPS-based security solutions.

Table 3-35.   Exam Required to Earn the Cisco IPS Specialist Certification

Cisco Network Admission Control Specialist

The Cisco Network Admission Control Specialist shows the skills necessary to install, configure, and operate the Cisco NAC appliance. By applying their knowledge of the Cisco NAC solution, the Cisco Network Admission Control Specialist demonstrates the skills and knowledge needed to effectively identify, isolate, and clean infected or vulnerable devices that attempt to access the network.

Table 3-36 describes the exam required to earn this certification.

Cisco VPN Security Specialist

The Cisco VPN Security Specialist certification recognizes security professionals with the skills and knowledge to configure, maintain, troubleshoot, and support various VPN solutions, using Cisco IOS Software and the Cisco ASA adaptive security appliance.

Table 3-37 describes the exams required to earn this certification.

Video Certifications

Cisco Video Specialist certifications validate skills for Cisco Video and Collaboration IT solutions. These certifications and related training align closely with the on-the-job performance needs of video IT, audio/video, and networking professionals seeking to specialize in the planning, designing, implementation, and management of video deployments.

Required Exam	Description
642-591 CANAC	This exam requires candidates to demonstrate knowledge of implementing a Cisco NAC appliance.

Table 3-36.   Exam Required to Earn the Cisco Network Admission Control Specialist Certification

Required Exams	Description
642-637 Secure v1.0	This exam assesses a candidate's knowledge and skills needed to secure Cisco IOS Software router- and switch-based networks, and provide security services based on Cisco IOS Software.
642-648 VPN 2.0	This exam tests a candidate's knowledge and skills needed to deploy Cisco ASA-based VPN solutions.

Table 3-37.   Exams Required to Earn the Cisco VPN Security Specialist Certification

Cisco Rich Media Communications Specialist

The Cisco Rich Media Communications Specialist certification validates an IT professional's ability to successfully design, implement, and support integrated voice, video, and web collaboration in a converged network.

Table 3-38 describes the exams required to earn this certification.

Cisco TelePresence Installations Specialist

The Cisco TelePresence Installations Specialist certification focuses on the job-performance needs of an Installation Professional seeking to master the physical deployment and construction of single-screen Cisco TelePresence systems (500, 1000, 1100, 1300).

Required Exams	Description
642-481 CRMC	This exam assesses the candidate's knowledge and skills to provide presales technical support, design, installation, configuration, and maintenance of Cisco rich media solutions based on Cisco Unified MeetingPlace Express and Cisco Unified Videoconferencing.
642-437 CVOICE v8.0	This exam assesses a candidate's knowledge of how to implement and operate gateways, gatekeepers, Cisco Unified Border Element, Cisco Unified Communications Manager Express, and QoS in a voice network architecture.

Table 3-38.   Exams Required to Earn the Cisco Rich Media Communications Specialist Certification

Required Exam	Description
642-188 ITI	This exam is used to assess the candidate's understanding of the physical installations of the Cisco TelePresence 500, 1000, 1100, and 1300 systems.

Table 3-39.   Exam Required to Earn the Cisco TelePresence Installations Specialist Certification

Topics include room readiness recommendations, physical assembly of single-screen systems, codec cabling, first-time setup, camera tuning, and installation of auxiliary devices such as document cameras. Resulting skills development enables network engineers and technicians to install the furniture; to construct the frame, table, stand, and wall mount; and to connect the cables and networking equipment for the Cisco TelePresence 500, 1000, 1100, and 1300 systems.

Table 3-39 describes the exam required to earn this certification.

Cisco TelePresence Solutions Specialist

The Cisco TelePresence Solutions Specialist certification focuses on the job-performance needs of a voice specialist or networking engineer who wants to specialize in the planning, design, implementation (PDI), and maintenance of Cisco TelePresence deployments. Tasks include assessing network paths for rich media, evaluating call-control design options, and configuring interoperability functions.

Table 3-40 describes the exam required to earn this certification.

Required Exam	Description
642-185 ITSI	This exam is used to assess a candidate's knowledge and skills in implementing Cisco TelePresence Solutions and how the solutions are physically installed.

Table 3-40.   Exams Required to Earn the Cisco TelePresence Solutions Specialist Certification

Where to Get Help

With the certification tracks ranging from Cisco to Microsoft to Novell, forward-minded, entrepreneurial individuals and organizations have found a niche to help the hopeful wireheads. If digging through stacks of white papers and dry texts is just too much to stomach, there are a number of interactive alternatives that can help you achieve that much-sought-after Cisco certification.

Websites

If you haven't already taken a peek into cyberspace, there are a number of websites out there willing to help you earn that Cisco Certification. Like any topic represented on the World Wide Web, sites range in their slickness, complexity, and usefulness. Some seem to have been slapped together as an afterthought; others are chock full of information and have a slick, professional layout and design.

Some sites simply require you to register; others charge a fee; and some others are completely free. Be wary of the websites where a group of people who recently took the test are sharing answers. It's akin to buying used college textbooks just so you can cut to the highlighted bits—how do you know the person who had the book before you knew what he was doing? It's the same deal for testing. Sometimes, posters will claim to have the exact test questions along with the correct answers. As attractive as this is, don't bet your testing fee on what an anonymous person out in the ether tries to tell you.

If you can't afford to set up a brand-new Cisco router in your living room, some sites offer access to test routers so you can experiment with commands and see their results. One such site is Clickx3, which isn't especially fancy, but is full of information for the CCNA exam (along with several other companies' certifications). Some sites, like Clickx3, offer this service for free; others charge for online lab time.

Table 3-41 lists a number of websites that can help you prepare for the certification.

Name	URL
CCPrep	www.ccprep.com
Certification Zone	www.certificationzone.com/cisco
Learn Key	www.learnkey.com
Boson	www.boson.com
Cisco	www.cisco.com/en/US/learning/index.html

Table 3-41.   Websites That Can Help With Certification Preparation

Classes

A number of independent learning centers offer classes to bone up for the Cisco Certification exams. The classes' format will guide what kind of educational experience you can expect.

Some classes are formulated around quarter and semester formats and require an hour or so a couple times a week, with the final exam in the form of the actual Cisco Certification exam. But for those who don't want to wait three or four months, there are accelerated courses—or "boot camps"—that can pound the information into your head in less than a week.

Don't worry too much—I'm quite certain no push-ups are required and not many dogfaces have had to push a rack of routers and switches up a muddy hill at 4 A.M. while calling cadence. Different boot camps are suited for different people. Some are very intense and are best for those with little or no experience. These usually require you to live, eat, and breathe Cisco. Still others are designed for people who have some previous experience and aren't nearly as severe.

Boot camps aren't cheap. In the real Army, you have to pay with blood, sweat, and tears. But for certification, the only price you'll pay is in cold, hard cash—many cost around $7,000 plus hotel and other transportation expenses (at least in the Army you get three hots and a cot).

It's in your best interest to compare boot camps and other training courses—first, to find the course that matches with your skill level and needs, and second to make sure you're actually learning, not just studying to pass the test. Without getting an understanding of the technologies and tools, you could still pass the tests. However, you would have the certification in name only, and would be in trouble the first time you had to do something that wasn't asked on the test.

Table 3-42 lists some companies offering Cisco classes and boot camps.

Don't forget your local community and technical colleges. Years ago, Cisco started a program through community and technical colleges to train certified techs. The courses emphasize learning, they are endorsed by Cisco (many other training programs are not), and you're likely to come away with more than you would at a boot camp. Not only will you get the training and the certification you're after, but you also get a bullet point for your resume, acknowledging your training. You may also score some college credit.

No matter what your Cisco certification goal or the means by which you choose to achieve that goal, the end result will be most beneficial. Certification puts you in a select class that understands and can be counted on to design, build, and maintain the plumbing of the Internet.

Name	URL
Global Knowledge	www.globalknowledge.com
CCPrep	www.ccprep.com
Intense School	www.intenseschool.com

Table 3-42. Cisco Boot Camps

PART II | Cisco Internetworking Tools

CHAPTER 4 | Routing Overview

A dizzying array of hardware, software, telecommunications media, and technical expertise goes into internetworking. Switches, hubs, firewalls, packets, gateways, ports, access servers, interfaces, layers, protocols, serial lines, LTE, DSL, SONET, frames, topologies—the list can seem endless. A route is defined as a course, way, or a road for passage or travel. So why then is routing the focus for this chapter? Because without a device that performs routing (usually simply called a "router," the device Cisco built its company on), all that fancy fiber-optic cable crisscrossing the globe is no more than high-quality melted sand encapsulated within protective sheathing. Without routing, internetworks could not exist. Routers are the devices that are required to interconnect LANs.

In the most basic terms, *internetworking* is about nothing more than linking computers and people through a maze of intermediary telecommunications lines and computing devices. This takes routing, which, in essence, involves just two fundamental missions: determine a path along which a link can be made, and transmit packets across that path. It is within these two functions—which take place inside a router—that internetworking becomes easier to understand. This is because the router itself must cut all the complexity down to a level it can deal with. The router does this by working with everything, one IP packet at a time.

The router used to be the centerpiece of internetworking. Not so in the present day. Today the *routing process* is the cornerstone that exists in almost every networking device. Large, corporate data centers and campuses are no longer the only users of multi-LAN environments. Each and every scenario involving the Internet today requires a device that performs routing on both ends. Internet, you say? Isn't that the place where the black-hatted, hacker cowboys live, and shouldn't we have a firewall inspecting that traffic? Sure thing, but guess what? That firewall is also a router. So are the DSL and cable Internet modems that ISPs need in your home or business to provide you with broadband connections. How about that Linksys "by Cisco" Wi-Fi access point you have at home that allows you to share your home Internet with friends on a guest network? You got it, it's a router. DSL and cable Internet, 4G cellular Internet? Absolutely, there are routing processes running on each and every one. The short version is this: Without routing, there would be no Internet.

Looked at in this way, the router is the basic fabric of internetworks. Indeed, without the router, the Internet as we know it couldn't even exist. This is because of the unique and powerful capabilities of routers:

- They can simultaneously support different protocols (such as Ethernet, SONET and others), effectively making virtually all computers compatible at the internetwork level.

- They seamlessly connect local area networks (LANs) to wide area networks (WANs), which makes it feasible to build large-scale internetworks with minimal centralized planning—sort of like Lego™ sets.

- They filter out unwanted traffic by isolating areas in which messages can be "broadcast" to all users in a network.

- They can act as simple security gateways by checking or "screening" traffic against access control lists (ACLs).

- They can also ensure transport reliability by providing multiple paths through internetworks.

- They can be configured to automatically learn about new paths and select the best ones, eliminating artificial constraints on changing internetworks.

In other words, routers make internetworks possible. They do so by providing a unified and secure environment in which large groups of people can connect. However, there are obstacles to bringing users together on internetworks, whether on a corporate intranet, a virtual private network, or the Internet itself. Figure 4-1 depicts how routing technology is the key to overcoming these obstacles.

The router's ability to support communications between a wide variety of devices is certainly its most important role. Way back when, the computer industry spent decades and millions of dollars debating how computers were to talk with each other. All the jostling, positioning, and open struggling to create compatibility between proprietary systems met with limited success. Yet, in less than a decade, TCP/IP internetworking became a common platform across which virtually all computer and network architectures could freely exchange information.

The router's ability to filter out unwanted remote traffic is also important to internetworking. If users are bombarded with volumes of unwanted messages, or if they feel their systems can be easily broken into, they will resist linking up to internetworks. Properly configured filtering and access control provided by routers can give users (devices) some of the basic protections necessary to effectively participate in internetworks.

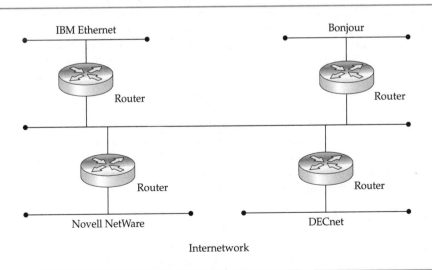

Figure 4-1. Routers make internetworks possible by overcoming incompatibility.

There are other important types of network devices besides the router, but understanding how a router works will go a long way toward your understanding of the whole of internetworking. Before you can learn how to configure and manage routers, however, you need to know the basics of what one is made of, and that is what you'll learn in this chapter. The following chapter provides a general review of Cisco router hardware and software.

How Routers Work

In a nutshell, routers do exactly what their name says: They route data from one network to another network, then another network, and so on, until data is delivered to its final destination. Routers can also act as rudimentary traffic cops, allowing only authorized computers to transmit data into the local network so that private information can remain secure. Routers can be used to support many types of network connections, from dedicated connections (such as Ethernet or leased lines) to dial-in connections. In addition to supporting these dial-in and leased connections, routers handle errors, keep network usage statistics, and oversee some security issues.

Routing for Efficiency

When you download a file from a File Transfer Protocol (FTP) server, it's the routing technology that ensures you are getting the file from a specific server and not from a different server hooked up elsewhere on the Internet. Routers direct the flow of traffic among, rather than within, networks. For instance, let's consider how routers can be used within a LAN to keep information flowing.

Design-O-Rama is a computer graphics company. The company's LAN is divvied into two smaller LANs—one for the animators and one for the administration and support staff, as shown in Figure 4-2. The two subdivisions are connected with a router. Design-O-Rama employs eight people—four animators and four other staffers. When one animator sends a file to another, the large file will use a great deal of the network's capacity. This results in performance problems for the others on the network.

To keep the animators from constantly slowing things down, the network was divided into two—one for the animators and one for everybody else. A router links the two networks and connects them both to the Internet. The router is the only device on the network that sees every message sent by any computer on either network. When an animator sends a file to a colleague, the router looks at the recipient's address and keeps that piece of traffic isolated on that LAN. On the other hand, if the animator wants to query the Human Resources department's server about vacation time, the router knows to direct those packets to the HR department's network segment.

Routers and the Internet

In our previous example, we examined how a router could be used locally. Now, let's broaden the scope of what routers do to include their functionality across the entire Internet.

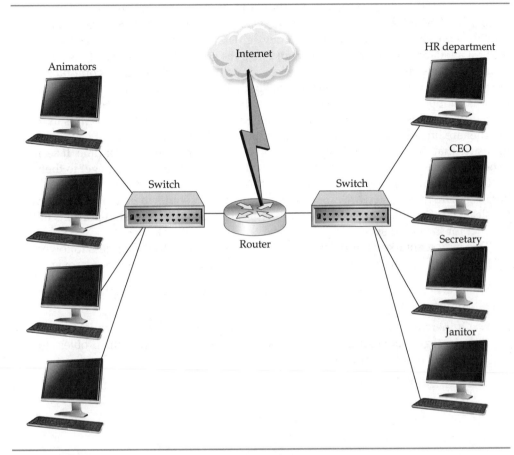

Figure 4-2.   Routers can be used to improve efficiency within a LAN.

For the sake of comparison, let's first talk about how a telephone call is routed across the country. Say its Aunt Sadie's birthday and rather than send an e-mail, you want to call her. When you make a long-distance call, the telephone system establishes a stable circuit between your telephone and Aunt Sadie's. The circuit may involve hopping through a number of steps, including fiber optics, copper wires, and satellites. This end-to-end chain ensures that the quality of the line between you and Aunt Sadie will be constant. However, if the satellite goes offline or work crews sever the fiber-optic cable, your conversation with Aunt Sadie will be cut short. The Internet avoids this problem by making its "calls" in an entirely different way.

Packets and Paths

Whatever information is sent across the Internet (e-mail, web page, and so on) is first broken into packets. The size of these packets will vary based on network parameters and other factors we'll cover later—for the purposes of discussion, let's say they are 1,500 bytes. The packets may be transmitted across a number of routers, each one sending a packet toward its destination device. The packets will be transmitted through the best available route. Each packet could take the same route, or none of the packets could take the same route. Once the packets show up at the destination computer, they are reassembled. This process goes so quickly that you wouldn't even know that the file was chopped into 1,500-byte packets and then reassembled.

Figure 4-3 illustrates how a packet-switched network operates. The routers in the Internet are linked together in a web. The packets follow the path of least resistance to ensure that they arrive at their destination in a reasonable amount of time. It seems logical that the packets would go through the least number of routers to get to their destination. However, sometimes the fastest route isn't the most direct one. This is because there may be network congestion or a slow link somewhere along the shortest (or "least hop") path. Routers can send the traffic around the congested portions of the Internet for increased speed and efficiency.

This may seem like a complicated system—as compared to the process followed when placing a telephone call—but the system works for two important reasons:

- The network can balance the load across different pieces of equipment on a millisecond-by-millisecond basis.

- If there is a problem with one piece of equipment in the network while a message is being transmitted, packets can be routed around the problem to ensure that the entire message is received.

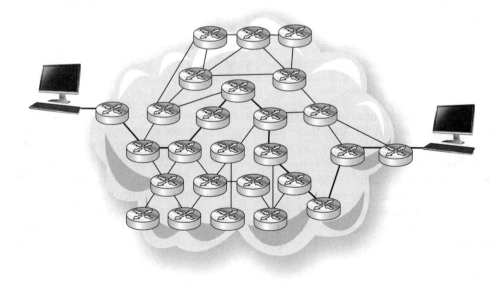

Figure 4-3.   Routers send packets across the perceived path of least resistance.

The routers that make up the main backbone of the Internet can reconfigure the paths that packets take because they look at all the information surrounding the data packet, and they tell each other about line conditions, such as problems sending and receiving data on various parts of the Internet.

All Shapes and Sizes

Not every router is responsible for the fate of packets whizzing across the Internet. Routers come in different sizes and do more or less, depending on how big and sophisticated they are. For instance:

- If you have enabled Internet Connection Sharing between two Microsoft Windows 8–based computers, the computer that is connected to the Internet is acting as a simple router. This router does very little—it just looks at data to see which computer it's meant for.

- Routers that are used to connect small offices to the Internet do more. They may be configured to enforce rules about security for the office LAN, and they generally handle enough traffic that they tend to be stand-alone devices.

- The biggest routers (the ones used to handle data at the major traffic points on the Internet) deal with a lot of information—millions of packets each second. These are stand-alone devices that look more like Maytag made them than a computer company.

Let's consider the medium-sized router—it's probably something likely to be humming away in a small room at a typical small or medium-sized business. To keep it simple, let's say that this router only has two places to deal with—your LAN and the Internet. The office LAN connects to the router through an Ethernet connection. The router might also have two connections to your company's ISP—a T3 and a DSL connection. For the most part, your traffic comes and goes over the T3 line. However, the DSL line is used in the event something goes awry with the T3 line. In fact, the router is configured to send data across the DSL line, because the configuration table has been programmed to switch over in case of an emergency.

This router is also tasked with another function—it can be a "screening" layer of security against outside attacks. Although firewalls are routinely used to prevent access, and are strongly recommended (you would be insane not to use one when connected to the Internet), an external router should also be configured with security in mind.

Optical Routers

In a conventional internetwork, information would be transmitted using twisted-pair copper wire across a WAN or even a LAN. As useful and utilitarian as twisted-pair cabling and an electrical network have been, fiber optics allow information to be transferred at immensely higher rates. In the past, when computers shared only brief conversations across the miles, electrical networks could handle the load. But now, as information is shared as it has never been shared before, there is a clear need for an upgrade in network capacities.

Comparing the bit rates in electrical networks to optical networks is like putting Woody Allen in a prison yard fistfight with Mike Tyson—there's just no comparison. The greatest things that optical networks have going for them is raw speed and huge capacity.

Common WAN links that move across electrical networks are T1 (1.544 Mbps) and T3 (45 Mbps). There are even serial circuits that are run across vDSL2 and presented to customers as bonded T1 interfaces (unbeknownst to them). On the LAN front, things get a little better. Most organizations use 100 Mbps, 1000 Mbps, or 10Gbps Ethernet. The top-of-the-line copper-based Ethernet clocks in at 10 Gbps; however, once fiber optics get into the race, look out. Although still rare, 100 Gbps Ethernet is now publicly available.

At their slowest, fiber-optic networks speed along much faster than a T1 or a T3. Once fiber shifts out of first gear, there ceases to be a comparison. When discussing optical networking speeds, you'll hear the terminology change from T1 or T3 to OC. OC stands for *optical carrier*. OC takes over where T leaves off. Once the optical carrier gets involved, speeds not only reach 1 Gbps, but even leave 1 Gbps in the rearview mirror.

Table 4-1 shows how optical networking line speeds increase.

As you can see, the speed rates in optical networks (not to mention their development) increase at an amazing velocity. Thanks to dense wavelength division multiplexing (DWDM), optical bandwidth will only increase, because more than one stream of data can be introduced on a single run of fiber. More on that in a moment.

Optical Technologies

The two prevalent technologies in the world of optical routing are SONET and DWDM. SONET (aka T1.105.06) is the oldest and most popular technology, whereas DWDM is somewhat of a new kid on the block, but supports capacities much greater than SONET. Let's examine these technologies in a little more depth.

Designation	Speed
OC-1	51 Mbps
OC-3	155 Mbps
OC-12	622 Mbps
OC-24	1.244 Gbps
OC-48	2.488 Gbps
OC-192	9.952 Gbps
OC-768	39.813 Gbps

Table 4-1.   Optical Networking Speeds

SONET The most basic and popular architecture for an optical network is the Synchronous Optical Network (SONET).

SONET is a standard for optical telecommunications transport developed by the Exchange Carriers Standards Association (ECSA) for the American National Standards Institute (ANSI), the body that sets industry standards in the United States for telecommunications and other industries. The comprehensive SONET standard is expected to provide the transport infrastructure for worldwide telecommunications for at least the next two or three decades.

NOTE In Europe, SONET is known by another acronym, SDH, which is short for Synchronous Digital Hierarchy.

SONET is so speedy that you could transmit an entire 650MB CD-ROM from New York to Seattle in less than one second. Not only is SONET fast, but it's also rather versatile. Voice calls from one office to another can be multiplexed along with data and fired out across the same fiber. Furthermore, because of the generous bandwidth SONET affords, compression and encapsulation into Internet Protocol (IP) packets is unnecessary. For comparison's sake, a single OC-3 connection can carry more than 2,000 simultaneous voice calls. In addition, all types of data can be multiplexed alongside the calls.

SONET offers a top-end bandwidth of OC-768 (39.813 Gbps) and can carry a diverse range of information. In addition to high speeds, SONET features bit-error rates of one error in 10 billion bits. Compare this with copper transmission methods that have bit-error rates of one error in 1 million bits.

DWDM In its beginning, SONET delivered bandwidth that was previously unimaginable. At the time, delivering OC-3 levels (155.52 Mbps) provided more bandwidth than anyone knew what to do with. Of course, those were in the mid-1980s, a decade before the Internet and high-bandwidth applications. Technology kept delivering faster and faster optical carriers. After OC-3, there were OC-12, OC-48, and beyond.

OC-192 (9.953 Gbps) is a popular speed for SONET; however, the next level, OC-768 (39.813 Gbps), is about the best SONET will be able to deliver. Sure, 20 years ago no one knew what a gigabit was, but now we do and we can't get enough of them. The problem is that 40 Gbps is about SONET's limit. The solution is a combination of DWDM and a new specification, G.709.

DWDM is a technique in which multiple signals can traverse a single strand of optical fiber. The lasers used in optical networking can be tuned to different wavelengths (think of them as different colors). As such, it is possible to put multiple colors on a single fiber. When the receiving router sees the various colors, it knows which colors to separate out for which data streams, as shown in Figure 4-4.

G.709 will eventually replace SONET, as its bandwidth starts at 10 Gbps, and SONET tops out at 40 Gbps. G.709 also allows for simpler management of the worldwide Net because it's designed to map within its protocol structure internally to 10G Ethernet (allowing it to scale with Ethernet to 100 Gbps today and further tomorrow), whereas SONET maps to the 1.5 Mbps E1 of yesteryear.

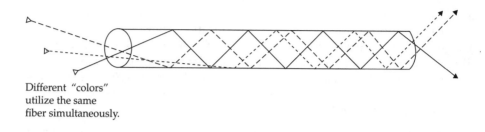

Different "colors"
utilize the same
fiber simultaneously.

Figure 4-4.   Multiple transmissions can be sent on a single fiber using DWDM.

Cisco's Optical Offerings

Cisco utilizes both SONET and DWDM with its optical routers. For example, the Cisco ONS 15600 optical router supports SONET/SDH technology. This carrier-class router supports speeds of 40 Gbps and is capable of transmitting up to 80 kilometers.

Cisco also provides a certain level of modularity with its devices. Rather than make a few models, with a predetermined number of ports set up for Gigabit Ethernet and another amount dedicated to SONET or DWDM, the company has developed cards and modules that can be plugged into a router, thus making it customizable. In other words, you can decide to load the router with SONET modules, DWDM modules, or any combination of optical and electrical you please.

IOS: The Internetwork Operating System

We usually don't think of an operating system as a file. After all, your PC's operating system is made up of many thousands of files (they sit in your directory with file extensions such as .sys, .exe, .drv, and .dll).

However, IOS is indeed contained in a single file. When you ship an IOS file somewhere, it holds everything necessary to run a router. Depending on the version, an IOS software image will have a footprint from 3MB to over 100MB in size.

NOTE   Less-sophisticated Cisco internetworking devices get their intelligence in the form of factory-installed software called *firmware*, which is a subset of IOS itself. It can be field-upgraded to keep the device's software current with the rest of the network.

IOS needs to be tightly constructed because copies of it, referred to as *system images*, are routinely shipped across internetworks. System images are uploaded and downloaded over routers in order to back up routers, upgrade their capabilities, and restart them after a failure. It wouldn't be practical to send thousands of 50MB files. Being able to send a single, small, self-contained IOS file makes effective network management possible.

IOS Feature Sets

Feature sets are packages that try to simplify configuring and ordering IOS software. There is no single IOS software product, per se. IOS is actually a common software platform on which a suite of IOS implementations is based, each one packaged to fulfill a specific mission. Cisco calls these IOS packages *feature sets* (also called *software images* or *feature packs*). When you order a Cisco router, you choose an IOS feature set that contains all the capabilities your particular situation requires. Most of these requirements have to do with maintaining compatibility with the various hardware devices and network protocols in the environment in which the router will operate.

As depicted in Figure 4-5, variants of the Cisco IOS software are defined two ways: by feature set and by release. Feature sets define the job a version of IOS can do; releases are used to manage the IOS software through time.

Cisco IOS feature sets are designed as follows:

- To be compatible with certain router platforms

- To enable interoperability between disparate networking protocols (Novell NetWare, IBM SNA, Bonjour, and so on)

- To provide functional features in the form of network services and applications for such things as network management, security, and multimedia

Packaging and selling IOS software in this way simplifies things for Cisco and customers alike. For the customer, having a single part number to order simplifies figuring out what software to buy. For Cisco, it helps the company's product engineers to figure out what goes where so that their support personnel figure out who has what. Remember, internetworking can get hopelessly complicated because the nature of the business is to enable disparate computer platforms and networking protocols to interoperate and coexist.

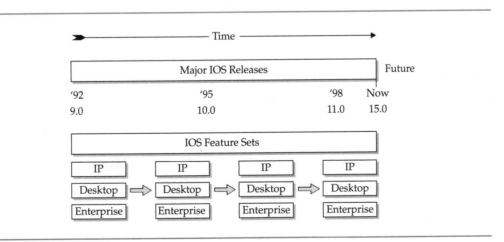

Figure 4-5.   IOS is arranged by releases and feature sets.

How Feature Sets Are Constructed   Because IOS feature sets have dependencies on the router hardware on which they run, two rules of thumb apply:

- You can't run all feature sets on all router platforms.
- Sometimes, specific features within a feature set will or will not run, depending on the router platform.

If you look at a Cisco product catalog, understanding Cisco's feature sets can seem tough at first glance. Feature sets do nothing more than put functionality groupings into logical packages that customers can use. All feature sets, in one way or another, derive their functionality from about a dozen categories, listed in Table 4-2.

Don't worry about the examples on the right side of this table or all the acronyms you don't know. The important thing here is to understand that IOS software's myriad features and functions can be grouped into about a dozen categories.

Cisco IOS feature sets try to combine features into groups most likely to match real-world customer requirements. Cisco offers dozens of point-product feature sets in the form of IOS software product numbers you can put on a purchase order. They are grouped by general characteristics into the four general feature set families shown in Table 4-3. Notice in Tables 4-2 and 4-3 that proprietary computer platforms, such as IBM, DEC, and Apple, and proprietary networking platforms, such as Novell

Category	Examples of Features
LAN support	IP, Novell IPX, Bonjour, Banyan VINES, DECnet
WAN services	PPP, ATM LAN emulation, Frame Relay, ISDN, X.25
WAN optimization	Dial-on-demand, snapshot routing, traffic shaping
IP routing	BGP, RIP, IGRP, Enhanced IGRP, OSPF, IS-IS, NAT
Other routing	IPX RIP, AURP, NLSP
Multimedia and QoS	Generic traffic shaping, random early detection, RSVP
Management	SNMP, RMON, Cisco Call History MIB, Virtual Profiles
Security	Access lists, extended access lists, lock and key, TACACS+
Switching	Fast-switched policy routing, Bonjour routing over ISL
IBM support	APPN, Bisync, Frame Relay for SNA, SDLC integration
Protocol translation	LAT, PPP, X.25
Remote node	PPP, SLIP, MacIP, IP pooling, CSLIP, NetBEUI over PPP
Terminal services	LAT, Xremote, Telnet, X.25 PAD

Table 4-2.   IOS Software Feature Categories

Feature Set	Target Customer Environment
IP Base	Basic IP routing
IP Voice	IP voice routing
Enterprise Base	High-end functionality for LANs, WANs, and management
Advanced Security	Enhanced security features
Enterprise Services	Includes the features of the Enterprise Base, along with voice services, ATM, and MPLS support
Advanced IP Services	Includes the functionality of IP Base and Voice, along with ATM, MPLS, and security support
Advanced Enterprise Services	Same as Enterprise, but with additional security features

Table 4-3.   iOS Feature Set Families

and SNA, drive much of the need for feature sets. Each Cisco router must deal with the customer's real-world compatibility requirements, which means being able to run with legacy hardware and software. Nearly all legacy architectures exist at the "network's edge"—which is to say most of the proprietary equipment with which IP must maintain compatibility sits either on LANs or on computers sitting on the LANs. This is where compatibility issues with proprietary legacy computer architectures or specialized platforms are manifested.

Tables 4-2 and 4-3 also show which software functionality groupings go into what IOS feature set products. For example, multinational enterprises are likely to be interested in IBM functionality, such as NetBEUI over PPP and Frame Relay for SNA, and would probably be interested in one of the Enterprise/APPN feature sets. By contrast, an advertising agency heavy into Apple and Windows would focus on the Desktop feature sets.

Grouping feature sets into families is Cisco's way of bringing a semblance of order to pricing policies and upgrade paths. Ordering a single IOS part number instead of dozens helps everybody avoid mistakes. Figure 4-6 depicts the process of feature set selection.

Last, feature sets are further grouped into software product variants:

- **Basic**   The basic feature set for the hardware platform.
- **Plus**   The basic feature set and additional features, which are dependent on the hardware platform selected.
- **Encryption**   The addition of an encryption feature atop either the Basic or Plus feature set. Cisco added a 256-bit AES in 12.2(13).

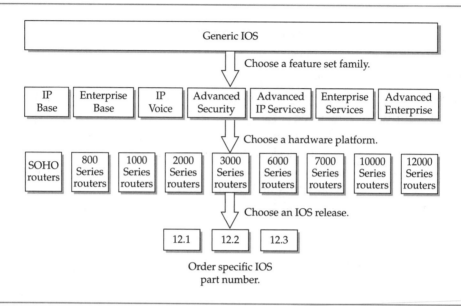

Figure 4-6. The process of configuring a specific IOS feature set involves selecting desired attributes.

The ultimate goal of feature sets is to guide you through the process of ordering, say, IOS Feature Set Enterprise 56 for a Cisco 7500/RSP running Release 11—without making a mistake that costs your network upgrade project a two-week delay.

The new platforms are shipping with a universal image. This image has all the features available and you enable features, data, security, UC, and switching by purchasing a license that unlocks the required feature.

The Anatomy of Cisco Release Numbers Cisco IOS software release numbers have four basic parts, as shown in Figure 4-7.

The first part is a major release (the "12" in Figure 4-7), which marks First Customer Shipments (FCS) of an IOS version of stable, high-quality software for customers to use in their production networks. Major releases are further defined by the following:

- **Stage** The "3" in Figure 4-7, which marks FCS of various major release stages (first release, general deployment release, short-lived release, and so on). Stage releases are often referred to in the future tense, when they are still planned but have not yet taken place.

- **Maintenance update** The "5e" in Figure 4-7, which denotes support for additional platforms of features beyond what was available in the major release's FCS.

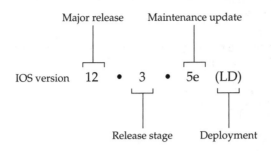

Figure 4-7. There are four major parts in an IOS release number.

The fourth part of the release number is the deployment. A mainline deployment (MD) release is for unconstrained use by all customers. Early deployment (ED) releases are used to deliver new functionality or technologies to customers to deploy in a limited manner in their networks. Limited deployment (LD) denotes a limited lifecycle between FCS and MD.

At any given time, there can be several major releases in use in the field. For example, five versions of IOS 12 are available, but 11.2 and 11.3 are still used. Most network managers are content to stick with a release they know works for them. Early adopters use advanced IOS releases because they need platform or feature support not available before. Most users are happy to let the early adopters help Cisco shake things out before general release.

NOTE The terms "version" and "release" are sometimes used interchangeably in connection with editions of IOS software. In this book, "version" is used to specify a particular release of a particular IOS feature set.

Using TFTP for IOS Backups and Updates

In the event of a network catastrophe, it is possible for a router's IOS system image to be corrupted or erased from flash memory altogether. Standard procedure is to maintain a backup image of every IOS version in use in the network being managed. These backup IOS images are maintained on TFTP servers or within network management applications, such as CiscoWorks and Cisco Prime (covered in Chapter 16).

TFTP stands for Trivial File Transfer Protocol. TFTP is a TCP/IP application derived from the early days of the Unix operating system. As you may have guessed, TFTP is a stripped-down version of FTP, the command many of you have used to download files over the Internet. IOS uses TFTP instead of FTP because it's speedier and uses fewer system resources.

So-called TFTP servers are computer platforms on an internetwork that store and download IOS system images and configuration files. It is recommended that more than one TFTP server be used to back up a network. This is in case the TFTP server itself goes down or the network segment connecting it to the devices it backs up becomes unavailable.

To load a new IOS image to a router's flash memory, use the **copy tftp flash** command, following the procedure shown here:

```
Router#copy tftp flash
System flash directory:
File  Length    Name/status
   1   4171336   c4500-j-mz_112-15a.bin
[4171400 bytes used, 22904 available, 4194304 total]
Address or name of remote host [10.1.10.40]? 10.1.10.40
Source file name? c4500-j-mz_112-15a.bin
Destination file name [c4500-j-mz_112-15a.bin]? <cr>
Accessing file 'c4500-j-mz_112-15a.bin' on 10.1.10.40...
Loading c4500-j-mz_112-15a.bin from 10.1.1.12 (via TokenRing1): [OK]

Erase flash device before writing? [confirm]yes
Flash contains files. Are you sure you want to erase? [confirm]yes

Copy 'c4500-j-mz_112-15a.bin' from server
   as 'c4500-j-mz_112-15a.bin' into Flash WITH erase? [yes/no]yes
Erasing device... eeeeeeeeeeeeeeee ...erased
Loading c4500-j-mz_112-15a.bin from 10.1.1.12 (via TokenRing1): ! !!!!!
!!!!!!!!!!!!!!!!!!!!!!!!!!!!!!!!!!!!!!!!!!!!!!!!!!!!!!!!!! !!!!!!!!!!
!!!!!!!!!!!!!!!!!!!!!!!!!!!!!!!!!!!!!!!!!!!!!!!!!!!!!!!!! !!!!!!!!!!!!!
!!!!!!!!!!!!!!!!!!!!!!!!!!!!!!!!!!!!!!!!!!!!!!!!!!!!! !!!!!!!!!!!!!!!!!!
!!!!!!!!!!!!!!!!!!!!!!!!!!!!!!!!!!!!!!!!!!!!!!!! !!!!!!!!!!!!!!!!!!!!!!!
!!!!!!!!!!!!!!!!!!!!!!!!!!!!!!!!!!!!!!!!!!!! !!!!!!!!!!!!!!!!!!!!!!!!!!!
!!!!!!!!!!!!!!!!!!!!!!!!!!!!!!!!!!!!!!!! !!!!!!!!!!!!!!!!!!!!!!!!!!!!!!!
!!!!!!!!!!!!!!!!!!!!!!!!!!!!!!!! !!!!!!!!!!!!!!!!!!!!!!!!!!!!!!!!!!!!!!!
!!!!!!!!!!!!!!!!!!!!!!!!!! !!!!!!!!!!!!!!!!!!!!!!!!!!!!!!!!!!!!!!!!!!!!!
!!!!!!!!!!!!!!!!!
[OK - 4171336/4194304 bytes]

Verifying checksum...  OK (0x29D5)
Flash copy took 00:00:30 [hh:mm:ss]
Router#
```

You can see that the TFTP server confirmed that it had the IOS system image before overwriting the one in the router's flash memory. Each exclamation point in the display indicates that a block of the file was successfully copied over the network from the server to the router.

NOTE   If you are copying a file to a TFTP server, be sure the name of the file that you are attempting to transfer already exists in the TFTP directory, unless you have configured the TFTP daemon to accept new files. Create the file on Unix systems using the **touch** command. On Microsoft platforms, open Notepad to create the file and save it under the filename.

Router Security

Router security is an important and dual-pointed topic. Access control is not limited to routers, and we'll have more on Cisco security issues in Chapters 8 and 9. We'll continue deeper into security practices and appliances in Chapter 10. For now, let's break router security down into the following sections.

Router Administrative Security

This consists of the security layers safeguarding the device itself. Beginning with physical access, access control protects the device from those who would subvert your traffic by simply powering it off or logging in to the router and then misconfiguring it for a denial-of-service attack. It will stop misguided individuals or systems from sending your traffic to the wrong location in order to capture it for nefarious purposes. Whoever can access your router's configuration can make changes that may be adverse or sublime. What parts of the configuration that individuals may change are the basis of access control talked about in Chapter 9. Who can audit the configuration and thus gain knowledge of your network via its routing tables are just as important in today's internetworks as making sure legitimate traffic continues to flow.

Router Network Security

Router network security is the practice of disallowing and allowing traffic between specific hosts, internetworks, interfaces, and so on. This can be implemented via routes, access lists, or the IOS firewall. Router visibility is also managed via network security. An important best practice for security on a router is to disable any unauthenticated information transfer about the devices and their configuration.

To achieve this, services such as Cisco Discovery Protocol (CDP) need to be disabled. For example, if Cisco Discovery Protocol (which is multicast at a layer 2) is enabled on a router, every adjacent device knows its IOS version, VTP information, and more. The less information about a device that is available, the less surface area and fewer vectors a hacker has to attack. If that router's neighbor is compromised, CDP will betray it and give the hacker free information. A router handles traffic-based security the opposite of a firewall. Its purpose is to get traffic from point A to point B; therefore, its security policy is "accept," unless denied by a lack of a route or an access control list.

Conversely, firewalls deny everything that isn't explicitly allowed. That isn't to suggest a router cannot participate in securing the traffic of an internetwork; it simply means that thoughtful consideration of numerous tools within the IOS software can be used for the same purpose. If a route doesn't exist between a hacker's PC and a target server, no access control list (ACL) or firewall is required.

ACLs are similar to a user list in that they explicitly permit or deny traffic from one subnet or host to another subnet or host. However, without a third-party service such as Cisco's Access Control Server, an ACL cannot be authenticated. The majority of ACLs are implemented as static entries on the router itself. An example is placing an ACL on the SSH configuration of a remote terminal session, stating that SSH clients must come from the specific IP address assigned to the network administrator for that router. Router encryption involves encrypting data in transit. Traditionally utilized across the public Internet, a router configured to use a Virtual Private Network (VPN) tunnel between itself and another router employs encryption techniques to keep the data between two or more points private. Using these encryption techniques between routers on internetworks, even when not on the public Internet, is becoming more and more prevalent within enterprises. Likewise, user-based VPN allows a user to work from an unsecured ISP connection and connect securely back to their corporation.

Routers aren't very visible on internetworks, mainly because they usually don't have addresses (such as www.yahoo.com and www.amazon.com). Routers don't need to have human-friendly addresses because normal internetwork users never need to know that a router is there; they just need the connectivity it provides them.

The only people who ever need to log in to a router directly are members of the network team responsible for managing it. In TCP/IP networks—the protocol on which most internetworks run—routers identify themselves to internetworks only with their IP addresses. For this reason, to log in to a router, you must first know that it exists and then what its IP address is. The network administrators responsible for the router will, of course, know this information and usually will have access control lists (ACLs) limiting who can connect for the management of that device installed on the router for security purposes.

NOTE   In many cases the loopback IP address of a network device is utilized for management purposes; in fact, the hostname for any IP address of such a device may be added to the enterprise's Domain Name System (DNS) for easy access by network admins by hostname.

The potential for abuse by hackers still exists. As you will learn in Chapter 16, routers constantly send messages to one another in order to update and manage the internetworks on which they operate. With the proper skills and enough determination, a hacker could discover a router's IP address and then attempt to establish a Telnet connection to it. Given that routers are the links that stitch internetworks together, it's easy to understand why Cisco and other internetwork equipment manufacturers design so many security measures into their products. As shown in Figure 4-8, security must restrict access to areas within an internetwork and to individual devices.

NOTE   Router passwords only control entry to the router devices themselves (along with what level of access you wish to allow). Don't confuse router passwords with the passwords normal internetwork users must type to enter certain websites or to gain admittance to intranets (private internetworks). Restrictions put on normal users are administered through firewalls and access lists, which are covered in Chapters 9 and 10.

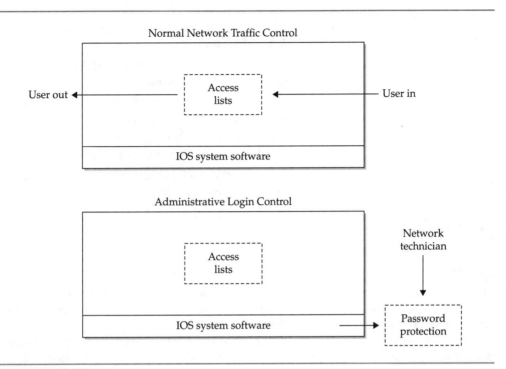

Figure 4-8. Security control is managed separately for network traffic and administrative login.

Router Passwords

Router passwords aren't intended only to keep out hackers. Frequently, password protection is administered on a router-by-router basis. Although a variety of authentication methods allow centralized administration of passwords, passwords to get into a router are often "local" in most smaller/mid-sized implementations. That means the user name and passwords necessary to administratively access the router are stored inside the router itself. Large internetworks that have dozens or even hundreds of routers—some more critical to network operations than others—may deploy a centrally managed solution. Still, there may be local passwords, so it's a common practice for network managers to allow only select network team members access to certain routers, or even to command levels within routers. Table 4-4 lists router passwords and what they do.

In Cisco routers, passwords are used to control access to:

- The router device itself
- The Privileged EXEC (enable mode) portion of the IOS software environment
- The use of specific IOS commands

Control Point	Password Type	What's Restricted
Console port	Line	Logging in to the router via a local line connected via the console port
AUX port	Line	Logging in to the router via a modem (or local) line connected via the auxiliary port
Network login	Line	Logging in to the router via a network connection using Telnet on a VTY line
Privileged EXEC	Enable or Enable Secret	Entry into the more powerful Privileged EXEC level of IOS environment

Table 4-4.   Overview of Router Passwords and Their Uses

Line Passwords

Line passwords are used to control who can log in to a router. They are used to set password protection on the console terminal line, the AUX (auxiliary) line, and any or all of the five virtual terminal (VTY) lines.

You must set at least one password for the router's VTY lines. If no Line password is set, when you attempt to log in to the router through Telnet, you will be stopped by the error message "Password required but none set." Remember, anyone on the Internet can conceivably telnet in to any router, so setting Line passwords will stop all but the best hackers from getting a foothold. Here, IOS is prompting for a password:

```
User Access Verification  Password: Router>>
```

When you enter passwords into IOS, no asterisks appear to mask the letters typed—something to which most of us are accustomed. In the preceding example, at the prompt Router>> (the router's hostname in this example), the correct password was entered, the host router was successfully logged in to, but no asterisks appear to the right of the password prompt. This might throw you off at first, but you'll grow accustomed to it.

NOTE   You may have noticed that the password examples in this chapter are not made person-specific with usernames. Although it is possible to have usernames with Enable and Enable Secret passwords, it is rarely done. This is because Enable and Enable Secret passwords are stored in router configuration files. Although using shared passwords is a security risk and can complicate overall management if someone who knows the password leaves, we still see many network managers who issue generic passwords to avoid the administrative nightmare of maintaining usernames/passwords across dozens or even hundreds of routers. For a best-practices approach, refer to Chapter 6 to find out how user accounts and passwords can be centrally maintained using TACACS+ and CiscoSecure Access Control Server.

Enable and Enable Secret Passwords

Once you get past the Line password, you are logged in to the router's IOS software environment. IOS is divided into two privilege levels: EXEC and Privileged EXEC (which is usually called Enable mode).

The EXEC level contains only basic, nondestructive commands. Being in Enable mode provides access to more commands. EXEC-level commands basically allow you to view diagnostic types of information about a router. Enable mode commands are more powerful in that they let you reconfigure the router's settings. These commands are potentially destructive commands, the **erase** command being a good example.

Two types of passwords can be used to restrict access to Privileged EXEC (Enable mode): the Enable password and the Enable Secret password. The idea of a "secret password" seems silly at first. *Of course* all passwords are secret, or at least they should be. What the Cisco engineers are alluding to here is the level of encryption used to mask the password from unauthorized users.

The Privileged EXEC Level of IOS   Enable and Enable Secret passwords both do the same thing: They restrict access to Privileged EXEC (Enable mode). The difference between the two is in the level of encryption supported. *Encryption* is a technique used to scramble data, making it incomprehensible to those who don't have a key to read it. Enable Secret passwords are scrambled using an advanced encryption algorithm based on 128 bits, for which there is no known decoding technique. Encryption for the Enable password relies on a less powerful algorithm. Cisco strongly recommends using the Enable Secret instead of the Enable password.

Enable Secret was introduced in 1997, so you may encounter some hardware and software that can only support Enable Passwords. When both are set, the Enable Secret password always takes precedence over the Enable password. IOS will only put the Enable password to use when running an old version of IOS software.

IOS passwords are stored in the configuration file for a router. Configuration files routinely cross networks as routers are updated and backed up. Having an Enable Secret password means that a hacker using a protocol analyzer (a test device that can read packets) will have a tougher time decoding your password. The following sample configuration file illustrates this:

```
version 12.4
service password-encryption
service udp-small-servers
service tcp-small-servers
!
hostname Router
!
enable secret 5 $1$C/q2$ZhtujqzQIuJrRGqFwdwn71
enable password 7 0012000F
```

Note that the encryption mask of the Enable password on the last line is much shorter than the encryption mask of the Enable Secret password (on the second-to-last line).

NOTE   Although these passwords are stored in an encrypted fashion in the router, enterprising hackers have come up with their own utilities to retrieve these passwords. Programs such as "Cain and Abel" allow someone to enter the encrypted password into the application and then retrieve the unencrypted password.

The Service Password-Encryption Command   Certain types of passwords (such as Line passwords) by default appear in cleartext in the configuration file. As such, you should avoid using them. You can use the service password-encryption command to make them more secure. Once this command is entered, each password configured is automatically encrypted and thus rendered illegible inside the configuration file (much as the Enable/Enable Secret passwords are). Securing Line passwords is doubly important in networks on which TFTP servers are used, because TFTP backup entails routinely moving config files across networks—and config files, of course, contain Line passwords.

Now that we've covered some of the basics of routing, how it is configured, and how it is secured (at a basic level), the next chapter takes a closer look at Cisco's specific router offerings and how devices other than routers can perform routing tasks.

CHAPTER 5 | Routing Platforms

R outer? We don't need no stinking router! Well, actually we do, but it needs to be understood that routing exists in many forms within the Cisco product line. Cisco produces many devices that support this all-important process we mentioned earlier—routing. The routing process is available on devices as small as the fanless, eight-port C3560, all the way through the ASA firewall line, data center Nexus 7000 switches, up to the service provider line of ONS 15600 ONS. Understandably so, certain advanced routing features such as Border Gateway Protocol (BGP) are not available on every device Cisco sells.

These devices start with routing and then build from there. Their primary purpose is routing; however, Cisco, through its many acquisitions and R&D, has integrated software-based firewalls, Power over Ethernet (PoE) enabled switch modules, video surveillance modules, Wi-Fi controllers, SIP gateways, and even analog voice service cards alongside its traditional repertoire of interface cards. Cisco views the router as a multifunction device, and why not? A router is required at every point a network crosses an ISP boundary.

Other platforms that enable routing with various levels of routing feature support are the ASA firewall line, every switch model above the 3500 series, and the Optical Transport Networks (OTN) series. This is not an exhaustive list, however.

Router Hardware

Now that we've identified routing as a process, we'll focus on the device Cisco built its business on—the traditional router.

At first glance, routers seem a lot like PCs. They have a CPU, memory, and—on the back—ports and interfaces to connect peripherals and various communications media. They sometimes even have a monitor to serve as a system console.

But there's one defining difference from a PC: the majority of routers are usually diskless. They don't even have optical disc drives. If you think about it, this makes sense. Routers exist just to route. They don't exist to create or display the data they transport. Routers have—as their sole mission—the task of filtering incoming packets and routing them outbound to their proper destinations. Of course, there are hard-disk-enabled add-on modules for capturing data passing *through* a router and enabling other features, but that is not the focus here.

Another difference is in the kind of add-on modules that can be plugged into routers. Whereas the typical PC contains cards for video, sound, graphics, and other purposes, the modules put into routers are generally strictly for networking (for obvious reasons). These are called *interface modules*, or just plain *interfaces*. When people or documents refer to a router interface, they mean an actual, physical printed circuit board that handles a particular networking protocol. E0 and E1, for example, probably mean Ethernet interface numbers 1 and 2 inside a router.

Interfaces are added according to the network environment in which they will work. For example, a router might be configured with interface modules only for

Ethernet. A router serving in a mixed LAN environment, by contrast, would have interfaces for both the Ethernet and Token Ring protocols, and if that router were acting as a LAN-to-WAN juncture, it might also have a T1 module.

Router Memory

Routers use various kinds of memory to operate and manage themselves. There are many variations on what the internals of a router look like (based on what they do and how they do it). Figure 5-1 depicts the layout of a motherboard in a Cisco router. This is a classic "old-school" router with a good layout for identifying the various parts. All Cisco router motherboards use four types of memory, each dedicated to performing specific roles.

Each Cisco router ships with at least a factory default minimum amount of DRAM and flash memory. Memory can be added at the factory or upgraded in the field. As a general rule, the amount of DRAM can be doubled or quadrupled (depending on the specific model), and the amount of flash can be doubled. If traffic loads increase over time, DRAM can be upgraded to increase a router's throughput capacity. This memory increase does not increase the router's throughput, but does allow it to perform more robust tasks such as maintaining larger routing tables.

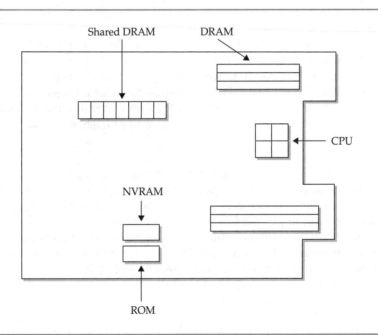

Figure 5-1.   Motherboards of Cisco routers are similarly designed.

RAM/DRAM

RAM/DRAM stands for random access memory/dynamic random access memory. Also called *working storage*, RAM/DRAM is used by the router's central processor to do its work, much like the memory in your PC. When a router is in operation, its RAM/DRAM contains an image of the Cisco IOS software, the running configuration file, the routing table, other tables (built by the router after it starts up), and the packet buffer.

Don't be thrown by the two parts in RAM/DRAM. The acronym is a catchall. Virtually all RAM/DRAM in Cisco routers is DRAM—dynamic random access memory. Non-dynamic memory, also called *static memory*, became obsolete years ago. But the term RAM is still so widely used that it's included in the literature to avoid confusion on the subject.

Cisco's near-smallest router, the ISR 860 series, ships with a maximum of 256MB of DRAM. At the other end of the spectrum, the CRS-1 router, one of Cisco's largest, supports up to 12GB.

NVRAM

NVRAM stands for nonvolatile RAM. Nonvolatile means memory that will retain information after losing power. Cisco routers store a copy of the router's configuration file in NVRAM (configuration files are covered later in this chapter). When the router is intentionally turned off, or if power is lost, NVRAM enables the router to restart in its proper configuration.

Flash Memory

Flash memory is also nonvolatile. It differs from NVRAM in that it can be erased and reprogrammed as needed. Originally developed by Intel, flash memory is in wide use in computers and other devices. In Cisco routers, flash memory is used to store one or more copies of the IOS software. This is an important feature, because it enables network managers to stage new versions of IOS on routers throughout an internetwork and then upgrade them all at once to a new version from flash memory.

ROM

ROM stands for read-only memory. It, too, is nonvolatile. Cisco routers use ROM to hold a so-called *bootstrap program,* which is a file that can be used to boot to a minimum configuration state after a catastrophe. When you boot from ROM, the first thing you'll see is the rommon>> prompt. ROMMON (for ROM monitor) harkens back to the early days of the Unix operating system, which relied on ROMMON to reboot a computer to the point at which commands could at least be typed into the system console monitor. In smaller Cisco routers, ROM holds a bare-bones subset of the Cisco IOS software. ROM in some high-end Cisco routers holds a full copy of IOS.

Router Ports and Modules

A router's window to the internetwork is through its ports and modules. Without them, a router is a useless box. The ports and modules that are put into a router define what it can do.

Internetworking can be intimidating, with the seemingly endless combinations of products, protocols, media, feature sets, standards—you name it. The acronyms come so fast and so hard that it might seem hopeless to try to learn how to properly configure a router. But choosing the right router product can be broken down into manageable proportions. Table 5-1 lays out five major requirement areas that, if met, will lead you to the best router solution.

Cisco obviously can't manufacture a model of router to match every customer's specific requirements. To make them more flexible to configure, routers come in two major parts:

- **Chassis**   The actual box and basic components inside it, such as power supply, fans, rear and front faceplates, indicator lights, and slots

- **Ports and modules**   The printed circuit boards that slide into the router box

Cisco's router product-line structure tries to steer you to a product—or at least to a reasonably focused selection of products—meeting all five requirement areas in Table 5-1.

Area	Description	Configuration Requirement
1	Physical	The router must be hardware-compatible with the physical network segment on which the router will sit.
2	Communication	The router must be compatible with the transport medium that will be used (Frame Relay, ATM, and so on).
3	Protocol	The router must be compatible with the protocols used in the internetwork (IP, IPX, SNA, and so on).
4	Mission	The router must provide the speed, reliability, security, and functional features the job requires.
5	Business	The router must fit within the purchase budget and network growth plans.

Table 5-1.   Five Major Factors in Selecting a Router

Finding the right router for your needs is basically a two-step process. The following illustrates the process of selecting a router for a large branch office operation:

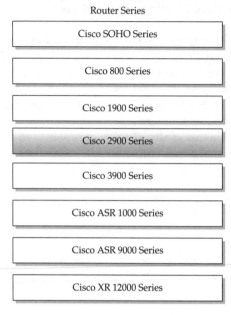

First, Cisco's routers are grouped into product families called *series*. Choosing a router product series is usually a matter of budget, because each series reflects a price/performance tier. Models within series are generally based on the same chassis, which is the metal frame and basic components (power supply, fans, and so on) around which the router is built. In this example, we'll select the Cisco 2900 series because it fits both the purchase budget and performance requirements for our large branch office.

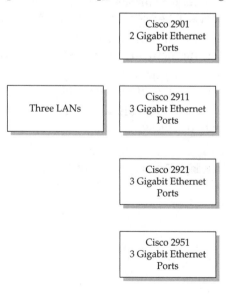

From the 2900 series, we'll take the Cisco 2911. The 2911 chassis is versatile enough to fit a lot of situations, making it a popular brand of branch office router. We'll also select the Cisco 2921 because it has three Ethernet ports. Also, our imaginary branch office will operate three subnets: one for the customer service office, one for production, and another for the front office. The three Ethernet ports will let us separate the departments, thereby isolating traffic.

NOTE   The term "port" can cause confusion if you're not careful. When speaking of hardware, *port* means a physical connection through which I/O can pass (a serial port, for example), but there are also so-called "ports" at the transport layer of network protocols. These "ports" are actually port numbers used to identify what network application packets contain. These ports (port numbers) are also referred to as TCP or UDP ports or "listeners," because they inform the receiver what's inside the message. Sample TCP-defined port numbers include Port 25 for Simple Mail Transfer Protocol and Port 80 for HTTP. Refer to the section in Chapter 2 titled "The Transport Layer" for more on TCP and UDP ports.

Router Packaging

Four major categories of modules can be configured into Cisco routers to support either LAN, WAN, or other feature connectivity:

- **Ethernet modules**   Support many of the Ethernet LAN variants on the market, including Novell NetWare, TCP, and UDP over IP.

- **Wireless LAN and WAN modules**   Include CDMA, HSPA, EVDO cellular modems, and Wi-Fi wireless LAN controllers.

- **WAN connectivity modules**   Support a wide variety of WAN protocols, some old and some new. Sample WAN technologies include newer protocols, such as DSL, DOCIS, ISDN, Frame Relay, Asynchronous Transfer Mode (ATM), as well as legacy protocols, such as SDLC and X.25.

- **Application modules**   Include support for voicemail, VoIP trunking, Services Ready Engines for hosting third-party applications, video surveillance, and much more.

Configuration options depend mainly on the specific Cisco router:

- Lower-end routers tend to be "fixed configuration" in that the modules are factory integrated only (preconfigured). The 1900 series is low end and modular.

- Midrange routers, such as the Cisco 2900 and 3900 series, are "modular" in that they can accept a variety of modules, often packaging different protocols in the same box. Many modules may be plugged into this class of routers' motherboards.

- High-end routers, such as the Cisco 7600 series and Cisco 12000 series, have buses (also called *backplanes*). Bus-based routers accept larger modules—usually referred to as *blades* or *cards*—that are effectively self-contained routers (they have their own CPUs, memory units, and so on).

The backbone of the Internet uses the third kind of router listed. Cisco's Gigabit Switch Router 12000 series is the kind of equipment used to run the Internet. These routers are designed and built like supercomputers. For instance, the 12000 series uses 400 MHz MIPS 7000 processors, which are the same kind of processors used in the computers that make special effects for the movies. Cisco's largest router—the 12816—can handle up to 1.28 trillion bits of information per second.

Cisco Router Models

Cisco offers different routers for different environments. For example, an ISP won't be too successful with a router that can only accommodate four or five users. Likewise, a small office doesn't need a $500,000 terabit router. The following sections explain the different types of routers Cisco offers.

SOHO Routers

SOHO is an industry term for very small network users—that is, small office/home office. Typical SOHO customers have only one or two LAN segments in their facility and an ISP connection to the Internet.

The linchpin of Cisco's SOHO strategy has been low-end routers. Allowing small companies to tap into ISPs router-to-router—instead of as dial-in users—has saved money on telephone connections, upgraded performance, and improved reliability. Today, these same routers allow the use of Internet connections and encrypted communications. Cisco's router capabilities changed to take advantage of new WAN technology, and as such their marketing plan from two decades ago is still intact. Table 5-2 outlines Cisco's SOHO product series. The term *series* here means a chassis that is variously configured at the manufacturing plant into several product models—usually depending on the printed circuit cards installed in them.

Product Series	Description
Cisco 861 Series	Ethernet connectivity. Includes IOS, firewall, and VPN encryption. Optional Wi-Fi access point.
Cisco 880 Series	Cellular and DSL connectivity options. Includes IOS and VPN encryption. Optional Wi-Fi access point, IPS, and firewall features.
Cisco 888 Series	Ethernet and DSL. Includes IOS and VPN encryption. Optional Wi-Fi access point, IPS, and firewall features.
Cisco 891 Series	Metro Ethernet and v92 modem. Includes IOS and VPN encryption. Optional Wi-Fi access point, IPS, and firewall features.
Cisco 892 Series	Metro Ethernet, cellular, ISDN. Includes IOS and VPN encryption. Optional Wi-Fi access point, IPS, and firewall features.

Table 5-2.   Cisco's SOHO Routers

SOHO products emphasize broadband technologies (DSL, cable, and ISDN) because small offices and home offices don't have dedicated WAN links connecting them to their ISP or enterprise internetwork.

Midrange Cisco Routers

The small-to-medium-sized network requires a wide variety of solutions. Cisco has several tiers of access router products designed to fit the customer's capacity needs and type of telecom link.

The series in Table 5-3 represent dozens of individual product numbers. Depending on the product series, various combinations of LAN technologies and WAN media can be configured. *Modular* means that the chassis can be upgraded in the field by inserting one or more modules. Every one of these devices is modular—that is, they can be ordered with additional enhanced high-speed WAN interface cards (EHWIC) such as T1, 3G cellular, serial, DSL, and cable modems. All of these routers support a similar connectivity feature set. Simply put, the higher the model number, the more connections and speed you get. The 1900 series does not integrate with Cisco's Unified Communications platforms, unlike its larger siblings.

Product Series	Description
Cisco 1800 Series	Ethernet access router to connect to ISDN, DSL, broadband. High-density router, offers support for 802.11 a/b/g technologies, multiple WAN interface options, and VPN capability.
Cisco 1900 Series	Modular Ethernet access router designed to connect to a broadband or ISDN WAN link. VPN encryption, VoIP (Voice over IP), and VoFR (Voice over Frame Relay) capability. Includes a base license for IOS firewall. Subscriptions for IPS available and content filtering available.
Cisco 2900 Series	Modular access router. Supports up to two Ethernet LAN segments, wireless (802.11 a/b/g) LANs, along with Cisco IP phones. Modular high-density router for dial-access or router-to-router traffic. Supports ISDN, serial, channelized T1, digital modems, and ATM links. Also supports voice/fax and Frame Relay.
Cisco 3900 Series	Geared toward medium-to-large businesses and enterprise branch offices, this model operates at up to T3 speeds and is capable of data, security, voice, video, and wireless functions. This series is modular and offers VPN capabilities.

Table 5-3. Cisco's Midrange Routing Solutions

Backbone Routers

When Cisco claims that over 70 percent of the Internet is run using its routers, these are the models they're talking about. The 7000 and 12000 series are big, resembling dorm refrigerators in shape and size, and have data buses into which *blades* (whole devices on a board) can be installed.

Because they're not access routers, Cisco's backbone routers can take as many users as they can handle packets. All seven product series (described in Table 5-4)

Product Series	Description
Cisco 2000 Series	One- or four-slot router marketed to power distribution and generation customers. This modular device has a hardened form factor and has no moving parts. Options include T1, DSL, 2G/3G/4G, and LTE cellular.
ASR 901/903	The ASR 900 series is intended for ISP distribution sites where broadband is distributed within neighborhoods.
ASR 1000	The Aggregation Services Router or "ASR" series is a newer offering that utilizes software-enabled services and Cisco's newest QuantumFlow processor. The ASR has displaced the 7000 series for WAN routing at a data center level. These routers include all the newest security features and are very fast, topping out at 100 Gbps of I/O.
Cisco 7600 Series	Three to 13 slots with 240 to 720 Gbps data rate per slot. This series offers a flexible, modular design, IP/MPLS services, and is an easy upgrade from the Cisco 7500 series. Offers up to 40 Gbps line speeds.
Cisco 10000 Series	Eight-slot Gigabit Ethernet switch router. Has a special card for an OC-48 WAN link. Offers IPSec and MPLS VPN and QoS capabilities.
Cisco 12000 Series	Six- or 15-slot, 40-Gigabit per-slot Ethernet switch router optimized for IP. Has special cards for OC-48 and OC-192 WAN links.
Cisco CRS-1 Series	Eight to 16 slots, powered by Cisco IOS XR software, which offers a self-healing, self-defending operating system. Supports fixed and modular line cards. It offers terabit speeds with OC-768 support.
ASR 9000	With a software set that virtualizes the edge, aggregation, and network distribution and includes all the best features of the CRS line, these routers are the next "big thing" in ISP-land. These rack-sized devices top out at 96 Tbps.

Table 5-4. Cisco's Series of Backbone Routers

are modular, letting customers install modules according to the LAN technology being run and the capacity needed. In fact, these routers can operate more than one protocol simultaneously, such as Ethernet and SONET. A *slot* is an electronic bay into which a printed circuit board module is inserted.

There is a specialized high-speed connection used on the high-end Cisco routers. HSSI stands for *high-speed serial interface,* a specialized I/O standard mainly used in conjunction with supercomputers. The behemoth Cisco 12000 router and uBR10012 router are carrier-class devices, in that local equipment carriers' telecommunications network operators use them in their back-office data-switching operations.

All the backbone Cisco routers have extensive capabilities for VPN, security, quality of service (QoS), and network management.

Switches

As mentioned earlier, a myriad of devices envelop the routing process. Cisco has developed many devices that can perform routing duties. The first we'll discuss beyond an actual router is the switch. Although we will go into further detail on switching and network design later, let's ponder this question now: Why would anyone want to add routing to a switch, or any other device that's not designed as a router?

Take a look at Figure 5-2. This diagram is what we call Cisco's "reference model." Cisco's documentation, training plans, books, and so forth all feed back into the

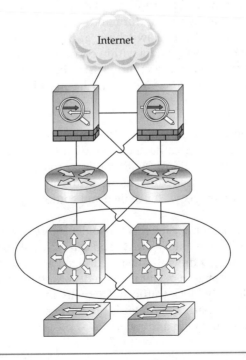

Figure 5-2. Cisco's reference model is the blueprint on which internetworking is built.

lifecycle of Cisco's reference model for networks. This means that in every project you work on, depending on the scale of deployment, you have a framework to "reference." Whether you're working on a greenfield project (such as a freshly built data center) or the migration of an existing L2 switched campus to MPLS, you always have this overarching plan from Cisco to refer to. This may have been a marketing plan 20 years past, but Cisco's strategy to deploy a router to each and every office and household globally is now the gold standard for building multiplatform, resilient internetworks.

The highlighted portion of Figure 5-2 is where the majority of routing questions could be answered. Wouldn't it be more efficient if that core distribution switch ran a routing process instead of passing all that traffic upstream to another device? If you said yes, you'd be correct.

As a matter of fact, some switches, like the 3560 line, can route all the way out at the edge now, allowing finite segregation of layer 3 traffic. It's one thing to allow layer 2 VLANs to talk to each other; it's an altogether different strategy to allow VLANs with routable traffic on them to communicate. This allows network engineers to plan for managing the unwieldy task of thousands of devices on a seemingly small network.

To put this in scale: Let's say a company of 1,000 employees has 1,000 PCs, 1,000 IP telephones, 10 IP video conference units, 50 printers, and 75 servers. What about the physical security systems—the card readers and the IP CCTV network? Now think about "bring your own device" initiatives and smartphones: The 1,000-employee network that started needing about 2,100 IP addresses just doubled to 4,000. This isn't excessive; this is a typical campus internetwork, and having the ability to create small subnets in any data closet instead of trunking all that traffic back to a campus core router can create huge efficiency and performance gains.

Another reason that these "layer 3 switches," as they have come to be called, is the need for a proliferation of Ethernet ports within corporate and ISP data centers alike. Interfaces in Cisco routers come at a premium cost, whereas a 3560X has 24 ports and each of them can be made routable via a properly licensed IOS image.

Firewalls

Firewalls also understand routing, although to a lesser extent. Unlike the layer 3 switches we've been discussing that have the same Multi-Protocol Label Switching (MPLS) and Border Gateway Protocol (BGP) routing protocols available to their routing processes as an actual router, Cisco firewalls are primarily a firewall. Their job is to only allow specified traffic first, inspect it for malice and conformity to its rules, and to block all others.

They segregate sections of internetworks, usually by VLAN but sometimes also by physical interface. In order to create a VLAN and thus a routed segment to be used as a demilitarized zone (DMZ), a firewall must be utilized as a DMZ and by its nature needs to have all traffic passing in or out inspected. A router can be used to create a DMZ, but because ACLs only block traffic, not actually inspect it, prior to passing the traffic on to its intended path, the router is not the best tool for this job. Figure 5-3 describes a packet flowing through a firewall.

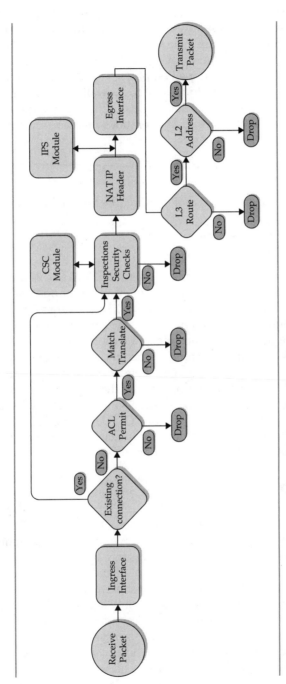

Figure 5-3.   Packets get disassembled passing through a firewall.

Firewalls live in between a public (or hostile) network, such as the Internet, and trusted internetworks. We see them sandwiched by data centers and the client PCs they serve. They also are utilized to limit the scope of an audit, eliminating access by employees to small internetworks where, for example, a credit card server may live and only two of those 1,000 aforementioned employees need access. All this takes a routing process, which the firewall performs. Cisco firewalls can—and do—understand a number of routing protocols, and as such can pass traffic accordingly, but they cannot participate in the large-scale Internet routing operations their cousins can.

Essential Files

In contrast to normal computers, Cisco routers have just two main files:

- The configuration file
- The Cisco IOS software

Cisco IOS software contains instructions to the router. IOS acts as the traffic cop, directing activity inside the router. IOS manages internal router operations by telling the various hardware components what to do, much like Windows 8 or Linux with a general-purpose computer. Customers cannot alter the contents of the IOS file.

The configuration file contains instructions to the router input by the customer, not Cisco. It contains information describing the network environment in which the router will run and how the network manager wants it to behave. In a phrase, the configuration file tells the router *what* to do; IOS tells the router *how* to do it.

As will be covered in the next chapter, routers also use dynamic files, which are not stored in the router's flash memory, NVRAM, or ROM. Dynamic files instead are built from scratch when a router is booted and are strictly reactive in the sense that they only hold live information, not operational instructions.

Communicating with IOS

You can gain access to a router either directly through the console or AUX ports or through a network using the Telnet, SSH (Secure Shell), HTTP, or HTTPS protocol. Network pros generally use SSH for security and convenience. Keep in mind that once a session is established, Telnet and SSH are essentially the same except for one important feature—SSH traffic will be fully encrypted and Telnet will not. Whatever method is used, you need to get into the IOS environment in order to review files and enter commands. Telnet and SSH clients are commonly available for all operating systems. A popular client is PuTTY, available for download at www.putty.nl. Once it's downloaded, you just need to double-click it to get started.

Notice in Figure 5-4 that either remote or local hosts can be accessed. The IP address selected in Figure 5-4 is for a router on the local area network (LAN) in the same office as the network administrator. One of the remote IP addresses would be used if the router were located at a remote site (that is, beyond the LAN). Even if you are on the same network with the router, a valid password must be entered in order to gain entry.

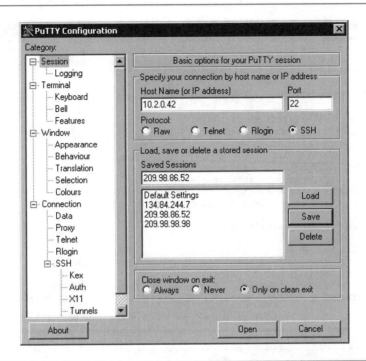

Figure 5-4. Configuration can be accomplished by logging on to a router through a Telnet connection.

Figure 5-5 shows an error condition that commonly befuddles beginners typing their first IOS commands (in case you ever encounter it). What's happening is this: When you enter text that IOS cannot interpret as a command, it assumes that the text is a symbolic name for an IP address. IOS has no choice in the matter. After all, one purpose of a router is to communicate with other routers, and no single router has all existing addresses on file. Here, the router attempts to send the symbolic address name to all addresses within its broadcast domain. Broadcasts are always addressed 255.255.255.255 (as you no doubt remember from Chapter 2). After ten seconds or so, the router gives up, displays an error message, and returns to the prompt.

NOTE If you enter a bad command into most computer operating systems, you get an error message. Give IOS a bad command, and it assumes the input is a network address and tries to Telnet to it. Normal operating systems know all possible input values that can go into them, but IOS doesn't have that luxury. It deals in network addresses, and routers never assume they know all possible addresses because networks change constantly. If you'd like to disable this feature and have the Telnet session time out immediately, issue **no ip domain-lookup** (assuming you don't have a valid need for domain lookup).

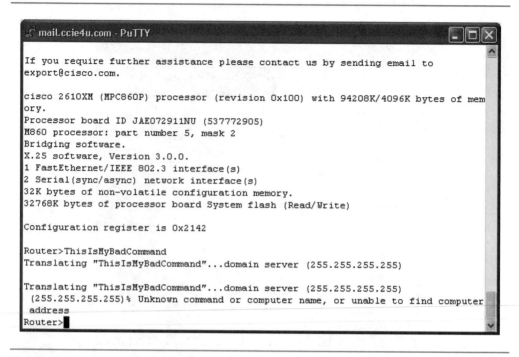

```
mail.ccie4u.com - PuTTY                                        _ □ X

If you require further assistance please contact us by sending email to
export@cisco.com.

cisco 2610XM (MPC860P) processor (revision 0x100) with 94208K/4096K bytes of mem
ory.
Processor board ID JAE072911NU (537772905)
M860 processor: part number 5, mask 2
Bridging software.
X.25 software, Version 3.0.0.
1 FastEthernet/IEEE 802.3 interface(s)
2 Serial(sync/async) network interface(s)
32K bytes of non-volatile configuration memory.
32768K bytes of processor board System flash (Read/Write)

Configuration register is 0x2142

Router>ThisIsMyBadCommand
Translating "ThisIsMyBadCommand"...domain server (255.255.255.255)

Translating "ThisIsMyBadCommand"...domain server (255.255.255.255)
  (255.255.255.255)% Unknown command or computer name, or unable to find computer
  address
Router>
```

Figure 5-5.   Entering a bad command results in an inadvertent broadcast message.

Meet IOS 12.4T (A.K.A. the "OLD" IOS)

IOS 12.4T features a number of enhancements that build on earlier releases of the IOS platform. There are hundreds of features in IOS, far more than we have space to cover here. That said, let's take a look at some of the highlights in IOS 12.4T versus older versions.

Cisco recommends upgrading to 12.4(24)T or 15 for customers who are using Release 12.4, because either of these provides maintenance for the 12.4 release once it reaches its end of engineering stage in January of 2013. Beyond that, however, it's a good idea to consider what features you plan on using and determine whether the new features in 12.4T or 15M are worth your while. A distinguishing fact about IOS versions is how the different versions relate to each other and the mainline of code. Mainline is the most stable version of IOS software. It includes the fewest features, but safest operation. Safety equals stability. Knowing this, we also have these facts:

- Cisco skipped mainline versions 13 and 14.
- 12.3T reached its final EOL date of support in January of 2012.
- 12.4(24)T is listed as the newest "old" IOS version.

- 12.3T was closer in function to 12.4 mainline than 12.3 mainline.

- 12.4T is closer in function to 15.0 mainline than 12.4 mainline.

- We still have a section in this book on 12.4T because of the millions of deployments that aren't utilizing 15M or 15T.

- Cisco has published an EOL statement for 12.4(22)T.

- Cisco has *not* published an EOL statement for 12.4(24)T but is encouraging customers whose hardware supports it to migrate to 15.

- The current recommended mainline is 15M.

Hardware Support

Cisco has bolstered the list of hardware supported in IOS 12.4(24)T. It includes the VPN Services Adapter, PVDM2 modules, additional 800 series routers, multiple interface HWICS, the ATM T3 module, G.SHDSL WICs, MFT ECAN, voice interface cards, HIMI interfaces, and more.

Broadband

Broadband includes DSL aggregation, MPLS features, and dial-like features. Broadband is certainly a more prevalent (and, of course, useful) technology, but some of these features may be a bit more specialized than the average IOS user will need to implement.

High Availability

IOS 12.4T offers enhanced availability through two features:

- **Cisco IOS Firewall**   Adds support for H.323 v3 and v4 to maintain high availability of mission-critical IP telephony calls while upholding high-level call experience.

- **Bidirectional Forward Detection (BFD) support for Cisco Integrated Services routers**   BFD is a detection protocol that is designed to provide fast-forwarding path-failure-detection times for all media types (L3 and L2).

Infrastructure

The infrastructure is enhanced in four areas:

- **Cisco IOS Embedded Event Manager 2.2**   Detects events and triggers local command-line actions within the router.

- **Embedded Resource Manager**   Allows the monitoring of internal resources and the performance of actions to improve router performance and availability. Network administrators can define thresholds to create notifications according to the real-time resource consumption.

- **Toolkit Command Language (TCL)**   Signing Toolkit Command Language was first introduced in Cisco IOS Software in 1994. Many components of Cisco IOS Software, such as EEM, ESM, and IVR, use TCL scripts. Signing of TCL scripts enables customers to execute only authenticated and approved scripts on the Cisco devices. It provides a mechanism for the customers to verify the source of the TCL scripts.

- **Call Home Service**   Imagine a network module fails on a Saturday, the router or switch it resides in runs diagnostics on the failed module, uploads that data to Cisco, and then notifies Cisco to open a service request needed to ship a replacement part. You get a notification this all happened and have the replacement module on your desk Monday morning. That's how the Call Home Service works in an optimal scenario. It requires a valid SmartNet maintenance contract, and not all devices support it today. However, the list is expanding. Generally speaking, devices sold beginning around 2010 support this service.

IP Mobility

IP mobility is enhanced as policy and application-based routing for Mobile Router Multi-Path Support Cisco Mobile Routers (MRs) running Cisco Mobile Network technology offer seamless network connectivity for devices connecting to them.

The IPv6 Access Control List Extensions for Mobile IPv6 is a new feature allowing IPv6 access control list (ACL) entries to match Mobile IPv6 (MIPv6), specific ICMPv6 messages, and packets containing the new and modified IPv6 extension headers. In addition, a new command is introduced to control the generation of ICMPv6 unreachable messages.

IP Routing

You would expect IP routing to really be the area with lots of new stuff, but it really isn't. Not much earth-shattering, anyway.

- **IOS BGP support for 4-byte autonomous system numbers (ASNs)**   An advance over the previous 2-byte limit increases the pool of available ASNs from 65,536 to 4,294,967,296.

- **Multi-VRF Selection using Policy-Based Routing (PBR)**   This is an extension of VRF Selection based on source IP address. This feature does not support MPLS.

IP Services

IP services include an assortment of enhancements:

- **DHCPv6 individual address assignment**   DHCP has been selected by the IPv6 community to fulfill automation functions within IPv6 beyond simple client address assignment. The new feature of allocating individual addresses is now supported for client, server, and relay functions.

- **IPv6 default router preference** Provides preference metrics for default routers. IPv6 DRP is the Cisco IOS implementation of RFC 4191, enabling a network manager to assign a priority to a router.

- **IPv6 Secure Neighbor Discovery (SeND) protocol** Designed to counter the threats of the ND protocol. SeND defines a set of discovery options for a device's neighbors and a pair of neighbor discovery messages. SeND also defines a new autoconfiguration mechanism to establish address ownership.

Management Instrumentation

There are a number of new SNMP Management Information Bases (MIBs). For more information on MIBs, flip ahead to Chapter 16. For now, here are some of the features:

- QoS's functionality has been bolstered in IOS 12.4T by the addition of Hierarchical Queuing Framework (HQF), which enables customers to manage their QoS at multiple levels of scheduling for applying QoS templates.

- Web Services Management Agent (WSMA) is a new management mechanism that can be utilized by network management systems (NMSs). It utilizes XML and SOAP, both standard web development toolkits. Users may access WSMA via SSHv2, HTTP, HTTPS, or Transport Layer Security (TLS) to access the entire set of CLI commands.

Security and VPN

Here are some highlights of security and VPN:

- **Access Control List (ACL) Syslog Correlation** A feature that provides a correlation mechanism for ACLs that can be used by Network Management System (NMS) tools to correlate the triggered syslog with the access control entry (ACE) within the ACL that triggered the syslog with deep granularity. This feature uses "tags" that are appended to the syslog.

- **IOS IPS signatures** These have been normalized so that they can be managed side by side with IPS sensors, modules, and ASA firewalls by Cisco Security Manager.

- **IOS Support for Lawful Intercept** Cisco IOS provides a cost-effective, yet powerful Communications Assistance for Law Enforcement Act (CALEA) compliant solution with the ability to monitor digital communications.

- **IOS SSL VPN Internationalization** IOS SSL VPN Internationalization deploys a framework to support multiple languages in the login and portal pages. Users may select their language preference for their session from a drop-down menu prior to logging in.

- **Cisco IOS Content Filtering** IOS Content Filtering is a subscription-based hosted solution that leverages Trend Micro's global TrendLabs™ threat database. It is supported on routers running the Advanced Security image.

This is by no means a complete listing of IOS 12.4T's features, but it hits on some of the highlights. Some of the new features are more advanced and may be off the radar for a beginner. However, if you want to see what sorts of features have been included in IOS 12.4T, go to www.cisco.com/go/ios. This site also details advances and features included in IOS since this book's publication.

Meet IOS Release 15 (A.K.A. the "New" IOS)

Cisco IOS Release 15 is the newest in the long lineage of the Internetwork Operating System. You may ask, where are Release 13 and Release 14? Well, Cisco skipped them entirely. Although we have no official story to tell, it's widely held in European cultures that 13 is an unlucky number—*triskaidekaphobia* is the fear of the number 13. On the other hand, 14 is 13's parallel on the Pacific rim, with many cultures in that region displaying *tetraphobia*, the fear of the number 4, to the extent that tail signals and ship designators may not utilize the number 4 per some government regulations. Query your favorite search engine for more details.

Release Schedule

IOS Release 15 is based on a shift in IOS architecture and a convergence of standardized schedules with an accelerated delivery of features. The most obvious change between IOS 12.4 and 15 is that Cisco has changed its approach to how they design IOS. We've only discussed 12.4M and 12.4T (Mainline and Technology) up to this point. However, Cisco also has other releases to develop and support—S for service providers, E for enterprises, B for broadband features, and X for special projects. What Cisco has done with Release 15 is to not only remove complexity on the customer's side of things but to streamline their own software development operations as well.

Previously, features were added seemingly in an ad hoc manner, with no regular schedule, per IOS train rebuild. Bug fix releases were produced in a similar fashion. One can see how it would be difficult to maintain momentum or even continue to innovate within a company the size of Cisco. With IOS Release 15, Cisco has established a specific release schedule. New mainline code appears on a set schedule of approximately every 20 months, with technology code (otherwise known as *feature releases)* becoming available in intervals three times a year between them.

This set schedule is supposed to bridge the fact that we had four years between mainline versions 12.4 and 15 and not allow it to happen again. The defined life and death of 15.0 and the release of subsequent versions 15.1 and so on, are part of the release model, as the next version is to be announced when the EOL announcement for the previous version is published. Since the availability of Release IOS 15 in 2009, Cisco has deviated from its plans to support only M and T versions of IOS. Service providers operating the 7000 series of routers were provided with a 15S release.

Change in Approach to Design

The aforementioned shift in schedule was likely predicated by a need to simplify the software development structure in order for Cisco to maintain the many software "trains" (Cisco defines a *train* as a vehicle for delivering software) meant to be deployed on the same hardware line. For example, IOS in a 2811 router was inefficient. From the customer perspective, it was more and more difficult to implement new features without incurring outages. Simply put, choosing which IOS image to use was no simple task, and implementing one caused network downtime.

With IOS Release 15, Cisco has made this process somewhat less complicated *and* gives the company an avenue to provide their shareholders additional revenue.

Here's what we get with IOS 15, which is multilayered:

- Consistent bug-fix rebuild schedules
- Consistent feature release schedules
- Broadened feature constancy
- Far more shared code, helped by software activation

These last two points mean more features embedded in more images. This makes it easier to choose which IOS to use and implement, right? That's the theory.

The IOS selection process now begins with a new "universal" IOS image. Feature sets are now "license enabled." No longer do you have to upgrade or migrate to a new IOS if you wish to utilize security or enterprise features; now you just have to "unlock" those features by licensing them. Should we thank Cisco, or is this new license-enforcement mechanism going to cost more overall? I'd imagine if one was so inclined to build an ROI statement for their company, they could determine that. Figure 5-6 depicts the Release 15 decision tree for pre-ISR2 models: 1800, 2800, 3800, and so on.

As you can see in Figure 5-7, the decision tree for the current ISR2 models (1900, 2900, 3900) is a bit more simplified.

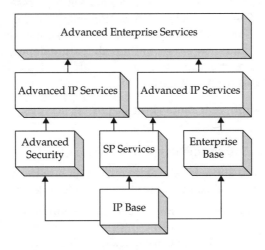

Figure 5-6.   Cisco's license enablement flow for pre-ISR2 routers with IOS Release 15

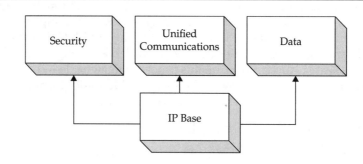

Figure 5-7. The license enablement flow for ISR2 and newer routers with IOS Release 15

Features, Features, Features

We now know that IOS Release 15 will have a consistent, accelerated upgrade schedule that helps us deploy new features sooner. Is this a good thing or a bad thing? You may be wondering how Cisco is finding all the bugs and fixing them before these accelerated release dates? The answer is, they aren't and cannot. Excessive acceleration of software development always increases the risk of writing software code and inadvertently creating flaws in that code. Those who create this new code may discover bugs but do not have the time required to test their fixes—or to even fix the bugs in the first place.

This is where a thorough evaluation of release notes and known bugs (now called "caveats") is warranted by a network engineer prior to delivering any recommendation on equipment or IOS software to utilize. Cisco's marketing message has been consistent since 2009. In utilizing Cisco IOS Release 15, customers will see operational savings because of fewer images to manage and deploy; they will enjoy simplified SW management, ordering, and greater flexibility with feature deployment.

Next are some features that came with the initial IOS Release 15.0(1)M on top of the grandfathered-in features from 12.4(24)T.

Licensing Cisco offers different models for acquiring licenses. Changes in the system include

- Try-and-buy features using temporary license keys.

- A software key to allow for simplified upgrading to the new feature set (versus the entirely new IOS install required with previous releases).

- Improved version and licensing tracking and compliance. CLI, XML, and SNMP allow for simplified license information gathering. The process is streamlined via an a la cart license packaging if bundles aren't flexible enough.

Cisco License Manager   Managing Cisco licenses has also been streamlined. Improvements include

- Rapid rollout of large license quantity
- Automated license deployment using templates
- Detailed license reporting
- Scaling up to 100,000 nodes

Deprecated Support   Cisco has also cut off support for several devices and technologies with IOS 15, including the following:

- Router models 2600XM, 3600, and 3700
- AppleTalk Phase I and II
- Service Selection Gateway (SSG)

Security Enhancements   Security is always a moving target, and Cisco's latest response toward beefing up IOS security includes

- A large number of simultaneous IPS signatures/lightweight IPS engines for signatures
- New default IOS IPS category signatures
- Chaining of traffic scanning (regular expression) tables for IPS
- DMVPN enhancements

Other New Features   Here are some of the other new features included in IOS 15:

- Automatic discovery and configuration of network services with SAF
- Graceful OSPF restart (RFC 3623; Helper mode only)
- Graceful restart for OSPFv3 (RFC 5187; Helper mode only)
- OSPF graceful shutdown
- BGP graceful restart per neighbor
- S-IS VRF support
- MPLS VPN (Inter-AS Option AB)
- BFD support for WAN interfaces
- BFD client for IPv4 static routes
- BFD VRF support
- Optimal routing path selection for an application by performance metrics using PfR and PIRO
- IGMP static group range support

- IPv4 and IPv6 multicast address group range support

- IP multicast load splitting—Equal Cost Multipath (ECMP) using S, G, and next hop

- PIM triggered joins

- Unified Border Element support for SRTP-RTP internetworking, which enhances VoIP security and interoperability with Cisco Unified Communications Manager

- UC Trusted Firewall Control version 2 and Cisco Unified Border Element (CUBE) support for SRTP-RTP internetworking

- Cisco UC Release 8.0 SAF support

- Per-flow application visibility in the network Flexible NetFlow and NBAR

- Embedded policy AAA bypass

Meet NX-OS

Cisco NX-OS was born of a need to integrate storage networks within data center internetworks. Many of the features inherent in NX-OS were ported from SAN-OS, which has been used to operate Cisco's storage area network (SAN) switches—the MDS 9000 line—for some time. Traditional Fibre Channel (which we will discuss in Chapter 13) utilizes the same physical (layer 1 on the OSI model) mechanisms as internetworks and the Internet in kind, but different protocols are implemented above layer 1, such as the Fibre Channel (FC) protocol, which encapsulates SCSI disk commands. As large quantities of network customers moved into the SAN space, data centers became crammed with fiber optic cables of different systems as well as the storage and network switches required for both. A lot of duplication of effort was (and still is) occurring.

Fibre Channel (FC) storage requires direct connectivity, so it goes without saying that unless you have fiber available, no storage network can be built—that is, until iSCSI, Fiber over IP, and other IP network-centric storage protocols came on the scene. Fibre Channel, unlike Ethernet, doesn't care for retransmitting frames. Storage area networks are inherently more expensive then IP data networks because of the need to build in redundancy *and* resiliency. *Redundancy* is having multiple nodes available in the case of a failure of another node; *resiliency* is the ability of a system to tolerate upgrades to parts of the system with causing service disruptions.

This is where the Nexus switch platform and its purpose-built operating system NX-OS come in. Much like IOS XR, the software services within IOS NX were built to be modular, so specific services can be upgraded with no downtime, if need be, using in-service software upgrades (ISSUs). These upgrades run in their own protected memory spaces for additional resiliency and security. Redundant hardware supervisor modules can be upgraded with zero impact using ISSU. NX-OS also understands Fibre

Channel, so when deploying a Nexus chassis switch system, you no longer need an MDS switch to handle FC traffic. That's all handled by modular licensing. Following are some of the features of NX-OS:

Hardware Support

- Nexus 7000, 6000, 5000, 4000, 3000, and 1000V series switches
- Nexus 2000 series fabric extenders
- Cisco MDS 9000 family storage switches
- UCS 6200 series fabric interconnects

New Technologies

- **Virtual device contexts**   Logical separation of route tables, permissions, and ports
- **Overlay transport virtualization (OTV)**   Encapsulates L2 inside L3 for transmission anywhere another Nexus switch or ASR 1000 series resides, thus enabling L2 extension via encapsulation between data centers. This is necessary to support the evolution of full data center virtualization.

Meet IOS XR

Although Cisco IOS is the most prevalent version of Cisco's operating system (be it 10.x all the way through 12.x), Cisco has also created a new operating system that could be looked at as more modular. In May 2004, Cisco released IOS XR for its CRS platform. In addition to the catchier name (inasmuch as an operating system name can be catchy), IOS XR delivers more modularity and features beyond its earlier incarnations.

Modularity

IOS XR's biggest feature is its modular architecture, which offers greater stability and easier management. Cisco is taking any transition slowly. At this point, IOS XR is only used on carrier-class routers, but one could certainly expect that some features will eventually make it into enterprise environments, assuming there is a supporting business requirement.

Current versions of IOS work as a single piece of executable code on the router. As customers demand various features, they are added to the operating system. This means the code requires more memory and system resources to execute.

IOS XR is designed more like a server. It incorporates an underlying operating system, and then services are added as separate processes. Ideally, this will make the operating system more reliable and faster.

The movement to new IOS architectures started late in 2004 as IOS High Availability (IOS-HA) was introduced for the Catalyst 6500 switch. This technology allows 6500s to run dual supervisor cards and failover without losing packets or experiencing any network disruption.

Speed and Efficiency

The move to this different operating system architecture is for a reason: The more features are added to IOS, the bigger and less efficient the operating system becomes. As such, the IOS XR architecture can include (or not include) features, as needed, thus making for a sleeker, sexier operating system. Current versions of IOS include millions of lines of code. IOS XR has around 80,000.

Having every feature under the sun is great to round out a device and be able to say, "Hey, it does all this ...." But the fact of the matter is that most clients don't need every feature IOS has to offer—and all those extra features just slow down the device.

Using IOS Commands

Any computer software environment has its quirks, and IOS is no exception. On one hand, IOS is a purpose-built operating system that has been stripped of all but the bare essentials in order to keep things simple and fast. That's a good thing, but you won't see the plush conveniences that the Mac, X-Windows (Unix/Linux), or Microsoft Windows graphical user interface (GUI) offers. On the other hand, IOS is one of the world's most widely distributed and important operating systems. So, everything you need to operate is inside, if you look.

The IOS Command Hierarchy

IOS has hundreds of commands. Some can be used anywhere in IOS; others only within a specific area. Even Cisco gurus haven't memorized all the IOS commands. So, like any good operating system, IOS arranges its commands into a hierarchy. Figure 5-8 is an overview of how IOS commands are structured.

The first division within IOS is between the User EXEC and Privileged EXEC levels. User EXEC, of course, contains only a subset of Privileged EXEC's commands. The less powerful User EXEC mode is where **connect, login, ping, show,** and other innocuous commands reside. These are in Privileged EXEC, too, but privileged mode is where the more powerful, and potentially destructive, commands—such as **configure, debug, erase, setup,** and others—are exclusively available.

Depending on the IOS feature set installed, there are many more commands in Privileged EXEC than in User EXEC. The commands in User EXEC mode tend to be "flat." In other words, they don't have branches leading to subset commands underneath, as the following example shows:

```
Router>connect ?   WORD  IP address or hostname of a remote system
<cr>
```

As a rule, User EXEC mode commands go, at most, just two levels deep. Being more powerful, Privileged EXEC mode commands can go deeper, as the following sample sequence shows:

```
MyRouter#show ip ?   access-lists         List IP access lists
   accounting             The active IP accounting database
   aliases                IP alias table
```

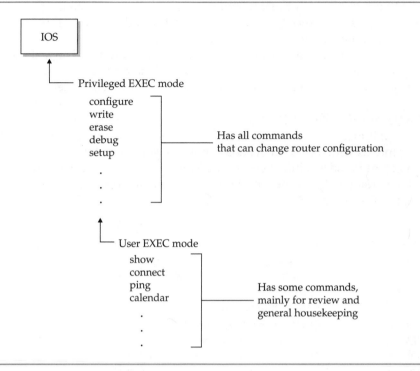

Figure 5-8.   The IOS command structure has two modes.

```
   arp                    IP ARP table
   .
   .
   .
```

The **show ip** command has many available arguments (subcommands):

```
MyRouter#show ip arp ?
H.H.H                  48-bit hardware address of ARP entry
Hostname or A.B.C.D  IP address or hostname of ARP entry
  Null                  Null interface
  Serial                Serial
  Ethernet              IEEE 802.3
  <cr>
```

Arguments can be modified by other arguments still deeper in the root command's "subcommand" tree:

```
My Router#show ip arp serial ?
  <0-3>  Serial interface number
  <cr>
```

For example, after you've pieced together a full command from the preceding options—**ip access-lists serial2,** for example—you would enter a carriage return after the "2" for serial line number 2.

Piecing together straightforward command lines is one thing. The real trick is knowing where to find arguments to root commands so that you can put together complete and correct command lines. This is where the IOS help system comes into play.

Traversing IOS with the Help System

IOS has a built-in, context-sensitive help system. *Context sensitive* means the help system responds with information based on where you are in the system at the time. You can get the broadest kind of context-sensitive help by simply entering a question mark at the prompt. Here, for example, is a listing of all the root commands available in the User EXEC level of IOS:

```
Router>>?
Exec commands:
  <1-99>            Session number to resume
  access-enable     Create a temporary Access-List entry
  access-profile    Apply user-profile to interface
  clear             Reset functions
  connect           Open a terminal connection
  crypto            Encryption related commands.
  disable           Turn off privileged commands
  disconnect        Disconnect an existing network connection
  enable            Turn on privileged commands
  exit              Exit from the EXEC
  help              Description of the interactive help system
  lock              Lock the terminal
  login             Log in as a particular user
  logout            Exit from the EXEC
  name-connection   Name an existing network connection
  ping              Send echo messages
  rcommand          Run command on remote switch
  release           Release a resource
  renew             Renew a resource
  resume            Resume an active network connection
  set               Set system parameter (not config)
  show              Show running system information
  ssh               Open a secure shell client connection
  systat            Display information about terminal lines
  tclquit           Quit Tool Command Language shell
  telnet            Open a telnet connection
  terminal          Set terminal line parameters
  traceroute        Trace route to destination
```

```
tunnel          Open a tunnel connection
where           List active connections
```

You can also get what some call "word help" by entering part of a command you don't know followed immediately by a question mark:

```
Router>>sh?
show
```

Word help is a great way to get definitions and is especially handy for figuring out what truncated commands are, as with **show** in the preceding example. Another way to get help on a partial command is to simply enter it, whereupon the system will come back with an instruction on how to obtain complete help on the command:

```
Router>>sh
% Type "show ?" for a list of subcommands
```

Notice that in help's suggested command (**show ?**) there's a space between the command and the question mark. As you've noticed by now, there's always a space between a command and its modifier (called an "argument"). Doing this in a help request is the way to ask for a list of the arguments available for the command. In the following example, the question mark asks for all arguments available for the **show** command:

```
Router>>show ?
  bootflash       Boot Flash information
  calendar        Display the hardware calendar
  clock           Display the system clock
  context         Show context information
  dialer          Dialer parameters and statistics
  history         Display the session command history
  hosts           IP domain-name, lookup style, nameservers,
                            and host table
  kerberos        Show Kerberos Values
  location        Display the system location
  .
  .
  .
```

Sometimes, using help in this way is called "command-syntax help," because it helps you properly complete a multipart command. Command-syntax help is a powerful learning tool because it lists the keywords or arguments available to you at nearly any point in IOS command operations. Remember, the space must be inserted between the command and the question mark in order to use command-syntax help.

In IOS, help plays a more integral role than help systems in normal PC or business application software packages. Those help systems (also context sensitive) are essentially online manuals that try to help you learn a whole subsection of the application. IOS help is terse: It just wants to get you through the next command line. That's refreshing. Most help systems nowadays seem to assume you're anxious to spend hours reading all about an entire subsystem when, in fact, you just want to know what to do next.

NOTE   Don't be confused by the **show** command's name. This command displays running system information. It is not an all-purpose command to "show" help information; the **?** command does that. The **show** command is used to examine router status.

Command Syntax

There's more to operating IOS commands than simply "walking rightward" through the root command's subcommand tree. To run IOS, you must learn how to combine different commands—not just modify a single command—in order to form the command lines it takes to do the heavy lifting that network administration requires. But IOS isn't rocket science, as the following sample sequence demonstrates:

```
MyRouter#config
Configuring from terminal, memory, or network [terminal]?
```

In the preceding prompt, we're entering config mode, and IOS wants to know if the configuration will be delivered through network download, copied from an image stored in the router's NVRAM memory, or typed from the terminal. We just as easily could have bypassed the prompt by concatenating the two commands into one command line:

```
MyRouter#config terminal
```

Don't let this throw you: We're not configuring a terminal, as IOS's phrasing seems to imply. In IOS command shorthand, **config terminal** means we're "configuring from a terminal." The next step is to "point" at the thing to be configured. We'll configure an interface:

```
MyRouter(config)#interface
% Incomplete command.
```

Instead of asking, "What interface would you like to configure?" IOS cruelly barks back that our command is no good. This is where some user know-how is required:

```
MyRouter(config)#interface GigabitEthernet0
MyRouter(config-if)#
```

IOS wanted to know what physical interface module was to be configured. We told IOS that port number 0 of the Gigabit Ethernet interface module was the one to be configured. The IOS prompt changes to:

```
MyRouter(config-if)#
```

where the "if" is shorthand for "interface." (Configuration modes are covered later in this chapter.)

> **NOTE**   Always keep track of the device you're pointing at when configuring. The IOS config prompt is generic and doesn't tell you at which network interface the **(config-if)#** prompt is pointed. IOS does not insert the interface's name into the prompt by default. The prompt may be changed on newer versions of the router IOS, but we've experienced some of the embedded tools not working flawlessly when the prompt is changed.
>
> Once pointed at the network interface to be configured, router configuration is simply a matter of supplying IOS the configuration parameters for that interface, which we'll cover in a few pages.

An understanding of how IOS syntax works, combined with the help system, is enough for anyone to begin entering correct command lines—with some time and hard work, of course.

Command Completion

Sooner or later, you'll encounter IOS command lines filled with seemingly cryptic symbols. Don't be intimidated by them; they are only commands that expert users have truncated to speed up the process of typing them—and maybe to impress people a bit. IOS is like DOS and most other editors in that it will accept truncated commands. But if the truncated command is not a string of letters unique to the command set, an error message will be generated. For example, if you type the first two letters of a command that another command starts with, you'll get an error message, such as the following:

```
Router#te
% Ambiguous command:   «te»
```

This error is displayed because IOS has three commands beginning with the letter string *te:* **telnet, terminal,** and **test.** If the intent was to telnet somewhere, one more character will do the job:

```
Router>>tel
Host:
```

> **NOTE**   If you run across a truncated command you don't understand, simply look it up by using word help in the online help system. Type the truncated command followed immediately by a question mark. Unlike with command-syntax help, when you're using word help, no space should precede the **?** command.

Recalling Command History

IOS keeps a running record of recently entered commands. Being able to recall commands is useful for avoiding the following:

- Having to type commands that are entered repeatedly
- Having to remember long, complicated command lines

The history utility will record anything you enter, even bad commands. The only limit is the amount of buffer memory you dedicate to keeping the history. Here's an example:

```
Router#show history
    test
    tel
    exit
    enable
```

More recently entered commands are toward the top of **show history** lists. They are not listed in alphabetical order.

Arrow keys can also be used to display prior commands. Using arrow keys saves having to enter the **show history** command, but this only shows prior commands one at a time. Press the UP ARROW (or CTRL-P) to recall the most recent commands first. If you're already somewhere in the sequence of prior commands, press the DOWN ARROW (or CTRL-N) to recall the least recent commands first.

Overview of Router Modes

Cisco routers can be in any one of seven possible operating modes, as illustrated in Figure 5-9. Three of them are startup modes. In the other four, network administrators are in either User EXEC mode or Privileged EXEC (enable) mode. Once inside Privileged EXEC, network administrators can make configuration changes either to the entire device or to a specific network interface.

You must keep track of what router mode you are in at all times. Many IOS commands will execute only from a specific mode. As can be seen in Figure 5-9, router modes get more specific—and powerful—as the user traverses toward the center of IOS. It pays to keep an eye on IOS prompts, because they'll always tell you which mode you're in.

The Three Types of Operating Modes

Cisco router operating modes exist to perform three general tasks:

- Boot a system
- Define what commands can be used
- Specify which part(s) of the router will be affected by changes made to the config file

Table 5-5 outlines the various IOS modes and what they are used for. As you become more familiar with Cisco internetworking in general, and the IOS software in particular, you will see that most of the action takes place inside the various configuration modes.

Mode Type	Purpose
Boot	*Setup mode* is used to make a basic working configuration file.
	RXBoot mode assists router boot to a rudimentary state when a working IOS image can't be found in flash memory.
	ROM monitor mode is used by the router if the IOS image can't be found or if the normal boot sequence was interrupted.
User	*User EXEC mode* is the first "room" one enters after login; it restricts users to examining router status.
	Privileged EXEC mode is entered using an Enable password; it allows users to change the config file, erase memory, and so on.
Configuration	*Global config mode* changes parameters for all interfaces.
	Config-command mode "targets" changes at specific interfaces.

Table 5-5.   Three General Kinds of IOS Software Modes

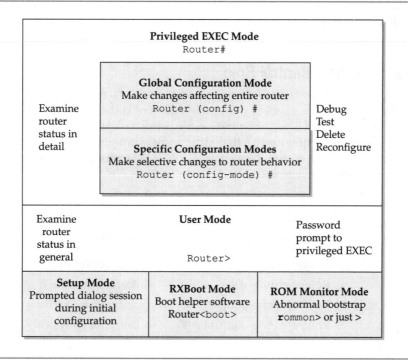

Figure 5-9.   Seven operating modes are made possible by Cisco routers.

Configuration Modes

Configuration modes differ from user modes by nature. The two EXEC modes define what level of IOS commands you may use. By contrast, configuration modes are used to target specific network interfaces—physical or virtual—to which a configuration change applies. For example, you would go into configure interface mode—identified by the **(config-if)#** prompt—in order to configure a specific Ethernet interface module. There are dozens of configuration modes in all, each targeting different parts of the configuration file. Table 5-6 lists eight of the most common configuration modes.

A look at Table 5-6 tells you that configuration mode is all about instructing IOS on what to do with packets flowing through the device. Some modes apply to packets flowing through specific connection points, such as interfaces, lines, and ports. The other IOS configuration modes deal with routing protocols and tables needed to handle that flow.

The Two Types of Config Files

There are two types of config files for every router: the running-config file and the startup-config file. As their names imply, the basic difference is that the running-config file is "live" in the sense that it is running in RAM. Any changes made to the running-config file go into effect immediately. The startup-config file is stored in the router's NVRAM, where the IOS bootstrap program goes to fetch the router's running configuration parameters when starting up.

After router-specific parameters have been changed, the **copy** command is used to save and distribute config file changes. As can be seen at the bottom of Figure 5-10, a master config file can be distributed to other routers through a TFTP server.

The Configuration File's Central Role

Managing a router involves installation, upgrades, backups, recovery, and other event-driven tasks, but the biggest part of router management is the care and feeding of a router's configuration file. The configuration file is the cockpit from which the network administrator runs the router and all the traffic going through it. As will be detailed in the next chapter, configuration files contain access lists, passwords, and other important router management tools.

Configuration Mode	Router Port Targeted	Applies To
Global	Router(config)#	Entire config file
Interface	Router(config-if)#	Interface module (physical)
Subinterface	Router(config-subif)#	Subinterface (virtual)
Controller	Router(config-controller)#	Controller (physical)

Table 5-6. Config Modes and the Parts of the Router Targeted

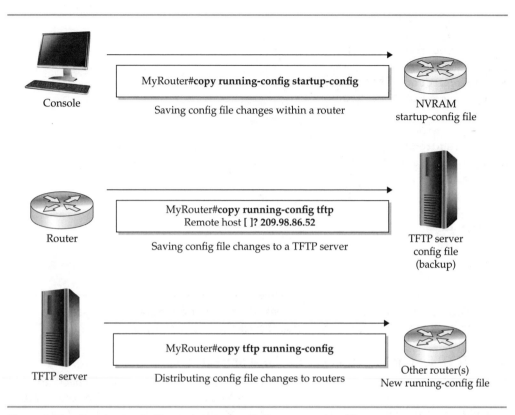

Figure 5-10. Running-config files and startup-config files are used in different ways.

Viewing the Configuration File

The most common way to examine the operational status of a router is to view its running configuration file. To view most anything in IOS is to ask for a view of the configuration. The main IOS command for viewing such information is the **show** command.

The following example uses the **show running-config** command to view a router's running configuration. There are two types of configuration files. The *running* configuration file is an image running in DRAM (main memory) at a given time. The *backup* or *startup-config* configuration file is stored in NVRAM and is used to boot the router.

```
Router#show running-config
Building configuration...
Current configuration:
!
version 12
```

```
service password-encryption
service udp-small-servers
service tcp-small-servers
! hostname Router
! enable secret 5 $1$C/q2$ZhtujqzQIuJrRGqFwdwn71
enable password 7 0012000F
! vty-async
! interface Serial0
  no ip address
no ip route-cache
no ip mroute-cache
shutdown
! interface Serial1
no ip address
.
.
.
```

 NOTE   Rather than pressing SPACEBAR repeatedly to read through a **show running-config** command, use a pipe and filter the output. There are several filters. Try **show run | ?**.

Using TFTP for Configuration File Backups and Updates

As with IOS system image backups and updates, TFTP servers are used to back up and update configuration files. For example, the **copy running-config tftp** command is used to back up the router's running configuration file (named tomtest, in this example) to a TFTP server using the following procedure:

```
Router#copy running-config tftp
Remote host []? 10.1.10.40
Name of configuration file to write [router-config]? test
Write file tomtest on host 10.1.10.40? [confirm]<cr>
Building configuration...
Writing test !! [OK]
Router#
```

Here are the other TFTP commands to back up or update configuration files:

- **copy tftp running-config**   Configures the router directly by copying from the TFTP directly into the router's DRAM

- **copy startup-config tftp**   Backs up the startup configuration from the router's NVRAM to the TFTP server

- **copy tftp startup-config**   Updates the router's startup configuration file by downloading from the TFTP server and overwriting the one stored in the router's NVRAM

Note that **tftp** goes *in front of* the file type—**running-config** or **startup-config**—to download (update from the server) and *behind* the file type to upload (back up to the server). Think of the **copy** command as copying *from* somewhere *to* somewhere.

> **NOTE**   All these commands may be run at once, but without an additional command telling the router not to pause for input, user intervention is required. This can be considered a safety mechanism because you could accidently copy from tftp to running-config! Entering **file prompt quiet** from configure mode will allow you to run a tftp copy string in one line.

We've taken a close look at Cisco's routers and their routing philosophy in this chapter. Although we touched briefly on router configuration, we take a much closer look at the task in the next chapter and discuss how you can configure your router for maximum efficiency and utility.

CHAPTER 6 | Configuring Routing

The router is the centerpiece of internetworking. It's the device that stitches networks together into internetworks and makes them useful. So, if you can learn how to manage routers properly, you can pretty much manage an internetwork. The network administrator's single point of control over router behavior is the configuration file, called the "config file" for short. The config file is one of only two permanent files on a router. The other is the IOS software, which is general in nature and cannot be altered by customers. The config file, then, is the network administrator's single point of control over the network. It's at the center of the router operations, with IOS referring to it hundreds of times per second in order to tell the router how to do its job.

Although the config file is the key tool, at first it can seem hard to understand. This is because the config file is unlike the kinds of files most of us are used to. You can't put a cursor inside one and edit it in real time like you would, say, a word processor document. You can't compile it and debug it the way computer programmers turn source code into executable code. Config files are modified by entering IOS commands and then viewing the new configuration to see if you achieved the desired results.

Communicating with a Router

Most users of internetworks don't communicate with routers, they communicate *through* them. Network administrators, however, must deal directly with individual routers in order to install and manage them.

Routers are purpose-built computers dedicated to internetwork processing. They are important devices that individually serve hundreds or thousands of users—some serve even more. When a router goes down, or even just slows down, users howl and network managers jump. As you might imagine then, network administrators demand foolproof ways to gain access to the routers they manage in order to work on them.

Routers don't come with a monitor, keyboard, or mouse, so you must communicate with them in one of three other ways:

- From a terminal that's in the same location as the router and is physically connected to it through a console cable (the terminal is usually a PC or workstation running in terminal mode)

- From a terminal that's in a different location than the router and is connected to it through a modem that calls another modem connected to the router with a cable (typically connected on the auxiliary port on the router)

- Through the network on which the router sits using terminal emulation software, such as Telnet, SSH, or web-based management consoles using HTTP or HTTPS

In large networks, network administrators are often physically removed from routers and must access them over a network. However, if the router is unreachable due to a network problem, or if there's no modem attached to the router itself, someone must go to its location and directly log in to the router. The three ways to gain administrative access to routers are depicted in Figure 6-1.

Even when network administrators manage routers in the same building, they still prefer to access them by network. For many organizations, it doesn't make sense to have a terminal hooked up to each router, especially when there are dozens of them stacked in a data closet or computer room. Also, it's much more convenient to manage them all from a single PC or workstation.

There are several ways to communicate with a router, each made possible by a particular communications protocol. Table 6-1 lists each method, the protocol, and how each is used.

The Console Port

Every Cisco router has a console port. It is there to provide a way to hook up a terminal to the router in order to work on it. The console port (sometimes called the management port) is used by administrators to log in to a router directly—that is, without a network connection. The console must be used to install routers onto networks because, of course, at that point there is no network connection to work through.

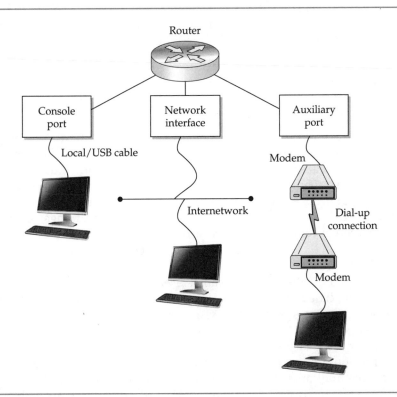

Figure 6-1.   Administrative access to routers is obtained in three different ways.

Access Method	Protocol	Communication Method
Console port	EIA/TIA-232	Serial line connection from local terminal.
Auxiliary port	EIA/TIA-232	Serial line terminal connection via modem.
USB 5-pin Type A	USB	Serial-line emulation via on-board USB serial adapter. When a USB connection is used, the traditional RS-232 port is inoperable.
Telnet/Secure Shell (SSH)	Telnet/SSH	Virtual terminal connection via TCP/IP network.
HTTP/HTTPS Server	HTTP/HTTPS	Web browser connection via TCP/IP network.
SNMP	SNMP	Simple Network Management Protocol; virtual terminal connection made via a TCP/IP network. (SNMP is covered in Chapter 13.)
WSMA	SSHv2, HTTP, HTTPS, TLS	Web Services Management Agent (WSMA) is a management mechanism that can be utilized by network management systems. It utilizes XML and SOAP.

Table 6-1.   How Network Administrators Access Routers

Long term, the console's role is to be there as a contingency in case of emergency. When a router is completely down—in other words, when it is no longer able to process network packets—it cannot be accessed over the network. If the router is up and processing packets, but the network segment through which the technician must access it is down, going over a network to fix the router is not an option. This is when the console port provides a sure way to log in to the router to fix things, or you have a special terminal server configured to allow access remotely.

Console Terminal Types

A standalone client, PC, or workstation can be used as a console. Console terminals must run a character-based user interface. They cannot run a graphical user interface (GUI), such as Microsoft Windows, Apple's OS X, or X-Windows. In order to use a PC or workstation as a console, you must use terminal emulator software. For example, one of the best-known terminal emulators is HyperTerminal, which shipped with versions of Windows previous to Windows Vista. As of that release, however, Microsoft no longer ships a serial-communication-capable console. Remember PuTTY, the SSH client we mentioned in an earlier chapter? There is also PuTTYtel, which is serial capable. One may start up PuTTYtel (or one of the many other terminal emulator products) and log in to the router from there. An example of a PuTTY configuration is shown in Figure 6-2.

Console Connector Types

Console ports in Cisco routers have used a variety of connector types (25-pin, RJ-45, 9-pin, and so on), but all provide a single terminal connection. A word of warning: Make sure you have the proper rollover cable—not an Ethernet cable—before trying to hook up a console terminal to work on a router. Many a network administrator has spent a half-hour fiddling with cables to finally find one that could connect to a router just to do 15 minutes of productive work.

 NOTE   Console ports on newer Cisco devices are usually labeled "Console" and are painted light blue—but not always. On some products, console ports are labeled "Admin," and on others they are labeled "Management." Don't be confused by this; they are all console ports. Also, newer models include an on-board USB serial adapter as fewer laptops include an RS-232 connection. When we refer to a serial connection, this on-board USB port can be utilized interchangeably.

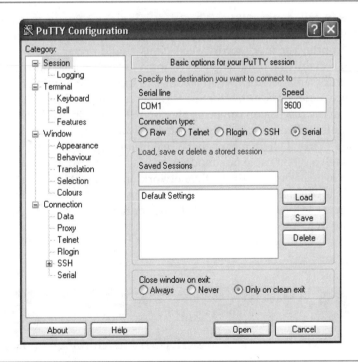

Figure 6-2.   A PuTTY connection can be used to configure Cisco routers.

The Auxiliary Port

Most Cisco routers have a second port on the back called the "auxiliary port" (usually called the "AUX port," for short). Like the console port, the AUX port makes possible a direct, non-network connection to the router.

How does the AUX port differ from the console port? The AUX port uses a connector type that modems can plug in to (console ports have connectors designed for terminal cables). If a router in a faraway data closet goes down, the network administrator asks somebody in the area to go to the router and plug in a modem so that it can be serviced remotely. In more critical configurations, a modem is often left permanently connected to a router's AUX port. Either way, the AUX port affords console-like access when it isn't practical to send a technician to the site to work on a router through a local console. Figure 6-3 shows the back of a Cisco 1841 router.

 NOTE   Cisco's smaller routers do not have AUX ports, only console ports. These devices support remote management logins by connecting a modem to the router using an auxiliary/console cable kit.

SSH/Telnet

Once a router is installed on a network, access to it is almost always made through a Secure Shell (SSH) connection or a nonencrypted Telnet session, not through the console or AUX ports. The more security conscious would prefer an SSH connection, and this should certainly be used when accessing a device over an untrusted network (which is practically any network when it comes to the type of administration one does with a piece of network infrastructure). In this section, we'll use the term "Telnet" but everything in the discussion can be applied to SSH, too, since it is essentially a secure form of Telnet. This connectivity is just simply a way to log in to a router as a virtual terminal. "Virtual" here means that a real terminal connection is not made to the device through a direct cable or a modem, as with the console or AUX ports. Telnet connections are instead made through the network. In the most basic terms, a real terminal session is composed of bits streaming one by one over a serial line. A virtual terminal session is composed of IP packets being routed over a network, pretending to be bits streaming over a serial line.

Figure 6-3.   Console and AUX ports on a Cisco 1841 router make direct, non-network connections possible.

Telnet is a network application, not a terminal emulator. It was developed in the early days of the Unix operating system as a way to log in to remote computers to manage them. Later, internetwork pioneers incorporated Telnet directly into the TCP/IP networking protocol as a way to get to and manage internetwork devices. A Telnet client and server ship with every copy of Cisco's IOS software and most computer operating systems.

When using Telnet to access a router, you do so over a virtual line provided by the Cisco IOS software. These are called VTY lines. Don't let the word "line" confuse you. It does not refer to an actual communications circuit; it means a virtual terminal session inside the IOS software. IOS supports up to various quantities of virtual terminal lines, from five on older versions (numbered VTY 0–4, inclusive), upwards, making it possible to have many virtual terminal sessions running on a router at the same time. This is probably design overkill, however. It's rare to have more than one virtual terminal session running on a router at the same time.

Cisco's IOS software is used mostly in character-based interface mode, which is to say that it's not a point-and-click GUI environment, as previously mentioned. Whether logging in to a router through the console port, AUX port, or Telnet/SSH, you are delivered to the character-based IOS software interface. The following shows character-based IOS output:

```
!
line con 0
   exec-timeout 0 0
 line aux 0
  transport input all
 line vty 0 2
  exec-timeout 0 0
  password 7 1313041B
  login line vty 3
  exec-timeout 5 0
  password 7 1313041B
  login line vty 4
  exec-timeout 0 0
  password 7 1313041B
  login
!
```

The preceding example is a listing of the seven IOS lines—*con* for console, *aux* for auxiliary, and *vty* for the virtual terminal. Here's what the seven lines are

- The console port, accessed through a local serial or USB cable connection
- The AUX port, accessed through a modem connection
- Five VTY lines, accessed through TCP/IP network connections

The HTTP Server User Interface

A more recent router access method is HTTP Server. Don't be misled by the name; no computer server is involved in using HTTP Server. The "server" in HTTP Server refers to a small software application running inside the Cisco IOS software. HTTP Server first became available with IOS Release 10.3. HTTP Server makes it possible to interact with the router through a web browser. Figure 6-4 shows an HTTP Server screen.

Like so many Cisco devices and applications, its user applications tend to change over time. Your device's interface may or may not look like the one in Figure 6-4. That said, the same basic functionality will be present. It will just be accessible through a slightly different interface.

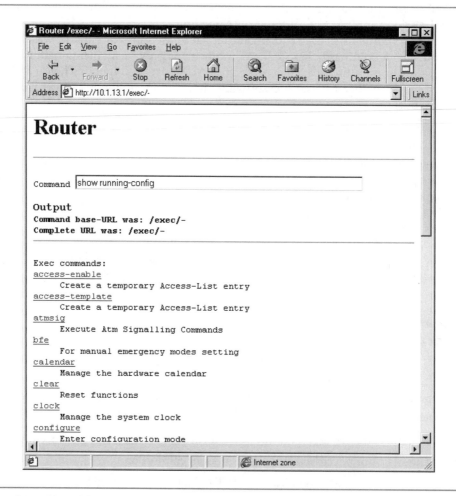

Figure 6-4.   Cisco IOS can be managed through an HTTP Server screen.

Using HTTP to handle IOS command-line input and output isn't particularly ergonomic. The majority of network administrators still prefer using the IOS software in character-based mode because it's faster and more direct than pointing and clicking. This is not unlike those old hands who jump into Microsoft Windows' MS-DOS prompt window to type system-level commands, but Cisco may gradually move IOS toward a graphical user interface for a couple of reasons. The most obvious reason to at least offer a GUI-based alternative to working with IOS is that Cisco devices are increasingly being tended to by non-experts. Another is that as complexity increases, the need for system visualization, even inside a single router, grows. Using visualization tools (to show load conditions, isolate errors, and so on) will, of course, require a browser instead of the old-fashioned "green screen" character-based command-line interface.

 NOTE   To use the command-line interface, you must know what commands to type. You may want to use HTTP Server to get started and phase over to character-based mode as you become comfortable with the IOS command structure.

Essential Router Commands

A few major root commands handle most tasks associated with configuring routers. They include the following:

- **show**   Examine router status.
- **configure**   Make changes to config file parameters.
- **no**   Negate a parameter setting.
- **copy**   Put config file changes into effect.

The **show** command is the bread-and-butter command of IOS. It's used to examine nearly everything about a router and its configuration. The following example shows who's logged in to the router, which is moment-to-moment information:

```
Router>show users
    Line       User      Host(s)              Idle       Location
   0 con 0               idle                 00:10:14
 194 vty 0     admin     idle                 00:01:13 192.168.1.99
 195 vty 1     admin     idle                 00:00:18 192.168.1.99
*196 vty 2               idle                 00:00:18 192.168.1.99
   Interface   User                  Mode     Idle       Peer Address
```

The **show** command can also be used to show information such as the version of IOS software installed:

```
Router>show version
Cisco IOS Software, 1841 Software (C1841-ENTBASEK9-M), Version 15.1(4)M3,
RELEASE SOFTWARE (fc1)
```

```
Technical Support: http://www.cisco.com/techsupport
Copyright (c) 1986-2011 by Cisco Systems, Inc.
Compiled Tue 06-Dec-11 15:26 by prod_rel_team
ROM: System Bootstrap, Version 12.4(13r)T5, RELEASE SOFTWARE (fc1)
Router uptime is 1 day, 6 hours, 9 minutes
System returned to ROM by reload at 18:28:04 UTC Sun Oct 28 2012
System image file is "flash:c1841-entbasek9-mz.151-4.M3.bin"
```

The **no** command is used to reverse an existing parameter setting. For example, if we turned on IP accounting for Fast Ethernet port number 1 and now want to turn it off, we point to that interface in configure interface mode—indicated by the **MyRouter(config-if)#** prompt—and then simply precede the command used to turn it on (**ip accounting-list**) with the **no** command, as shown here:

```
MyRouter(config-if)#no ip accounting-list
```

Any IOS command can be turned off using the **no** command syntax.

Knowing how to navigate within an operating system environment is always half the battle. This is especially so in command-line interfaces, because there are no graphical icons to show the way. Table 6-2 lists the commands used to move around within the IOS environment.

"Hot key" commands are useful because some config-file command lines can get long and complicated.

Command	Purpose
Enable	Move from User EXEC to Privileged EXEC mode.
Disable	Return to User EXEC mode from Privileged EXEC mode.
Exit	Exit configuration mode or terminate a login session.
CTRL-A	Move to the start of a command line.
CTRL-B or ARROW	Move backward one character position.
CTRL-F or ARROW	Move forward one character position.
CTRL-Z	Exit or quit a process (such as a login or a multipage display).
ESC-B	Move to the beginning of the prior word (good for making corrections).
ESC-F	Move to the beginning of the next word.

Table 6-2.   IOS Navigation Commands

Password Recovery

Sometimes situations occur that make it necessary to recover a router's password. Two of the most common such situations are

- A password is forgotten, and a record of it cannot be found.
- A router is bought used, and it came with passwords on it.

Password recovery naturally involves somehow getting into the router's configuration file to find the lost password, change it, or erase the entire configuration file and reconfigure the router from scratch.

The trouble is that the configuration file sits inside the Privileged EXEC (enable mode) level of IOS, which itself is password protected. For that reason, recovering a password means getting to the unconfigured version of the IOS software. This is why password recovery procedures are so involved.

There are several procedures for recovering passwords from Cisco routers, depending on whether a Line or Enable password was lost, the model of router hardware, and the version of IOS software. All the procedures involve resetting settings that tell the router how to boot. Older Cisco routers use physical hardware jumpers, so you need to go inside the router box to reset them. Newer Cisco routers have "soft jumpers" called configuration registers, where settings can be changed. A sample configuration register setting is 0x2102. The first four bits (0–3) are the ones that select the boot mode:

- When the four bits are 0000 (0), the router will enter rommon> mode upon reboot.
- When the four bits are 0001 (1), the router will boot from the IOS system stored in ROM.
- When the four bits are 0010 (2) through 1111 (F), the router will look to the configuration file in NVRAM to find which IOS system image to boot from.

Recovering Enable Passwords

Two procedures are used to recover Enable passwords (Enable and Enable Secret). The one to use depends on the router model, and sometimes on the CPU or IOS software version the router runs on. If you don't find what you need here, a quick search of the Cisco website for the term "password recovery" should help you find a specific procedure.

To recover a password, you must get to the rommon> prompt to recover Enable or Enable Secret passwords, and the test-system>> prompt to recover a Line password. This is done by sending a Break signal from the console terminal to the router to interrupt the normal boot process.

NOTE The router may not respond to the Break signal sent from PC terminal emulators. You must understand how the terminal emulator you're using generates Break signals. In some emulators, Break is generated with the ALT-B key combination; in others, CTRL-B. Check the help documentation for your emulator if you have problems interrupting the router's boot process with Break.

Getting to the rommon> Prompt

For either of the two procedures to recover Enable/Enable Secret passwords, the first part—getting to the **rommon>** prompt level of IOS—is the same:

1. Attach a terminal, or a PC running terminal emulation software, to the router's console port using these settings:

   - 9600 baud rate
   - No parity
   - One stop bit
   - No flow control

2. Go to the > prompt and type the **show version** command. (Remember, you lost either the Enable or Enable Secret password, which only locks you out of Enable mode, not out of the IOS entirely.)

```
TN3270 Emulation software.

2 FastEthernet/IEEE 802.3 interface(s)
4 Serial network interface(s)
128K bytes of non-volatile configuration memory.
4096K bytes of processor board System flash (Read/Write)
4096K bytes of processor board Boot flash (Read/Write)

Configuration register is 0x2102
```

3. The last line of the **show version** display is the configuration register. The factory default setting is usually 0x2102; sometimes it is 0x102. Write down the settings in your router for later use.

4. Reboot the router by turning off the power and then turning it back on.

5. Press the BREAK key on the terminal (or combination of keys required to send Break from your terminal emulator) within 60 seconds of having turned the router back on.

6. The **rommon>** prompt—without the router's name showing—should appear.

Now that you've gotten to the **rommon>** prompt, the battle of password recovery is half won. From this point on, the router model will determine what you need to do to recover the password (in some cases, the IOS version and CPU also come into play). From here, there are two ways that the password recovery process can proceed. Again, check for your router's model at www.cisco.com. It'll tell you which procedure your particular model uses. Most often, you'll be following procedure 2.

Enable Password Recovery Procedure 1 If your router model requires that you follow procedure 1 for password recovery, follow these steps:

1. Type **o/r 0x2142** and then press ENTER at the > prompt. This loads from flash memory without loading the router's configuration file.

2. Type **i** at the prompt and then press ENTER.

3. You will be asked a series of setup questions. Answer **no** to each question, or press CTRL-C to skip this sequence altogether.

4. At the **Router>** prompt, type **enable.**

5. Type **configure memory** or **copy startup-config running-config**. This copies the NVRAM into memory.

6. Type **copy startup-config nvram:startup-config.bak**. This will create a backup of your current startup configuration.

7. Type **write terminal** or **show running-config**, which shows the router's configuration. In this case, it will show that all the interfaces are currently shut down. Additionally, you will see the passwords, either encrypted or unencrypted. Unencrypted passwords can be reused, whereas encrypted passwords must be changed with a new password.

8. Type **configure terminal** and make any desired changes. Now the prompt will be **hostname(config)#**.

9. To change a given password, type **enable secret <password>** to change the Enable Secret password, for instance.

10. On each interface, type the **no shutdown** command.

11. Type **config-register 0x2102** (or whatever value you wrote down in step 2).

12. Press CTRL-Z or END to exit configuration mode. The prompt should now be **hostname#**.

13. Type **write memory** or **copy running-config startup-config** to save your changes.

14. Type **Reload** to restart the router with the Cisco IOS software booting from flash memory.

Enable Password Recovery Procedure 2 Use this procedure for routers that must use password recovery procedure 2:

1. Type the **confreg 0x2142** command at the **rommon>** prompt. (Note that **confreg** is not a mistyping of **config**. It stands for configuration register.) When the "Do you wish to change configuration?" prompt appears, answer **yes**.

2. Type **reset** at the **rommon 2>** prompt. The router will reboot, but ignore the saved configuration.

3. A number of setup questions will appear. Type **no** for each one. Alternatively, you can press CTRL-C to skip the initial setup sequence.

4. Type **enable** at the **Router>** prompt. This will put you into Enable mode, and you'll see the **Router#** prompt.

5. Type **copy startup-config nvram:startup-config.bak**. This will create a backup of your current startup configuration.

6. Type **configure memory** or **copy startup-config running config**. This copies the nonvolatile RAM into memory.

7. Type **write terminal** or **show running-config**. These commands show the router's configuration, and will show that all the interfaces are currently shut down. Additionally, you will see the passwords, either encrypted or unencrypted. Unencrypted passwords can be reused; encrypted passwords must be changed with a new password.

8. Type **configure terminal** and make any desired changes. Now the prompt will be **hostname(config)#**.

9. To change a given password, type **enable secret <password>** to change the Enable Secret password, for instance.

10. On each interface, type the **no shutdown** command.

11. Type **config-register 0x2102** (or whatever the previously noted configuration register value was).

12. Press CTRL-Z or END to exit configuration mode. The prompt should now be **hostname#**.

13. Type **write memory** or **copy running-config startup-config** to save your changes.

14. Type **Reload** to restart the router with the Cisco IOS software booting from flash memory.

Recovering a Line Password

The router must be forced into factory diagnostic mode in order to recover a lost Line password. Refer to the hardware installation/maintenance publication for the router product for specific information on configuring the processor configuration register for factory diagnostic mode. Table 6-3 summarizes the hardware or software settings required by the various products to boot into factory diagnostic mode.

Once the router has been forced into factory diagnostic mode, follow these steps:

1. Type **yes** when asked if you want to set the manufacturer's addresses. The **test-system>** prompt appears.

2. Type the **enable** command to get the **test-system> enable** prompt.

Recovery Procedure	Platforms Using Procedure
Change the setting to 0x8000 to boot into factory diagnostic mode. Use the **reload** command to restart; then change the configuration settings back to 0x2102 when finished.	Cisco AS5100, AS5200, AS5300 Cisco 1600 series, 2500 series, 3000 series, and 3600 series
Set the jumper in bit 15 of the configuration register, restart, and then reset the jumper when finished.	Modular products

Table 6-3. Configuration Register Settings to Enter Factory Diagnostic Mode

3. Type **config term** and then **show startup-config**. You should now be looking at the system configuration file. Find the password and write it down. Do not attempt to change the password.

4. Restart the router.

5. Use the recovered Line password (the one you wrote down) to log in to the router.

Recovering Passwords from Older Cisco Routers

To recover passwords from legacy Cisco routers, it is necessary to change the configuration register setting using a hardware jumper switch. Those procedures are not covered here. Refer to www.cisco.com to find password-recovery procedures for legacy products listed in Table 6-4.

Recovery Procedure	Legacy Cisco Platforms Using Procedures
Technique 3	IG routers running software earlier than Cisco IOS 9.1
Technique 4	CGS, MGS, AGS, AGS+, and any Cisco 70x0 Series running ROMs earlier than Cisco IOS 10.0
Technique 5	500-CS Communication Servers
Technique 6	Cisco 1020

Table 6-4. Cisco's Password-Recovery Procedures for Legacy Router Protocols

Step-by-Step Router Configuration

A router can be configured via one of the following methods:

- Using the preloaded CCP Light
- Entering changes directly to a router's running-config file
- Downloading a new config file from a TFTP server
- Setting up the config file from scratch

The best way to learn how to configure a router is to set one up from scratch. We'll step through setup mode here, not because the procedure is performed that often, but because it's an excellent way to review the fundamentals of router configuration.

Setup Mode

Setup is, essentially, an interactive script run to get the router up to a basic level of operation. If the device is new (and therefore has never been configured) or if the config file in NVRAM has been corrupted, the IOS software defaults into setup mode to rebuild the config file from scratch. Once that's accomplished, setup mode can be exited and the router rebooted in normal IOS mode, whereupon a complete config file can be built. Setup mode doesn't run by itself; a network administrator must be present to respond to setup's long sequence of questions about how to configure the router. Also, given that the router isn't configured, you cannot run setup through a network connection. Setup must be run through either the console or AUX port.

A router doesn't have to be new or corrupted for you to run setup. Setup can also be useful in non-emergency situations. Network administrators sometimes use setup when a config file has become so jumbled that it makes more sense to start anew—sort of like a blank sheet of paper. Used in this way, the parameter settings given as answers during a setup session overwrite the existing config file.

Setup mode is entered using the **setup** command. But before starting, hook your PC's COM port to the router's console port. Then start whatever terminal emulator software you prefer to use (remember, you'll be logged in to the router's operating system, not your PC). The following instructions assume you're running on a Microsoft Windows PC and have installed the PuTTY suite. Otherwise, you'll need to know how to start your terminal emulator. This shouldn't be a problem, because if you're running Apple, you're familiar with the App Store; if you're running X-Windows from a Unix/Linux computer, you don't need our advice on such a trifling technical issue in the first place.

We have two scenarios:

- If this device is fresh out of the box (post circa 2010), you'll likely be staring at some jargon about a default password and using a browser to configure the device. You can skip that part and just run setup from step 1.

- If this is an existing device, you may also just log in and run setup. If you'd like to "clean" its configuration prior to running setup, the needed command is **erase startup-config** or **erase /all nvram:** and then **reload**.

Here are the steps to follow:

1. Click the Start button.

2. Select All Programs | Putty | Putty.

3. The Putty configuration window will open.

4. Click the Serial radial button and enter your COM port (generally COM1).

5. Press ENTER, and you should be looking at the router's prompt. If you erased the config, the device will be prompting you to run setup (yes/no); if this is the case, skip to step 7.

6. Go into Privileged EXEC mode by entering **enable** and then the Enable Secret password (**setup** is essentially a configuration command, and config files cannot be modified from the user EXEC level of IOS).

7. Type **setup**, and setup mode is started.

Once setup is started, a banner appears with command instructions, an option to quit, and an option to review a summary of the interface modules on the router, as shown here:

```
The following code Router#set
*Mar  3 04:58:46.167: %SYS-5-CONFIG_I: Configured from console by con-
soleup


          --- System Configuration Dialog ---

Continue with configuration dialog? [yes/no]: y

At any point you may enter a question mark '?' for help.
Use ctrl-c to abort configuration dialog at any prompt.
Default settings are in square brackets '[]'.


Basic management setup configures only enough connectivity
for management of the system, extended setup will ask you
to configure each interface on the system

Would you like to enter basic management setup? [yes/no]: y
Configuring global parameters:

  Enter host name [Router]:
```

If you decide to proceed, setup starts by configuring global parameters. This is basic information, such as giving the router a name and passwords. If it's a new router, or if the config file in NVRAM has been corrupted, you must enter new parameters for these things, as shown next:

```
Configuring global parameters:

   Enter host name [Router]: MyRouter

   The enable secret is a password used to protect access to
   privileged EXEC and configuration modes. This password, after
   entered, becomes encrypted in the configuration.
   Enter enable secret: test

   The enable password is used when you do not specify an
   enable secret password, with some older software versions, and
   some boot images.
   Enter enable password: test1
```

You can see by looking at the following example that setup automatically detects interface modules physically present in the router's slots. It presents the available interfaces and asks which one we want to use to connect to the management network. In this case, we've chosen the Fast Ethernet connection.

```
Current interface summary


Interface       IP-Address      OK? Method Status
Protocol
FastEthernet0/0  unassigned      YES unset  administratively down down
Serial0/0        unassigned      YES unset  administratively down down
Serial0/1        unassigned      YES unset  administratively down down

Enter interface name used to connect to the
management network from the above interface summary: FastEthernet0/0

Configuring interface FastEthernet0/0:
   Use the 100 Base-TX (RJ-45) connector? [yes]:
   Operate in full-duplex mode? [no]:
   Configure IP on this interface? [no]:
```

Once this selection has been made, the router shows the completed command script. The following configuration command script was created:

```
hostname MyRouter
enable secret 5 $1$gAi3$BXI873YTi..MOL0NIl5X11
enable password test1
```

```
line vty 0 4
password test2
no snmp-server
!
no ip routing

!
interface FastEthernet0/0
no shutdown
media-type 100BaseX
half-duplex
no ip address
no mop enabled
!
interface Serial0/0
shutdown
no ip address
!
interface Serial0/1
shutdown
no ip address
!
end


[0] Go to the IOS command prompt without saving this config.
[1] Return back to the setup without saving this config.
[2] Save this configuration to nvram and exit.

Enter your selection [2]: 2
```

If you go ahead, setup then takes a few seconds to "build" the config file (as we said earlier, config files are not edited interactively like a word processor file). Once the build is done, you're delivered to IOS in "normal mode" and advised that if you want to continue configuring, you must do so using the **config** command:

```
[OK]
```

Once the setup session is done, a basic configuration file has been created. From there, you would follow normal procedure and use the **configure** command to input a complete configuration file.

Giving a Router an Identity

Taking the time to name and document each router properly helps make networks easier to manage. Identifying information can be assigned via the following methods:

- Giving the router a meaningful name
- Individually documenting router interfaces
- Putting a message of the day (MOTD) on the router

You will frequently see the name "Router" used in configuration examples. Don't let that confuse you; "Router" is not a mandatory part of the Cisco IOS prompt. A router could just as easily be named "MainOffice" or "R23183" or anything else. Routers should be given meaningful names that inform network administrators where the router is and what it does. You must be in global configuration mode and use the **hostname** command to change the device name, as shown here:

```
Router(config)#hostname MyRouter
MyRouter(config)#
```

Because the new name was input into the running-config file, the new router name MyRouter is used immediately in the next command prompt. However, unless you use the **write** or **copy** command to store the new name (or any other change) in NVRAM, if the router is rebooted, IOS would come back up using the old name.

NOTE The term "host" can confuse computer industry veterans new to internetworking. In the computer applications world, a host is a full-fledged computer system acting as a server, and network devices are nodes. In the internetworking context, host can mean any networked device, including routers, switches, and access servers, in addition to servers. We try to keep all this clear by referring only to computers as "hosts" and calling network equipment "devices." However, you should be aware that the term "host" can take on different meanings in internetworking documents.

A router interface can be specifically documented using the **description** command. Using descriptions is a great way to keep track of the network (and users) serviced by an interface. This may not sound like much, but big networks have thousands of interfaces, and they are reconfigured frequently. To enter an interface-specific description, you must first go to that interface (in this example, FastEthernet0/0):

```
MyRouter(config)#interface FastEthernet0/0
MyRouter(config-if)#
```

Then enter the **description** command followed by the description:

```
MyRouter(config-if)#description Fast Ethernet for finance department
MyRouter(config-if)#
```

Descriptions can be up to 240 characters in length. To close the loop, the description can be seen in part of the config file for the interface:

```
MyRouter(config-if)#
MyRouter#show running-config
.
.
.
interface FastEthernet0/0
 description Fast Ethernet for finance department
```

Router names and interface descriptions are only seen by network administrators. A third router identification tool—the message-of-the-day banner—is a way to announce information to all terminals connected to a router. MOTD banners are a good way to make sure housekeeping announcements are seen by all users on the network. Banners are commonly used to warn against unauthorized use, announce scheduled system downtime, and make other types of announcements. Use the **banner motd** command to put a banner on a router:

```
MyRouter(config)#banner motd $MyRouter will be down tonight$
```

The dollar sign was arbitrarily chosen for use here as the delimiter marking the start and end of the banner message. Any character can be used; just make sure to use a character that will not appear in the banner text itself.

The banner will display whenever someone either logs directly in to the router or hits the router from a web browser:

```
MyRouter will be down tonight
User Access Verification
Password:
```

Fancy multiline banners can be built using extended mode commands for VT terminals. VT is a de facto standard for terminal programming from Digital Equipment Corporation (which was later acquired by Compaq Computer, which was then acquired by HP).

CAUTION   Do not put any sensitive information in MOTD banners, because anybody can see them. In addition, there could be both security and legal implications if a "Welcome to . . ." message greets a hacker who is breaking into your network.

Examining Device Status

Examining network interfaces is a basic technique for getting critical status information. The **show interface** command does this.

Keepalive messages are sent by interfaces to one another at the data link layer to confirm that the virtual circuit between them is still active. Table 6-5 summarizes what the various status reports mean (using an interface named Ethernet1 as an example).

Cisco Discovery Protocol

Cisco has a proprietary troubleshooting tool called the Cisco Discovery Protocol (CDP). It ships with all Cisco equipment, including routers. CDP is used by devices to discover and learn about one another. It is media and protocol independent. Cisco devices use CDP as a way to advertise their existence to neighbors on a LAN or on the far side of a WAN connection. Think of CDP as a sort of "show configuration" command for a neighborhood of Cisco routers and other devices—a way for devices to tell anyone who will listen about their version (both software and hardware), hostname, number, and type of interface information (IP address, duplex, VTP domain, VLAN power draw).

CDP runs at the data link layer in order to be compatible with devices running different network layer protocols (IPX, IP, Bonjour, and so on). CDP can communicate with any physical media supporting the Subnetwork Access Protocol (SNAP), including LANs, Frame Relay, and ATM media. SNAP is a protocol designed to let devices pass messages within a subnetwork, allowing them to keep track of what's operating in the neighborhood.

CDP is automatic. You can connect any combination of Cisco devices, power them up, stand back, and let them automatically identify one another—even prior to being assigned network addresses. CDP is able to do this using a proprietary standard called the Cisco Proprietary Data-Link Protocol. Figure 6-5 shows how CDP spans otherwise incompatible protocols.

CDP is enabled by default in all Cisco devices. It works by having all Cisco devices in a directly connected network pass CDP frames to one another. The key to understanding CDP's outer limit lies in the words "directly connected." CDP can discover devices beyond a LAN, but only as long as the WAN connection does not go through any non-Cisco (and therefore non-CDP) devices to make the connection. CDP frames must be able to pass through internetwork connections in order to keep extending the map of what's connected to CDP's home LAN.

Message	Meaning
Ethernet1 is up, line protocol is up	Running okay
Ethernet1 is up, line protocol is down	Interface okay, but no active connection
Ethernet1 is down, line protocol is down	Interface problem
Ethernet1 is administratively down, line protocol is down	Disabled

Table 6-5.   Interface Status Report Definitions

High-level protocols	TCP/IP Novell Bonjour DECnet Others IPX
Cisco Proprietary Data-Link Protocol	Discover other Cisco devices, show information about them
SNAP	Ethernet Token Ring ATM Frame Others Relay

Figure 6-5. CDP bypasses incompatible protocols to keep track of networks.

Use the **show CDP** command to see what its current operating settings are:

```
MyRouter>show CDP
Global CDP information:
        Sending CDP packets every 60 seconds
        Sending a holdtime value of 180 seconds
```

Asking for command-syntax help for the **show CDP** command displays the kind of information CDP can provide:

```
MyRouter>show CDP ?
  entry      Information for specific neighbor entry
  interface  CDP interface status and configuration
  neighbors  CDP neighbor entries
  traffic    CDP statistics
  <cr>
```

The most common usage of CDP is to show other devices directly connected to the device requesting the CDP information:

```
vsigate>show cdp neighbors
Capability Codes: R - Router, T - Trans Bridge, B - Source Route
Bridge, S - Switch, H - Host, I - IGMP, r - Repeater
```

```
Device ID              Local Intrfce      Holdtme      Capability
Platform               Port ID
tacacsrouter           Fas 0              168          R
3640                   Fas 0
Switch.gallifrey.loc   Eth 1              129          S
WS-C2960               Fas 0/1
vsitest7               Fas 1              169          R
RSP2                   Fas 6/0
```

To look in greater detail at a specific neighbor, use the **show cdp entry** command:

```
vsigate>show cdp entry vsitest7
-----------------------
Device ID: vsitest7
Entry address(es):
  IP address: 10.1.12.2
Platform: Cisco RSP2,  Capabilities: Router
Interface: Ethernet1,  Port ID (outgoing port): Ethernet6/0
Holdtime : 138 sec

Version :
Cisco IOS Software, 3600 Software (C3640-JK9O3S-M), Version 12.4(3b),
RELEASE SOFTWARE (fc3)
Technical Support: http://www.cisco.com/techsupport
Copyright (c) 1986-2005 by Cisco Systems, Inc.
Compiled Thu 08-Dec-05 22:10 by alnguyen
```

As you can see, CDP is able to gather fairly detailed configuration information on devices remotely. It was designed to be an efficient, low-overhead protocol so as not to gobble precious bandwidth and thereby slow down Cisco's entire product line. Because CDP is proprietary, it is able to gather a lot of information using a tiny amount of overhead. Because of this, other vendors that interoperate with Cisco on a large scale have taken to reading the CDP data. For example, using a vSphere console from VMWare, you can read CDP information about what ports your ESXi hosts are patched into. This could present a security issue for some environments. Other tools exist for discovering "locally connected" devices. The SNMP network management tools are great for centralized management, but gather less-granular configuration information than CDP can on Cisco devices without significant effort (SNMP is covered in Chapter 16).

Changes in IOS from Release 12.4 to Release 15

We introduced IOS Release 15 in Chapter 5. There are many, many commands that are similar between the two versions; for example, all of the general setup and password-recovery commands listed previously within this chapter are transportable from Release 12.4 to 15. This bodes well for folks who have knowledge of IOS 12 (and earlier versions) because this know-how is also transferrable. There are, however, newer features within Release 15 that simply did not exist in 12.4—and with new features come new commands. Although this book is a beginner's guide and we do not want to delve too deeply into details about the complexities of VRFs, MPLS, or IP SLA, some commands you do need to be aware of involve the aforementioned licensing that IOS Release 15 brings to the table. The root of these commands is **show license**:

```
Router#show license ?
```

As with the many varieties of **show** commands, **show license** includes several variables, as detailed in Table 6-6.

We've shared that the **show** command helps us see statistics and how a router is configured. The mirror command to **show license**, of course, is simply **license**. The following are some basic steps to deploying a license file to your router.

You'll first need to obtain your product authorization key (PAK) and pull the unique device identifier (UDI) off your router so you can obtain your license from Cisco's licensing portal at http://www.cisco.com/go/license. The PAK should have been sent to you with your router; if not, contact your reseller.

```
Router#show license udi
Device#   PID              SN            UDI
-----------------------------------------------------------------
*0        CISCO1841        BGH1324P34N   CISCO1841: BGH1324P34N
```

Variable	Description
EULA	Display end user license agreement information
agent	Show license agent information
all	Show license all information
call-home	Show license call-home information
detail	Show license detail information
feature	Show license feature information
file	Show license file information
right-to-use	Show license right-to-use information
statistics	Show license statistics information
status	Show license status information
udi	Show license UDI information
|	Output modifiers

Table 6-6.   License Command Variables

Now that you have your PAK and your UDI, follow the prompts on the website to obtain your license file. The license files may be uploaded using any of the methods listed or managed via the GUI tool Cisco License Manager. CLM is intended to be deployed within larger networks because it's a server-based service. The command is

```
Router#license install ?
```

In this case, the "?" represents a variable. For instance, the command could read like so:

```
Router#license install tftp://license_file_name
```

The variables you can use with the **Router#license install ?** command are listed in Table 6-7.

You may be asked to accept the end user license agreement (EULA). Obviously, you have no choice here if you want to use the product before you. Accept the EULA and issue a **show license** to validate your work.

You may also want to add comments about this license:

```
Router#license comment add IPS "Installed 10.1.2011"
```

Variable	Description
archive	Install from archive: file system
flash	Install from flash: file system
ftp	Install from ftp: file system
http	Install from http: file system
https	Install from https: file system
null	Install from null: file system
nvram	Install from nvram: file system
pram	Install from pram: file system
rcp	Install from rcp: file system
scp	Install from scp: file system
syslog	Install from syslog: file system
system	Install from system: file system
tftp	Install from tftp: file system
tmpsys	Install from tmpsys: file system
xmodem	Install from xmodem: file system
ymodem	Install from ymodem: file system

Table 6-7.   Router#License Install Command Variables

An alternative license installation method is to use Cisco's call-home mechanism. This requires your router to have functioning DNS and HTTPS Internet access. This method is a bit more intrusive (that is, too slow) to utilize in mass deployments because you're required to enter a CCO user ID, password, name, address, ZIP Code, company name, your cousin's girlfriend's bank card PIN number, e-mail address… you get the point.

Using Applications to Help Configure Routers

So far in this chapter, we've dealt with configuring routers by hand. For some time, Cisco has provided a "thick-client" configuration tool with each of its routers. The most current incarnation of this tool is its Cisco Configuration Professional (CCP). It is a workstation-hosted, web-based GUI that helps simplify router configuration and deployment. Flip back to earlier in this chapter for more information on router setup using the basic HTTP Server user interface.

In addition to CCP, Cisco provides Cisco Configuration Assistant, an application that is specific to Cisco Smart Business Communications System (SBCS) devices such as the Unified Communication (UC) 500 series of combo devices (a switch/router/AP), the 500 series of routers and access points, the SPA300/SPA500 IP phones, and the Unified IP phone 6900 and 7900 series. This tool (and the network devices it supports) are meant for small business offices of not more than 100 nodes.

We'll quickly run through configuring a router using the CCP tool. In doing this, we'll cover some router configuration concepts not discussed during the setup procedure.

Both tools use a graphical user interface to assist with the task of getting routers up and running. Neither tool addresses large or complex internetworking problems. A separate suite of products called Cisco Prime is used for enterprise internetwork modeling and management. Configuration Assistant and Configuration Professional are meant for use by small-to-medium internetworks only.

Cisco Configuration Professional

Cisco Configuration Professional (CCP) is the latest device management tool. Access is handled through a Telnet and HTTP connection or an HTTPS and SSH connection for secure communication between the web browser–based user interface and the device being managed. Best of all, it's downloadable for free and works with almost all routers. There is also an embedded web browser–based version (CCP Express) that comes preinstalled on the newest routers, such as the 890 and the 1900, 2900, and 3900 models. CCP Express only allows for a basic list of parameters within the device to be set when compared to CCP.

To make life easier, Cisco Configuration Professional offers what Cisco calls "task-based smart wizards" to help with everything from initial configuration to more complicated WAN/LAN and security configurations. It's a logical step forward in device management for small and medium-sized businesses, and also useful for enterprise branch offices environments, where CiscoWorks LMS or Prime might be the primary configuration management tool and Cisco Configuration Professional is used for troubleshooting or to allow read-only access to the device for local personnel. The download and additional information can be found at www.cisco.com/go/ccp.

CCP also employs SSL and SSH connections to allow administrators to easily configure routers remotely.

When you start CCP Express, you see a screen like the one in Figure 6-6. It gives you a quick snapshot of the status of your router, including the following information:

- Model
- IOS version
- Interface and connection configuration information

Figure 6-6.   The CCP Express home page shows a summary of router information.

To display additional information, click on the About link in the upper-right corner. This displays the CCP Express version. Click on Hardware Details and Software Details for even more information. These are shown in Figures 6-7 and 6-8, respectively.

As stated previously, CCP Express allows for basic interface and router configuration. Now let's take a look at the other, more useful version of the tool: Cisco Configuration Professional. The first thing you're going to see when starting up CCP after installing it to your PC is a "Manage Community" screen. CCP defines groups of routers as a community. This is shown in Figure 6-9.

Clicking on the Router Status button will provide information about memory, versions, and features. The Device Information screen is shown in Figure 6-10.

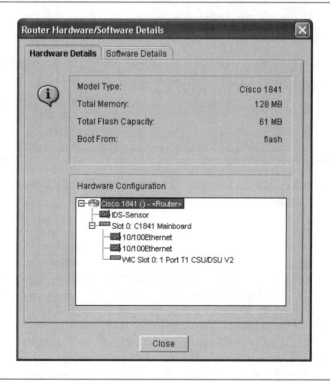

Figure 6-7.   The Hardware Details tab provides model, memory, Flash capacity, and boot details.

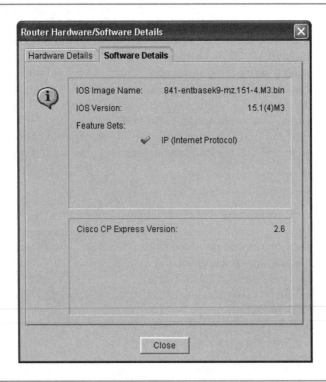

Figure 6-8.   The Software Details tab provides IOS image information, CP Express information, and the features available for your router.

Wizards

Wizards are used in CCP to help configure the various features of your Cisco router. These wizards are helpful, because you can configure the features simply by pointing and clicking, rather than try to figure out the cryptic command line.

Launching one of the wizards is similar to the countless other wizards you've probably used with a Windows system. For example, to configure the serial line, we start the Serial WAN Connection Wizard by selecting Serial from the radial menu and then clicking on Create New Connection. Its starting screen is shown in Figure 6-11.

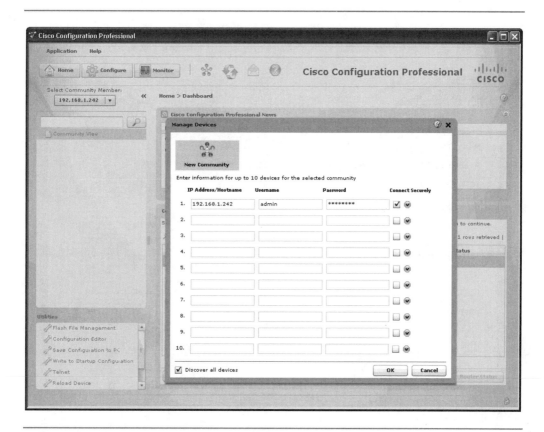

Figure 6-9. This window is used to create a community, add routers and credentials, and allow discovery.

Once we've selected the interface we wish to configure (in this case, we'll use the serial line), we are taken to another page—this one asking what type of encapsulation we want to configure. As Figure 6-12 shows, we're given the option between Frame Relay, Point-to-Point Protocol, and High-Level Data Link Control.

After choosing our encapsulation type, we're taken to another screen, shown in Figure 6-13, that asks us for the connection's IP address and subnet mask.

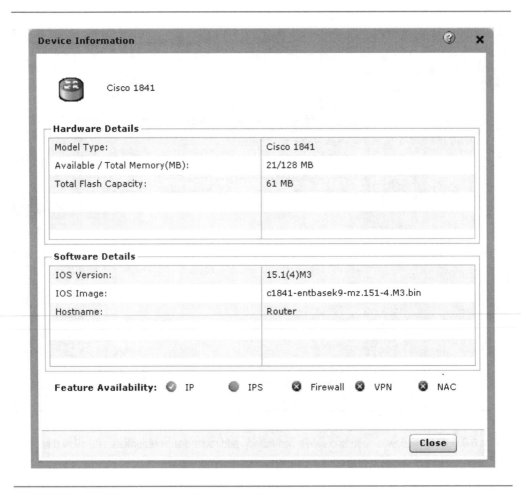

Figure 6-10. Basic router information can be examined.

Once the wizard is done gathering information from you, it turns your choices and instructions into a configuration file for the router.

The command line isn't totally out of the picture. The fact of the matter is that once you configure your router or a feature on the router, CCP takes what you've selected and turns it into IOS code.

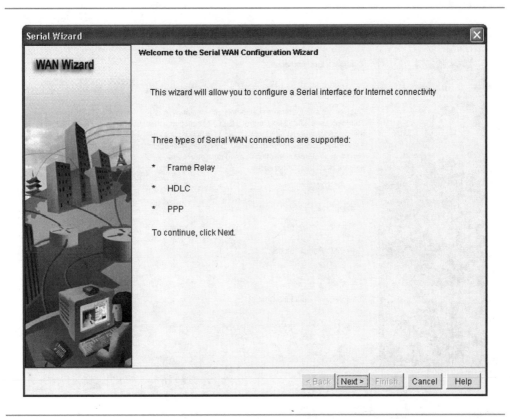

Figure 6-11. Starting the Serial WAN Connection Wizard

Monitoring and Troubleshooting

CCP also lets you monitor your router so that you can observe real-time metrics. For instance, the screen in Figure 6-14 shows a number of useful details. We can examine the CPU usage, total memory used, and flash memory used. Furthermore, we can examine the status of each connection, showing us whether it is up or down and how much bandwidth is being used.

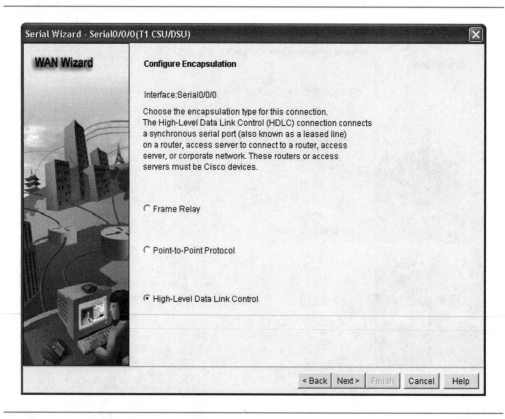

Figure 6-12.   Choose the encapsulation type that best meets your needs.

To get even more in depth, clicking Interface Status in the left column of icons launches a tracking tool that allows you to monitor such details as the following:

- Bytes in and out
- Packets in and out
- Errors
- Bandwidth usage

This tool is shown in Figure 6-15.

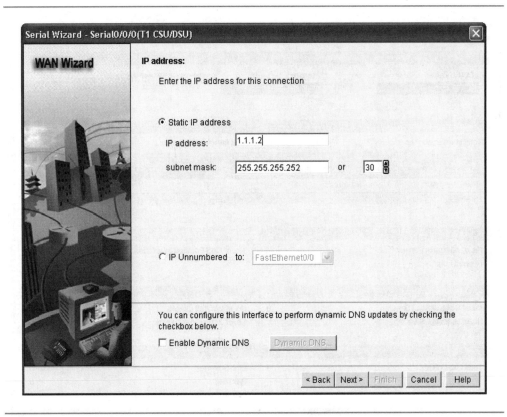

Figure 6-13. Enter the connection's IP address and subnet mask.

Firewall Configuration

CCP also allows you to quickly configure a firewall on your router. The Firewall Wizard can walk you through the steps needed to implement varying levels of security.

Another feature of CCP is the Router Security Audit. When you launch this tool, CCP examines your router's configuration and tells you where security needs to be bolstered. An example is shown in Figure 6-16.

Once this tool has examined your router and identified any weaknesses, you can check individual issues, which can then be automatically corrected by CCP, as shown in Figure 6-17.

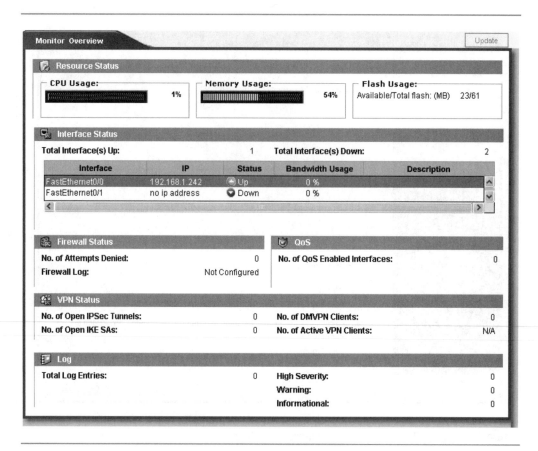

Figure 6-14.   CCP allows monitoring of various router details.

Configuring a New Device

Another useful feature of CCP is the ability to configure either a new router or one that has had its configuration erased. Once you learn all the appropriate commands to enter into a new router in order to set it up in preparation for use with CCP, this bit may be unnecessary. But until that day, this is a handy feature indeed.

First, connect the device using a serial cable (or USB serial) to your PC/laptop. Then select Setup New Device from the application menu. Be patient: CCP needs to poll all our serial ports to find the router. This is shown in Figure 6-18.

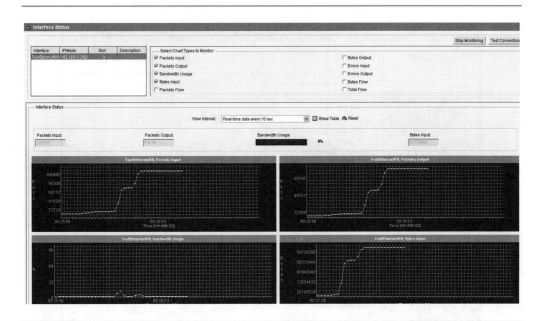

Figure 6-15. The Interface Status tool allows you to track interface statistics.

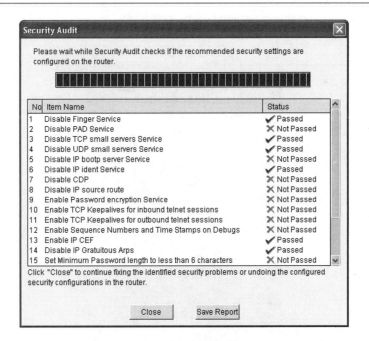

Figure 6-16. The Router Security Audit tool examines the router's security configuration.

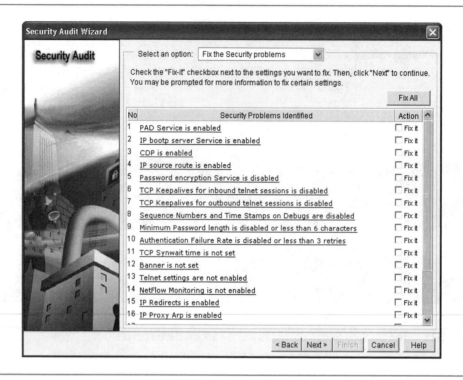

Figure 6-17. CCP features semi-automated security audit fixes.

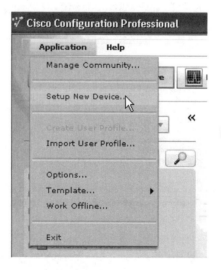

Figure 6-18. CCP will poll all your serial ports to find the router, so this step will take some time.

Next, you'll be asked to configure the device with the IP device's IP address, username, password, and any other items you'd like delivered as part of your initial setup into the text box. This is shown in Figure 6-19.

When setup is complete, you'll see a screen like the one in Figure 6-20.

Now navigate back to the community section. Your device will be part of "New Community." You can remove it from that area and add it to another if you have a preexisting group of devices.

Summary and Review of Cisco Configuration Professional

Cisco Configuration Professional is a step above its predecessor Cisco Router and Security Device Manager (SDM). Although the new tool has similar functionality, it has a cleaner interface and is far more stable. SDM was prone to hang up and lock for no apparent reason. CCP has exhibited none of these symptoms. As we've shown, the serial deployment tool works. The ability to configure enterprise features relatively quickly is a huge boon to the network administrator of a small or medium-sized business. These staffers are under constant pressure to get their tasks done and move on to the next request.

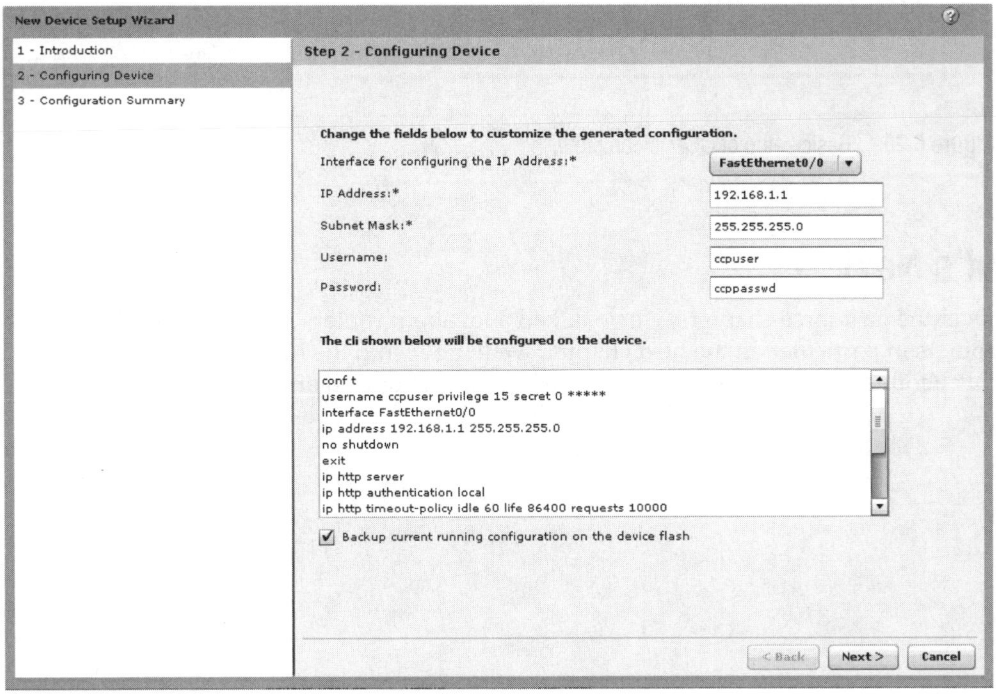

Figure 6-19.   CCP asks you for basic router information.

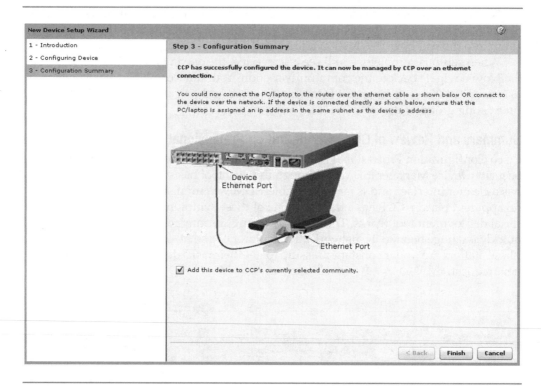

Figure 6-20. Basic setup of CCP is complete.

What's Next

Over the past three chapters, we've talked a lot about routers in general and Cisco routers in particular. In the next chapter, we'll move into the heart of your LAN and talk about switches—the devices that help connect your organization at the local level.

CHAPTER 7 | Switches

The three previous chapters discussed routers, which operate between networks. An internetwork is, by definition, a collection of local area networks connected by routers. In other words, a packet that has to traverse one or more routers has traveled across an internetwork. Eventually, that packet will arrive at the destination network—home of the destination IP address.

But what then? At that juncture, the message has gotten past the last router and must worm its way through the destination network's wiring. In other words, it must drop out of the internetwork cloud and look not for yet another router interface, but for the specific connection port into which the destination host is plugged. Because most PCs and servers do not have network connections directly to a router, there is one last leg of the journey.

So, hosts don't have their own router ports. Well, hosts—PCs and servers, for example—need to hook up to networks somehow. The router is designed to connect networks to other networks, so it is of little use when it comes to physically connecting hosts. That's where switches come in. Switches provide local connectivity to hosts, and are the building blocks with which LANs are pieced together.

The last leg of a message's journey takes place inside a building or within an office campus. Here, the transition must be made from the internetworking cloud's telecom lines, down into the cabling strung through the walls and ceilings of the building, all the way out to a wall plate, and finally to the host device itself. This final stage requires making the transition to the destination host's physical address. This address is called the *media access control address*, or *MAC*. The IP address gets you to the neighborhood, whereas the MAC address gets you to the front door of the house. MAC addresses should always be unique, and they identify the actual NIC (network interface card) connecting the destination device to its LAN. They serve as a kind of serial number for a physical device, so any device on any network in the world can be uniquely identified.

But a one-step shift from a worldwide IP address down to an individual host's MAC address would be too abrupt. There needs to be an intermediary step separating the high-speed router level from slow-speed NICs. Having no buffer zone would, in effect, put side-street traffic onto the interstate highway. Even if NICs and hosts were lightning fast, a middle level would still be necessary just to make things manageable. A switch provides that intermediary step. Figure 7-1 shows where switches fit in.

In this chapter, we delve into that zone sitting between the desktop and the router that links it to the LAN. This is the realm of cables and connectors. We realize eyes tend to glaze over when talk turns to cable plants and patch panels, as if these things are for some reason best left to the building janitor, but the subject of local connectivity is not as mundane as you might think. As high-tech networking equipment inches outward from the backbone toward the desktop, deciding how to connect individual hosts and workgroups has become strategic to the big picture of enterprise internetworking. Technology advances are happening quickly in the field of local connectivity. Thus, it's important that you understand the basics of this subject area, including some specifics on how Cisco switches work.

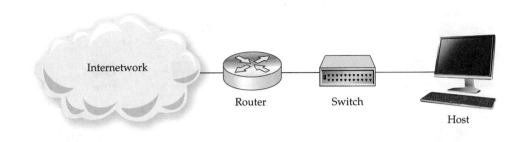

Figure 7-1. Switches mediate between backbones and hosts.

Network Topologies

The physical layout of a network is referred to as its *topology*. Thirty or so years ago, there was little, if any, choice in designing a network's topology.

Although there were (and are) many ways to do it, let's look at a typical "old-school" LAN. To build a LAN, you ran a fat coaxial cable called a *Thicknet* through your building and tapped hosts directly into it. The Thicknet cable was the network backbone. Connecting hosts directly to the network backbone resulted in a so-called bus topology. A *bus* is a cable (or a printed circuit board acting like a cable), and a *bus topology* is where most or all of a network's devices are connected to a single cable—which is like having everybody's driveway empty into one major thoroughfare instead of side streets. Two typical early network topologies are depicted in Figure 7-2.

As network technology developed, topologies evolved a bit with the introduction of terminal servers, which made it possible to indirectly connect dumb terminals to the LAN. This was a good thing, because it gave individual users easy access to more than one minicomputer or mainframe. Another advance was the introduction of a thinner kind of coaxial cable called *Thinnet*, which was cheaper and far easier to work with than Thicknet cabling. But these improvements were only incremental; network layouts were still basically a bus topology.

The trouble with physical bus topologies was that if something failed along the trunk, the whole network went down (or at least a big part of it). Another drawback was that connecting hosts meant crawling into the ceiling plenum, finding the trunk cable, making the tap, dropping a second cable from the tap down to the device, and then testing the connection to see if it worked. Not only were early networks prone to failure and hard to install, but the equipment was also bulky and expensive.

Things have changed a lot since then. Nowadays, most hosts are connected to networks through switches. Switches give network administrators more choices in both the physical and logical layout of networks. They are modular in the sense that devices and hosts can be added without having to change anything on the network backbone. But above all, switches do away with physical bus topologies by allowing the easy installation and management of multiple LANs. Today, network designers use star topologies in place of one overtaxed LAN.

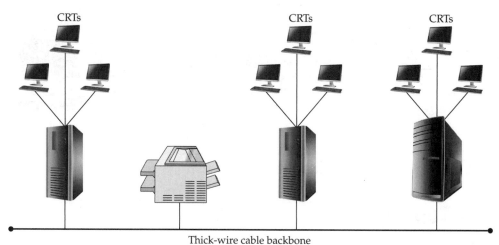

Thick-wire cable backbone

Early LAN Topology

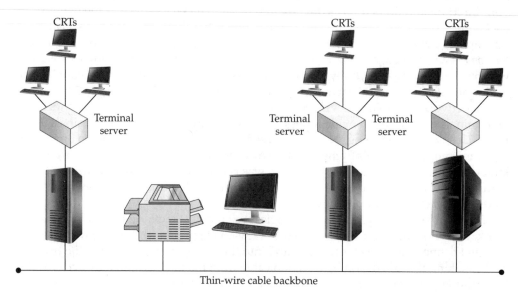

Thin-wire cable backbone

Early LAN with Terminal Servers

Figure 7-2. Early network topologies employed thick- and thin-wire connections.

NOTE   The term "LAN" can be confusing. In the old days, a LAN was a central trunk running through a building with everything on the network connected directly to it. Today, that same building might have dozens of switches serving as host connection points, with the switches, in turn, connected to a backbone. Any shared network medium is a LAN. A switch is a shared medium, and so is the backbone's central trunk cable. Even experts use the term "LAN," or "local area network," to loosely describe a local network composed of multiple LANs. To avoid confusion, in this book, we use the term "LAN segment" to describe a shared network medium, which is the basic building block of network topologies. A LAN segment is defined by a switch or cable. Nowadays, the term "LAN" most often refers to a collection of LAN segments within a building or campus.

Breaking things up into smaller LANs makes it easier to meet current needs and still leave room for future change and growth. Network segmentation improves network performance by isolating traffic. Users within a workgroup or department are most likely to send messages to one another, so putting them on their own LAN segment means others won't get caught in their traffic. Reliability is better, because what happens on one LAN segment doesn't affect the overall network; the fault is isolated within the segment where the trouble started. Network administrators can better identify where the trouble is because of the transition points between LAN segments—an important feature in complicated networks. Also, the modularity of hierarchical networks naturally enhances security and manageability because devices can be grouped in ways that best fit management needs.

NOTE   Logically, each switch port is a LAN segment. LAN segments are the individual parts of a LAN separated by a networking device such as a switch.

For all these reasons, networks today use switches to concentrate multiple hosts into a single network connection point—an approach called the *star configuration*. Star configurations are the building blocks with which hierarchical networks are constructed. Figure 7-3 shows common variations on the basic star topology.

In stark contrast to the bad old days of trunk pulling and cable dropping, connecting a host to a network now is as simple as plugging in a phone-style jack. Each star-topology building block meets certain needs:

- A small business or department might use just one switch to form a LAN—in effect, putting the entire network inside a box—which is called a *single-star topology*. With switches, backbone cabling is no longer necessary to form small networks.

- A *star-hierarchy topology* is used to make more connection ports available within an office. Plugging outlying switches (access switches) into a master switch (Distribution or Core switch) gives more hosts a place to plug in without having to pull additional cable into the area.

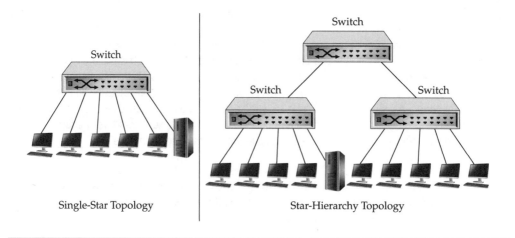

Figure 7-3.   The star topology is the network's basic building block.

NOTE   The terms "backbone" and "central trunk" evoke the image of a single, unbroken span of cable. In reality, most backbones are made up of many cable spans spliced together. At the other extreme, some backbones aren't made up of cable at all, but instead are contained inside a box entirely on circuit boards, which is called a *collapsed backbone.* By definition, though, a backbone is the part of a network that acts as the primary path routing traffic between LAN segments. In general, only switches and routers are connected directly to backbones. In large networks, a backbone usually runs at a higher speed than the LAN segments it connects.

The topology of a network is, of course, most closely tied to the enterprise's geography— who's on what floor, which server sits where, and so on, but other considerations also come into play. Table 7-1 lists network design factors and how they affect decisions about what to do when designing a network.

Network design decisions are most often constrained by the amount of money to be spent and by such logistical issues as how long the enterprise plans to stay in a building. Platforms, on the other hand, are always strategic and are usually a condition that network designers have little or no control over. If the enterprise is heavily invested in Novell NetWare or IBM SNA or Apple, the network equipment must adapt to the hardware and software platforms already installed.

Nowadays, however, no matter what your budget is or which platforms you're using, segmenting networks is not only an option, it's the preferred design approach.

Factor	Network Design Consideration
Preexisting cable plant	To save time and money, network designers frequently try to run networks over wiring already installed in the walls and ceiling spaces of a building. Sometimes, they have no choice, and the type of network devices that can be used is dictated by preexisting cabling.
Performance goals	Projected network traffic loads and end-user "need for speed" can influence the class of network devices and cabling plant used.
Platforms	The installed base of network operating systems and computer platforms frequently dictates network design decisions.
Security	Topology layout is often used as a way to help enforce security.

Table 7-1.   Topology Design Factors (Besides Geography)

The Importance of Network Domains

The *domain* is one of the most fundamental concepts in internetworking. Although the term has many uses, for our purposes, what is important are the two most basic kinds of domains: the collision and the broadcast domain.

LAN segments run over shared media. In physical terms, member hosts in a LAN segment share a switch. To stave off the electronic chaos that would otherwise ensue from sharing a medium and "talking" all at once, some form of control must be enforced over access to it. This is called *media access control* (from whence the MAC address takes its name, as mentioned earlier).

NOTE   For the literal-minded out there who are thinking that the name should be "medium access control" because LANs, by definition, share only a single switched segment, you're right—to a point. Keep in mind, though, that MAC addresses are routinely exchanged between segments. Besides, somehow "medium access control" sounds half-hearted in the world of strict networking rules.

Ethernet Collision Domains

Ethernet uses the CSMA/CD (Carrier Sense Multiple Access/Collision Detection) method. Ethernet lets network hosts randomly contend for bandwidth. A host may send a message at will, but if it collides with a message sent by another host, both must back off and retry after a random wait period. An Ethernet collision domain is any segment or port in which collisions can take place. The more traffic there is on a collision domain, the more likely it is that collisions will occur. Increased collisions, in turn, result in hosts spending more and more time futilely attempting to retransmit.

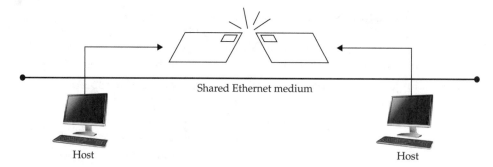

The majority of new LAN installations are Ethernet, so throughout the remainder of this chapter, we'll focus on Ethernet switches.

NOTE There are three kinds of messages in IP-based networks, all ending in "cast": A *unicast* message is a message sent to a single network address, a *multicast* is a single message copied and sent to a specific group of network addresses, and a *broadcast* message is sent to all nodes on a network. IPv6 networks, you might recall, introduce a fourth kind of message, called *anycast*. Anycast messages are transmitted by a host to the closest destination host.

Broadcast Domains

A *broadcast domain* is a set of all stations (network devices and hosts) that will receive any broadcast message originating from any device or host within the set. The key differentiation between broadcast and collision domains is that they are defined by the type of message they encompass. Collision domains encompass messages of any kind, whereas broadcast domains encompass only broadcast messages. As the lower-left part of Figure 7-4 illustrates, for two switches to join in the same broadcast domain, they must somehow be internetworked (routers usually block broadcasts).

The right side of Figure 7-4 shows how broadcast domains can be very different in switched networks. Using switch technology, a broadcast domain can be specifically configured through logical connections instead of physical ones. This is called a *virtual LAN*, or *VLAN* for short. The "virtual" in VLAN means that the LAN's domain is not defined by a physical connection. In fact, VLANs usually aren't even local at all (more on that in the section "VLANs," later in the chapter).

Collisions waste bandwidth because they abort transmissions. In contrast, broadcast messages indeed reach their destinations, but are still wasted bandwidth if the receiving hosts discard them as irrelevant. Obviously, then, broadcasts also play a central role in traffic congestion. Think of broadcast domains as internetworking's version of the ZIP code: the more addresses within a ZIP code, the longer it takes to deliver all the mail. Internetworking is no different. The larger the broadcast domain is, the slower the network tends to be.

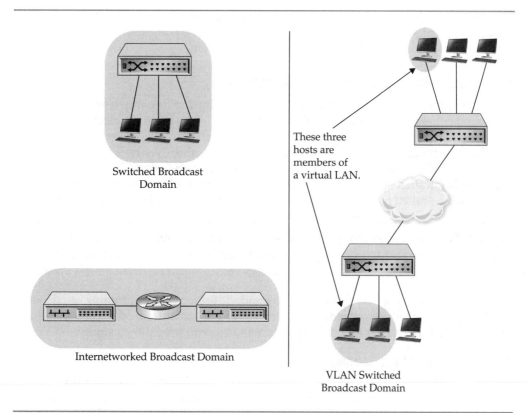

Figure 7-4. Broadcast domains are implemented differently.

The Need to Segment Networks

LAN segments should be kept small in order to help guarantee throughput speed by limiting the frequency of collisions. Small is also good when it comes to network flexibility, security, and maintainability. The trend is to divide networks into more and more LAN segments as network bandwidth comes under increasing strain. More users are becoming members of networks, and, on average, individual users are generating more network traffic. In addition, the mix is changing to more bandwidth-intensive applications, such as graphics, voice, and video. All this has combined to push network managers to deliver more bandwidth by both installing faster networking media and breaking up networks into ever smaller segments.

Network managers are doing both, but demand for bandwidth is outstripping the ability of network manufacturers to create faster technology, so network infrastructures are being reconfigured to incorporate more hierarchy and segmentation. This trend is reinforced as the cost of the hardware needed to segment networks plummets.

The trend's greatest reinforcement is that the tools needed to integrate and manage heavily segmented networks have improved significantly. These tools are so good, in fact, that switches are being used to "microsegment" networks into tiny LAN segments.

Cabling Defines Network Speed and Distance

You can't appreciate traffic management without understanding the basics of road building. So, before we go into how Cisco switches address these problems, it's necessary to learn about the physical media over which networks operate: the cabling.

The most fundamental fact about wired networks is that they run over either two kinds of physical transport media: copper wire or fiber-optic cable. The vast majority of all LANs installed in the world today are on some form of copper wire. Fiber-optic cabling—often called *fiber* or *glass* for short—is mostly used for high-speed backbones.

 NOTE   Though copper and fiber are the most prevalent types of connecting equipment in the datacenter, wireless has become the most common way to connect laptops, tablets, phones, and other user devices to the network. We talk about wireless connectivity and networking in Chapter 11.

The proliferation of network users and bandwidth-hungry applications has driven the industry to introduce a steady stream of newer and faster transport technologies. A review of network cabling and terminology will help you keep things straight.

A Brief History of LAN Cabling

As mentioned, the earliest LANs ran over Thicknet coaxial cables. Thicknet was costly and hard to work with, so in the mid-1980s, Thinnet coaxial cable (also called *Cheapernet)* became more popular. When used to run 10 Mbps Ethernet, Thinnet has a maximum length of 185 meters. Thinnet LANs can be extended beyond that distance using repeaters to link segments. (*Repeaters* are devices placed along a LAN cable to amplify electrical signals and extend maximum operating length. Simple repeaters are rarely used now.) Also, coaxial cable requires that there be a certain minimum amount of spacing between connections, which cramps topology design choices.

Hubs were introduced in the late 1980s. Also called *concentrators*, hubs make hierarchical network topologies possible and simplify the installation and management of a cable plant. Hubs also hastened the introduction of a new type of cabling called *twisted-pair*, which is inexpensive and easy to work with. One of the reasons using twisted-pair became possible is that its relatively short operating limit of 100 meters is extensible using hubs. For example, an office space 300 meters in length could be wired with twisted-pair by placing two hubs into the topology.

LAN Cabling Today

Most larger networks today use a combination of fiber and twisted-pair. Twisted-pair is used to connect hosts to switches, whereas fiber is used for network backbones. Thanks to technological advances, even though twisted-pair uses less copper and shielding than Thinnet coaxial cable, it supports faster data rates. About the same time twisted-pair was taking over desktop connectivity, fiber-optic cabling established itself as the preferred medium for high-speed network backbones. Fiber is used to connect floors or major areas within an office building, and twisted-pair is used to connect LAN segments spanning from the backbone. As Figure 7-5 depicts, switches funnel the LAN segments into the backbone through various star-hierarchy configurations. "Backbone" is a relative term, however. For example, the fiber trunk interconnecting the buildings of a campus LAN is referred to as its *backbone*, whereas the cable connecting the floors of one of the buildings is referred to as a *riser.*

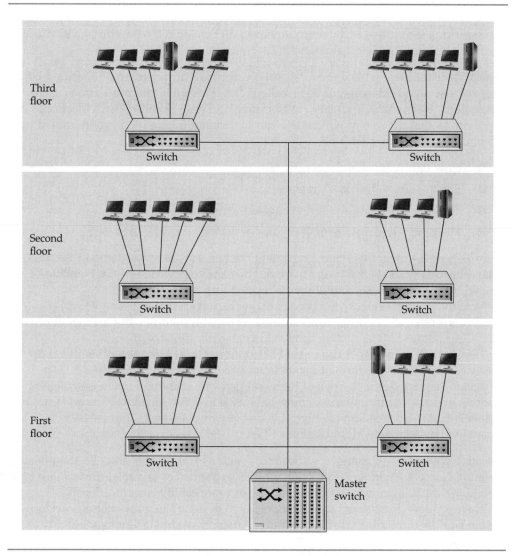

Figure 7-5.   Enterprise networks today combine fiber and twisted-pair cable media.

Twisted-pair cable comes in two basic types:

■ **STP (shielded twisted-pair)** A two-pair cabling medium encased in shielded insulation to limit electromagnetic interference of signals.

■ **UTP (unshielded twisted-pair)** A four-pair cabling medium not encased in shielding. UTP is used in most networks.

Generally, the more tightly twisted the copper wire strands are, the less likely it is there will be interference or signal loss. As its name suggests, STP has shielding to protect content on the wires. UTP, on the other hand, has no shielding. Because UTP is fast, reliable, and inexpensive, it has become the predominant type of cabling used in networking today. Use of the more expensive STP is limited to environments made hostile by high levels of electromagnetic interference.

Cabling Specifications Table 7-2 explains the categories of twisted-pair specified by an international standards organization called TIA/EIA (Telecommunications Industry Association/Electronics Industry Association). These cabling specifications are important in that the rate at which data can be reliably transmitted is determined by a combination of factors, such as:

■ How tightly twisted the copper wire is

■ The quality of the cable's copper

■ The type of insulation used to encase the cable

■ The design and quality of the cable connectors

In Table 7-2, Categories 3 and 5 represent the lion's share of twisted-pair networks today—especially Cat 5. But keep an eye on the relative newcomers, Cat 6 and 7. As bandwidth needs increase, so will their adoption rate.

Note that higher category numbers indicate higher speeds. Most new LAN installations use Cat 6 in order to accommodate Gigabit Ethernet, but many still run on older Cat 3 because it's so widely installed in network infrastructures.

The alternative to copper cabling is fiber-optic cabling. Although it's employed mostly as a backbone medium, it's sometimes used all the way out to the desktop for demanding applications, such as high-end graphics, although lower-cost Gigabit Ethernet over copper is now more commonly used in those scenarios. The advantage of fiber is that it can sustain very high speeds over long distances, but its use is constrained by relatively high costs.

Network Technologies Cabling specifications, such as Cat 6 or 7, describe the physical medium. *Network specifications* describe what is to happen over a medium and are built around the capabilities and limitations of one or more cabling specifications.

There are several Ethernet specifications, each designed to guarantee efficacy on the physical medium over which it operates. Any networking technology's ability to

Category	Cable Description	Cable Application
Cat 1	Traditional telephone cable.	Not usable for networking; no longer installed for telephones.
Cat 2	Four twisted-pairs.	4 Mbps; not recommended for networking.
Cat 3	Four twisted-pairs with three twists per foot, rated up to 16 MHz.	10 Mbps Ethernet and 4 Mbps for Token Ring; also used for new telephone cabling.
Cat 4	Four twisted-pairs, rated up to 20 MHz.	16 Mbps; used for Token Ring.
Cat 5	Four twisted-pairs with eight twists per foot, rated up to 100 MHz.	100 Mbps; used for Fast Ethernet; fast becoming ubiquitous in networked buildings.
Enhanced Cat 5	Four twisted-pairs with eight twists per foot, but made of higher-quality materials and rated up to 200 MHz.	Rated to have up to twice the transmission capability of regular Cat 5.
Cat 6	Four twisted-pairs with eight twists per foot, but made of higher-quality materials. Rated to support Gigabit Ethernet.	Rated to have up to six times the transmission capability of regular Cat 5.
Enhanced Cat 6	Four twisted-pairs, with eight twists per foot. Used for 10GBASE-T Ethernet.	Standard for 100 meter distances.
Class F (Cat 7)	Four twisted-pairs, made of high-quality materials. Rated up to 600 MHz.	Super-fast broadband applications such as Gigabit Ethernet; allows multiple applications operating at different frequencies.
Class F_A (Enhanced Class 7)	Four twisted pairs in braid-screened cable. Rated up to 1,000 MHz.	Superfast applications such as 10 Gigabit Ethernet and broadband video.

Table 7-2.   TIE/EIA Twisted-Pair Specifications

function properly depends on how well matched it is to the physical medium. The faster a network must run—or the greater the distance over which it will operate—the better the underlying cable plant must be.

Network specification names seem mysterious until you've been introduced to the logic behind them. The following illustration breaks down the name of the Ethernet 10BaseT specification.

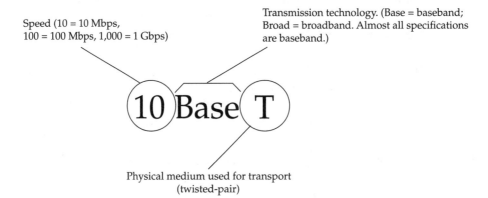

Speed (10 = 10 Mbps, 100 = 100 Mbps, 1,000 = 1 Gbps)

Transmission technology. (Base = baseband; Broad = broadband. Almost all specifications are baseband.)

Physical medium used for transport (twisted-pair)

Sorting out the various network specifications shows that some types of media are used only for certain speeds, some are legacy specs no longer used in new installations, and others are specs that never quite caught on. Table 7-3 lists network specifications (mostly Ethernet) in their approximate order of importance, based on:

- Percentage of new LANs being installed
- Percentage of all installations
- Probable future importance as a technology

The specifications reflect the worldwide trend toward Ethernet technologies.

Table 7-3 shows that many network specifications are either old or are contending standards that meet with limited market acceptance. The trend in networking technology is, of course, toward ever faster speeds running over cheaper cabling plant. Not including high-speed backbones, most new LANs today use 1000BaseX Fast Ethernet running over Cat 6 or 7 cabling.

Gigabit Ethernet won the backbone war with ATM and FDDI. ATM initially supplanted FDDI, probably due in part to the recent sharp increase in the demand for multimedia applications, but 1000BaseX—commonly known as Gigabit Ethernet—is the current popular medium. Planners not only like Gigabit Ethernet's rated speed of 1,000 Mbps, but they also like its compatibility with most installed Ethernet networks. Chapter 2 discusses competing network technologies in detail.

LAN Spec	Description
10BaseT	10 Mbps Ethernet using UTP Cat 3, 4, or 5 cabling; used for most new installations during the 1990s; in the process of being eclipsed by 100BaseT; 100-meter limit.
100BaseTX	100 Mbps Fast Ethernet using UTP Cat 5 cabling; most new installations going in now are 100BaseT; 100-meter limit.
100BaseFX	100 Mbps Fast Ethernet using two strands of multimode fiber-optic cable per link; most new high-speed backbones are 100BaseFX; 400-meter limit.
FDDI	100 Mbps Fiber Distributed Data Interface token-passing LAN using either single-mode or multimode fiber-optic cabling (or sometimes either STP or UTP copper, called CDDI, for Copper Distributed Data Interface); 100-kilometer limit over fiber, 100-meter limit over copper.
ATM	622 Mbps Asynchronous Transfer Mode over fiber-optic cabling; popular as a backbone for its sustained throughput and its proven ability to move multimedia applications at speed.
1000BaseFX	1 Gbps Gigabit Ethernet over fiber-optic cabling; however, 1000BaseX is now being reengineered to run over Cat 5 copper (to be called 1000BaseTX).
10GBASE-SR	Designed to support short distances for multimode fiber with a range of 26, 300, or 400 meters, depending on which type of fiber is used.
10GBASE-LRM	Designed to support distances up to 220 meters on multimode cable.
10GBASE-LR	Designed to support single-mode fiber for distances up to 10 kilometers.
10GBASE-ER	Designed to support single-mode fiber with distances of up to 40 kilometers.
10GBASE-LX4	Designed to support multimode fiber of up to 300 meters or 10 kilometers on single-mode fiber.
10GBASE-CX4	Uses four-lane InfiniBand connectors for distances of up to 15 meters.

Table 7-3.   LAN Specifications with Cable Types and Distance Limits *(continued)*

LAN Spec	Description
10GBASE-T	Provides 10 Gigabit connections spanning 55 meters (Cat 5e or 6) or 100 meters (Cat 6a or 7).
100VG-AnyLAN	100 Mbps Fast Ethernet and Token Ring using UTP Cat 3, 4, or 5 cabling; developed by Hewlett-Packard; can be run over any existing 10BaseT networks.
10Base2	10 Mbps Ethernet using Thinnet coaxial cabling; widely installed in the 1980s; eclipsed by 10BaseT; 185-meter limit.
10Base5	10 Mbps Ethernet using Thicknet coaxial cabling; widely installed in 1970s and 1980s; 500-meter limit.
100BaseT4	100 Mbps Fast Ethernet using four pairs of UTP Cat 3, 4, or 5 cabling; 100-meter limit.
10BaseFB	10 Mbps Ethernet using fiber-optic cabling; used as a LAN backbone (not to connect hosts directly); two-kilometer limit.
10BaseFL	10 Mbps Ethernet using fiber-optic cabling; two-kilometer limit, one-kilometer with FOIRL (Fiber-Optic Inter-Repeater Link, a precursor signaling methodology that FL replaces).
10BaseFP	10 Mbps Ethernet using fiber-optic cabling; used to link computers into a star topology without using repeaters; 500-meter limit.
10Broad36	10 Mbps Ethernet using broadband coaxial cable cabling; 3.6-kilometer limit.
40GBASE-KR4	40 Gbps Ethernet; one-meter limit.
40GBASE-CR4	40 Gbps Ethernet over copper; 10-meter limit.
40GBASE-SR4	40 Gbps Ethernet over multimode fiber optical cabling; 150-meter maximum.
40GBASE-LR4	40 Gbps Ethernet over single-mode fiber; 10-kilometer limit.
40GBASE-FR	40 Gbps over pair of single-mode fiber; two-kilometer limit.
100BASE-CR10	100 Gbps using twin-ax copper cabling; seven-meter limit.
100GBASE-SR10	100 Gbps using laser-optimized multimode filer (LOMF) at 850nm; 125-meter limit.
100GBASE-LR4	100 Gbps using single-mode optical fiber at 1,310nm; 10-kilometer limit.
100GBASE-ER4	100 Gbps using single-mode optical fiber at 1,550nm; 40-kilometer limit.

Table 7-3. LAN Specifications with Cable Types and Distance Limits

NOTE Ever wonder how data travels over a cable? In simple terms, electrical pulses going over a wire are measured for plus or minus voltages to track signals. Special encoding schemes—for example, the Institute of Electrical and Electronics Engineers (IEEE) schemes for Fast Ethernet and Gigabit Ethernet— are used to translate data from identifiable bit patterns represented by the voltage fluctuations. Fast Ethernet uses a three-level encoding scheme to track data; Gigabit Ethernet uses a five-level encoding scheme. The two major problems facing network communications are return-loss and near/far-end crosstalk. Without getting bogged down in engineering details, *return-loss* is when a signal echoes back to the transmitter, confusing it. *Crosstalk*, on the other hand, is when signals leak between wire pairs, creating electrical noise. Network engineers are always looking for improved encoding schemes to squeeze more bandwidth into smaller wires.

Straight-Through vs. Crossover Cables and Devices

Network hardware documentation frequently refers to *straight-through* cables and *crossover* cables. Network devices have transmitter (TX) pins and receiver (RX) pins. In a straight-through cable, the wire pair does not cross from TX to RX between interfaces. In a crossover cable, however, wire pairs are crossed over from TX to RX between connections. You must use crossover cables to connect similar hosts with identical interfaces. If a straight-through cable is used, one of the two devices must perform the crossover function. If neither device has a crossover connector, then a crossover cable must be used. In other words, signals must be crossed over either in one of the devices or in the cable. Figure 7-6 illustrates the two ways.

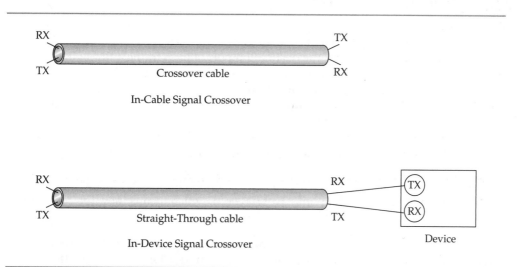

Figure 7-6. Signals can be crossed over either in the cable or in the device.

Think of a signal traveling RX-to-RX or TX-to-TX as being like a conversation in which two persons mouth words, but no sound reaches their ears. Crossing over signals between devices makes networking possible by moving the signal from "mouth (TX) to ear (RX)."

Cisco Switches

It's no exaggeration to say that switched network technology is revolutionizing how internetworks are designed and what they can do for users. Over the past decade, switches have begun pushing internetworks to size scales and service levels many considered infeasible not long ago.

But what exactly are switched networks? How do they work? As Cisco likes to put it, "Switches deliver shared bandwidth." How can the switches do this? The answer is in the electronics:

- They run at very high speeds because they operate at the data-link layer (layer 2) instead of at the network layer (layer 3), where routers operate. This enables switches to process traffic without creating bottlenecks.

- They have many of the capabilities of a router, but sit between the host and the backbone, instead of between backbones as routers do. Switches can take control of traffic at or near its source, whereas the router usually doesn't take over until the message is ready to begin its trek to a remote LAN. Taking control at the source takes much of the randomness out of network operations.

How an Individual Switch Works

Almost all computer advances in one way or another come down to miniaturization and speed, and the network switch is no different. Switches are smart and fast enough to read both the source port and the destination port of each frame and "switch" messages between the two (thus the name). This is shown in Figure 7-7.

Much like routers, switches examine destination and source addresses as messages pass through. Switches differ from routers in that they're looking at layer-2 MAC addresses instead of layer-3 IP addresses.

The switch provides a shared media LAN into which hosts can connect. But the switch is at the same time able to assume packet-sorting duties, for two reasons:

- Switches have more powerful electronics than their predecessors, the hubs.

- They operate at the data-link layer (layer 2), which means they don't have to dig as deep into messages as layer-3 routers.

Beefed-up electronics give the switch the ability of a speed reader, but although switches are smart, they're not nearly as smart as routers. The switch is, in effect, given a lighter reading assignment than routers because it handles traffic at layer 2.

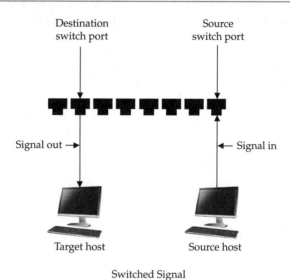

Figure 7-7.   Switches deliver signals to a specific port.

To illustrate this, Figure 7-8 traces a message through a hypothetical switched network. The first step takes place between the host sending the message and its switch port. To do this, the switch reads the incoming message's destination MAC address and instantly moves it to the outbound port it associates with that destination MAC.

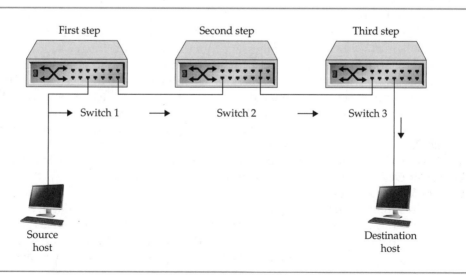

Figure 7-8.   How a message moves through a switched network.

Because the message is switched to a targeted outbound port instead of being replicated to all ports, it encounters no collisions. This makes more bandwidth available and moves messages at faster throughput speeds.

The same process holds for the message's second step. As the message pours out of the outbound port on Switch 1, it has dedicated bandwidth (no collisions) over the cable connecting it to the port in Switch 2. The switching process again repeats itself through the third step, all the way out to the destination host.

When a switch receives a message seeking an address it doesn't know, instead of dropping the message, the switch transmits the message to all its ports. This process is called *flooding*, which is necessary for discovery-type messages. For example, Dynamic Host Configuration Protocol (DHCP) is used by a host when it boots up to locate nearby services, such as network printers. Without flooding, switches could not support broadcast messages sent by DHCP and other utilities.

Switched Networking Basics

How is it possible to have dedicated bandwidth all the way through a multiple-device network connecting hundreds of hosts? The answer is that switched networks balance intelligence with raw power.

In simplified terms, routers move messages through an internetwork to their destinations by working from left to right across the destination's IP address, as depicted in the following illustration.

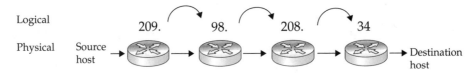

In a general sense, as the message hops between routers, it checks the routing table maintained in each new router, trying to match the next part of the destination IP address. When it finds a match, the message moves through the internetwork to the router whose location is represented by that matched IP address information. Sooner or later, the message arrives at the router serving as the gateway to the destination host.

In sharp contrast, a message must find its way through a switched network without the luxury of hierarchical IP addresses. Switched networks operate using MAC addresses, which are considered to be flat in topology. A MAC address—also called a *physical address*—is a sort of network serial number assigned to a host's NIC. The first half of every MAC address is a vendor code (also known as an *organizationally unique identifier, or OUI)* signifying the manufacturer of the NIC; the second half is the serial number of the actual device. If you move a device to the other side of the world, its MAC address remains unchanged. Switched networks are completely flat in that, because they rely solely on MAC addresses, they essentially think all devices and hosts are attached to the same cable. Beyond the friendly confines of the home LAN, a MAC address is a small clue. How, then, do switched networks manage to deliver messages?

MAC address column   Switch ports associated with MAC addresses

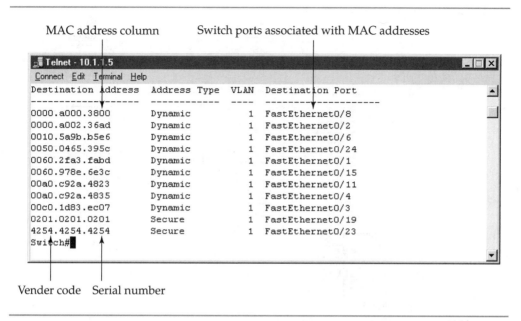

Vender code   Serial number

Figure 7-9.   The content of a switch's dynamic address table is topologically flat.

When a switch is turned on, it begins building a dynamic address table. It does so by examining the source MAC address of each incoming frame and associating it with the port through which it came. In this way, the switch figures out what hosts are attached to each of its ports. Figure 7-9 shows a dynamic address table.

The switch also discovers and maps the surrounding neighborhood using Cisco Discovery Protocol (CDP), which was covered in Chapter 6. The switch uses CDP to discover nearby switches. CDP only talks to those switches it is directly connected with. However, as Figure 7-10 shows, that doesn't matter. MAC addresses are passed back through a chain of cooperating switches until they reach the switch building its dynamic address table.

Switches drop unused MACs after a default period of five minutes. The dynamic address table isn't as smart as routing tables, which use all types of costing algorithms to choose optimal paths. A switch simply places the most frequently used MACs toward the top of its dynamic address table. Together, these two procedures guarantee that the switch's network path-finding intelligence is at least fresh, and more likely to be reliable.

Designing Switched Internetworks

Even if a switch's dynamic address table could identify a path through a large switched internetwork, if that path required hundreds or even just dozens of hops, it would be too slow. Two technologies have been developed to solve this problem: switched backbones and multilayer switching.

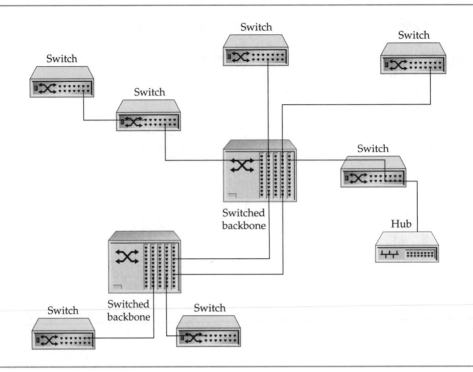

Figure 7-10. The switches share physical address information to determine paths through networks.

Switched Backbones

Switched backbones are high-end switches used to aggregate bandwidth from other switches. The idea of a switched backbone is for it to have the biggest dynamic address table of all. Switched backbones are frequently configured with multiple high-end switches, both for purposes of redundancy and in order to attain blazingly fast throughput rates. The point here is to illustrate how the backbones can be enhanced.

It'd be neat to tell you that switched backbones are fat, high-tech cables strung atop towering pylons in electrical utility power grids, or that they're meshed networks of very fast and expensive T3 high-speed data circuits. But they're not. Even the biggest of the big switched backbones is an unglamorous collection of refrigerator-like boxes cabled together, quietly humming away in a computer room somewhere.

A switched backbone's job is to concentrate what would otherwise be many hops into a single hop through a single backbone LAN. Switched backbones pack large amounts of memory and throughput into a single configuration. Not all switched backbones are behemoths. A switched backbone might be a device about the size of a pizza box sitting in a rack in a data closet. Remember, a backbone by definition is a relatively fast LAN interconnecting other LANs.

Although switched backbones aren't absolutely necessary in smaller networks, they probably are in very large ones. You might remember when AOL's network collapsed. After the headlines faded, gurus lambasted AOL for having stuck with its mostly router-based topology for too long.

Switched backbones are implemented using any of three technologies:

- ATM (Asynchronous Transfer Mode)
- Fast Ethernet or Gigabit Ethernet
- 10 and 40 Gigabit Ethernet

These days, the new data center configurations use 10 Gigabit Ethernet (individually or bonded) between the backbone switches. However, it won't be long before 40 Gigabit Ethernet surpasses 10 Gigabit Ethernet in new data center implementations.

Many large internetworks inevitably have subnets implementing a variety of technologies. For this reason many switches, such as Cisco's Catalyst 6500 family of switches, feature any-to-any switching between Gigabit, Fast Ethernet, and 10 Gigabit Ethernet.

Aggregating bandwidth, of course, means rolling up traffic from a number of access switches into another larger and faster switch (or group of switches). Because switched networks deal only in MAC addresses, this cannot be done by hierarchical routing. The workaround is to create levels of switches through uplink ports. Figure 7-11 depicts how this configuration funnels the traffic from many hosts through the host switch out to the backbone switch.

This configuration technique enables designers to create a power hierarchy in lieu of a logical hierarchy. Switched networks aggregate traffic into the bandwidth of a single switch to help keep traffic flowing. Described in basic terms, this is accomplished by a switched backbone machine having more switches connected directly to it and thus building a much larger dynamic address table.

The ability of each of Cisco switches to aggregate bandwidth into a high-speed intelligent backbone relies on most or all of the advanced switching technologies introduced in Table 7-4.

The technology central to Cisco's switched backbone strategy is something called EtherChannel, which is a bus technology. Strictly speaking, a bus is a cable (or a printed circuit board functioning like a cable). What makes EtherChannel a full-blown technology is that it's an integrated package of high-speed cabling, connectors, controllers, software, and management tools designed to sustain high switching throughput rates. EtherChannel provides bandwidth scalability in increments from 200 Mbps to 160 Gbps.

EtherChannel works by allowing logical groups of ports to serve as high-speed connections between switches sitting in the same location. An EtherChannel group can have up to 16 member ports, depending on the chassis model. Ports are usually grouped to service a specific VLAN, which is why EtherChannel is central to Cisco's switched network strategy: Aggregating bandwidth means interconnecting switches to switch servers that hold ever-larger dynamic MAC address tables. Large-volume streams of switched messages flow within VLANs. EtherChannel is where the logical

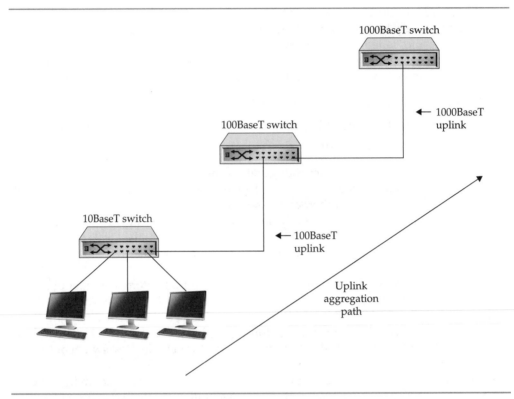

Figure 7-11. Uplink ports aggregate traffic into the switched backbone.

meets the physical. It funnels a VLAN's traffic through a dedicated high-speed bus into a collapsed switched backbone running at about the same speed. Balanced bus-to-switch throughput speed is increasingly referred to as a *switch fabric*, in which ports, and even stack units, share a common dynamic address table. For example, EtherChannel combines the bandwidth of separate ports into a single port. That is, a 600 Mbps EtherChannel is really six 100 Mbps interfaces.

An added benefit is that EtherChannel groups provide load balancing and redundancy. If one port is overloaded or fails, traffic loads are transparently shifted to other ports in the group. EtherChannel is a design architecture Cisco is now using to deliver multigigabit capacity. The technology implements IEEE 802.3 standards as Fast EtherChannel, Gigabit EtherChannel, and 10 Gigabit EtherChannel products, respectively.

Multilayer Switching

Multilayer switching is a hybrid of routing and switching technologies. Even the best-designed switched networks must still use routers at some level. The hierarchical

Technology	Description
Address cache	Also called MAC cache—the maximum number of MAC addresses a switch can maintain in its dynamic address table, which is a function of a combination of factors, including DRAM and CPU capacity.
Wirespeed	Also called *forwarding rate*—the rate at which a switch can pick up a stream of packets from an incoming cable, usually expressed in packets per second (pps).
Backplane (switch fabric)	The data rate of the switch's bus, which services CPU, memory, and I/O controllers, expressed in megabits per second (Mbps) or gigabits per second (Gbps).
IP Multicast	Certain message types tend to be multicast, where, for example, one copy of a message is sent to 1,000 hosts instead of 1,000 copies being sent. Doing this through a switched network requires a switch with sufficient processing power, memory capacity, bus speed, and software to handle such large MAC addressing transactions. IP Multicast is becoming an important switch technology as the world moves to the type of traffic that lends itself to multicast messaging, such as video on demand.

Table 7-4.   Key Switching Technologies

topology of layer-3 IP addressing has a much better "aim" than switched network schemes, given that routers use hierarchical addresses instead of flat MAC addresses. This is why network designers are using multilayer switches to augment switched networks with the capabilities of a router to identify and utilize optimal paths to destinations. To top it off, it makes sense to integrate the functions into a single hardware platform wherever possible. Fewer hops and "moving parts" help keep things speedy and available. Depending on the manufacturer, multilayer switching is also called *IP switching, layer-3 switching, shortcut routing,* or *high-speed routing.*

Operators of very large internetworks—mainly corporations running big intranets—are offering services in which users can click a hyperlink in one place and suddenly create a message demanding information or services from a faraway server. As users increasingly move about an internetwork to use its remote services, strain is put on the capacity of its routers. Properly implemented, multilayer switching can deliver tenfold throughput improvements at heavily traveled connection points. This is because most switches can make a routing decision and transmit the data much faster than a router.

Multilayer switching works by first determining the best route or routes through an internetwork using layer-3 protocols and then storing what it finds for later reference. Users who come along later wanting to travel that route do so through switches, bypassing the router (and the bottleneck it would cause).

Even if multilayer switching technology is not integrated into a switched network, some routing should still be used to provide some form of hierarchical topology to the network. This is necessary, not only to maintain network-wide performance, but also to enhance security. Switches will not displace routers from internetworks in the foreseeable future.

VLANs

In a switched network, a host can participate in a VLAN (virtual local area network). Much as a group of hosts becomes a member of a physical LAN by plugging into a shared switch, it becomes part of a virtual LAN by being configured into it using switched network management software. In switched networks built using Cisco equipment, VLANs are created and maintained using the embedded configuration software or IOS.

NOTE Another way to think about a VLAN is to think of it as an IP subnet. The two are synonymous.

Within a VLAN, member hosts can communicate as if they were attached to the same wire, when, in fact, they can be located on any number of physical LANs. Because VLANs form broadcast domains, members enjoy the connectivity, shared services, and security associated with physical LANs.

Basing LANs on logical parameters instead of on physical topology gives network administrators the option to align domains to parallel, geographically dispersed workgroups. Even temporary exigencies can be accommodated using VLANs. For example, if two computer programmers needed to run a week's worth of tests involving heavy upload and download activity, they could be temporarily configured into a VLAN so as not to drag down the network's performance for other members of the normal VLAN.

Domains are usually arranged by department or workgroup. However, the trend toward dynamic organizational structures in the business world has made planning and maintaining modern networks somewhat tougher than it would otherwise be. Contemporary business phenomena, such as virtual offices, distributed teams, reorganizations, mergers, acquisitions, and downsizing, cause near-constant migration of personnel and services within networks. Figure 7-12 outlines what a VLAN topology might look like.

But VLANs are more than just an organizational convenience. They are a necessity in switched networks in order to logically extend broadcast domains beyond the physical topology. Don't forget that using only MAC addresses causes a flat network topology. VLANs ameliorate most flat topology problems by creating virtual hierarchies.

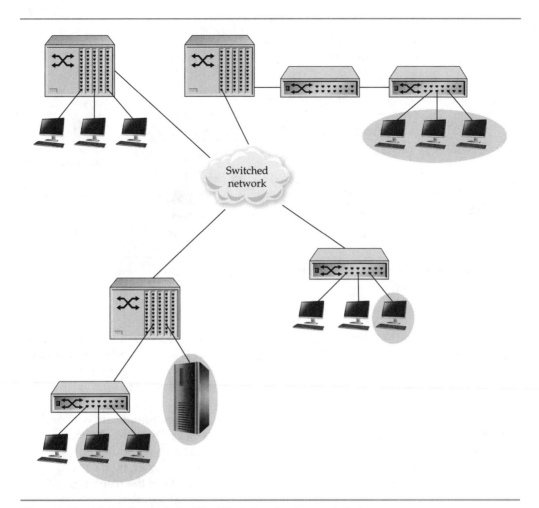

Figure 7-12.   VLAN offers unlimited flexibility in functional network design.

Largely, VLANs are created using Cisco switches. However, if a device on one VLAN needs to communicate with a device on a second VLAN, it is necessary to get a router (or layer-3 switch) involved. This is because two or more VLANs can't communicate with each other (that sort of defeats the purpose of the VLAN) without a little help from a layer-3 device.

Consider the network shown in Figure 7-13. In this example, there are two switches connecting four VLANs. Switch 1 has been configured with VLAN A and VLAN B. Switch 2 has been configured with VLAN C and VLAN D.

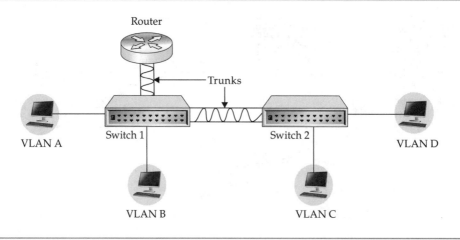

Figure 7-13. Routers are used to allow VLANs to communicate.

VLANs A and B are sent through a single port (this is called *VLAN trunking)* to the router and through another port to Switch 2. VLANs C and D are trunked from Switch 2 to Switch 1, then through Switch 1 to the router. This trunk is able to carry the traffic from all four VLANs. That single connection to the router allows it to appear on all four VLANs.

Because the VLANs are connected to the router, they can communicate with each other through the trunking connection between the two switches, using the router. For instance, if a file is located on a computer on VLAN D and a computer on VLAN A needs access to it, the data must travel from Switch 1 to the router, then back to the Switch 1, and then on to Switch 2. In simple terms, because of the trunking, both computers and the router think they are on the same physical segment.

SmartOperations

In 2012, Cisco introduced a new set of features for Catalyst switches called Cisco Catalyst SmartOperations. It is a set of technologies and features used to simplify network planning, deployment, monitoring, and troubleshooting.

SmartOperations combines Catalyst features and IOS to help get switches up and running faster and more efficiently than before. The SmartOperations toolkit includes the following:

■ Smart Install is a transparent technology to configure the IOS Software image and switch configuration without user interaction. It uses dynamic IP address allocation and the assistance of other switches to install the switch.

- Auto Smartports automatically configures devices connected to the switch port, allowing autodetection and activation of the device onto the network as soon as it is plugged in.

- Smart Configuration provides management for a group of switches from a single interface. It adds the ability to archive and back up configuration files to a file server or switch.

- USB file storage and console used for file backup and distribution.

- Smart Troubleshooting is a host of debugging diagnostic commands and system health checks within the switch.

SmartOperations deployment tools include the following:

- Automatic QoS (AutoQoS), which simplifies QoS configuration in Voice over IP (VoIP) networks. It issues commands to detect Cisco IP phones, classify traffic, and enable queue configuration.

- Dynamic Host Configuration Protocol (DHCP) autoconfiguration of multiple switches through a boot server simplifies switch deployment.

- Port autonegotiation automatically selects half- or full-duplex transmission mode.

- Dynamic Trunking Protocol (DTP) enables dynamic trunk configuration across all switch ports.

- Automatic Media-Dependent Interface Crossover (MDIX) automatically adjusts data transmission if an incorrect cable type (crossover or straight through) is installed.

- Unidirectional Link Detection Protocol (UDLD) and Aggressive UDLD allow unidirectional links to be disabled when incorrect fiber cabling is attached.

- Voice VLAN keeps voice traffic on a separate VLAN for easier administration and troubleshooting.

Cisco's Switched Network Products

Cisco's main line of switched network solutions is its Catalyst Switches, delivered in over a dozen different series of products. With the vast options available, you can "have it your way," at least when it comes to high-performance switching. The Catalyst line is similar to Cisco routers in that it includes fixed-configuration desktop models and configurable Plug-and-Play modular chassis models. The switch line goes all the way up to the ASR and CSR "dormitory refrigerator" packages with high-speed buses into which many cards can be inserted—each card packing as much as other fully configured Catalyst models.

In keeping with well-established trends in the networking marketplace, most Cisco LAN switches are Ethernet products. The lineup of Catalyst-switched backbone products incorporates the diversity of technologies competing at that level, with support for Fast Ethernet, Gigabit Ethernet, and ATM.

Most Cisco switches run a full-blown image of the IOS software, different only in that it's tuned for switching rather than routing. Most Catalyst switches offer the regular command-line interface, but some have a menu-driven interface.

Cisco switched network products are packaged to do the following:

- Deliver seamless migration from legacy technologies, with tools such as 10/100/1000 autosensing and high-speed uplink ports
- Enable interoperation between diverse technologies, such as ATM and Ethernet
- Facilitate bandwidth aggregation through scalable configurations and powerful switch fabric technologies
- Be manageable using remote monitoring, configuration, and security tools

The following sections describe the line of Cisco switches, which were current as of the time this was written. Refer to www.cisco.com for current catalogs of information on Cisco switches and other products.

Modular Switches

Cisco's line of modular switches are designed for campus and data center environments and can be modified through a number of supervisors, line cards, service modules, fabric modules, and power supplies. These switches are very customizable, which makes them ideal for environments with very specific needs—or those environments with changing needs.

Switches can also be tweaked to scale from 10 to 40 to 100 Gigabit speeds. These switches also support such features as the Cisco Virtual Switching System to ease switch management.

This type of switch is also beneficial from an investment standpoint: It allows for incremental upgrades, rather than having to buy brand-new equipment when the organization's needs change. Table 7-5 lists Cisco's current line of modular switches.

Fixed Configuration Switches

Fixed configuration switches differ from modular switches in that they have already been configured with all the core hardware they need and are ready to be deployed to the environment where they are best suited. These switches are less expensive options and can be easily installed.

NOTE Additional equipment can be added to these switches, including power supplies, fans, and expansion modules, but the switches are ready to use right out of the box.

Table 7-6 lists Cisco's line of fixed configuration switches.

Compact Switches

Cisco's compact switches are small switches designed for use outside the wiring closet and not part of huge infrastructure installations. These switches are targeted at retail,

Product	Description
Nexus 7000	Cisco's top-end data-center-class product line. Designed for highly scalable 1, 10, 40, and 100 Gigabit Ethernet networks. Over 17 Terabits per second (Tbps) capacity and 550 Gbps per slot. Three switches in this line offering 4, 9, 10, or 18 slots. Utilizes NX-OS.
Catalyst 6500	Cisco's most robust Catalyst switch. This series offers integrated service modules that provide high-speed services including integrated wireless, firewalling, intrusion detection, application control, SSL termination, and network analysis services. Six models offer chassis with 3, 4, 6, 9, or 13 slots. Offers Power over Ethernet (PoE), PoE Plus, 10/100 Fast Ethernet, and 10/40 Gigabit Ethernet as well as 10GBASE-T and DS0 to OC-192 WAN interfaces.
Catalyst 4500	Its scalability and customization allows backward and forward compatibility, thus maximizing return on investment. Offers sophisticated Quality of Service (QoS), PoE, and PoE Plus. There are four modular models in this series, offering 3-, 6-, 7-, and 10-slot chassis.

Table 7-5.   Cisco's Line of Modular Switches

hospitality, education, and enterprise customers. Compact switches are Gigabit and Fast Ethernet switches that are designed for unified communications, wireless, and IP video. Table 7-7 describes Cisco's current line of compact switches.

Fabric Extender Technology

Fabric Extenders serve as remote line cards for a parent Cisco Nexus switch (Nexus 5000 or 7000 series switches). These devices behave as extensions of the parent switch. These switches offer the following benefits:

- Architecture flexibility
- Scalable server access
- Simplified operations

Table 7-8 describes Cisco's current line of fabric extender technology.

Product	Description
Nexus 5000 Series	Consolidates separate LAN, SAN, and server cluster networks into a single Ethernet fabric called Unified Ports. 10 Gigabit Ethernet, Fibre Channel, Fibre Channel over Ethernet (FCoE). There are three models in the series, offering 32, 48, or 96 ports and one or three expansion slots.
Catalyst 4500-X Series	Wire-speed performance of up to 800 Gbps. Three models offering 16 to 40 10 Gigabit Ethernet ports. Ports scalable from 1 to 10 Gigabit Ethernet Mode. Hot swappable AC or DC power supplies.
Nexus 3000	Three models offering 16, 48, or 64 ports. Ultra-low latency. Same switch architecture for 1/10/40 Gigabit Ethernet is ideal for large-scale configurations that require consistency. Features include virtual port channel, Precision Time Control Boundary Clock, and Configurable Control Plane Policing.
Catalyst 4900 Series	Compact form-factor (one to two rack units). Four models with 40 or 48 10/100/100 Base-T ports. One model with 28 Gigabit Ethernet (fiber) ports. Hot-swappable AC or DC power supplies
Catalyst 3850 Series	Five models offering 24 or 48 10/100/1000 Gigabit Ethernet ports. 480 Gigabit Ethernet backplane. Stackable. AdvancedPoE.
Catalyst 3750-X Series	Five models offering 24 or 48 ports. Stackable for ease of scalability. IPv4, IPv6, and multicast routing. Advanced PoE.
Catalyst 3750v2 Series	Four models offering 24 or 48 ports. Multilayer, stackable switches aimed at branch offices and mid-market organizations. Up to nine switches can be stacked. PoE.

Table 7-6.   Cisco's Current Line of Fixed Configuration Switches *(continued)*

Product	Description
Catalyst 3560-X Series	Five models offering 24 or 48 ports. Stackable. Enables IP Telephony, wireless services, and video. PoE.
Catalyst 3560V2 Series	Targeted at small enterprise LANs. Five models with 24 or 48 10/100/ ports. Able to use Cisco's IP Base or IP Services. Supports Cisco EnergyWise.
Catalyst 2960-S Series	12 models. 10 and 1 Gigabit Ethernet uplink capability. 24 or 48 Gigabit Ethernet ports. PoE. USB storage for file backup, distribution, and simplified operations.
Catalyst 2960 Series	Seven models with 16, 24, or 48 Fast Ethernet ports. Targeted at entry-level wiring closets and small branch office networks. Enhanced security features.

Table 7-6. Cisco's Current Line of Fixed Configuration Switches

Product	Description
Catalyst 3560-C Series	Five models with 10 or 14 ports Features IP Base software PoE Enhanced security features
Catalyst 2960-C Series	Five models with 10, 12, or 14 ports Features LAN Base software PoE

Table 7-7. Cisco's Current Line of Compact Switches

Product	Description
Nexus 2000 Series	Eight models with 24 or 48 fabric extender host interfaces. Designed to provide connectivity for rack and blade servers, as well as converged fabric deployments. Usable for different connectivity solutions, including: ■ 100 Megabit Ethernet ■ 1 Gigabit Ethernet ■ 10 Gigabit Ethernet (copper and fiber)

Table 7-8.   Cisco's Current Line of Fabric Extenders

Blade Switches

Blade switches are designed to scale out virtualized x86 architectures built on high-density blade servers. The Cisco Nexus 4000 series is an all-10-Gbps Fibre Channel over Ethernet (FCoE) switch.

Table 7-9 describes Cisco's current line of blade switches.

Cisco ONS

For switching needs that are more robust than a conventional switching model, Cisco relies on optical networking technology via its Cisco ONS series of devices.

When we think of "switching," we think of rows of client computers connected to a switch that is also connected to servers. However, that model doesn't fit every organization's needs; some require something beefier and with more geographical coverage.

Enter optical metropolitan area networks (MANs).

 NOTE   MANs are somewhat of a hybrid between a LAN and a WAN.

Product	Description
Nexus 4000 Series	20 10-Gigabit Ethernet ports Enhanced server virtualization Fault tolerance

Table 7-9.   Cisco's Current Blade Switch Line

LAN technologies offer high data rates, but are limited in distance (typically 100 meters or less) between nodes. WAN technologies offer greater distances between nodes (hundreds or thousands of miles between), but the data rates are low (typically 2 Mbps or less). MANs fit into the middle ground between having a LAN that goes fast for a very limited distance and a WAN that goes far, but with low data rates. A lot of service providers now offer MAN connectivity to allow a network to reach a distance of up to about 50 km, but at relatively high speed (usually around 100 Mbps).

For an organization, the common use of a MAN is to extend their LAN connectivity between offices that are within the same city or urban area. The organization can pass their Ethernet frames to the service provider MAN; the service provider will carry their frames across the MAN and then deliver the frames to the destination site.

What the customer sees is that the MAN looks like one big Ethernet link between their offices. The different sites could belong to the same IP subnet, and from the customer's viewpoint, no routing was required between their sites. The customer can also send their Ethernet frames to the service provider, and the service provider can route the traffic off to the Internet through the MAN.

Let's use an example of a clinic with geographically disparate offices, but with the need to share and transfer large amounts of data between offices.

Mrs. McGillicuddy goes to see her regular doctor, Dr. Abner Murphy, at the Coon Rapids, Minnesota location. After pulling up her high-definition MRI results, Dr. Murphy suggests that Mrs. McGillicuddy go see his colleague, Dr. Lilly, at a clinic 20 miles away. When she gets there, Dr. Lilly checks not only those MRI scans, but also exams that were taken three, five, and even ten years prior. Because the clinics are on the same MAN, pulling up information from one office, making changes to a file, and so forth, are easily done at other locations within the network.

Cisco's gear operates at different locations within a MAN:

- **Metro edge**   The metro edge is the boundary between the MAN and end users or customers.

- **Metro core**   The metro core is where the data really gets flowing and high speeds and bandwidths are necessary. This is where the critical "thinking" of the MAN goes on.

Cisco offers different technology to perform tasks in varying roles and capacities within a MAN. Table 7-10 describes those technologies.

Configuring and Managing Cisco Switches

Cisco Catalyst switches can be configured using either the IOS command-line interface or a web interface, such as the Visual Switch Manager (VSM) or Cisco Network Assistant (CNA). Which to use is a matter of user preference; neither configures anything the other doesn't. If you use the command-line interface, the normal rules apply as far as using Telnet to log in through the Console port. For simplicity's sake, we'll use Cisco Network Assistant to explain Cisco switch configuration and management.

Product	Description	Location
ONS 15600 Multiservice Switching Platform (MSSP)	Simplifies bandwidth management by allowing service providers to integrate metro core and metro edge networks. Combines the duties of multiple metro systems, including SONET multiplexers and digital cross-connect network components. Offers four OC-192 ports per card. Up to eight OC-192 cards or 32 OC-192 ports per shelf assembly.	Metro core
ONS 15400 Multiservice Provisioning Platform (MSPP) and Multiseries Transport Platform (MSTP) Series	Best for service providers and enterprises that need bandwidth and cost savings. Delivers voice, video, and data. Supports DS-1, DS-3, and EC-1 along with 10/100/1000 Mbps Ethernet and SONET transport through OC-192.	Metro core
ONS 15300 Series	SONET multiservice provisioning platforms (MSPPs). Best for service providers who want to offer differentiating services. Supports Gigabit Ethernet, 101000 Ethernet, DS1/E1, and DS3/E3 services	Metro edge
ONS 15200 Series Metropolitan DWDM Systems	Three platforms in the series. Provides optical services to customer premises. Delivers Gigabit Ethernet and OC-48 in a one-rack unit size.	Metro edge

Table 7-10.   Cisco's Current Line of ONS Equipment

Cisco Network Assistant

There are many ways to configure Cisco's switches—they can be as involved as complex, yet powerful, command-line options, or as simple as a helpful point-and-click interface. Cisco Network Assistant (CNA) is an example of the latter. CNA is meant for overall network configuration and management, but we'll talk about it here for its switch-specific attributes.

CNA 5.0 is a PC-based network management application for small- and medium-sized organizations with networks of up to 250 users. The tool features network management and device configuration capabilities from a centralized location.

How much does this application cost? That's the best part. It's free.

Features

CNA utilizes a GUI (graphical user interface), so Cisco switches, routers, and access points can be easily configured and managed. CNA's features include

- Configuration management
- Troubleshooting information
- Inventory
- Event logging
- Network security
- Password synchronization
- IOS upgrades

CNA manages communities of devices. Communities are groupings of up to 40 networked devices. The devices use the Cisco Discovery Protocol (CDP) to identify qualified network devices ("qualified" means that they are Cisco devices). Once a device has been added to the community, it becomes a member device.

Because each member device is individually managed, monitored, and configured, it must have its own IP address.

Communities might sound a lot like clusters. However, there are some important distinctions between the two. First, clusters can only support up to 16 devices, whereas communities can support 40 devices. Second, only switches are clusterable. Communities allow the inclusion of APs, routers, switches, and other network devices.

In addition, CNA can communicate securely with each device in a community. In a cluster, secure communications are only possible between CNA and the command device—the primary switch in the cluster.

Communities offer more failover support than clusters. If a command device fails, CNA won't be able to manage any other devices in the cluster. However, using communities, CNA is able to manage any other device in the community in the event another device fails.

Installation

Installing CNA is simple and free of charge. All you need is an account at www.cisco.com. Don't worry, a www.cisco.com account is also free; you just need to fill out some online forms and you'll be able to download CNA in no time.

Feature	Requirement
Processor	1 GHz
Memory	1 GB
Hard drive space	50 MB
Colors	65,536
Screen resolution	1,024 × 768
Supported operating systems	Windows 7 (64-bit and 32-bit) Windows Vista (64-bit and 32-bit) Windows XP Professional, Service Pack 3 (64-bit and 32-bit) Windows 2008 (64-bit and 32-bit) Windows 2003 Server (64-bit and 32-bit) Macintosh OS X

Table 7-11. System Requirements for Cisco Network Assistant 4.0

System Requirements

Before you download CNA, you must ensure that the computer you'll be running it on is up to speed. Table 7-11 outlines the system requirements.

How to Install

To install CNA, follow these steps:

1. Go to www.cisco.com/go/NetworkAssistant.

2. Locate and download the CNA installer: cna-windows-k9-installer-5-0.exe.

3. Double-click the installer on your computer and follow the onscreen instructions to complete installation and setup.

4. Once installation is complete, double-click the Cisco Network Assistant icon on your desktop or locate it on your Start menu.

Views

You have two ways to look at your community and devices. CNA offers the Front Panel view and the Topology view.

Front Panel View

The Front Panel view is used to manage the port settings and configuration details for one or more devices. The Front Panel view of a Cisco Catalyst 2960 switch is shown in Figure 7-14.

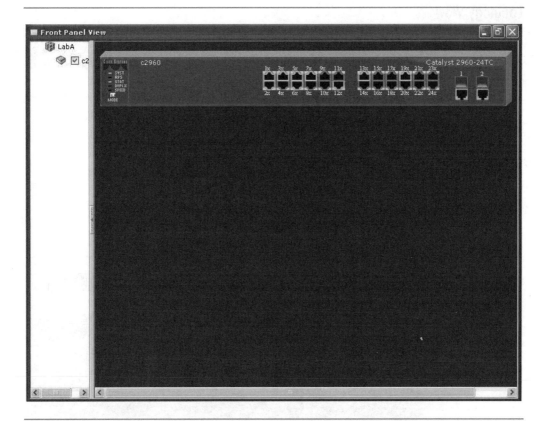

Figure 7-14. Cisco Network Assistant's Front Panel view gives an overview of your device's status.

To access the Front Panel view, click Front Panel on the toolbar or select Monitor | View | Front Panel.

This displays the front panel of the device. If the device belongs to a community, all the devices that were selected the last time the Front Panel view was displayed appear for that community. If the device is a command device of a cluster, cluster members that were selected the last time the view was selected are displayed.

The Front Panel view allows you to perform the following tasks:

- Rearrange devices
- Select and configure devices
- Configure individual ports
- Configure multiple ports on multiple devices simultaneously

Topology View

Whereas the Front Panel view allows you to examine a specific device or devices, the Topology view shows the entire membership of your community or cluster. The Topology view is the default view. If you need to switch back to the view once in Front Panel view, click Topology view on the toolbar or select Monitor | View | Topology.

The Topology view allows you to see VLAN links as well as add or remove devices from the community. Figure 7-15 shows the Topology view of a small network with a switch and an AP.

Interaction

CNA allows you to configure and manage devices in several ways. This section explains the various ways you can interact with CNA.

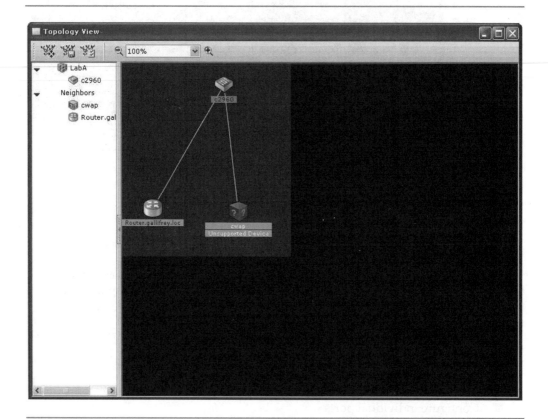

Figure 7-15.   Cisco Network Assistant's Topology view shows a diagram of your network's managed devices.

Guide and Expert Mode

The two fundamental ways to interact with CNA are either through Guide mode or Expert mode.

Guide mode is oriented more toward beginners—it walks you through configuration and management steps one at a time. Expert mode, on the other hand, presents all the configuration options at once. By default, CNA is in Expert mode. Clicking a feature on the Feature bar that shows a signpost icon, as shown in Figure 7-16, takes you to Guide mode. If you select a feature without this icon, you will be in Expert mode.

Figure 7-16. Signpost icons on the Feature bar show items that can be managed in Guide mode.

Wizards

CNA also offers a number of wizards to help with configuration and management. Wizards are like Guide mode in that they are meant to simplify the configuration process. However, they are unlike Guide mode in that they do not prompt you for every bit of information. Rather, they prompt you for minimal information and fill in the blanks with default settings.

Smartports Advisor

Smartports Advisor uses predefined settings, or *roles,* for devices. When CNA starts, it checks to see if Smartports have already been applied to the device. If they have not been applied, CNA will ask you if you want those roles applied to your devices.

Smartports can help you configure your devices with optimal security, availability, quality of service, and manageability.

Smartports Advisor shows you the devices to which you are connected, and then the ports to which Smartports roles have been applied are shown. It also shows the ports to which Smartports roles could be applied.

Communities

Once you've installed and started CNA, you can connect to an existing community or device. You can also create a new community.

Connecting

When you start CNA, use the Connect dialog box, as shown in Figure 7-17, to connect to a specific device or an existing community:

- To connect to a specific community, click the Connect to a New Community option.

- To connect to a specific community, click the Connect To option and then select the community from the drop-down menu.

- To connect to an existing cluster, select the command device's IP address from the drop-down menu.

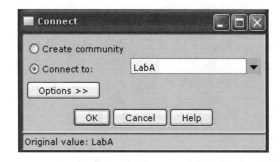

Figure 7-17.   The Connect dialog box allows you to select which community you'll connect to.

Click the **Options** button to do the following:

- Communicate with a standalone device or cluster command device using HTTPS rather than unsecure HTTP
- Use an HTTP port other than 80
- Connect with read-only access

Once you've selected the community you want to access, you'll be prompted for a username and password.

If you are connecting to a cluster, CNA asks you if you'd like to convert the cluster to a community. You simply enter the cluster command device's IP address, and CNA will convert it. Don't worry if you want to retain the cluster's properties. CNA will not delete that information, and you can still use it as part of a cluster.

Discovery

When CNA starts, you enter the IP address of one of your devices, as shown in Figure 7-18. Then, using CDP, CNA will discover all the Cisco devices in your network. CNA can discover devices across multiple networks and VLANs, assuming they have valid IP addresses.

Once CNA has discovered all the devices on your network, you can sort through them to place them into the community or communities you desire.

NOTE   You won't need hostnames for devices when using CNA. However, IOS automatically assigns switches the hostname of "Switch." You might want to rename your switches before running CNA, simply to make it easier to know which switch is which.

You will be prompted for passwords only when an already entered password does not work on a given device. For example, if you have 20 devices and they all have the same password, you will only have to enter the password once. However, if they all have different passwords, you'll have to enter 20 different passwords.

Creation

The information in the previous sections is useful when connecting to an existing community, but you'll likely need to create your own community before you start.

Communities can be created in one of three ways:

- Discovering and adding devices
- Creating them manually
- Converting a cluster

Discovering and Adding Devices   To generate a list of candidate devices and then add them to your community, follow these steps:

1. Start CNA.
2. Select Connect to a New Community in the Connect dialog box.

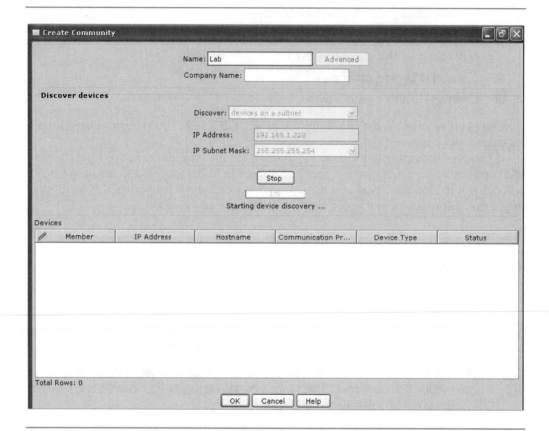

Figure 7-18. Enter the IP address of one of your devices to start the discovery process.

3. Click Connect.

4. In the Create Community window, enter a name for your community.

5. If you want to select an HTTP port other than 80, click the Advanced button and then click OK.

6. Enter the IP address for a device in your network.

7. Click Discover Neighbors.

8. In the Devices Found list, select devices you wish to remove.

9. Click Remove.

10. To add the remaining devices to your new community, click Add All to Community.

Adding Members Manually   There are two ways in which you can manually add member devices to a community:

- In the Create Community window, enter the device's IP address and then click Add to Community.
- The second way utilizes the Topology view. Right-click a candidate device's icon and then select Add to Community from the resulting context menu.

NOTE   Members of a community are labeled green, whereas candidate devices are cyan.

Converting a Cluster   If you want to convert a cluster to a community from the application, you can do so by clicking Configure | Cluster | Cluster Conversion Wizard.

Using CNA

Once you're connected to your community, using CNA is simply a matter of navigating the GUI. In this section, the configuration and management of a Catalyst 2950 switch is examined.

There are many ways to get to the different settings and windows described in this section. We'll turn our attention to the leftmost pane (also called the Feature bar) in CNA. This contains the various settings we can manage, but many can also be set by clicking an icon at the top of the screen or from within a context menu somewhere within the application. For the sake of consistency, we'll talk about the attributes as they are accessed from the Feature bar.

Configure

The Configure portion of the CNA tool allows you to manage several features, as detailed here.

Ports   This window allows you to manage port settings and EtherChannels. Figure 7-19 shows the Configuration Settings tab of Port Settings. Making a change is as easy as right-clicking an attribute and selecting the new setting from the drop-down menu.

The Runtime Status tab shows the current status of the device. Selecting EtherChannels allows you to manage EtherChannel settings for this device.

Security   Port security is managed with this setting. This window has two tabs:

- **Security Configuration**   This is used for checking port security settings and configuring a secure port. Secure ports are ports where a user-specified action initiates whenever an address-security violation occurs.
- **Secure Address**   This is used for adding, removing, or managing secure addresses. Secure addresses are MAC addresses that are forwarded to only one port per VLAN.

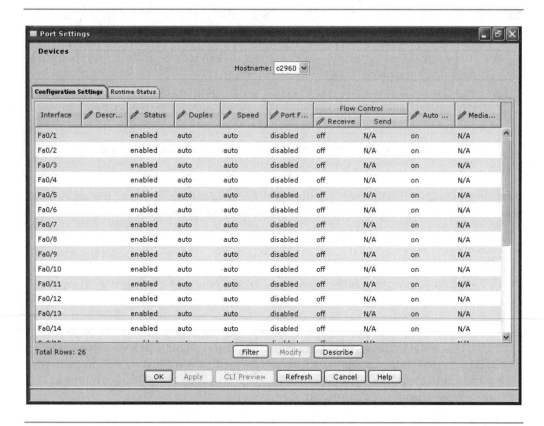

Figure 7-19.   Port Settings is where you can manage attributes of your device's ports.

To manage this setting, select a device from the Hostname list whose security settings you want to manage. You can filter the results of the list by clicking **Filter** and using the Filter Editor window.

Quality of Service   The device's Quality of Service (QoS) settings are managed with this attribute. Incoming packets contain a Class of Service (CoS) value (0 to 7) or a Differentiated Services Code Point (DSCP) value (0 to 63).

You decide which marker you want to trust and what default CoS value to assign a packet if it contains no marker. This is done by selecting Trust Settings under the Quality of Service setting. The resulting window is shown in Figure 7-20.

Switching   This attribute allows you to configure various features of your switch. The features here are similar to the configuration capabilities of Cluster Management Suite

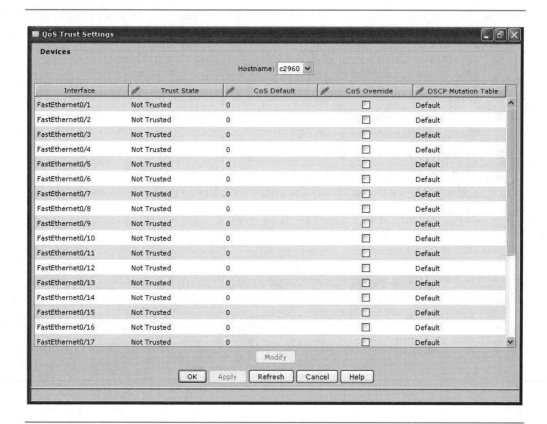

Figure 7-20. Quality of Service management in Cisco Network Assistant helps control network traffic flow.

(CMS), which was covered in Chapter 5. CNA simply provides another way to configure these settings. It also provides an environment in which you can apply consistent configuration settings across all or select devices in a community.

For more information on configuring a switch, flip back to Chapter 5.

Device Properties   The Device Properties setting allows you to manage such device basics as IP address, gateway information, and usernames and passwords.

Monitor

The Monitor section of the Feature bar allows you to review various bits of information and statistics about your device. There are two portions of the Monitor attribute: Reports and Views.

Reports   The Reports setting lets you review statistics for your device. Information includes:

- **Inventory**   Gives a listing of devices in your community, along with device type, serial number, MAC address, IP address, and IOS version.

- **Port statistics**   Gives information about port transmit and receive rates.

- **Bandwidth graphs**   Provides line and bar charts depicting bandwidth usage, like the one shown in Figure 7-21.

- **Link graphs**   Provides line and bar charts depicting link statistics.

- **ARP**   Provides a table linking the device and its MAC address to its IP address. The table also shows the age of the entry in the table, its encapsulation method, and the device interface.

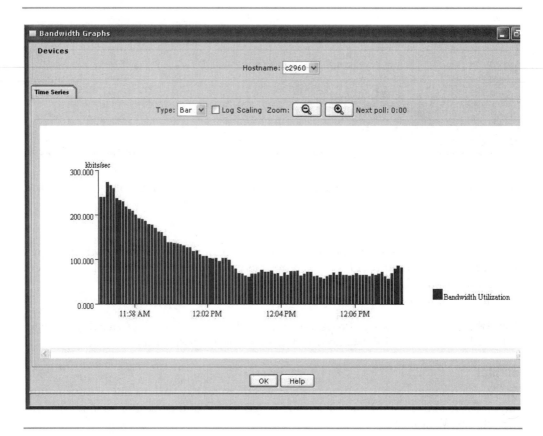

Figure 7-21.   The Bandwidth graphs show line and bar charts detailing bandwidth usage.

Views Views allows you to review system events and messages. For example, the Event Notification setting will alert you to events that CNA deems important. Such events include

- A device with a high temperature
- A device with a broken fan
- A port with a duplex mismatch
- An unknown device on the network

System messages can be configured to send you an e-mail when a message is generated.

Troubleshoot

If you're having trouble with a device, the Troubleshoot attribute offers a Ping and Trace feature. You can trace on a layer-2 or layer-3 route. A layer-2 route determines the source-to-destination network path of a layer-2 device. A layer-3 trace determines the path that a packet travels in a layer-3 network, but does not include information about layer-2 devices. The Ping and Trace window is shown in Figure 7-22.

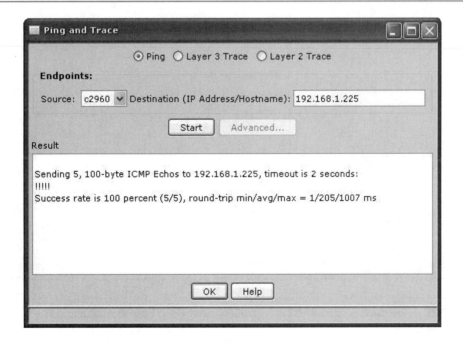

Figure 7-22. Cisco Network Assistant provides Ping and Trace services to help with troubleshooting.

Maintenance

The final attribute is Maintenance, where you can manage the functionality of CNA. One of its best features is the ability to upgrade software for devices in your community. Click Software Upgrade, and the window shown in Figure 7-23 opens.

This allows you to select specific devices in your community that you wish CNA to upgrade. When you select Upgrade Settings, you specify where on your computer or in the network the updated file is located. Your devices' upgrade files can be found on www.cisco.com.

Configuration Archive stores old community and device configurations, and System Reload saves the current device configuration and restarts the device.

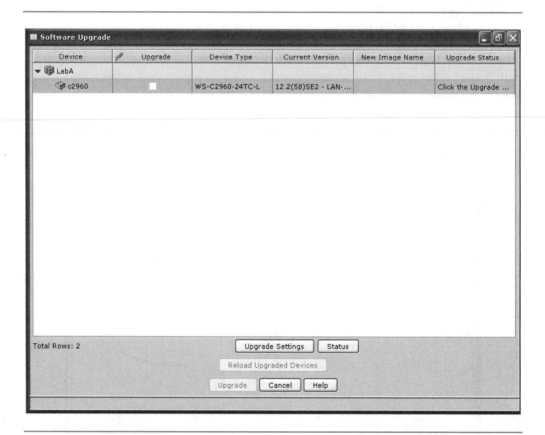

Figure 7-23.   Your devices' firmware is easily upgraded using Cisco Network Assistant.

CHAPTER 8 | Security Overview

The concept of network security may seem somewhat of a moving target—or several moving targets. When we talk about "security," we know what we *want*, but describing it and making it happen can be different matters altogether. Network security has a natural conflict with network connectivity. The more an autonomous system opens itself up, the more risk it takes on. This, in turn, requires that more effort be applied to security enforcement tasks.

On top of that, add departmental budget constraints (and the personnel cuts that many companies have seen in recent years), and even reasonable security solutions might seem impossible to attain. Four trends have increased the bite that security takes out of the IT department's overall budget:

- Internetworks have gotten bigger and more complicated.

- New threats are always emerging; they are far more complicated than they used to be.

- The typical network security system is usually not a system at all, but is a patchwork of vendor-specific tools (sound familiar?).

- Regulations and industry standards make specific demands of security measures. If your network does not meet minimum standards, you could be faced with serious fines.

Network security is so pervasive a consideration that even network management consoles raise concerns. Some, for good reason, are worried about whether the SNMP infrastructure itself is secure enough. After all, stealing the right SNMP community string would give a hacker a roadmap to an entire internetwork's configuration, and unless you've been living in a cave, you know about computer viruses spreading in various forms: e-mail bombs, Trojan horse Java applets, denial-of-service (DoS) attacks, social engineering (hyper-targeted spear phishing), and other worrisome new threats to computer security. Suffice it to say that a lot of time, money, and effort go into network security.

NOTE   SNMP stands for Simple Network Management Protocol and, as you have probably deduced, it is used for network management as a means for gathering information from various devices on a network. There are three versions, aptly named SNMPv1, v2, and v3. Versions 1 and 2 used community strings, a "secret" name that was used to allow or deny access to SNMP information. This was sent in the clear and was easily compromised. SNMPv3 finally provided an authentication mechanism along with the ability to encrypt SNMP information so that the information cannot be read in transmission.

In Chapter 9, we'll talk about Cisco's Internet access and security products. Just as a head's up, the focus will be mainly on how firewalls—and even routers—monitor internetwork traffic at the packet level to provide security. This type of "network-layer" security operates at the OSI layer people associate with IP addresses.

But a second kind of security operates at the *people* level. This kind of security, called *user- or identity-based security*, employs passwords and other login controls to authenticate users' identities before they are permitted access. There are two basic types of user-based security:

- End-user remote access to services and servers, including ISP dial-up connections, HTTPS encrypted portals, social media sites, e-mail systems, and VPN clients

- Network administrator access to network devices, where technicians log in to IOS on various kinds of network devices in order to work on them

Security is the third major control system in internetworking, along with network management systems and routing protocols. Although the three control systems have distinct missions, you'll see a familiar pattern:

- **Embedded commands**   Application commands built directly into IOS that are used to configure individual devices to participate in a larger network control system

- **Dedicated control protocol**   A communications protocol that coordinates the exchange of messages needed to perform the network control system's tasks

- **Server and console**   A server to store the messages and a workstation to provide the human interface through which the network control system is operated

Figure 8-1 illustrates the common architecture shared by network control systems. Looking at the figure, you see two new names listed next to SNMP—TACACS and RADIUS. These protocols are used for security, not management like SNMP, but they're generally similar in how they operate in that they are protocols used to communicate information across a network. In the case of SNMP, data is gathered from network devices and stored in a central database, and a console is used to configure devices from a central management workstation. Network management and security systems differ in what they do, but are similar in how they use a network to communicate.

The third internetwork control system, routing protocols, differs sharply. Routing protocols don't use servers because the information (route tables) is transient and doesn't need to be stored on disk. Additionally, they don't use consoles because they are largely self-operating.

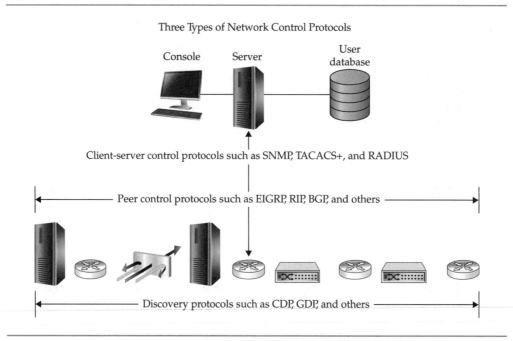

Three Types of Network Control Protocols

Console   Server   User database

Client-server control protocols such as SNMP, TACACS+, and RADIUS

Peer control protocols such as EIGRP, RIP, BGP, and others

Discovery protocols such as CDP, GDP, and others

Figure 8-1.   Internetwork control systems, including security, share certain features.

Overview of Network Security

We'll talk about two kinds of network security here. One kind is enforced as a background process not visible to users; the other is in your face:

- **Traffic-based security**   Controls connections requested by a network application, such as a web browser or an FTP download

- **User-based security**   Controls admission of individuals to systems in order to start applications once inside, usually via username and password

One kind of traffic-based security is the use of firewalls to protect autonomous systems by screening traffic from untrusted hosts. Another kind of traffic-based security is router access lists, used to restrict traffic and resources within an autonomous system. User-based security is concerned with people, not hosts. This is the kind of security with which we're all familiar—login-based security that asks you for a username and password.

The two types complement one another, yet operate at different levels. Traffic-based security goes into action when you click a button in a web browser, enter a command into an FTP screen, or use some other application command to generate network traffic. User-based security, on the other hand, asserts itself when an individual tries to log in to a network, device, or service offered on a device.

Traffic-Based Security

Traffic-based security is implemented in a Cisco internetwork by using firewalls or router access lists. This style of security—covered in Chapter 7—focuses mainly on source and destination IP addresses, application port numbers, and other packet-level information that can be used to restrict and control network connections.

Until fairly recently, firewalls have focused strictly on guarding against intruders from outside the autonomous system. However, they're now coming into use in more sophisticated shops to restrict access to sensitive assets from the inside. Access lists have been the traditional tool used to enforce intramural security.

Access List Traffic-Based Security

Routers can be configured to enforce security in much the same way firewalls do. All routers can be configured with access lists, and they can be used to control what traffic may come and go through the router's network interfaces. What exactly an access list does is left to how it's configured by the network administrator.

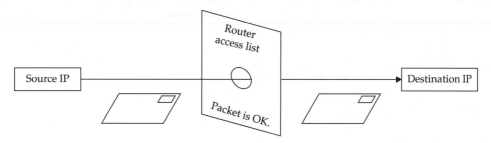

Access lists can be used to improve network performance by isolating traffic in its home area, but more commonly, access lists are used to "screen" traffic and to perform rudimentary firewall-like restrictions on network traffic.

Firewall Traffic-Based Security

Packet-filtering firewalls are basically beefed-up routers that screen processes according to strict traffic management rules. They use all sorts of tactics to enhance security: address translation to hide internal network topology from outsiders; application layer inspection to make sure only permitted services are being run; even high/low counters that watch for any precipitous spikes in certain types of packets to ward off denial-of-service (DoS) attacks such as SYNflood and FINwait.

Firewalls intentionally create a bottleneck at the autonomous system's perimeter. As traffic passes through, the firewall inspects packets as they come and go through the networks attached to its interfaces.

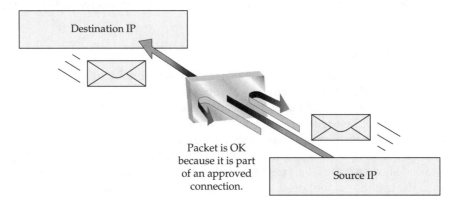

Firewalls read source and destination host addresses and port numbers (for example, port 80 for HTTP) as well as establish a context for each permitted connection. The context comes in the form of a session, where packets with a certain address pair and port number must belong to a valid session. For example, if a user tries to connect to a web server to download a file, the firewall will check the user's source IP address and the application service requested before permitting the packets to pass. If the traffic is permitted, the user will be allowed to connect to the web server. If not, the traffic will be denied and the connection will not be allowed.

Think of traffic-based security as being like those "easy pass" automated tollbooths on major toll roads. Vehicles are funneled through a gateway where a laser reads each electronic ID, barely slowing the flow of traffic. Once a car is allowed to pass, nothing has been done to inspect what might have been in the trunk of that car—more on deep packet inspection of the "trunk" later.

User-Based Security

User-based security evokes a different picture—this one of a gate with a humorless security guard standing at the post. The guard demands to know who you are and challenges you to prove your identity. If you qualify, you get to go in. More sophisticated user-based security systems also have the guard ask what you intend to do once inside and issue you a coded visitor's badge, giving you access to some areas, but not others.

Thus, user-based security is employed where a person must log in to a host, and the security comes in the form of a challenge for the username and password. In internetworking, this kind of security is used as much to keep bad guys from entering network devices, such as routers or switches, as it is to restrict access to payload devices, such as servers.

Unlike firewalls, however, user-based security is nearly as concerned with insiders as outsiders. That security guard at the gate has colleagues on the inside to make sure nobody goes into the wrong area. You know the routine—there are employee badges and there are visitor badges, but the employee badges let you go more places.

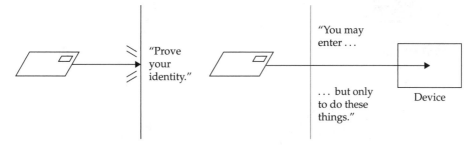

Login/password authentication is generally required on every network device and all servers. Because user-based security mechanisms are software, not hardware, they can be deployed at will within an internetwork with little impact on performance or budget. The trade-off is how much inconvenience you're willing to put network users through, having to log in to gain access to various services. User-based security has four major applications:

- To grant remote employees access to the enterprise internetwork
- To grant onsite employees access to protected hosts and services within the internetwork
- To let network administrators log in to network devices
- To let ISPs grant subscribers access to their portals

Because a lot of user-based security involves connections allowing remote access to corporate resources, WAN technologies play an important role. The two most important pieces of authenticating WAN connections are access servers and dial-in protocols.

Access Servers

Entering an internetwork through a dial-in connection is almost always done through an access server. The access server is a dedicated device that fields phone calls from remote individuals trying to establish a connection to a network. Access servers are also called *network access servers* or *communication servers*. Their key attribute is to behave like a full-fledged IP host on one side, but like a modem on the other side. Figure 8-2 depicts the role access servers play in remote connections.

NOTE Although resources such as DSL, cable, and the various 4G cellular technologies are displacing analog modem dial-in service like wildfire, there are enough analogies between access servers used for dial-in modems and the other connectivity that they service that it is justified we discuss them in this book.

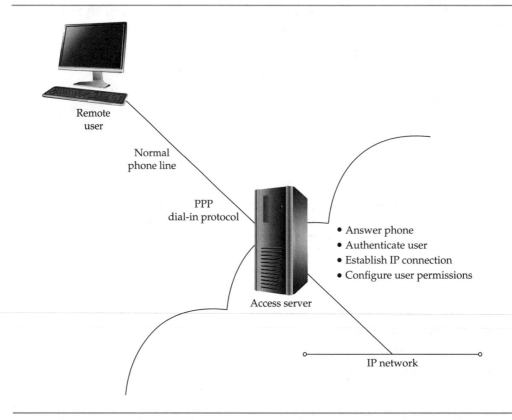

Remote user

Normal phone line

PPP dial-in protocol

- Answer phone
- Authenticate user
- Establish IP connection
- Configure user permissions

Access server

IP network

Figure 8-2. Access servers are dedicated to supporting remote dial-in connections.

When you connect to an internetwork's host from the enterprise campus, you usually do so over a dedicated twisted-pair cable that is connected to a hub or a switch. To make that same connection from afar, you usually do so over a normal telephone line through an access server—a device that answers the phone call and establishes a network connection. Besides making connections for remote dial-in users, access servers can also be used to connect remote routers.

User-Based Security for Local Connectivity When you turn on your PC and log in at work, you're usually not dealing with TACACS+ or RADIUS. The username and password prompts are coming from your local server. Most LAN servers run Windows Server, Linux, Unix, or Novell platforms. They have security subsystems and user databases of their own to authenticate and authorize users. RADIUS isn't used because, among other things, it's a dial-in password protocol. TACACS+ isn't used because it controls entry into the Cisco network devices themselves—routers, switches, and access servers—in addition to providing dial-in security, much like RADIUS.

In this chapter, discussions of local or "in-network" connections refer to network administrators logging in to IOS to work on a Cisco network device.

User-Based Security for Remote Connectivity   Small office and home office users may connect to their enterprise internetworks through an access server, making it perhaps the most basic device in any wide area network. Low-end access servers are inconspicuous desktop devices resembling a PC without a monitor. When your cellular hotspot, cable modem, or DSL router dials in to your ISP to get into the Internet from home, the connection request (although you never interact with it) is also answered by an access server. As you might imagine, an ISP's computer room is jammed with rack-mounted high-density access servers to handle connections made from thousands of subscribers. (As a reminder, *high density* means many ports per device.)

Access servers are intelligent devices that handle other tasks in addition to making a line connection. They provide special services to accommodate configurations frequently encountered in enterprise internetworks:

- **Routing service**   Run by access servers called *access routers,* this service makes it seem as if the dial-in user is sitting directly on the campus network. The key feature of access routers is dial-on-demand routing (DDR), which makes it possible to route traffic from a remote LAN to the main network over low-cost, dial-up phone lines.

- **Terminal service**   Many WAN connections still use terminal protocols. For that reason, most access servers support terminal protocols such as IBM's TN3270, Unix's rlogin, and Digital Equipment's Local-Area Transport (LAT). A PC could run terminal emulation software to make such a connection.

- **Protocol translation**   A remote user may be running a virtual terminal protocol and then connect to a system running another virtual terminal protocol. Most access servers still support protocol translation.

As computing infrastructure improves, terminal service and protocol translation are declining in use. In contrast, access routers are increasing in popularity as small offices build LANs of their own and turn to DDR for convenience and savings.

Dial-In Protocols

It may seem like no one uses dial-in Internet access anymore, but the exact opposite is true, especially if you live in a rural area. Additionally, if you have Internet access on your smartphone, a cellular Wi-Fi hotspot, a cable modem, or DSL in your home or office, you are a dial-in subscriber—the difference is it's not user interactive any longer. Your devices are "auto-dialing" for you so you don't have to. This short section, however, is focused on traditional telco-based connections.

As you've learned by now, there's a protocol for just about every major internetworking task. Making dial-in network connections work properly presents special problems, because most telephone company infrastructure was designed to handle voice, not high-speed data. Dial-in protocols exist to handle the point-to-point dial-in connections over normal telephone lines:

- **PPP**   Point-to-Point Protocol is the de facto standard for remote dial-in connections to IP networks; virtually all dial-in connections to the Internet use PPP. Most PPP connections are over asynchronous lines, but a growing number are made over ISDN in areas where it's available.

- **SLIP**   Serial Line Internet Protocol is also used to make point-to-point dial-in connections to IP networks from remote sites. SLIP is the predecessor to PPP, but is still in use in some quarters. You may also encounter a SLIP variant called CSLIP (Compressed Serial Line Internet Protocol).

In the old days, to make a remote connection, you dialed in to a PBX or terminal server to connect to a mainframe or minicomputer as a dumb terminal. With the rise of internetworking in the 1980s, network-attached terminal servers took over the job of taking dial-in calls. As demand for remote computing grew, simple terminal connections were replaced by those made using the SLIP protocol. By that point, many desktops had PCs instead of terminals, but they emulated terminals in order to make dial-in connections. The boom in demand for Internet connectivity drove the market to replace SLIP with PPP, a protocol even more capable of computer-to-computer communications over phone lines. PPP brought better error detection, compression, and authentication support. It also allowed for multilink connectivity—double your throughput anyone? For our purposes, we'll assume PPP as the dial-in protocol unless otherwise noted. There is another technology, developed in the early 1990s, that is also referred to as a terminal server—and that is Microsoft Terminal Services, since renamed Remote Desktop Services. Microsoft TS supported direct dial-in modems, whereas Microsoft RDS today is deployed on the Internet over IPSec or SSL VPN using a layer-3 encrypted tunnel. It's important to not confuse the Unix style of terminals discussed throughout this book with Microsoft TS/RDS.

Authentication, Authorization, and Accounting

The framework for user-based security is called authentication, authorization, and accounting (AAA), pronounced *triple-a*. The AAA framework is designed to be consistent and modular in order to give network teams flexibility in implementing the enterprise's network security policy.

NOTE   Network security systems, such as CiscoSecure Access Control Server (ACS), control access to LAN segments, lines, and network applications such as HTTP and FTP. Network access devices—usually access servers and access routers—control access to these network-based services, but an additional layer of security is sometimes configured into the server platform once it is reached. For example, an IBM mainframe will enforce security policies using its own mechanisms, although that mainframe may reference the same LDAP user directory that ACS does. Security for computer platforms and major application software packages is still performed using self-contained security systems resident in the application server, in addition to the network access device security measures covered in this chapter.

Overview of the AAA Model

AAA's purpose is to control who is allowed access to network devices and what services they are allowed to use once they have access. Here is a brief description of the AAA model's three functional areas:

- **Authentication**   Validates the user's identity as authentic before granting the login

- **Authorization**   Grants the user the privilege to access networks and commands

- **Accounting**   Collects data to track usage patterns by individual user, service, host, time of day, day of week, and so on

Thankfully, the acronym makers put the three functions in sequential order, making the AAA concept easier to pick up: First, you're allowed to log in (your identity is authenticated). Then you have certain privileges to use once you're in (you have predetermined authorizations). And, finally, a running history is kept on what you do while logged in (the network team keeps an account of what you do).

The philosophy is to let network teams enforce security policy on a granular basis. Most AAA parameters can be put into effect per LAN segment, per line (user), and per protocol (usually IP).

AAA is a clearly defined security implementation framework that everybody can understand. The architecture is defined down to the command level. Indeed, the AAA concepts are actual IOS commands. Starting an AAA process on a Cisco device involves using the **aaa** prefix followed by one of the three root functions, such as **aaa authentication**. A whole AAA command line might read **aaa authentication ppp RemoteWorkers TACACS+ local**, for example. The purpose of AAA is to provide the client-side command structure on which CiscoSecure relies.

The following explains how to enable AAA on a Cisco router or access server:

1. Enable AAA by using the **aaa new-model** global configuration command.

2. If you decide to use a separate security server, configure security protocol parameters such as RADIUS, TACACS+, or Kerberos.

3. Define the method lists for authentication by using an AAA authentication command.

4. Apply the method lists to a particular interface or line, if required.

5. Optionally, you can configure authorization using the **aaa authorization** command.

6. Optionally, you can configure accounting using the **aaa accounting** command.

AAA Modularity

A security policy is a set of principles and rules adopted by an enterprise to protect system resources, confidential records, and intellectual property. It's the network manager's responsibility to implement and enforce the policy, but in the real world, security policy can get dragged down into the mire of office politics, budget constraints, and impatience. An end-user manager can have a lot of clout as to how the policy will be conducted on his or her turf. After all, the company, not the IT department, funds the network. Consequently, there can be a lot of variance among security policies—even within an enterprise's internetwork.

This means that security policies must be highly adaptable. CiscoSecure ACS tries to satisfy this need with modularity—the ability to separately apply security functions by secured entity, independent of how they are applied to other resources. The AAA architecture gives you the option to implement any of the three functions independent of the other two. This includes whether they're activated on a device, which security protocol is used, and what security server or user database is accessed.

Authentication Controls   The **aaa authentication** command validates a user's identity at login. But once you're authenticated, exactly what can you access? That depends on the type of access being made:

- If you're a network administrator logging in to a switch to tweak its config file, the authentication gets you into that switch's IOS command prompt.

- If you're an employee sitting inside the enterprise and you were authenticated by a router, you get into a protected host to run Windows- or browser-based internetwork client-server applications.

- If you're a telecommuter and an access server authenticated you, you're admitted to your enterprise's internetwork to run the same client-server applications.

- If you dialed in to the Internet from home, as a member of the general public, you were authenticated by one of your ISP's many access servers, and you enter the World Wide Web.

Authentication must protect three destination environments: the Internet, the internetwork, and, most of all, the internal operating system of the devices over which internetworks run. Figure 8-3 illustrates access types and destination environments.

The scenario of the network administrator logging in to IOS devices is unique. In Cisco internetworks, that type of access is usually authenticated using TACACS+. Network administrators access a device's IOS environment in order to perform device maintenance tasks.

Users also require different dial-in services. Although almost everybody uses PPP nowadays, there still can be different requirements. Depending on the local network from which the call is made, different PPP services may be required, such as IP, IPX, NetBEUI, or just a plain terminal connection.

Whatever the issues may be, different requirements often call for a variety of authentication methods to be used in the same internetwork. CiscoSecure ACS lets the network manager employ any of the major dial-in protocols and authentication techniques. In addition, it supports the ability to apply these different tools by network interface or line—even on the same device.

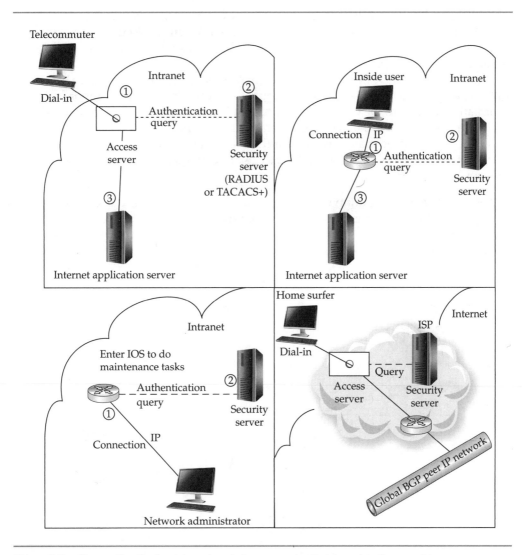

Figure 8-3.   User authentication takes place in four scenarios that open into three worlds.

Authorization Controls   AAA authorization limits services to the user. In other words, if authorization has been activated on a secured entity using the **aaa authorization** command, users must be explicitly granted access to it.

The person's user profile is usually stored in the security server and sometimes also in the device's local user database. When the administrator logs in to the device and his or her user profile is checked, the device configures the authorizations to know what commands to allow the administrator to use during that session. Commands can be authorized by IOS command mode (the MyRouter: versus MyRouter# prompts) or by specific commands within a mode. Figure 8-4 lays out some of the various forms authorizations can take.

Authorization can be more complicated than authentication. After you've been authenticated, the security server must supply the access device configuration information specific to the user—for example, which networks the user may access, which application traffic may be run, which commands are okay to use, and so on. Without centralized maintenance of authorization information, it wouldn't be practical to assign authorizations by user. (It's hard enough just to keep usernames and passwords up to date.)

Accounting Controls   Accounting doesn't permit or deny anything, but instead keeps a running record of what users do. AAA accounting is a background process that tracks the person's logins and network use. Figure 8-5 shows how AAA security accounting tracks resource usage.

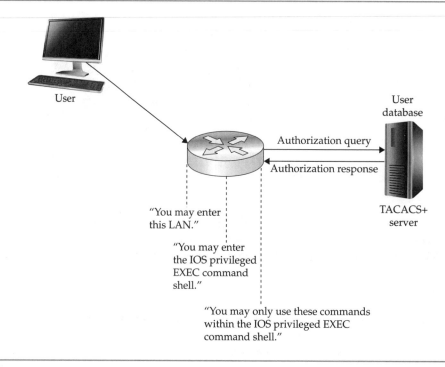

Figure 8-4.   Authorizations can be enforced by network, command mode, and even by command.

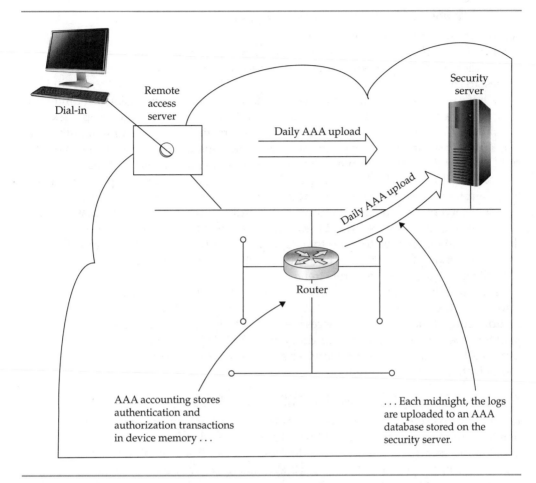

Figure 8-5.   AAA accounting is a background process that tracks a user's network activity.

AAA accounting reflects events as they take place in entering systems and using services. Thus, the accounting commands more or less mirror the others. For example, accounting tasks can be enabled by system, command mode, network device interface, protocol, and connection—just like authorization commands.

NOTE   By default, AAA defines IOS as having two command modes: the user EXEC mode (sometimes also called Shell) and the privileged EXEC modes. The IOS **level** command can be used to further divide things up into 16 command levels (numbered 0–15), so access to commands can be authorized on a more fine-grained basis.

Trends Leading to Client-Server Security Systems

As with most network control systems, AAA uses the client-server model to manage security. In other words, there is a central security server holding the user profile information used by client access devices to enforce security. When a user makes a request to connect to a network, line, or service, the client device queries the server to check if it's okay. Centralization is necessary, because it's no longer feasible to administer security one access device at a time; there are simply too many of them to keep track of.

In the 1970s, a natural by-product of remote users dialing in to central mainframes was that user security profiles (accounts, passwords, and authorizations) were stored right there on the same computer where all the services sat. This made it easy for the security system to check on user permissions. Then, in the 1980s, departmental minicomputers became popular, spreading computers out into the organization. Terminal servers were invented to provide the additional entry points the distributed topologies required, but user databases were now spread across many access devices—making it much tougher to maintain the security system. By the time IP-based networking took off, it became apparent that security information had to be centralized. Figure 8-6 depicts this trend.

The rise of internetworking demands that an enterprise offer dial-in access throughout the organization. Doing so presents problems for enforcing consistent security controls across so many access servers. The AAA architecture is Cisco's game plan for meeting these challenges. Additionally, TACACS+ and RADIUS servers are capable of integrating with such services as Microsoft's Active Directory, allowing for centralization of AAA information.

AAA's Two Security Protocols: TACACS+ and RADIUS

It's possible to use AAA security on a standalone basis, with no central security database. In the real world, few do this because it would require the extra effort of maintaining security parameters on a device-by-device basis—a labor-intensive and mistake-prone proposition. IOS supports standalone security because, in some cases, a security server is unavailable—for example, in a very small internetwork or during the period of time when a security server is being implemented but is still not operable.

AAA configures access devices as clients. Client devices include access servers, routers, switches, and firewalls. The clients query one or more security servers to check whether user connections are permitted. To do this, a protocol is needed to specify rules and conventions to govern the exchange of information. AAA security can use two protocols to handle client-server security configurations:

■ **RADIUS** A security protocol used mainly for authentication. RADIUS stands for Remote Authentication Dial-in User Service. RADIUS is an industry standard under the auspices of the IETF (Internet Engineering Task Force). It utilizes UDP and is susceptible to command sniffing. Also, only the password is encrypted.

■ **TACACS+** A proprietary Cisco protocol that is largely the equivalent of RADIUS, but with stronger integration of authorization and accounting with

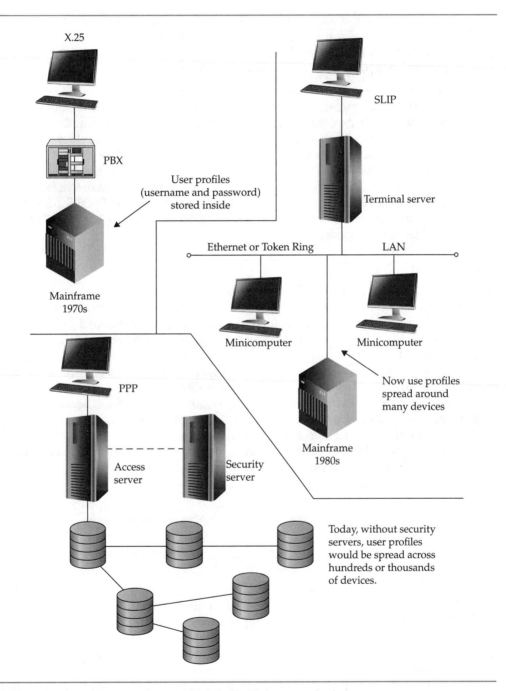

Figure 8-6.   Security systems have evolved along with the computing industry.

authentication. TACACS stands for Terminal Access Controller Access Control System. Cisco has submitted TACACS+ to the IETF for consideration as a security protocol standard; however, the draft expired. TACACS+ utilizes TCP and encrypts password and command payload.

NOTE There exist many security protocols, but a third security protocol called Kerberos (coincidently named for the three-headed guard dog of Hades that is also known as Cerberus) needs to be mentioned. Developed at MIT, Kerberos is an open standard for secret-key authentication that utilizes Advanced Encryption Standard (AES) cryptographic algorithm. Microsoft, for example, integrated Kerberos into Windows 2000 way back when. Although more difficult to implement and administer, Kerberos is gaining in popularity in internetworks more sensitive to security. Its key benefits are that it can function in a multivendor network like RADIUS, but it doesn't transmit passwords over the network (it passes so-called "tickets" instead). IOS includes Kerberos commands in its AAA framework.

How AAA Works

AAA is the security infrastructure of IOS devices. AAA commands are located in the IOS privileged EXEC mode. Each client device is configured for security using the AAA commands from global configuration mode. Properly configured, the device can then make use of the CiscoSecure server using the TACACS+ or RADIUS security protocols—or both.

In fact, AAA commands can be used standalone to secure a device. In other words, the device can use a local user database stored in NVRAM on the device itself, instead of one on a RADIUS or TACACS+ server. However, this is rarely done, because it entails maintaining and monitoring user security data in hundreds, or even thousands, of device config files instead of in a single database.

TACACS+ and RADIUS are client-server network protocols used to implement client-server security over the network. In that sense, they are the equivalent of what SNMP is to network management.

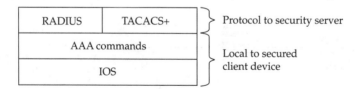

A user database changes every time users are added or deleted, passwords are changed, or authorizations are modified. Separating the user database from device config files reduces the number of places updates must be made. Most internetworks use a primary server and one or two alternate security servers, leaving only a few places in which user profile databases need to be updated.

Ensuring that the user databases contain identical data is called *database synchronization*. This can be done automatically by configuring Replication Partners in CiscoSecure ACS.

In the scenario with three security servers, the three user databases would be configured as replication partners, and the CiscoSecure ACS would automatically synchronize user profile records between the three on a scheduled basis.

In addition to the user profiles, the server can synchronize any of the following:

- User and group database
- Group database only
- Network Configuration Device tables
- Distribution table
- Interface configuration
- Interface security settings
- Password validation settings
- EAP-FAST master keys and policies
- CNAC policies

The AAA Approval Process

AAA works by compiling attributes that specify a user's permissions. In the AAA context, an *attribute* is a pointer to an entity (or object) to which the person may have access. For example, an authentication attribute might be a specific LAN segment to which the person is permitted access. An authorization attribute might be the limit on concurrent connections the person may have open at one time.

When a user attempts to connect to a secured service, the access device checks to see if the user has clearance per the security policy. It does so by sending a query to the server database to look for a match. The secured access device knows what to query for based on its config file parameter settings, and the query is used to verify that the user has permission to do whatever is being attempted.

Attribute-Value Pairs   The query contains the attributes that are mandatory for the requested service, as defined in the access device's config file. The server processes the query by searching for the same attributes in the user's profile in the user database. The search is for so-called attribute-values. An attribute, called an *attribute-value pair* (or *AV pair*) in TACACS+ terminology, is a fancy term to describe the representation of a network entity that is secured.

For example, in someone's user profile, the password is an attribute, and the person's actual password, *imreallyme*, is the value paired with it. When the user enters the password, the access device handling the login first knows to check for a password, because to do so is set as a parameter in the device's config file. By checking the person's user profile, it looks for a match between the value entered into the password prompt and what's on file in the user database for the username the person entered. Figure 8-7 shows the AAA procedure for handling a user's request for a connection.

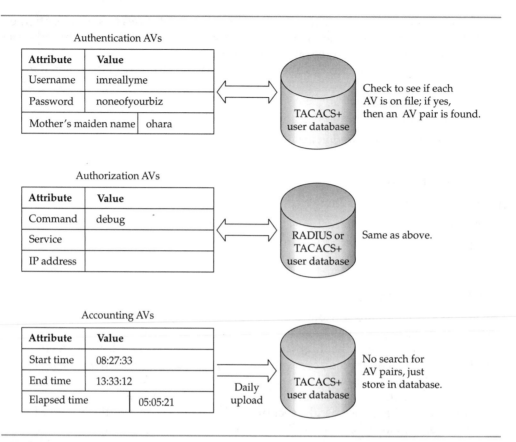

Authentication AVs

Attribute	Value
Username	imreallyme
Password	noneofyourbiz
Mother's maiden name	ohara

Check to see if each AV is on file; if yes, then an AV pair is found.

TACACS+ user database

Authorization AVs

Attribute	Value
Command	debug
Service	
IP address	

Same as above.

RADIUS or TACACS+ user database

Accounting AVs

Attribute	Value	
Start time	08:27:33	
End time	13:33:12	
Elapsed time		05:05:21

Daily upload

TACACS+ user database

No search for AV pairs, just store in database.

Figure 8-7.   User access requests are granted if attribute-values are matched in the user profile.

How AAA Handles Authentication Transactions   When the connection is established, the access device contacts the security server and displays a user prompt. The user enters the information (usually just a username and password), and the protocol (RADIUS or TACACS+) encrypts the packet and sends it to the server. The server decrypts the information, checks the user's profile, forms and encrypts the response, and returns the response to the access device.

The rules of AAA approval are fairly simple: If an ACCEPT is returned, the requested connection is made. If a REJECT is returned, the user's request-for-connection session is terminated. But if an ERROR is returned and the access device is configured for multiple security servers, the query is then forwarded to an alternate server. If that server also fails to return a response, the process continues until the query runs out of servers. At that point, if the access device has been configured with a second method, it will iterate through the process again, first trying for approval with a query to the primary security server, and so on. If the access device exhausts authentication methods, it terminates the user's request-for-connection session.

The CONTINUE response is another optional configuration parameter that prompts the user for additional information. The prompts can be anything the network administrator arbitrarily defines. For example, prompting users for their mother's maiden name is a common challenge.

NOTE   A daemon (pronounced *DI-men* or *DAY-men*, depending on your age) is a process that runs on a server to perform a predefined task, usually in response to some event. The term comes from Greek mythology, in which daemons were guardian spirits. Daemons are called services in Windows parlance. A TACACS+ daemon sits on the security server and fields authentication or authorization queries from client access devices. It does so by searching the user database for required AV pairs and returning the results to the client in TACACS+ packets.

Authorization Transactions   If the user is authenticated, the daemon is contacted to check for authorization attributes on a case-by-case basis. Figure 8-8 depicts how authentication and authorization work together.

Authorization attributes can be issued for such services as connection type (login, PPP, and so on), IOS command modes (User EXEC or Privileged EXEC), and various connection parameters, including host IP addresses, user timeouts, access lists, and so on. Authorization is, by nature, more sophisticated than authentication. More information than just username and password is involved, and the attributes have a state. For example, the Maximum-Time attribute requires the server to keep tabs on how long the user has been connected and to terminate the session when the value (number of seconds) for the user has been exceeded.

Authentication Protocols

CiscoSecure ACS supports a number of authentication mechanisms. Also called *password configurations* or *password protocols,* authentication protocols make sure you are who you say you are when logging in to a system, and they can utilize physical tokens, personal certificates, or just cleartext passwords. Here are four major authentication mechanisms supported by AAA in use today:

- **ASCII**   American Standard Code for Information Interchange is the oldest authentication protocol. ASCII is a machine-independent technique for representing English characters, and has many other uses besides authentication. ASCII authentication requires the user to type a username and password to be sent in cleartext (that is, unencrypted) and matched with those in the user database stored in ASCII format.

- **CHAP**   Challenge Handshake Authentication Protocol provides the same functionality of PAP, but it is much more secure because it avoids sending the password and other user information over the network to the security server. There are several varieties of CHAP.

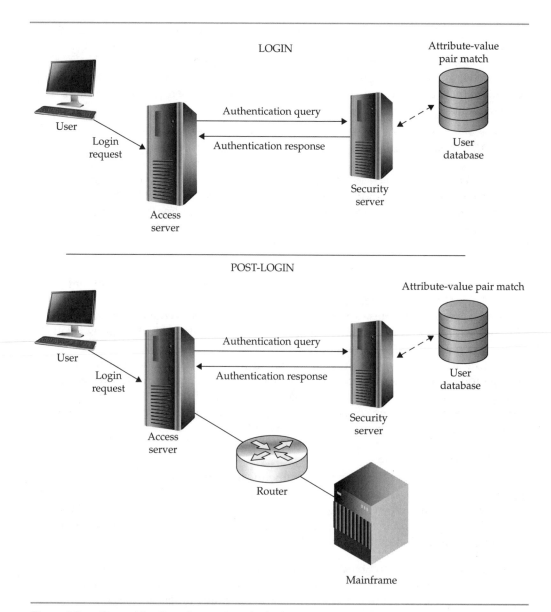

Figure 8-8.   Once authenticated, a user's authorizations are cleared as needed.

- **Physical token**   This authentication technique uses one-time passwords and a physical device one must have in their possession in order to authenticate. That device can hold an encrypted certificate or generate a number every 60 seconds that is used in conjunction with a token server that ACS validates your identity against. An older method involves a token-card that is an electronic device that's a bit larger than a credit card. The card is used to generate an encrypted password that must match one filed for the user in the token-card database residing on the security server. The encrypted password is good for only one use; thus the name *token*. Physical token–based authentication systems provide the best access security. One variation of this scheme is to have the token server send SMS messages to a cellular phone, effectively turning that phone into a physical token.

■ **Extensible Authentication Protocol**   EAP is an authentication *framework* that is mostly seen in wireless networks in various configurations corporate networks.

NOTE   Lightweight Extensible Authentication Protocol (LEAP) is Cisco proprietary and shares many commonalities with WEP and MS-CHAP. It is not recommended for use any longer. Companies are deploying certificate-based authentication schemes such as Protected Extensible Authentication Protocol (PEAP) based EAP-MSCHAPv2. PEAP wraps your EAP authentication conversation in a TLS encrypted tunnel. Figure 8-9 shows how a PEAP authentication occurs.

Legacy versions of ACS using TACAS+ also supported NASI (NetWare Asynchronous Services Interface), an authentication protocol built into Novell LANs. Another vendor-specific password protocol is ARAP (AppleTalk Remote Access Protocol), with a double challenge-response authentication mechanism that goes CHAP one better by making the security server authenticate *itself* to the client as well. In addition, there are subtle variations in how the PAP protocol works with Windows operating systems. We only mention these for reference—you are not likely to run into them in the field nowadays.

Security comes at a cost—mostly in the form of increased inconvenience to users, but there's also additional expense to deploy and administer security measures. For example, CHAP requires some extra hardware and expertise, and physical tokens are cumbersome to deploy. Can you imagine the giant social network Facebook mailing token-cards to every new user and administering a token database system? The added expense and logistical complexity of advanced authentication protocols can discourage their adoption.

Physical token–based systems used to be the prevue of high-security networks in the military, R&D, banking, or other security-conscious environments, but no longer. Corporate internetworks are far more likely to use physical tokens today because there are simply too many ways a simple password-based system can be compromised. The vast majority of corporate internetworks utilizes physical tokens for network administration at a minimum and ramp it up from there.

Methods and Types

Certain pieces must be put in place before security can be enforced. As you just saw, the access device must be configured to query one or more security servers for authentication and authorization, and the user database must have profiles containing attributes that

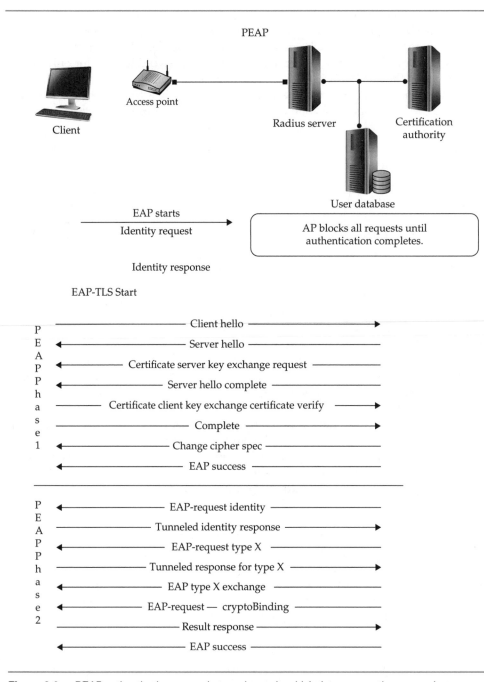

Figure 8-9.   PEAP authentication occurs in two phases in which the conversation occurs in an encrypted tunnel.

define what the user is permitted to do on the network. But what exactly happens when the query hits the TACACS+ or RADIUS database? What steps are taken to verify the user's identity and figure out what services that person is permitted?

AAA command statements in an access device's config file tell the device what to do when a user tries to log in. The root AAA commands **authentication**, **authorization**, and **accounting** are used in conjunction with various keywords to code config file instructions on how connection attempts are to be handled. As mentioned earlier, these instruction parameters are modular in that they can be applied per user and per service. The instructions are implemented in the access device's config file using methods and types:

- A *method* is a prepackaged computer program that performs a specific function. For example, **radius** is a method to query a RADIUS server.

- A *type* is the entity to which the method applies. For example, a **radius** method is applied to a **ppp** type so that when a user attempts to make a connection using the PPP protocol, the access device queries its RADIUS server to authenticate the person's identity.

Because there are almost always multiple security parameters set for a device, AAA configurations are referred to as *named method lists*. They're called *named methods* because they are named by the administrator in the device config file and applied to one or more specific secured entity types. Figure 8-10 shows how named method lists and types work together to enforce security.

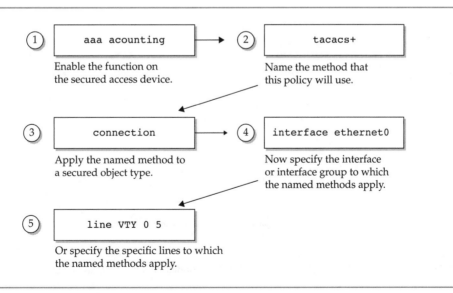

Figure 8-10.   Named method lists enforce security policies in access device interfaces.

NOTE   There are unnamed methods in the form of the default method list. If an interface or line has no named method list configured, a default method list is automatically put into force for it. To have no AAA security, it must be explicitly configured this way by using the none method. The command would look like aaa accounting none. Cisco makes it hard to have no security in force.

Named method lists are entered into the config file of the access device being secured—usually an access server or a router. IOS applies methods in the sequence in which they appear in the configuration, initially trying the first method and then turning to the following ones until an ACCEPT or REJECT is returned. Figure 8-11 explains a typical named method list.

The last part of the AAA configuration in Figure 8-11 specifies lines because authentication deals with individual users. Traffic-based security can be applied on the interface level because the firewall or router monitors information in the header of each packet—a process that is done either to all or none of the packets passing through an interface. By contrast, user-based security controls individuals as they make a remote network connection through an access server or log in to IOS inside a router or switch within the network. Each of these two scenarios involves using a line.

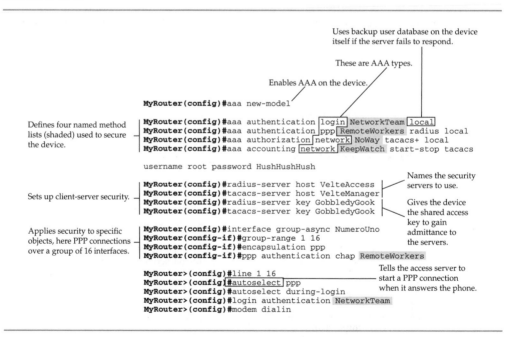

Figure 8-11.   The basic parts of a device security configuration model contain a number of settings.

AAA Authentication Methods and Types   AAA has several methods to authenticate user identity. Only one method may be used per user line (except when the **Local** method is configured as backup to one of the three client-server methods). Table 8-1 lists Cisco's authentication methods.

The list of AAA methods in Table 8-1 varies slightly according to the password mechanism being used. Remember that AAA is an architectural model that must be adapted to differences in the way other vendors design their products. For example, AAA supports Guest and Auth-Guest methods for the password protocol in Apple's ARAP.

It's possible to configure different authentication methods on different lines within the same access device. For example, you might want to configure PPP connections to query the user database on a RADIUS server, but to check the local user database for login connections made from the console or AUX ports.

IOS Command Keyword	AAA Authentication Method
Group RADIUS	Authenticates using the RADIUS protocol and user database.
Group TACACS+	Authenticates using the TACACS+ protocol and user database.
Group *group name*	Authenticates using a subset of RADIUS or TACACS+ servers for authentication as defined by the **aaa group server radius** or **aaa group server tacacs+** command.
Krb5	Authenticates using the Kerberos 5 protocol and user database. (Note: Kerberos can only be used with the PAP password protocol.)
Krb5-telnet	Uses Kerberos 5 telnet authentication protocol when connecting using Telnet.
Local	Authenticates using a user database stored in memory in the access device, or for backup if the security server does not respond.
Line	Authenticates using the Line password for authentication.
Local-case	Authenticates using case-sensitive local username authentication.
Cache *group name*	Authenticates using a cache server group.
Enable	Authenticates using Enable Secret passwords in the access device's config file.
None	Uses no authentication.

Table 8-1.   Authentication Methods in IOS

Connection Types   Because authentication is applied to user lines, named authentication methods are applied to connection types. A *connection type* is the communications protocol used to make a connection. To explain, remote connections to ISPs and internetworks nowadays are usually PPP connections. But when a network administrator logs in to IOS in order to work on a device, that connection is through a Telnet session (if over the network) or through a terminal emulator (if over the console or AUX port). Table 8-2 explains the authentication types.

The following sample statement illustrates a serial interface on an access server being configured to use TACACS+ to authenticate persons making PPP network connections:

```
MyAccessServer(config)#aaa new-model
MyAccessServer(config)#aaa authentication ppp MyList tacacs+ local
MyAccessServer(config)#interface serial0
MyAccessServer(config-if)#ppp authentication pap MyList
MyAccessServer(config)#tacacs-server host 10.1.13.10
MyAccessServer(config)#tacacs-server key DoNotTell
```

The **aaa new-model** command activates (enables) the AAA inside the device's IOS software. Then the statement specifies that a TACACS+ security protocol be used and that the local user database should be used if the TACACS+ server fails to respond. The **interface serial0** command points the configuration to all lines on the access server's serial network interface named serial0. The **ppp authentication pap MyList TACACS+ local** command specifies that the PAP password protocol be used for PPP connections and applies the named method list **MyList** to be used as the test.

The next statement specifies that the TACACS+ server resides on the host computer at IP address 10.1.13.10. The next line specifies that the encryption key **DoNotTell** be

IOS Command Keyword	AAA Authentication Type
Login	Line connections made to Ethernet or Token Ring network interfaces using Telnet, or to console or AUX ports using virtual terminal (VTY)
PPP	Dial-in line connections made to serial network interfaces using Point-to-Point Protocol
SLIP	Dial-in line connections made to serial network interfaces using Serial Line Internet Protocol
ARAP	Dial-in line connections made to serial network interfaces using AppleTalk Remote Access Protocol

Table 8-2.   Entity Types Secured by AAA Authentication Methods

used for all communications between the security server and the client access device being configured here. The shared encryption key also must be configured on the security server(s) with which the client access device will communicate.

> **NOTE**   Three types of protocols play a major role in AAA: dial-in protocols such as PPP, security protocols such as RADIUS, and password protocols such as CHAP. Dial-in protocols are network protocols that handle signals over phone lines, keeping the IP packets together between the access server and the remote user. Security protocols provide the client-server messaging system to the centralized user database. Password protocols are relatively simple mechanisms to deal with the person logging in. Some dial-in protocols incorporate their own password protocol—ARAP, for example.

AAA Authorization Methods and Types   AAA has seven methods for authorization. There are actually eight, but the **none** method is a request not to do any authorization procedure. Table 8-3 explains the AAA authorization methods. Each method is a keyword for use as an argument with the root **aaa authorization** command. These, in turn, are applied to secured entity types.

IOS Command Keyword	AAA Authorization Method
Group TACACS+	Sends a message requesting authorization information from the TACACS+ server.
Group RADIUS	Sends a message requesting authorization information from the RADIUS server.
If-authenticated	Allows access to the requested function if the user has already been authenticated. (*If* here is the word *if*, as in "depending on," not the mnemonic IOS uses for network interface in the config prompt.)
Local	Uses the local user database to execute the authorization program.
Krb5-instance	Uses an instance defined in the Kerberos instance map.
Cache *group name*	Authorizes using a cache server group.
Group *group name*	Authorizes using a subset of RADIUS or TACACS+ servers for accounting as defined by the **server group** *group-name* command.
None	Does not execute any authorization methods on this access device.

Table 8-3.   AAA's Eight Named Methods for User Authentication

As mentioned, RADIUS and TACACS+ can coexist on the same access device. Depending on the connection being attempted and how the device is configured, the client will query either the RADIUS or the TACACS+ servers, which are separate user databases.

The **if-authenticated** command waives authorization if the user has already been authenticated elsewhere. This is important, because during a single session a user may make dozens of connections to entities secured by AAA authorization (such as IOS command modes), and it would be unwieldy for the client device to query the TACACS+ or RADIUS server each time.

Generally, a device's local user database contains only usernames and passwords. Remember that network devices don't have hard disks, and they must store permanent information in NVRAM memory, already burdened with storing a boot image of IOS and even daily AAA accounting logs. For this reason, local user databases generally do not hold authorizations for users. Therefore, if a security server were unavailable when a user logged in, that person would likely be unable to access any services configured to require authorization. Figure 8-12 shows how a local user database coexists with the server database(s).

If no authorization is to be executed on a secured entity, this should be explicitly configured by using the **none** command. Otherwise, the IOS software will automatically put the default authorization methods into force. The five types of secured objects to which AAA authorization methods can be applied are explained in Table 8-4.

The five authorization entity types can be broken down into two pairs:

- The EXEC and Command methods each deal with access to IOS commands.

- The Network and Reverse Access methods both deal with connections, but those that go in different directions.

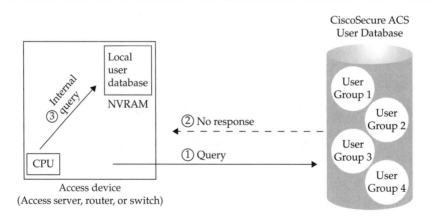

Figure 8-12.   A user database can be stored in the access device's NVRAM for local use.

Type	AAA Authorization Type
Network	Applies method to network-related service requests, including direct login connections (via console or AUX), Telnet connections (via IP or IPX), or dial-in connections (via PPP, SLIP, or ARAP).
Reverse Telnet	Applies method to Telnet sessions in which the user attempts to connect from the secured access device to another host—a common maneuver by a hacker who has broken into a network device.
EXEC	Applies method to sessions in the User EXEC command mode and can be applied by user, date, and start and stop times.
Commands	Applies method to restrict access to specific commands. Command methods must be applied to an IOS command-level group. There are two default groups: numbers 0 and 15 (user EXEC and privileged EXEC modes, respectively). The Command method can be applied by user, date, and start and stop times.
Configuration	Downloads the configuration from the AAA server.

Table 8-4. IOS's Five Authorization Types

On Cisco access devices, the **aaa authorization config-commands** command is enabled by default. That way, the device has security right out of the box, in case the administrator installs it without configuring security. The following example statement illustrates a router being configured to require authorization for any type of network connection. This would apply, for example, whether the connection was being made through a console TTY login, a Telnet VTY login, or a PPP dial-in login:

```
MyRouter(config)#aaa new-model
MyRouter(config)#aaa authorization network NetTeam group tacacs+ local
```

The preceding command specifies that the TACACS+ security protocol be used to check users against the NetTeam named method list and to use the local user database for backup. By default, this authorization is applied to all network interfaces on the device (as opposed to authentication methods, which must be applied to specific lines).

But, as mentioned earlier, sometimes having authorizations stored on the device itself isn't practical. To accommodate this, the restriction could be loosened using the **none** command to allow a network connection if the TACACS+ server fails to respond:

```
MyRouter(config)#aaa authorization network NetTeam group TACACS+ none
```

In the preceding command, the user's identity must have already been authenticated with a password to get this far into the AAA configuration. The **none** command goes into effect only when the TACACS+ server fails to respond. The following code statement configures a somewhat more sophisticated authorization:

```
MyRouter(config)#aaa authorization commands 15 SeniorTechs group TACACS+
MyRouter(config)#line vty 0 5
MyRouter(config-line)#authorization commands 15 SeniorTechs
```

The preceding statement shows an example of configuration by line, as opposed to network interface. Here, the six virtual terminal (VTY) lines are secured. In this example, the named method list SeniorTechs is declared as necessary for an administrator to use IOS command level 15 in this device. We mentioned earlier that the IOS **level** command can be employed to authorize the use of a group of commands. By default, all Privileged EXEC mode commands are grouped into level 15, and all User EXEC mode commands are grouped into level 0. Therefore, the preceding code snippet specifies that only administrators with user profiles configured with the SeniorTechs attributes will be permitted to use the Privileged EXEC commands.

Accounting Methods and Types   AAA accounting methods configure user activities to be tracked within a secured access device. Accounting methods gather data from TACACS+ and RADIUS packets and log it. Table 8-5 explains how the two work.

Notice that the only accounting methods are the security protocols themselves. This is because accounting data is, by default, collected for the entire device. The reason for the two methods is that the accounting data must travel either in TACACS+ or RADIUS packets to the server (AAA accounting isn't done without servers).

AAA has six secured accounting entity types, slightly different from those for authorization. Table 8-6 explains them.

The **system** accounting keyword only collects a default set of variables. It cannot be configured to collect only certain events. The reason for this is that a system event simply happens—a user does not request permission to cause it. An example of a system event would be a network interface going down at 11:32:28 Thursday, January 9, 2013. AAA accounting does not automatically associate the system event with a security transaction, but comparing accounting and authorization logs for that date and time would make it easy for a system administrator to figure out who the culprit was.

Command Keyword	AAA Accounting Method
TACACS+	Logs accounting information on TACACS+ in the CiscoSecure ACS database
RADIUS	Logs accounting information on RADIUS in the CiscoSecure ACS database

Table 8-5.   Accounting Methods

Command Keyword	AAA Accounting Type
Network	Applies the method to network connections, usually a PPP connection, but methods can also be named for logins, SLIP, or ARAP connections.
Auth-proxy	Provides information about all authenticated-proxy user events.
EXEC	Provides information on all User EXEC mode terminal sessions within the access device's IOS environment. EXEC accounting information can be collected by user, date, and start and stop times.
Commands	Provides information on any commands issued by users who are members of an IOS Privileged EXEC mode. Command accounting information can be collected by user, date, and start and stop times.
Connection	Provides information on all outbound connections attempted from the secured access device in sessions made using the Telnet, rlogin, TN270, PAD, and LAT terminal protocols.
System	Provides information about system-level events, such as reboots.

Table 8-6.   AAA Accounting Types That Track Asset Usage for Five Security Entity Types

Like authorization, AAA accounting named method lists must be applied to all network interfaces they are meant to secure and then applied to an indicated accounting type. For example, the command

```
MyRouter(config)#aaa accounting network group group name TACACS+
```

configures IOS to keep track of all SLIP and PPP connections made over a network interface that are authorized using TACACS+.

Accounting is a little more complicated in how it tracks requests, though. AAA accounting relies on so-called accounting notices to gather data. An *accounting notice* is a special packet notifying the accounting method of an event. This information is recorded in the accounting log file for upload to the appropriate security server. One of three AAA accounting keywords must be used to specify exactly when during the service request process the notices are to be sent. The terminology can get a bit confusing, but Figure 8-13 will help you visualize how the three work:

- **Stop-only**   For minimal accounting. Have RADIUS or TACACS+ send a stop recording accounting data notice at the *end* of the requested service. Stop-only accounting is good only for tracking who went where. This is important information for security purposes.

- **Start-stop**   For more accounting. Have RADIUS or TACACS+ send a start accounting notice at the *beginning* of the requested service and a stop accounting notice at the end of the service. Start-stop accounting yields the elapsed time of a connection.

- **Wait-start** For maximum accounting. Have RADIUS or TACACS+ wait until the start notice is received by AAA accounting *before* the user's request process begins. Most regard wait-start as overkill and an inconvenience to users, so its use is limited to highly sensitive services. This is used in older versions of IOS.

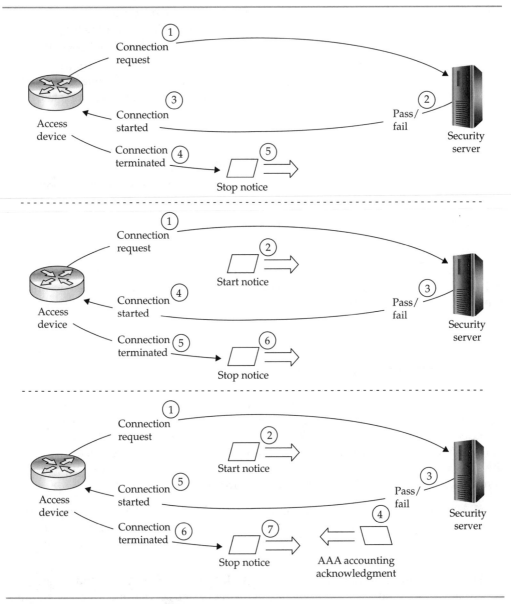

Figure 8-13. AAA accounting can use any of the three methods to track user activity.

To select a method, include any one of the three keywords as arguments to the root **aaa accounting** command in the configuration statement. The three options give differing levels of accounting control. For example, if an administrator requests entry into a secured device's User EXEC mode, the stop-only process records only the end of the administrator's session within User EXEC mode. The start-stop process records the beginning and the end of the session. The wait-start process ensures that no connection is made prior to the accounting notice having been received and acknowledged.

- **none**   No accounting
- **start-stop**   Record start and stop without waiting
- **stop-only**   Record stop when service terminates

The following example shows an AAA accounting configuration. Lines 2, 3, and 4 show all three AAA functions being configured together, the normal practice in the real world.

```
MyAccessServer(config)#aaa new-model
MyAccessServer(config)#aaa authentication login NetTeam local
MyAccessServer(config)#aaa authentication ppp RemoteWorkers group TACACS+
local
MyAccessServer(config)#aaa authorization network NetTeam group TACACS+ local
MyAccessServer(config)#aaa accounting network WeWillBillYou none
MyAccessServer(config)#
MyAccessServer(config)#tacacs-server host BigUnixBox
MyAccessServer(config)#tacacs-server key JustBetweenUs
MyAccessServer(config)#
MyAccessServer(config)#interface group-async 1
MyAccessServer(config-if)#group-range 1 16
MyAccessServer(config-if)#encapsulation ppp
MyAccessServer(config-if)#ppp authentication chap RemoteWorkers
MyAccessServer(config-if)#ppp authorization NetTeam
MyAccessServer(config-if)#ppp accounting WeWillBillYou
```

The accounting commands are woven in with the others to give you an idea of how statements really look. As configured here, full start-stop accounting records will be logged for all network connections made by the network team through any of the 16 asynchronous ports on the device, MyAccessServer.

Exactly what gets logged depends on how the named method list WeWillBillYou is configured. Most network managers, at a minimum, would use the **network** command to account for connection times. Generally speaking, the command-oriented parameters **exec** and **commands** are useful only for security audits.

RADIUS and TACACS+ Attributes

A security protocol is largely defined by the attributes it supports. After all, security tools define the raw material used to operate the user-based security system. RADIUS and

TACACS+ are separate protocols packaged into the AAA command structure within IOS. The major differences between the two come into play inside the user database, where each user has a security profile containing attributes that define what that person may do. As separate technologies, RADIUS and TACACS+ have their own attributes.

RADIUS is an open standard under the auspices of the IETF and defines nearly 60 attributes. We won't list them all here, but Table 8-7 shows several to help you see what's involved in user-based security.

RADIUS Attribute	Description
User-Name	The name of a person's user profile account. For example, Anne Marie's username might be "amarie."
User-Password	The secret passcode created by the person.
CHAP-Password	The encrypted value returned during the challenge-handshake exchange. This is the user name mixed with a random number called a *challenge*.
NAS-IP Address	The IP address of the access server requesting authentication. (Recall that NAS stands for *network access server*, the same thing as an access server.)
NAS-Port	The physical port number on the access server. This includes the various types of interfaces possible, such as asynchronous terminal lines, synchronous network lines, ISDN channels, and other types of interfaces.
Service-Type	The service requested or granted—for example, an administrator might request the **enable** command in IOS in order to enter the Privileged EXEC command mode.
Login-Port	The TCP port with which the user is to be connected—for example, port 80 for HTTP web browsing.
Acct-Session-Id	A unique accounting identifier used to match start and stop notices in an accounting log file.
Acct-Session-Time	The number of seconds the user remained connected.
Acct-Authentic	The way the user was authenticated, whether by RADIUS, the local user database, TACACS+, or Kerberos.

Table 8-7.   RADIUS Attributes Used to Enforce User-Based Security

Seventeen RADIUS attributes are so-called vendor-proprietary attributes. These are items that vendors can customize to extend functionality within their products. Table 8-8 shows a few Cisco extensions to give you an idea of what vendors like to customize.

TACACS+ has over 50 attributes (attribute-value pairs). Although TACACS+ and RADIUS both support the three AAA functions, TACACS+ is more sophisticated. For example, it has attributes such as Tunnel-ID to help secure VPN connections. This is why internetworks that use RADIUS for authenticating dial-in users will frequently use TACACS+ for authorization and accounting. Table 8-9 shows sample TACACS+ attributes to give you a feel for the protocol.

The sampling of AV pairs in Table 8-9 shows two areas in which TACACS+ is stronger than RADIUS. First, TACACS+ offers stricter internal security than RADIUS by locking down commands and access lists. The first thing a hacker would do upon breaking into an IOS device would be to make new entries into its access lists, which makes file transfers possible. These AV pairs not only help to stop hackers, they also let the network manager specify which devices, IOS commands, or access lists individual administrators may work with. Locking out certain team members helps avoid configuration errors.

The second area in which TACACS+ is stronger is protocol support. For example, TACACS+ has AV pairs to enhance security of VPNs, which are exploding in popularity. As would be expected, TACACS+ also has accounting attributes to go along with the areas where it expands beyond RADIUS. For example, the **cmd5x** AV pair lets you keep track of which IOS commands an administrator uses while working on a device. This can be useful information for diagnosing how a configuration error was made.

Cisco-Specific RADIUS Attribute	Description
Password-Expiration	Specifies a time interval or event that forces the user to create a new password.
IP-Direct	The Cisco device will bypass all routing tables and send packets directly to a specified IP address. For example, IP-Direct might be used to make sure a user's WAN connection goes through a firewall.
Idle-Limit	Specifies the maximum number of seconds any session may be idle.

Table 8-8.   Cisco Extensions to the RADIUS Standard

TACACS+ AV Pair	Description
service5x	Specifies the connection service to be authorized or accounted. For example, **aaa authorization service5ppp** would be used to authorize a person to make a remote PPP connection to a device. Another example would be **service5shell** to let an administrator get into a device's Privileged EXEC command mode.
protocol5x	A protocol is a subset of a service. For example, a PPP connection might use TN3270, VINES, Telnet, or other protocols. A key protocol nowadays is VPDN (Virtual Private Dialup Network). The AV pair **protocol5vpdn** would let a remote dial-in user establish an encrypted connection to the enterprise's VPN network.
routing5x	Specifies whether routing updates may be propagated through the interface used for the connection.
priv-lvl5x	Specifies the IOS command mode the person may use. For this to work, commands must first be grouped using the **level** command.
acl5x	Restricts connection access lists on a device. Connection access lists are also called *reflexive access lists* and are used to track sessions.
inacl5x, inacl#5x, outacl5x, outacl#5x	Four AV pairs restricting access to per-user inbound and outbound access lists placed on an interface.
tunnel-id	Specifies a username for establishing remote VPN connections.
gw-password5x	Specifies the password placed on the home gateway into the VPN. Must be used with **service5ppp** and **protocol5vpdn**.

Table 8-9.   TACACS+ Authentication and Authorization AV Pairs

Dynamic Access Lists

Let's take a quick look at access lists as they relate to TACACS+ and RADIUS. Access lists are normally used to filter traffic at the packet level. In other words, when a connection is attempted through a router interface, packet headers are inspected for prohibited IP addresses or application port numbers, and traffic is passed or blocked. These are called extended access lists, and they're discussed in Chapter 9. To review here, such access lists are *extended* in that they can filter based on network application port numbers and/or source/destination instead of just addresses. They're also called *static* extended access lists, because the **permit** and **deny** commands are blindly enforced, regardless of the user. To make an exception for a particular person, an administrator would need to go into the router's config file and edit the list for that interface.

Dynamic access lists are configured using so-called lock-and-key commands. By employing these, a user who would otherwise be blocked can be granted temporary access to a network or subnet through a Telnet session over the Internet.

The Telnet session is opened to a router configured for lock-and-key. The dynamic access list prompts the user for authentication information. As with other user-based security protocols, lock-and-key can be configured to check against a user database on the router itself (local) or against a user database maintained on a TACACS+ or RADIUS server. If authenticated, the user is automatically logged out of the Telnet session and can start a normal application, such as a browser.

Lock-and-Key Using a Local User Database

The following sequence of code snippets shows how lock-and-key could be configured on a router using a locally maintained user authentication file. To start, a particular network interface on the router is declared, along with a subnetted IP address. The **ip access-group** command places the just-named interface and networks under the control of access list 103:

```
MyRouter(config)#interface ethernet1
MyRouter(config-if)#ip address 209.198.208.30 255.255.255.0
MyRouter(config-if)#ip access-group 103 in
```

The keyword **in** specifies that access control be applied only to inbound connections (lock-and-key can also be used to restrict outbound connections).

In the following statement, the first entry of access list 103 allows only Telnet connections into the router. The second entry of access list 103 is ignored until lock-and-key is triggered whenever a Telnet connection has been established in the router. The keyword **dynamic** defines access list 103 as a dynamic (lock-and-key) list.

```
MyRouter(config)#access-list 103 permit tcp any host 209.198.207.2 eq telnet
MyRouter(config)#access-list 103 dynamic InCrowd timeout 60 permit ip any any
```

This is the key juncture. If so configured, an attempted Telnet connection to the router causes it to check against its local user database to see if the user and password are valid for lock-and-key access to the router. If validated, the **timeout 60 permit ip any any** statement gives the user 60 minutes to use the router as a connection between any two IP addresses.

Finally, an **autocommand** statement creates a temporary inbound access list entry (named InCrowd in the previous statement) at the network interface Ethernet1 and line 0 on the router. The temporary access list entry will time out after five minutes.

```
MyRouter(config)#line vty 0
MyRouter(config-line)#login local
MyRouter(config-line)#autocommand access-enable timeout 5
```

The temporary access list entry isn't automatically deleted when the user terminates the session. It will remain configured until the timeout period expires.

Dynamic access lists can also be configured to authenticate users against a user database maintained on either a TACACS+ or RADIUS server. This, in effect, turns a router into an access server through which a user can gain entry into an internetwork, but only by logging in through a Telnet session.

Best Practices

Cisco has some beefy security measures—and it shouldn't come as any surprise. As the company that arguably built the Internet, they have a huge stake in staying secure. But while they have put some solid measures in place to facilitate secure networks, it is ultimately up to you, the networking professional, to ensure that your own network is secure.

Cisco will help, but you have to take the ball and run with it. In addition to utilizing the tools provided with your Cisco gear, there are other procedures and habits that you should get used to making a part of your job. In this section, we'll talk about some of the things you can do to proactively stay on top of your network's security.

Reviewing Logs

Your Cisco security devices have a great tool that is somewhat of an afterthought to many professionals—security logs. Regrettably, these logs are often only used *after* an incident, when they can—and should—be reviewed regularly to check for any signs of trouble.

The Problem

There are many places on your network where security logs are generated, including:

- Routers
- Firewalls
- Intrusion detection and prevention systems
- Switches
- Clients
- Operating systems
- Applications

Ideally, you'll take time each day to examine those logs. The sorts of things you should look for include (but are not limited to):

- Password hacking
- Large numbers of login failures

- Malware attacks
- Port scans
- Denial-of-service attacks
- Excessive errors on network devices

But it's hard to make the time to review all those logs each day, especially when there is so much other work on your plate. It's like brushing your teeth: Take the time to do it now, or you'll have to make the time to visit the dentist.

Although there are plenty of obstacles to regularly reviewing logs, such as lack of staffing and logs located in disparate places, developing a plan to review those logs is an important way to get yourself in the habit.

The Plan

To begin, you first need to create a policy that will define what your organization wants to get out of log management. It sounds like the sort of advice you'd hear from a guy in a cheap suit at a business seminar at an airport hotel, but there is a good reason for it—the policy gives you and your organization guidance. Without it, there's no guarantee you and everyone else in your department won't be working toward the same goal.

To that end, generate a policy that addresses these details:

- Log generation
- Log storage
- Log analysis
- Log disposal

When you're deciding how to generate logs, be selective in the information you collect. Logs can be generated on hundreds of metrics. But if you are collecting things you don't need, then you're wasting time looking at that data. Data collected should match up with the objectives you've established in your policy.

Reviewing logs from your most critical systems is necessary. Less critical systems can be reviewed less often. Be sure to have a tool in place that will pull all your log information into a single location and then compare entries from different sources to identify relationships.

Some other security log tips:

- Secure your log archives. This is especially important if you're trying to reconstruct what led to a security incident or if—sorry to have to say it—litigation is involved.
- Make sure the clocks on all the systems from which logs are culled are synchronized. This is important when you're trying to make events from different systems match up.
- Revisit your log system often—make sure you're getting the data you need and review the data you're collecting to find out if there's anything you should be reviewing, but aren't.

Location	Log Entry
Traffic allowed on firewall	`Built...connection` `access-list...permitted`

Traffic blocked by firewall	`access-list...denied`
	`deny inbound`
	`deny...by`

Bytes transferred	`Teardown TCP connection ...duration ...` `bytes`
Bandwidth and protocol usage	`Limit...exceeded` `CPU utilization`
Detected attack activity	`Attack from`

User account changes	`User added`
	`User deleted`
	`User priv level changed`

Administrator access	`AAA user`
	`User...locked out`
	`Login failed`

Table 8-10.   Things to Look for in Your Security Logs

The Process

Tons of bits of data can be collected by your Cisco devices. Table 8-10 lists some of the things that should make you raise an eyebrow.

Securing Protocols

Routing provides the information needed to get traffic from part of a network to another and is highly scrutinized for security vulnerabilities. Securing the routing protocol is a very important—but often overlooked—part of routing security.

The following are some common methods of breaching routing protocol security.

Disrupting Peering

Peering disruption attacks are efforts to attempt to deny network resources to authorized network users. The good news is that these sorts of attacks are not very effective. Once the routing protocols realize that their route is not very efficient, they will rebuild the route. For instance, if a session exists between two Open Shortest Path First (OSPF) protocol routers, and a peering attack brings them down, they will—by their nature—rebuild the route once the attack has stopped.

Rigging Routing Information

A subtler way to attack a routing system is to attack the information carried within the routing protocol, including the topology and reachability information, in an effort to misdirect traffic. Normally, this sort of attack creates a denial of service or causes traffic to follow a path it normally wouldn't.

Misdirecting to Monitor

Organizations that routinely encrypt data when it passes through a public network might find themselves under attack because it is simply easier to redirect that traffic with false routing information than it is to break the encryption on the traffic stream.

Making Traffic Go Away

An attacker might just want to prevent traffic from getting to its rightful destination. To that end, they can create a black hole. The attacker can build a black hole by pulling traffic to the attacking machine and then simply discarding it.

NOTE   This is a riskier method of attack, because it exposes the host.

Solutions

The first place to protect from hackers is the routers themselves. It's easier for hackers to compromise routers that aren't sending out a lot of packets than it is to attack routers that have very active relationships with other routers.

In addition to the routers themselves, data can also be attacked on the wire. The best way to protect it is to authenticate routing protocol packets using Message Digest Algorithm 5 (MD5) or IP Security (IPSec) signatures.

Unauthorized devices added to the network are another source of concern, but can be protected against. When we talk about a cryptographic signature, there are three parts to it: the key, the routing data being transmitted, and the encryption hash. If the routing data has changes in transit, the receiver will not be able to receive the data, so the information will be discarded.

Physical Security

Technology not only makes the Internet possible in its functionality, but it has also added to the ability to keep it secure. But it isn't all on technology's shoulders. There are a number of things you can—and should—do to ensure that security exists even beyond your networking gear. It isn't just evildoers on the other end of the Internet who are causing difficulty.

Secret Agent Doyle

Physical security isn't very sexy. Sure, it's sexy when you watch a spy movie and Agent 009 quietly breaks into the Evil Megalomaniac's lair, gets around a series of laser sensors, attaches a gadget (that doubles as a cork screw) to the mainframe, and then downloads all that information in a matter of seconds. But in reality, physical security is sort of a humdrum task of making sure only authorized people have physical access to your systems.

The truth is that computers connected to the Internet are open to attack. Routers allow their passwords to be reset, server software–based security can be bypassed, and passwords can be stolen.

And not everyone breaking into a computer system is a cyber terrorist—they can just be a curious employee named Doyle who wants to poke around the system and try to give himself more access to his PCs. Another consideration isn't the pure evil or malevolence of someone breaking in in an effort to steal company secrets. Sometimes an employee might be trying to "help" by plugging in an unauthorized wireless access point so that they can use their laptop from the courtyard. Nice as it is to see them take the initiative, this can create a huge chink in your security armor.

Importance

Although we spend a lot of time talking about the mechanisms within Cisco gear to keep networks secure, all that is for naught if someone can walk in and get right to the computers and servers in your network. In fact, once the information has been downloaded, it can create an opening that hackers can keep using for years to come.

If an intruder can gain physical access to a server and access the server's hard drive, then they can reboot the server and install a new version of the operating system, establishing new rules for access. Once they've got access to the file system, they can extract a password file that gives the usernames and passwords to every user in the system.

 NOTE   This can be equally problematic when you realize that most people use the same password for the many different systems of which they are members. Compromise the password once, and likely a user's access to multiple systems has been compromised.

Locks

The popular answer to the question "What's mankind's greatest invention?" is always "the wheel." But "the lock" hardly ever gets mentioned, and that's unfortunate, because the lock does a lot of really important work—especially where the physical security of computer networks is involved.

We're not talking about something as simple as a padlock on the server room door. Although that's better than nothing, it's best to go beyond simple key locks. Keys can be lost, stolen, and copied—that creates a problem when you're trying to manage access to your servers. One disgruntled employee with a key can compromise the whole thing.

A better option is to use card access to get in the server room. Using a card access system (or a fob or a keypad) generates an audit trail. You will have a record of who went in to the server room—you can even set it up to allow access for certain people only at certain times.

It's also wrong to assume that all your servers are in one, central location. Branch offices might not have their own server room, and those servers might be sharing space with other equipment and be accessible by other employees. They might be in a corner of a closet, in the break room, or anywhere else they can be shoehorned in. Servers and other networking gear are built to standard specifications so that they will fit in a 19-inch rack, and those racks can be locked, thus keeping busy fingers away from them.

Keep Current on Your Devices

As much as we'd like to think that they are, no company is invulnerable to security risks—not even Cisco. Although they aren't bulletproof, they are responsive when threats are made to their products. Cisco's Product Security Incident Response Team (PSIRT) may conjure images of techies in dark sunglasses and white HAZMAT suits (emblazoned with the Cisco logo) sliding down a fire pole and rushing into the Ciscomobile, in response to a klaxon. But PSIRT is Cisco's measured response to security threats in its products.

The website shows two tabs:

- **Cisco Security Advisories**   This tab is a clearinghouse—listed from newest to oldest—of security vulnerabilities. It lists the title of the threat, the version it applies to, when it was first announced, and when it was last updated. Next to that information is space for six icons that indicate what methods Cisco is using to address the issue. The icons indicate how Cisco is communicating the advisory via the following:

  - Cisco Security Advisory
  - Cisco IPS Signature
  - Cisco Applied Mitigation Bulletin
  - Blog
  - Event Response
  - Alerts

  This tab is also searchable, so if there is a specific product or technology you need information about, you can narrow it down based on keywords.

- **Cisco Security Responses**   This tab provides a means to address less severe problems that affect network security or issues and that require a response to information posted to a public discussion forum. Cisco publishes these responses if a third party makes a public statement about a Cisco product vulnerability that Cisco has previously addressed or when the nature of the issue does not warrant the visibility of a Cisco Security Advisory.

NOTE   PSIRT isn't unique to Cisco. Many tech companies have their own Product Security Incident Response Teams to address newly discovered security threats.

To keep up on Cisco's PSIRT, you can visit their website (they maintain a list of all their PSIRT efforts). It can be found at www.cisco.com/go/psirt.

It goes without saying (and is certainly a cliché) that network security is extremely important and necessary. However, understanding that security is important and understanding how to actually implement it are two different things. To be sure, an entire book could be (and many have been) written on the subject of network security in general and Cisco security in particular. The objective of this chapter was to show you various details behind some of the important components in securing your internetwork. In Chapter 9, we'll talk about some specific tools Cisco offers in the realm of network access and security.

CHAPTER 9 | Access Control

Although Cisco's bread and butter is in the world of making the physical boxes that make internetworks work, there are also important technologies going on under the hoods of those devices. In addition to the few pounds of silicon and steel, there's also a fair amount of software and brainpower behind how those devices work.

In this chapter, we'll take a closer look at some of that brainpower and how it has been applied to keep your networks safe.

Cisco SecureX Architecture

Oh, how times have changed. In the past, employees would show up to work, sit down at their desks, break out their pencils, and get ready for the day. Then the computer revolution came along and those same workers found computers on their desks. These days, workers come in and they've got not only their company-issued desktop or laptop computer, but also smartphones and tablet computers. And that has changed the demands of network security.

In its 2011 Annual Security Report, Cisco notes: "Ten years ago, employees were assigned laptops and told not to lose them. They were given logins to the company network, and told not to tell anyone their password. End of security training. Today, your 'millennial' employees—the people you want to hire because of the fresh ideas and energy they can bring to your business—show up to their first day on the job toting their own phones, tablets, and laptops, and expect to integrate them into their work life. They also expect others—namely, IT staff and chief information officers— to figure out how they can use their treasured devices, anywhere and anytime they want to, without putting the enterprise at risk. Security, they believe, is not really their responsibility: They want to work hard, from home or the office, using social networks and cloud applications to get the job done, while someone else builds seamless security into their interactions."

Overview

We're definitely changing the way we do business, and Cisco recognizes a need to change the way network security is delivered. To address the dynamic needs of network security, Cisco introduced SecureX.

The main goal of SecureX is to make networks more aware of policy and threats, no matter where the threats to the endpoint reside. SecureX distributes security and interweaves it into the network fabric, along with bringing in context-aware security intelligence.

There are many changes to network security that SecureX was developed to counter, including:

- **BYOD**   Bring Your Own Device (BYOD) describes the current state of technology where the endpoint isn't just the company-issued PC or laptop. Rather, with smartphones and tablets more prevalent, these devices are finding their way into corporate networks. And it isn't just so that workers can check their e-mail or play *Angry Birds*—they are performing work on those devices. They probably aren't using those devices while sitting at their desks, but they can whip them out in the break room, on a business trip, or even during their commute. The point is, these devices and their functionality are out there, and SecureX aims to keep your network secure even with these devices in the mix.

- **Virtualization and cloud computing**   In years past, your organization's data was maintained on a few pieces of humming equipment locked away in the server room. That's not the case anymore—and for good reason. Where data is located isn't as important as its availability. With a growing trend toward green IT, thus resulting in lower energy costs (as well as operational costs) to the organization, more and more of those ubiquitous server rooms are no longer growing in size—in fact, they're moving out of the building completely. But as servers are being virtualized and outsourced to the cloud, there comes a new set of security concerns.

- **Network traffic**   Rich media has caused an explosion in network traffic. This video data isn't just for fun, it's necessary for online collaboration. On top of that, remote users need access to the data center, thus driving up the demand on network resources.

- **Crafty hackers**   When a new piece of technology comes out, it falls to the networking professional to know how it works—especially its security features. Regrettably, not all networking professionals can keep up on all the bells and whistles of their new toys—but hackers can (and they do). After all, it's their job. As change comes to networks, the bad guys keep up on the ins and outs of network security, for their benefit.

When networks change—especially at a fundamental level—there is only so much that traditional network security can do to keep things protected. Because the face of computing has changed so much in recent years, there is a need to manage security in the face of those new technologies, like cloud computing, virtualization, and mobile computing. To mitigate those threats, security has to move its focus from IP addresses and ports, and security policies need to fall more in line with business rules.

To that end, Cisco has added context-aware security features to its ASA CX firewall lineup.

Cisco SecureX Framework

SecureX is built in to a number of Cisco's recent devices. As a collective, SecureX gathers and analyzes data before applying it to your network's needs. It does its work based on three core pillars:

- Cisco Security Intelligence Operations (SIO)
- Context-aware policy and enforcement
- Integrated network and security management

Cisco Security Intelligence Operations (SIO)

Cisco has tweaked its approach to network security. Rather than simply looking at a lone attack, they are instead looking at the attacker. Because attacks are dynamic and constantly changing, examining the attacks is more of a reactive response. Rather, global correlation is Cisco's new approach.

Cisco likens it to police at the scene of a crime. They don't just talk to one witness; they talk to as many as possible to find out what really happened. Also, some witnesses are more (or less) credible than others, so their account of what happened is weighed accordingly.

To that end, Cisco developed its global Security Intelligence Operation (SIO), which has the following features:

- 1TB of data received each day.

- 700,000 globally linked sensors constantly monitor e-mail, web traffic, IPS, and firewalls, sharing their data.

- Over US$100 million spent in threat R&D.

- 500 PhDs and engineers worldwide working around the clock.

- Over 8 million rule updates and 7,000 signatures.

This information is distilled into a metric that is used by Cisco's IPS devices. Those devices are also part of the global intelligence network, sharing what they learn and adding to the SIO information database.

SIO provides insight into real-time security threats, as well as a database of threat information that's more than 10 years old. Threat data is collected and analyzed by a series of Cisco security operations centers, spanning more than 750,000 network, web, and email collection points.

NOTE Although Cisco's IPS and firewall devices have been providing information to SIO, the addition of AnyConnect allows as many as 150 million endpoint-scanning elements to contribute data to SIO.

Using this information, SIO can analyze potential new treats, looking for such things as:

- Brand-new websites, with the URL only being registered a couple days earlier
- URLs hosted in Russia
- URLs in hostile e-mails
- Domain typos
- SPAM blacklists
- Numbers being used instead of letters in the domain
- Senders using dynamic IP addresses

Although none of these are instantly indicative of a dangerous site, they are issues that should be considered and added to the overall threat level of a questionable site. SIO also weighs positive factors in their overall ranking of a potential threat. Sites are ranked between –10 and +10.

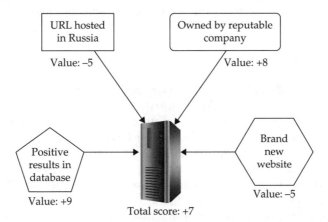

Cisco IPS adds anomaly detection and visibility into all major protocols with their anti-evasion techniques. If it all looks good, the information is passed along to Cisco's signature analysis engine, which scans for network, operating system, and application vulnerabilities.

Context-Aware Policy and Enforcement

At an organizational level, SecureX ties security policies to business operations based on five parameters:

- User identity
- Application
- Access device
- User and device location
- Time of access

The policies are dynamic, which means that security policies will adapt and change as those context parameters change. Further, those policies can be applied across all access methods (wireless, local, or VPN), and once a device has been authenticated and meets the security policy, anywhere that device is used (or a user accesses the network), those security policies will be applied. Whereas SIO provides global context for security threats, TrustSec (discussed later in this chapter) provides local context for security.

Integrated Network and Security Management

Once all these network security components are in place, SecureX also gives you a way to manage your security details. The security management tools allow network administrators to deploy specialized security, where needed, and provide a means of monitoring security controls from other network management tools.

Identity Management

Previously, in Chapter 8, we laid out the two types of network security. Traffic-based security is exactly what it sounds like: security based on allowing or denying network traffic to and from specific segments within internetworks. User-based security can be a modest undertaking, such as creating a user ID and a password to be manually entered by a user, or a far more complicated subject involving large, centralized repositories of users and devices. In this chapter, we'll go further in depth and describe how the different varieties of Cisco Secure Access Control Server (ACS), Network Admission Control (NAC), and the new Identity Services Engine (ISE) work separately, or together, to provide both of these pieces across your internetwork. These tools are all part of a group of tools that form Cisco's TrustSec solution, which—in marketing terms—is an "intelligent access control solution" that utilizes "contextual" security information to control access to resources.

What is contextual security information? *Context* is usually defined as words that help describe another word, so what Cisco means here is information that helps describe another piece of information. A user's ID, their group memberships, their PC's group memberships, where they are entering the network (Wi-Fi, VPN, or LAN), and what resources they are attempting to access within the network are all pieces of information assembled to formulate an accept or deny response by the network to that user.

NOTE   Cisco is all about the context. You'll note that that word is used throughout the TrustSec solution, SecureX framework, and all other security nomenclature produced by Cisco. The first time we heard the term *context* from Cisco was several years ago, and the now-retired PIX firewall had a feature added to it called a "context." In the context of a PIX or ASA, the "context" is considered a logical segmentation of the firewall; however, in the context of Cisco's security architecture, "context" has a different context altogether.

Cisco has embedded TrustSec software services into network gear beyond the ASA firewall line so that nearly every switch, router, and wireless controller understands and can participate in some part of the TrustSec solution. Of course, unless one deploys the latest and greatest Nexus switches, the newest security services and features aren't available. For example, Security Group ACLs are not available on all network devices.

Cisco TrustSec

The Cisco TrustSec intelligent access control solution combines the deployment of ACS, NAC, and ISE to provide granular control of traffic within a Cisco-based internetwork, utilizing real-time, identity-based contextual security information.

TrustSec allows for the following:

- Identity-aware networking
- Compatibility with 802.1x
- Role-based grouping of devices and users
- Policy-based network control
- Utilization of Active Directory or other LDAP sources
- Utilization of AAA databases
- Data confidentiality utilizing 802.1AE (a.k.a. MACsec)
- Internetwork device AES encryption (when using Nexus switches)
- Security group tags (SGT) that tag each packet with identity information
- Security group access control lists (SGACLs) that allow or deny packets based on SGT

Table 9-1 shows a list of TrustSec-enabled devices.

Switches	Catalyst 2960 Series
	Catalyst 3560 Series
	Catalyst 3750 Series
	Catalyst 4500 Series
	Catalyst 6500 Series
	Nexus 7000 Series
	Nexus 5000 Series
	Nexus 2000 Series
LAN Controllers	Wireless LAN Controllers
Routers	Integrated Services Router—Generation 2 (ISR-G2)
	Cisco ASR 1000 Series Aggregation Services Routers

Table 9-1.   Devices Supporting TrustSec

Cisco Secure Access Control Server (ACS)

ACS has been a stalwart companion of Cisco network administrators since around 1992. Having been originally developed for the Solaris platform, ACS only supported TACACS+. A Windows version was created and sold under the name EasyACS in 1997—again only supporting TACACS+. Version 2 saw a renaming to the current Cisco Secure ACS moniker (for both Unix and Windows NT) and the addition of RADIUS.

Although they shared a revision number and a name, they retained separate development teams until the year 2000. As such, their interfaces had diverged. ACS for Unix's WebUi was AAA protocol driven, requiring an in-depth knowledge of AAA. ACS for Windows was more user friendly, allotting internetwork administrators a menu-driven WebUi and the ability to configure much of the ACS system without knowing AAA in extreme detail. With the dawning of version 3.1, we saw an integration of both features and the browser-based interface, and ACS for Unix was depreciated.

ACS for Windows 3.2 added the concept of Network Admission Control (NAC). With version 4 we saw ACS *appliances* for the first time. Called "Solution Engines," these devices were among the first in a long line of management servers developed and sold by Cisco. Generally speaking, at that time they were partnerships with OEM server suppliers. The Cisco Secure Access Control Server Solution Engine 4.0 was a Windows-based "appliance." The customer didn't have to provide Windows software or licensing, nor did they have to provide the hardware (Cisco handled that piece via OEM license agreements).

Some of this OEM'ing is still occurring today, but by and large Cisco has developed its own line of x86-based servers (a.k.a. Solution Engines) that we see deployed within security management and other areas of the Cisco product line. Time went by with no major changes to ACS; .dot revisions added features but the package wasn't changed significantly until recently. There was a diverging of the code base within ACS, with the advent of version 3.2, because there was a major push by Cisco to migrate as many customers as possible to the Windows version.

Fast-forward a few years to today: Similar to most modern Enterprise IT platforms, ACS software developers (or perhaps their management) have recognized the power and flexibility of Linux and have begun to shift back to a Unix-based system. ACS is once again a Unix-based system; however, this time its developed for Linux.

The ACS Solution Engines, as well as the VMWare soft appliances produced by Cisco on version 5.4, both run on top of a Linux-based OS. The Windows versions are on their way out the door. Unless an extension is granted, support for ACS for Windows 4.2 ends in 2014. Table 9-2 describes all the current flavors of ACS and their purpose.

ACS is still marketed for its original purpose, but several varieties of identity management solutions are available from Cisco, depending on how and what you need to authorize onto what parts of your network.

Version	Description
Cisco Secure ACS View	Software reporting tool for Windows Server and VMWare ESX. EOL (end of life)
Cisco Secure ACS 4.2	Ex-flagship product that featured new Extensible Authentication Protocol (EAP) options. Cisco Secure ACS for Windows EOL
Cisco Secure ACS 5.4	Appliance or VMWare template Rule-based policy-model allowing network access control based on dynamic network conditions Linux based Integrates view

Table 9-2.   Cisco Secure ACS Versions

Cisco Network Admission Control (NAC)

The most significant feature additions to ACS came when the security landscape began to shift from the simple user-based identification everyone was familiar with to a more comprehensive view of the threatscape—desktop machines became as much a threat as compromised user accounts.

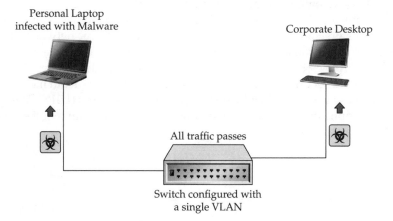

With the advent of machine compromise, Network Admission Control (NAC) was added to ACS in order for ACS to function as a central authentication source for machines and users. Port-based MAC authentication of devices was the first step. A switch that has its ports configured with this feature will disable those ports when a device is connected that is not authorized to do so. This eliminates a fair amount of threat from one's own network ports, behind the Internet firewalls, but all too often a corporate resource that is compromised is allowed onto the network.

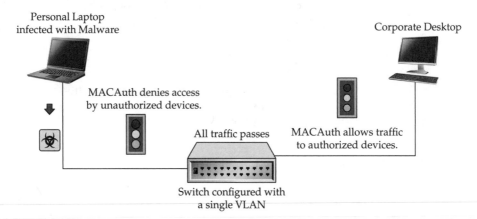

The next step up the security ladder is to validate that those machines aren't compromised in any way by using Network Admission Control to a higher degree. NAC allows switches deployed in corporate offices to ask the ACS server permission for computers to attach to the network via MAC authentication. A NAC-enabled switch can also dynamically place that device into a "remediation" VLAN prior to actually allowing that device onto the production internetwork.

While residing on the remediation VLAN, a NAC appliance can scan that device for a list of items preconfigured by the NAC administrator. This network admission prerequisite list could consist of nothing more than an operating system version scan for inventory purposes, or a far more complicated scan that determines if that PC has all the required security software the corporation's security team has specified. Antivirus database updates, Host Intrusion Prevention Services (HIPS), Windows service packs, application patches, a hostname, Windows domain membership, and anything that NAC administrator needs to look for before allowing that device on the production VLAN can be discovered prior to the device being allowed onto the production network, where a compromised PC could infect or attack the other computers.

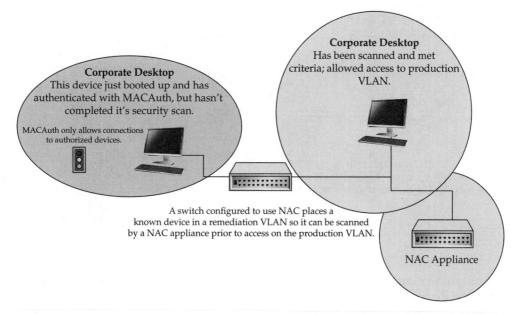

Corporate Desktop
Has been scanned and met criteria; allowed access to production VLAN.

Corporate Desktop
This device just booted up and has authenticated with MACAuth, but hasn't completed it's security scan.

MACAuth only allows connections to authorized devices.

A switch configured to use NAC places a known device in a remediation VLAN so it can be scanned by a NAC appliance prior to access on the production VLAN.

NAC Appliance

The NAC server can take one of several actions, depending on the results of its scan. It can simply report the noncompliance and allow the device, it can deny the noncompliant device, or it can trigger an automated response from a company's PC management system (LanDesk or Altiris, for example)—or any combination of those.

Alerting the PC management system for remediation is the gold standard to be reached for—it is the pinnacle of automation. Once that device has been updated, the PC management system can notify the NAC server to rescan it for access to the production network. Once this system of automation is in place, all the NAC administrator or desktop staff must do is maintain the patch database and watch the logs. In theory, they no longer need to lose sleep about the security of their PCs.

Once the device is granted a status of "clean," the NAC server will tell the switch it's okay to migrate that device from the remediation VLAN to the production internetwork VLAN.

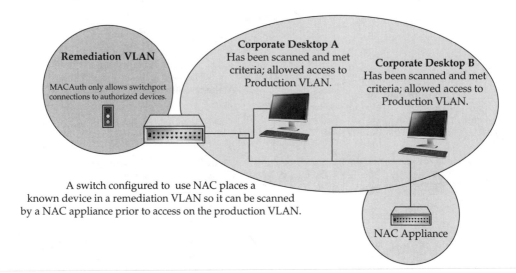

A switch configured to use NAC places a known device in a remediation VLAN so it can be scanned by a NAC appliance prior to access on the production VLAN.

Here's a simple analogy: The true purpose of NAC can be thought of as using MAC address authentication before a device is allowed into the parking garage of a condo where the device was invited to a party, and then having a household robot come by to make sure its shoes are clean, that it's wearing the "happy birthday" shirt mailed out with the invitation (it *is* a surprise party), and that the device isn't carrying a contagion (or a weapon) before it is allowed into the house to join the party.

Identity Services Engine (ISE)

ACS created a central database for authentication and allows for filtering on RADIUS or TACACS+ permissions and basic Network Access Roles (NAR) creation. NAC goes a few steps further and validates a device's security posture as it's powering up and attempting to connect to the network. Between these two security devices, your edge network is covered fairly well.

These things are great, but what about all the other devices in the middle of your network? Typical IP traffic flows from end user station (endpoint) to server and back again. How many devices does that traffic pass through in a typical internetwork? For example, you have a switch at a branch clinic connected to a router or ASA that connects the branch with the corporate data center for the hospital. In turn, it is connected to perhaps one or more switches or routers before the user's requested intranet resources are connected to a website, e-mail server, or IP telephony server.

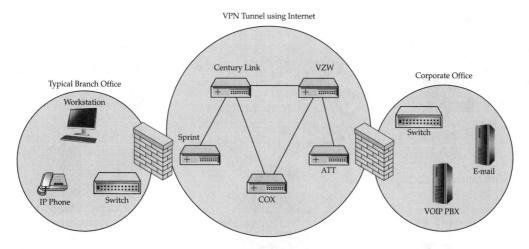

The key thought in the previous paragraph is that there are one, two, or even dozens of devices in the "middle" of that IP conversation. Why should all of those devices simply pass the traffic? Why shouldn't they be more intelligent? Usually core network devices sit (mostly) idle. When an intranetwork is designed, it's designed for peak traffic patterns, which is 5 percent of the week, generally during the A.M. rush and in the middle of the night when server backups are run.

This leaves an enormous amount of underutilized resources within those expensive, corporate assets. If those devices were allowed to assist in the security of the network, wouldn't that make them that much more valuable? The idea behind the Identity Services Engine is the core of Cisco's SecureX framework—every piece of network equipment should be able to assist in some way with internetwork security. This idea isn't new, but it certainly wasn't possible until now, considering the low cost of high-performance CPUs built in to network equipment today, which simply didn't exist 20 years ago.

The ISE is a policy-driven security clearinghouse. Whereas ACS and NAC are very specific about source, destination, and where you enter the network, ISE concerns itself with which traffic patterns are allowed once you enter the network. An example is a medical records server that should only be accessible to doctors at your branch clinic, and not the lab technicians. ACS can allow a corporate-owned Wi-Fi laptop onto the network, NAC can make sure that device is clean, but the Identity Services Engine can tell every switch, router, and firewall beyond that clinic's branch switch whether it's a doctor's laptop or lab technician's, and whether or not that traffic pattern is allowed.

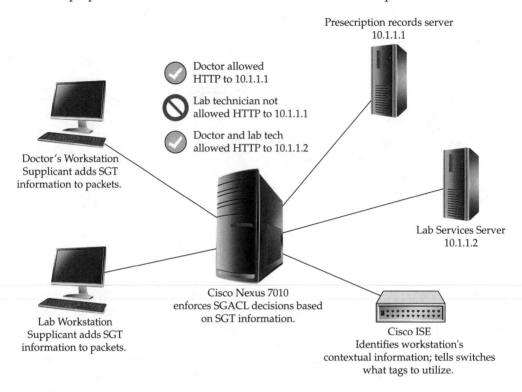

The Access Lists

The simplest form of network security technology is the access list. It's not much of a firewall anymore, but it is certainly useful in a variety of situations. Also called an *access control list (ACL)*, or *filter*, the access list is a basic component of any firewall's configuration. As the name implies, the access list restricts certain traffic from gaining access to a network. It provides a basic level of network security by filtering packets according to these criteria:

- **Source and destination IP address** The IP address from which the packet originated and is addressed

- **Source and destination port number** The port number from which the packet originated and is addressed

- **Source and destination protocol number** The protocol number from which the packet originated or is addressed

Cisco calls these *extended access lists*—the extension being the port number, protocol number (source and/or destination), and/or destination IP address. Early Cisco products used only source addresses, which were referred to as *standard access lists*. But don't be misled by this terminology: Extended access lists are the basic type of access lists being used now.

NOTE Port numbers (also called *network ports* or just *ports*) aren't physical interface ports like S0 or E3. Messages sent using the TCP or UDP transport-layer protocols (layer 4) use port numbers to identify which application protocol the transmission will run. For example, the number for HTTP (WWW) is port 80; SMTP's port is 25; and FTP's port is 20 and 21.

Network administrators create access lists in the router's configuration file. One access list is created for each network interface. If an interface handles traffic in multiple network protocols—for example, IP, IPX, and Bonjour—each network protocol has its own access list format. Therefore, a separate access list must be created for each protocol to run over that network interface. Regardless of the network protocol used, each criterion (access rule) occupies a line on the list. Figure 9-1 depicts how access lists work. This example uses a router restricting the flow of traffic between departments within an organization.

As each packet attempts to enter an interface, its header is examined to see if anything matches the access list. The router is looking for positive matches. Once it finds a match, no further evaluations are performed. If the rule matched is a *permit* rule, the packet is forwarded out a network interface on the other side of the router. If the matched rule is a *deny*, the packet is dropped right there at the interface.

If a packet's evaluation runs all the way to the bottom of the access list without a match, it is dropped by default. This mechanism is called the *implicit deny rule*, which provides an added measure of security by dealing with conditions not anticipated in the access list.

The router evaluates the packet one rule at a time, working its way from the top line to the bottom. The bottom part of Figure 9-2 is an example taken from a router's access list. Each line in the list is a rule that either permits or denies a specific type of traffic. The top of Figure 9-2 charts the parts of a rule's statement, starting with the **access-list** command followed by various modifiers. Keep in mind that this example is for IP; syntax varies slightly for IPX, Bonjour, and other non-IP network protocols.

A cohesive access list is created by using a common access list name at the beginning of each statement for an IP access list. Each statement must declare a transport protocol, such as the Transmission Control Protocol (TCP), the User Datagram Protocol (UDP), or the Internet Control Messaging Protocol (ICMP). If the rule involves a network application, the statement must first declare a transport protocol and end with the application protocol. In the sample rule at the top of Figure 9-2, the transport protocol is TCP, and the application protocol is HTTP.

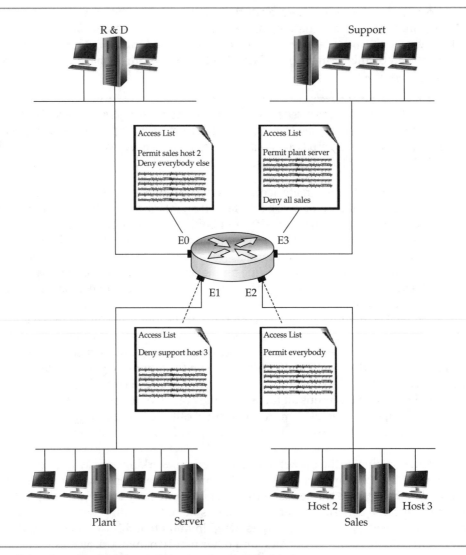

Figure 9-1. An access list filters packets at each router interface.

Keep in mind that ACLs can have other protocols as well:

- **AHP**   Authentication Header Protocol
- **EIGRP**   Cisco's Enhance Interior Gateway Routing Protocol (EIGRP) routing protocol
- **ESP**   Encapsulation Security Payload

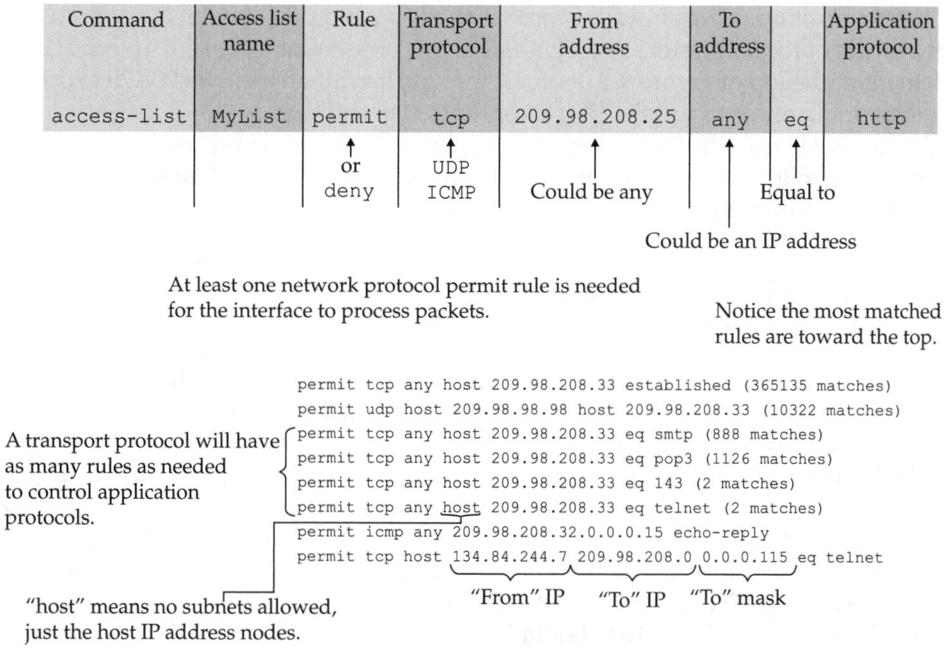

Command	Access list name	Rule	Transport protocol	From address	To address		Application protocol
access-list	MyList	permit	tcp	209.98.208.25	any	eq	http

or
deny

UDP
ICMP

Could be any

Equal to

Could be an IP address

At least one network protocol permit rule is needed
for the interface to process packets.

Notice the most matched
rules are toward the top.

A transport protocol will have
as many rules as needed
to control application
protocols.

```
permit tcp any host 209.98.208.33 established (365135 matches)
permit udp host 209.98.98.98 host 209.98.208.33 (10322 matches)
permit tcp any host 209.98.208.33 eq smtp (888 matches)
permit tcp any host 209.98.208.33 eq pop3 (1126 matches)
permit tcp any host 209.98.208.33 eq 143 (2 matches)
permit tcp any host 209.98.208.33 eq telnet (2 matches)
permit icmp any 209.98.208.32.0.0.0.15 echo-reply
permit tcp host 134.84.244.7 209.98.208.0 0.0.0.115 eq telnet
```

"From" IP   "To" IP   "To" mask

"host" means no subnets allowed,
just the host IP address nodes.

Figure 9-2. Access list statements are security rules.

- **GRE** Cisco's Generic Routing Encapsulation (GRE) tunneling
- **ICMP** Internet Control Message Protocol
- **IGMP** Internet Gateway Message Protocol
- **IP** Any Internet Protocol
- **IPINIP** IP in IP tunneling
- **NOS** KA9Q NOS compatible IP over IP tunneling
- **OSPF** Open Shortest Path First (OSPF) routing protocol
- **PCP** Payload Compression Protocol
- **PIM** Protocol Independent Multicast
- **TCP** Transmission Control Protocol
- **UDP** User Datagram Protocol

To apply a rule to incoming traffic, you must put the outside host's IP address in the *from* position, which always precedes the *to* position. This order is reversed so as to restrict outbound traffic. The modifier **any** is used to indicate all networks. The statement at the top of Figure 9-2, then, is saying, "Permit host 209.98.208.25 to access any network in order to run the HTTP application over TCP."

The access list is activated on an interface by using the **access-group** command, as shown in the following code snippet. The first line "points" the IOS to serial0 interface, and the second line applies access list 100 to all incoming traffic trying to enter through serial0:

```
MyRouter(config)#interface serial0
MyRouter(config-if)#ip access-group 100 in
```

Routers look for matches between packet header content and the interface's access list. A catch would be a source address, destination address, protocol, or port number. If the matched rule is a permit rule, the packet is forwarded. If, however, a deny rule is matched, the packet is dropped without evaluating against any rules further down the list.

An access list can have as many filtering rules as desired, with the practical limit being the amount of router memory you wish to use for security filtering instead of productive routing. Because access list rules are evaluated from top to bottom, the most frequently encountered matches should be put toward the top of the list so as not to waste router CPU cycles.

Keep in mind that an access list alone doesn't turn a router into a firewall. The majority of access lists are used for basic traffic management within internetworks. However, you could physically configure a router as a choke point so that all traffic must pass an access list, thereby making it into a lightweight firewall. This is frequently done to restrict access among networks making up an internetwork. In fact, standard IOS has dozens of security-oriented commands beyond the **access-list** command that are also used in Cisco's firewall products. However, relying on the access list as the centerpiece of a firewall configuration results in questionable security.

Network Address Translation

Cisco's IOS software has a capability called Network Address Translation (NAT) used by routers and firewalls to mask internal network addresses from the outside world. As discussed in Chapter 2, IP allows the use of private addresses instead of registered IP addresses—for example, 10.1.13.1 instead of 209.78.124.12. This is done for a variety of reasons, but mainly it's done to conserve addresses (sometimes called *address space*), because there simply aren't enough IP addresses to uniquely number all the hosts, devices, and LANs in most internetworks. It's possible to run an internetwork without private addresses, but it's rarely done.

As packets are forwarded to the outside, NAT overwrites the internal network address in the source address field with a full IP address. This is done from a pool of registered IP addresses made available to NAT, which then assigns them to outbound connections as they're established. NAT maps the inside local address to the pool address, deletes the mapping when the connection is terminated, and reuses the pool address for the next outbound connection that comes along. As you can see at the top of Figure 9-3, NAT translation takes place on a one-to-one basis. Therefore, although NAT hides internal addresses, it does not conserve address space.

The bottom of Figure 9-3 shows that NAT can also be configured to use just one registered address for all internal hosts making outside connections. This function is called Port Address Translation (PAT), which differs from NAT by translating to one global outside address instead of to individual outside addresses. PAT provides additional security by making it impossible for hackers to identify individual hosts inside a private internetwork because everybody appears to be coming from the same host address. Beyond enhancing security, PAT also conserves address space.

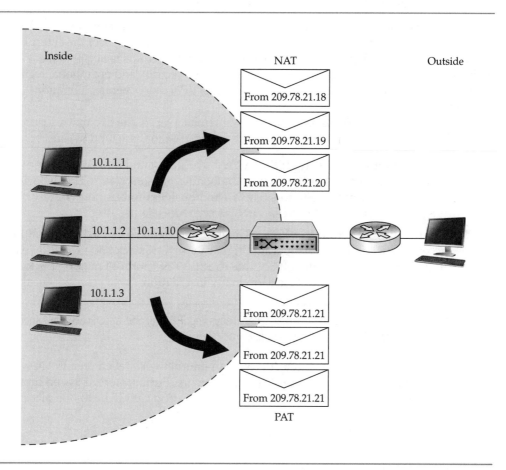

Figure 9-3.   Internal host addresses can be translated one-to-one or to a global address.

Address translation is an example of the value of context-based session tracking. Without the ability to keep track of which session each packet belongs to, it wouldn't be possible to dynamically assign and map internal addresses to the public addresses.

Virtual Private Networks

What is a virtual private network (VPN)? As so often happens in the computer business, marketing hype can muddle an otherwise clear term. In the case of VPNs, some confusion exists over what's *virtual* in a VPN—the privacy or the network? Here's the two-part definition of a virtual private network:

- VPN topology runs mostly over *shared* network infrastructure, usually the Internet, and has at least one private LAN segment at each end point.

- VPN sessions run through an encrypted connection.

To operate through encrypted connections across the Internet, the network segments at each end of a site-to-site VPN must be under the administrative control of the enterprise (or enterprises) running the virtual network. In practical terms, this means that the endpoint routers and firewalls must be under a common security and operational regimen. Above all, the devices (router, firewall, and client) in a VPN must operate a common encryption scheme.

There are many technologies one may utilize to build a VPN. The two that are primarily utilized by enterprise network designers and thus of interest to Cisco (and us) are:

- **Internet Protocol Security (IPSec) VPN** The oldest and most widely deployed VPN protocol, IPSec has been utilized globally for many years. The de facto standard for corporate site-to-site (S2S) and business-to-business (B2B) VPNs, it is also used for remote access VPN via software clients.

- **Secure Socket Layer (SSL) VPN** Generally recognized as the better remote access client solution, SSL operates higher in the OSI stack and is slightly easier to deploy and manage than IPSec due to SSL VPN "portals" making thick client deployments unnecessary on many installations.

 NOTE Continuing through this chapter, when discussing IPSec or SSL specifically, we'll specify. If we are meaning VPN in general, we will not.

Traditionally, long-distance connectivity to an internetwork relied on a WAN with a leased line. These leased lines were slow and insecure. Furthermore, a leased line is simply not an option for an individual who is traveling and cannot be in one place long enough for a leased line to be justified. The following are some reasons why VPN have made an impact on the leased-line market:

- **Lower costs for WAN connectivity**   Leased lines require expensive transport bandwidth and backbone equipment. In addition, VPNs do not need in-house terminal equipment and access modems.

- **Network and corporate agility**   Relatively speaking, S2S IPSec VPN links are easy and inexpensive to set up, change, and remove. S2S VPN also allow interoperability between vendors. Because of this, an organization's communications infrastructure won't be traumatized when a VPN is installed, reconfigured, or removed. Furthermore, the availability of the Internet ensures that you can interconnect your company utilizing IPSec VPN nearly anywhere on the globe.

- **Remote access**   Because of its availability utilizing the Internet, subscribers anywhere on an IPSec and/or SSL VPN may have the same level of access and view of central services, such as e-mail, internal (intranet) websites, voice and directory services, HR, financial systems, security, and so forth.

What Composes a VPN?

Think of VPNs as wide area networks that operate, at least partly, over insecure networks such as the Internet. Like most WANs, a VPN could provide a mixture of access types, as shown in Figure 9-4.

IPSec VPNs are steadily taking over the role of WANs in enterprise networking. All or part of a VPN can be an intranet, an extranet, or a remote access vehicle for telecommuters, mobile workers, as well as automated systems requiring encrypted communications, like ATM machines. VPN provides a much quicker return on investment than traditional WAN. A significant number of VPNs are now owned and operated by Internet service providers, who parcel out their VPN bandwidth to enterprises. This has enabled corporations to implement simplified private IP routing via MPLS worldwide, rather than having to interconnect sites with complicated publicly routed NAT. Take this example of ISP-provided VPN: A company may now deploy a router with an inexpensive T1 link in London, and unknown to the network admin managing that simple T1 link, that very same T1 on the backside is tied into an ISP-managed VPN connection that comprises his company's private MPLS cloud.

Encryption and other security measures largely define an IPSec VPN. This is for the simple reason that running enterprise WANs over the Internet is easy and inexpensive, but not feasible without appropriate security. Thus, security is part of what makes up a VPN. It is also defined by a suite of Internet compatible access servers, network appliances (such as firewalls), and internetwork management techniques.

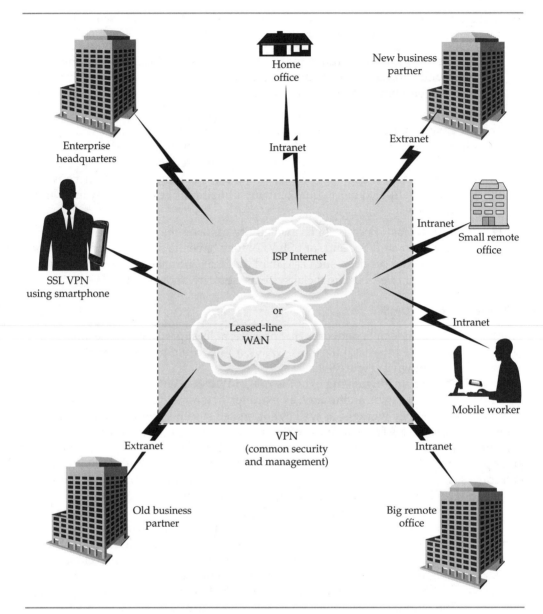

Figure 9-4.   VPNs are encrypted WANs that come in variations.

NOTE Network traffic encryption is a technique that scrambles the format of data in such a way that it can only be read by a system holding an authorized key with a mathematical formula needed to unscramble the payloads. (Packet headers are left unscrambled so that they can be routed.) IPSec utilizes Encapsulating Security Payload (ESP). In the context of our discussion in this section of the book, ESP encryption and decryption take place between two peer encrypting routers, called peer routers. (Note that firewalls can also handle encryption.) Peer routers share a secret algorithm key used to unscramble the payload. Peer routers must authenticate each other before each encrypted session using Digital Signature Standard (DSS) keys (unique character strings). When a signature is verified, the peer router is authenticated and the encrypted session begins. The actual scrambling is done using a temporary encryption key, which must be exchanged in the connection messages between the peer routers. When the encrypted session is over, the key is discarded. The algorithm providing the key could be derived from numerous standards. Advanced Encryption Standard (AES) is the most common. Data Encryption Standard (DES) is no longer recommended.

The components making up a IPSec VPN are

- **Tunneling** Point-to-point connections over a connectionless IP network—in essence, a set of predetermined router hops taken through the Internet to guarantee performance and delivery.

- **Encryption** The scrambling of an IP packet's contents (but usually not the header) to render it unreadable to all but those with a key to unscramble it. (Keys are held by authorized VPN senders and receivers only.)

- **Encapsulation** Placing a frame inside an IP packet to bridge dissimilar networks (the IP packet is unpacked on the other side), effectively allowing tunneling to take place across otherwise incompatible VPN network segments.

- **Packet authentication** The ability to ensure the integrity of a VPN packet by confirming that its contents (payload) weren't altered en route.

- **User authentication** User authentication, authorization, and accounting (AAA) capabilities enforced through security servers, such as TACACS+, RADIUS, or Kerberos.

- **Access control** Firewalls, intrusion detection devices, and security auditing procedures used to monitor all traffic crossing VPN security perimeters.

- **Quality of Service (QoS)** Cisco's QoS is a set of internetwork management standards and functions to ensure interoperability of devices and software platforms, and to leverage the platform to guarantee end-to-end network performance and reliability.

The components making up the two types of SSL VPN are

- **Web browser-based** An SSL VPN begins with a website where internal resources are published called a "portal." The device the portal is installed upon functions at the transport layer and acts as an application reverse proxy to remote users.

- **Tunneling** The second type of SSL VPN, tunneling is achieved by a lightweight, downloaded client "shim." Point-to-point connections over a connectionless IP network—in essence, a set of predetermined router hops taken through the Internet to guarantee performance and delivery.

- **Standardization** Unlike IPSec, which is deployed with minor variations by many diverse vendors, SSL is highly consistent globally.

- **Encryption** SSL has been widely deployed for securing web-based applications in the form of HTTP Secure (HTTPS). Even newbie computer users are aware of the padlock symbol shown on secure websites, even if they do not understand this means the site is protected by SSL.

- **Encapsulation** Placing an IP packet inside an SSL tunnel to bridge dissimilar networks (the IP packet is unpacked on the other side), effectively allowing tunneling to take place across otherwise incompatible VPN network segments. Layer 3 encapsulation is only utilized when tunneling.

- **Packet authentication** Message authentication coded (MAC'ed) to ensure the integrity of a VPN packet by confirming that its contents (payload) weren't altered en route.

- **User authentication** User authentication, authorization, and accounting (AAA) capabilities enforced through security servers, such as LDAP, TACACS+, RADIUS, or Kerberos.

- **Access control** Firewalls, intrusion detection devices, and security auditing procedures used to monitor all traffic crossing VPN security perimeters.

 NOTE The name "SSL VPN" is actually a misnomer. The IETF renamed SSLv3 to Transport Layer Security (TLS); however, SSL as a term is so pervasive that TLS is still referred to as SSL by many.

This list shows how a VPN is as much about *seamlessness* as security. All of these items work in silent concert. Forcing network administrators or users to go through multiple steps to accomplish simple tasks would make using a VPN as infeasible as poor security. In practical terms, therefore, a VPN must be configured using hardware and software devices with these required characteristics.

Cisco's Solution

To deliver VPN functionality, Cisco has used a broad sword to make a name for itself. Rather than focus on just the hardware side of the issue, Cisco developed an integrated solution relying on both hardware and software.

The Cisco solution doesn't put all of its VPN eggs in one basket. In addition to routers and ASA firewalls enabled with VPN functions, they have software designed to make use of that extra functionality. The following sections take a closer look at Cisco's hardware and software, and how the two can be used together to deliver VPNs for remote access, intranets, and extranets.

Hardware

To deliver VPN functionality, Cisco has built VPN features into a number of its router models. For instance, the Cisco 1905 Integrated Services Router (part of the ISR G2 line) can be used to connect small branch sites to a corporate core via VPN. The 1905 is packaged to perform high-speed encryption and deliver tunnel-routing services in a single package. VPNs have traditionally been software-based solutions. However, by building equipment with VPN hardware-accelerated functionality in mind, Cisco has improved VPN services over software solutions. For example, Cisco has added VPN acceleration functionality to Cisco 2900 and 3900 series routers, making VPN functionality and performance far greater than software solutions alone.

Some of Cisco's VPN-enabled hardware is listed in Table 9-3.

Cisco VPN Client

Though Cisco is building VPN functionality into its hardware, they haven't forsaken the software end of the solution. A Cisco VPN connection can begin at a piece of equipment that has no connection to a piece of Cisco hardware. With a Cisco AnyConnect VPN Client version installed on a Windows, Linux, or OS X–based PC, a telecommuter, remote office, or traveler can connect across any internetwork with their own VPN tunnel.

Product	Description
Cisco 800 Series Routers	For the SOHO market SSL VPN for secure remote access Broadband
Cisco 1900 Series Routers	For the branch office market Integrated 802.11n access point
Cisco 2900 Series Router	For the branch office market Up to 350 Mbps WAN performance Voice+video-ready digital signal processors (DSPs)
Cisco 3900 Series Router	For the large branch office Scalable 350 Mbps WAN performance
Cisco SA500 Series Security Appliances	For small businesses Combines firewall and IPS Up to 85 Mbps VPN capability
Cisco ASA 5500 Series Adaptive Security Appliances	For medium- to large-sized businesses Built to counter a host of security threats

Table 9-3.   Some of Cisco's VPN-Enabled Hardware

The client, which can be placed on these devices anywhere in the world and whose traffic traverses the Internet just like any other traffic, finds its way to its home router or ASA firewall unscathed and securely.

Requirements   The AnyConnect VPN client is available for:

- Windows XP, Vista, 7, 8, and x64 versions of the same
- Linux (Intel)
- Mac OS X 10.6 and higher
- Apple iOS 4.1 and higher
- Android 4.0 and higher
- Android 2.3 and 3.0 devices that are jailbroken

On Windows, installation of AnyConnect is a simple process of double-clicking an icon on the installation CD-ROM or downloading and installing it from the corporate SSL VPN portal. Once the client is installed, it sits quietly in an icon at the bottom of the screen until it is needed. iPhone and Android users may download the client from their respective stores.

Features   Under the hood, Cisco's AnyConnect VPN client features a number of tools aimed at ensuring safe, stable IPSec and/or SSL tunneling. Some of the major features include

- The network administrator can export and lock the security policy.
- The client is IPSec and SSL compliant and can be configured to use either of these exclusively or make a determination on its own as to which is best for the environment it finds itself in.

  It also supports

  - Tunnel Mode or Transport Mode security
  - 3DES, MD5, AES-256, and 3DES-168 algorithms
  - NSA Suite B algorithms
  - IKEv2 using ESP3
  - 4,096-bit RSA keys
  - SHA-256 and SHA-384
- It's compatible with most Windows, Mac, and Linux communications devices, including LAN adapters, modems, PCMCIA cards, and so on.
- It can be centrally configured for ease of use.

- It's compatible with X.509 Certificate Authorities, including:
  - Windows Certificate Services
  - VeriSign and other managed service PKI for SSL
  - A GUI to make security policy and certificate management user-friendly
- It's transparent when in use.

Digging a Tunnel

When a combination of Cisco's VPN-enabled hardware and software come together, that's when the strength of the Cisco VPN solution is evident. For instance, when a Cisco ASA 5512 firewall is used, the ASA can create and/or terminate VPN tunnels between other ASAs, between the ASA and any Cisco VPN-enabled router, and between the ASA and the Cisco AnyConnect VPN client—all simultaneously.

The following scenarios explain how different VPN needs can be met.

Remote Access

The most basic VPN comes when a user needs to access the network from a remote location. For instance, if a salesman is traveling and needs to access information on the company's network, he need only initiate a VPN back to the home office.

IPSec VPN   Let's look at how an IPSec remote access connection can be made. Figure 9-5 shows a pet food company's headquarters located in St. Paul, Minnesota, and a salesman, who is on a business trip in Boise, Idaho, and accompanying him is a corporate-owned laptop. To access his company's network, the remote user will be connected through a secure tunnel that is established through the Internet using the AnyConnect VPN client his IT staff installed. This allows the salesman to access internal information as if his computer was physically connected to the corporate LAN, anytime, anywhere he has an Internet connection.

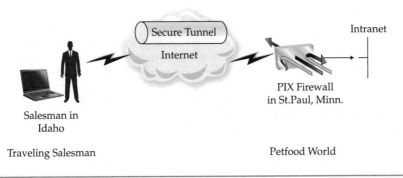

Figure 9-5.   A remote user utilizes a VPN to access the corporate network.

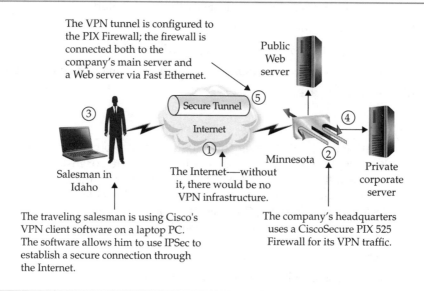

The VPN tunnel is configured to the PIX Firewall; the firewall is connected both to the company's main server and a Web server via Fast Ethernet.

Public Web server

Secure Tunnel

Internet

Salesman in Idaho

The Internet—without it, there would be no VPN infrastructure.

Minnesota

Private corporate server

The traveling salesman is using Cisco's VPN client software on a laptop PC. The software allows him to use IPSec to establish a secure connection through the Internet.

The company's headquarters uses a CiscoSecure PIX 525 Firewall for its VPN traffic.

Figure 9-6.   These are the hardware components of a remote access VPN connection.

In Figure 9-6, we add the hardware elements that will make the VPN possible. In this scenario, we used an ASA firewall as the VPN device on the company's end. This same scenario can be configured with a router in place of the ASA firewall. Using the same construction, one of Cisco's VPN-enabled routers could be used in place of the ASA, eliminating the need for the "extra" T1 router in the diagram; however, regulation compliance, change control, and so on, may dictate otherwise.

NOTE   Refer back to Table 9-3 for a list of Cisco's VPN-enabled hardware.

Of course, your internetworking needs and your means will feature prominently in your decision between an ASA firewall and a router. For maximum security, you should use the firewall; the advanced logging alone is worth the difference.

SSL VPN   A far more common scenario these days is the use of the SSL VPN portal. Let's look at that salesman scenario again; this time we'll let him use his own PC rather than a corporate asset. Just for fun we'll send him to someplace warm, like California. Again, to access his company's network, the remote user will be connected through a secure tunnel that is established through the Internet, but that tunnel is between his browser (not his PC's network stack) and the ASA.

The primary difference is the user interaction and the resources the user is able to connect with (for instance, users have limited access to organizational resources and can only connect to web-based applications). Rather than having a full, routable tunnel requiring a corporate IT-maintained piece of software (AnyConnect) on his personal PC, now the ASA performs reverse proxy on his applications, making his experience faster and his company safer. When there is no full tunnel, malware and other Internet badness cannot pass through the tunnel unnoticed. Figure 9-7 shows how a secure SSL VPN login session is started.

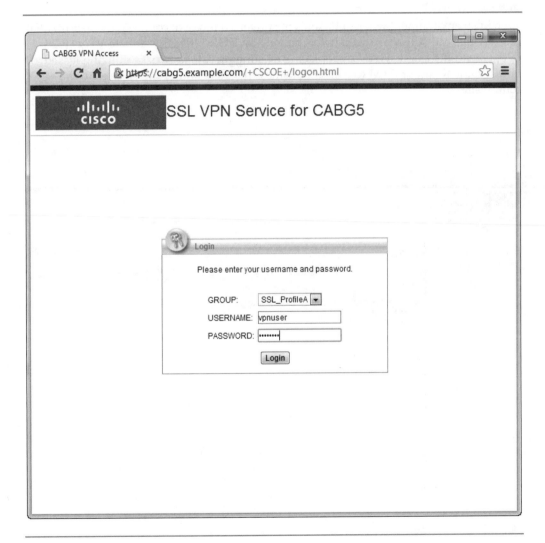

Figure 9-7.   Starting a secure SSL VPN login session

Cisco SSL VPN is configurable on both ASA and routers. Again, you'll have to choose what exactly your goal is and whether it's within your budget to have separate devices. One primary reason to choose an ASA when using an SSL VPN is the many extra features available to the portal administrator, and the ability to separate duties within platforms.

Figure 9-8 shows a VPN being made.

The previous IPSec configuration example works well for the "traveling salesman with a corporate laptop" scenario, but VPN -functionality can also be established between two companies or a company and a branch office.

Site-to-Site Access

Even in an environment where a WAN is the preferred mode of connectivity, a substantial cost savings can still be realized by employing an IPSec VPN. Site-to-site VPNs (S2S or B2B) extend the classic WAN by replacing existing private networks utilizing leased lines, Frame Relay, or ATM to connect business partners and branch offices to the central site.

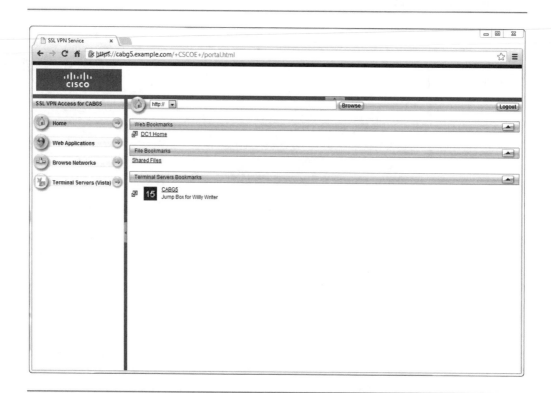

Figure 9-8.   A VPN connection is made.

In this capacity, IPSec VPNs don't change the requirements of private WANs, such as support for multiple protocols, reliability, and extensibility. Rather, they meet these requirements, but are more cost-effective and flexible. To deliver private WAN-style capabilities on a budget, site-to-site VPNs can use the Internet or Internet service providers by utilizing tunneling and encryption for privacy, and, in some cases, Quality of Service for reliability. The following scenario shows how an IPSec VPN can be established between a company's headquarters and a remote office (intranet) or between two business partners (extranet).

In this example, let's show how two business partners can link their respective networks together across the Internet. Figure 9-9 shows the headquarters of HydroDynamics, which needs to provide network access to extranet partner, Johnson Pneumatics. The two offices are connected through a secure IPSec tunnel, which connects through the Internet. Employees at Johnson Pneumatics are able to access the web server of their business partner across the country. Figure 9-10 shows the hardware and software details of the IPSec VPN link between HydroDynamics and Johnson Pneumatics.

As you can see, connecting two business partners or a branch office through VPN is much easier and less expensive than a WAN. By safely and securely tunneling though the Internet, connectivity can be delivered without taking too much of a bite out of an organization's bottom line.

Group Encrypted Transport VPN

Group Encrypted Transport (GET) VPN bears worthy mention. This is a newer mechanism that allows large-scale deployments of encryption between routers on a corporate network using a shared key server resource (see Figure 9-11). This method of deployment is often managed by an MPLS provider, rather than the customer, directly on their premises. By utilizing group properties via the open IETF standard Group Domain of Interpretation (GDOI), network engineers can secure their routed private networks that, due to distance, are forced to utilize an ISP provided WAN connection rather than their own private fiber.

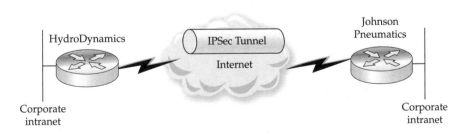

Figure 9-9.   Business partners can use IPSec VPNs to link their organizations.

The Fast Ethernet interfaces at
HydroDynamics are connected
to both a private corporate server
and a public Web server.

One of the Fast Ethernet
interfaces of Johnson
Pneumatics' router is
connected to a PC client.

The IPSec tunnel joining the
companies is configured on a serial
interface on both companies' routers.

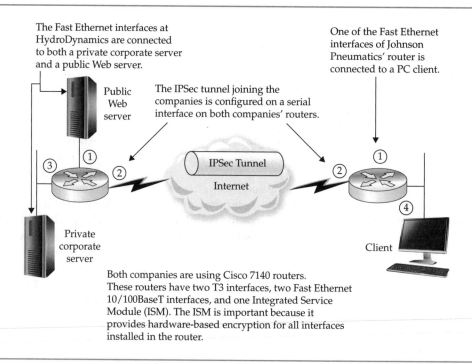

Public
Web
server

IPSec Tunnel

Internet

Private
corporate
server

Client

Both companies are using Cisco 7140 routers.
These routers have two T3 interfaces, two Fast Ethernet
10/100BaseT interfaces, and one Integrated Service
Module (ISM). The ISM is important because it
provides hardware-based encryption for all interfaces
installed in the router.

Figure 9-10.   These are the hardware components of a site-to-site VPN solution.

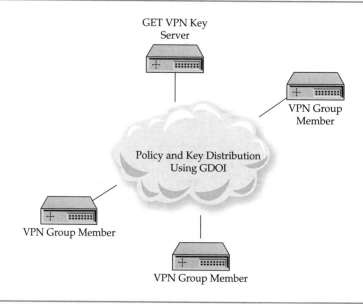

GET VPN Key
Server

VPN Group
Member

Policy and Key Distribution
Using GDOI

VPN Group Member

VPN Group Member

Figure 9-11.   GET VPN simplifies encryption management within corporate WANs.

Summary

In this chapter, we talked a lot about the mechanics behind how security tools are used and how access is granted or prohibited. In the next chapter, we'll look at the tools Cisco offers for network and internetwork security.

CHAPTER 10 | Security Appliances

All this discussion of security protocols, theory, and practices really comes together in the appliances used for managing network security. Cisco offers a number of devices that help secure your network. Although it may seem that one device should be able to do it all (and Cisco is probably working on that, anyway), the current state of internetworking requires specific tools for specific jobs.

In this chapter, we'll take a look at Cisco's security toolbox and discuss how those specialized tools are used. First, we'll spend a fair amount of time discussing firewalls—probably the most visible and utilitarian device for internetworking security. Although firewalls are the most prevalent device for network security, we'll also take a look at some of the specialized devices that Cisco offers to mitigate security on other fronts, including intrusion prevention systems (IPSs), integrated services routers (ISRs), and some specialized modules that plug into modular switches and routers.

Firewalls

A *firewall* is a traffic control point between a private network and one or more public networks. It's a gateway that selectively decides what may enter or leave a protected network. To do this, a firewall must be the sole gateway between the network it protects and the outside. If traffic can go around a firewall, the security it provides is worthless. A basic tenet is that all inbound and outbound traffic must pass through the firewall. A normal router could serve as a rudimentary firewall if it were configured as a choke point. Figure 10-1 shows how a firewall acts as a funnel through which all traffic must pass.

There is a necessary trade-off between security and network performance. If you substituted cars and trucks for IP packets in Figure 10-1, you'd see traffic from several highways squeezed through a single on-ramp. If security weren't a concern, to boost performance, private internetworks would be surrounded on all sides by routers.

Firewall Basics

In simple terms, a firewall is a traffic filter. Traffic enters through one network interface and leaves through another, and in basic firewalls, messages are handled at the network layer (layer 3) of the seven-layer OSI model. Higher security application-filtering firewalls handle messages and filter at layer 7 as well.

Firewalls operate by intercepting and inspecting each packet that enters any of their network interfaces. The inspections vary according to the firewall's sophistication and how tight the security policy is. But the goal is always to identify a match between each packet's contents and the security rules the firewall has been programmed to enforce. The basic steps of intercepting and inspecting packets are shown in Figure 10-2.

There's nothing fancy about how a firewall intercepts traffic. It does so by funneling all traffic entering its network interfaces over a single path (called a *data bus* in computer terminology). By having all traffic pass through the firewall's internal data

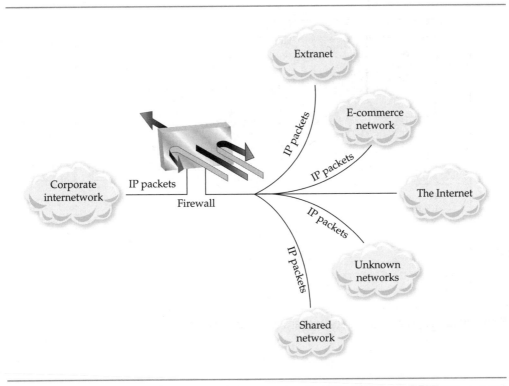

Figure 10-1. A firewall is partly defined by its position as a traffic bottleneck.

bus and memory, software running on the central processing unit (CPU) is given the opportunity to check each packet against the security rules it has been programmed to enforce.

The actual inspection on a packet filtering firewall is done by reading the packet's header for conditions that match rules set up in security tables. Security tables usually include dozens of rules, each designed to explicitly accept or reject specific kinds of traffic by applying a pass/fail test to the packet. If the packet passes, it's forwarded to its destination. If it fails, the packet is dropped at the network interface and ceases to exist.

Firewalls Map Out a Defensive Landscape

Routers tend to take a friendly view of the world. They focus on addresses and the best routes for delivering messages to them. By contrast, firewalls take a militaristic view of things, where addresses are still important, but for inspection and clearance instead of delivery. Firewalls define the world as either inside networks or outside networks, with the division made according to what lies beyond the security perimeter. The security

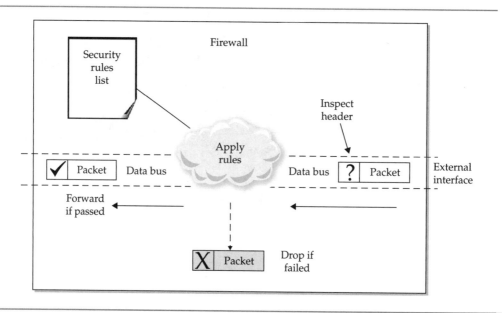

Figure 10-2.   Firewalls inspect all packets and apply security rules to them.

perimeter itself is established by one or more firewalls placed between the secured network and the outside. The firewall places every network it encounters into one of three classifications:

- **Trusted network**   Inside the security perimeter and under complete administrative control of the enterprise.

- **Untrusted network**   Outside the security perimeter and known to the firewall, but beyond the enterprise's administrative control.

- **Unknown network**   A network that the firewall has received no information or instructions about—this includes almost the entire Internet. Of course, unknown networks are untrusted networks.

The security perimeter is drawn right down the middle of the firewall, with the physical configuration of the device itself defining what's internal and external. The network interfaces on the firewall are designated as internal (*inside*), external (*outside*), and *DMZ* (in some cases) interfaces. The network attached to each interface, in turn, takes on its interface's designation. In Figure 10-3, for example, network 10.1.13.0 is attached to an inside interface is therefore defined as being inside the security perimeter, and thus a trusted network.

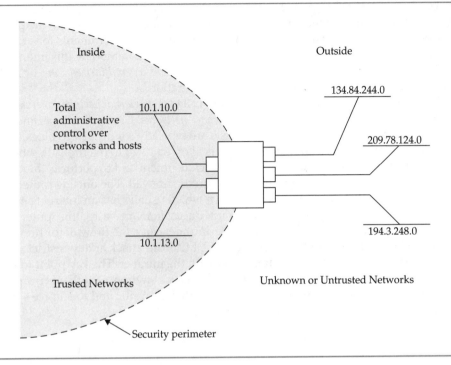

Figure 10-3.   Firewalls define security perimeters and classify networks accordingly.

In terms of network security, *administrative control* is the ability to do such things as assign IP addresses, issue user accounts and passwords, and maintain network device configuration files. Usually, the network media—LANs and WANs—over which a secured network operates are owned and controlled by the enterprise. The major exception to this is the VPN, which runs mostly over intermediate network segments that are operated by somebody else but that are still regarded as trusted networks.

Security Is a Matter of Policy, Not Technology

Internetwork security isn't just a matter of how much control you can exert; it's also how much you *choose* to exert. Much like the trade-off between security and performance, a trade-off also exists between security and connectivity. In theory, any LAN could have an externally impenetrable security posture by simply having all routers, switches, and modems leading to the outside unplugged.

But enterprises are compelled to connect to the outside because the benefits of connectivity outweigh the risk it brings. In fact, almost all businesses are now connected to the most unknown and dangerous public network of all: the Internet. Every time you hit a company's website to look up information, download software, or place an order, that enterprise has taken a calculated risk by letting you access some part of its system. Most enterprises need to open their internal networks to the public to at least some degree. Businesses do it to sell and support, governments to serve, and educational organizations to teach. Firewalls try to help accommodate this intentional security compromise by defining a middle ground called a *demilitarized zone,* or *DMZ* for short. Figure 10-4 shows a typical DMZ configuration.

LAN segments on the firewall's outside are called the *external perimeter networks,* and ones on the inside are called *internal perimeter networks.* Usually, each perimeter network has a router attached, and access lists are typically configured to block some "bad" traffic. However, the bulk of the traffic is allowed to go to the firewall, where it can do its job of inspecting the traffic for malicious intent and to perform "block or allow" enforcement based on rules defined on the firewall. The outside router is often referred to as the *screening* or *shield router,* which usually has an Internet service provider (ISP) attached to at least one of its interfaces; in many cases, this router is provided by the ISP. In addition to Internet-to-intranet duty, the firewall (or firewalls) is also called upon to protect the servers in the DMZ from attack and to restrict what those servers are allowed to communicate with on the intranet. The key point to understand is that a firewall is a critical part of a secure environment that is purpose-built to protect the intranet and the DMZ from malicious traffic and to enforce specific security rules as defined by its owner (or administrator).

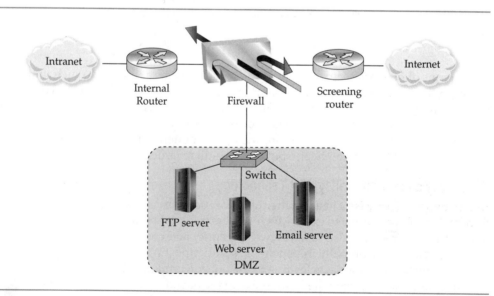

Figure 10-4.   Many firewall configurations include a DMZ to run public servers.

How Firewalls Work

Security rules can be defined globally so that they apply to the entire firewall, and other more specific rules can be defined and applied to a specific network interface. This is true whether the firewall is a router trying to serve as a firewall or a high-tech dedicated device, such as the Cisco ASA or the popular (but now retired, yet still very prevalent) Cisco PIX Firewall. Generally speaking, each packet or flow is inspected and then filtered based on rules applied to the specific network interface card through which it entered the firewall. The act of configuring a firewall, then, is largely a matter of assigning security rules to each firewall interface.

The Access List Is the Most Basic Internetwork Security Tool

The simplest form of network security technology is the access list. It's not much of a firewall anymore, but it is certainly useful in a variety of situations. Also called an *access control list (ACL)* or *filter*, the access list is a basic component of any firewall's configuration. As the name implies, the access list restricts certain traffic from gaining access to a network. It provides a basic level of network security by filtering packets according to these criteria:

- **Source and destination IP address**   The IP address from which the packet originated and is addressed

- **Source and destination port number**   The port number from which the packet originated and is addressed

- **Source and destination protocol number**   The protocol number from which the packet originated or is addressed

Cisco calls these *extended access lists*—the extension being the port number, protocol number (source and/or destination), and/or destination IP address. Early Cisco products used only source addresses, which were referred to as *standard access lists*. But don't be misled by this terminology: Extended access lists are the basic type of access lists being used now.

NOTE   Port numbers (also called *network ports* or just *ports)* aren't physical interface ports like S0/0 or Gi3/1. Messages sent using the TCP or UDP transport-layer protocols (layer 4) use port numbers to identify which application protocol the transmission will run. For example, the number for HTTP (WWW) is port 80; SMTP's port is 25; and FTP's port is 20 and 21.

Network administrators create access lists in the router's configuration file. One access list is created for each network interface. If an interface handles traffic in multiple network protocols—for example, IP, IPX, and Bonjour—each network protocol has its own access list format. Therefore, a separate access list must be created for each protocol to run over that network interface. Regardless of the network protocol used, each criterion (access rule) occupies a line on the list. Figure 10-5 depicts how access lists work. This example uses a router restricting the flow of traffic between departments within an organization.

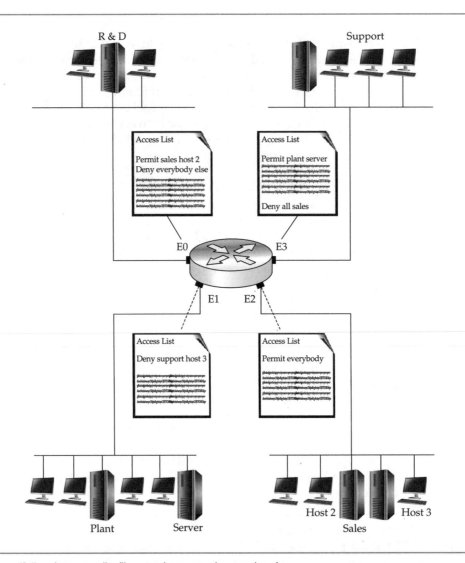

Figure 10-5. An access list filters packets at each router interface.

As each packet attempts to enter an interface, its header is examined to see if anything matches the access list. The router is looking for positive matches. Once it finds a match, no further evaluations are performed. If the rule matched is a *permit* rule, the packet is forwarded out a network interface on the other side of the router. If the matched rule is a *deny*, the packet is dropped right there at the interface.

If a packet's evaluation runs all the way to the bottom of the access list without a match, it is dropped by default. This mechanism is called the *implicit deny rule*, which provides an added measure of security by dealing with conditions not anticipated in the access list.

The router evaluates the packet one rule at a time, working its way from the top line to the bottom. The bottom part of Figure 10-6 is an example taken from a router's access list. Each line in the list is a rule that either permits or denies a specific type of traffic. The top of Figure 10-6 charts the parts of a rule's statement, starting with the **access-list** command followed by various modifiers. Keep in mind that this example is for IP; syntax varies slightly for IPX, Apple's Bonjour, and other non-IP network protocols.

A cohesive access list is created by using a common access list name at the beginning of each statement for an IP access list. Each statement must declare a transport protocol, such as the Transmission Control Protocol (TCP), the User Datagram Protocol (UDP), or the Internet Control Messaging Protocol (ICMP). If the rule involves a network application, the statement must first declare a transport protocol and end with the application protocol. In the sample rule at the top of Figure 10-6, the transport protocol is TCP, and the application protocol is HTTP.

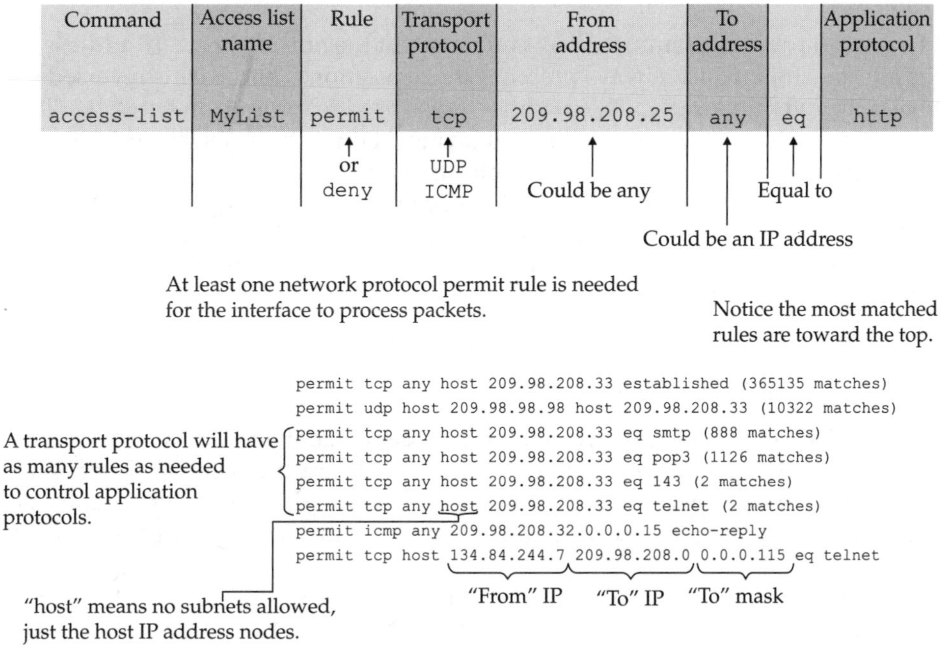

Command	Access list name	Rule	Transport protocol	From address	To address		Application protocol
access-list	MyList	permit	tcp	209.98.208.25	any	eq	http

```
permit tcp any host 209.98.208.33 established (365135 matches)
permit udp host 209.98.98.98 host 209.98.208.33 (10322 matches)
permit tcp any host 209.98.208.33 eq smtp (888 matches)
permit tcp any host 209.98.208.33 eq pop3 (1126 matches)
permit tcp any host 209.98.208.33 eq 143 (2 matches)
permit tcp any host 209.98.208.33 eq telnet (2 matches)
permit icmp any 209.98.208.32.0.0.0.15 echo-reply
permit tcp host 134.84.244.7 209.98.208.0 0.0.0.115 eq telnet
```

Figure 10-6.   Access list statements are security rules.

Keep in mind that ACLs can have other protocols as well:

- **AHP**   Authentication Header Protocol
- **EIGRP**   Cisco's Enhance Interior Gateway Routing Protocol (EIGRP) routing protocol
- **ESP**   Encapsulation Security Payload
- **GRE**   Cisco's Generic Routing Encapsulation (GRE) tunneling
- **ICMP**   Internet Control Message Protocol
- **IGMP**   Internet Gateway Message Protocol
- **IP**   Any Internet Protocol
- **IPINIP**   IP in IP tunneling
- **NOS**   KA9Q NOS compatible IP over IP tunneling
- **OSPF**   Open Shortest Path First (OSPF) routing protocol
- **PCP**   Payload Compression Protocol
- **PIM**   Protocol Independent Multicast
- **TCP**   Transmission Control Protocol
- **UDP**   User Datagram Protocol

To apply a rule to incoming traffic, you must put the outside host's IP address in the *from* position, which always precedes the *to* position. This order is reversed so as to restrict outbound traffic. The modifier **any** is used to indicate all networks. The statement at the top of Figure 10-6, then, is saying, "Permit host 209.98.208.25 to access any network in order to run the HTTP application over TCP."

The access list is activated on an interface by using the **access-group** command, as shown in the following code snippet. The first line "points" the IOS to serial0 interface, and the second line applies access list 100 to all incoming traffic trying to enter through serial0:

```
MyRouter(config)#interface serial0/0/0
MyRouter(config-if)#ip access-group 100 in
```

Routers look for matches between packet header content and the interface's access list. A catch would be a source address, destination address, protocol, or port number. If the matched rule is a permit rule, the packet is forwarded. If, however, a deny rule is matched, the packet is dropped without evaluating against any rules further down the list.

An access list can have as many filtering rules as desired, with the practical limit being the amount of router memory you wish to use for security filtering instead of productive routing. Because access list rules are evaluated from top to bottom, the most frequently encountered matches should be put toward the top of the list so as not to waste router CPU cycles.

Keep in mind that an access list alone doesn't turn a router into a firewall. The majority of access lists are used for basic traffic management within internetworks. However, you could physically configure a router as a choke point so that all traffic must pass an access list, thereby making it into a lightweight firewall. This is frequently done to restrict access among networks making up an internetwork. In fact, standard IOS has dozens of security-oriented commands beyond the **access-list** command that are also used in Cisco's firewall products. However, relying on the access list as the centerpiece of a firewall configuration results in questionable security.

NOTE The following link is a good read that'll get you started thinking about all the things you'll need to learn about in order to operate an IOS device securely: http://www.cisco.com/en/US/tech/tk648/tk361/technologies_tech_note09186a0080120f48.shtml.

Firewalls Track Internetwork Sessions

Firewall technology builds on access lists by keeping track of sessions. This technology is called *stateful* or *context-based* packet filtering, because an individual packet can be handled based on the larger context of its connection (not to be confused with Cisco's firewall virtualization, known as *security contexts,* nor with the contextual identity information discussed in Chapter 9). This type of filtering uses what some call *reflexive access lists,* so named because their contents dynamically change in reflexive response to the state of individual sessions (whether the session was initiated from an inside host, how long it's been running, and so on). Figure 10-7 shows how context-based firewalls track sessions.

NOTE TCP and UDP are protocols running at the transport layer (layer 4) of the seven-layer OSI reference model. TCP stands for Transmission Control Protocol, a connection-oriented protocol designed to deliver full-duplex communications with guaranteed delivery. The bulk of IP traffic goes through TCP connections. UDP stands for User Datagram Protocol—a no-frills, low-overhead, connectionless protocol that has no guaranteed delivery or error correction. UDP is used by relatively simple applications such as TFTP (Trivial File Transfer Protocol). A third transport protocol is ICMP (Internet Control Message Protocol), a specialized protocol used by applications such as **ping** and **traceroute**. Transport protocols are covered in Chapter 2.

The astute reader might wonder how a firewall can track UDP sessions, given that UDP is a so-called connectionless transport protocol lacking the formal handshakes and acknowledgments of TCP. UDP filtering works by noting the source/destination address and port number of the session, and then guessing that all packets sharing those three characteristics belong to the same session. Because timeout periods are so brief for UDP sessions (usually a fraction of maximum times set for TCP sessions), the firewall almost always guesses right.

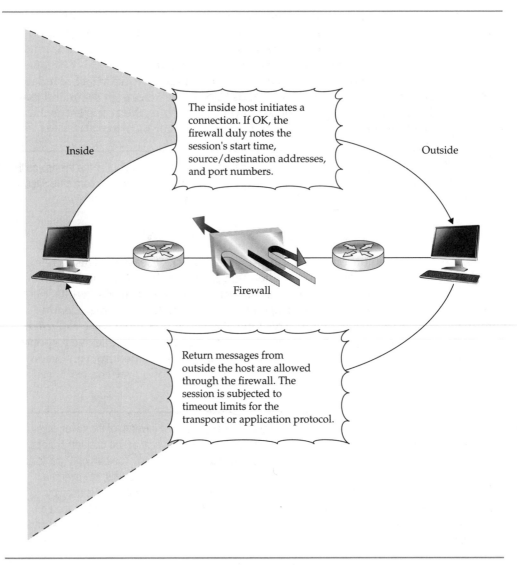

The inside host initiates a connection. If OK, the firewall duly notes the session's start time, source/destination addresses, and port numbers.

Inside

Outside

Firewall

Return messages from outside the host are allowed through the firewall. The session is subjected to timeout limits for the transport or application protocol.

Figure 10-7.   Context-based firewalls track connection states.

Using Global Addresses to Hide Internal Network Topology

Cisco's IOS software has a capability called Network Address Translation (NAT) used by routers and firewalls to mask internal network addresses from the outside world. As discussed in Chapter 2, IP allows the use of private addresses instead of registered IP addresses—for example, 10.1.13.1 instead of 209.78.124.12. This is done for a variety of reasons, but mainly it's done to conserve addresses (sometimes called *address space)* because there simply aren't enough IP addresses to uniquely number all the hosts, devices, and LANs in most internetworks. It's possible to run an internetwork without private addresses, but it's rarely done.

As packets are forwarded to the outside, NAT overwrites the internal network address in the source address field with a full IP address. This is done from a pool of registered IP addresses made available to NAT, which then assigns them to outbound connections as they're established. NAT maps the inside local address to the pool address, deletes the mapping when the connection is terminated, and reuses the pool address for the next outbound connection that comes along. As you can see at the top of Figure 10-8, NAT translation takes place on a one-to-one basis. Therefore, although NAT hides internal addresses, it was not intended to conserve address space when utilized as a front end to server-based services. Other, application-level, URL-based redirection tools are intended for this purpose.

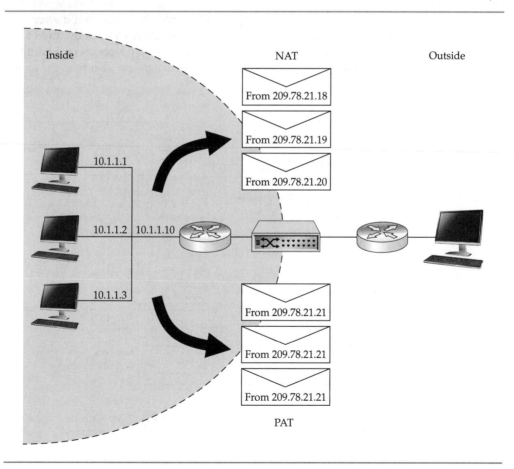

Figure 10-8.   Internal host addresses can be translated one-to-one or to a global address.

The bottom of Figure 10-8 shows that NAT can also be configured to use just one registered address for all internal hosts making outside connections. This function is called Port Address Translation (PAT), which differs from NAT by translating to one global outside address instead of to individual outside addresses. PAT provides additional security by making it impossible for hackers to identify individual hosts inside a private internetwork because everybody appears to be coming from the same host address. Beyond enhancing security, PAT also conserves address space.

Address translation is an example of the value of context-based session tracking. Without the ability to keep track of which session each packet belongs to, it wouldn't be possible to dynamically assign and map internal addresses to the public addresses.

Proxy Servers

A *proxy server* is an application that acts as an intermediary between two end systems. Proxy servers operate at the application layer (layer 7) of the firewall, where both ends of a connection are forced to conduct the session through the proxy. They do this by creating and running a process on the firewall that mirrors a service as if it were running on the end host. As Figure 10-9 illustrates, a proxy server essentially turns a two-party session into a four-party session, with the middle two processes emulating the two real hosts. Because they operate at layer 7, proxy servers are also referred to as *application-layer firewalls.*

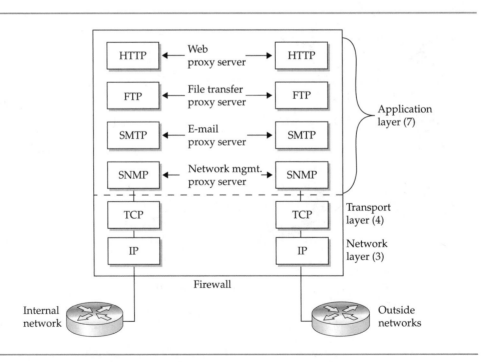

Figure 10-9.   Proxy-server technology is the basis for advanced firewalls.

A proxy service must be run for each type of Internet application the firewall will support—a Simple Mail Transport Protocol (SMTP) proxy for e-mail, an HTTP proxy for web services, and so on. In a sense, proxy servers are one-way arrangements running from one side of the network to the other. In other words, if an internal user wants to access a website on the Internet, the packets making up that request are processed through the HTTP server before being forwarded to the website. Packets returned from the website, in turn, are processed through the HTTP server before being forwarded back to the internal user host. As with NAT, the packets go to the external web server carrying the IP address of the HTTP server instead of the internal host address. Figure 10-9 depicts a firewall running several proxy servers at once.

Because proxy servers centralize all activity for an application into a single server, they present the ideal opportunity to perform a variety of useful functions. Having the application running right on the firewall presents the opportunity to inspect packets for much more than just source/destination addresses and port numbers. This is why nearly all modern firewalls incorporate some form of proxy-server architecture. For example, inbound packets headed to a server set up strictly to disburse information (say, an FTP server) can be inspected to see if they contain any write commands (such as the **PUT** command). In this way, the proxy server could allow only connections containing read commands.

Proxy server is another technology possible only in context-based firewalls. For example, if a firewall supports thousands of simultaneous web connections, it must, of course, sort out to which session each of the millions of incoming packets with port number 80 (HTTP) belong.

Dual-Home Configurations

A *dual-homed* firewall configuration is typically implemented with the ability to route traffic turned off between the network interface cards, without inspecting it. A dual-homed configuration forces all traffic to go through a proxy service before it can be routed out another interface, which is why proxy-server firewalls use dual-homed configurations, as depicted on the left side of Figure 10-10. Another use of dual homing is when you want users on two networks—say, the R&D and Sales departments—to access a single resource but don't want any traffic routed between them. Then any routing capabilities between the two interfaces would be disabled. The configuration on the right in Figure 10-10 shows this.

Using a dual-homed configuration this way doesn't create a firewall gateway, per se, because inbound traffic isn't headed anywhere beyond the server. It's just an easy way to have one server take care of two departments that shouldn't exchange traffic. It's also a way of making sure traffic isn't exchanged, because routing services are turned off inside the router.

Event Logging and Notification

Record keeping is an important part of a firewall's overall role. When a packet is denied entry by a firewall, the event is duly recorded into a file called *syslog* (industry shorthand for *system log)* or to a proprietary logging system based on the firewall manufacturer.

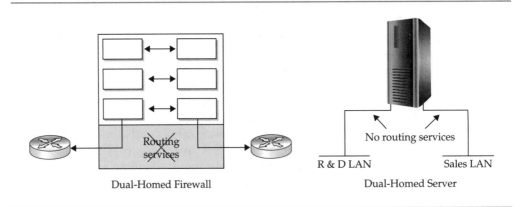

Figure 10-10.   Dual-homed configurations turn off routing services within the device.

Most firewalls can be configured to upload log information to a logging server elsewhere on the network, where it can be analyzed against the enterprise's security policy.

Firewalls can also be configured to generate alert messages if specified thresholds are surpassed. In more sophisticated network operations, these alerts are immediately directed to a manned console so that the network team can respond to the event by any number of measures (usually shutting down the network interface where the apparent security breach is taking place).

The IOS Firewall Feature Set

The IOS Firewall is a value-added option to the Cisco IOS software. It is purchased as a so-called IOS *feature set* (feature sets are covered in Chapter 4). IOS Firewall is used to turn a standard Cisco router into a fairly robust firewall by adding several security functions over and above the basic traffic filtering of standard IOS software:

- **Zone-Based Policy Firewall (ZFW)**   Functioning exactly the way it sounds, ZFW assigns interfaces to zones, with the security policy dictating what traffic is allowed to pass between which zone's border, and whether to pass, drop, or inspect it.

- **IOS Firewall (IFW)**   The predecessor to ZFW and previously known as Context-Based Access Control (CBAC), IFW is a form of traffic filtering that examines application-layer (layer 7) information, such as HTTP, to learn about the state of TCP or UDP connections. IOS Firewall functions are invoked when the ZFW policy action is "inspect."

- **Address Translation (PAT and NAT)**   Disguises internal IP addresses by inserting disguised source addresses on packets sent outside the firewall. PAT and NAT hide internal network topology from hackers.

- **Security server support**   The router can be configured as a client to TACACS+, RADIUS, or Kerberos security servers, where usernames and passwords can be stored in such a server's user authentication database.

- **Denial-of-service attack detection**   Detects the traffic patterns characteristic of so-called *denial-of-service (DoS)* attacks and sends alert messages. (Denial-of-service attacks attempt to deny service by overwhelming a network with service requests, such as illegal e-mail commands or infinite e-mails.)

- **Network-Based Application Recognition (NBAR)**   Recognizes many different applications and can use special services based on them.

- **Java blocking**   The ability to selectively block Java messages from a network. (Java applets are downloadable self-operating programs, and applets can be programmed to harm any host system unfortunate enough to execute them.)

- **Encryption**   The ability to make a packet's contents incomprehensible to all systems except those provided with a cipher (key) to decrypt it.

- **Neighbor router authentication**   A command by which a router can force a neighboring router to authenticate its identity or to block all packets routed from it.

- **Security alerts and event logging**   Messages alerting network administration of a security problem, and the logging of all security events for later collation and analysis.

- **VPN and QoS support**   Provides tunneling and QoS (Quality of Service) features to secure VPNs. This feature provides encrypted tunnels on the router while ensuring strong security, service-level validation, intrusion detection, and advanced bandwidth management.

- **Audit trail**   Provides you with a number of features for detailed tracking. It records the timestamp, source host, destination host, ports, duration, and total number of bytes transmitted for detailed reporting. It is configurable based on applications and features.

- **Dynamic port mapping**   Permits CBAC-based applications to be run on nonstandard ports. This allows network administrators to customize access control for selected applications and services.

- **Firewall management**   Firewalls are configured with a user-friendly interface that provides step-by-step help through network design, addressing, and IOS Firewall security policy configuration.

- **Integration with Cisco IOS software**   This feature set seamlessly interacts with Cisco IOS features, integrating security policy features.

- **Policy-based multi-interface support**   User access can be controlled based on IP address and interface. Access is determined by the security policy.

- **Redundancy/failover**   Automatically routes traffic to a secondary router in the event of failure.

- **Time-based access lists** Security policy can be established based on time of day and day of the week.

- **Intrusion prevention system** An inline detection system that responds to suspicious activity. The router can be configured to log the event, send a message to the system administrator, or deny access to the IP address of the attacker.

- **Authentication proxy** Security policies can be established on a per-user basis.

Zone-Based Policy Firewall

When Cisco announced Zone-Based Policy Firewall, they made a departure from how the IOS "Classic" Firewall (CBAC) had previously been configured with regard to firewalling subnetted locations. Because policy was now assigned to traffic passing between zones rather than interfaces, much more granularity and flexibility became available. Before ZFW, every interface had its own policy assigned in the same way traditional ACLs were managed. This made writing policy potentially very complicated and thus was limiting to the platform. Simplifying writing firewall policy was the primary driver for ZFW. After all, who wants to buy a firewall with 16 interfaces if each interface (and thus sub-interface) requires individual policy management? Through the creation of zones—groups of interfaces, subnets, and so on—policy is much easier to write and maintain. New default rules were added as well, including the following:

- When two interfaces are not members of zones, traffic passes freely.

- When one interface is a member of a zone and another interface is not a member of any zone, traffic will never be allowed between them.

- If two interfaces are members of two different zones, traffic will not be allowed until explicitly defined by policy.

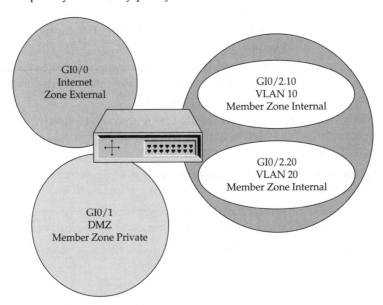

NOTE   It's important to realize that the results of these new defaults are the opposite of all IOS ACL configurations we have discussed previously. All traffic assigned to zones is denied unless explicitly allowed.

The final major change worth mention is the introduction of a new configuration policy language known as Cisco Class-based Policy Language (CPL). This language is very much analogous to Cisco's QoS mapping language involving class maps and policy maps.

How IOS Firewall Works

Under the covers, the inspect engine that runs the packet inspection hasn't changed much over time. What has changed is the way policy is managed. Whether newer zone-based commands or the elderly interface pair-based ones are used, the inspect engine is the most important piece of the IOS Firewall. This collection of bits was previously known as Context-Based Access Control (CBAC), but Cisco's marketing has seen fit to rename it to simply Cisco IOS Firewall (IFW). IOS Firewall is a set of IOS commands that can be used to inspect packets much more closely than normal access lists. IFW works by tracking outside connections initiated from inside the firewall. IOS Firewall identifies sessions by tracking source/destination IP addresses and source/destination port numbers gleaned from the packets. When a response returns from the session's remote host in the form of inbound traffic, IFW determines the session to which the inbound packets belong. IFW, in this way, maintains a dynamic list of ongoing sessions and is able to juggle security exceptions on a moment-by-moment basis. This dynamic list, called the *state table*, tracks the state of valid sessions through to termination. The IFW state table maintains itself by deleting sessions when concluded by users or dropping them after a maximum allowable period of inactivity called a *timeout*. Timeout values are specified by the network administrator for each transport protocol. Figure 10-11 depicts the IOS Firewall process.

IFW uses the state table to make dynamic entries and deletions to the access list of the interface. Source/destination address or port numbers normally blocked by the access list are momentarily allowed, but only for a session IFW knows to be a valid session initiated from inside the firewall security perimeter. IFW creates openings in the firewall as necessary to permit returning traffic. Once the session shuts down, the access list's prohibition is put back in effect until another session calls from the IFW state table, asking for a temporary exception of its own.

NOTE   Zone-based policy is far easier to manage than plain-old CBAC-based policy. We wouldn't recommend anyone use CBAC-style rules unless their router only had two interfaces with no chance of growth.

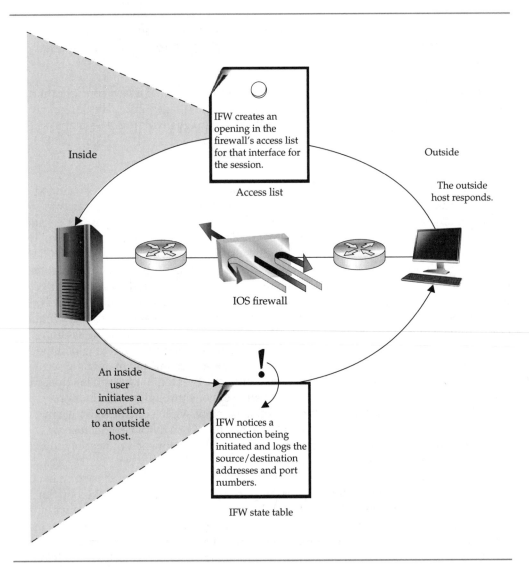

Inside

IFW creates an opening in the firewall's access list for that interface for the session.

Access list

Outside

The outside host responds.

IOS firewall

An inside user initiates a connection to an outside host.

IFW notices a connection being initiated and logs the source/destination addresses and port numbers.

IFW state table

Figure 10-11.   IOS Firewall creates temporary openings based on connection status.

You might think that the router would be overwhelmed by the sheer complexity of it all, but remember that state tables and access lists are managed on a per-interface basis. Each interface on a Cisco router running IOS Firewall has its own access list, inspection rules, and valid sessions. Good firewall-configuration design can cut down a big part of the complexity you must deal with by grouping similar traffic types or sources onto specific network interfaces.

Major IOS Firewall Functions

IOS Firewall selectively enforces security rules based on the context of each session. To pull this off, IOS Firewall must inspect packets much more closely than simple access lists do. For this reason, the IOS Firewall software is granular in its application of inspection rules. *Granular* here means inspection rules are applied much more selectively than the "all-or-nothing" permit/deny scheme used in access lists. This makes the firewall more flexible and a tougher security barrier to crack. We won't delve into IOS Firewall inspection features too deeply since this is a beginner's book, but a quick review will illustrate how firewall technology works at the packet inspection level:

- **SMTP inspection** Many of the worst virus attacks inject themselves into secured internetworks through e-mail. Beyond just inspecting each packet for the SMTP port number, IOS Firewall inspects SMTP packets for illegal commands. Any SMTP packet containing a command other than the 12 legal SMTP commands will be discarded as subversive.

- **Java inspection** Some network security policies prohibit downloading Java applets from outside networks because of their potential destructive power. A security policy mandating that all internal users disable Java in their web browsers is unenforceable. IOS Firewall allows you to block incoming Java applets at the firewall and also to designate a list of trusted (friendly) external sites from which downloaded Java applets will not be blocked (or you could permit applets from all sites except sites explicitly defined as hostile).

- **H.323 inspection** NetMeeting is a premier H.323 protocol application that requires the use of a second channel (session) in addition to the H.323 channel maintained in the CBAC state table. IOS Firewall can be configured to inspect for a generic TCP channel in addition to the H.323 channel to allow NetMeeting connections to operate through the firewall.

- **RPC inspection** The IOS Firewall RPC (Remote Procedure Call) inspection command accepts the entry of program numbers. For example, if the program number for NFS (Network File System Protocol) is specified in an RPC command, NFS traffic may operate through that firewall interface.

Configuring IOS Firewall

Address translation is configured in IOS Firewall using the **nat** and **pat** commands. Typically, the first step of configuring IOS Firewall is to set up translations so as to mask internal IP addresses from the outside world. Sample configurations for NAT and PAT are given in the next part of this chapter, which covers the ASA Firewall.

Context-based security is configured in the IOS Firewall by creating inspection rules. Inspection rules (also called *rule sets)* are applied to access lists governing specific firewall network interfaces. Configuring IOS Firewall, then, is done mostly using two variations of two commands:

- **access-list** A command used to define the basic access rules for the interface
- **ip inspect** A command used to define what IFW will look for at the interface

The access list specifies which normal rules apply to traffic entering the interface, and is used to tell the interface which network applications (port numbers) are prohibited, which destination addresses are blocked, and so on. CBAC inspection rules dynamically modify the access list as necessary to create temporary openings in the IOS Firewall for valid sessions. CBAC defines a valid session as any TCP or UDP connection that matches its access-list criteria.

In addition to creating temporary openings in the firewall, CBAC applies inspection rules to detect various kinds of network attacks and generate alert messages, which are usually sent to the network management console.

NOTE   One of the best-known denial-of-service attacks is SYNflood, so named for the SYN bit used to initiate a three-way handshake that sets up TCP connections. SYNflood attacks try to drown the target network in a flood of connection attempts—thereby denying legitimate hosts network service. A command called **ip inspect tcp synwait-time** is used by the network administrator to tell IOS Firewall how long an unrequited SYN bit is retained before being discarded. By not letting SYN bits pile up, the **ip inspect tcp synwait-time** command can be used to thwart this type of DoS attack.

IOS Firewall can be configured one of two ways, depending on whether the firewall configuration includes a DMZ. Figure 10-12 depicts this. The configuration on the right of Figure 10-12 shows the access list pulled back to the inside of the firewall.

Configuring IOS Firewall on the internal interface relieves the firewall from having to create and delete context-based rule exceptions for traffic hitting the DMZ's web (HTTP) server and DNS (Domain Name System) server. With this arrangement, IFW can still selectively control access to HTTP and DNS services by internal users, but it doesn't have to worry about connections hitting the DMZ servers.

NOTE   IOS Firewall is a feature within Cisco IOS software, so normal IOS conventions apply. To configure IOS Firewall, you must first gain access to the router through console, Telnet, SSH, or the web browser interface. Enter Privileged Exec command mode and then enter configuration mode, with the **firewall(config-if)#** prompt pointing to the interface to which the IFW configuration will apply.

The first step in configuring the IOS Firewall interface is to create an access list. To define an access list, use the following command syntax:

```
Firewall(config)#ip access-list standard access-list-name-or-number
Firewall(config-std-nacl)#permit ....
```

If a permit rule is matched, the packet is forwarded through the firewall. Deny rules are defined using the same syntax:

```
Firewall(config)#ip access-list standard access-list-name-or-number
Firewall(config-std-nacl)#deny ....
```

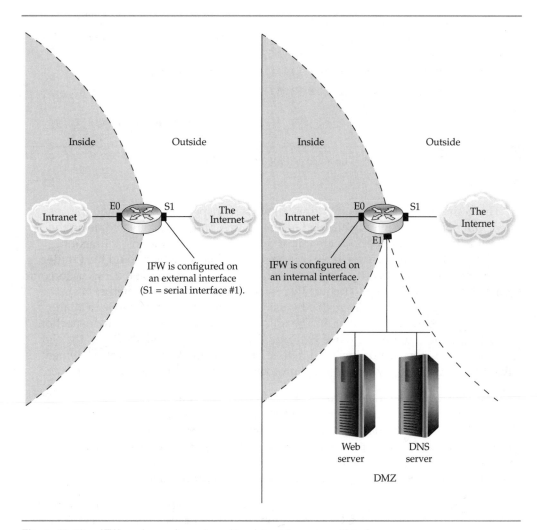

Figure 10-12.   IFW can be configured on either internal or external interfaces.

If a deny rule is matched, the packet is dropped. Figure 10-13 shows a sample access list 100. This access list will be applied to the Ethernet0 firewall interface. Access list 100 permits all traffic that should be inspected by IFW. The last line of the access list is set up to deny unknown IP protocols that a hacker might attempt to use.

The second step in configuring IFW is to define a set of inspection rules with the **ip inspect name** command, using the following syntax:

```
Firewall(config)#ip inspect name inspection-name protocol [timeout
seconds]
```

SMTP is OK if outbound to a management host.

```
access-list 100 permit tcp any 179.12.244.1 eq smtp
access-list 100 permit tcp 209.43.23.201 any eq 80
```

One internal host is OK for HTTP.

Figure 10-13.   This access list sets up traffic on Ethernet0 for IFW inspection.

This command syntax tells IOS Firewall what to inspect packets for and the maximum period of inactivity allowed before closing any session created using the inspection rule. Timeout periods are important in IFW configurations. If timeout limits are set too high, the state table could become bloated, which could hurt router performance and even security. On the other hand, if timeouts are set too low, users could become frustrated at having to frequently reset connections made to Internet hosts.

A set of inspection rules is created by using the same *inspection-name* in all the commands to be included in the set. The following code snippet shows an inspection rule set being built under the name ExtRules. By sharing the name ExtRules, the eight **ip inspect name** commands included in this set can be invoked in a single statement. Table 10-1 gives the keywords used for protocol inspection commands.

```
Firewall(config)#ip inspect name ExtRules ftp timeout 2000
Firewall(config)#ip inspect name ExtRules smtp timeout 3000
Firewall(config)#ip inspect name ExtRules tftp timeout 60
Firewall(config)#ip inspect name ExtRules http java-list 99 timeout 3000
Firewall(config)#ip inspect name ExtRules udp timeout 15
Firewall(config)#ip inspect name ExtRules tcp timeout 2000
```

The timeout limits in the preceding example allow TCP applications about three to five minutes to respond, and UDP applications a minute or less. This reflects the fact that UDP applications are more concerned with causing minimal network overhead than with session integrity. The timeouts set for TCP and UDP are overridden in sessions running an application protocol. For example, any TFTP backup session running through this firewall would have the 60-second timeout limit set for TFTP in force (preempting the 15-second limit set for UDP-only sessions).

Although it's true that timeouts help conserve system resources, the primary reason for configuring them in a firewall is security. The less time you give a hacker's attack program to try to worm through the firewall's interface, the better your internetwork security is. However, timeouts can't be set at too tight of a tolerance, or legitimate users will have to make several attempts to connect. Like everything else in internetworking, timeout strategy is a balancing act.

Protocols	Keyword
	Transport Layer
Terminal Control Protocol (TCP)	Tcp
User Datagram Protocol (UDP)	Udp
Internet Control Message Protocol (ICMP)	Icmp
	Application Layer
Application Firewall	appfw
CU-SeeMe	cuseeme
ESMTP	smtp
FTP	ftp
IMAP	imap
Java	http
H.323	h323
Microsoft NetShow	netshow
POP3	pop3
RealAudio	realaudio
RPC	rpc
SIP	sip
Simple Mail Transfer Protocol (SMTP)	smtp
Skinny Client Control Protocol (SCCP)	skinny
StreamWorks	streamworks
Structured Query Language*Net (SQL*Net)	sqlnet
TFTP	tftp
Unix r commands (rlogin, rexec, rsh)	rcmd
VDOLive	vdolive
WORD	User-defined application name; use prefix -user

Table 10-1.   Keywords in IOS Firewall's ip Inspect and Access-List Commands

Although the inspection set and the ACL don't have anything directly to do with each other, both are applied to the interface. So the last step in configuring an IOS Firewall interface is applying an inspection rule set to the access list. The ACL will then be modified by IFW in accordance with the inspection set. The following snippet taken from the config file for firewall interface FastEthernet0/0 shows the inspection set ExtRules and access list 89. The rules have been applied to inspect and filter inbound traffic.

```
interface fa0/0
 description gallifrey.loc Extranet Gateway
 ip address 209.78.124.12 255.255.255.248
 ip broadcast address 209.78.124.1
 ip inspect ExtRules in
 ip access-group 89 in
```

Without inspection rules to modify access lists, IOS Firewall behavior would revert to that of a normal router running normal access lists.

IOS Firewall Session Management Features

By now, you've seen how important time is to firewalls. This is not unlike the head of security in a bank maintaining strict control over how long the safe door may stay open as people enter and leave it. For obvious reasons, the security chief would frown on employees loitering about the safe door.

The max-incomplete Session Commands   Like the bank's security chief, network administrators fret over connections pending at the firewall's interfaces—especially the outside interfaces. These incomplete connections are called *half-open sessions*. A rising number of half-open sessions at the firewall may indicate that a denial-of-service (DoS) attack is under way. IOS Firewall has several commands, called TCP intercept commands that intercept DoS attacks before they can overwhelm a firewall's network interface.

IOS Firewall uses the **ip inspect max-incomplete** command to track and control half-open sessions. For TCP, *half-open* means that a session has not yet reached the established state. (In fact, it's entered into the IFW state table as a pending request to start a session.) A UDP session is deemed half-open when traffic is detected from one direction only. (Remember, UDP is a connectionless protocol.)

IFW monitors half-open sessions both in absolute numbers and in relative trends. Once every minute, IFW totals all types of half-open sessions and weighs the total against an allowable threshold specified in the config file (500 half-open requests is the default limit). Once the threshold is exceeded, IFW begins deleting half-open requests from its state table. It will continue deleting them until it reaches a minimum threshold, whereupon operations are returned to normal. The following code snippet shows a typical configuration of the **max-incomplete high** command. It's a good practice to keep the high-low spread narrow so IFW can make frequent use of this control feature.

```
Firewall(config)#ip inspect max-incomplete high 1000
Firewall(config)#ip inspect max-incomplete low 900
```

The inspect one-minute Command   The other command to control half-open sessions is the **inspect one-minute** command. Instead of acting on the number of existing half-open connections, the amount of new half-open sessions is what's measured. It works much like the **max-incomplete** command. Here's a sample configuration (using the default values):

```
Firewall(config)#ip inspect tcp one-minute high 900
Firewall(config)#ip inspect tcp one-minute low 400
```

Other TCP Intercept Commands   IFW has other commands to thwart DoS attacks. As mentioned earlier, the **ip inspect tcp synwait-time** command controls SYNflood attacks by deleting connection requests with SYN bits that have been pending longer than a specified time limit. (The default is 30 seconds.) The **ip inspect tcp finwait-time** command similarly controls FINflood attacks. (FIN bits are exchanged when a TCP connection is ready to close; its default is five seconds.) The **ip inspect tcp max-incomplete host** command is used to specify threshold and timeout values for TCP host-specific DoS detection. It limits how many half-open sessions with the same host destination address are allowed and how long IFW will continue deleting new connection requests from the host. (The defaults are 50 half-open sessions and 0 seconds.) Finally, generic protection is given by configuring the maximum idle times for connections with the **ip inspect tcp idle-time** and **ip inspect udp idle-time** commands (with default limits of 1 hour and 30 seconds, respectively).

ASA Firewall OS's Adaptive Security Algorithm

The Adaptive Security Algorithm is roughly equivalent to IOS Firewall's Context-Based Access Control. Both serve as the central engine for their respective firewall products. This is beneficial, because network administrators are familiar with the environment and its basic commands (**configure**, **debug**, **write**, and so on). But ASA has a very different set of firewall-specific commands, and its architecture is radically different from that of IOS Firewall. ASA enables Cisco's firewall appliances to implement tighter security measures and to scale to higher-capacity gateway sizes.

 NOTE   What's an algorithm? The term makes it sound as if writing one would involve quantum physics with a dash of quadratic equations thrown in. But algorithms aren't anything mysterious. An algorithm is nothing more than a carefully crafted set of rules rigorously applied to a repetitive process that is logically able to handle variable conditions. Yes, some algorithms contain mathematical equations, but most don't. Computers make heavy use of algorithms because nearly everything in computing is repetitive and driven by variables.

The Security Level Command

The cliché is that the world is painted not in black and white, but in shades of gray. So, too, for the world of internetwork security, where the "good guys versus bad guys" model falls short, because almost *everybody* is regarded as suspect. The trend in truly powerful network security, then, is the capability to designate networks and hosts as a spectrum of security levels instead of merely as "inside" or "outside."

ASA Firewall's **security-level** command lets you specify relative security levels for interfaces both inside and outside of the firewall. Applying relative security levels on an interface-by-interface basis lets you draw a far more descriptive security map than you would be able to by defining all networks as either inside or outside.

To configure a firewall's interfaces with relative security levels, you enter a **security-level** command for each interface. Additionally, you must use the **nameif** command to identify the interface you wish to manage.

You can choose any value for a security level between 0 and 100, and no two interfaces on an ASA Firewall may have the same level. The common practice is to assign levels in tens, as shown in the following code snippet, which identifies eight interfaces in three security zones:

```
firewall(config)# interface ethernet 0/0
firewall(config-if)# nameif inside
firewall(config-if)# security-level 100
firewall(config-if)# ip address 10.1.10.10 255.255.255.0
firewall(config-if)# no shutdown
firewall(config-if)# interface ethernet 0/1
firewall(config-if)# nameif outside
firewall(config-if)# security-level 0
firewall(config-if)# ip address 10.1.20.10 255.255.255.0
firewall(config-if)# no shutdown
```

The way security levels work is that, by default, *all* traffic from a higher security level is permitted to a lower security level. In this context, the application of rules is simplified, and traffic for a given host, for example, can use a security level lower than what was assigned to it. A connection being made from a higher level to a lower network is treated by the software as outbound; one headed from a lower-level interface to a higher level would be treated as inbound. This scheme enables the network administrator to apply rules on a much more granular basis.

Because each zone has its own security scale, the option exists to implement intrazone security checks. For example, access lists could apply restrictions on traffic flowing between hosts attached to the two DMZ networks. Some possible uses of security levels are depicted in Figure 10-14.

As with the IOS firewall and other firewalls, packets may not traverse the ASA Firewall without a connection and a state. The Adaptive Security Algorithm checks inbound packets using the following rules:

■ When moving between a higher security level and a lower security level, all outbound connections are permitted except those configured as denied in outbound access lists.

■ Static outbound connections can be configured using the **static** command, bypassing the dynamic translation pools created using the **global** and **nat** or **pat** commands.

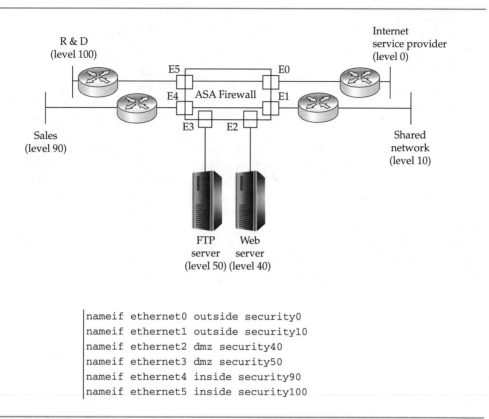

```
nameif ethernet0 outside security0
nameif ethernet1 outside security10
nameif ethernet2 dmz security40
nameif ethernet3 dmz security50
nameif ethernet4 inside security90
nameif ethernet5 inside security100
```

Figure 10-14.   The security-level command draws a more detailed and powerful security map.

ASA Firewall Translation Slots

As with the IOS Firewall, address translation and session tracking are at the center of the architecture. But the ASA Firewall uses a more formal system to implement IP address translation. Instead of simply creating a new translation and dynamically entering it into a reflexive access list, like IOS Firewall, ASA assigns a *slot* to the new connection.

To help manage slot consumption, you can specify a slot limit when configuring interfaces with the **nat** command. In this way, network administrators can prevent individual network users from consuming too many translation slots.

NOTE   Did you know that some applications use more than one connection at a time? For example, FTP takes two connections. A web browser (which runs the HTTP application protocol) can take up to four or more connections, depending on whether it's in the process of loading a page or other objects, such as Java applets. So don't think of Internet connections in terms of something the user consciously decides to start and stop. Sessions are launching and quitting without our even knowing it. Older versions of Microsoft Internet Explorer were said to consume up to 20 TCP connections per user! Imagine what's going on with the current, multitab modern browsers.

We'll run through a simple ASA firewall configuration to showcase some of the commands. Whole books have been written about firewalls, so we'll only cover those commands that will help you understand basic ASA Firewall operations. The ASA Firewall runs a special version of IOS, so the usual IOS command conventions apply. Figure 10-15 shows a three-interface ASA configuration with one shield router, one inside shield router, and one DMZ server attached. The configuration incorporates global address translation, restrictions on outbound traffic, and an outbound static route with an inbound conduit. In our case, we're using an ASA 5505 with a base license, which limits administrators to utilizing VLANs rather than interfaces directly.

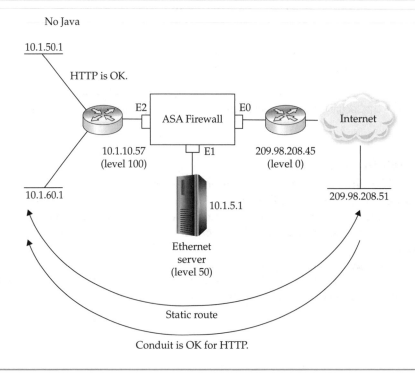

Figure 10-15.   This three-interface ASA firewall supports a static route with a conduit.

The setup is similar, however, on the larger units where you may be configuring trunks and interfaces directly.

> **NOTE**   A lot of ASA Firewalls out there are configured in a similar manner to this—what we have here will give you a good idea of what's in use. Keep in mind that commands are updated, old ones removed, and new ones added as new software is introduced. Security software, in general, is updated frequently. Always refer to the documentation specific to your actual hardware and software setup.

The first step is to go into configure interface mode, pointing at each VLAN interface as its being configured:

```
Firewall.enable
Password:******
Firewall#config t
Firewall(config)#
```

Then, **interface vlan** commands are used to give VLANs security zones and levels, and those VLANs are then assigned to physical interfaces:

```
Firewall(config)#interface vlan 1
Firewall(config-fi)nameif inside
Firewall(config-fi)security-level 100
```

Rinse and repeat for other VLANs:

```
Firewall(config)#interface vlan 2
Firewall(config-fi)nameif outside
Firewall(config-fi)security-level 0
Firewall(config)#interface vlan 3
Firewall(config-fi)nameif DMZ
Firewall(config-fi)security-level 50
```

Next, physical **interface** commands determine the Ethernet specification that the interfaces will operate (autosensing 10/100 Mbps):

```
Firewall(config)#interface ethernet0/0
Firewall(config-if)# speed auto
Firewall(config)#interface ethernet0/1
Firewall(config-if)# speed auto
Firewall(config)#interface ethernet0/2
Firewall(config-if)# speed auto
```

Routable interfaces must be identified with IP addresses and masks, which is done using **ip address** commands. Notice that the private internal IP addresses are used for the DMZ and inside interfaces (10.1.5.1 and 10.1.10.57):

```
Firewall(config)#interface vlan 1
Firewall(config-if)# ip address 209.98.208.45 255.255.255.240
Firewall(config-if)interface vlan 2
Firewall(config-if) ip address DMZ 10.1.5.1 255.255.255.0
Firewall(config-if) interface vlan 3
Firewall(config)#ip address 10.1.10.57 255.255.255.0
```

NOTE You may recognize some of these commands from working on routers or switches. This is due to Cisco's ever-marching-forward int. You know that ASA Firewalls are zone based, but they also are object based, as of version 8.3. Observe that the names you gave to the interfaces previously (outside, DMZ, and inside) are now put to use.

The **nat** command is used to let all users residing on the networks of these two inside interfaces make outbound connections using a shared, translated IP address. Specific pools or addresses may be utilized to make NAT more granular. In this case, "source dynamic" signifies that the source to be translated is the original requesting IP.

```
Firewall(config)# nat (DMZ,outside) source dynamic any interface
Firewall(config)# nat (inside,outside) source dynamic any interface
```

A **static** statement is used to create an externally visible IP address. An accompanying **conduit** statement permits a specified host or network—a business partner, for example—through the ASA Firewall. The following sample statement permits users on an outside host access through the firewall to server 10.1.60.1 through TCP connections for web access. The **eq 80** clause specifies that the TCP connection must be running (equal to) port 80—the port number for the HTTP application protocol. The **any** modifier lets any external host attach to 10.1.60.1.

First, create the object with an embedded NAT address:

```
Firewall(config)# object network host2nat
Firewall(config-network-object)# host 209.98.208.51
Firewall(config-network-object)# nat (DMZ,outside) static 10.1.60.1
```

Now we need a corresponding ACL entry to allow HTTP from the outside:

```
Firewall(config)# access-list outside_access_in extended permit
tcp any object host2nat eq www
```

This statement using the **outbound** command creates an access list that permits an inside host web access (port 80), but forbids it from downloading Java applets. ASA uses the **outbound** command to create access lists and the **apply** command to apply them. Notice that the port number for Java is represented by the text string **java** instead of a port number. Using names instead of numbers is possible for some newer application-layer protocols such as Java. It's obviously a lot easier to remember names instead of a cryptic number. The **outgoing_src** option denies or permits an internal address the ability to start outbound connections using the services specified in the **outbound** command:

```
Firewall(config)#outbound 10 permit 209.98.208.22 255.255.255.255 80
Firewall(config)#outbound 10 deny 209.98.208.22 255.255.255.255 java
Firewall(config)#apply (DMZ) 10 outgoing_src
```

There are many other commands to use when configuring a ASA Firewall. Indeed, in most internetworking environments, there are several more that *must* be configured to get the firewall working properly. Properly configuring an ASA Firewall with multiple servers, protocols, access lists, and shield routers would take days. The possible configurations are endless. But the simple statements we just went through demonstrate that configuring even a firewall—one of internetworking's most complex devices—isn't rocket science. It can get pretty deep, but it's just a matter of taking things one interface at a time, one command at a time.

ASA OS 9

The latest version of the ASA Firewall OS software is version 9, and it offers a variety of improvements and upgrades over previous versions of the software. Some of its features include

- **IPV6 enhancements**   Support for IPv6 VPN connections added to an outside interface using SSL and IKEv2/IPSec protocols; also added are NAT64, OSPFv3, Unified ACL for IPv4 and IPv6, DHCPv6 relay, and more.

- **Remote access enhancements**   IPV6 addressing, name service, split-tunneling, and more are now supported by ASA for AnyConnect clients.

- **Cisco Cloud Web security**   Provides content scanning and other malware protection service for web traffic.

- **Network security integration**   Cisco TrustSec is implemented, allowing security group-based policy enforcement.

- **Resiliency and scalability**   Dynamic routing in Security Contexts using EIGRP and OSPFv2. Site-to-site VPNs are supported in multicontext mode; different contexts may now run in different modes. Increased maximum connection limits for service policy rules, from 65,535 to 2,000,000.

- **Management and serviceability**   Management is enhanced with such features as the **traceroute** command, which allows you to trace a packet's route to its destination, and the **packet-tracer** command, which allows you to examine the packet as it moves through the appliance. ASA OS 9 also includes improvements to its handling of IPv6 addressing.

- **Encryption standards improved**   Next Generation Encryption proposed standard (RFC 6379 defines the Suite B cryptographic suites) is included.

Many other major elements go into firewall configuration. One example is configuring two firewalls—one as the primary gateway server and the other as a hot backup box to which traffic will go if the primary server fails (configured using the **failover** command). Another is configuring the firewall to integrate with a security server, such as TACACS+.

Adaptive Security Appliances

For a long time, Cisco Secure PIX Firewall was Cisco's premier product for firewall duties. In 2008, Cisco discontinued the line and replaced it with their Adaptive Security Appliance (ASA) line. However, it looks like it might be quite awhile before the PIX is no longer used: It was so prevalent that it's still out there, being upgraded and maintained—at least until mid-2013 when all support ends. Both are *security appliances*—they have the sole task of acting as the internetwork's bouncer, but they do things a bit differently than a firewall.

The IOS Firewall feature set is targeted at more price-sensitive customers or for duty in cordoning off access within enterprise networks. PIX/ASA was positioned by Cisco to compete head-to-head with the major firewall products on the market. ASA Firewall differs from IOS Firewall in these ways:

- **Integrated hardware/software** ASA Firewall is an integrated package on a hardware platform purposely built for heavy-duty firewall service. It doesn't come as a separate software package.

- **Adaptive security algorithm** Neither a packet filter nor an application proxy firewall, ASA implements a stateful inspection and cut-through architecture that delivers higher performance.

> **NOTE** *Cut-through processing* is a technique that allows a connection (HTTP, FTP, or Telnet) to be authorized and permitted once at the application layer. Then all packets that follow it, for that session, are filtered at the network layer.

- **Integrated VPN option** Virtual private networks are natively supported; however, a plug-in processor card optimally configures VPNs supporting the advanced Internet Protocol Security (IPSec) encryption and Internet Key Exchange (IKE) standards.

Network administrators are increasingly turning to purpose-built devices, such as Cisco Secure ASA Firewall to meet their network security needs. The electronics and software in the ASA Firewall are tuned specifically to balance advanced security functionality with the need for high-throughput performance. ASA Firewall and dedicated products like it are called *network appliances*—the hip, new term for devices built to serve a narrowly defined networking function. The most obvious advantage of using a firewall appliance is that the IOS software doesn't have to split its time between filtering and routing.

Beyond the appliance versus firewall-enabled router debate, Cisco positioned PIX and ASA as real-time embedded systems against competitors' firewall appliances based on Unix platforms. The argument is that Unix-based firewall appliances must pay a price in performance and in security. The reasoning is that a general-purpose operating system kernel such as Unix not only has latencies and overheads inappropriate for firewall duty, but also inherent security holes that hackers could use to break into the firewall itself.

The ASA is designed to secure an entire organization, no matter what its size. Additionally, it can secure a segment of a business, while still consolidating security mechanisms and reducing operating costs.

The Cisco ASA 5500 series provides the following network-based features:

- Worm and virus prevention
- Spyware and adware prevention
- Network-traffic inspection
- Hacker prevention
- Denial-of-service prevention
- Identity based (context) rules

These features all come together with on-device security event correlation.

Application security provides inspection and control for dynamically protected networked business applications. These services include the control of bandwidth-intensive peer-to-peer services and instant messaging, URL access control, protection of core business applications, and a number of application-specific protections for VoIP and multimedia. The Cisco ASA appliances can act as hardware VPN clients, simplifying management, along with hardware-accelerated SSL and VPN services.

The ASAs are managed using the Cisco ASA software services. The latest release of the software (version 9) includes 49 new security enhancements. Some of the most significant bolster application-layer firewall services with external databases such as ScanSafe. The continued integration of Cisco security services (the previously discussed TrustSec) and IP telephony services (Unified Communications is discussed in an upcoming chapter) are integral to Cisco's end-to-end marketing approach.

Application-layer firewall services help protect applications, including web, e-mail, VoIP, instant messaging, and Microsoft networking protocols.

Cisco SA500 Series Security Appliances

The Cisco SA500 Series security appliances are all-in-one security devices for organizations with fewer than 100 members. These devices combine firewall, VPN, and IPS, along with e-mail and web security features. Employees working either locally or remotely can take advantage of these features. Table 10-2 compares these devices.

Model	Description
SA520	Firewall: 200 Mbps IPSec VPN: 65 Mbps 4 LAN ports 2 SSL VPN seats, upgradable to 25 50 IPSec VPN tunnels
SA520W	Firewall: 200 Mbps IPSec VPN: 65 Mbps 4 LAN ports 2 SSL VPN seats, upgradable to 25 50 IPSec VPN tunnels Wireless 802.11 b/g/n
SA540	Firewall: 300 Mbps IPSec VPN: 85 Mbps 8 LAN ports 50 SSL VPN seats 100 IPSec VPN tunnels

Table 10-2. Cisco's SA500 Line of ASA Devices

Small Office and Branch Office

Cisco's small office and branch office line of ASA routers is targeted at small businesses and large enterprise branch offices. These routers are available in a range of sizes and performance capabilities, based on specific network, budget, and security needs. Table 10-3 compares the models Cisco offers for this market.

Internet Edge

ASA routers for the Internet edge market are targeted at small businesses or large enterprises with several branch offices. These routers are designed to fit the needs of a small office, yet are able to deliver enterprise-strength security. Table 10-4 compares Cisco's models at this level.

Enterprise Data Center

Cisco's router models for the enterprise data center are designed to be dynamic. They are able to evolve, spanning multiple platforms, technologies, and means of deployment (including physical and virtual). Table 10-5 compares Cisco's ASA routers at this level.

Feature/Model	ASA 5505	ASA 5510	ASA 5512-X	ASA-5515-X
Firewall throughput	160 Mbps	300 Mbps	1 Gbps	1.2 Gbps
Maximum firewall connections	10,000/25,000	50,000/130,000	100,000	250,000
Maximum firewall connections per second	4,000	9,000	10,000	15,000
Maximum 3DES/AES VPN throughput	100 Mbps	170 Mbps	200 Mbps	250 Mbps
VLANs	Three (trunking disabled) or two (trunking enabled)	50/100	50/100	100

Table 10-3.   ASAs Designed for Small and Branch Offices

Feature/Model	ASA 5520	ASA 5525-X	ASA 5540	ASA 5545-X	ASA 5550	ASA 5555-X
Firewall throughput	450 Mbps	2 Gbps	650 Mbps	3 Gbps	1.2 Gbps	4 Gbps
Maximum firewall connections	280,000	500,000	400,000	750,000	650,000	1,000,000
Maximum firewall connections per second	12,000	20,000	25,000	30,000	33,000	50,000
Maximum 3DES/ AES VPN throughput	225 Mbps	300 Mbps	325 Mbps	400 Mbps	425 Mbps	700 Mbps
VLANs	150	200	200	300	400	500

Table 10-4.   Cisco's ASAs Typically Found at the Internet Edge

Feature/Model	ASA 5585-X with SSP10	ASA 5585-X with SSP20	ASA 5585-X with SSP40	ASA 5585-X with SSP60
Firewall throughput	4 Gbps	10 Gbps	20 Gbps	40 Gbps
Maximum firewall connections	1,000,000	2,000,000	4,000,000	10,000,000
Maximum firewall connections per second	50,000	125,000	200,000	350,000
Maximum 3DES/AES VPN throughput	1 Gbps	2 Gbps	3 Gbps	5 Gbps
VLANs	1,024	1,024	1,024	1,024

Table 10-5.   Cisco's ASA Devices Used in Enterprise Data Centers

Cisco ASA CX Context-Aware Security

As we have gotten more dependent on the Internet and its functions, the need for security has continually evolved. Networks are complex, and in order to secure your network, you must consider a number of variables and factors in order to build the right security tool. Because of this, Cisco has introduced ASA CX context-aware security. It extends the ASA platform with greater visibility and control, allowing enterprises to employ more of the applications and devices they need to make their organizations more powerful.

Visibility   Cisco ASA CX context-aware security provides security administrators a new level of visibility, when it comes to their network traffic flow. They can see what resources users connected to the network are using, along with which devices and applications are in use.

With this information in hand, security administrators can make decisions based on what they are seeing. Further, Cisco AnyConnect gives information about the type and location of a mobile device before it can access the network. It also uses global threat intelligence from Cisco Security Intelligence Operations (SIO) to provide malware protection.

Control   ASA CX also operates at a very granular level, to provide precise control. It blocks port- and protocol-hopping applications (such as Skype) and other peer-to-peer applications so that security is ensured, while requiring fewer policies to be written.

ASA CX is also deeply entrenched with unique social networking controls. It recognizes more than 1,000 applications and 75,000 micro applications. This enables organizations to allow access to specific portions of an application (such as Facebook for business) while disabling other components (such as Facebook's *Farmville*).

Model/Feature	ASA CX SSP-10	ASA CX SSP-20
Memory	12 GB	24 GB
Disk storage	600 GB	600 GB
Hot-swappable hard disk?	Yes	Yes
Flash memory	8 GB	8 GB

Table 10-6.   Cisco's ASA Devices

ASA CX allows security administrators to see which types of devices are trying to access the network, which operating systems they are using, and where they are located. By being able to see this information, administrators can allow specific devices while still maintaining high levels of network protection.

Other features include the following:

- **Identity-based firewalling**   Delivers differentiated access control based on users and user roles.

- **Device-type-based enforcement**   Determines which types of devices (iPads, Android devices, and so forth) are accessing the network and manages which devices are (and are not) allowed to connect.

- **URL filtering**   Used for determining which websites can and cannot be accessed through the network, thus providing more control for the administrator.

- **Cisco Prime**   Preloaded with Cisco Prime Security Manager, Cisco Prime is an intuitive management solution that simplifies the management of context-aware firewalls.

Table 10-6 compares the two models of Cisco ASA CX SSPs.

Both ASA CX-SSP-10 and SSP-20 are supported on Cisco ASA 5585-X platforms running Cisco ASA software and are managed using Cisco Prime Security Manager.

Access Routers

Access to your network can come in many ways. Access servers serve dial-in needs, for instance. However, branch offices, small offices, telecommuters, and road warriors may need higher performance and more robust access to the network. As such, access for these connections can be facilitated using access routers. Access routers are a subset of Cisco's router offerings.

Overview

Cisco's access router line provides the functionality for remote workers who need more powerful access to the network. To facilitate these connections, access routers include beefed-up security and performance features. Access routers offer secure Internet and network access through a variety of high-speed WAN access technologies. Benefits of these access routers include the following:

- High-speed broadband and leased-line access

- Multiservice data/voice integration applications

- Integrated security capabilities, with IPSec VPN, a stateful inspection firewall, and intrusion detection

- Modular higher-end models, providing design and deployment flexibility

Cisco's line of access routers covers the gamut of organizational needs, offering models from SOHO use to medium-sized businesses to huge enterprise deployments.

In addition to traditional router duties, access routers provide enhanced security, manageability, and the quality of service (QoS) necessary for such applications as video-conferencing, e-learning, VPNs, and online collaboration.

An important feature of the access routers is their QoS capabilities. Because the routers will be asked to channel VoIP, multimedia content, and other applications that would suffer from packet latency, QoS is a necessary mechanism. These capabilities result in smoother, jitter-free conversations and transmissions than without QoS in place.

Models

Cisco offers a number of access routers with varying levels of features. The lower-end access routers are fixed in their configuration—that is, they simply plug into a WAN connection, like a DSL line. However, when you start moving up the ladder of Cisco's access router products, there are more opportunities for modularity. They can be configured to operate on an OC-3 connection or T1 connection, for example, depending on which cards and modules you use to tweak them out.

Cisco offers eight models of access routers in two series:

- The Cisco 1900 series of access routers is targeted at small to medium businesses. This series, with six models, offers a number of IPSec VPN, stateful firewall, and intrusion detection capabilities.

- The Cisco 3900 series of Integrated Service Routers offers two models: the Cisco 3925 and the 3945 Integrated Service Router G2. They are an integral part of Cisco AVVID (Architecture for Voice, Video, and Integrated Data). Because they use IOS, they are highly configurable and offer QoS and security features to branch offices.

Cisco Cloud Web Security

Security is an ever-evolving topic, and one area in which Cisco has moved to keep up with the times is in the realm of cloud security. In December 2009, Cisco acquired ScanSafe for US$183 million and kept it as a separate business unit. In September of 2012, the service was renamed Cisco Cloud Web Security.

Cisco Cloud Web Security provides cloud-based web security services and controls for all sizes of organizations. The technology integrates with ASA Firewalls and ISR routers. Cisco Cloud Web Security is powered by Cisco Security Intelligence Operations (SIO), which is a cloud-based service that detects and blocks threats in real time. SIO utilizes detection technologies, automated machine-learning heuristics, and sundry scanning engines to provide a detailed view of each web request and its associated security risk.

The technology allows the safe use of web-based and social networking applications within the enterprise, while still keeping the organization's network infrastructure safe. As such, organizations can make use of social media (Facebook, for instance) and allow beneficial applications, without blocking an entire site. Controls allow organizations to provide access to applications that are suitable while blocking those that are deemed harmful.

 NOTE In addition to managing inbound web traffic, Cisco Cloud Web Security also helps prevent web-based leaks of confidential or personal data.

How Cisco Cloud Web Security Works

Internet traffic is redirected to the Cisco Cloud Web Security service, where it is scanned for malware and where user-based policy is enforced. When a user wants to go to a website, the URL request is routed to the nearest Cloud Web Security data center. Cisco uses several detection technologies and scanning engines to detect and block known and unknown web malware.

Via the Cisco AnyConnect Secure Mobility 3.0 client, Cisco Cloud Web Security provides remote workers as well as smartphone, tablet, and bring-your-own-device (BYOD) users with the same level of security as on-site employees using client computers.

Example of Cisco Cloud Web Security

Cisco Cloud Web Security isn't just limited to organizations with people already on the payroll—it can protect an organization in a public setting as well. For instance, consider a coffee shop—a bastion of people eager to jump on public Wi-Fi with their smartphones, tablets, and laptops. Although this is good for business, it also poses threats.

This access—although necessary for business—increases the likelihood of a customer visiting a website with inappropriate or unwanted content within the boundaries of the establishment. As such, the business needs to be able to block unwanted content from being accessed via its network.

The tool allows businesses not only to block unfavorable content, but also to see what sorts of websites customers are visiting, allowing them to utilize that information for business growth. For instance, if customers are looking for information about the music being played in the coffee shop, information about that music can be provided on the shop's web page, providing another opportunity to make the shop appeal to customers.

Cisco Security Manager

Security threats abound on the Internet in many different forms. Whether threats come from viruses, hackers, or denial-of-service attacks, the network administrator has had to keep on his or her toes to avoid trouble. To mitigate those problems, security has become somewhat of a patchwork affair—VPNs are used for one function, firewalls another. The Cisco Security Manager (CSM) aims to bring security together so it can be centrally managed rather than the piecemeal affair it is now.

CSM provides security management using different views. A device-level view allows you to see all of the devices on a network and the policies that can be set and managed for each. CSM's policy view allows for the creation and management of policies based on specific organizational needs.

This allows not only organization-wide policies to be established, but if there are specific hotspots within the organization that need additional attention, they can be established and managed. Furthermore, the network administrator can also establish policies for various links across the network.

The CSM also provides a topology-centric view, which provides a visual representation of the network that scales through linked network maps, allowing the administrator to manage policies from this level. These views provide the administrator with an integrated framework to manage security services such as firewalls, VPNs, and intrusion prevention services.

NOTE   The Cisco Security Manager used to be part of a larger tool called the Cisco Security Management Suite—the other component involved was Cisco Security MARS. MARS used to collect, correlate, and report security events, but Cisco has since discontinued MARS. Reporting duties are now performed by SIO.

Integrated Services Router

Another security device is Cisco's Integrated Services Router (ISR G2). This router differs from the modular routers we talked about previously. Modular routers, as you recall, give you the flexibility to expand your router to suit your network needs. This is done by offering different modules that can be added (or removed) depending on your needs. But ISRs optimize themselves for secure and concurrent transfer of data, voice, and images at wire-speed. They provide flexibility on services such as security, unified communications, data, and wireless.

 NOTE Cisco offers the ability to add specific security features to their modular devices as well. We'll talk about those modules and the devices to which they apply in the next section.

The Right Tool for the Right Job

What's the benefit of ISRs over modular routers? The biggest advantage to using an ISR is that you don't need to buy any extra hardware to handle different functions. This gives you greater control of the network and affords better security. Here are some examples:

- Setting up a firewall on an ISR eliminates the need to set up a separate firewall server.
- Enabling the DHCP services eliminates the usage of a computer as a DHCP server.
- Both wired and wireless networks can be managed with an ISR.

Optimally, you'll configure your ISR to perform both encryption and decryption services, thus adding an additional layer of protection to your network.

ISRs are especially useful if you have a large network or if you are connecting multiple, smaller networks. For instance, if your organization has a LAN, a WAN, and Internet connections, an ISR can make all three work together in harmony. The ISR is especially useful to protect your internal network from attackers who might come from the Internet portion of your network.

By activating the ISR's firewall features, you add another layer of protection. Further, you don't need to install policies for specific network clients—the router will not allow a client access to the unauthorized portions of the network.

Additionally, ISRs provide the sorts of services that in a traditional network would require extra hardware. Computers, IP phones, and wireless devices can share a single, secure network connection using an ISR. This is ideal for organizations that want multiple services, but only want to buy one, lone device.

Network management is also simplified. The LAN can have a variety of devices using both wired and wireless connections and communicate within the network and to external networks.

Models

Cisco offers seven series of ISRs, split into two generations of ISRs. Table 10-7 compares the features of the different series of ISRs.

You'll notice from Table 10-7 that there are currently two generations of ISRs. Although both are still available, obviously Cisco is moving away from the first generation and pushing the second. However, both are perfectly useful devices, especially where network and budgetary considerations are concerned. Table 10-8 shows the primary differences between both generations of ISRs.

Series	Description	Generation
Cisco 860, 880, and 890 Series ISR	Suited for enterprise branch offices or small businesses. Fifteen models. Cisco unified voice, video, and data communications. Built-in WAN optimization.	2
Cisco 1900 Series ISR	Suited for branch offices growing in size. Three models. Two Gigabit Ethernet WAN ports. One available integrated service module slot (1941 and 1941W only). Up to 11 modular LAN switch ports. Intrusion prevention features.	2
Cisco 2900 Series ISR	Suited for branch offices growing in size. Four models. Three Gigabit Ethernet WAN ports. One integrated service module slot. Up to 50 modular LAN switchports. Intrusion prevention features.	2
Cisco 3900 Series ISR	Suited for branch offices growing in size. Four models. Up to four Gigabit Ethernet WAN ports. One integrated services module slot (on 3925 and 3945 models only). Up to 98 modular LAN switch ports. Intrusion prevention features.	2
Cisco 1800 Series ISR	Suited for branch offices. Eight models. Eight 10/100 Mbps switch ports. Up to 50 VPN tunnels for fixed platform models, up to 800 VPN tunnels for modular platforms.	1
Cisco 2800 Series ISR	Suited for branch offices. Four models. Two 10/100/1000 Mbps built-in routed ports. Up to 64 10/100 Mbps switch ports. Up to 1,500 VPN tunnels.	1
Cisco 3800 Series ISR	Suited for branch offices. Two models. Up to two 10/100/1000 Mbps built-in routed ports. Up to 112 10/100 Mbps switch ports. Up to 2,500 VPN tunnels.	1

Table 10-7.   Cisco's ISR Line

Feature	Cisco ISR	Cisco ISR G2
WAN performance	Up to 45 Mbps with services	Up to 350 Mbps with services
Network processor	Single	Multicore
Service module performance and capacity	1X and 160GB storage	Up to 7X with dual core and 1TB storage
Onboard DSPs	Voice only	Voice and video-ready DSPs
Switch modules	Fast Ethernet with Power over Ethernet (PoE)	Fast Ethernet/Gigabit Ethernet with POE+
IOS image	Multiple images	Single universal IOS image
Services delivery	Hardware coupled	Services on demand
Redundancy	Single motherboard	Field-upgradeable motherboard
Energy efficiency	EnergyWise	EnergyWise with slot based controls

Table 10-8.   The Second Generation of ISRs Offers Improvements over the First Generation

Specialized Modules

A couple series of Cisco's devices (specifically the 6500 series switches and the 7600 series routers) are upgradable with service modules that perform specific, security-based tasks. One might think that these levels of security are only necessary for routers or other layer-3 devices. But security at the layer-2 level is an often-ignored (but very necessary) place to ensure network security exists.

Although the model seems like a pristine view of networking (this happens at layer 2, and this happens at layer 3), hackers don't care—they will look for any way into the network and will take advantage of any security hole available to them. Layer-2 attacks are one of the first things a hacker will utilize after getting a foothold within a single computer inside the network.

As such, it is important to keep your switches safe and secure. These modules allow you to configure modular switches and routers for tasks that are unique to your organization's needs.

Firewall Services Module and ASA Service Modules

Designed for large enterprises and service providers, the Firewall Services Module (FWSM) and ASA Service Modules apply firewall services in a single module. The modules can be installed inside Catalyst 6500 switches and 7600 series routers, and allow any VLAN on the switch to be passed through port-based firewall security running inside the switching infrastructure.

Both the FWSM and ASA Service Module (SM) are based on Cisco PIX technology and use the PIX operating system, a secure, real-time operating system. The module enables organizations to manage multiple firewalls from the same management platform.

The modules monitor traffic flows using application inspection engines to provide network security. They dictate the security parameters and enable the enforcement of security policies through authentication, access control lists, and protocol inspection. Table 10-9 explains some of the FWSM's features.

The FWSM provides additional features that can help reduce costs and organizational complexity, while allowing ease of management for multiple firewalls:

■ **Completeness of security**   Every port in the switch or router is afforded the security of the firewall.

■ **Resource manager**   Allows organizations to limit the resources allocated to security rules so that it does not conflict with others.

■ **Seamless integration**   Its transparent firewall feature enables the FWSM to act as a layer-2 bridging firewall to ensure minimal changes in network topology. Also, the FWSM allows any port on the device to operate as a firewall port and integrates firewall security inside the network infrastructure.

■ **Ease of use**   The FWSM uses the PIX Device Manager (PDM), a GUI that can be used for management and configuration. The FWSM can also be managed using the Adaptive Security Device Manager V5.2F.

A great attribute of the FWSM is that it allows multiple, virtualized firewalls on one physical hardware platform. Administrators can configure, deploy, and manage these firewalls as if they are on separate devices. Virtualization reduces the number of physical devices on the network, reducing the cost and complexity to the organization.

Feature	Firewall Services Module Capabilities
Throughput	5 Gbps (up to 20 Gbps when chassis is fully loaded).
Connections	1,000,000 concurrent.
Virtual firewalls	250 per unit.
Expandability	Four FWSMs can be installed on a single chassis.
OS	Cisco ASA Firewall.

Table 10-9.   FWSM Capabilities

Because of the sheer number of virtual firewalls available (250 per unit), large enterprises and service providers can create distinct policies for different customers or departments, depending on the need.

Cisco Wireless Service Module (WiSM2)

Wireless is another important area to consider when planning and deploying network security. Organizations implementing wireless VPNs also have distinct needs. Specifically, once authenticated, anonymous clients are allowed onto an access point, which is normally connected directly to an internal switch.

The Cisco Catalyst 6500 Series/7600 Series Wireless Services Module (WiSM2) is a member of the Cisco Wireless LAN Controller family, and provides security and ease of use for wireless LANs (WLANs). It affords network managers the ability to easily control and manage their WLANs.

WiSM2 works in conjunction with Cisco's Aironet access points and the Cisco Wireless Control System (WCS) to support data, voice, and video applications. WiSM2 is an important part of the Cisco Unified Wireless Network (for enterprises) and Cisco ServiceMesh (for service providers), and provides real-time communication between access points and other wireless LAN devices to provide a secure wireless environment.

Security features of WiSM2 include

- 802.11i Wi-Fi Protected Access 2 (WPA2), WPA, and Wired Equivalent Privacy (WEP).

- 802.1X with multiple Extensible Authentication Protocol (EAP) types, including Protected EAP (PEAP), EAP with Transport Layer Security (EAP-TLS), EAP with Tunneled TLS (EAP-TTLS), and Cisco LEAP.

- In Cisco WLANs, access points serve as air monitors, communicating real-time information about the wireless domain to Cisco wireless LAN controllers. Security threats are quickly identified and communicated to network administrators via WCS. This allows the information to be analyzed and action can be taken based on that information.

WiSM2 utilizes the 802.11 a/b/g/n standards, so organizations can deliver the wireless solution that is best for their needs. Additional features include

- Connections for up to 1,000 access points and 15,000 clients.

- Ability to update 500 access points at a time.

- Wireless LAN intrusion protection and location. Detects rogue devices and wireless threats and also locates these devices, thus allowing administrators mitigate threats.

- Identity-based networking. Networks have a multitude of security rules. WiSM2 supports those flavors of security, including:

  - Layer 2 security 802.1X (PEAP, LEAP, EAP-TTLS), WPA, 802.11i (WPA2), and Layer 2 Tunneling Protocol (L2TP)

  - Layer 3 security IP Security (IPSec) and web authentication

  - VLAN assignments

  - Access control lists (ACLs)

  - QoS

  - Authentication, authorization, and accounting (AAA) as well as RADIUS authentication

  - Cisco Network Admission Control (NAC)

  - Guest tunneling, to ensure that guest users are able to access a corporate network only by passing through a corporate firewall

Intrusion Prevention System

Firewalls are important components of network protection, but organizations of all sizes need a complete lineup of security services. An important piece of that puzzle is an intrusion prevention system (IPS).

NOTE   IPSs have their roots in intrusion detection systems (IDSs). And it only seems logical—why just detect an intruder when you can prevent their attacks in the first place? Cisco still offers a couple models of IDS devices, but seems to be discontinuing them fast. That sort of duty is now being performed by IPS devices.

The core of Cisco's IPS technology is in its Security Intelligence Operations (SIO) underlining that we talked about in Chapter 9. To refresh your memory, SIO is an enormous, dynamic database of threats that Cisco continuously monitors and updates, delivering your IPS devices the most up-to-date information available. In fact, every IPS that Cisco sells can be part of the database.

Online threats are continuously graded and then uploaded to Cisco, where that information is disseminated to IPS devices around the world. The fact that each IPS is part of this notification network makes it a robust—and highly effective—way to monitor threats.

Cisco has developed a number of IPS devices—from standalone units to plug-in modules. Like so many other Cisco devices, the IPS you need will depend on your organization's size, networking infrastructure, and threats you are trying to mitigate. Table 10-10 describes Cisco's IPS products.

Product	Description
IPS 4300 Series Sensors	Two models. Up to 1.5 Gbps average inspection throughput. Part of the Cisco SecureX architecture. Attacker visibility updated every 15 minutes through Global Correlation reputation feeds.
IPS 4500 Series Sensors	Two models. Up to 5 Gbps average inspection throughput. Up to 8,400,000 connections. Part of the Cisco SecureX architecture. Delivers hardware-accelerated inspection.
Catalyst 6500 Series Module	IDSM-2 module plugs into popular Catalyst 6500 series switch chassis. 500 Mbps. 5,000 new TCP connections per second. 5,000 HTTP transactions per second. 50,000 concurrent connections. Supports up to 500,000 concurrent connections. Inspection of traffic in layers 2–7 protects the network from policy violations, vulnerability exploitations, and so on.
ASA 5500 Series	Fifteen models with entries in small and branch offices, Internet edge, and enterprise data center. Up to 300,000 firewall connections per second. Between 150 Mbps and 20 Gbps throughput. Between 25 and 10,000 AnyConnect or clientless VPN user sessions.
ISR Series Routers IPS Solution	Two models, compatible with seven different Cisco ISRs. Suited for small and medium-sized businesses and enterprise branch offices. Can monitor up to 75 Mbps of traffic. Dedicated processor maximizes performance. Supports T1, T3, DSL, ATM, Fast Ethernet, and Gigabit Ethernet.

Table 10-10. Cisco's IPS Devices

Summary

Network security is an ever-changing, ever-moving target. Given all the ways attackers think up to go at a network, it's more likely than not that Cisco will continue to evolve these devices, if not introduce completely new devices and technologies. Although everyone knows that securing their network is important, it's not a job that can easily be done with a single device or piece of software. Given your network and what's going on with it, you might need to take a multifaceted approach and involve different sorts of devices at different places on your network.

CHAPTER 11 | Cisco Unified Wireless

C onventionally speaking, internetworking has always been accomplished by plugging cables into different electronic boxes and then letting the packets fly. But one of the latest, greatest additions to networking gives packets their own wings. They need no longer be constrained by the physical limit of the twisted-pair wiring. The era of wireless networking is upon us.

Introduction to Wireless Networking

With all the advances in conventional, wired networking, it was only a matter of time before someone looked up into the sky and wondered, "What about wireless?" Truth be told, someone asked that question about 25 years ago, but the practical, functional result of that question has only been realized in the last few of years.

In this section, we take a look back at where wireless networking came from, how it works, and how you can benefit from it.

The Roots of Wireless Networking

To understand better the wireless networking of today, it's important to know its history and how we've gotten here from there.

The most popular LAN technology in the world is Ethernet. It is defined by the Institute of Electrical and Electronic Engineers (IEEE) with the 802.3 standard. Ethernet has provided an evolving, widely available, high-speed networking standard. Initially, Ethernet provided 1 Mbps transfer rates, and then 10 Mbps transfer rates, which then grew to 100 Mbps, and then 1, 10, and 40 Gbps, and now 100 Gbps. Because IEEE 802.3 is an open standard, there is a broad range of suppliers and products for Ethernet users. The standard ensures a certain level of interoperability, no matter what the product or vendor.

The first wireless LAN (WLAN) technologies weren't as speedy as Ethernet at the time. They operated in the 900 MHz band and only clocked in at about 2 Mbps, max. Furthermore, they were proprietary in nature, which eliminated any common communication between different vendors' products. In spite of these obstacles, wireless networking managed to carve out a respectable niche for itself in vertical markets such as retail and warehousing. It was useful in these environments, because the mobility and flexibility of the technology was necessary in environments where the workers used handheld devices for such activities as inventory management and data collection.

Aironet, a wireless networking company, realized the need for wireless networking and began pushing for standards in 1991.

NOTE Cisco acquired Aironet in 2000 and uses its technology as the cornerstone of its WLAN products. We talk about Cisco's acquisition and their Aironet devices later in the chapter.

By establishing standards, they argued, wireless LANs would gain broad market acceptance. The next year, WLAN developers began working on products that operated in the unlicensed 2.4 GHz frequency band. This new technology was especially appealing to two particular markets:

- **Health care**   Wireless networking made it possible to transfer patient data to mobile computing devices. Rather than tote a computer from exam room to exam room, wireless networking puts patient information at a health care professional's fingertips.

- **Schools**   Not being constrained by wires made it possible for schools that were constructed without wiring conduits (remember the days) to construct computer networks without having to punch holes in walls and string cabling between floors.

In June 1997, the technology that serves as the core standard for the WLANs we know today was developed. The IEEE released the 802.11 standard for wireless local area networking. The standard supports data transmission in infrared light and two types of radio transmission within the unlicensed 2.4 GHz frequency band: Frequency Hopping Spread Spectrum (FHSS) and Direct Sequence Spread Spectrum (DSSS).

 NOTE   We'll get deeper into 802.11 specifics later in the chapter.

Benefits

If the simple ability to perform networking functions without being tethered to a switch or a hub isn't enough to stir your soul, let's take a closer look at the abilities of wireless data transmission, along with a few situations in which wireless networking is beneficial.

What It Can Do

Besides the "gee-whiz, this is kewl" aspect of a computer network that operates without wires, a number of important factors make wireless networking a useful, productive technology:

- **Mobility**   With WLANs, users can get real-time access to their LAN from virtually anywhere (depending on the range and any obstacles and interference). This ability comes without having to be hardwired into the network. This mobility gives users the freedom to access the network from almost anywhere at any time.

- **Reduced cost-of-ownership**   Even though start-up costs for WLAN hardware are more than the cost of a traditional LAN, when the complete, lifecycle expenses are considered, WLAN expenses can be considerably lower. The greatest long-term cost benefits are seen in dynamic environments where there are frequent equipment moves and changes.

- **Scalability**   WLANs can be easily configured in a number of networking topologies to meet the needs of specific applications and installations. Configurations are highly flexible, can easily be changed, and range from simple peer-to-peer networks that are ideal for a few users to full infrastructure networks of thousands of users that enable roaming across a broad area.

- **High-speed data rates**   WLAN transmission speeds are starting to be comparable to wired networks. Users can access information at up to 300 Mbps, which is on par with conventional wire speeds. Though not yet touching the 1 Gbps and 10 Gbps that are possible in wired networks, wireless has a respectable, functional speed.

- **Interoperability**   Manufacturers (such as Cisco) who build their products using the 802.11 standard ensure functionality with other compliant equipment or brands within the network.

- **Encryption for high-speed LAN security**   Through the incorporation of WPA and WPA2 schemes, network security can be ensured. WPA/WPA2 serves access points, mini-PCI cards, PCI Express cards, USB adapters, and so on.

- **Installation speed and simplicity**   Before wireless technology, connecting computers to a LAN required stringing and plugging in a mess of wires. The task could be further complicated if the wiring needed to be strung through walls or between different floors. Wireless technology simplifies and speeds up the installation process.

- **Installation flexibility**   Because WLANs aren't restricted by the physical barriers that constrain wired LANs, wireless networks can provide network access to those users and workstations where connecting to a LAN is simply impossible.

- **Tablets and smartphones**   Several years ago, smartphones and tablets weren't as prevalent as they are now, and they didn't have wired capability—remember Palm Pilot serial sync stations? With the pervasiveness of tablets, smartphones, and other gadgets within the enterprise, wireless is a must in most organizations because most every device now utilizes Wi-Fi for connectivity.

- **Bring Your Own Device (BYOD)**   On top of corporate sanctioned devices, BYOD has brought a whole new slew of wireless requirements to the enterprise. Separating corporate data from Guest Wi-Fi is a must.

Applications

Given the continually changing face of technology and its applications, it almost seems silly to pigeonhole a specific technology into specific fields. However, the following list will give you an idea of how wireless technology can be used in a number of different fields. Again, this list should not be considered as the extent of wireless's capabilities—

your own circumstances and situations will be the best guide as to whether you benefit most from a wireless or wired networking:

- **Corporate**   With a WLAN, corporate employees need no longer be tethered to their desks. By using laptops equipped with wireless NICs (network interface cards), they can take full advantage of e-mail, file sharing, and web browsing, regardless of where they are in the office or business campus.

- **Hospitality and retail**   Hospitality services such as restaurants can use WLANs to enter and send food orders to the kitchen, directly from the table. Retail stores can use WLANs to set up temporary cash registers for special events, such as the day after Christmas or the start of a sale.

- **Manufacturing**   WLANs link factory floor workstations and data collection devices to a company's network. They are mobile on the work floor and don't require more cabling on the factory floor.

- **Warehousing**   WLANs connect handheld and forklift-mounted computer terminals with barcode readers and wireless data links. This technology is used to enter and maintain the location of a warehouse's inventory.

- **Education**   Schools, colleges, and universities benefit from mobile connectivity by enabling students, faculty, and staff with notebook computers to connect to the academic institution's network for collaborative lessons, and to the Internet for web browsing and e-mail. Furthermore, wireless technology can save desperately needed classroom space by making portable computer labs a reality.

- **Financial**   Financial traders can use a handheld PC with a WLAN adapter to receive pricing information from a database in real time and to speed up and improve the quality of trades.

- **Health care**   By using wireless handheld PCs, health care professionals have access to real-time information and can increase productivity and quality of patient care by reducing treatment delays, roaming from patient to patient, and eliminating redundant paperwork and decreasing transcription errors.

This is just the tip of the iceberg on how wireless networking can be used. To be sure, as technology changes the face of business, more and more uses for wireless networking will be apparent.

WLANs

A WLAN is just what the acronym suggests—a LAN that is accessed without having to be physically tethered to a server, switch, hub, or any other networking device. Using radio frequency (RF) technology, WLANs transmit and receive data out of midair, eliminating the need for conventional, wired connections. WLANs are becoming more and more popular in a number of specialized fields, including health care, retail, manufacturing, warehousing, and academia. These domains have benefited from the productivity gains of using handheld PCs and notebook computers to transmit and receive real-time information with the centralized network. WLANs are gaining recognition as a general-purpose network connectivity solution for a broad range of business users.

In this section, we'll take a closer look at how wireless networking is deployed in a practical manner. Then we'll look at some of the core technologies fueling wireless networks. Finally, we'll gaze into our crystal ball and try to predict where wireless networking is going in the future.

How They Work

Like cordless telephones, WLANs use electromagnetic radio waves to communicate information from one location (your laptop, for instance) to another (an access point), without having to use any physical medium to transfer the message. Figure 11-1 illustrates this.

> **NOTE**   Radio waves are often referred to as *radio carriers* because their function is delivering energy to a remote receiver. The transmitted data is superimposed on the radio carrier so that it can be extracted at the receiving end. This is known as modulation of the carrier by the transmitted information.

Once data is added onto the radio carrier, the radio signal spills over, occupying more than a single frequency. This happens because the frequency—or bit rate—of the modulating data adds to the carrier.

This may seem to present a problem, especially in environments where several computers will be trying to access the wireless device. In reality, however, multiple carriers function just fine in the same area, as long as the radio waves are transmitted on different frequencies. In order to collect data, a radio receiver tunes in just one specific radio frequency, as shown in Figure 11-2, while ignoring all others.

In a WLAN, the device that physically connects to the wired LAN is a *transceiver* (a combination of a transmitter and receiver) and is commonly called an *access point*.

Figure 11-1.   WLANs communicate information like cordless telephones.

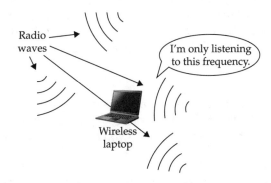

Figure 11-2.   Wireless devices tune out unwanted frequencies and focus on the relevant one.

The access point receives, buffers, and transmits data between the WLAN and the wired network. As shown in Figure 11-3, another way to think about an access point is to consider it as a wireless hub—a single access point can serve dozens of clients. Depending on the range of the access point, clients can be located within a few feet or up to 1,500 feet away from it. Optimally, the antenna for the access point would be situated high above the floor. However, the antenna could be located anywhere space permits.

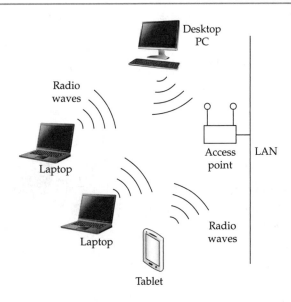

Figure 11-3.   Access points serve as wireless hubs, connecting one—or many—wireless devices to the LAN.

To connect to the access point, client computers use WLAN adapters, which are integrated within laptops, PCs, smartphones, and tablets. In the past they were small, plug-in PC cards for notebooks and expansion cards for full-size desktop computers. These modules have built-in antennas and transceiver components.

Architecture

Wireless LANs can be as simple as two computers talking to each other or as complex as hundreds of computers in one location connecting to computers in a building miles away. Let's take a look at the three basic ways you can build your wireless networks.

Peer-to-Peer

The simplest, most basic wireless network consists of at least two PCs equipped with wireless adapter cards. As shown in Figure 11-4, no access point is needed; whenever these two computers get within range of each other, they form their own independent network. This is called a *peer-to-peer network* or *ad-hoc network*. On-demand networks like this are extremely simple to set up and operate. They require no administration or preconfiguration; however, in this case, each computer would only have access to the resources of the other computer, but not to a central server or the Internet.

This type of network is ideal for home networking or small businesses for spontaneous networking.

In-Building

Much like a conventionally wired network, in-building WLAN equipment consists of a PC Express card, Personal Computer Interface (PCI), PCI Express (PCI-E), and/or Universal Serial Bus (USB) client adapters, as well as access points.

To extend the range of your WLAN, as shown in Figure 11-5, or to increase functionality, access points can be used in the network's topology and will also function as a bridge to a wired Ethernet network.

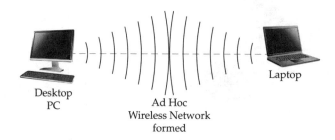

Figure 11-4.   Peer-to-peer, or ad hoc, networks connect individual devices.

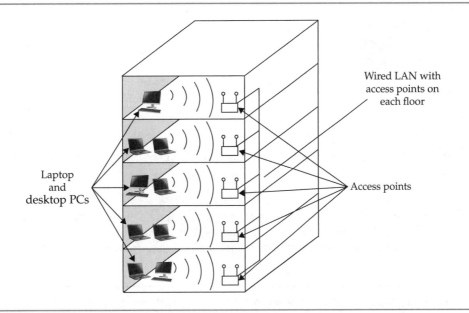

Figure 11-5.   By using multiple access points, the availability of the LAN can be increased.

By applying WLAN technology to desktop systems, an organization is afforded the flexibility that is simply impossible with a conventional LAN. Clients can be deployed in places where running cable is simply impossible. Furthermore, clients can be redeployed anywhere at any time. This makes wireless ideal for temporary workgroups or fast-growing organizations.

Installing an access point can extend the range of a wireless network. It would essentially double the range at which the devices can communicate. Because the access point is connected directly to the wired network, each client has access to the server's resources, as well as to other clients. Like hubs in a wired network, each access point can accommodate several clients—exactly how many depends on how many transmissions are involved and the nature of those transmissions. It's not uncommon for access points to handle up to 50 clients.

NOTE   Be aware, however, that more clients connecting to an access point cuts into the amount of traffic that an access point can handle. If an access point is handling 40 clients, don't expect it to be as speedy as an access point being used by only 10 clients.

Repeaters, as shown in Figure 11-6, look and act just like access points, but with one important exception—they are not tethered to the wired network. Repeaters extend the range of the network by relaying signals from a client to an access point

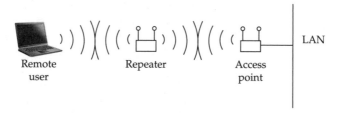

Figure 11-6.   Repeaters are simply access points configured to extend the range of a WLAN.

or another repeater. Repeaters are necessary because signals weaken the farther they are from their receiving point. If you have clients that are far from the wired network, repeaters can be strung together in order to pass along data from the clients to an access point.

 NOTE   Most access points can be set up as repeaters (sometimes called *extenders*). Those access points wouldn't be plugged into the network, they would be installed so that distant clients could still access network resources.

Building-to-Building

The ultimate achievement in wireless networking comes when networks are extended between buildings in different cities. By using a wireless bridge, networks located in buildings miles away from each other can be connected into a single network.

When networks are connected between buildings with copper or fiber, any number of obstacles can put the skids on a project. Roads, rivers, and politics can break a project. A wireless bridge makes physical and ideological barriers a nonissue. Transmission through the air in accordance with 802.11 requires no license and no right of way.

For deployments that do not offer a wireless alternative, organizations routinely fall back to WAN technologies. However, leasing a line from a telephone provider presents a number of headaches:

- Installation is expensive and takes a long time to set up.

- Monthly fees are expensive for high bandwidth. The additional rub is that by LAN standards, WAN speeds are very slow. This is because telephone lines were designed and built for voice, not data.

One can purchase and install a wireless bridge in a single afternoon, and the cost is comparable to a T1 installation charge alone. Even better, there is no monthly charge—once a wireless connection is made, there are no recurring charges. Furthermore, wireless bridges provide bandwidth from a technology rooted in data, not voice.

To make your building-to-building network happen, you need two directional antennas and a clear line of sight between them. Let's suppose you had a WLAN in Building A (the headquarters) and wanted to extend it to a satellite office in Building B, 10 miles away in a neighboring city. As shown in Figure 11-7, you could install a directional antenna on the roof of each building, with each antenna targeting the other. Building A's antenna is connected to your main LAN through an access point. The antenna on Building B is similarly connected to an access point to that facility's LAN. This configuration brings the two LANs, located miles apart, together into one, common LAN.

NOTE   We talk about the different types of antennas (including directional antennas) that Cisco offers later in this chapter.

Because of their mobility and ease of installation, WLANs have a significant leg up on conventional LANs. They provide networking opportunities that would not be available to wired networks, and are not much more expensive in the long run.

Technologies

A number of technologies make wireless data transmission and receipt possible. Many of them have their roots in cellular telephony, whereas others have been designed solely with wireless networking in mind.

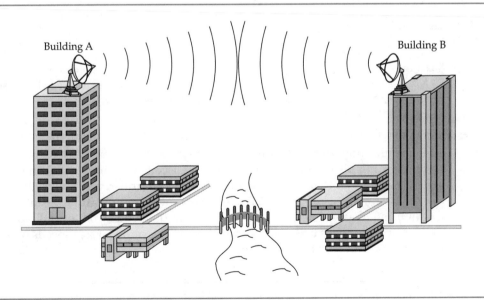

Figure 11-7.   Wireless bridges bring two networks—located miles apart—together.

In this section, we take a closer look at three of the most popular technologies and how they impact your wireless networking needs. These technologies cover short-range data communications, long-range data transfer, and how the Internet can be accessed using cellular phones.

802.11

The core technology allowing WLANs to communicate is the IEEE 802.11 standard. The IEEE 802.11 working group was formed in the early 1990s to develop a global standard for wireless LANs operating in the unlicensed 2.4 GHz frequency band. As we mentioned earlier, the first incarnations of 802.11 supported up to 2 Mbps.

The 802.11x standard offers different variations on the protocol for different speeds, frequency of operation, and range. The 802.11x LAN is based on architecture that is similar to the design of cellular telephone networks. Wireless LANs (WLANs) operate by connecting an access point to the server, whereas client computers are fitted with wireless adapters. These adapter cards can be installed in desktop or laptop computers, as well as in other networking devices, including print servers. Many laptops come with wireless capabilities built in.

Three types of 802.11x networks are germane to our discussion:

■ **802.11a**   Using this specification, devices transmit at 5 GHz and send data up to 54 Mbps. Although the speed is good, the range of 802.11a devices suffers, because it is limited to somewhere around 75 feet in a typical environment.

■ **802.11b**   Using this specification, devices transmit at 2.4 GHz and send data at up to 11 Mbps. This was the first commercially available wireless network. The speed wasn't great, but it made it possible to connect devices without being tethered by Cat 5 cabling. You'll see 802.11b in legacy devices, as it has been supplanted by the speedier 802.11g.

■ **802.11g**   This specification handles data communications at speeds of up to 54 Mbps and utilizes the same frequency as 802.11b devices (2.4 GHz). Because they operate on the same frequency, 802.11g is an easy upgrade path from existing 802.11b deployments.

■ **802.11n**   The latest incarnation of the wireless specification is 802.11n, which is currently seen in devices from laptops to smartphones to tablet computers. It is also the standard that allows Cisco to offer many of the next-generation features that it is able to offer (such as CleanAir, which we will discuss later in this chapter). 802.11n features multiple-input multiple-output (MIMO) antennas—which means it operates simultaneously on several radio frequencies. It utilizes both the 2.4 and 5 GHz bands and features speeds of up to 600 Mbps with four times the range of 802.11g gear.

 NOTE   There are other variations of the 802.11x standard (802.11c, 802.11d, and so forth, up through 802.11i). However, the rest of these variations really don't have anything to do with the current state of Cisco wireless networking.

For easier understanding of these three protocols and how they stack up against each other, we've enumerated their similarities and differences in Table 11-1.

There are two different ways to configure an 802.11 WLAN:

■ Ad hoc

■ Infrastructure

Let's take a closer look at each of these types of WLAN infrastructure.

Standard	802.11a	802.11b	802.11g	802.11n
Speed	54 Mbps	11 Mbps	54 Mbps	600 Mbps
Cost	Moderately expensive.	Inexpensive, although you'll be hard pressed to find a new 802.11b card today.	More expensive than 802.11b, but less expensive than 802.11a.	Most expensive, but most widely deployed.
Frequency	5 GHz. This band is uncrowded and can coexist with 802.11b and g networks.	2.4 GHz. This band is crowded and interference might occur with cordless telephones, microwave ovens, and other devices.	2.4 GHz. This band is crowded and interference might occur with cordless telephones, microwave ovens, and other devices.	Both 2.4 and 5 GHz. The 2.4 GHz band is crowded, but operation in the 5 GHz band allows some breathing room.
Range	100 feet indoors.	115 feet indoors.	125 feet indoors.	200 feet indoors.
Radio Compatibility	Incompatible with 802.11b and g networks.	Most prevalent deployment.	Interoperates with 802.11b, but incompatible with 802.11a.	Interoperable with 802.11b and g networks, making it a good fit to augment the most prevalent existing networks.

Table 11-1.   The Attributes of 802.11 a, b, g, and n Networks

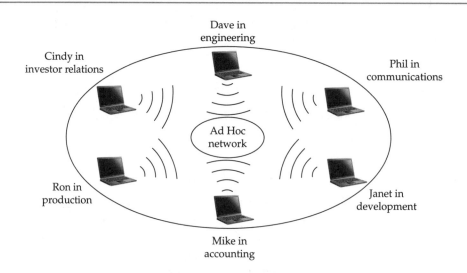

Figure 11-8. The 802.11x standard for wireless networking makes an ad-hoc network around a conference table possible.

Ad hoc In the ad-hoc network, computers are brought together to form a makeshift network, like a peer-to-peer network. As Figure 11-8 shows, there is no hierarchical structure to the network and no need for an access point. Everything is mobile and every node is able to communicate with every other node. A good example of how this would appear in the real world is to think of a meeting where everyone brought his or her own laptop.

Infrastructure The second type of connection, shown in Figure 11-9, comes more closely in line with a conventional LAN topology. This design uses fixed network access points with which mobile nodes can communicate. The access points can be placed within range of each other to expand the range of the network.

802.11 Design

802.11 was developed with three needs in mind:

- The need for a media access control (MAC) and physical layer specification for wireless connectivity for portable fixes and roaming stations
- The need for wireless connectivity to automatic machinery, equipment, or stations that require fast connectivity
- The need to offer a global standard

It's the third requirement that led the IEEE to embrace 2.4 GHz as the preferred frequency. It's an unlicensed frequency band reserved for industrial, scientific, and medical use on a global basis.

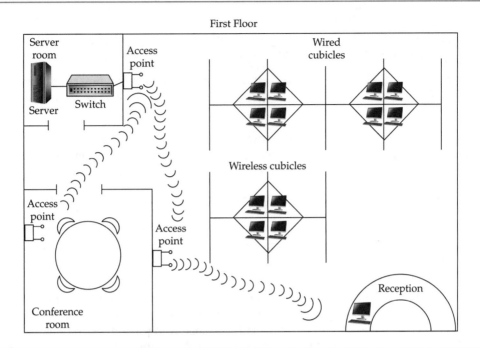

Figure 11-9.   In this example, the floor plan of a company's first floor shows how access points can be deployed.

The Mechanics   The 802.11 LAN is based on an architecture that is similar to the design of cellular telephone networks. By using a comparable network design, wireless networks have reaped the same benefits as cellular, while providing high data rates.

- **Cells and sets**   An 802.11 LAN is subdivided into cells, and each cell is referred to as a *basic service set (BSS)*, which is the coverage area of an AP. Each BSS is controlled by an access point. But, because a single access point may not be capable of fulfilling the entire network's wireless needs, several access points can be connected to a common backbone. When a configuration of several access points is used, this is called a *distribution system*. No matter how large or small the network, no matter how many nodes are connected, the grouping of wireless equipment is viewed as a single IEEE 802.11 network to upper layers of the OSI Reference Model. In 802.11 terminology, the upper layers of the OSI Reference Model are referred to as an *extended service set.*

- **The physical layer**   The 802.11 protocol covers the physical and media access control. But instead of a lone type of media, 802.11 supports four kinds of media: frequency-hopping spread spectrum, direct-sequence spread-spectrum, orthogonal frequency division multiplexing (OFDM), and infrared. A single MAC layer supports all three physical layers. In addition, the MAC layer provides a link to the upper-layer protocols. These functions include fragmentation, packet retransmission, and acknowledgments.

By basing wireless networking on cellular architecture, wireless devices can join, leave, or roam from cell to cell much like cellular telephones do. The heart of each cell is an AP.

Making the Connection   When it comes down to actually connecting to an access point or another computer, two methods are used. The first involves a station joining an existing cell; the second involves the process of moving from one cell to another:

- **Joining an existing cell**   There are three different times when a wireless device will try to access an existing access point or another wireless device: when the device is powered up, after exiting sleep mode, or when it enters a new area. With each situation, the device needs to obtain synchronization information. But how does a device know that there are other wireless devices with which it can interconnect? With two different methods of scanning:
    - **Active scanning**   This type of scanning requires the device to attempt to locate an access point that can receive synchronization information from that device. This is accomplished by transmitting probe request frames and waiting for a probe response packet, which is transmitted by an access point.
    - **Passive scanning**   Devices can listen for a beacon frame that is periodically transmitted from each access point. The beacon frame contains synchronization information, so a device can use this for synchronization.

    The following steps describe how a device locates another device and then associates with it.

    1. After a device locates an access point and gathers synchronization information, it exchanges authentication information. The device and the access point exchange a shared key with each other, ensuring one has the right to talk to the other.

    2. Once a device has been authenticated, the two machines begin the association process. Under the association process, information about the device and the capabilities of available access points are analyzed. The current location of the device is determined and the best access point is assigned to the device. Naturally, if there is only one access point, the association process is a done deal.

- **Roaming**   In the last scenario, the device was connected to the access point and wasn't likely to move. The connection was made, and the device was most likely associated with that access point until the user logged off. However, if you are in a situation in which a device would be moving from one cell (access point or other wireless device) to another, that is called *roaming*. Figure 11-10 illustrates this process.

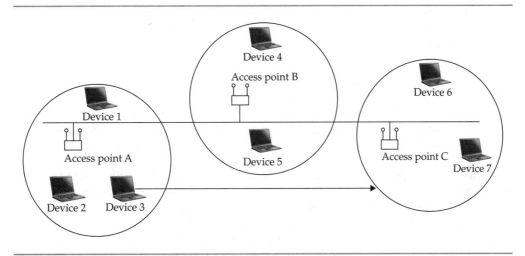

Figure 11-10. Roaming with a wireless device means moving from one cell to another.

Though much like roaming with a cellular telephone, there are two important differences between the technologies. First, 802.11 supports the transmission of packets that have a specific destination address, sequence, and fragment identification. This facilitates LAN roaming because the transition between cells is at a much slower pace—walking versus driving in a car in a cellular phone environment.

Next, if there is a brief interruption in service, it is not as damaging to a voice conversation as it is in a WLAN environment. This is because with a WLAN, once packets are sent, an upper-level protocol sets a time prior to each transmission. If the timer expires without the transmitting station receiving an acknowledgement, it will resend the packets. Conversely, in a cellular telephone network, if there is an interruption in the call, voice is simply lost and there is no mechanical effort to resend it. With a WLAN, however, interruptions can mean slower times because of retransmissions.

Cells know that roaming will occur, because as a device moves away from an access point, the device will observe that the signal is getting weaker. The device will use its scanning function to try and find an access point with a stronger signal. Once a new access point is found, the device will send a reassociation request. Then the new access point will send a message to the device's former access point to inform it of the new association. If the device does not receive a response to the request, it will scan for a new access point.

Security

For a long time, the standard security method used for wireless networking was the Wired Equivalent Privacy (WEP) option to the 802.11 standard. Vendors support 128-bit key lengths. The longer the key length, the greater the level of security. However, in 2001, it was discovered that one could crack WEP encryption by capturing millions of packets and running them through one of a small number of tools available for the task. Then, in 2004, a new method was posted that allowed WEP to be cracked with as little as a few hundred thousand captured WEP packets. Now there are so many tools available for cracking WEP that it's no longer considered secure, and its use is discouraged.

 NOTE Although we recognize that a lot of access points and workstations in the field only support WEP, for security's sake, you should make every effort to use WPA, or more preferably WPA2.

Introduced in 2003, Wi-Fi Protected Access (WPA) can be used with an 802.1x authentication server. In a typical setup, the server distributes a different encryption key to each authenticated user. It can also be set up with a pre-shared key (PSK) mode that is similar to WEP in that every user uses the same passphrase.

WPA and WPA2 are designed to use 802.1x authentication. Beyond the encryption, this provides a stronger means of security than WEP. Whereas WEP is used to encode data, WPA encryption with 802.1x is used to either allow or deny a client from accessing the network.

Price

Prices have significantly dropped in recent years, and there is no indication that there will be any slowdown. Cost savings are circular in nature—as demand for the technology increases, it is less expensive for the units to be manufactured. This, in turn, attracts more customers to wireless technology, which increases demand, which makes it less expensive to manufacture, and so on and so on. It is unlikely that the price of enterprise-grade wireless networking equipment will be less than conventional wired gear in the near future; however, once the price of cabling and labor are factored in, the two technologies' prices are almost competitive. In the next few years we will start to see the proliferation of 802.11ac and 802.11ad, which are theoretically capable of 500 Mbps per station and 7 Gbps (yes, Gbps), respectively. Once that happens, Wi-Fi will no longer be a supplemental albeit required technology. Considering today's MSRP of about $1,000 for a Cisco Aironet 3600, the fact that enterprises need lightweight AP controllers and that switches are still required to backhaul most access points, it's not likely that wired networks are going away entirely for some time—at least until wireless backhaul speeds increase significantly enough to offset the cost.

Cisco Wireless Networking

Cisco didn't get to be the internetworking big boy by sitting around and hoping good fortune would hit them on the head. Instead, they have taken steps to stay on the cutting edge of internetworking technology. Some of their research and investments have paid off, whereas others have become costly lessons for the development team.

In this section, we'll look at how Cisco has embraced wireless and has groomed it as the technology for the new millennium. Then we'll talk about the wireless networking products Cisco has to offer.

Philosophy

It should come as no surprise that Cisco has not only embraced wireless networking technology, but is also leading the charge. The company's recent acquisitions have come at a great time as the WLAN market heats up and user demand for high-speed access to corporate networks is greater than ever.

Naturally, some of the market's heat is due to Cisco's own behavior. In March 2000, Cisco acquired wireless LAN vendor Aironet Wireless Communications for $799 million. In February 1999, Cisco and Motorola announced a $1-billion partnership to develop a framework for Internet-based wireless networks. To cement the standards over which wireless networks operate, in October 1999, Cisco formed a partnership with 10 giant companies to drive standards for broadband wireless Internet services. In November of that year, Cisco introduced its first products based on those standards.

Cisco continues to broaden its wireless market saturation by continual acquisitions. In 2003, Cisco acquired Linksys Group for $500 million. This move brought Cisco more customers from the SOHO/consumer market. Home networks were expected to grow from US$2.7 billion in 2002 to over US$7.5 billion in 2006.

NOTE   Cisco is getting out of the consumer market, having announced the selling off of Linksys to Belkin in January 2013.

Then, in 2005, Cisco bought Airespace, Inc., for $450 million. This allowed Cisco to reach even more potential business wireless customers through Airespace's access points, management tools, and software. The Airespace appliances (controllers) and software allow for centralized configuration and intelligent management of thousands of access points. The intelligence piece is the key here. It includes things that standalone (a.k.a. autonomous) access points cannot handle on their own. Fast reauthentication of stations moving between APs, a self-contained wireless intrusion prevention system (IPS), automatic signal strength and channel interference controls, site heat mapping, templating of rollouts—this software is the primary reason Cisco dominates the market. Wireless controllers are the linchpin of enterprise networking today. More on those later.

In 2007, Cisco bought a company called Cognio, a maker of spectrum and interference analysis technologies. Later, this would be the bedrock on which Cisco's CleanAir technology is built.

2012 has seen Cisco retain a dominant leadership role in Wi-Fi deployments worldwide. Edging out its competition (the number-two spot is nearly half of Cisco's market share of 55 percent) and gaining said share by roughly 2 percent annually for several years. Cisco is both a driver for and a recipient of the benefits of the enterprise Wi-Fi market, which is projected to hit US$5 billion in 2015.

For Cisco, a company that built its fortune and dominance on the wire-line market, the move to wireless was a natural progression—plus a way to keep its thumb in developing areas.

Cisco's Offerings

With all Cisco's acquisitions, it is able to offer a host of product lines serving different types of business clients as well as home and small business users through its Linksys unit. Let's pay special attention here to Cisco's business offerings.

Autonomous vs. Lightweight

Let's start with a definition. The industry has moved entirely away from autonomous access points. An access point that is a standalone unit, similar to what is utilized on a SOHO or home network, is considered *autonomous*. An autonomous access point doesn't get its configuration from a central server. Everything from the interface used to configure the device, to where the configuration is stored can be found on the autonomous access point—it is entirely self-contained. That's fine for a few APs, but this model of deployment simply will not scale to dozens, hundreds, or thousands of units. A central mechanism for managing APs had to be imagined and designed. That's where *AP controllers* that manage *lightweight APs (LWAPs)* come in. A lightweight AP doesn't weigh any less, it simply has no local configuration and doesn't make any decisions for itself. When a lightweight AP boots, it contacts a controller, downloads the latest OS image, and then proceeds to download its configuration. Once an LWAP has joined a controller, it passes all decision making about almost everything to that controller. All authentication, radio configuration, and client traffic is routed back to the controller for delegation.

Access Points

Access points, as shown in Figure 11-11, are the hardware devices used to connect wireless clients to the network. Typically speaking, an access point simply plugs into a switch and then wireless devices connect (or *associate*) to the AP, allowing them to use the network. The core of Cisco's access point product line is the Aironet devices. These devices may run an autonomous config, or far more commonly can be deployed as LWAPs.

Cisco offers access points in all shapes and size. For example, you can get an access point that will handle 802.11b/g connections, but there are also access points that work in tri-mode. That is, access points such as the Aironet 1130AG include two radios that are able to communicate with both 802.11b/g and 802.11a or use the 802.11a radio as a backhaul connection. This type of backhauling is referred to as *mesh wireless*, which is becoming prevalent not only in use outdoors, as typically has been seen for years, but also indoors.

Table 11-2 compares Cisco's various series of indoor Aironet access points.

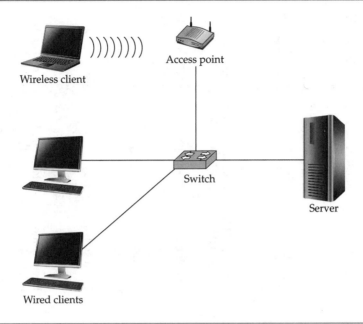

Figure 11-11.   Access points are connected to the network to allow wireless clients to access network resources.

Outdoor Wireless

These days, wireless networking isn't limited to indoor applications. There are more and more calls for its use outdoors. As a bit of a curveball, those outdoor implementations need to operate as well as their indoor brethren, but also be able to handle matters unique to them, including:

- Dealing with RF interference from external sources
- Data and physical security
- Maintenance
- Integration with existing networks

To alleviate these issues, Cisco's outdoor wireless access points feature 802.11n enhanced RF capabilities that heighten performance. With the inclusion of Spectrum Expert Wi-Fi analysis tools within certain access points Cisco created CleanAir. With CleanAir, access points are able to identify radio interference, automatically change channels, and optimize the signal to avoid further interference. Also, administrators are able to better view the surrounding wireless spectrum and use the information to optimize each access point's radio configuration. We'll talk more about CleanAir later in this chapter.

Features	1130AG Series	1140 Series	1240AG Series	600 Series	1600 Series	2600 Series	3600 Series
Target	Small or midsize offices	Small, midsize, or large offices	Non-office locations	Remote worker	Small or midsize offices	Small, midsize, or large offices	Midsize or large offices
Ideal site	Homes, indoor offices	Indoor offices, small warehouses	Warehouses, bus and taxi garages	Homes	Indoor offices, small warehouses	Indoor offices, midsize warehouses	Large offices, midsize or large warehouses
Optimized for crowded areas?	No	Yes	No	No	No	Yes	Yes
Number of radios	Dual (2.4 GHz and 5.0 GHz)	Dual (2.4 GHz and 5.0 GHz)	Dual (2.4 GHz and 5.0 GHz)	Dual (2.4 GHz and 5.0 GHz)	Dual (2.4 GHz and 5.0 GHz)	Dual (2.4 GHz and 5.0 GHz)	Dual (2.4 GHz and 5.0 GHz)
Maximum data rate per radio	108 Mbps	300 Mbps	54 Mbps	300 Mbps	300 Mbps	450 Mbps	1.3 Gbps (with additional radio module)
Max clients/Max ClientLink clients	20/No ClientLink support	25/Basic ClientLink support	15/No ClientLink support	15/No ClientLink support	128/32	200/128	200/128
CleanAir	No	Yes	No	No	CleanAir Express	Yes	Yes
Rogue access point detection	Yes	Yes	Yes	No	Yes	Yes	Yes
Antennas	Internal	Internal	External	Internal	Internal and external	Internal and external	Internal and external
Supports mesh	Yes	Yes	Yes	No	No	Yes	Yes

Table 11-2. Cisco's Series of Access Points

As you might imagine, access points meant for outdoor applications are designed with specific usage needs and environmental conditions in mind. Cisco's Aironet 1500 Series Outdoor Access Points offer 802.11n capacity along with self-healing and self-optimizing technologies. They offer a flexible and scalable mesh for mobility across metropolitan-sized areas, campuses, and manufacturing yards. These devices support multiple-device and multiple-network application delivery, including video surveillance and 3G and 4G data delivery, along with public and private Wi-Fi access.

NOTE   In case power is unexpectedly cut off, these models offer optional internal battery backups.

Table 11-3 compares Cisco's various models of outdoor access points.

Client Adapters

Laptops and desktop PCs need some way to communicate with the wireless access points, and, to that end, Cisco makes a line of CardBus client adapters that allow you to connect that PC to the network.

These adapters were very important—and big sellers—when they were first introduced a decade ago. However, because every laptop and many PCs now come with a wireless adapter built in, there isn't much market for these devices anymore.

Cisco announced the end-of-life status of its Aironet CardBus and PCI client adapters, saying it would stop selling them in May 2013. Chances are it would be cheaper to buy a new PC with built-in wireless capabilities than to try and make an old PC work on the wireless network. What Cisco does offer in the realm of enhanced

Features	1552E/EU	1552C/CU	1552I	1552H	1552S
Type	External antennas	Cable modem	Internal antennas	Hazardous	Sensor networks
Antennas	E: External, dual band EU: External, single band	C: Internal CU: External, single-band	Internal	External dual-band	External dual-band
CleanAir	Yes	Yes	Yes	Yes	Yes
ClientLink	Yes	Yes	Yes	Yes	Yes
Data rate	300 Mbps	300 Mbps	300 Mbps	300 Mbps	300 Mbps
Rogue access point detection	Yes	Yes	Yes	Yes	Yes
Wi-Fi standards	802.11a/b/g/n	802.11a/b/g/n	802.11a/b/g/n	802.11a/b/g/n	802.11a/b/g/n

Table 11-3.   Cisco's Outdoor Access Point Line

client connectivity is its ClientLink 2.0 feature available on some access points. Also, the previously discussed AnyConnect client has a purchasable plug-in called Network Access Manager that allows customers to manage what wireless networks its clients may connect to. This module provides the detection and selection of the optimal layer-2 access network and performs device authentication for access to both wired and wireless networks.

NOTE   Additionally, if the computer you want to connect wirelessly needs a wireless adapter, it's probably so old it is of little use to your network, anyway. That said, if you still need a wireless adapter for a client, your best bet is to look somewhere like eBay—you can get used client adapters cheap.

ClientLink 2.0

Bring Your Own Device (BYOD) is an acronym Cisco uses to talk about the proliferation of users bringing non-company client devices to the network. Those devices then use wireless resources to join the network. In the past few years there has been an explosion in smartphones, tablets, and similar devices that are not always "company issued." Further, because users are bringing their own devices, there is no uniformity of make or model. As such, there is a hodgepodge of devices out there.

And it's not only the devices. It's also different wireless standards used to connect.

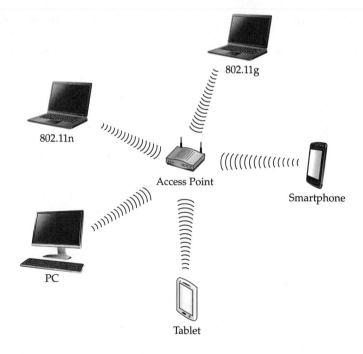

ClientLink 2.0 specializes in mixed-client networks, making sure that clients operating at different specifications are connecting optimally. The current prevalent standard for 802.11 is the 802.11n standard. However, since wireless took hold in the enterprise, there have been a number of variations—at different speeds and capacities—and there is enough legacy equipment out there that they can't simply be ignored. Although those devices are still welcome on the network, if not managed properly, they can slow down and hinder connectivity for 802.11n clients. ClientLink 2.0 seeks to smooth out connectivity for all clients, as well as increased network capacity.

Signal Received   When wireless data is transmitted indoors, the signal tends to take a circuitous path to its destination. That is because there are obstacles between the access point and the receiver. Although there are walls, cabinets, and other obstacles blocking a direct path between access point and receiver, there are also other obstructions that allow the signal to bounce off on its way to the receiver. This phenomenon is known as *multipath propagation,* and is shown in Figure 11-12.

The makers of 802.11n planned for this and, to that end, utilize multipath propagation to the technology's benefit. 802.11n transmitters and receivers have multiple antennas to maximize reliability of the signal. And, because of the additional radios and antennas involved, it allows 802.11n to be more robust than prior-generation 802.11a/g systems.

ClientLink 2.0 uses this technology to deliver optimal throughput and capacity. It uses multiple antennas to focus transmissions specifically to 802.11a/g clients. Access points such as the Aironet 2600 and 3600 series use four antennas to improve performance for 802.11a/g/n networks.

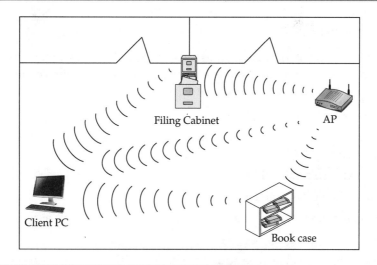

Figure 11-12.   Multipath propagation means that, because of the environment, the signal will arrive several times, a fraction of a second apart.

Beamforming   ClientLink 2.0 utilizes a technology that Cisco calls *beamforming*, which improves the signal-to-noise ratio (SNR) by making it easier for clients to hear the access point.

The wireless channel works both ways, meaning that the signal from the access point to the client and from the client to the access point are operating on the same frequencies and under that same environmental conditions. As such, the access point can learn about the connection from the data sent back from the client. That data can be used to tweak various settings in the transmission to ensure that the best signal is received by the client. Optimizing the transmission reduces the number of retries, improves data rates, increases the overall capacity of the system, and makes more efficient use of the system.

ClientLink 2.0 is available on Aironet 1600, 2600, and 3600 series access points.

WLAN Controllers

We stated previously that the software within Cisco's wireless controllers is the reason why Cisco has garnered such a large share of the Wi-Fi market. These controllers are the center of the wireless LAN operation. They are the devices on which configuration and control information is stored and then sent out to the lightweight access points.

WLAN controllers maintain such information as:

- Security policies
- Intrusion prevention
- Radio frequency (RF) management
- QoS (Quality of Service)
- Mobility
- AP configuration

But WLAN controllers don't just hand out configuration information. They are able to respond to environmental and usage changes to keep wireless connectivity and throughput high. WLAN controllers allow

- Dynamic assignment of channels to reduce interference
- Interference detection, followed by network optimization to reduce interference
- Automatic load balancing
- Coverage holes detected and corrected
- Automatic power adjustment across the network to specific access points

Table 11-4 compares Cisco's line of wireless LAN controllers.

Wireless controllers can also be added to some models of switches and routers, such as the Catalyst 6500 and 7600 series, using a Cisco Wireless Services Module (WiSM) add-on module. These modules allow administrators to support multiple WiSM and

Features	2500 Series	ISR G2 Controller	5500 Series	WiSM2	8500 Series	Flex 7500 Series
Usage	Small or midsized businesses	Small or midsized businesses	Midsize to large businesses	Midsize to large businesses	Large enterprises and service providers	Large number of branches
Form factor	Desktop	Module for Integrated Services Router	One rack unit (RU) appliance	Blade for Catalyst 6500 series (up to seven per chassis)	One RU appliance	One RU appliance
Cisco Network Access Control	Yes	Yes	Yes	Yes	Yes	Yes
Access control lists (ACLs)	Yes	Yes	Yes	Yes	Yes	Yes
Workgroup bridge	Yes	Yes	Yes	No	No	No
Access points managed	5–50	5–50	12–500	100–1,000	300–6,000	300–6,000
Number of access point groups	30	30	500	500	6,000	2,000
Access points per group	25	25	25	25	100	100
WLANs	16	16	512	512	4,096	512

Table 11-4.   Cisco's Wireless LAN Controllers

thus thousands of LWAP within one single chassis. A single 6513 can fit 11 WiSM, and each WiSM can support 500 LWAP and 10,000 clients, for a total of 5,500 LWAP and 110,000 clients. Impressed yet?

Wireless Integrated Routers

When Cisco introduced wireless products about 15 years ago, their offerings were simple—an access point and a client adapter. In the years since then, wireless has gone from being a novel feature to one that's crucial to business. Cisco has added a multitude of products and services (along with some innovative new technologies) to feed this demand.

Because wireless is so important, it is no longer a simple, small add-on device. Now, wireless capabilities are built in to a number of the company's switches and routers, most notably its Integrated Services Routers.

These models also include wireless LAN capabilities that can handle both 802.11a/g and 802.11n. Also, connected access points can be easily managed with features included in these devices.

Antennas

Cisco's access points are made with specific needs in mind. However, those access points can be further customized to suit your specific needs through the inclusion of specific antenna types. Cisco makes different styles of antennas to serve these specific needs.

Omnidirectional Omnidirectional antennas are connected to the access point via short plenum cabling. The antennas are ceiling-mounted to serve a large, circular area. These antennas can be used both indoors and outdoors. When mounted outdoors, they are typically installed on a mast to provide the most geographically dispersed coverage area.

Examples of omnidirectional antennas include

- Warehouses
- Outdoor seating areas
- Retail areas
- Places where vehicles must upload data

Figure 11-13 shows an example of omnidirectional antenna usage.

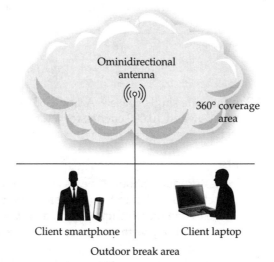

Figure 11-13. Omnidirectional antennas are used in areas where 360-degrees of coverage is needed.

Cisco offers eight models of omnidirectional antennas operating in 2.4 and 5 GHz bands. Some models are designed for either indoor or outdoor use, whereas some can serve both environments.

Dipole   Like omnidirectional antennas, dipole antennas serve a large circular area. The antennas can be bent to better serve a particular area, especially if the antennas are mounted on a wall or ceiling.

> **NOTE**   Cisco sells these antennas in three colors: black, white, and gray. The gray antennas are shorter than the black and white and do not bend. They are best suited for spaces where you don't want the antenna projecting out.

Examples of places where dipole antennas are ideal include

■ Conference rooms

■ Hotels

■ Medical environments

Because dipole antennas service a circular area, rooms off a hallway can receive coverage as well. Cisco offers eight models of dipole antenna made for 2.4 or 5 GHz applications. Figure 11-14 shows how a dipole antenna can be used.

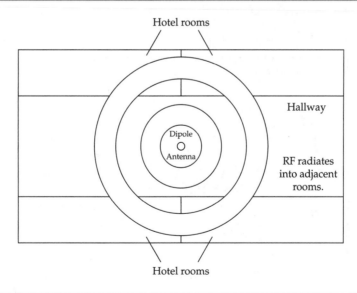

Figure 11-14.   Dipole antennas can be used to service areas such as hotels and medical facilities.

Directional Antennas

Unlike the other two types of antennas, directional antennas do not cover large, 360-degree areas. Rather, they are used to hone in a very specific area. It focuses all the radio energy in one direction, rather than in a broad circle.

Examples of places were this type of antenna is ideal include

- Point-to-point bridge connections between buildings
- Down hallways
- In warehouses with high shelving
- Mines
- Facilities where the wireless signal needs to be confined to a tight beam for security reasons

Cisco offers five models of directional antennas. Figure 11-15 shows how directional antennas are used.

Dual-Band Antennas   Cisco's latest generation of Aironet access points—the 3600 and 1550 series—require dual-band antennas. This is because they use the multiple-input multiple-output features (MIMO) of the 802.11n specification. As such, the number of radio transceivers per frequency band has increased. These antennas—Cisco offers seven models—support these transceivers while keeping the number of antennas low. Each dual-band antenna can transmit and receive both 2.4 and 5 GHz signals simultaneously. Figure 11-16 shows how dual-band antennas are used.

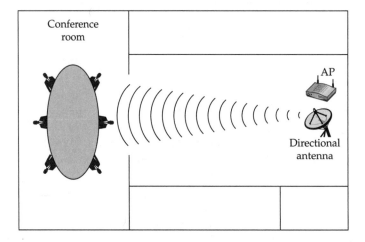

Figure 11-15.   Directional antennas are used in environments where a specific area needs coverage.

Figure 11-16.   Dual-band antennas make use of both 2.4 and 5 GHz frequencies, which is part of the 802.11n specification.

 NOTE   Many other brands of antennas are available for a much lower cost. As long as the installation specs are followed, Cisco will support an AP utilizing a non-Cisco antenna. Just be wary of very generic antennas if you go that route, and use a reputable vendor.

CleanAir

In the past, investigating sources of wireless interference and problems was largely a matter of investigative legwork and head scratching. Cisco has made the process much easier with its CleanAir technology. CleanAir is a system-wide feature of the Cisco Unified Wireless Network, which mitigates problems by detecting and locating sources of RF interference and then automatically making adjustments to the network to avoid said interference. With more and more devices relying on spectrum for proper operation, a crowded spectrum can result in the following:

- Speed slowdown
- Loss of signal
- An affected coverage area

Identifying RF interference used to require specialized and expensive tools and trainings, but CleanAir makes the process of avoiding interference simpler and less expensive.

Sources of interference might be threats to your network (such as rogue access points) or simply benign things (such as microwave ovens). For instance, as shown in Figure 11-17, perhaps Mom and Pop Amalgamated keeps losing wireless connectivity in its conference room. They might be unaware that nearby CompuGlobalMegaWare uses the same channel for its wireless bridge, and that signal passes straight through the conference room. The result is intermittent interference with company A's access points.

CleanAir can identify that interference, automatically change channels, and optimize the signal to avoid further interference. It also provides visibility of the wireless spectrum and delivers complete integration within Cisco wireless network to optimize the network and avoid interference.

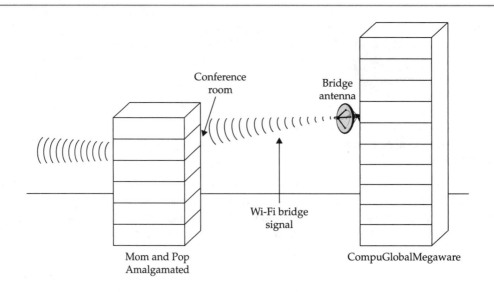

Figure 11-17.   The Wi-Fi signal in Mom and Pop Amalgamated's conference room is constantly disrupted because of the wireless bridge link between CompuGlobalMegaware's buildings.

Air Quality   CleanAir collects information from your access points, aggregates the data, and generates a map of interference sources and what they're coming from, and then stores historical data. Data is compiled into map points showing spectrum quality at different levels:

- Access point
- Floor
- Building
- Campus

Air Quality alerts can be sounded when air quality falls beneath a given threshold.

CleanAir can be configured to enforce security policies. For instance, what if your company prohibits the use of wireless video cameras? When CleanAir detects a wireless camera, it redirects data traffic to a different channel and then locates the camera on the CleanAir map so that IT staff can get rid of the offending hardware, physically. CleanAir allows you to mitigate interference sources to help protect the integrity of your network.

Air Quality reports can also be used to show sources of interference, such as microwave ovens, for instance, and resolve problems caused by interference. This also allows you to proactively avoid problems before they occur. For instance, you can view real-time spectrum data from all your access points. For even further analysis, some access points include Spectrum Expert Wi-Fi analysis tools that enable wireless surveys. These tools previously required an administrator to load up a laptop with sniffing software and a special WLAN card and literally walk around looking for interfering signals. Today an administrator can tell an LWAP with this tool set to reboot in sniffer mode and run the exact same analysis—and the admin can be anywhere in the world running a survey!

Security   CleanAir can also be used to ensure that system resources are not being misused. For instance, at a coffee house—where there is already a wireless infrastructure in place for customers to access the Internet—CleanAir knows which Wi-Fi devices are allowed on the network, so when it detects an access point operating on a nonstandard channel, CleanAir is able to locate that access point and display it on a map. Because of this ability, store management is able to determine that an employee has set up a rogue access point for his or her own nefarious purposes.

Access Point Configuration

Up to this point, we've talked about wireless basics, concepts, company positioning, and the comprehensive products and technologies that Cisco has to offer. In this section, however, we'll take a more hands-on approach, and actually set up and configure a WLAN.

Installing a switch or router generally means finding rack space in the server room, sliding the device in, and connecting cabling. It's somewhat of a different game for access points.

As we noted, two basic pieces of equipment are involved in a wireless network— the access point and a wireless adapter. The wireless adapter (which we'll talk about in a few pages) is the mobile component. This is the one that you plug into a laptop and can move around your organization. With the limitation of the AP's range, that piece of hardware can be anywhere in your organization.

Conversely, to afford yourself the flexibility to have highly mobile clients, you must locate the access point in the optimal location.

Site Survey

Many organizations employ site surveys. This is an exercise in which an access point is temporarily placed and bandwidth analyzer taken throughout the office to find the best and worst spots for connectivity. Bandwidth analyzers are expensive, and if you want to do it yourself, this task is generally undertaken with a rented analyzer. However, because a bit of a learning curve is involved with a bandwidth analyzer, it's better to hire someone with both the analyzer and the knowledge to do it for you.

When it's done, a site survey can tell you the following information:

- Ideal location for access points
- Bit rates and error rates in different locations
- Whether the number of access points you're planning to deploy is adequate
- The performance of applications on the WLAN

AP Placement

When you're conducting a site survey, the first step is to place the AP. Initially, situate the access point as close to its final position as possible. This can help solve any placement problems that could occur after the access point is finally mounted.

In most office environments, access points should be mounted at ceiling height. In warehouses and other sites with high ceilings, it's best to mount them between 15 and 25 feet.

At this height, however, you probably don't have electrical outlets conveniently located. As such, this is an excellent time to use Power over Ethernet (PoE). PoE can be added to your Cisco network using a power injector, such as a line-power patch panel, and it is also part of many Cisco switches (Catalyst switches, for example). As the name suggests, it delivers power to the downstream device using the same Ethernet cabling used to deliver data. PoE is a great option to consider when connecting remotely placed access points or when a power outlet is not conveniently located.

There's no reason your access point has to be located on the corner of a desk or affixed to the wall. You may find it aesthetically and strategically advantageous to place your access point within the ceiling plenum. That said, you should place your antennas outside of the ceiling plenum for optimal connectivity, but the access point can certainly make that its home. If you do opt for a ceiling plenum-located device, you should select one that is designed for remote antenna configuration.

NOTE   Check your local fire codes. You likely need plenum-rated access points and cabling if they're to be placed above the ceiling tiles.

Interference

Interference is a major consideration in the placement of your access point. You need to be cognizant of such sources of interference as photocopiers, microwave ovens, cordless telephones, and anything else that operates on the same frequency as your access point.

NOTE   If you are using Cisco equipment that uses CleanAir technology, interference worries are lessened, because it tells you what the problem is and shows you, on a map, where it is.

Just to make life more interesting, the 802.11g standard (if that's the equipment you're using) works in the 2.4 GHz band—the same band that other unlicensed devices operate on. As such, if your office has cordless phones that operate in this band, you might encounter some interference.

Also, since Wi-Fi has become more prevalent, you may experience problems, because a neighbor may already be using a Wi-Fi device. If this is the case, you might need to change channels.

Saying that 802.11g networks offer 11 channels is somewhat misleading. With 802.11g networks, it's necessary to move five complete channels away from another device to avoid interference. Normally, 802.11g networks operate on channels 1, 6, and 11. 802.11a networks, on the other hand, have more usable channels from which to choose, so you have more options if a neighbor is using 802.11a gear.

After you perform a site survey, check your error rates and connectivity. If the results aren't satisfactory, place the access point somewhere else and try again. This can be a long and somewhat tedious task, but if you approach it with an eye toward possible sources of interference and ideal placement, you should be able to locate the best site for your access point reasonably quickly.

Initial Autonomous AP Settings

Setting up an access point might seem like it should be a daunting task—after all we're mixing computer networking with radio transceivers, so we're combining two sciences. Truth be told, you can make wireless networking as complex—or as simple—as you want.

Cisco Aironet access points allow you to get extremely granular with your settings for both network and radio transceiver functions. You can manage the size of packets, the transmission power, and a host of other settings. These details are managed through many, many subpages on the Aironet configuration page. Cisco has made its access points not only powerful, but easy to use as well. The basic settings can be easily set up using two express setup pages—if you are not using any advanced features, that is.

 NOTE   As with the majority of Cisco's GUI tools, the CLI is not only easier, it's usually faster. Web-based management tools are sometimes viewed as security holes as well. In our travels, we usually see customers disabling non-encrypted WebUi.

In this section, we'll cover those initial setup pages as well as a basic configuration for a "corp" and a "guest" SSID. However, if you need more detailed and powerful control of the AP, that's a little outside the scope of what we're covering here—you can find out about those settings at Cisco's website.

 NOTE   For this demonstration we are using a Cisco Aironet 1140 access point running an autonomous IOS. Although the details will vary from model to model—and certainly from software update to software update—the steps are shown here as a basic guideline to how Cisco access points are configured. Expect that yours will be subtly different.

Express Setup

The Express Setup page is accessed by opening a web browser and entering the IP address of your AP. When you first log on to your AP, you'll see a status page like the one shown in Figure 11-18.

For our example, we're using a Cisco Aironet 1140 AP. This tells us how many clients are associated (connected) to the AP, the AP's IP address, the status of its network interfaces, an event log, and so forth.

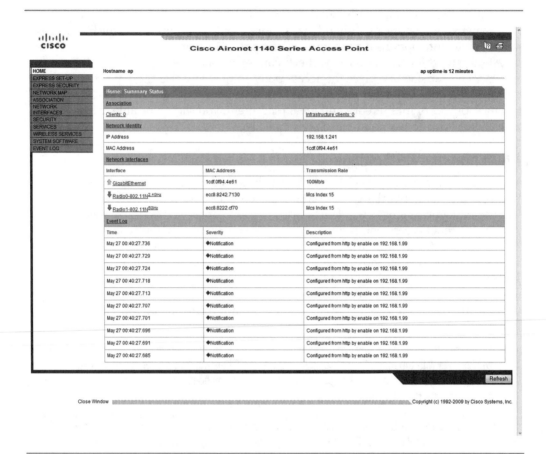

Figure 11-18. Once you've logged on to a Cisco AP, the home page shows you an overview of device settings.

To get to the Express Setup page, click the link on the left side of this screen. The resulting Express Setup page is shown in Figure 11-19.

This page allows you to manage such details as the following:

- Host name.
- How the AP's IP address is acquired—whether through dynamic host configuration protocol (DHCP) or statically.
- The device's IP address.
- IP subnet mask.
- Default gateway.
- SNMP community.

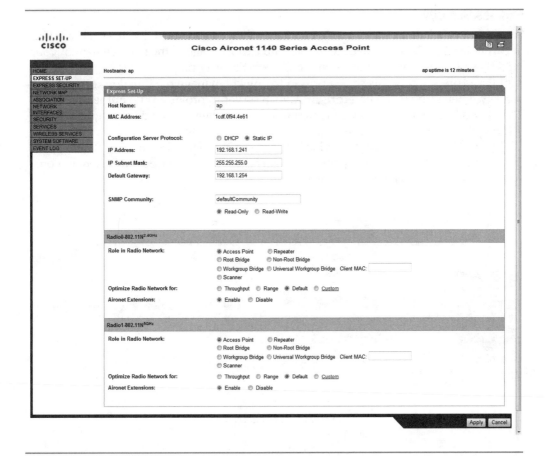

Figure 11-19.   The AP's Express Setup page allows management of the most prevalent access point settings.

■   Whether the access point is an access point root or a repeater.

■   Options for access point performance optimization.

■   Whether Aironet Extensions are enabled or disabled. Enabling Aironet Extensions is ideal if yours is an all-Cisco environment.

NOTE   Aironet Extensions provide enhanced capabilities when other Aironet devices are used. However, in environments where other wireless products are used, it's best not to enable Aironet Extensions. These extensions may also be viewed as a security issue to an IT auditor.

When you've entered or configured all this information, click the Apply button in the lower-right corner of this page, and the settings will be applied to the AP.

Express Security

Security is such an important issue in internetworking in general and wireless networking in particular that Cisco has dedicated a second express page to the management of your AP's security. It is managed through the Express Security page.

Like Express Setup, this screen is used to quickly manage the functions of your AP's security when utilizing an enterprise RADIUS server to provide WPA authentication. The details can be managed in more depth from elsewhere on the device, but for initial setup, this is a convenient place to go.

Figure 11-20 shows this page, which is accessed through a link on the left side of the Aironet AP's configuration pages. You can access this page from anywhere in your AP's configuration by clicking the link at the left.

Figure 11-20. An Aironet AP's Express Security page allows management of security settings.

This page allows you to do the following:

- Establish your AP's Security Set Identifiers (SSIDs). SSIDs indicate which wireless network an access point is part of.
- Enable and specify VLANs.
- Set up security protocols:
  - WEP (including specifying WEP keys)
  - WPA using an authentication source
  - 802.1X
- View a table showing your AP's SSIDs.

This page is a quick way to set up the initial WEP keys and to select between different security features that you would have to establish elsewhere in your AP's configuration file.

Let's talk about how you can set up and manage the two most prevalent forms of access point security WEP keys: WPA and 802.1x.

Security

The easiest and most basic security measure (and also the least secure) on an access point is the WEP key. This is a series of alphanumeric characters entered into both the access point and your client. When a client tries to connect to the AP, it must have the correct key or it will be unable to connect. Although this shouldn't be your sole means of security, it should at least be set if no other security measures are in place.

 NOTE   WEP keys are weak and easily broken. That said, enabling WEP is better than nothing. Believe it or not, many organizations don't set any sort of security mechanism, providing an open door into their network. You should enable WPA2 or 802.1x. Failing that, at the very least, enable WEP.

WEP Keys

You can perform more detailed WEP key tasks by following these steps:

1. On the Aironet 1140 AP, click Security on the left side of the window.
2. When the Security section expands, click Encryption Manager. This displays the screen shown in Figure 11-21.
3. This screen allows you to manage your WEP key settings:
   - Encryption Mode contains settings to disable WEP, enable WEP, or establish cipher settings.
   - Encryption Keys is the section in which up to four WEP keys and their lengths are entered. The WEP keys are not shown as you enter them. This is a security measure, but it also makes it difficult to tell if you've mistyped a character. Enter a key on each line if you plan on rotating through WEP keys.

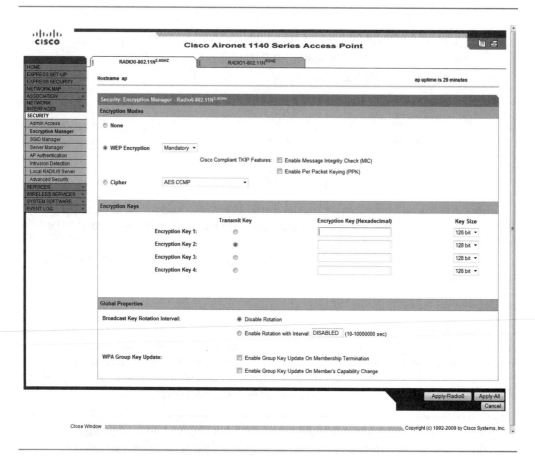

Figure 11-21.   The Encryption Manager is used to set up and manage your AP's encryption.

■ Global Properties is used to manage the behavior of your WEP keys. Here, you can select whether to rotate between keys and how long the interval is between each rotation and how keys are to be managed within your group.

4. Because the Aironet 1140 access point has both 2.4 and 5 GHz radios, these settings can be applied to either radio, or both. In this case, clicking Apply-Radio0 would establish these settings for the 2.4 GHz radio. Clicking Apply-All sends the settings to both radios.

WPA and WPA2

To answer the shortcomings of WEP, Wi-Fi Protected Access (WPA) was introduced by the Wi-Fi Alliance in 2003.

WPA combines both authentication (using an authentication server) and encryption to secure the connection. WPA enhanced WEP by using automatically changing encryption keys, using the Temporal Key Integrity Protocol (TKIP).

There are two flavors of WPA you might hear about: WPA and WPA2. For the most part, they provide the same functionality. The main difference between the two is the encryption method used. WPA uses an RC4 stream cipher, employing a 128-bit key and a 48-bit initialization vector (IV). When an IV (the larger the better) is used in conjunction with TKIP's key rotation mechanism, it becomes harder and harder to compromise the system's encryption.

WPA2 replaces RD4 with AES, which is a beefier encryption method. Whether WPA2 is available on your clients and access points will depend on which firmware version you are using.

 NOTE WPA was designed as an intermediate step toward 802.1x authentication. One of the main reasons was that the development and finalization of 802.1x took much longer than anticipated, and during that time, organizations became more and more worried about security weaknesses.

WPA also made wireless transmissions more resilient. Not only does the system provide authentication and encryption, but it also improves a payload's integrity. The cyclic redundancy check (CRC) in WEP is insecure, and it is possible to alter the payload or update the message CRC without first knowing the WEP key. WPA uses a message integrity code (MIC). The MIC used in WPA utilizes a frame counter, preventing replay attacks, which is another weakness of WEP.

Let's take a walk through the process of setting up WPA2 on your AP. Before we begin, however, we're making the assumption that you have a working LEAP, EAP, or PEAP configuration.

To start, navigate to your access point's Encryption Manager. We're using a Cisco Aironet 1140 AP. These steps will be similar to whatever Cisco access point you're using, but don't be surprised if there are some subtle differences based on your access point model and what firmware version it's running.

The Encryption Manager, shown in Figure 11-22, is accessed from the AP's home page by selecting Security | Encryption Manager.

From there, follow these steps:

1. Select the Cipher option.

2. Select AES CCMP from the drop-down menu.

3. Clear Encryption Key 1.

4. Select the Transmit Key option next to Encryption Key 2. (The results of these steps are shown in Figure 11-22.)

5. Click the Apply-Radio# button at the bottom of the page.

6. The SSID Manager must be set up next. On the leftmost menu, select SSID Manager. The SSID Manager is shown in Figure 11-22.

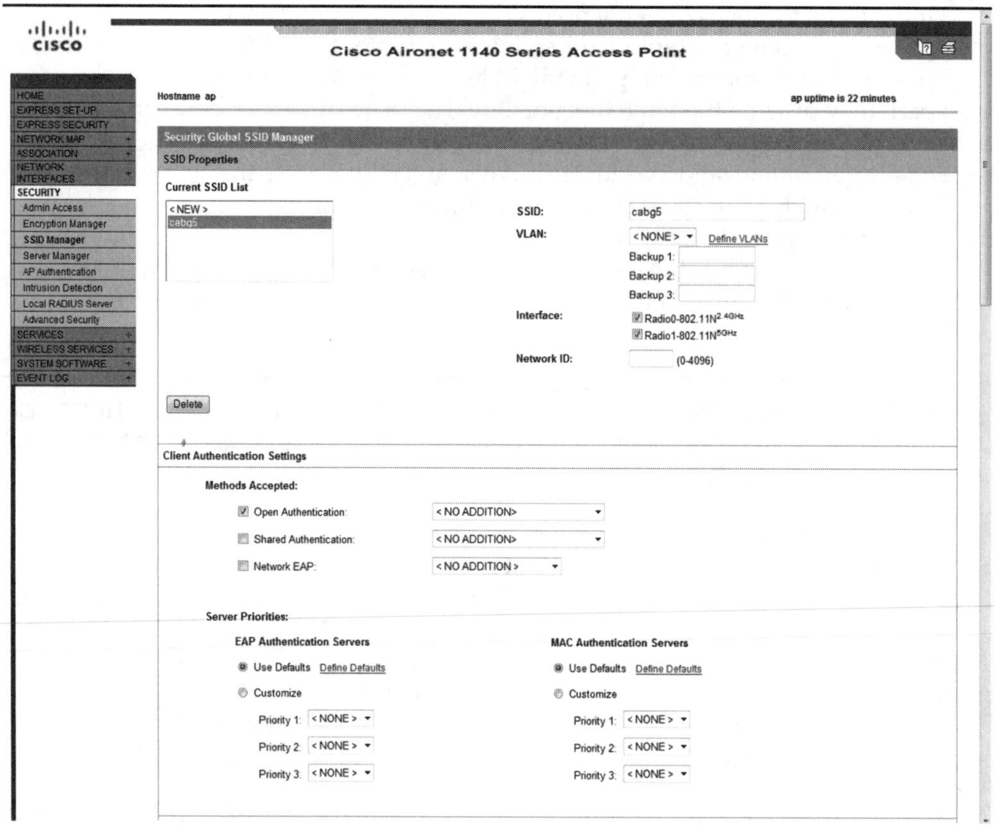

Figure 11-22. The SSID Manager can be configured by selecting it from the Security menu on the left of the page.

7. Select the desired SSID from Current SSID List.

8. Based on what type of clients will be connecting to the AP, select the authentication method to use. Table 11-5 lists the types of clients and what selection you should choose.

9. Under Client Authenticated Key Management, choose Mandatory from the drop-down menu.

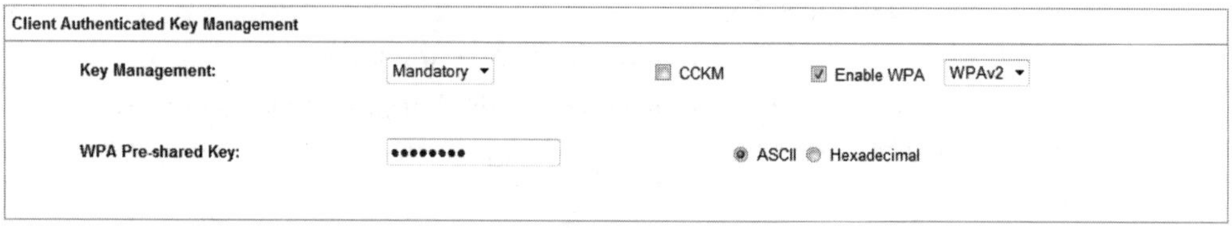

Client Type	Authentication Method
Cisco clients	Use Network-EAP
Third-party clients, including Cisco Compatible Extension (CCX) clients	Use Open Authentication with EAP
Both Cisco and third-party clients	Use both Network-EAP and Open Authentication with EAP

Table 11-5.   Authentication Methods for Client Types

10. Select the Enable WPA check box.

11. Select WPAv2 from the drop-down list.

12. Enter your data into the Pre-Shared Key field.

13. Click Apply-Radio# at the bottom of the page.

WPA2 configuration can be verified by clicking Association from the leftmost menu on your AP's home page and then clicking the client's MAC address. If WPA2 has been properly configured, AES will be displayed.

802.1x

WEP is quick and easy, but it can also be cracked by a dedicated hacker. 802.1x authentication provides a stronger means of security.

 NOTE   In order to set up 802.1x authentication, you must have a RADIUS server on your network.

To configure 802.1x authentication, follow these steps:

1. Click Express Security from the menu on the left of the AP's configuration screen.

2. Under Security, you establish whether you want no security, a static WEP key (along with a place to enter the key), EAP authentication, or WPA authentication.

3. To set up LEAP, PEAP, EAP-TLS, EAP-TTLS, EAP-GTC, EAP-SIM, and other 802.1x/EAP-based protocols, click the relevant option next to EAP Authentication. To use WPA, click the WPA Authentication option.

4. In the boxes next to EAP Authentication or WPA Authentication, enter the name of the RADIUS server and the secret that will be shared between the access point and the RADIUS server.

5. Click Apply.

These settings allow for a quick configuration of 802.1x authentication. For more control over your AP's handling of 802.1x, click Security from the menu on the left. This allows you to do such things as specify backup RADIUS servers, enable accounting, manage the authentication port, and several other details.

Corp and Guest Wi-Fi Example

Here is a common configuration that utilizes two SSIDs with the guest broadcast and the corp hidden, and both assigned to two separate subnets. Cisco access points are layer-2 devices, so accessing multiple networks from one AP requires a VLAN trunk configuration on the AP and the connected switch. We'll be using VLAN 100 for the corporate network and VLAN 101 for the guest network. Both of these need to have a default gateway attached to the switch. Substitute your WPA2 PSK and enable passwords.

Also, due to the way autonomous APs handle bridging on trunks, we've created a bridge group (5), assigned it to gi0, and then disabled it. It's not possible to remove it from the gi0 interface without some minor trickery. It's easier to reassign it and ignore it.

This configuration also follows the best practice of using HTTPS for the WebUi and SSH for the remote management connections. Simply delete your startup from NVRAM, reload the copy, and paste this config into a terminal. Of course, you need to change the management IP and VLANs to something on your network.

```
<<Switch config>>
interface FastEthernet0/X
 switchport trunk native vlan 100
 switchport trunk allowed vlan 100,101
 switchport mode trunk
 switchport nonegotiate

<<Access Point>>
no service pad
service timestamps debug datetime msec
service timestamps log datetime msec
service password-encryption
hostname cwap
!
logging rate-limit console 9
enable secret 0 your_enable_password
aaa new-model
username admin privilege 15 secret 0 your_admin_password
no ip domain lookup
dot11 syslog
dot11 ssid corp
    vlan 100
    authentication open
    authentication key-management wpa version 2
    wpa-psk ascii 0 your_corp_psk
```

```
dot11 ssid guest
   vlan 101
   authentication open
   authentication key-management wpa version 2
   guest-mode
   mbssid guest-mode
   wpa-psk ascii 0 your_guest_psk
!
crypto pki trustpoint TP-self-signed-261377633
 enrollment selfsigned
 subject-name cn=IOS-Self-Signed-Certificate-261377633
 revocation-check none
 rsakeypair TP-self-signed-261377633
crypto pki certificate chain TP-self-signed-261377633
bridge irb
!
interface Dot11Radio0
 no ip address
 no ip route-cache
 encryption vlan 100 mode ciphers aes-ccm
 encryption vlan 101 mode ciphers aes-ccm
 ssid corp
 ssid guest
  antenna gain 0
 mbssid
 station-role root
!
interface Dot11Radio0.100
 encapsulation dot1Q 100 native
 no ip route-cache
 bridge-group 1
 bridge-group 1 subscriber-loop-control
 bridge-group 1 block-unknown-source
 no bridge-group 1 source-learning
 no bridge-group 1 unicast-flooding
 bridge-group 1 spanning-disabled
!
interface Dot11Radio0.101
 encapsulation dot1Q 101
 no ip route-cache
 bridge-group 101
 bridge-group 101 subscriber-loop-control
 bridge-group 101 block-unknown-source
 no bridge-group 101 source-learning
 no bridge-group 101 unicast-flooding
```

```
 bridge-group 101 spanning-disabled
!
interface Dot11Radio1
 no ip address
 no ip route-cache
 encryption vlan 100 mode ciphers aes-ccm
 encryption vlan 101 mode ciphers aes-ccm
 ssid corp
 ssid guest
 !
 antenna gain 0
 dfs band 3 block
 mbssid
 channel dfs
 station-role root
 bridge-group 5
 bridge-group 5 subscriber-loop-control
 bridge-group 5 block-unknown-source
 no bridge-group 5 source-learning
 no bridge-group 5 unicast-flooding
 bridge-group 5 spanning-disabled
!
interface Dot11Radio1.100
 encapsulation dot1Q 100 native
 no ip route-cache
 bridge-group 1
 bridge-group 1 subscriber-loop-control
 bridge-group 1 block-unknown-source
 no bridge-group 1 source-learning
 no bridge-group 1 unicast-flooding
 bridge-group 1 spanning-disabled
!
interface Dot11Radio1.101
 encapsulation dot1Q 101
 no ip route-cache
 bridge-group 101
 bridge-group 101 subscriber-loop-control
 bridge-group 101 block-unknown-source
 no bridge-group 101 source-learning
 no bridge-group 101 unicast-flooding
 bridge-group 101 spanning-disabled
!
interface BVI5
 no ip address
```

```
 no ip route-cache
 shutdown
!
interface GigabitEthernet0
 no ip address
 no ip route-cache
 duplex auto
 speed auto
 no keepalive
bridge-group 5
 no bridge-group 5 source-learning
 bridge-group 5 spanning-disabled
!
interface GigabitEthernet0.100
 encapsulation dot1Q 100 native
 no ip route-cache
 bridge-group 1
 no bridge-group 1 source-learning
 bridge-group 1 spanning-disabled
!
interface GigabitEthernet0.101
 encapsulation dot1Q 101
 no ip route-cache
 bridge-group 101
 no bridge-group 101 source-learning
 bridge-group 101 spanning-disabled
!
interface BVI1
 ip address 192.168.1.10 255.255.255.0
 no ip route-cache
!
no ip http server
ip http secure-server
bridge 1 route ip
!
line con 0
line vty 0 4
 password 0 your_vty_password
transport input ssh
int dot11radio 0
no shut
int dot11radio 1
no shut
End
```

Antenna Placement

There are two types of APs—one that employs internal antennas (such as the Aironet 1130AG AP) and one that uses external antennas (such as the Aironet 1240AG AP).

Those requiring external antennas aren't designed that way to be inconvenient; rather, they provide greater flexibility in their use and deployment. That said, there are some important considerations to keep in mind when connecting an external antenna to your AP: The antenna should be located as closely to the access point as possible. The further the antenna is from the AP, the more signal reduction you can expect. For example, if you are placing antennas to cover an outside courtyard, don't place the access point in the server closet inside the building. In this case, it's best to place the access point outside in a weatherproof housing (or buy a weatherproof access point from the start), so it'll be closer to the antenna.

The type of antenna cabling you use is also important. Signal loss will be affected by the type of cabling. You can expect about 6 dB of loss for every 100 feet of cable. The thicker the cable you use, the better. The trade-off, however, is that thicker cable costs more money and is more difficult to run.

The type of wireless access point you use will also be a factor. If you are using an 802.11a AP, cable loss will become more significant because cable loss increases with higher frequencies. As such, you can expect more loss between antennas with an 802.11a access point than you would with an 802.11g access point.

We've only looked at how to configure your network's access points. Given the number of different client devices out there—especially when BYOD gets involved—it would be impossible to cover all the ways to configure them. What's most important is to ensure client devices have the correct WPA keys to access the network.

Summary

Wireless networking has come a long way in a few short years. It has gone from being a "Hey, isn't that cool" way of connecting to an integral part of enterprise networking. In the next chapter, we'll move on and take a closer look at another area where wireless has its tendrils—Voice over IP (VoIP).

PART III | Cisco Business Solutions

CHAPTER 12 | Cisco VoIP

A t the core of Cisco's offerings are its popular routers, switches, and servers. These are the meat and potatoes of Cisco's internetworking empire. Given the constantly changing face of business in the Internet world, Cisco is staying on the cutting edge of technology and networking needs by embracing current business technologies and investing in what they think will be popular technologies of the future.

One such area is the field of business communications. For many years, communications had been handled via a plain old phone sitting on the corner of a desk, e-mail, or simply shouting over a cubicle wall. The challenger to these methods of communication is Voice over IP (VoIP). VoIP provides a way to merge telephone services into an organization's IP network. The benefits of this come not just from a monetary standpoint (organizations can save a lot of money when they implement VoIP solutions, especially when we consider local, long-distance, and international tolls). VoIP can make communications smoother and easier as well as integrate with just about any corporate service you can think of.

In this chapter, we take a closer look at Cisco's IP contact products and services, including VoIP and its Cisco Unified Communications system, which has changed the way businesses communicate.

VoIP

If music, video, and other multimedia content can be delivered across internetworks, why not conduct telephone conversations across the internetwork? It probably comes as no surprise that Cisco has a whole line of products to enable VoIP interaction.

One of the biggest benefits to VoIP is something that will appeal to everyone across your organization: cost savings. Consider the benefits reaped by the Minnesota Department of Labor and Industry. The department's phone system was cobbled together from five proprietary systems. After exploring their replacement options, in the Fall of 2000, the department decided to pursue a VoIP solution and installed a system with 300 phones at a cost of $435,000.

After three years, the benefits were enormous. The department cut their monthly phone bill by more than half—from $21,700 to less than $10,000. In 2003, seven more locations were added to the department's VoIP deployment and, currently, almost every branch of the Minnesota government is riding the VoIP bandwagon.

As popular as it's becoming, VoIP isn't always a perfect way to get rid of your organization's desktop telephones, but it is a viable technology that is rapidly evolving. There is a good chance you will, if you have not done so already, use VoIP to communicate with a branch office, or even an old high school friend living on the other side of the continent. Companies such as Vonage (www.vonage.com) sell residential VoIP with unlimited long-distance and local calls for US$29.99 per month. Skype (www.skype.com) even offers *Jetsons*-style video calling around the world. For instance, you can start Skype on your PC in America and have a video conversation with your friend in Switzerland—for free.

It's quite possible that you already have VoIP equipment in your home because the traditional cable television companies have converted to IP streaming media systems and have been selling IP-based voice services for some years. In this section, we delve into the issues and technology surrounding VoIP, and then look at Cisco's solutions and equipment to deliver telephony across IP networks.

Introduction to VoIP

One of the early promises of the Internet was the prospect of making free long-distance telephone calls. In theory, calls would be encoded by one computer, transmitted through the Internet, and then decoded by the receiver. Furthermore, there would only be the need for one type of network—the Internet Protocol (IP) network. This would do away with the need for both dedicated voice and data networks. In practice, however, this technology had a long way to go.

The main problem was one of resources. In order for the call to go through, packets had to be received in the correct order; otherwise, Internet phone calls would come through as gibberish. Too often, packets were received in a random order. The result was delay, packet loss, and jitter, ultimately making the calls hard to understand and revealing the system to be something other than the panacea all had hoped for.

How a VoIP Call Works

Just what happens when you make a VoIP call? Let's take a look at the process, shown in Figure 12-1, by following the steps by the numbers:

1. The receiver is picked up and a dial tone is generated by the Private Branch Exchange (PBX).

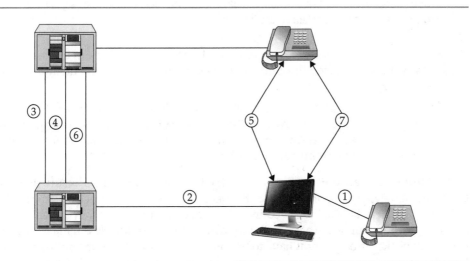

Figure 12-1.   The numbered steps demonstrate how VoIP works.

NOTE   A PBX is a device located within an organization that routes incoming telephone calls to the desired extension. It also supplies additional features, such as voicemail or call forwarding. We'll talk more about PBXs throughout this chapter.

2. The user dials the telephone number. (The numbers are stored by the PBX.)

3. Once enough digits are entered to match a configured destination pattern, the telephone number is mapped to the IP host. This step is accomplished using the dial plan mapper. At this point, the IP host has made a connection to either the destination telephone number or a PBX that will complete the call to its destination.

4. A transmission and reception channel are established when the session application runs a protocol such as Session Initiation Protocol (SIP) or the H.323 session protocol. (We talk about SIP and H.323 in more detail later in this chapter.) If a PBX is managing the call, it forwards the call to the destination telephone. If Resource Reservation Protocol (RSVP) has been configured, the RSVP reservations are made.

NOTE   RSVP "clears a path" across the routers between the two telephones. Cisco calls this "reserving resources." RSVP is one way to achieve the desired quality of service over an IP network.

5. The codecs are enabled for both ends of the connection, and the conversation proceeds using RTP/UDP/IP as the protocol stack.

NOTE   *Codecs* are hardware or software devices that translate analog voice signals into IP packets that can be transmitted across the network.

6. Any call-progress indicators (or other types of signals that can be carried in-band) are connected through the voice path once the end-to-end audio channel has been established.

7. As soon as the phone call has ended (once either end hangs up), the RSVP reservations are torn down (if RSVP is used), the connection is broken, and the session ends. At this point, each end becomes idle, waiting for an "off hook" signal or an incoming IP phone call.

In addition to transporting the packets, the IP network must also ensure that the conversation is transported across the media in a manner that delivers the best voice quality. If packets are received in a different order than how they're sent out, the conversation will be garbled and, ultimately, choppy and useless. Finally, the IP telephony packet stream might have to be converted by a gateway to another format.

This is necessary for the sake of interoperation with either a different IP-based multimedia system or if the phone call is terminating on the conventional public telephone system.

Building VoIP Networks

The three basic types of VoIPs are designed around the user's specific needs and suit a specific market:

- **Simple toll bypass**   The most basic, straightforward use for VoIP involves using it to make telephone calls without having to use the public switched telephone network (PSTN). This is ideal if you just want to use IP to transport calls between branch offices within the corporate network. The design requires minimal change to existing PBX, cabling, and handset infrastructures. What's more, it's relatively easy to develop and has no PSTN integration issues to worry about.

- **Total IP telephony**   This design relegates your existing voice systems to the dumpster. No longer will desktops have conventional telephone handsets, which are traded in for IP telephones that plug into Ethernet ports. You'll use LAN servers to provide the majority of the features your PBX now provides. This is the Holy Grail of VoIP and not a journey to begin on a whim.

- **IP-enabled PBXs**   This solution isn't as gutsy as total IP telephony, but you still get a mélange of functionality. You don't have to change the existing cabling or handsets, but you will upgrade the PBXs so that your organization's core systems can speak IP telephony protocols. PBX users will be able to communicate with other IP telephony users, but the limitation is that your PBXs will have to rely on IP telephony gateways to communicate with the conventional, public telephone system.

The easiest solution to implement is simple toll bypass, so let's take a closer look at how that works, and then we'll add some of the elements from the other two design concepts.

Simple Toll Bypass

VoIP toll bypass solutions are reasonably easy to implement. Before we start making changes, let's take a closer look at what you're likely to be starting with. Figure 12-2 shows three interconnected PBXs.

A PBX is a device located within an organization that connects phone calls coming in on trunk lines from the PSTN to their designated extensions. PBXs are also able to switch calls to extensions located on other connected PBXs. Most PBX interconnections are digital, and might even be E1 circuits (similar to a T1, but offering more channels and specifically coded by the provider for voice traffic instead of data), which are dedicated for the sole purpose of interconnecting PBXs. Typically, however, they are channels set up on a Time Division Multiplexing (TDM) backbone. The TDM divides bandwidth between voice and data.

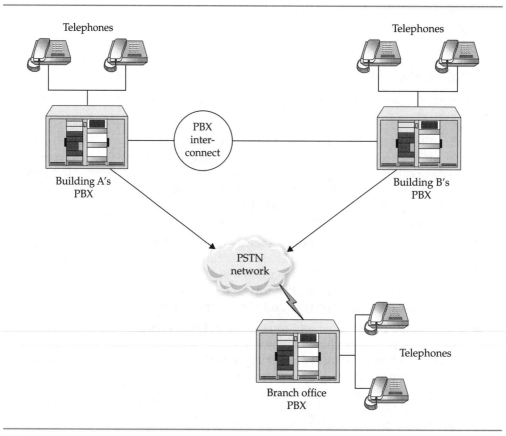

Figure 12-2. This existing telephone network is common to many organizations.

The problem in having both dedicated voice and multiservice TDM lines is that bandwidth must be permanently allocated for each voice circuit, even though the voice circuits are not always in use. A better way to manage resources is to split traffic into packets so that all traffic can be commingled and use bandwidth more efficiently. This is where VoIP makes its entrance.

The easiest way to deploy a VoIP solution is to simply unplug the lines to the PBX and plug them into a separate unit that converts the voice signaling and transport into an IP format. These units (such as the Cisco ATA 187 Analog Telephone Adapter) are referred to as a *VoIP relay* and connect into a router for transport over an IP network, as illustrated in Figure 12-3.

You do not, however, have to buy a separate VoIP relay and router. Several Cisco routers (the 1900, 2900, and 3900 series, for instance) provide direct PBX interfaces. But if you want a separate VoIP relay and router, you can certainly configure your VoIP solution that way.

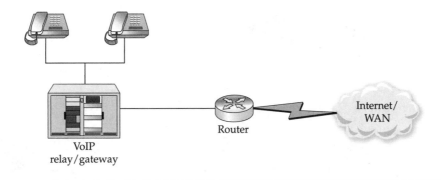

Figure 12-3.   Connecting telephones to a VoIP relay and router provides VoIP connectivity.

No matter which route you choose, you must address three basic design concerns:

- Make sure that the VoIP gateway will relay sufficient signaling information to support the features in use on the PBXs.

- Make sure you know which standards your solution is using. Even though some products promise H.323 compliance, there are still a number of proprietary schemes.

- Make sure you figure out how you're going to supply the necessary voice quality. This issue comes down to a combination of which encoding scheme you use and the QoS capabilities of your network.

VoIP Solution

The toll bypass system we just discussed is a straightforward, cost-saving scenario that you can hook up with little or no headache. But if you want to get adventuresome, consider the design in Figure 12-4.

In a full IP telephony solution, all end-user devices (PCs and phones) are connected to the LAN. The telephone that users will come to know and love can be one of two types:

- Hardware IP phones that look and act just like regular telephones, except they are plugged into the network

- Software IP phones that rely on client software running on the PC

Consider Figure 12-5. If, for instance, Keith in Custodial Services wants to call Pat in Accounting, he picks up the IP phone and they communicate across LAN A using an IP connection. However, if Keith needs to order a drum of floor wax, his call goes through the network using IP connection B and then is linked to a gateway. The *gateway* (such as the Cisco 1861E Integrated Services Router) is a device that links VoIP calls to the public phone network.

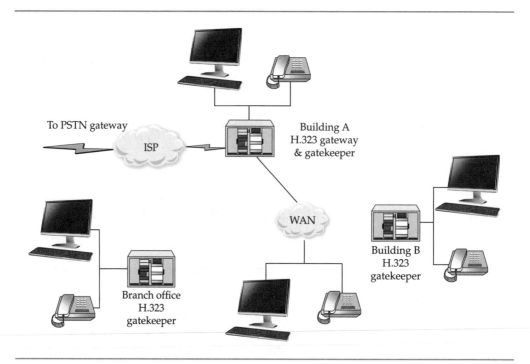

Figure 12-4.   With a full-blown IP telephony solution, both PCs and phones are connected to the LAN.

Finally, there are servers that support IP telephony. These servers provide both basic call setup functions as well as the advanced features users have come to expect from traditional PBXs, such as voicemail, call hold, and call forwarding. Let's take a closer look at IP phones, gateways, and servers.

At its simplest, an IP telephone can be set up by plugging in a speaker and a microphone to the PC. However, people have come to expect their telephones to look and feel like telephones. As we mentioned earlier, there are hardware and software IP phones. That "telephone feel" can be accomplished with a telephone that speaks IP and that can be plugged directly into a switch. Alternatively, users can simply plug a specially designed handset into their PC to take advantage of the software solution.

Later in this chapter, we'll talk about the Cisco Unified Communications system. Many of the IP phones for that solution not only look like "normal" telephones, they also have *Jetsons*-like video screens and displays on them.

Each of these phones offers the same sorts of features that a telephone connected to a PBX offers. Naturally, there are some disadvantages to these solutions. Hardware IP phones will need a jack on the switch (watch out, you can run out of connections fast), and they also need a power supply. Many switches, such as the Cisco Catalyst 3560 and 2960, can provide that power over the spare pair of wires inside an Ethernet cable (PoE).

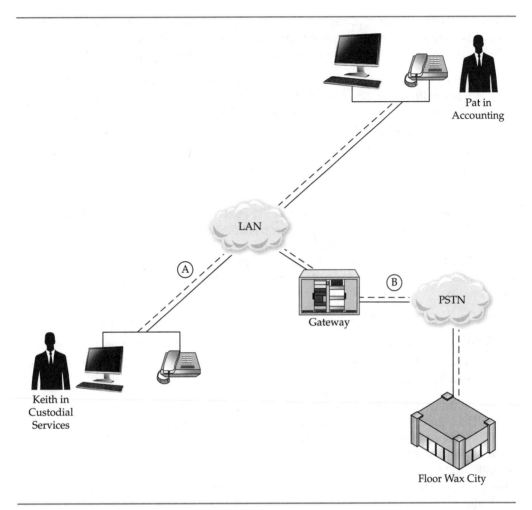

Pat in
Accounting

LAN

A

B

PSTN

Gateway

Keith in
Custodial
Services

Floor Wax City

Figure 12-5. IP telephone calls are connected inside and outside the IP network with different pieces of equipment.

These hardware phones today generally include a small two-port switch so you can daisy-chain your PC to the phone and then the phone to the switch, thereby saving switchports.

These pitfalls can be avoided by using a software-based IP telephone. This can be done by plugging a telephone into a serial or USB port, or you can plug a plain-old desktop analog telephone into a PC card or external adapter. We'll talk more about some of Cisco's VoIP phones and softphones later in this chapter.

If you decide to use a software-based IP telephone (a.k.a. softphone), you must also get client software that can support IP telephony. The software can be a standalone product, a standards-based product (make sure you buy one that matches your phone's standards), or part of a package such as Microsoft's Communicator.

You should keep the following three issues in mind when selecting an IP telephone:

- When considering hardware IP telephones, make sure the phone won't limit your ability to integrate with the desktop environment. For example, you need to ensure you have enough bandwidth and device ports to support both computers and VoIP.

- Make sure that the phones support appropriate codec and signaling standards.

- Make sure that the phone and your network will be able to share QoS priorities.

Gateways serve as interfaces between PSTN telephone calls and IP telephony. PSTN consists of two separate networks—one for transporting the voice conversations and one for transporting signaling information (using the SS7 protocol).

Let's pause for a moment to consider some of the basics of the public telephone system that will be important to know for the sake of understanding gateway functionality:

- **Central Office**   Where local phone lines first connect into the public network

- **Central Office Switch**   The local switch in the Central Office

- **Tandem Switch**   Switches that interconnect between Central Office Switches in a local area network

A Central Office Switch connects both voice and SS7 signaling trunks, which connect to Signal Transfer Points (STPs). STPs are the message switches that route SS7 signaling information. These two trunks are kept separate because doing so facilitates the setup and teardown of voice calls. It also streamlines the network during periods of peak usage. SS7 is also necessary for the provisioning of 800 and 888 numbers, and makes such perks as call forwarding, caller ID, and last-call return possible.

Using SS7 is not necessary for an IP Telephony to PSTN Gateway connection, as long as there is in-band signaling on voice trunks, but this provides only for a telephone call from an IP telephony device to a telephone on the PSTN network. If additional functionality (such as call forwarding and the like) is desired, another gateway is needed: the SS7-to-IP Telephony Gateway.

Cisco offers a number of gateway products for use in VoIP solutions, including its AS5300, AS5400, and AS5800 Series Universal Gateways. In addition, a number of routers include gateway functionality, from the 800 Series up to the 7500 Series.

A basic IP telephone call occurs when one IP telephone connects to another. However, a number of "behind-the-scenes" functions must be managed, including such features as call routing and billing. These functions cannot be performed by either of the end users; rather, they must be performed by an IP telephony server (or several servers, depending on the size of the network). Under the H.323 protocol, this set of functions is performed by a gatekeeper. We'll explain H.323 and the gatekeeper in more detail later in this chapter in the section "H.323." We'll also talk about the newer protocol, Session Initiation Protocol (SIP). Gatekeepers may also include support for such extras as voice messaging and voice conferencing in the same IP telephony server.

Encoding

When you speak into a telephone, you cause air molecules to move, which bounce off a microphone and are converted into an electrical signal, which is sent across the network, where it vibrates the speaker on the other telephone. Those vibrations move air molecules, which complete the transformation from sound into electricity and then back into sound.

With VoIP, another layer must be added to this process. It isn't enough for the electrical signal to be transported; it must be converted from an analog to a digital format. This conversion is exactly like the difference between records (remember them?) and compact discs.

An analog wave is pictured in Figure 12-6, where A represents what sound looks like when it first moves through a microphone. Next, the wave (B) is sampled at regular intervals, the signal is sampled, and the numbers (C) are converted into a series of 0's and 1's. This process is called *voice encoding,* and the piece of software or device used to encode (then later to decode) the signal is called a *codec.* Obviously, the more frequent the sampling interval, the better the sound quality. However, the more frequent the sampling interval, the more bandwidth will be devoured.

A good rule of thumb to use when sampling is to sample at a rate at least 2.2 times the maximum frequency represented in the underlying signal. The human voice uses frequencies ranging from 300 Hz to about 4 KHz. For the sake of simple math, we can use a sampling rate of 8,000 times per second. If, for each sample, we use 8 bits to represent the signal strength, then we'll need a bandwidth of 8 bits, 8,000 times per second, or 64 Kbps. This is called Pulse Code Modulation (PCM) and is the most popular way to encode voice on public telephone networks.

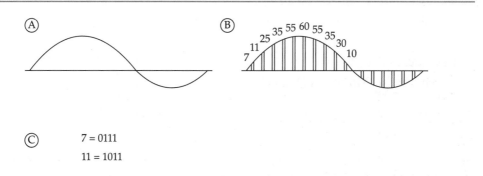

Figure 12-6.   An analog wave is converted into a digital datastream by measuring regular "slices."

Codecs provide varying qualities of speech. This quality is not a finite amount, but is rather subjective. What one person might think is perfectly clear speech might sound too muddy and electronic to someone else. The way to make the subjective world of sound quality more objective is through the use of the mean opinion score (MOS). Like a group taste-testing a new kind of ketchup, listeners are brought together to judge the quality of a voice sample; then they rate the sound quality on a scale of 1 to 5, with 1 being "bad" and 5 being "excellent." These scores are then averaged to provide the MOS for that sample.

Table 12-1 compares the different codecs, their bit rates, compression delay, and MOS rankings.

In Table 12-1, the bit rate is used to describe the amount of data sent per second. Remember, the larger this value, the better the overall quality. You'll notice that the code with the highest bit rate—G.711—rated the highest MOS score.

Second is the compression delay. This is the amount of time it takes, in milliseconds, for the signal to be encoded. This is an important factor to consider when selecting a codec, because lengthy encoding times will cause conversations to be difficult to understand.

Compression Method	Bit Rate (Kbps)	Compression Delay (ms)	MOS Score
G.711 Pulse Code Modulation (PCM)	64	0.75	4.1
G.726 Adaptive Differential Pulse Code Modulation (ADPCM)	32	1	3.85
G.728 Low-Delay Code Excited Linear Prediction (LD-CELP)	16	3 to 5	3.61
G.729 Conjugate-Structure Algebraic-Code-Excited Linear-Prediction (CS-ACELP)	8	10	3.92
G.729 x 2 Encodings	8	10	3.27
G.729 x 3 Encodings	8	10	2.68
G.729a CS-ACELP	8	10	3.7
G.723.1 Multipulse, Multilevel Quantization (MP-MLQ)	6.3	30	3.9
G.723.1 Algebraic Code Excited Linear Prediction (ACELP)	5.3	30	3.65

Table 12-1.   VoIP Codec Comparison

There is no "best" codec to use. Depending on your need, you will have to balance these variables to get the best solution. Even though G.711 has the highest MOS score, it also consumes the most amount of bandwidth. G.723 consumes ten times less bandwidth than G.711 and is a close third in terms of MOS score. However, it takes 40 times longer to compress the signal with G.723 than G.711. These are all balls you'll have to juggle when selecting a codec for your VoIP solution.

Quality of Service

Encoding isn't the only way to ensure voice quality. By virtue of the way IP networks operate, it's important that the packets containing VoIP information arrive and are decoded in the same order in which they were sent, and without delays in excess of 150 milliseconds (ms). Otherwise, the conversation will be a nonsensical mélange of gibberish.

In essence, QoS (Quality of Service) is a means to ensure that prioritized packets (such as those containing VoIP information) speed through the network ahead of packets from other, less critical applications.

Packet prioritization is usually less important to data networking, which is mostly tolerant to variable network performance. As such, networks weren't designed to ensure that packets are received expeditiously or in order—something most data applications didn't worry about too much. However, without QoS mechanisms in place, random and slow delivery is the death of VoIP.

It is helpful to discuss how QoS can be implemented with VoIP in mind. From a design standpoint, you have two considerations when establishing how to provide your desired level of QoS. First, you must determine the capabilities of your router infrastructure and what upgrades you would have to make to support your desired QoS levels. Next, you must make sure that the IP telephony end systems will work with your QoS mechanisms.

H.323

A number of protocols are important in the world of VoIP. H.323 is an umbrella recommendation from the International Telecommunications Union (ITU), which establishes standards for multimedia communications over LANs that do not have a QoS mechanism in place. Unfortunately, these kinds of networks are the norm in most organizations, which include packet-switched TCP/IP and over Ethernet of all kinds. As such, the H.323 standard is an important technology for LAN-based applications for multimedia communications. The standard covers a range of technologies, including standalone devices and embedded personal computer technology, as well as point-to-point and multipoint conferences. In addition to hardware, H.323 addresses such management and control functions as call control, multimedia management, and bandwidth management.

Importance of H.323

The H.323 standard is all inclusive, yet it remains flexible and can be applied to basic voice handsets or to full video-conferencing workstations. There are a number of reasons that H.323 is a popular protocol for VoIP:

- H.323 establishes multimedia standards for the most prominent IP-based networks. It is designed to compensate for the highly variable LAN latencies that exist in IP-based networks. By using H.323, multimedia applications can be used without having to overhaul the whole network.

- IP LANs are getting more and more powerful. From speeds of 10 Mbps, then 100 Mbps, and now 10 Gbps, more networks are able to provide the bandwidth that H.323 applications demand.

- PCs continue to get more powerful because of constant improvements in processors, memory, and multimedia accelerator chips.

- If you need to communicate between two different kinds of networks, the H.323 standard allows for internetwork functionality.

- Increased manageability of networking can limit the amount of bandwidth that is devoured with multimedia activity. With H.323, network administrators can restrict the amount of network bandwidth available for conferencing. To be more efficient with network resources, H.323's support of multicasting reduces bandwidth consumption.

- In a field thick with proprietary technologies, H.323 has the benefit of many computing and communications companies supporting it. Intel, Microsoft, Cisco, and IBM are some of the biggest names backing H.323.

Key Benefits of H.323

H.323 stands out as the most popular way to conduct VoIP conversations for a number of reasons:

- **Codec standards**   H.323 defines standards for compression/decompression of audio and video data streams. This ensures that data will be readable if it is transmitted between the products of two different vendors.

- **Network independence**   H.323 is designed to run on top of common network architectures. As network technology evolves and as bandwidth management techniques have improved, H.323-based solutions have been able to take advantage of those enhanced capabilities.

- **Platform and application independence**   Like all standards, H.323 is not the sole purview of any single hardware or operating system vendor. Furthermore, H.323 isn't restricted to PCs alone. H.323-compliant platforms come in a number of forms, including videophones, IP-enabled telephones, and cable TV boxes.

- **Multipoint support**   Multiconferencing is already supported by H.323, which can support conferences with three or more endpoints without requiring special equipment. However, including multipoint control units (MCUs) will provide a more powerful environment for hosting multipoint conferences.

■ **Bandwidth management**   Because the traffic generated by audio and video applications is bandwidth intensive, the potential exists to clog even the most robust networks. H.323 addresses this problem with bandwidth management tools. Using the management devices, network managers can set limits on the number of concurrent H.323 connections within their network, or they can restrict the amount of bandwidth available to H.323 applications. With proper resource management, no network need ever be slowed down.

■ **Multicast support**   For situations where a number of people will receive the same broadcast, H.323 supports multicast transporting. For instance, in the case of a CEO broadcasting an address to a number of branch offices, H.323 multicast sends a single packet to all the branch offices. While the data is still on the company's headquarters network, the data is not duplicated, thereby saving resources. Compare this to *unicast,* which sends multiple point-to-point transmissions, and *broadcast,* which sends to all destinations. Employing unicast or broadcast is an inefficient use of the network, because packets are replicated unnecessarily. Multicast transmission uses bandwidth more efficiently because all stations in the multicast read the same data stream.

■ **Flexibility**   Not all users' computers are created equal. However, using an H.323-compliant device allows conferences to be conducted across a network that includes a variety of endpoints, each with different capabilities. For instance, a teleconference can be listened to by a user whose computer is enabled only for VoIP.

■ **Internetwork conferencing**   In the last example, we talked about H.323 as a means to communicate over networks with different devices, but H.323 isn't limited to the boxes on desktops. H.323 can also be used across different kinds of network architectures, and uses common codec technology from different videoconferencing standards to minimize transcoding delays and thus deliver the best results.

H.323 defines four major components for a network-based communications system: terminals, gateways, gatekeepers, and multipoint control units.

Terminals

Terminals are the endpoint devices that clients use. The specification requires that all terminals support voice communications, but video and data are optional. H.323 specifies how different audio, video, and data terminals will work together.

In addition, all H.323 terminals must support H.245, which is a mechanism used to negotiate channel usage and capabilities. Terminals must also support three other components:

■ The Q.931 protocol for call signaling and call setup

■ Registration, Admission, and Status (RAS), a protocol used to communicate with a gatekeeper

■ Support for RTP/RTCP for sequencing audio and video packets

Optional components in an H.323 terminal are video codecs, data-conferencing protocols, and MCU capabilities.

Gateways

The main function of a gateway is to serve as a translator between H.323 conferencing endpoints and PSTN networks. This function includes translation between transmission formats and between communications procedures. Furthermore, the gateway also translates between different audio and video codecs, and performs call setup and clearing on both the LAN side and the switched-circuit network side.

But gateways are an optional component in an H.323 conference. You don't need a gateway if you're not connecting to other networks, since endpoints can communicate directly with other endpoints on the same LAN.

As complete as the H.323 standard is, several gateway functions are left open for the manufacturer to determine. For example, the standard does not establish how many terminals can connect through the gateway.

Gatekeepers

Whereas gateways were an optional piece of the H.323 pie, gatekeepers are an extremely crucial component. A gatekeeper is the central point for all calls within its zone and provides call control services to registered endpoints.

Gatekeepers perform three important control functions:

- Address translation from LAN aliases for terminals and gateways to IP addresses.
- Bandwidth management. For instance, if the network administrator has set a limit on the number of concurrent H.323 connections or a threshold on bandwidth usage, it is the gatekeeper that can refuse more connections once the threshold is breached.
- Access control to the LAN for H.323 terminals and gateways.

Gatekeepers serve the optional function of routing H.323 calls. Routing calls through a gatekeeper allows them to be managed more effectively and efficiently. This feature is especially important at the service provider level, because they need the ability to bill for calls placed through their network. This can also help balance network resources, because a gatekeeper capable of routing H.323 calls can make decisions about managing multiple gateways.

A gatekeeper is not required for a functional H.323 system. However, if a gatekeeper is present on the network, terminals must use their address translation, admissions control, bandwidth control, and zone management services.

Multipoint Control Units

For conferences among three or more users, the multipoint control unit (MCU) is employed. An MCU consists of a multipoint controller (MC), which is required, as well as multipoint processors (MPs). MC and MP capabilities can be housed in a dedicated component or be part of other H.323 components.

The MC handles H.245 negotiations between all terminals and establishes the common audio and video capabilities. The MC is used to manage conference resources by determining which of the audio and video streams can be multicast.

However, the MC does not directly control any of the media streams. This task is the purview of MP, which mixes, switches, and processes audio, video, and data.

SIP

An alternative to H.323 that has picked up steam in the VoIP community is the Session Initiation Protocol (SIP). SIP is the IETF (Internet Engineering Task Force) standard for multimedia conferencing over IP. SIP is an ASCII-based, application-layer control protocol that establishes, maintains, and terminates calls between two or more terminals.

Table 12-2 highlights some of SIP's functionality.

Function	Description
Resolving the location of target endpoints	SIP supports address resolution, name mapping, and call redirection.
Establishing the media capabilities of the target endpoint	This is achieved by using the Session Description Protocol (SDP). SIP determines the "lowest level" of common services between the endpoints, and communications are only conducted using the media capabilities supported at both ends.
Determining the availability of the target endpoint	If a call cannot be completed because the target is not available, SIP figures out if the target is already on the phone or did not answer in the allotted number of rings. Finally, it returns a message explaining why the call was unsuccessful.
Establishing a session between the originating and target endpoint	If the call can be completed, SIP establishes a session between the endpoints. SIP also supports mid-call changes, such as the addition of another endpoint to the conference or the changing of a media characteristic or codec.
Handling the transfer and termination of calls.	SIP supports the transfer of calls from one endpoint to another. During a call transfer, SIP simply establishes a session to a new endpoint and terminates the session between the transferee and the transferring party.

Table 12-2.   SIP Functionality

SIP is a peer-to-peer protocol, which means that it doesn't need a dedicated server to manage the sessions. The peers in a session are called user agents (UAs). A UA serves one of two roles in a conversation:

- **User Agent Client (UAC)**   Client applications that initiate the SIP conversation request

- **User Agent Server (UAS)**   Server applications that contact the user when an SIP request is received and then return a response on behalf of the user

An SIP endpoint can function both as a UAC and UAS. However, they only function as one or the other on any given conversation. An endpoint will function as a UAC or UAS depending on which UA initiated the request.

The physical components of an SIP network can be split into two categories: clients and servers. SIP clients include

- **Phones**   These devices can act as either a UAS or UAC. Softphones and Cisco SIP IP phones can initiate SIP requests and respond to requests.

- **Gateways**   These devices control call functions. Gateways provide a number of services, including translating functions between SIP conferencing endpoints and other terminal types. This includes translation between transmission formats and between communications procedures. The gateway also performs call setup and teardown.

SIP servers include

- **Proxy server**   This server provides such functionalities as authentication, authorization, network access control, routing, reliable request retransmission, and security. Proxy servers receive SIP messages and forward them to the next SIP server in the network.

- **Redirect server**   This server tells the client about the next hop that a message should take. Next, the client contacts the next-hop server or UAS directly.

- **Registrar server**   This server processes requests from UACs to register their current location. Often, registrar servers are co-located with a redirect or proxy server.

SCCP

SIP is somewhat of a juggernaut—inasmuch as a VoIP protocol could be considered a juggernaut. In early 2006, Cisco took a step back from its proprietary Skinny Client Control Protocol (SCCP) and allowed the popular SIP protocol to be used as part of its far-reaching Cisco Unified Communications system.

SCCP is now owned and defined by Cisco as a lightweight protocol for session signaling with Cisco Unified Communications Manager (formerly CallManager). SCCP is used to communicate between IP devices and Cisco Unified Communications Manager. Examples of SCCP clients include the Cisco 7900 series of IP phones, Cisco IP

Communicator softphone, and the Wireless IP Phone 7920, along with the Cisco Unity voicemail server.

SCCP is a proprietary terminal control protocol developed by Selsius Corporation and bought by Cisco in the late 1990s. It acts as a messaging set between a skinny client and Cisco CallManager.

Cisco had been backing SCCP (and it still does), but has allowed SIP functionality to be added to more recent VoIP solutions. This is beneficial, because it allows third-party equipment and technology to be part of a Cisco VoIP solution; in fact, the 9900 series only supports SIP.

Implementation

VoIP can be implemented in several different ways within your organization. Whether you are dealing with a telecommuter connecting from home, or a branch office with a small complement of workers, all the way to a large branch office, there are a number of ways to configure a network to enable VoIP capabilities.

Let's take a closer look at these scenarios and talk about how to design and build VoIP-enabled networks.

Telecommuter

The Internet provides exceptional opportunities to decentralize your office. Rather than pack everybody into an endless beehive of cubicles, technology has made it possible for workers to limit their commute to a walk across the living room carpet. By using VoIP technology, telecommuters can communicate with the central office—or anywhere else for that matter—without affecting their own home telephone bill. VoIP solves a lot of problems for telecommuters and the organization's IT staff. The most important problem it solves is the need for independent circuits for both voice and data.

As Figure 12-7 shows, by providing a single data circuit and VoIP equipment, both voice and data can be integrated into a single circuit. They can be so well integrated, in fact, that the telecommuter can call the company operator (just by dialing 0), the voicemail system, and other telephone resources. Long-distance fees can be reduced by letting the telecommuter place VoIP calls to remote offices.

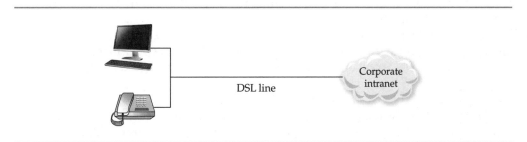

Figure 12-7. Combining voice and data into a single circuit saves money and resources.

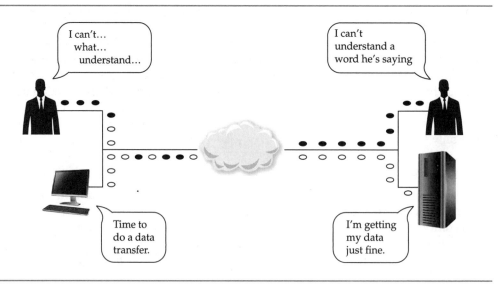

Figure 12-8.   Sending data and VoIP at the same time can disrupt a phone call.

But VoIP isn't without some headaches. The tallest wall to telecommuter and SOHO (small office/home office) VoIP involves bandwidth and network management. Users need enough bandwidth to accommodate VoIP traffic while simultaneously prioritizing, fragmenting, and queuing other data to protect the integrity of the voice transmission. If, as shown in Figure 12-8, a VoIP call gets stuck in the middle of a large file transfer, the call will wind up sounding like you're talking to an alien George Lucas thought up for a *Star Wars* movie. This isn't as large a problem as it was fifteen years ago when DSL and cable internet connections were less than 1 Mbps.

Another issue to consider is that circuits to telecommuters and SOHOs must maintain full-time connectivity during business hours; otherwise, calls to the user's equipment may not be established. For instance, some VoIP devices try to gauge latency to a remote system before establishing the call. Some systems are so sensitive that ISDN's call setup times may be too long, resulting in rejected calls.

The best solution for these issues—packet prioritization and full-time connectivity—all but require using at least flat-rate ISDN or DSL (Digital Subscriber Line). However, your basic-rate ISDN is only a 128 Kbps link, whereas DSL can exceed 10 Mbps.

Branch Offices

The best place to implement a VoIP solution is at the branch office level. Branch offices are ideal because they generally contain a small number of users and don't generate voluminous amounts of traffic. Furthermore, these offices are the sites most likely to benefit from the toll-free advantages of VoIP as a replacement for long-distance services. Branch offices typically use high-speed lines such as DSL, cable, or a T1 for connectivity. A sample configuration is shown in Figure 12-9.

As with anything, there are few instances where everything will fall into place perfectly. For instance, your organization's branch offices may house several hundred people, and implementing VoIP can create some infrastructure challenges. Furthermore, if your remote office is already equipped with a PBX, there isn't much need to add new equipment. Also, if your organization routes long-distance calls across a fixed-cost dedicated circuit, there may not be much cost savings back to the headquarters.

Where VoIP really makes a name for itself as a long-distance alternative is in connecting offices over the Internet. Your organization will recognize considerable cost savings by buying guaranteed services from an ISP and then routing VoIP calls across that connection, rather than paying long-distance fees or buying your own dedicated network.

By implementing a VoIP deployment in a branch office, you can also use your corporate dialing plan, voicemail, and other features for less money than the cost of an additional PBX.

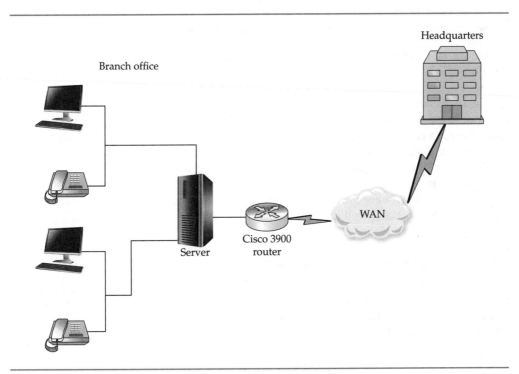

Figure 12-9.   Branch offices are great places to implement VoIP solutions.

Cisco Unified Communications

The Internet used to be such a quiet and peaceful place—just heated which-*Star-Trek*-captain-was-better debates and Yahoo.com. But in the two decades since its real explosion, it has become so much more than a forum to discuss Kirk vs. Picard. Now, the Internet is such a part of all of our lives. We use it for daily entertainment; we use it as part of our work; we use it in places that we aren't even aware that we're using it. And, with such ubiquity, there is a need for the pieces to fit together cleanly and seamlessly.

To that end, Cisco points to its Unified Communications products to connect people and information. Unified Communications aims to accomplish such goals as the following:

- To connect co-workers, partners, vendors, and customers to get and share the information they need
- To access and share video, across platforms and devices
- To improve communications
- To allow users easy access to the corporate network, no matter what device they're using
- To help organizations of all sizes communicate more effectively

Figure 12-10 shows how Cisco Unified Communications' components of presence, location, and call-processing intelligence work together to deliver the next generation of business communications.

Cisco Unified Communications is an open and extensible platform for real-time communications. It utilizes the computer network as a service platform to help users reach the correct resource the first time and by delivering presence and preference information to the organization's users.

As you might imagine, it would be impossible for one appliance or software tool to do it all. Cisco Unified Communications is composed of dozens of different pieces of hardware and software that you can use to build your own, ideal, communications solution. In this section, we'll take a look at what Cisco has to offer in its Unified Communications portfolio.

Cisco Unified Communications Manager

The heart of Cisco's Unified Communications efforts is its Cisco Unified Communications Manager (CUCM), formerly known as Cisco Unified CallManager and Cisco CallManager. It is a software-based call-processing system.

The manager tracks the organization's VoIP network components, including:

- Phones
- Gateways

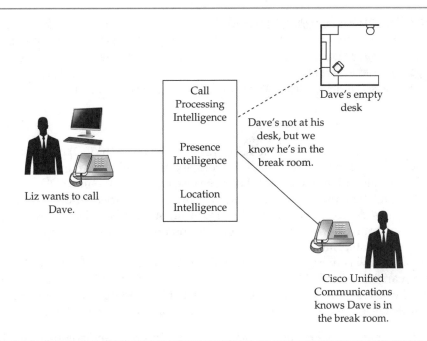

Figure 12-10. Cisco Unified Communications is based on three components.

- Conference bridges
- Voicemail boxes
- Transcoding resources

CUCM uses SCCP as the communications protocol for signaling the system endpoints, such as IP phones. Once the call is signaled, it uses H.323 or SIP to pass signaling along.

CUCM can manage up to 30,000 IP phones utilizing 20 servers, which combines the following:

- A publisher
- Two TFTP servers
- Sixteen subscribers
- Nine media resource servers

CUCM is installed on a Cisco Media Convergence Server (MCS) or other Cisco-approved hardware (such as a VMWare virtual machine). It is configured through a web browser, and large imports, exports, and changes can be made through the Bulk Administration Tool (BAT).

> **NOTE** CUCM is compatible with the following browsers on the PC: Internet Explorer 6.0 or later and Mozilla Firefox version 3.x, 4.x, and 10.x. It is compatible with the following browsers on the Mac: Safari 5.x or Mozilla Firefox version 4.x or 10.x. The following Internet browsers are officially supported to access the Enterprise License Manager interface: Firefox version 8, 9, and 10, Internet Explorer version 8 and 9, Chrome version 15, 16, and 17, and Safari version 5.1.

Version 9.0

Cisco expands its assimilation of the Bring Your Own Device (BYOD) philosophy with CUCM. Cisco looks to the change in work styles brought about by BYOD for its latest implementation of CUCM. That's because the explosion in BYOD brings a new paradigm where users are relying on their own—and varied—devices more than company-issued devices. That means the organization must be able to allow users to communicate from anywhere using any device and on any network—and it has to be cost effective, reliable, and secure.

CallManager was first introduced in 1997 when it was called Selsius-CallManager. Over the years it has gone through different names and versions, and in 2012 CUCM version 9.0 was released. Version 9.0 builds on what its predecessor (version 8.6) offered with several voice and video enhancements, including the following:

- A centralized tool for license management, reporting, and compliance. Mobile convergence enhancements help integrate mobile and desk phones using IP Multimedia Subsystem (IMS) integration.

- Systems are bridged, thus improving interoperability for endpoints.

- The end-user dialing system provides future-proofing for call-control platforms.

- Third-party endpoints are integrated into the Cisco Unified Communications environment using the Cisco Extend and Connect feature.

- Enhanced E911 features for emergency call rerouting.

Table 12-3 lists more improvements to CUCM 9.0

Cisco Unified Communications Manager Express

Cisco Unified Communications Manager Express (CME)—formerly Cisco Unified CallManager Express—is an implementation of CUCM for small- and medium-sized businesses as well as enterprise branch offices. It is an IOS-based IP-PBX and provides call control and voice applications for those environments. It supports Cisco IP phone endpoints using SCCP and SIP.

CME provides call-processing duties to Cisco Unified IP Phones for branch office and retail environments. It allows Cisco Integrated Services Routers (ISRs) to deliver unified communications features that users need when they rely on voice and video communications. CME allows the deployment with just IOS software.

Feature	Improvement
Platform improvements	Optimization for higher density per Cisco Unified Communications Manager virtual machine. Platform Administrative Web Service (PAWS) interface, allowing applications to perform their own upgrades on multiple Cisco Unified Communications Managers, thus centralizing software versioning and allowing remote upgrades.
Cisco Unified Communications Session Management Edition	Extend and Connect is a new device type on CUCM, showing remote devices and delivering features and services. Improved end-to-end round-trip time between the nodes in a Session Management Edition (SME) cluster to the degree that nodes can exist in several continents. Administrators can specify codecs for outbound SIP trunks and inbound PSTN SIP trunks.
Telephony feature enhancements	The ability to make encrypted calls when using the Extension Mobility Cross Cluster (EMCC) feature. Pause in Speed Dials allows users to configure the phone speed-dial button with strings. The ability to queue calls using different methods. The phone has a Start/Stop recording key. E911 is available for remote workers on hardware IP phones.
Mobility	Video calling now included. The ability to participate in a video conference via Wi-Fi and cellular modes—the conference sessions can be moved between mobile and desk phones. Consistent user experience for VoIP and cellular modes for mobile devices.

Table 12-3.   Cisco Unified Communications Manager 9.0 Improvements

CME is an IP telephony solution that is capable of handling between 24 and 450 phones, depending on the router model. The best part of CME is that it runs on Cisco routers and does not require separate hardware. If you have a Cisco router, adding CME to your organization is as simple as upgrading your IOS. Once that's done, you can configure and use it right away. Because CME is modular, it is extremely flexible.

When the IP phones boot up and register with CME, CME will assign each IP phone with its own extension. The IP phones and CME router use SCCP to communicate.

When calls are placed between two IP phones under the control of CME, SCCP is used to set up the call.

NOTE SCCP is not used between the two phones, but rather between each phone and the CME router.

Once the call is established, the Real-time Transport Protocol (RTP) is used to carry the audio stream. RTP is used to carry voice inside of IP packets. RTP is a common protocol used to carry traffic that is sensitive to jitter, such as voice and real-time video. RTP is carried inside of a UDP segment, which is then carried inside an IP packet. When the call has concluded, the IP phones are hung up and a signal is sent from each IP phone back to CME to let it know that their call is done and they are ready for a new call.

For all VoIP networks, Cisco recommends isolating VoIP traffic from data traffic, no matter the size of your network or how beefy your network infrastructure is. This is an effort to reduce jitter that would result from comingling voice and data on the same network. Isolating VoIP traffic is accomplished by the creation of a separate VLAN meant specifically for voice traffic. Cisco switches are built to automatically identify and prioritize VoIP traffic. This design ensures that VoIP packets will be placed in a higher QoS queue than other traffic, thus minimizing or eliminating problems with delay and jitter.

Benefits of CME include

- Service delivery through a single voice and data platform for all branch-office needs. ISRs provide QoS, network security, encryption, firewall, and network modules that deliver content networking and enhanced VPN services.

- Delivery of telephony features for the retail office, including multimedia capabilities through XML and Java.

- The CME Services Interface application programming interface (API) allows for the development of computer telephony integration with CME and third-party applications. This enables call monitoring, call control, and call provisioning with any CME SCCP endpoint.

- Any sized organization can utilize advanced call center capabilities.

Cisco Unified Communications Manager is for larger sites and Cisco Unified Communications Manager Express is for branch-office locations where local call processing is required without a dependency on the WAN.

IOS software is used to configure and administer Cisco Unified Communications Manager Express.

Cisco Unified Communications Manager Session Management Edition

The third flavor of Cisco Unified Communications Manager is its Cisco Unified Communications Manager Session Management Edition (CM Session Management Edition). The Unified CM Session Management Edition is essentially the same as Cisco Unified CM, but the software has been improved to suit its new usage model. Unified

CM Session Management Edition isn't concerned with the end user per se—rather, it is more designed for managing trunk-to-trunk connections.

Overview   CM Session Management Edition is, basically, a Cisco Unified Communications Management (CUCM) cluster with trunk interfaces only and no IP endpoints. This allows aggregation of multiple unified communications systems.

> **NOTE**   Multiple unified communications systems that are centrally managed are also known as *leaf* systems.

CM Session Management Edition is used for the migration and deployment of multiple PBXs and phones to a Cisco Unified CM cluster with IP phones and few trunks. The Unified CM Session Management Edition cluster can start with several trunks and third-party PBXs and, over time, migrate to a native Cisco Unified CM Cluster deployment with thousands of IP phones.

Unified CM Management is on version 8.0 of this tool, and this version supports the following features:

- H.323 Annex M1 intercluster trunks
- SIP intercluster trunks
- SIP trunks
- H.323 trunks
- MGCP trunks
- Voice calls
- Video calls
- Encrypted calls
- Fax calls

Unified CM Session Management Edition can also be used to connect third-party telecommunications systems such as IP PSTN connections and PBXs.

> **NOTE**   Cisco recommends testing the third-party hardware and its connection before being placed into a production environment.

Usage   Cisco advises that Unified CM Management Session is best deployed in these sorts of scenarios:

- **Creating and managing a centralized dial plan**   Instead of configuring each unified communications system with different dial plans, Unified CM Management Edition allows the system to be configured so that each leaf is configured with a simplified dial plan. Unified CM Management Edition maintains the centralized dial plan and connectivity information of all the other unified communications systems.

- **Centralize applications**   Commonly used applications—such as conferencing—can be connected directly to the session management cluster.

- **Need for centralized PSTN access**   PSTN systems can be aggregated to one or more centralized IP PSTN trunks.

Cisco Business Edition

The Cisco Unified Communications Manager Business Edition is a solution integrating media processing and unified messaging on a single appliance. Cisco has combined everything onto a lone appliance to make it cost effective as well as easy to set up, manage, and use. Besides just the sheer ease of use, the goal is to reduce total cost of ownership and allow easy transition from older telephony systems to Cisco's Unified Communications solution.

Cisco Unified Communications Manager Business Edition is meant to deliver enterprise-level communications and collaboration tools to your organization. Cisco Unified Communications Manager Business Edition comes in three models: 3000, 5000, and 6000 for small-, medium-, and large-sized organizations, respectively.

Table 12-4 compares the appliances and the environments for which they are aimed. Cisco Unified Communications Manager Business Edition consists of the following components:

- **Cisco Unified Communications Manager Version 7.1**   The media-processing engine of Cisco Unified Communications Manager Business Edition. This extends telephony features to packet telephony network devices such as IP phones, media processing devices, and VoIP gateways.

Feature	Business Edition 3000	Business Edition 5000	Business Edition 6000
Maximum number of users	300	500	1,000
Maximum number of mailboxes and voicemail ports	300 mailboxes and 21 voicemail ports	500 mailboxes and 24 voicemail ports	1,000 mailboxes and 24 voicemail ports
Number of remote sites	9	20 (centralized call processing, with Cisco Unified Survivable Remote Site Telephony [SRST])	100

Table 12-4.   Comparison of Cisco Unified Communications Manager Business Edition Appliances

- **Cisco Unity Connection Version 7.1** The unified messaging application in Cisco Unified Communications Manager Business Edition. It integrates messaging and voice-recognition functions to provide access to calls and messages across the organization.

- **Cisco MCS 7828 Unified Communications Manager Business Edition Appliance** An appliance for Cisco Unified Communications Manager Business Edition 6.0 or later. It is a key part of a fully built, expandable architecture for high-quality communications deployments.

IP Phones

IP telephony within Cisco Unified Communications includes both individual telephones and call-processing applications. Although the IP Communicator and Cisco Unified Personal Communicator provide ways to do it all with a computer, some people just really want to use a good, old-fashioned telephone. Cisco offers 24 phones across five series Cisco Unified IP Phones.

 NOTE Saying that Cisco offers 24 IP phones is a bit misleading, because it is a snapshot in time. Their offerings fluctuate as new phones are introduced and old phones are retired. Although this statement is true as of this writing, their offerings will likely be different by the time you read this. What's important to get from the following tables is the general trend in their offerings.

Tables 12-5 through 12-8 compare the various models within the series.

Feature	6901	6911	6921	6941	6945	6961
Integral switch	No	10/100	10/100	10/100	10/100/1000	10/100
Display	None	Paper label	396×81	396×162	396×162	396×162
Touchscreen	No	No	No	No	No	No
Speakerphone	No	Yes	Yes	Yes	Yes	Yes
Extension mobility	No	No	Yes	Yes	Yes	Yes
Supports expansion module	No	No	No	No	No	No
Unified video camera	No	No	No	No	No	No
Signaling protocols	SCCP	SCCP	SCCP/SIP	SCCP/SIP	SCCP/SIP	SCCP/SIP

Table 12-5. Comparison of Cisco IP Phones Models 6901–6961

Feature	7911G	7915	7916	7921G	7925G	7925G-EX
Integral switch	10/100	N/A	N/A	N/A	N/A	N/A
Display	192×64	Grayscale	Color	16-bit graphical	16-bit graphical	16-bit graphical
Touchscreen	No	No	No	No	No	No
Speakerphone	Yes (listen only)	N/A	N/A	Yes	Yes	Yes
Extension mobility	Yes	N/A	N/A	Yes	Yes	Yes
Supports expansion module	No	N/A	N/A	No	No	No
Unified video camera	No	N/A	N/A	No	No	No
Signaling protocols	SCCP/SIP	N/A	N/A	SCCP	SCCP	SCCP

Table 12-6. Comparison of Cisco IP Phones Models 7911G Through 7925G-EX

Feature	7931G	7937G (Conference Station)	7942G	7945G	7962G	7965G
Integral switch	10/100	No	10/100	10/100/1000	10/100	10/100/1000
Display	192×64	255×128	4-bit grayscale	16-bit graphical	4-bit graphical	16-bit graphical
Touchscreen	No	No	No	No	No	No
Speakerphone	Yes	Yes	Yes	Yes	Yes	Yes
Extension mobility	Yes	Yes	Yes	Yes	Yes	Yes
Supports expansion module	No	No	No	No	Yes	Yes
Unified video camera	No	No	No	No	No	No
Signaling protocols	SCCP/SIP	SCCP	SCCP/SIP	SCCP/SIP	SCCP/SIP	SCCP/SIP

Table 12-7. Comparison of Cisco IP Phones Models 7931G Through 7965G

Feature	7975G	8941	8945	8961	9951	9971
Integral switch	10/100/1000	10/100	10/100/1000	10/100/1000	10/100/1000	10/100/1000
Display	Digital, 16-bit graphical	Digital, 16-bit graphical	Digital, 16-bit graphical	Digital, 24-bit graphical	Digital, 24-bit graphical	Digital, 24-bit graphical
Touchscreen	Yes	No	No	No	No	Yes
Speakerphone	Yes	Yes	Yes	Yes	Yes	Yes
Extension mobility	Yes	Yes	Yes	Yes	Yes	Yes
Supports expansion module	Yes	No	No	No	No	Yes
Unified video camera	No	No	No	No	Yes	Yes
Signaling protocols	SCCP/SIP	SCCP	SCCP/SIP	SIP	SIP	/SIP

Table 12-8. Comparison of Cisco IP Phones Models 7975G Through 9971

Cisco Unified Communications Gateways

As we touched on earlier, in order to make VoIP work, the network must have a VoIP gateway. These are appliances that convert voice and fax calls between the PSTN and an IP network. Gateways compress and decompress, prioritize, route, and signal data.

Cisco offers a number of different types of gateways for VoIP needs. Let's take a closer look at their gateway offerings. Table 12-9 compares some of Cisco's gateway devices.

TelePresence

We touched on TelePresence just briefly in Chapter 1. TelePresence, as you might remember, is a teleconferencing tool that is used to make the process of meeting much more streamlined, interpersonal, and—ultimately—effective. Cisco notes that the solution is not only effective in terms of productivity, but also in cost savings.

The idea is that rather than spend the time and money to go to a meeting on the other side of the country (or the world, for that matter), you can rent out a TelePresence conference room for an hour or two (or if you have one of the desktop models, just fire it up) and have the conference with much more immediacy and without all the mucking around of travel.

Product	Description
800 Series Integrated Services Routers	Five models. Designed for small- and medium-sized businesses. Integrates voice, call processing, voicemail automated attendant, conferencing, transcoding, and security. Integrated eight ports 10/100 Ethernet switch. Some models offer 802.11g/n. PoE to power IP phones.
2900 Series Integrated Services Routers	Four models. Two to three integrated 10/100/1000 Ethernet ports with one port capable of RJ-45 or SFP connectivity. One to two service module slots. Four Enhanced High-Speed WAN Interface Card slots. Two to three onboard digital signal processor (DSP) slots. One internal service module slot for application services. PoE and Cisco Enhanced PoE.
3900 Series Integrated Services Routers	Up to four 10/100/1000 Ethernet WAN ports. Two of the 10/100/1000 Ethernet WAN ports can support Small Form-Factor Pluggable–based connectivity in lieu of RJ-45 ports, enabling fiber connectivity. Two service module slots. Three integrated Enhanced High Speed WAN Interface Card slots. PoE and enhanced PoE.
1000 Series Aggregation Services Routers	Six models. Targeted at high-end branch offices, enterprise WANS, or large enterprises. Between 1 and 24 shared port adapters. One or two route processor slots.
VG2000 Series Gateways	Three models. Used for small-, medium-, and low-density analog gateway solutions. Used for analog phones, fax, modems, and speaker phones. Between 2 and 144 FXS ports.
AS5400 Series Universal Gateways	Three models. Two fast Ethernet or two Gigabit Ethernet ports. Seven card slots. PCI card slot for future expansion.

Table 12-9.   Comparison of Cisco Gateways

The smallest models can be added to an existing flat-panel monitor or are standalone devices that can sit on your desk, whereas the largest one is composed of three, 64-inch high-definition displays that can accommodate conferences of up to 18 people.

These aren't cheap devices, by the way—the small SX20 costs around US$9,000 while the top end TX9000 starts off at US$299,000. Because these are so pricey, the top-end models are typically not something a company would buy—although it can be cost-effective for some Fortune 500 companies to build their own TelePresence theaters.

Normally, however, there are Cisco-owned TelePresence theaters where you simply rent time to go in for your conference and save the effort and expense of getting on an airplane and checking into a hotel.

The most visible of the TelePresence devices are its endpoints. These are the devices with the monitors, video cameras, and control pads attached. This is, ultimately, what these devices are all about. After all, that's where these devices' functionality is involved—how many attendees can be in a conference and the speed and resolution of the session.

Table 12-10 compares Cisco's line of TelePresence endpoints.

Can't decide if it's worth it to your business to start using TelePresence? Cisco has come up with a handy calculator that will show just how much greenhouse gas you're eliminating. And while that's nice, warm, and fuzzy—there's a more solid metric that can help with your decision: cold, hard cash. This calculator gives you an estimate on how much money you would save each year by using TelePresence versus hopping on a plane and doing your meetings the old-fashioned way.

The tool is accessed at http://www.cisco.com/web/applicat/TPcalcul/home.html. Alternately, a mobile site can be found at http://www.telepresencecalculator.com/Mobile.aspx.

Collaborations

Although this chapter is about VoIP and Cisco's implementation of it, we would be remiss if we didn't touch on the collaboration applications that fall under the broad umbrella of Cisco Unified Communications. Cisco offers collaboration tools that serve three distinct markets.

Cisco Jabber

Cisco Jabber is a unified communications application that combines presence, instant messaging, voice and video, voice messaging, desktop sharing, and conferencing into a single experience on all sorts of devices, including smartphones, tablets, PCs, and Macs.

Jabber provides a simple way for workers to find the right person for whom they're searching, to determine what device they have available, and then to collaborate using that device. Jabber also allows users to elevate their IM conversation to voice, video, or desktop sharing on the fly. Further, users can access these abilities whether they are in the office or on the road.

The idea behind Jabber is that users will be able to work from a variety of platforms and locations that are most convenient for them, thus allowing for faster and more effective collaboration.

Feature	SX20	EX Series	MX Series	TX1300 Series	TX9000 Series
Design	Used on existing flat-panel display. Connects simply—like connecting a DVD player. Provides up to 1080p60 resolution.	Standalone units. Two products in the series. Either 21-inch or 21.5-inch LCD monitor. Provides up to 1080p30.	Standalone units. Two products in the series. 42-inch or 55-inch LCD monitors. Simple, 15-minute installation. Floor stand or wall mountable. 1080p60 resolution.	Standalone units. Two products in series. 47-inch or 55-inch LCD monitors. 1080p60 resolution. Pedestal or wall mountable.	Standalone units. Two products in the series. Uses three 65-inch HD screens. 1080p60 resolution. Pedestal or wall mountable.
Application	API available over IP. Dual-display option available. HD content capable using 1080p15.	All-in-one tool used to move between individual work to a teleconference with colleagues. Integrated with Cisco Unified Communications Manager.	Used for small group meetings. Standards-based systems for connectivity to any type of system (from PC video to immersive TelePresence).	Used for up to six participants Triple camera cluster activated by voice-activated switching HD capable up to 30 frames per second	Used for up to 6 or 18 participants Gives continuous, whole room coverage with no field-of-view overlap Three HD camera cluster
Performance	H.323/SIP up to 6Mbps. Ability to add up to three additional callers. Two USB ports for future expansion.	H.323/SIP up to 6Mbps. Bluetooth support. Up to two USB ports for future expansion.	H.323/SIP. Bluetooth support for future expansion. RJ-45 for service.	H.323/SIP. RJ-45 Ethernet port. Internal four-port switch.	H.323/SIP. RJ-45 Ethernet port. Internal four-port switch.
Security	Management using HTTPS and SSH. IP administration password. Menu administration password. Disable IP services. Network settings protection.	Management via HTTPS and SSH. IP administration password. Menu administrator Menu password. Disable IP services. Network settings protection.	Management through HTTPS and SSH. IP administration password. Menu administration password. Disable IP services. Network settings protection	Management through HTTPS and SSH. IP administration password. Menu administration password. Disable IP services. Network settings protection	Management through HTTPS and SSH. IP administration password. Menu administration password. Disable IP services. Network settings protection

Table 12-10. Comparison of Cisco TelePresence Endpoints

WebEx

Cisco takes a bite at Skype and online meetings with its WebEx solution, which facilitates high-definition videoconferences. Once the meeting has started, it is easy to share information and work collaboratively. You can show other attendees information on your computer—files, apps, your whole desktop. Then you can turn the focus over to another participant who can do the same things.

In 2011, Cisco updated the software to support HD video and tighter interoperability with Cisco TelePresence products—including two-way video with Cisco's own Cius tablet and both the Apple iPad and iPhone. This service comes with a monthly price tag. Cisco offers meetings for up to eight people for $19 a month. This is a reduced price from its introduction—the standard package formerly offered up to 25 people in a meeting for $49 a month.

WebEx Social

Think of Cisco WebEx Social as the Facebook of enterprises. Cisco WebEx Social (formerly Cisco Quad) is an enterprise collaboration tool combining social networking, content creation, and real-time communications. Employees can connect with the people and resources they need to finish projects. WebEx Social allows greater collaboration between departments and geographies.

Feature of WebEx Social include

- **Unified post**   A simplified way for users to create and share content as well as receive feedback.

- **Bi-directional e-mail notification**   Create a post or reply to one from your e-mail client.

- **Enterprise social networking**   Used to find experts, join discussions, and access "tribal" knowledge. The tool includes profiles, dynamic communities tagging, and expert Q&A.

- **Unified communications integration**   Allows you to integrate with real-time communications tools, including video, voice, IM, and WebEx conferencing.

- **Microsoft Office integration**   Documents can be updated or published directly from Microsoft Word, Excel, and PowerPoint. Versions can be tracked and co-authors included in documents. You can also participate in WebEx Social conversations while working on the documents.

Summary

VoIP is such a moving target—especially these days. As smartphones and tablets have become the norm in recent years, there's going to be even more demand to use those devices in a VoIP or collaborative manner. And let's not forget the old standby—the common desk phone. Long gone are the days of rotary dials and big, clunky handsets.

Much more is expected of today's office phone, and there's no lack of Cisco products and services to address those needs.

In the next chapter, we move deeper into the organization's infrastructure and look at the data center and virtualization. In addition to VoIP, all those BYOD gadgets need something to get their data from. And it's not only Millennials trying to look cool while working at the local Starbucks—there are a number of solid reasons for embracing the data center and virtualization. We'll look at them next.

CHAPTER 13 | Data Center and Virtualization

In the previous chapter, we talked about how the amalgamation of voice and data into a single circuit is a goal for many organizations' internetworks. As more and more data, voice, and video cross the network, there will be a larger demand for storage. Unfortunately, conventional means of data storage—disk arrays and tape backups connected to the server—just aren't enough to keep up with the task.

Furthermore, with the moniker "Information Age" comes the burden of storing data in all sorts of sizes and compositions. It wouldn't be so bad if the term "information" were limited to pages of the printed word, punctuated with the occasional photograph. In recent years, however, "information" has evolved to mean rich multimedia content, mixing graphics, sound, and even high-definition video. Those video and sound files are becoming lengthier and with greater detail, which means larger-sized files. Organizations aren't just storing the data for archival use, either. This information is routinely accessed either internally or served up to website visitors. For example, just look at the proliferation of television programs, movies, and music that can be bought online and streamed to a consumer's computer or media device. According to Eric Schmidt, Executive Chairmen of Google, "Between the birth of the world and 2003, there were 5 exabytes of information created. We now create 5 exabytes *every 2 days.*" That quote is circa 2010. The good news is that there's more multimedia on the horizon. The bad news is that organizations dealing with this content need to find a way to store it and serve it as efficiently as possible.

As wonderful as multimedia is, the storage requirements of these files take their toll. Conventional network server storage gear is finding itself incapable of maintaining all this information. If that weren't enough, transferring large amounts of data creates its own problems because network bandwidth is continually challenged with other loads.

Having endured for two decades, the parallel Small Computer System Interface (SCSI) bus that has facilitated server-storage connectivity for LAN servers imposed limits on network storage. Modern versions of SCSI such as SAS (Serial Attached SCSI) have included improvements (for example, removing the loop requirements of parallel SCSI). However, although SCSI connections are fine for desktop computers and LANs, they are not robust enough for large-scale storage needs by themselves.

Organizations have a few popular options when it comes to mass storage, including the following:

- **Direct attached storage (DAS)**   With this option, an organization's active data is maintained on disk drives that are connected to computer servers. This becomes wasteful when a company has several servers running multiple applications, however, because DAS becomes inefficient: Some of the servers' drives can run out of space, while others have lots of unused space. DAS is also referred to local storage.

- **Network-attached storage (NAS)**   With this option, organizations remove storage systems from servers to make better use of storage space and to make networks more modular, thus making repairs and upgrades easier. For instance, one NAS solution involves disk drives with hardware and software that make the file system available across an IP network (most commonly via NFS, iSCSI, or FCoIP). The data is pooled in one location. This makes backing up, archiving, and retrieving data faster and easier. This is ideal for some scenarios, and NAS performance is governed by the network speed and specific protocols. We'll examine some NAS solutions at the end of this chapter.

- **Storage area network (SAN)** This is a more complex, powerful, and expensive storage option. SANs connect servers and storage on their own networks using a fiber-optic network utilizing the Fibre Channel protocol.

In this chapter, we'll first talk about the generalities of SANs and how you can design a SAN for your own internetworking needs. Then we'll talk about Cisco's SAN solution.

Storage Area Networks

One solution to the storage dearth is implementing a SAN. SANs are networks designed, built, and maintained with one purpose in mind: to store and transfer data. Enterprise storage overall is a burgeoning field, with perennial impressive growth.

Storage Needs

With the popularity of the Internet and the massive increase in e-commerce, organizations had to scramble for a means to store vast amounts of data. A very popular way to maintain terabytes of information employs SANs, which interconnects storage devices with Fibre Channel switches. Even though server data storage is cheap—you can add a 2TB hard drive for a couple hundred dollars—this is a reactive response to storage shortages. By creating a patchwork of systems with large groups of local hard drives, your internetwork's overhead escalates, and you slowly lose control.

SANs, on the other hand, allow you to manage all your storage needs in a proactive manner while maintaining the high availability that you need. Figure 13-1 shows an example of how a LAN and a SAN work together.

As organizations and their computing needs grow, so will their reliance on data storage. For instance, as more and more companies add server farms to manage their internal and external affairs, the more reliable the internetwork must be. To ensure high availability, servers sharing storage pools in a SAN can fail over with no hiccup in service. Furthermore, because fiber optics supplant copper as the backbone of SANs, disaster recovery is pared down from several hours to a few minutes or less.

By combining LAN networking models with the core building blocks of server performance and mass storage capacity, SANs eliminate the bandwidth bottlenecks and scalability limitations imposed by previous SCSI bus–based architectures. In addition to the fundamental connectivity benefits of SAN, the new capabilities, facilitated by SAN's networking approach, enhance its value as a long-term infrastructure. These capabilities, which include clustering, topological flexibility, fault tolerance, high availability, and remote management, further elevate a SAN's ability to address the growing challenges of data-intensive, mission-critical applications.

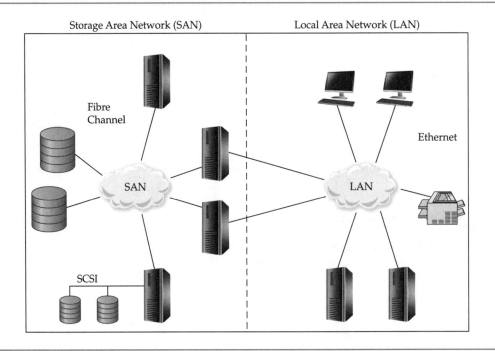

Figure 13-1.   SANs and LANs operate independently, but are still able to mesh together.

There are three primary components of a storage area network:

- **Interface**   The interface is what allows storage to be external from the server and allows server clustering. SCSI, Fibre Channel, iSCSI, Fibre Channel over Ethernet (FCoE) and Fibre Channel over IP (FCIP) are common SAN interfaces.

- **Interconnect**   The interconnect is the mechanism these multiple devices use to exchange data. Devices such as hubs, routers, gateways, and switches are used to link various interfaces to SAN fabrics.

- **Fabric**   The platform (the combination of network protocol and network topology) based on switched SCSI, switched fiber, and so forth. The use of gateways allows the SAN to be extended across WANs.

Fibre Channel

Fibre Channel is an industry-standard, high-speed serial interface for connecting servers and storage systems. Fibre Channel provides attachment of servers and storage systems across distances up to 100 km (which is about 4,000 times farther than parallel SCSI interfaces). This allows the storage facilities to be located on another floor, another building, or in another city.

Fibre Channel carries 25 times more bandwidth than SCSI (8 Gbps versus 320 Mbps). In addition, Fibre Channel supports multiple standard protocols (such as TCP/IP and SCSI) concurrently over the same physical cable. This is useful because it simplifies cabling and keeps down infrastructure costs. Because Fibre Channel allows standard SCSI packets to be transported across fiber-optic lines, existing SCSI devices can be maintained and used alongside Fibre Channel devices.

NOTE Although Fibre Channel is most often used with fiber-optic connections, it can still be used with copper wiring. However, there are more speed and distance limitations imposed on copper deployments than on fiber. In addition, copper can suffer performance degradation due to electromagnetic interference.

For the sake of reliability through redundancy, Fibre Channel SANs should be built around SAN switches. This ensures that no single point of failure exists and that performance bottlenecks are ameliorated. This should sound familiar, because it is a key consideration when designing a LAN.

Fibre Channel Layers

The Fibre Channel standard contains five layers. Each layer is responsible for a specific set of functions. If you think back to Chapter 2, you might notice some commonalities between Fibre Channel and the OSI model. In the Fibre Channel model, the layers are numbered FC-0 through FC-4.

Table 13-1 describes the different layers of the Fibre Channel model, and Figure 13-2 illustrates this stack.

Layer	Description
FC-0: Physical Layer	Defines cabling, connectors, and the signaling controlling the data. This layer is akin to the OSI physical layer.
FC-1: Transmission Protocol Layer	Responsible for error detection, link maintenance, and data synchronization.
FC-2: Framing and Signaling Protocol Layer	Responsible for segmentation and reassembly of data packets that are sent and received by the device. Additionally, sequencing and flow control are performed at this layer.
FC-3: Common Services Layer	Provides services such as multicasting and striping.
FC-4: Upper Layer Protocol Mapping Layer	Provides the communication point between upper-layer protocols (such as SCSI) and the lower Fibre Channel layers. This layer makes it possible for more than SCSI data to traverse a Fibre Channel link.

Table 13-1. Layers in the Fibre Channel Stack

FC-0: Physical Layer
FC-1: Transmission Protocol Layer
FC-2: Framing and Signaling Protocol Layer
FC-3: Common Services Layer
FC-4: Upper Layer Protocol Mapping Layer

Figure 13-2.   The Fibre Channel Stack contains five layers.

Although the stacks are different (not the least of which is that the OSI model has seven layers, whereas Fibre Channel has five), each layer in the model relies on the layer immediately above or below it.

As Fibre Channel utilizes the layer format, products and applications performing at one layer are compatible with products and applications residing at another layer, which is what the OSI model does.

Going the Distance

SCSI storage solutions have to be located next to the server because its range is limited to 25 meters. This can prove to be troublesome, especially if space in a server room is at a premium. Because Fibre Channel allows for long-distance locations between servers and storage devices, the two pieces of equipment can be up to 100 km apart.

Three technologies can be added to Cisco SAN devices to provide Fibre Channel connectivity. These technologies employ different laser wavelengths to garner varying levels of bandwidth and distance. Those wavelengths are

- **Short wavelength (SWL)**   Providing connectivity up to 500 meters

- **Long wavelength (LWL)**   Providing connectivity up to 10 km

- **Coarse Wavelength Division Multiplexing (CWDM)**   Providing connectivity up to 100 km

In practice, however, the ability for data to travel long distances can be useful if a storage center is constructed to maintain all the data for several departments. Furthermore, several servers located at one campus could send their data to a central storage facility in a separate building. This allows for the creation of modular and scalable storage pools.

Increased Connectivity

Using Fibre Channel also simplifies the connectivity of multiple systems accessing a shared storage device by overcoming the limitations of parallel SCSI, including distance and number of devices per bus. Fibre Channel supports eight times more devices per loop than parallel SCSI. In practice, however, it may not be realistic to put so many devices on a single loop. However, the capability now exists for large numbers of servers to access storage devices such as RAID arrays and tape libraries.

Other SAN Protocols

In addition to Fibre Channel, you need to be aware of a couple of other SAN protocols. These protocols are useful in designing and deploying the optimal SAN, and can be used as part of your SAN solution. Let's talk about two of the currently prevalent protocols (iSCSI and FCIP) and rub our crystal ball for a look at the future of the SAN protocol iFCP.

iSCSI

The first protocol is the basket in which Cisco seemed to put all of their eggs several years ago—Small Computer System Interface over IP. In essence, this simply transports data in the SCSI protocol across TCP/IP networks. SCSI is the language of disk drives, and iSCSI is a protocol that encapsulates SCSI commands and data for transport across IP networks. It is beneficial because it interoperates with existing applications and operating systems, as well as with LANs and WANs.

Products that use iSCSI allow hosts on an IP network to connect across Gigabit Ethernet networks to Fibre Channel or SCSI storage. IP storage networks are built directly on top of existing IP networks. It didn't take off like Cisco had originally hoped, but don't read this to mean that iSCSI is a dead technology. It is still a viable protocol and used in many of Cisco's (and other vendors') SAN devices. In fact, iSCSI and Fibre Channel are both prevalent in SAN deployments.

FCIP

Next is FCIP, or Fibre Channel over IP. FCIP represents two distinct technologies (storage networking and long-distance networking) merged together. FCIP combines the best attributes of both Fibre Channel and the Internet Protocol to connect distributed SANs. FCIP encapsulates Fibre Channel and sends it over a TCP socket.

FCIP is considered a tunneling protocol because it makes a transparent point-to-point connection between geographically disparate SANs, utilizing IP networks. FCIP relies on TCP/IP services for connectivity between SANs over LANs, MANs, and WANs. TCP/IP is also tasked with congestion control and management, as well as with data error and data loss recovery. The benefit of all this is that organizations can leverage their existing technology investments by extending the Fibre Channel fabric over an IP link.

iFCP

Just to confuse matters with FCIP, another SAN protocol is iFCP, which stands for Internet Fibre Channel Protocol. Even though the letters are the same (though in a different order, to really confuse things), the technology is rather different. iFCP allows an organization to extend Fibre Channel across the Internet using TCP/IP. This sounds a lot like FCIP, but that is where the similarities end. Whereas FCIP is used to extend a Fibre Channel fabric with an IP-based tunnel, iFCP is a movement away from current Fibre Channel SANs toward the future of IP SANs.

iFCP gateways can complement existing Fibre Channel fabrics or completely supplant them. iFCP allows organizations to create an IP SAN fabric, minimizing the Fibre Channel component and maximizing the use of the TCP/IP infrastructure. iFCP can also be used to facilitate migration from a Fibre Channel SAN to an IP SAN.

Fibre Channel over Ethernet

Fibre Channel over Ethernet (FCoE) is a recent network storage protocol. It maps Fibre Channel directly over Ethernet while being independent of the Ethernet forwarding scheme. The FCoE specification (a subset of the FC-BB-5 standard) replaces the FC0 and FC1 layers of the Fibre Channel stack with Ethernet. This protocol allows hosts to run what is referred to as "dual-stacking," meaning a host can access a SAN and an IP network with one card. Of course, the Ethernet switch they are patched into must understand dual-stacking, and the Nexus line performs this task quite well.

NOTE   Some implementations of FCoE combine both the Ethernet NIC and Fibre Channel HBA into a single, 10-Gbps interface card that is called the Converged Network Adapter.

Advanced Technology Attachment over Ethernet

The newcomer to the mix is Advanced Technology Attachment over Ethernet (AoE), which was created by the developer of the PIX Firewall. How's that for a technology switch? AoE runs on layer-2 Ethernet and therefore is non-routable, but uses far less CPU overhead than iSCSI. Designed to be lightweight and as unrestricted as possible, AoE's specification is about 20 times shorter than iSCSI, making it easy to deploy and integrating several "automatic" features that are not as easily configurable when using iSCSI.

Designing and Building a SAN

When it comes down to designing and building a SAN, it's necessary to consider several important factors before plugging fiber into routers and switches. You should consider such issues as what kind of applications you'll be using, the best design for the backbone (think resiliency, resiliency, and resiliency), how you'll configure your topology, and what mechanisms you'll use to manage your SAN. Let's take a closer look at each of these issues.

Application Needs

When developing and designing a SAN, the first step is to figure out which applications will be served. No matter if you're designing a common data pool for a bank of web servers, a high-performance data-streaming network, or something else to meet your needs, you must pay special attention to the SAN infrastructure. You have to take into consideration such issues as port densities, distance and bandwidth requirements, and segmentation. These are all variables affected by the application.

NOTE   In a mixed environment, it's important to evaluate the platforms that will compose the SAN. Hardware and software support for SANs varies, depending on which platforms you use. Once you have addressed these fundamental questions, you can begin constructing the SAN.

A SAN's construction is similar to a typical Ethernet infrastructure. A SAN comprises a few basic components: the Fibre Channel disk storage and tape libraries (physical or virtual), fiber switches, host bus adapters (HBAs), and some form of SAN management.

NOTE   An HBA is a device that connects a server to your other storage devices.

Backbone

As you design your SAN, a critical architectural hardware decision is whether to use arbitrated loop or switched fabric:

■ **Arbitrated loop**   Shares bandwidth and employs round-robin data forwarding. At one time, it was the only choice for SAN backbones. This method of deployment has largely been relegated to history since hubs have all but disappeared.

■ **Switched fabric**   Dedicates full bandwidth on each port and allows simultaneous data transfers to a single node.

Your choice will be decided based largely on your scaling and performance needs. If you have modest storage needs, a simple switch with one VSAN should be enough to get the job done. On the other end of the spectrum, larger storage environments almost demand fiber switches.

In small groups or SOHOs (small office/home office), a good foundation is a Fibre Channel hub in an arbitrated-loop configuration. Hubs are well suited for this environment because they provide a high level of interoperability for a reasonably low price. Hubs support an aggregate bandwidth of 100 Mbps. Hubs can support up to 127 devices, but for optimal results, you should limit it to about 30 devices. Furthermore, because the per-port costs of a switch are higher than those of a hub, a hub is best to fan out the core switch ports to the connecting servers.

> **NOTE**   Hubs are barely hanging on in terms of use, but they are still out there and at least worth a mention.

One of the main reasons hubs are limited in their scalability is because of the way devices are added into the loop. In order to recognize other devices in the loop, each loop must perform a loop initialization (LIP) sequencer when it is first attached to the network. When this action is performed, the loop is suspended while the entire membership on the loop acquires or verifies the port addresses and is assigned an arbitrated loop physical address. Although the recognition process is quite fast, time-sensitive traffic (such as VoIP and data backups) can be negatively affected by these performance speed bumps.

On the other hand, hubs are useful because they are inexpensive, easy to configure, and interoperate well with other hubs and other vendors' products.

Fiber

If SANs are so fantastic, why did mass-adoption within medium-sized businesses take as long as it did? The main factor that has brought SANs into play as a viable technology beyond the "big boys' data centers" is the use of switched fiber.

Fiber switches support 8 Gbps full-duplex on all ports. Unlike hubs, which, as we mentioned earlier, require an LIP, a fiber switch requires nodes connected to its ports to perform a "fabric logon." The switch is the only device that sees this logon, and this allows devices to enter and exit the fabric without providing an interruption to the remaining devices.

Devices on an arbitrated-loop hub, which is cascaded off a switch, are not fundamentally compatible with other devices on the fabric. Unlike a switched LAN environment, devices in a switched SAN environment must perform a fabric logon to communicate with other devices. However, those devices that are not built with fabric support usually cannot operate over fabric, because they don't perform a fabric logon. Rather, they use an LIP.

Configuration

Just as in a LAN, there are several ways to configure switches, providing different levels of performance and redundancy. In a SAN, the basic configuration design is the tree-type model. In this scheme, switches cascade off one another and fan out throughout the SAN, as shown in Figure 13-3.

The main problem with this model is its scalability constraints due to the latency inherent with the single-port interface. This also limits bandwidth and is not ideal because it can be a single point of failure. This type of design is best as an alternative to fiber hubs for a SAN that has just a single-tier cascade.

For larger, more intricate SANs, the best choice for both high availability and performance is the mesh model. The mesh makes a large network of switches: Each switch is connected to every other switch, thereby eliminating the opportunity for a

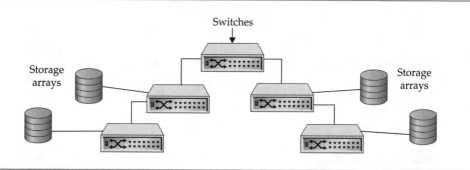

Figure 13-3.   The tree model is the basic topology for a SAN.

single point of failure. The mesh also reduces bottlenecks and latency. The mesh model is illustrated in Figure 13-4.

A mesh isn't perfect. The biggest problem is that it doesn't scale very efficiently. As you can tell, as more switches are added, the number of ports required to connect to all the available switches will use up most of the ports on each of the switches. Given that limitation, the mesh's strength is a good choice for midsize SANs with five or fewer switches requiring a maximum guaranteed uptime and optimal performance.

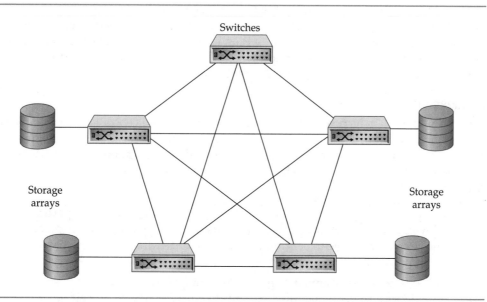

Figure 13-4.   A mesh eliminates bottlenecks and single points of failure.

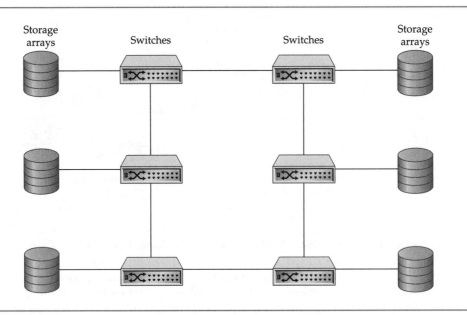

Figure 13-5.   Connecting to two other devices reduces bottlenecks and increases scalability.

Scalability and redundancy are brought together in the next model, as shown in Figure 13-5. To ensure a redundant data path, each switch is connected to two other switches. Each switch has two different paths through the SAN, thereby eliminating a single point of failure. This configuration is an ideal solution for enterprise-class SANs. In larger and mission-critical SAN deployments, the most prevalent SAN design is dual fabrics, containing both primary and alternate paths.

Management

For a SAN to work at its peak, all the components need to be centrally managed. SAN management is mainly a security device that ensures servers see only the intended devices and storage arrays, reducing the chance for data corruption. There are two basic ways to manage your SAN's hardware: port-level zoning and logical-unit-level (LUN-level) zoning.

■ *Port-level zoning* is similar to a virtual LAN (VLAN). Port zoning partitions devices based on which ports they are using on the hub or switch. Attached nodes won't be able to communicate unless individual ports are shared in a common zone.

■ *LUN-level zoning* is similar to port-level zoning; however, it increases the granularity, thereby making it possible to partition nodes by their device ID. LUN-level zoning gives you more flexibility when it comes to communicating with devices on the edge of a SAN.

> **NOTE** We'll talk more about zoning with Cisco devices later in this chapter and include a discussion of virtual SANs (VSANs).

Data storage can be an ever-changing environment. Storage needs may differ drastically from one day to the next. Happily, however, managing a SAN is helpful, because it gives you the ability to dynamically allocate storage to the different pools without having to reboot the servers in your storage cluster. In addition, you can add more storage to your SAN and reallocate it as you wish, again with no interruption.

Storage Options

When it comes to deciding what you'll use as the storage component of your SAN, you don't have an abundance of options. An easy option, especially if you already have SCSI or SAS RAID or disk shelves, is to buy an external SCSI-to-fiber bridge. A bridge will allow you to connect almost any SCSI device to your SAN. The downside of this is that you waste all the speed that a natively attached fiber device would deliver. Some bridges can push as high as 1,200 Mbps, nowhere near the native speed of Fibre Channel.

This leads to the second option: native fiber-attached storage. Fibre Channel storage is far and away more popular and—as is the case with technology—the price is coming down. Fiber storage can push 8 Gbps (and 16 Gbps is around the corner), but even though prices are coming down, they aren't nearly as inexpensive as a SAS RAID solution. Cost-wise, the hard drives are on a par with SAS drives. It's the external Fibre Channel RAID controllers, at anywhere from $8,000 to $50,000, that jack up the price. Something else is at work as well: 10 Gbps Ethernet is faster. Working out the math on the protocol overhead, we see that 8Gb Fibre Channel uses 8b/10b encoding. This means that 8 bits of data get encoded into 10 bits of transmitted information with the 2 bits used for data integrity. 1Gb FC is actually 1.0625 Gbps so 8Gb FC would be 8×1.0625, or a useable bandwidth of 8.5Gbps. 8.5 times .80 equals 6.8Gb of usable bandwidth on an 8Gb FC link. When running these same calculations on 10 Gbps Ethernet, we see a huge difference. 10Gb uses 64b/66b encoding. For every 64 bits of data, only 2 bits are used for integrity checks. Although this lowers the overall protection of the data in theory, and increases the amount of data discarded in case of failure, the actual number of data units discarded due to failing transactions is minuscule. For a 10Gb link using 64b/66b encoding, that leaves 96.96 percent of the bandwidth for user data, or 9.7 Gbps. Completing this thought, 8Gb FC equals 6.8Gb usable, whereas 10Gb Ethernet equals 9.7Gb usable, and 9.7 minus 6.8 equals 2.9 Gbps more usable bandwidth. It's no wonder FC is losing market share to FCoE.

Backup

Fiber-optic backups are just the things for administrators who manage networks with copious amounts of data. Not only can they offload backups from the network, but they can also share a single library among multiple servers scattered throughout several different departments. Furthermore, resources can be allocated to the departments that have the greatest backup needs. In addition to drives, tape libraries can use SCSI-to-fiber bridges, but more commonplace today is for these devices to be directly attached via FC. Though tape libraries don't come close to the speed of drives and may seem a waste of fiber resources, many implement tape libraries into their SANs because backups are easier to perform.

Routers in a SAN are intelligent devices that can execute a direct disk-to-tape backup without the middleman of the server processing the information first; they also allow for bridging islands of SANs together via an IP network. As you can imagine, backing up information without taxing the server not only releases the server to perform other tasks, but it also reduces backup times by removing any bottlenecks that might occur as the data filters through the server. Furthermore, routers have the technology integrated with them to handle error recovery, as well as the capability to report problems to the backup software. This functionality has been integrated into a SAN device called a "director," which is an FC switch with a very high port count that also integrates the router, IP presentation, chassis management, and a myriad of other features that used to be standalone appliances.

Cisco MDS Switches and Directors

Cisco's SAN solution is its MDS switches and directors. Introduced in 2003, the MDS devices are Cisco's entry into the world of SANs and SAN management. But not only has Cisco developed its own line of gadgetry, the company has also brought some new and interesting tools, technologies, and software. In this section, we take a closer look, first, at the technologies at play behind Cisco's SAN solution. Then, we'll look at the specific hardware Cisco offers for SAN switching. Finally, you can't just hook all this hardware together and expect it to work—Cisco offers a couple of software packages to ease the configuration and management of its SANs.

Technologies

In addition to the core tools at play in SANs that we discussed in the last section, Cisco adds some other technologies to its SAN solution. Although some philosophies are common with other vendors' SANs, Cisco dishes up some new ideas, such as virtual SANs, trunking, and its own take on SAN security. Let's examine these technologies in more depth.

VSANs

Think back to Chapter 7 and our discussion of virtual LANs. The same sort of logic is at play behind virtual SANs (VSANs) and zones.

VSANs—which started as a proprietary Cisco technology and has since become an industry standard—allows independent logical fabrics to be defined from a set of one or more physical switches. VSANs are isolated from other VSANs and function as a separate and independent fabric, with their own set of fabric services, such as naming, zoning, routing, and so forth.

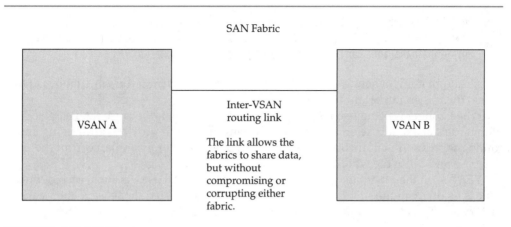

Figure 13-6. Inter-VSAN routing allows data to be transferred between VSANs but without compromising them.

In order to transfer data traffic between VSANs, Cisco's MDS line employs a technique called *inter-VSAN routing*, which enables the transfer of data among sources and destinations on different VSANs, as shown in Figure 13-6, but without compromising the VSANs by merging them into a single fabric. This ensures that data can be shared between VSANs, but without affecting the VSANs' scalability, reliability, and security.

In addition, inter-VSAN routing works across WANs using FCIP. This allows routing features to be used across long distances, which is ideal for organizations that have their assets spread across disparate locations that are not connected via private fiber.

The ability to connect VSANs across a WAN link is useful, because isolated fabrics in remote data centers can be interconnected. In addition, VSANs supplement the switch's scalability and creation of multiple SAN "islands," which eliminates the need for a separate switch for different applications.

Zoning

Zoning is another method allowing limitations on users' access to storage devices. While the users are all, technically, accessing the same devices, they are only granted permission to utilize portions of specific devices. The benefit here should be obvious: security is increased and network traffic is minimized.

Zones are a segment of SAN fabric and are used to connect groups of servers with storage devices for routine processing, but can be changed as needed. For instance, the zones can be reconfigured to allow occasional backups to storage devices residing outside the individual zones. Only members of a zone have access to it.

NOTE   Zone sets are groups of zones that interoperate on the fabric. Each zone set can accommodate up to 8,000 zones. All devices in a zone see only devices assigned to that zone, but any device in that zone can be a member of other zones in the zone set.

Although it might sound like VSANs and zones are cut from the same fabric, so to speak, there is an important distinction between the two.

When zoning is being used, segmentation is not complete, because it takes place within the same database on the switch enforcing zones and provides addressing and routing services. A malfunctioning node on one zone can, for example, corrupt the database and cause the whole SAN to crash.

VSANs, on the other hand, are able to segment the database. As such, each defined zone is its own unique storage network with its own dedicated database. That means that if one VSAN has trouble, it doesn't affect other VSANs on the same switch.

NOTE   As a reminder, a LUN is an identifier used on a SCSI bus to distinguish among devices (logical units) with the same SCSI ID. In a SAN or NAS environment, a LUN is a virtual disk carved out of a single disk or array, presented to the host via iSCSI, FC, and so on.

In a SAN, storage devices are typically zoned at the device level or LUN level:

- **Device level**   Each connected host is restricted to using another device's specific interface and all devices attached to that device, such as LUNs, entire RAID arrays, or specific disk drives.

- **LUN level**   This allows the administrator to make device-level zoning even more granular by limiting access from a host with access to another's interface to a specific device behind that interface, normally a disk LUN. A LUN zone could be spread out over a number of physical hosts. As Figure 13-7 shows, devices could easily be the home of several zones.

Although zoning is a great tool for managing resources, establishing zones should not be taken lightly. Like building a house, one doesn't just stumble to the hardware store, grab a few two-by-fours, a box of nails, some shingles, and then start hammering away. Zones must be carefully planned to ensure that the best use of the SAN's storage and the network's bandwidth is considered. Additionally, once zones have been put in place, it is more difficult to move storage space from one group of users (in Zone A, for instance) to another group of users (in Zone B). If this is undertaken, it is often necessary to reboot, which will cause network disruption. Even worse, there will be security holes because users in both zones might end up with access to the moved storage space, so be cautious when planning and implementing zone merges.

QoS

Quality of Service (QoS) is an important attribute of the MDS switch line. In earlier versions of Cisco SAN-OS (we'll talk about this operating system in more detail later in this chapter), traffic was only segmented based on whether the traffic was control data

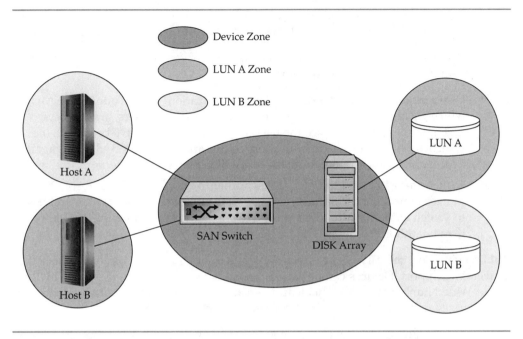

Figure 13-7.   Zones can be configured to access resources on different devices.

or traffic data. In more recent releases of the operating system, QoS allows classification of traffic. For example, QoS can be applied so that data for latency-sensitive traffic has higher priority over throughput-sensitive applications such as data warehousing.

MDS switches provide the following QoS mechanisms:

- **Priority queuing**   Levels of priority are assigned to different types of traffic. Latency-sensitive traffic is granted higher priority than other types of traffic.

- **Fibre Channel Congestion Control (FCC)**   This is a flow-control mechanism used to ease congestion on FC networks. Essentially, any switch in the network can identify congestion, sample frames from the congested queue, and then send messages about the problem upstream to the source. The switch closest to the source of the congestion can either forward the frames to other switches or limit the flow of frames from the port causing the problem.

Security

As with any internetworking device or technology, security is an essential consideration. It may be especially important in SANs, where so much of your organization's data is moving around and being warehoused. The last thing you want is some thug getting into your company's archives and causing mischief.

MDS switches have a number of security features, meant to keep your data safe and secure. Let's take a closer look at the MDS switch's line of security mechanisms.

Authentication   The MDS switches provide the first layer of security through authentication methods. Authentication comes in two forms:

- **User authentication**   Authentication, authorization, and accounting (AAA), which we talked about in Chapter 6, is used to validate users, grant access, and monitor activities. Once the user's ID and password have been sent, the switches perform local authentication, comparing the user's credentials against a local database, or remotely, using a RADIUS or TACACS+ server.

- **Switch-to-switch and host-to-switch authentication**   The Cisco SAN-OS utilizes Fibre Channel Security Protocol (FC-SP) for switch-to-switch and host-to-switch authentication. This is used to stifle any disruptions that would occur if an unauthorized device tried to connect to the fabric.

Port Security   Port security ensures that only an authorized device can be connected to a given switch port. Devices can be a host, target, or switch and are identified by their World Wide Number (WWN). This feature ensures that the SAN is not violated by an unauthorized device attempting connection to a switch port.

VSAN Access Control   Roles can be assigned based on the limitations of a specific VSAN. For instance, the network administrator role can be authorized for configuration setup and management duties. VSAN administrators, on the other hand, can be granted permission only to configure and manage specific VSANs. This is a useful tool because it limits disruptions to the SAN. Rather than a misconfiguration affecting the entire SAN, it would be localized to the VSAN where the change was made.

Role-Based Access   Going hand-in-hand with user authentication is role-based access. This mechanism limits access to the switch based on the specific permissions level granted to that user. The user can be granted full access to the device, or specific read and write levels of each command can be managed.

SPANs

A unique feature in the Cisco MDS 9000 line is the switched port analyzer (SPAN). SPAN monitors network traffic using a Fibre Channel interface. Traffic through a Fibre Channel interface can be replicated to a port known as a SPAN destination port (SD port). Any of the switch's Fibre Channel ports can be configured as SD ports. When an interface is in SD port mode, it cannot be used with normal data traffic. A Fibre Channel Analyzer can be attached to the port to monitor SPAN traffic.

As the name suggests, Remote SPAN (RSPAN) allows you to monitor traffic for SPAN sources in switches throughout a Fibre Channel fabric. The SD port of a remote switch is used for monitoring. Normally, the remote switch is different from the source switch, but is attached to the same fabric. The MDS 9000 family of switches allows for the remote monitoring of traffic from any switch in the fabric as if it were the source switch.

SPAN is noninvasive because SD ports do not receive frames; they just transmit copies of the SPAN source traffic and do not affect the redirection of network traffic. In addition, VSANs can be specified as a SPAN source. All supported interfaces in the selected VSAN are included as SPAN sources. SPAN traffic can be monitored in two directions:

- **Ingress** This refers to traffic entering the switch fabric through a source interface. This traffic is copied to the SD port.

- **Egress** This refers to traffic exiting the switch fabric through a source interface. Like the ingress traffic, this is also copied to the SD port.

When a VSAN is selected as a source, then all physical ports, as well as PortChannels, are used as SPAN sources. TE ports are included when the port VSAN of the TE port is the same as the source VSAN. TE ports are ignored if the configured allowed VSAN list has the source VSAN but the port VSAN is different.

Trunking

Harkening back to our discussion of VLANs is the term *trunking.* Trunking exists within the world of SANs in much the same way that it does in the world of VLANs. Trunking refers to an interswitch link (ISL) carrying more than one VSAN. Trunking ports send and receive extended ISL (EISL) frames, as shown in Figure 13-8. These frames contain an EISL header, which carries VSAN information. Once EISL is enabled on an E port, that port becomes a TE port.

 NOTE ISL is a Cisco proprietary protocol that maintains VSAN information as traffic flows between source and destination.

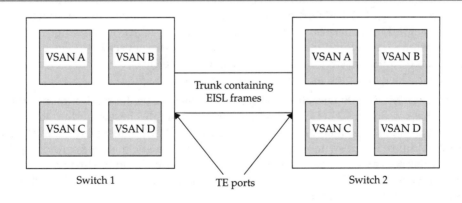

Figure 13-8. Trunking in a SAN combines multiple VSAN conversations.

PortChannel

Multiple Fibre Channel ports can be aggregated into a single, logical port, providing high aggregated bandwidth, load balancing, and link redundancy. This is known as *PortChannel,* which allows the aggregation of up to 16 physical ports into a single logical port.

PortChannel is a useful technology because it increases the aggregate bandwidth on an ISL or EISL by distributing traffic among all links in the channel. Additionally, traffic is load-balanced across multiple links. This traffic is identified by source ID (SID), destination ID (DID), or the originator exchange ID (OX ID).

PortChannel also provides redundancy for its links. If one link fails, that traffic is shifted to the remaining links. Furthermore, if a link fails, the upper protocol does not perceive the link as having failed. Rather, it simply has less bandwidth with which to work. As such, the routing tables are not affected by a link failure.

Hardware

The Cisco family of MDS products includes three Cisco MDS 9500 Series Multilayer Directors and two models of Cisco MDS 9100 Multilayer Fabric Switches, in addition to several modules providing customized functionality. These devices provide intelligent network services for SANs, including VSANs, security, traffic management, diagnostics, and a centralized management environment.

Let's take a closer look at the devices in Cisco's MDS line of multilayer storage switches.

MDS 9500 MultiLayer Director Switches

The Cisco MDS 9500 MultiLayer Director switches are modular devices aimed at large data center environments. They provide a high level of scalability, security, and management.

The MDS 9500 Series includes three multilayer switches:

- ■ **Cisco MDS 9506 Director**   Targeted at data center environments and consisting of 192 8-Gbps ports and six slots on the chassis, two of which are reserved for supervisor modules. Four switching or services modules can be installed, providing Fibre Channel or Gigabit Ethernet services. The backplane can be directly plugged into four switching modules, two supervisor modules, two clock modules, and two power supplies.

- ■ **Cisco MDS 9509 Director**   Targeted at large data center environments, the chassis contains 336 Fibre Channel ports on a single chassis, and up to 1,008 in a single rack. It also has nine slots, two of which are reserved for supervisor modules. Seven switching or services modules can be installed, providing Fibre Channel or Gigabit Ethernet services. The backplane can be directly plugged into seven switching modules, two supervisor modules, two clock modules, and two power supplies.

	MDS 9506	MDS 9509	MDS 9513
Available Slots	6	9	13
8 Gbps Fibre Channel Ports per Chassis	192	336	528
iSCSI and FCIP Ports per Chassis	24	48	60
Rack Units	7	14	14
Chassis per Rack	6	3	3
Fibre Channel Ports per Rack	1,152	1,008	1,584

Table 13-2.   Comparison of the Cisco MDS 9500 Series

■ **Cisco MDS 9513 Multilayer Director**   Cisco introduced this switch in August 2002, but then pulled it off the market—turns out the world wasn't ready for this much switch. It reintroduced the switch in the spring of 2006. The Cisco MDS 9513 Multilayer Director is a 528-port Fibre Channel device aimed at companies who want to consolidate their SANs and oversubscribing ports on smaller switches. The switch features 13 slots and 528 8-Gbps Fibre Channel ports. It also supports iSCSI and FCIP protocols.

The supervisor modules on these directors provide high-availability and load-balancing features. A second supervisor module is available for the sake of redundancy. In addition, the autosensing Fibre Channel ports support ISL (E ports), EISL (TE ports), loop (FL and TL ports), and fabric (F ports) connections.

The Directors' small form-factor ports (SFP) are hot-swappable and can be configured for short-wavelength (500 meters) or long-wavelength (10 kilometers) connections. The ports are also individually configurable for both FCIP and iSCSI.

Table 13-2 compares the features of the Cisco MDS 9506, the MDS 9509, and the MDS 9513.

MDS 9000 Fabric Switches

The "little brothers" to the MDS 9500 Series are the Cisco MDS 9000 switches. These use a similar architecture and software structure as the 9500 Directors. However, whereas the 9500s are fully modular in design, the 9000 Series is semi-modular. Within this family are two series: the Cisco MDS 9222i Fabric Switch and the Cisco MDS 9100 Series.

Cisco MDS 9222i Multiservice Modular Switch   The Cisco MDS 9222i Multiservice Modular Switch uses both Fibre Channel and IP in a single module for a strong service delivery. The switches support up to eighteen 8 Gbps Fibre Channel interfaces and four Gigabit Ethernet ports for FCIP and iSCSI service.

The integrated VSANs and inter-VSAN routing allows for a large-scale, multisite SAN topology. The ability to utilize FCIP with the MDS 9222i switches provides a number of benefits, including:

- Simplification of data protection and mission performance by enabling backup, remote replication, and other recovery services over a WAN.

- Cisco MDS 9000 family capabilities are possible, including VSANs, advanced traffic management, and network security across remote connections.

Benefits of iSCSI services include

- The ability to connect to Ethernet-attached servers is much less expensive than only being able to connect through Fibre Channel.

- Storage is enhanced and more widely available through the consolidation of IP and Fibre Channel block storage.

The MDS 9222i switch is modular and supports the line of MDS 9000 family switching or services modules outlined later in this chapter.

Cisco MDS 9100 Series   Small- and medium-sized SANs are served with the Cisco MDS 9100 Series of Fibre Channel switches. The switches (Models 9124 and 9148 support 24 and 48 ports, respectively) are fixed in terms of their expandability. Like their higher-powered brothers, the 9100 Series provides high levels of scalability, availability, security, and management.

The MDS 9100 Series includes built-in SAN management tools (useful for management of one or many fabric devices), including a command line and a GUI tool, which we will talk about later in this chapter.

The common architecture and software structure is an important consideration when discussing the Cisco MDS devices. Because they share a common design, it is easy to migrate from a smaller device to a larger device or to add new switches to your fabric. In addition, like any switches, the device can be purchased and installed based on a specific need within the organization.

For example, a small-to-medium-sized organization can use the Cisco MDS 9120 to construct its first SAN as it moves from a direct-attached to a networked-storage solution. Larger organizations might use the 9120 for specific application or business functions.

Modules

Like many other Cisco products, the MDS 9000 family (save the 9100s) can be customized and configured based on your organization's particular needs. As such, a number of modules can be installed in the devices. The following sections explain these various modules and how you can best use them in your SAN deployment.

The Cisco MDS 9500 Series Supervisor-2 Module   The Cisco MDS 9500 Series Supervisor Module provides nondisruptive software updates and hardware redundancy for optimal availability. It can automatically restart a failed process before that process is detected at the system level. This is ideal because it reduces the number of resets to the module. However, in cases where a reset is needed, the unit's backup module will have taken over to eliminate disruption to the SAN.

With two supervisor modules installed, a 9500 Series Director can provide 1.44 Tbps of switching bandwidth. It also provides 1, 2, 4, or 10 Gbps autosensing Fibre Channel ports.

Cisco MDS 9000 Family Fibre Channel Switching Modules Cisco MDS 9000 Family Fibre Channel Switching Modules (there are five of them) are 4-, 24-, 32-, and 48-port devices. Each is a hot-swappable Fibre Channel tri-rate multiprotocol module, as well as a coarse wavelength division multiplexing (CWDM) module. Individual ports can be configured with short- or long-wavelength SFPs, providing connectivity of 500 meters and 10 kilometers, respectively.

The CWDM SFP provides even great distances between devices of up to 100 kilometers. The module's interfaces operate at up to 10 Gbps. The ports can be configured to operate as:

- E ports
- F ports
- FL ports
- FX ports
- Span destination (SD) ports
- ST ports
- TE ports
- TL ports

The Cisco MDS 9000 Family IP Storage Services Node IP services can be added to the MDS 9000 family of switches through use of the Cisco MDS 9000 Family IP Storage Services Node. This module allows traffic to be routed between an IP storage port and any other port on an MDS 9000 family switch. In addition to the services available through other storage service modules (including VSANs, security, and traffic management), the Cisco MDS 9000 Family IP Storage Services Node uses IP to provide cost-effective connections to more servers and locations. This module provides FCIP and iSCSI IP storage services:

- **FCIP** Provides data protection by enabling backup, remote replication, and disaster recovery across WAN connections, using FCIP tunneling. WAN resources are optimally utilized by tunneling up to three ISLs on a single Gigabit Ethernet port. In addition, SAN complexity is ameliorated because a remote connectivity platform is not needed.

- **iSCSI** One of the best attributes of the iSCSI features of the IP storage services module is the capability to use Fibre Channel SAN-based storage to IP-based servers. This is much less expensive than just using Fibre Channel. Storage and utilization are increased because IP and Fibre Channel are consolidated for storage purposes. Furthermore, iSCSI allows the usage of legacy storage applications.

The Cisco MDS 9000 18/4-Port Multiservice Module   This module delivers multiprotocol and distributed multiservice convergence. The module offers eighteen 5 Gbps Fibre Channel ports and four Gigabit Ethernet IP storage services ports. The module supports the MDS 9222i switch and the MDS 9500 series switches.

Other highlights of the module include

- Virtual fabric isolation with VSANs and Fibre Channel routing
- Serves as a platform for intelligent fabric operations, including Storage Media Encryption, Data Mobility Manager, and EMC Recoverpoint

Software

There are three ways to manage MDS switches: from the command line or one of the GUI tools on the Cisco MDS 9000 Device Manager and Cisco Prime Data Center Network Manager for SAN (DCNM). We'll talk about DCNM for LAN (previously known as LMS, or "the network piece of Cisco Prime Infrastructure") in Chapter 14, but the spoiler for now is that Cisco has made huge leaps in the arena of management in the last couple of years. They have successfully unified CiscoWorks LAN Management Solution (LMS), Cisco Wireless Control System (WCS), and Cisco Fabric Manager (FM) under the heading Cisco Prime Infrastructure. Prime has a unified login, and it centralizes all of these tools into one dashboard. For the SAN management discussion, we're referring to Prime DCNM for SAN (DCNM-SAN). This is shown in Figure 13-9.

The command-line interface (CLI) is similar to the CLI used for managing Cisco's other switches and routers. The GUIs, on the other hand, provide a graphical representation of your SAN, its status, and the devices on the SAN. Before talking about the CLI and GUI, it's helpful to understand the operating system behind the MDS family: Cisco NX-OS.

Cisco NX-OS

As we discussed in Chapter 5, Cisco NX-OS is the operating system for the Cisco MDS line of SAN devices. It provides storage networking features, including nondisruptive upgrades, multiprotocol integration, VSANs, traffic management, diagnostics, and unified SAN management.

The latest version of the operating system, Cisco MDS 9000 NX-OS 5.2, includes support for a standalone version of Device Manager, a Java-based graphical management tool. This tool is great when SAN switches are not plentiful in your environment

Figure 13-9.   The Cisco Data Center Network Manager for SAN is now integrated into the Prime Infrastructure family.

(for example, just one HA pair in one data center). In this way, Device Manager is much like Cisco Configuration Professional. It provides a quick way to set up interface pairings, VSANs, trunks, and so on. The third alternative provides three important improvements: centralized management of multiple fabrics; continuous health, discovery, and monitoring; and performance monitoring.

Furthermore, security in NX-OS is enhanced through switch-to-switch and server-to-switch authentication using Fibre Channel Security Protocol (FC-SP). This protects against intrusion from unauthorized devices. It also employs TACACS+ for authentication, authorization, and accounting of switches.

CLI

The first way to manage a Cisco MDS 9000 switch is by using a serial RJ-45 connection on the supervisor module. This connection, like the connections made on other Cisco routers and switches, provides access to the CLI.

Whether you choose to use the CLI or Device Manager for initial setup will depend largely on your personal taste and preferences. However, there are some instances when one or the other will be preferable. For example, the CLI might be optimally employed when:

- Initial setup routines are performed
- Running **debug** and **show** commands for diagnostics and troubleshooting
- Writing and running configuration scripts

When the MDS device is connected to power locally for the first time, the system enters a setup routine that aids in the initial configuration of the device. This step must be completed before you are able to connect to the switch remotely via SSH/Telnet or can manage it with the Cisco Device Manager/DCNM-SAN.

The CLI parser gives command help, command completion, and the ability to access previously executed commands. Entering commands is similar to the process used when entering commands into other Cisco switches. For example, the following command would be used to send a message to all users on the network that the system will be shutting down for maintenance:

```
switch# send Shutting down the system in 5 minutes. Please log off.
```

To enter the configuration mode, simply enter the following on the MDS switch:

```
switch# conf t
switch(config)#
```

Once in configuration mode, the device can be managed using a number of commands. Table 13-3 contains a brief list of some of these commands and an explanation of what they do.

Command	Description
Fcc	For configuring FC Congestion Control
Fcdomain	Used to enter the fcdomain configuration mode
QoS	Establishes the priority of FC control frames
Radius-server	For configuring RADIUS parameters
Vsan	Used to enter the VSAN configuration mode
Zone	Used to enter zone configuration commands

Table 13-3.   Several Configuration Commands Used in the CLI

The Cisco Data Center Network Manager for SAN

If you perhaps have many MDS switches, you might want to manage your MDS fabric using a GUI that actively collects information about your environment and lets you see all your devices through one interface. In this case, Cisco has provided the Cisco Data Center Network Manager for SAN (DCNM-SAN). DCNM-SAN is a Java- and SNMP-based network fabric and device management tool that shows real-time views of the fabric and installed devices. Cisco DCNM-SAN is an alternative to the CLI for most switch-management operations and requires an additional license as well as a server to run it on.

Cisco DCNM-SAN gathers information about the fabric topology and then sends SNMP queries to the SNMP agent running on the switch to which the DCNM-SAN server is connected. Once the switch has discovered all connected devices, it replies. It gathers this information using data from its FSPF database, as well as from the name server database.

DCNM-SAN is used to discover and view the fabric's topology as well as manage zones. It is also useful for the management of the following items:

- Zones and zone sets
- VSANs
- Port channels
- Users, roles, and much more

The GUI uses many views to manage your network fabric. As you can see from the dashboard in Figure 13-9, there are many views of your environment. These include health, performance, inventory, reporting, configuration, and administration of the system. Here are some examples of drilling down into device detail:

- **Module View**   Displays a current exhibit of device configuration and performance conditions for a single device.

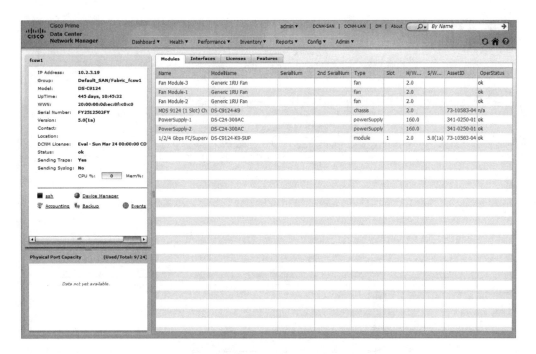

■ **Interface View** Displays the current status of the interfaces, including multiple devices.

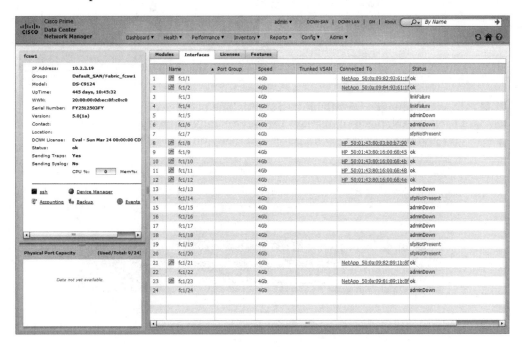

- **Fabric View** Displays the current status of the network fabric, including multiple devices.

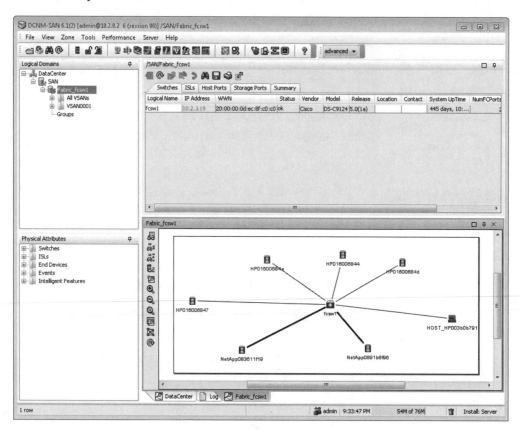

- **Device Manager** Available as a standalone package or integrated with DCNM-SAN, this tool displays the Device and Summary Views of the fabric and grants access to Quick Config and many other useful tools.

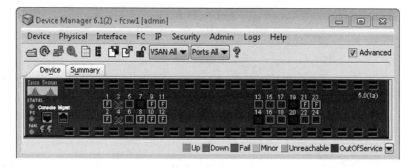

- **Summary View**   Displays a summary of switches, hosts, storage subsystems, and VSANs connected to your MDS switch. It displays a summary of different port activity as well as FC and IP neighbor devices.

Interface	Description	VSAN(s)	Mode	Connected To	Speed	Rx	Tx	Errors	Discards	Log
fc1/1		1	F	0x9b1700, NetApp_50:0a:09:82:93:61...	4 Gb	0	0	0	0	
fc1/2		1	F	0x9b1100, NetApp_50:0a:09:84:93:61...	4 Gb	0	0	0	0	
fc1/8		1	F	0x9b1d00, HP_50:01:43:80:03:b0:b7:9...	4 Gb	3	0	0	8	
fc1/9		1	F	0x9b2200, HP_50:01:43:80:16:00:68:45.	4 Gb	0	0	0	0	
fc1/10		1	F	0x9b1f00, HP_50:01:43:80:16:00:68:4b.	4 Gb	0	0	0	0	
fc1/11		1	F	0x9b2000, HP_50:01:43:80:16:00:68:48.	4 Gb	0	0	0	0	
fc1/12		1	F	0x9b2100, HP_50:01:43:80:16:00:68:4e.	4 Gb	0	0	0	0	
fc1/21		1	F	0x9b1c00, NetApp_50:0a:09:82:89:1b:...	4 Gb	0	0	0	0	
fc1/23		1	F	0x9b1b00, NetApp_50:0a:09:81:89:1b...	4 Gb	0	3	0	0	

Private Cloud

Without a doubt, the network and computing strategy with the greatest buzz in recent years has been "the cloud." In essence, cloud computing is simply offloading your computational functions to a vendor who handles all the duties and responsibilities that you need. The vendor pays for the computational infrastructure, maintains it, and then rents it to you.

There are pros and cons to this model. On the plus side, it is less expensive for you to rent network resources from a vendor than to install new servers when you need more computational capacity. On the other hand, however, if the vendor's network (or the Internet between you and the vendor) is out, then you can't get access to those resources.

Happily, however, major outages seem to be few and far between. But there is another downside: Someone else has access to all of your sensitive data. True, that can all be handled with solidly worded terms of service and bloodthirsty lawyers, but Cisco means to even remove that issue with somewhat of a gray-area compromise: a private cloud.

With Cisco's Private Cloud, you maintain the equipment to provision your own cloud services, and need not rely on the network resources and capacity of others to facilitate your cloud needs.

NOTE   Obviously this model leaves off one of the most important reasons to use cloud computing resources—cost. Your organization will have to pay for the infrastructure required to build the cloud, but the resources are yours to do with as you wish, and you need not worry as much about the safety and security of your network.

Cloud computing isn't just a single offering. Cloud computing has been customized and offers very specific services for whatever the client needs. These services are typically described as *"service name-as-a-service."* Here are some examples:

- Infrastructure-as-a-service (IaaS)
- Platform-as-a-service (PaaS)
- Software-as-a-service (SaaS)
- Network-as-a-service (NaaS)
- Storage-as-a-service (STaaS)
- Security-as-a-service (SECaaS)
- Data-as-a-service (DaaS)
- Database-as-a-service (DBaaS)
- Test environment-as-a-service (TEaaS)
- Desktop virtualization
- API-as-a-service (APIaaS)
- Backend-as-a-service (BaaS)

The three most prevalent services are

- **Software-as-a-service**   End-user applications delivered on demand over a network on a pay-per-use basis
- **Platform-as-a-service**   Used by software development companies to run their software products
- **Infrastructure-as-a-service**   A number of features, including servers and disk drives that can be provisioned on demand

Cisco's Private Cloud is Infrastructure-as-a-service (IaaS) and, once installed, is very easy to create and manage new virtual network resources.

Cisco Unified Computing System

The hardware component of Cisco's Private Cloud solution is the Cisco Unified Computing System (UCS). UCS is composed of several different types of servers, fabric interconnects, and fabric extenders. What UCS is really intended for is to simplify the data center into one homogenous, manageable system. UCS integrates servers, switching, routing, SAN/NAS access, and cabling all into one platform. The UCS blade centers are designed to be connected by a top of rack (ToR) piece of network gear called a network or fabric extender. Much like Cisco's reference design for networks across campuses, the extenders are the distribution points for that rack. These extenders are then tied back to the central data center core (a.k.a. the Nexus), and now you know where the Nexus line acquired its moniker.

These components can be pieced together as a greenfield deployment or added as your system requires additional resources. Table 13-4 describes the various components in the UCS solution and what feature they include.

Component	Product	Description
Blade Servers	UCS B-Series Blade Servers	Up to two Intel Xeon Series multicore processors. Two front-accessible, hot-swappable SAS hard drives. Double-data-rate 3 (DDR3) memory. Up to 384GB RAM. Up to four full-width servers or eight half-width servers per chassis.
Rack Servers	UCS C-Series Rack Servers	Intel Xeon E7-4800 processor. Up to 2TB RAM. Up to 12 small form-factor SAS or SATA hot-plug hard drives of solid state drives (SSD). Two 1/10 Gb Ethernet LAN ports and two 10/100/1000 Ethernet ports.
Fabric Interconnects	UCS 6200 Series Fabric Interconnects and UCS 2200 Series Fabric Extenders	Fabric Interconnects: Up to 1920 Gbps throughput. Up to three expansion modules. Fabric Extenders: Up to eight 10 Gbps fabric ports. Up to 80Gb throughput.
UCS Management	UCS Manager UCS Central	Allows you to manage all hardware and software system components and configuration across multiple chassis and rack servers and thousands of virtual machines through policy-driven architecture.
Virtual Interface Card	Cisco UCS Virtual Interface Card 1280 Cisco UCS Virtual Interface Card 1240 Cisco UCS Virtual Interface Card 1225 Cisco UCS M81KR Virtual Interface Card Cisco UCS P81E Virtual Interface Card	Provides acceleration for operational modes introduced by server virtualization.

Table 13-4.   Cisco UCS Components

Cisco Intelligent Automation for Cloud

The software component of Cisco's Private Cloud solution is Cisco Intelligent Automation for Cloud Starter Edition. It allows you to provision your network resources through a simple point-and-click interface for both physical and virtual servers. It allows you to start off provisioning virtual and physical machines. Then, as your organization's needs grow, you can expand your deployment with additional virtual machines, or simply increase the amount of resources allocated to existing machines.

There are two main components of Cisco Intelligent Automation for Cloud:

- **Cisco Cloud Portal**   This is the user interface, service catalog, and lifecycle management tool for ordering IT resources.

- **Cisco Process Orchestrator**   This is the engine that automates workflows and requests to fulfill those requests.

Enterprise storage is a burgeoning technology and one that many organizations are expected to embrace in the coming years. Although Cisco has a solid solution in its MDS line of switches, look for the company to expand its SAN offerings in the years to come. There is little doubt of the growing need for SANs and advanced storage, and this should be an interesting time for anyone involved in the storage arena.

CHAPTER 14 | Cisco Content Networking and Video Solutions

As the Internet continues to be a place rich with multimedia, it's apparent that an organization's single server cannot bear the entire burden on its own. For example, when thousands of users from around the country try to access the multimedia content at a site located on a server in Kansas City, the results will be less than optimal.

However, if the content of that server were to be replicated and co-located in Seattle, New York, Chicago, Atlanta, Kansas City, and Reno, then users could get faster access to the material with fewer burdens on the network. This type of network is known as a *content delivery network* (*CDN*) and has gained popularity with organizations that seek high availability from their internetworks. CDN is responsible for the explosion of streaming solutions such as YouTube and Netflix—you name it, and it's probably distributed content.

Content Delivery Networks

Not only is the content more readily available by virtue of the fact that several servers are hosting it, but with an integrated CDN in place, a content provider can publish content from origin servers to the network edge. This frees resources on the servers, making the content easier, faster, and more efficient to locate and transfer to the user.

In this section, we talk about CDNs, how they work, and how they can be configured to help your organization. In addition, we take a close look at Cisco's CDN solution, which involves several pieces of hardware and some specialized management software.

Meet the CDN

A CDN is an overlay network of content, distributed geographically to enable rapid, reliable retrieval from any end-user location. To expedite content retrieval and transmission, CDNs use technologies such as caching to push content close to the network edge. Load balancing on a global scale ensures that users are transparently routed to the "best" content source. "Best" is determined by a number of factors, including a user's location and available network resources. Stored content is kept current and protected against unauthorized modification.

When an end user makes a request, content routers determine the best site, and content switches find the optimal delivery node within that site. Intelligent network services allow for built-in security, Quality of Service (QoS), and virtual private networks (VPNs).

The CDN market is exploding. Fueling the growth is demand for Internet services such as web and application hosting, e-commerce, multimedia applications, but mostly streaming media. While user demand for such services mounts, the challenge for service providers comes in scaling their already congested networks to tap into these higher-margin opportunities.

CDN Needs

A CDN allows web content to be cached—or stored—at various locations on the Internet. When a user requests content, a CDN routes the request to a cache that is suitable for that client. Specifically, it's looking for one that is online, nearby, and inexpensive to communicate with.

Which organizations will get the best results from a CDN? As with any technology and its usability, this is a loaded question. As we've seen time and time again, the only thing that limits how a technology is used is the imagination. However, those who would benefit most from a CDN are those who have an abundance of high-demand files or rich multimedia that would cause a strain on a single network.

However, there is a great deal of merit in using CDN principles to ensure reliability in case of a catastrophe. For instance, if you are storing content in caches in three different states, a natural disaster in your home state won't mean doom for your internetwork. Rather, users will still be able to access your information from one of the other two caches.

Using a CDN doesn't mean that all your data will be spread across the Internet. You can control where your content is located on the CDN and who will have access to it. Specified content is assigned to particular caches, and only those caches are authorized to store that material. By controlling where content is cached, you increase the likelihood that requested content will be present in the cache. This is because there is enough room in the cache to store all the authorized content. Furthermore, controlling content yields better performance results, because you can ensure that a particular cache is handling only the load associated with the content it is authorized to store.

Cisco CDNs allow service providers to distribute content closer to the end user and deal with network bandwidth availability, distance or latency obstacles, origin server scalability, and traffic congestion issues during peak usage periods. The system also enables businesses to expedite application deployment across private networks.

A CDN isn't a replacement for a conventional network. Rather, it's used specifically for specialized content that needs to be widely available. Dynamic or localized content, on the other hand, can be served up by the organization's own site, avoiding the CDN, whereas static and easily distributed content can be retrieved from the nearest CDN server. For instance, the banner ads, applets, and graphics that represent about 70 percent of a typical web page are easily offloaded onto a CDN.

How It Works

The need for a CDN is especially apparent when it comes to multimedia content. Because multimedia is such a bandwidth hog, a lone server cannot possibly tend to multiple, concurrent requests for rich multimedia content.

Figure 14-1 shows the basic design of a CDN.

Let's say you're surfing the Internet and want to watch a video that is online at Content Delivery Networking's website (a.k.a. www.cdning.com). Because that particular

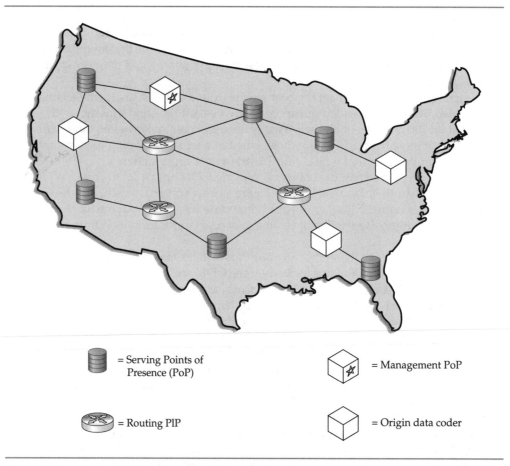

Serving Points of Presence (PoP)

= Management PoP

= Routing PIP

= Origin data coder

Figure 14-1.   A basic CDN deployment contains a number of components.

video is so popular, they have it deployed on their CDN. Here's what happens when you click the video's icon:

1. The browser requests the URL of www.cdning.com/video.mpg.

2. The workstation issues a DNS lookup for the IP address of www.cdning.com to a local DNS proxy server.

3. The local DNS server does not have the IP address for www.cdning.com cached, so it queries the DNS hierarchy to determine who the authoritative DNS server is. Then it sends the request to that DNS server.

4. If the environment has been properly configured, the query ultimately ends up at the Content Router, because its IP address is provided back to the DNS proxy server, which, in turn, sends that IP address back to the original requestor (your workstation).

5. The net effect is that the process has resulted in a substitution of the real IP address for the content engine. Now the browser can request the actual file associated with the URL www.cdning.com/video.mpg.

6. Once the file request is received, the content engine (CE) checks to see if it has a cached copy. If it does, it is sent to the requesting browser. If this copy is not on the CE, the CE will fetch the file from the original site (the www.cdning.com website), cache it, and send a copy to the requesting browser.

On the next request for content associated with www.cdning.com, the IP address should be cached so that a client request is quickly resolved to a good CE. If the address is no longer cached, the steps would be repeated to find the CE, and then it would provide the content. If the content was no longer deemed to be fresh, or if it was no longer there, then the entire process would be repeated.

Cisco's Solution

CDNs come in a variety of shapes and configurations, based largely on the vendor and the need. Cisco's CDN solution utilizes several components, each performing its own specific function in the larger machine. Those components include

- Content engine
- Content routing
- Content edge delivery
- Content switching
- Intelligent networking
- IP multicasting

No matter what the data being transferred—from a text file to streaming media—the content is delivered using these technologies.

Content Engines

Cisco's content engines are content networking products that accelerate content delivery, and are where the Application and Content Networking System (ACNS) software is housed. A content engine is a device that caches content in a CDN to serve end-user requests. A collection of content engines makes up a CDN.

 NOTE   ACNS is explained later in this chapter.

In the past, Cisco produced individual content routers and Content Distribution Managers (CDMs). However, this functionality has now been incorporated into its line of content engines.

NOTE Content engines can be configured as content engines, content routers, or content delivery managers. They cannot, however, be configured to perform two or more functions. That is, a content engine cannot be configured as both a content engine and a content router. It must be configured as one or the other.

The Cisco content engine works with your existing network infrastructure to complete your traffic-localization solution. Content engines offer a broad range of content delivery services for service providers and enterprises, including streaming media, advanced transparent caching service, and employee Internet management. The latest iteration has added virtualization as well. Some of these devices can run a virtual "blade" (a.k.a. virtual machine) using Windows 2008.

NOTE After activating a virtual blade on a Wide Area Virtualization Engine (WAVE) device, a disk partition designated for the virtual blade is created. This partition cannot be removed without reloading the WAVE using a factory restore disk. The CPU, memory, and disk allocated are not dynamic either; they are dedicated to the virtual blade—even when the virtual blade is powered off.

The Cisco content engine product line covers a broad range of environments, from service provider "Super Points of Presence (sPoP)" down to small enterprise branch sites. Cisco's content engine product line includes

- **WAVE 8541**   This content appliance is for sPOP and large enterprise sites and was designed around two Intel Xeon E5645 Hex-Core processors, 96GB RAM, and a RAID 5 array with 8× 600GB disks for a total of 4.2TB of storage. This device has 10GB NICs available in WAAS mode only and supports 150,000 TCP connections.

- **WAVE 7571**   This content appliance is for large enterprise sites and was designed around two Intel Xeon E5620 Quad-Core processors, 24GB RAM, and RAID 5 array with 8× 450GB disks for a total of 2.2TB of storage. This device has 10GB NICs available in WAAS mode only. It supports 60,000 TCP connections.

- **WAVE 7541**   This content appliance is for large enterprise sites and was designed around two Intel Xeon E5620 Quad-Core processors, 24GB RAM, and a RAID 5 array with 6× 450GB disks. This device has 10GB NICs available in WAAS mode only. It supports 18,000 TCP connections.

- **WAVE 694**   Designed for large branches, this engine comes with 600GB of RAID 1 SAS storage and 16GB RAM, with a 16GB upgrade available. The engine uses a 2.67 GHz Intel Xeon X3450 Quad-Core processor. The Cisco WAVE-694 is available with Cisco WAAS software or Cisco ACNS software and is licensable for six virtual blades and Windows streaming media. An optional redundant power supply is available as well as additional network interfaces.

■   **WAVE-594**   This engine comes with a 500GB SATA disk and 8GB RAM, with a 4GB upgrade available. The engine uses a 2.4 GHz Intel Xeon X3430 Quad-Core processor. The Cisco WAVE-594 is licensable for four virtual blades and Windows streaming media. A redundant power supply, a redundant 500GB disk, as well as additional network interfaces are available options.

■   **WAVE-294**   This engine comes with 250GB of storage and 4GB RAM, with a 4GB upgrade available. It is geared as an entry-level edge platform for branch offices. It's licensable for two virtual blades and Windows streaming media.

Content Routing

Content routing is the mechanism that directs user requests to the CDN site. This allows for high scalability and reliability. Routing is based on a set of real-time variables, including delay, topology, server load, and policies (such as the location of content and a user's authorization). Content routing enables accelerated content delivery and adaptive routing around broken connections and network congestion. Cisco's content routing products interoperate with intelligent services in the network infrastructure, thereby ensuring content availability and providing global load balancing.

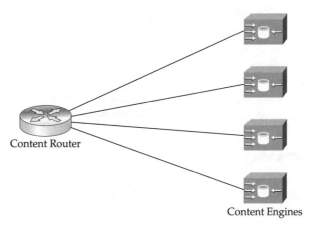

Content Router

Content Engines

The content router nodes are deployed at strategic locations within the network. Their functionality includes

■   Real-time content request processing using standard DNS by redirecting user requests to an appropriate content engine based on geographic location, network location, and network conditions

■   Redundant configuration for multi-network and wide-area fault tolerance and load balancing

Cisco provides a multitude of content routing protocols that enable enterprises and service providers to build content delivery networks. These protocols enable communication about content state among Cisco networking products. These protocols, which include Director Response Protocol (DRP), Dynamic Feedback Protocol (DFP), Web Cache Control Protocol (WCCP), and Boomerang Control Protocol (BCP), allow Cisco's products to work as a single, seamless system.

As with CDMs, Cisco used to produce specific content router appliances. However, those models have also been discontinued and their capabilities rolled into content engines.

Content Edge Delivery

For the speediest delivery of content, content edge delivery (performed by content engines) distributes content from the edge of the network to the end user. Cisco's CDN solution allows service providers to define and expand the edge of their network anywhere, from a small number of data centers near the network core, out to the network edge and just inside the firewall of a customer.

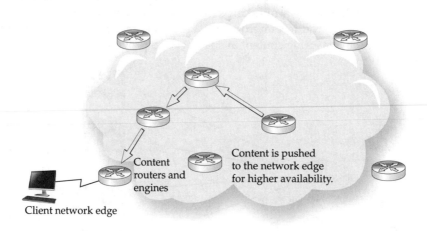

The content engines are located at the network edge, storing and delivering content to users. Other functionality includes

- Content delivery to end users and other content engines based on the Cisco content routing technology

- Self-organization into a mesh routing hierarchy, with other content engines forming the best logical topology based on current network load, proximity, and available bandwidth

- Storage of content replicas

- Endpoint servers for all media types

- Platform for streaming media and application serving

Once the right network foundation is in place, network caches are added into strategic points within the existing network, thereby completing the traffic-localization solution. Network caches store frequently accessed content and then locally fulfill requests for the same content, thus eliminating repetitive transmission of identical content over WAN links.

Content Switching

Content switching is used to intelligently load-balance traffic across delivery nodes at PoPs or distributed data centers based on content availability, application availability, and server load. Intelligent content switching adds an additional layer of protection against flash crowds and ensures transaction continuity for e-commerce applications in the face of system stoppages. Intelligent content switching also allows for customization of content for select users and types of data—and data centers. An Application Control Engine (ACE) has the capacity to direct traffic to multiple data centers or simple columns within one data center.

When Cisco first got into the CDN game, it did not develop switches that were meant just for CDNs. Rather, CDN functionality was originally included as a component of other types of Cisco switches. Cisco has developed its Application Control Engines to be standalone units and to fit inside a 6500 or 7600 switch chassis. The ACE has the functionality to work in cooperation with the other devices in the Cisco CDN solution:

- **ACE 4700 Series Application Control Engine Appliance** The Cisco ACE4710 provides load-balancing and content-switching functions with granular traffic control based on customizable Layer 4 through 7 rules, with support for both IPv4 and IPv6 addresses, virtual IP addresses (VIPs), and server farms. This device has a fixed configuration, offers 4 Gbps aggregate throughput (depending on a license purchase and four 1 Gbps Ethernet ports. This appliance can conduct up to 7,500 SSL transactions per second. In order to scale higher, you simply add more appliances.

- **ACE 6500 Bundle** This card may be inserted into a Catalyst 6500 or 7600 chassis individually or alongside other service modules. It supports one million concurrent TCP connections, 165,000 Layer 4 connection setups per second, and 1.25 million packets per second.

Intelligent Network Services

The heartbeat of CDN is intelligent network services. This provides such functions as security, QoS, VPNs, and multicast. The Cisco CDN system integrates with existing content-aware services, which are required to build intelligent CDNs.

Key services that content intelligence provides include

- Content routing
- Traffic prioritization for content
- Services that scale economically and respond appropriately to unpredictable flash crowds
- The ability to track content requests and respond with content updates and replication

Because the functionality of a CDN is dependent on processing a number of variables, intelligent network services are crucial to maintaining an efficient, effective CDN.

IP Multicasting

IP multicasting is a bandwidth-efficient way to send the same streaming data to multiple clients. Applications that benefit from IP multicasting include videoconferencing, corporate communications, and distance learning. Rather than consume large amounts of bandwidth by sending the same content to multiple destinations, multicast packets are replicated in the network at the point where paths separate. This results in an efficient way to conserve network resources.

How It Works   IP multicasting is ideal when a group of destination hosts are receiving the same data stream. This group could be composed of anyone, anywhere. It could be a training video sent to all new hires at a company's headquarters, or it could be updated benefits information sent, simultaneously, to the Human Resources departments at numerous branch offices. The hosts can be located anywhere on the Internet or on a private network.

We'll now examine the different types of transmission services in order to nail down, more precisely, what is going on in a multicast. Let's first consider the different types of network traffic—unicast, multicast, and broadcast—shown in Figure 14-2:

- **Unicast**   Applications send one copy of each packet to the users requesting the information. If one user is linking to the web server and requesting information, this isn't so bad. However, if multiple users want the same content, this gobbles up system resources as the same packets are sent to each user simultaneously. That is, if there are 30 users requesting the same content, 30 copies of the data will be sent at the same time.

- **Broadcast**   Applications can send one copy of each packet to a broadcast address. That is, the information is sent to everyone on the network. Although this preserves bandwidth, because the same content is being routed to everyone (rather than multiple copies of the content being sent at once), it also suffers when various users neither want, nor need, to see the content.

- **Multicast**   Applications send one copy of the packet and address it to a group of selected receivers. Multicast relies on the network to forward packets to the networks and hosts that need them. As such, this controls network traffic and reduces the quantity of processing performed by the hosts.Multicasting has a number of advantages over unicasting and broadcasting. Although unicasting is an effective way to bring content to a single host, when the same content must be sent to multiple hosts, it can cripple the network by consuming bandwidth. Broadcasting, on the other hand, is a good way to conserve network resources (a single copy of the data is sent to every user on the network). However, although this resolves bandwidth-consumption issues, it is not useful if only a handful of users need to see the information.

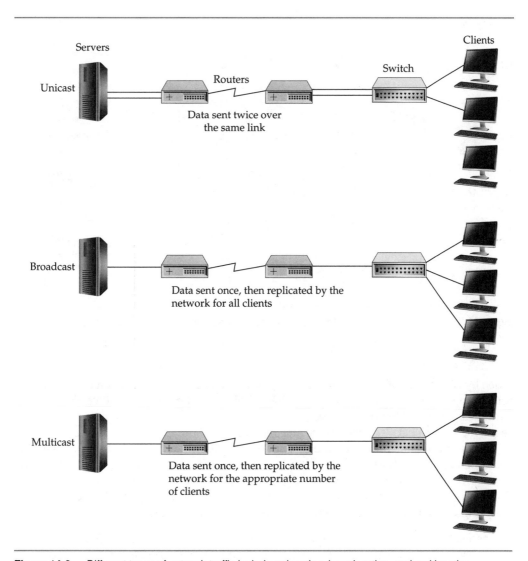

Figure 14-2. Different types of network traffic include unicasting, broadcasting, and multicasting.

IP multicasting solves the bottleneck problems when data is being transferred from one sender to multiple destinations. By sending a lone copy of the data to the network and allowing the network to replicate the packets to their destinations, bandwidth is conserved for both sender and receiver.

Figure 14-3 shows how IP multicast delivers data from one source to multiple, appropriate recipients. In this example, users want to watch a videocast training them on a new application. The users let the server know they are interested in watching the

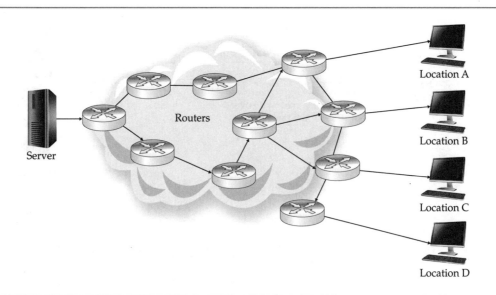

Figure 14-3.   Multicast distribution trees send content to the appropriate network segments.

video by sending an IGMP (Internet Group Management Protocol) host report to the routers in the network. The routers use PIM (Protocol Independent Multicast) to create a multicast distribution tree. The data stream will be delivered only to the network segments that lie between the source and receivers.

Users opt in to be part of a group by sending an IGMP message. IGMP is a layer-3 protocol, allowing a host to tell a router that it is interested in receiving multicast traffic for a particular group or groups. IGMP version 2 added the ability to leave a group. This made it easier for routers to know that a given host was no longer interested in receiving the multicast, thus freeing up more network resources.

Addressing   Addressing is an important component in the world of IP multicasting. Once a client opts in to be part of a group, the content is delivered to a single IP address. When the data is sent to that IP address, the network, in turn, delivers it to everyone who agreed to be in the multicast group. By using a single IP address, the network can handle the task of channeling data to the appropriate clients.

The Internet Assigned Numbers Authority (IANA) manages the assignment of IP multicast addresses. It has assigned the Class D address space for use in IP multicast applications. Class D address space falls between 224.0.0.0 and 239.255.255.255. There are no host addresses within the Class D address space because all hosts in the group share the group's common IP address.

However, this doesn't mean that one multicast address will suit each and every need. Within the Class D address space, IP addresses have been subdivided for specialized use. The following examines how the Class D address space is further stratified:

- **224.0.0.0 through 224.0.0.255**   For use only by network protocols on a local network segment. Packets with these addresses should not be forwarded by a router. Rather, they stay within the LAN segment and always are transmitted with a TTL value of 1.

- **224.0.1.0 through 238.255.255.255**   Called *globally scoped addresses,* these addresses are used to multicast data from the source and across the Internet.

- **239.0.0.0 through 239.255.255.255**   Called *limited scope* or *administratively scoped addresses,* these addresses are tied to an organization. Routers are configured with filters to prevent multicast traffic in this range from leaving the private network. Also, within the organization, this range of addresses can be subdivided within internal boundaries, thus allowing the reuse of addresses on smaller domains.

Another means of multicast addressing is called *GLOP addressing.* RFC 2770 suggests that the 233.0.0.0/8 address range be reserved for addresses by organizations that already have an Autonomous System Number (ASN) reserved. The ASN of the domain would then be converted and be made part of the second and third octets of the 233.0.0.0/8 range to generate a static multicast address for that organization.

 NOTE   An ASN is a globally unique identifier for an Autonomous System. Autonomous Systems are groups of networks that have a single routing policy managed by the same network operators.

For instance, an organization with an ASN of 24545 would have a multicast IP address of 233.95.225.0. This conversion first takes the ASN (24545) and converts it into hexadecimal. The hexadecimal value is separated into two octets and then converted back to decimal to provide a subnet that is reserved for ASN 24545 to use.

ACNS

A CDN is a constantly changing environment. Content engines, content switches, and content routers are added and removed, and the content housed on those devices is in a constant state of flux because content providers come and go. New routed domains are defined, old ones are removed, and assignments of routed domains to content engines change.

Cisco Application and Content Networking System (ACNS) software is targeted at organizations and service providers deploying CDNs. ACNS 5.3 is the latest version of this software, which runs on content engines and the Cisco Wide Area Application Engine (WAE), combining content networking components into a common application for the content distribution manager, content engine, and content router. This application is useful for both small and large CDN deployments.

ACNS is the core application behind Cisco's CDN and IP video solutions. It allows content and video to be transmitted from the data center to remote locations, including:

- Secure web content
- Web application acceleration
- Business video
- Point-of-sale video and web kiosks

 NOTE   ACNS can also be used to deliver antivirus updates and security patches across a network.

ACNS can manage CDN deployments of up to 2,000 content engines and 1,000,000 prepositioned items in content engines. ACNS software pulls content from a web server or an FTP server and sends it directly to the content engines.

ACNS combines demand-pull caching and prepositioning to accelerate the delivery of web applications, objects, files, and media. ACNS runs on Cisco content engines, CDM, and content routers.

In an IP video environment, ACNS can be used with the Cisco IP/TV components to capture and deliver MPEG video with synchronized presentation, program creation, and scheduling.

In a CDN environment, content engines can be used with the ACE 4700 Series Application Control Engine, the Catalyst 6500 Series Content Switch Module, and the Secure Sockets Layer (SSL) switching modules for reverse-proxy caching, thereby offloading back-end servers.

 NOTE   Reverse-proxy caching is explained later in this chapter.

ACNS benefits from a number of features, including the ability to configure the system to run both cache and CDN applications simultaneously. Network administrators can also upgrade ACNS software, or they can downgrade to a previously installed version if they determine the new version is not as useful as a previous installation. ACNS also allows for disk provisioning, providing the management of disk space for HTTP caching and for prepositioned content.

Wide Area Application Engine

The Cisco Wide Area Application Engine (WAE) series is a line of network appliances for providing access to applications, storage, and content across a WAN. WAE is used in conjunction with ACNS and Cisco Wide Area File System (WAFS) software (we'll talk about that in the next section). These products and technologies allow LAN-like access to applications and data across the WAN. Some benefits of this solution include

- Enterprise applications, such as enterprise resource planning (ERP), customer relationship management (CRM), and intranet portals

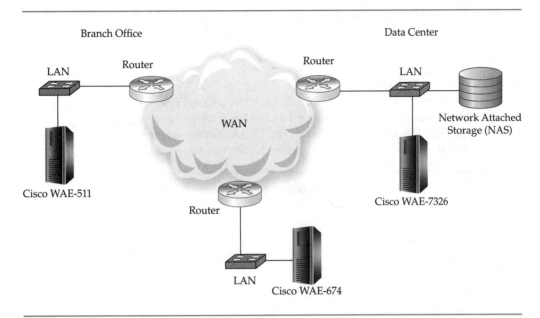

Branch Office

Data Center

Figure 14-4.   WAEs reduce storage burden on branch offices, centralizing it at a data center.

- Real-time videoconferencing
- Storage

Furthermore, WAE allows branch offices to be able to utilize infrastructure across the WAN, including servers, backup, and storage, with only a WAE appliance placed at each branch. This is illustrated in Figure 14-4.

WAE application engines include

- **Cisco WAAS Modules for Integrated Service Routers**   Two modules may be inserted into the various ISR G2 routers. The SM-SRE-710-K9 and SM-SRE-910-K9 may be purchased and licensed for use as WAE nodes. These devices provide the most basic WAAS functionality.

- **Cisco WAE-674 Wide Area Application Engine**   This device is based on an Intel 2.0 GHz Xeon Quad-Core processor and is aimed at small offices. The unit comes with 4GB RAM and is expandable to 8GB. It has three Serial Attached SCSI disk drive bays for between 300 and 600GB of storage capacity.

- **Cisco WAE-7341 Wide Area Application Engine**   The next step up is the Cisco WAE-7341. Using a 2.33 GHz Intel Xeon Quad Core processor, the WAE-7341 has more memory than the 674, with 12GB included (none optional). The unit has four Serial Attached SCSI disk drive bays and can store between 300GB and 900GB total capacity.

■ **Cisco WAE-7371 Wide Area Application Engine** Cisco's topline WAE is the WAE-7371. It uses two Intel Xeon processors and 24GB of memory. It supports six 300GB SAS hard drives, for a total capacity of 1.5TB.

Cisco Wide Area File System

Another component of Cisco's WAN CDN solution is Cisco Wide Area File System (WAFS). It eliminates WAN latency and bandwidth limitations, and strives to give WAN users LAN-like speed and bandwidth. This technology helps the consolidation of branch-office data into central file servers in the organization's data center.

NOTE WAFS used to be its own, standalone technology, but it is now a part of WAAS.

Benefits

By centralizing an organization's data, rather than keeping it all scattered in branch offices, the following benefits can be realized:

■ **Lower costs** File and print services at branch offices replace unreliable and expensive tape backup and file servers.

■ **Improved data protection** Data generated at branch offices is sent to the data center in real time. This improves data protection, management, and storage efficiency.

■ **Reduced administration** Data can be centrally managed at the data center.

■ **Fast file access and sharing** With LAN-like speeds now on a WAN, remote users can enjoy increased productivity.

WAFS uses new protocol optimization technologies to give branch and remote office users LAN speeds, thereby reducing WAN latency, bandwidth, and packet-loss limitations.

Branch offices consolidate their file servers and storage into central file servers or network-attached storage (NAS) devices at the organization's data center.

How It Works

WAFS uses protocol optimizations, including:

■ Latency mitigation

■ Object caching

■ Metadata caching

■ WAN transport optimizations

This ensures the operation of standard file-system protocols, such as Common Internet File System (CIFS) with Windows and Network File System (NFS) with Unix. It also maintains file integrity and security policies.

WAFS runs on the Cisco Wide Area Application Engines outlined in the previous section. In addition to the WAE appliances, WAFS runs on the router-integrated network module.

Within a WAFS solution, each node can be configured with one or more services:

- **Edge file engine** Used at branch offices to replace file and print servers, this engine allows users to enjoy near-LAN speeds with read and write access to the data center.

- **Core file engine** Used at the data center and connected through the LAN to NAS devices, this engine is responsible for providing aggregation services for edge file engines.

- **Cisco WAFS Central Manager** Provides web-based management and monitoring of all WAFS nodes.

NOTE Though the WAE appliances can be configured with any service, only the router-integrated network module can be configured as an edge file engine.

Figure 14-5 shows an example of how these services are deployed.

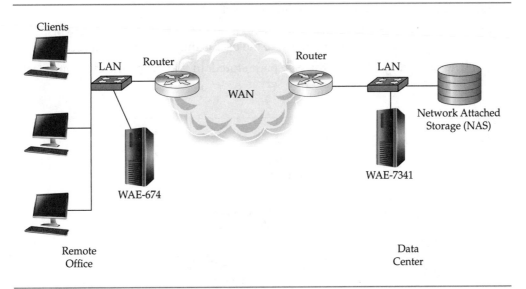

Figure 14-5. WAE appliances are configured for specific content duties within the network.

Caching

For years, Internet traffic has been growing at a breakneck pace. Because of the sheer amount of traffic coursing across the Internet and intranets, congestion has gotten worse. ISPs and organizations are being challenged to deal with this problem, because it is difficult to ensure QoS and deliver content to clients efficiently and affordably. By localizing traffic patterns on your existing network, you get a double bonus—not only is content delivered more quickly, but also the freed resources are available for additional traffic.

Content delivery is accelerated by locally filling content requests, instead of having to go across the Internet to fetch the information. This ensures the content is delivered quickly, and you don't have to worry about bottlenecks beyond your control. Traffic localization reduces the amount of redundant traffic on your WAN connections. This allows additional network resources for more users and for new services (VoIP, for example).

In order to achieve this solution, it is necessary to have a network that enables transparent redirection technologies such as Web Cache Communication Protocol (WCCP). With this technology in place, network caches are added to key locations in the network to realize the traffic localization solution. Network caches store frequently accessed content and then serve it locally to deliver requests for the same content, but without having to go back across the Internet or WAN to get them. Obviously, this relieves congestion because repeated transmissions no longer need to be sent out. Figure 14-6 illustrates this process:

1. Using a web browser, a user requests a web page.

2. The network examines this request and then redirects it to a local network cache. This is done transparently so the user is unaware of the redirection.

3. The cache may not have the web page stored. In that event, the cache makes its own request of the original web server.

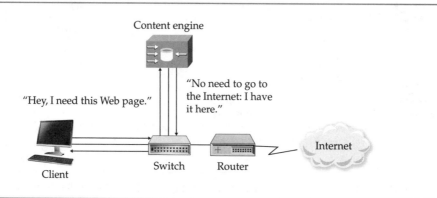

Figure 14-6. Web caching stores frequently accessed web pages locally.

4. The original web server delivers the requested web page to the cache, which then re-sends it to the user. The cache stores a copy of the page in case it is needed later.

5. When another user requests the same web page, the cache now has the page on hand and the request is fulfilled locally.

6. The cache delivers the web page to the user locally. This eliminates the need to use WAN bandwidth and delivers the content much more quickly.

Web Cache Communication Protocol

Though we mentioned several CDN protocols earlier in this chapter, Cisco's proprietary protocol for enabling transparent caching throughout a network—Web Cache Communication Protocol (WCCP)—has become the protocol on which Cisco's solution is built. This protocol uses HTTP redirects to provide functionality. The first version of WCCP allowed communicating with just one router, did not support multicasting, and was limited to HTTP traffic. The current version is WCCP v2 and resolves the shortcomings of version 1.

WCCP uses UDP port 2048, operating through a generic routing encapsulation (GRE) tunnel between the router and the content engine (or content engines). Once the content has been delivered, either from the content engine or the source web server, the HTTP packets are delivered and are not altered.

The content engines maintain a list of routers with which they have WCCP communications. When the content engine identifies itself to the routers, it shares its list of routers. In turn, the routers reply with a list of content engines that they see in the *service group*. As soon as all the devices know about one another, one content engine becomes the lead engine and determines in what way packets will be redirected.

The content engines send *heartbeats* to the routers every ten seconds through a GRE tunnel. If there is a cluster of content engines and one of the engines fails to send a heartbeat within 30 seconds, the router informs the lead content engine that the engine is missing and its resources must be reallocated to the remaining engines.

 NOTE   We'll talk more about the specific resources in a cluster and what clustering is later in this section.

Freshness

An obvious concern when using caching is the issue of freshness. How can you be sure that the page you're looking at contains the most current information? That is, what prevents the content engine from storing last Friday's visit to a newspaper website for perpetuity?

Each web page is made up of a number of web objects, and each object has its own caching parameters that are established and managed by the web page authors and HTTP standards. So, for example, our newspaper website will have new content, but things like the toolbars, navigation buttons, and the masthead are likely to be cacheable. As such, when the content engine stores the newspaper's website, it stores the elements that are not likely to change and then goes out to cull the new content. Content engines deliver fresh content by obeying HTTP caching standards (which we'll talk about in a moment) and allowing the administrators to decide when content should be refreshed from the source web servers.

Web authors can establish to what degree to allow caching. In HTTP, caching parameters for each object on a website can be managed. Content can be set up for caching based on three settings:

- The content is noncacheable.

- The content is cacheable (the default setting).

- The content is cacheable, but it will expire on a given date.

HTTP 1.1 introduced a freshness mechanism called If-Modified-Since (IMS), which ensures cached data is up to date. Content engines send an IMS request to the destination web server when the engine receives a request for cached content that has expired or when it receives IMS requests from clients where the cached content is older than a percentage of its maximum age. If the content on the destination web server determines that the content in the engine has not been updated, it sends a message to the content engine to go ahead and serve its stored data to the client. If the content has been updated and is no longer fresh, the content engine will retrieve the new content.

But freshness is not just in the hands of the web page creators. Network administrators can control the freshness of web objects in their content engines. Content engines have a parameter called the *freshness factor* that can be configured by the network administrator. This determines just how quickly content expires. When an object is stored in the cache, a TTL value is computed. That value is

TTL = (current date − last modified date) * freshness factor

If the content has expired, based on the aforementioned formula, the web data is refreshed in the cache the next time an IMS request is issued.

To establish a modest freshness policy, the freshness factor can be set to a small value (such as .05) so that objects will expire more quickly. This will, however, cause more bandwidth to be consumed as pages are refreshed. Setting the freshness factor higher will cause less bandwidth to be consumed.

NOTE   Freshness can also be managed by the client. The client can click the browser's Reload or Refresh button. This will cause a series of IMS requests asking for web objects that have been refreshed. Alternatively, SHIFT-Refresh or SHIFT-Reload causes content engines to be bypassed and have the content sent directly to the client from the web server.

Content Engine Caching

There are three primary ways in which content can be cached in Cisco's solution: transparent, proxy style, and reverse proxy style. The most common means of caching utilizes the transparent style of caching. However, the other methods are also useful to understand because they may be more relevant and useful for your organization's needs.

Transparent Caching

The first method of caching is known as transparent caching. We outlined the steps involved in this type of caching already. In essence, a web browser requests a web page. That request first runs through the WCCP-enabled router, where it is analyzed. If the router determines that a local content engine has the desired content cached, it sends the request to the content engine, which delivers the content back to the browser. If it isn't cached, the content engine goes to the Internet to fetch and store the page.

Because this method utilizes a WCCP-enabled router, the content engine functions transparently to the browser. Clients need not be configured to be pointed to a specific proxy cache. Because the content engine is transparent to the network, the router acts in a "normal" role for traffic that does not have to be redirected.

Using a CSS switch, however, the client's request need never reach the router. In larger deployments, it makes better sense to have a CSS switch to make decisions as to whether particular content has already been cached locally. Furthermore, large deployments might employ several content engines and data would be stored in each device, based on a uniform resource locator (URL).

HTTPS   The whole process of caching seems straightforward enough, especially if someone is requesting static content. However, there is a slew of content on the Internet, on your intranet, or possibly traversing a dynamic WAN link. For instance, there are times when a user's web page request will have to go to the intended web server. The concept of caching is not thrown out the window in these cases. Let's consider what happens when a Secure HTTP (HTTPS) session is initiated:

1. The user initiates an HTTPS session. It is taken by the WCCP-enabled router and sent on to the content engine.

2. The content engine, configured as an HTTPS server, receives the request from the router.

3. A Secure Sockets Layer (SSL) certificate is obtained from the destination web server by the content engine and then sent back (through the content engine) to the client to negotiate an SSL connection.

4. The client sends HTTPS requests within the SSL connection.

5. The content engine analyzes the request. If the information is in its cache, HTTP request processing occurs. If the content is in the content engine's cache (also known as a *cache hit*), it sends the desired content back using the SSL connection.

6. If the content is not stored within the content engine (also known as a *cache miss*), it establishes a connection to the destination web server and requests the content through the SSL connection.

7. If possible, the content engine will cache the information and then send a copy back to the client through the SSL connection.

Content Bypassing   Sometimes the content engine simply has to be avoided in order to get the session that the client needs. Though mechanisms are in place for establishing HTTPS sessions, not all secure conversations can be accepted through the content engine.

Some websites rely on IP authentication and, as such, won't allow the content engine to connect on the client's behalf. Content engines can use authentication traffic bypass to avoid service disruption. Authentication traffic bypass is used automatically to create a dynamic access list for client/server pairs.

When a client/server pair goes into authentication bypass, it is bypassed for a set amount of time. The default setting is 20 minutes, but that value can be changed, depending on the organization's need.

Nontransparent/Proxy-Style Caching

The nontransparent or *proxy-style* caching is known to the client, whereas transparent caching happens without the client's knowledge that it is occurring. With proxy caching, the proxy cache performs the DNS lookup on the client's behalf. Proxies are used for different protocols, such as HTTP, HTTPS, FTP, and so forth. Consider the network in Figure 14-7.

The client has been configured to use a proxy server for HTTP requests. Normally, port 8080 is used, but different ports can be configured for the protocol you wish to manage. The IP address of the proxy is also configured on the client. In the example, we're using address 10.1.100.100. Let's follow this method of caching step by step:

1. HTTP requests for content are directed to the proxy.

2. If the proxy cache does not have the content, the proxy performs the DNS lookup for the destination website.

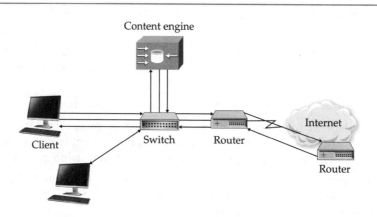

Figure 14-7.   Proxy-style caching works on the client's behalf.

3. When the DNS has been resolved, the proxy requests the content from the destination web server and then retrieves it.

4. The content is stored in the cache before being forwarded to the client. This ensures that the next time the content is requested, the cache will have it.

Proxy caching is useful because the cache can be anywhere in the network. Furthermore, a measure of network security is provided in that only the client contacts the proxy, so the firewall rules can be stricter, allowing only the proxy to work through the firewall.

Reverse Proxy Caching

In the aforementioned proxy cache method, the proxy server is a proxy for the client. In the reverse proxy method, the proxy server acts as a proxy for the server. Reverse proxy caches also store selected content, whereas transparent and proxy methods store frequently requested content.

There are two cases in which reverse proxy caching is desirable:

■ Replicating content to geographically disparate locations

■ Replicating content for the sake of load balancing

In this scenario, the proxy server is set up with an Internet-routable IP address. That is, clients go to the proxy server based on DNS resolution of a domain name.

WCCP Servers   Consider the cache deployment in Figure 14-8. The content engine works with a WCCP-enabled router and is configured for reverse proxy service for a web server. In this scenario, the router interface linked to the Internet has an IP address of 192.168.1.100. HTTP requests sent to this server are first sent to the router interface

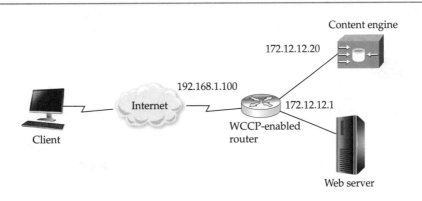

Figure 14-8.   Reverse proxy caching with WCCP-enabled routers places the content engine in front of the web server.

at 172.12.12.1. Once the HTTP request has been received at this interface, the router redirects the request to the content engine (with an IP address of 172.12.12.20). In this case, the content engine is in front of the web server, helping reduce the amount of traffic on it. If the information requested is not in the content engine, it sends a request to the web server to locate the content.

CSS Switches   Now consider the cache deployment in Figure 14-9. Here, the content engines are deployed with a WCCP-enabled router and a CSS switch. A user sends a request for web page content. This is accepted at the CSS switch's virtual IP address. When the CSS switch takes the request, it forwards the request to the content engine. If the content engine does not have the requested data, the content engine will forward a request to the web server.

Multiple Content Engine Deployment

Content engines can be located at multiple points throughout an organization for optimal caching performance. For instance, consider the organization in Figure 14-10. In this case, the organization is served by three content engines. The first handles caching for the Customer Service department at the organization's headquarters; the second handles caching for the Production department in a branch office.

If a client in the Customer Service department sends a web page request that can be accommodated by the first content engine, it will be served by that device. If that content engine cannot fulfill the request, it passes the request to the end web server. Before it gets to the destination web server, the request is considered by the content engine at the main Internet point of access. This provides another chance for the

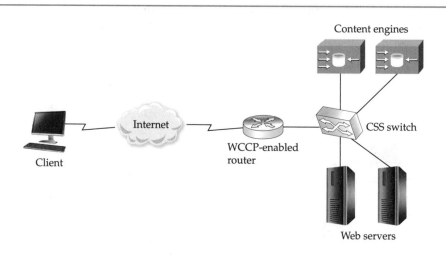

Figure 14-9.   In a reverse proxy scenario with CSS switches, the content engines are checked first before the request is forwarded to the web server.

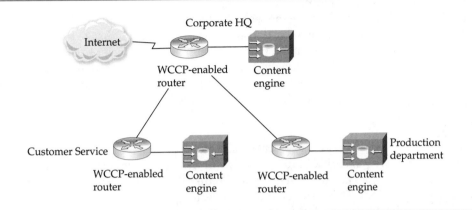

Figure 14-10.   Content engines at different levels in an organization provide greater content availability.

content to be served before having to go out onto the Internet or across a WAN. If this content engine is able to fulfill the request, it is unnecessary to go onto the Internet. In the event someone at the branch office had requested the page, it might still be located on content engine number three, at corporate headquarters.

This scenario is especially useful for Internet service providers. With a content engine serving a number of clients, if common websites are requested, it is unnecessary to keep getting the page from the Internet. Instead, it can be served up locally by the content engine.

Clustering

Another way to manage high traffic levels is through clustering. This simply means that multiple content engines are set up together. For instance, one Cisco Content Engine 7325 can support in excess of 155 Mbps of traffic and up to 936GB of data. However, if a second 7325 is added, then the cluster can handle more than 310 Mbps throughput and 1.87TB of data. Up to 32 content engines can be clustered together.

When a new content engine is added to the organization's cluster, the WCCP-enabled router detects the new device and reallocates resources for the new content engine.

Content engines use so-called "buckets." WCCP-enabled routers redirect traffic to content engines using a hashing procedure based on the incoming request's destination IP address, and the request is sent to one of 256 buckets. Using a hashing technique, requests are spread evenly across all 256 buckets and, therefore, to all content engines in the cluster.

When a new content engine is added to the cluster, the WCCP-enabled router detects the new engine and then the number of buckets is reconfigured, based on the total number of content engines. For example, let's say your organization has two content engines. Each engine would contain 128 buckets. If a third is added, then each engine is reconfigured to contain 85 or 86 buckets.

However, because a brand-new content engine won't have any content when it is added, it will suffer frequent cache misses until it has built up its storage. This problem is initially ameliorated, because the new content engine sends a message to others in the cluster, seeking the requested content. If another engine in the cluster has the content, it will be sent to the new engine. Once the engine decides that it has gotten enough content from its cohorts (based on parameters established by the network administrator), it will stop bothering its peers for content requests and instead query the end server.

Reliability

Clustering is not only a good way to balance the load of caching requests, it also is a good way to ensure reliability. In the event one of the content engines in a cluster goes down, the WCCP-enabled router steps in and redistributes that engine's load across the remaining engines. The system continues operating, but with one less content engine. Certainly, this is not ideal from an availability standpoint, but at least the system remains accessible until the failed content engine can be restored.

If the entire cluster fails, then the WCCP-enabled router will stop bothering with caching, sending web requests to their destination web servers. To end users, it will appear as though it is simply taking longer for web content to arrive.

As you have probably noticed by now, there seems to be a lot of responsibility placed on the shoulders of the WCCP-enabled router. If an engine in a cluster goes down, it is easy enough to redistribute its load to the other engines. But what happens if the WCCP-enabled router fails? In such an event, and assuming the pieces are in place before a failure, a WCCP-enabled, Multigroup Hot-Standby Router Protocol (MHSRP) router pair provides routing protection. This is known as *WCCP multihoming*.

Consider the network in Figure 14-11, where two WCCP-enabled routers are depicted. In the event one of these routers fails, the other would step in to take over for its failed brother, redirecting web requests to the content engine cluster. The network in

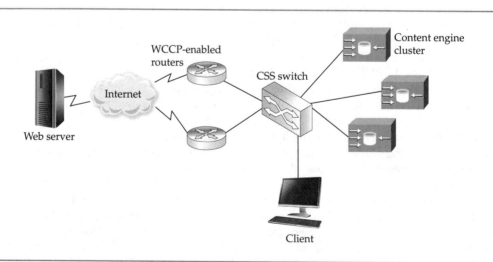

Figure 14-11.   Multihoming provides reliability in addition to load balancing.

Figure 14-11 is fully redundant, because it employs both a content engine cluster and WCCP multihoming.

Bypassing

Multihoming and clustering are good ways to plan for problems. However, as effective as they are, they aren't perfect. There might be a time when the entire cache system must be avoided. There are two scenarios in which the cache system is bypassed.

Overload Overload bypassing is used when there is a sudden surge of web traffic and the content engine or cluster is simply overwhelmed. When this happens, the content engine is able to sense when it is overloaded and refuses additional requests until it can handle those already backlogged. Thus, incoming web requests are simply forwarded to their destination web servers, whether or not the content is stored in the content engine. The content engine continues to refuse requests until it determines that not only has the overload situation been averted, but also it does not expect to become overloaded again if it takes in new requests.

If the content engine is so besieged with requests that it cannot communicate with the WCCP-enabled router and share status messages, the router will logically remove that engine from the cluster, reallocating its buckets to other engines in the cluster.

Client If a client needs to be authenticated to the website using the client's IP address, authentication will fail if the content engine's IP address is seen and not the client's IP address. In such cases, the content engine will allow clients to bypass the engine and connect directly to the destination web server.

Consider the exchange in Figure 14-12. In this figure, the client is attempting to access a web server that insists on authentication. First, the request is funneled through the

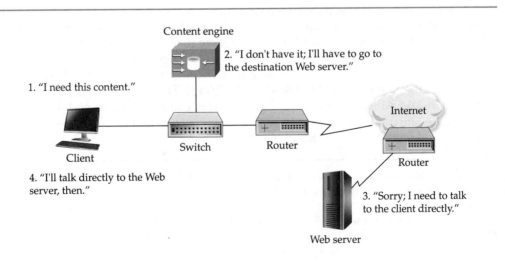

Figure 14-12. If need be, the client can bypass the caching infrastructure and go directly to the source.

content engine. Seeing that the information is not stored locally, it is forwarded on to the destination web server. If error codes are returned to the content engine (for instance, a 401-unauthorized request or 403-forbidden), the engine will automatically enter client bypass mode and allow the client to interact directly with the destination web server. In addition, the content engine will store the destination IP address along with the client IP address. The next time the client attempts to access that web server, the content engine will automatically enter client bypass mode.

Content Delivery Network Federations

Looking ahead, we'll quote Scott Puopolo, Vice President of Global Service Provider Practice for Cisco: "Whether driven by live sports or blockbuster movies, the explosive demand for Internet video keeps rising. Increasingly, consumers want it all, and they want it on any device, at any time. Indeed, by 2015, Cisco projects a *quadrupling* of IP traffic, 90 percent of which will be video." It's very likely we'll see CDN providers change their current business model as they are currently deployed and share their content among each other by implementing CDN federations or partnerships. Cisco has been attempting to get companies to move in this direction since 2011.

If you think the golden days of internetworking are behind us, you haven't seen anything yet. The future is bright, as technologies and protocols are able to handle more and more. As networks become more intelligent, we can expect to see more services delivered, with special attention paid to network conditions and the specific needs of the content.

Video

When Cisco sold its first router—and for years to come after that—the Internet was just about sending data packets, comprising relatively small files, from here to there. As the Internet has matured, we rely on it for so much more than passing small files. These days, video is a major component of the Internet and its capabilities.

According to Cisco's Visual Networking Index in 2011, by 2014 video will exceed 91 percent of the global Internet traffic. Overall IP traffic is expected to grow four-fold from 2009 to 2014. Much of that growth is expected to come from video and the rise of video-enabled mobile device. Further, an hour of high definition video requires several gigabytes of storage and network bandwidth.

NOTE   To further understand the relevance of video on the Internet, consider this: Consumers add 35 hours of video to YouTube every minute.

When you consider the video-streaming application features of so many operations—Netflix, broadcast TV, Hulu, and so forth—you can see why video is such an important consideration. So important, in fact, that its relevance is not at all lost on Cisco.

In recent years, Cisco refocused its energies on five priorities:

- Core (including routing, switching, and services)
- Collaboration
- Data center virtualization and cloud
- Video
- Architectures for business transformation

And video is the biggest growth driver for IP traffic, Cisco's core networking business. As such, Cisco offers a number of video solutions, appealing to different markets. Let's take a closer look at these markets and see how Cisco is serving them.

Video Entertainment

The first, most obvious place video is relevant is as an entertainment source. But in the twenty-first century, video has changed vastly from its early black-and-white days on television sets humming with the sound of busy vacuum tubes. These days, video isn't limited to five channels in the living room, or even dad's den.

Now, entertainment is accessed through flat screen TVs, on smartphones, computers, and tablets—and it can be accessed from virtually anywhere. In order to remain competitive, service providers and media companies must be able to deliver video on these screen options—they also must be able to offer unique experiences on those devices and figure out how to monetize those experiences.

Cisco Videoscape Unity is Cisco's solution for delivering and monetizing video. This allows service providers and media companies to deliver new, synchronized multiscreen video experiences. These include a multiscreen cloud digital video recorder (DVR), enabling consumers to restart shows, catch up on past programs, and play back DVR-captured content from anywhere, on any screen.

With Videoscape, video operators have an open software platform that speeds the delivery of immersive multiscreen video experiences that advance their service.

Features

Videoscape offers several unique features that make video more compelling and interesting:

- **Multiscreen cloud DVR**   Cloud-driven video recording with capture and storage in the cloud instead of the end device. Consumers can restart shows, catch up on past programs, and play back DVR-captured content from anywhere, on any screen.

- **Video Everywhere**   Broadens the TV Everywhere proposition with unified search, discovery, and viewing functions to allow consumers to watch premium live and on-demand content on any (service provider managed or unmanaged) connected device regardless of location.

- **Connected video to any device in the home**   Cisco's Connected Video Gateway serves as a single entertainment hub, with back-end management of IP and Quadrature Amplitude Modulation (QAM) video, for distributing video content and metadata to any IP-connected device in the home, while providing a unified user experience.

- **IP Video over Cable**   Gives consumers expanded choice of content and IP video services, with faster delivery of on-demand and interactive offerings, across a wider range of service provider managed devices, and with the flexibility to add unmanaged devices.

Details

Cisco announced its Videoscape TV services delivery platform at the Consumer Electronics Show in 2011. Videoscape Unity was created by integrating Cisco Videoscape with the assets and business model of NDS, Cisco's video software and content security and experience provider (acquired by Cisco in 2012). The new platform comprises a set of cloud, network, and client-based components, connected by open interfaces.

> **NOTE**   Cisco acquired the NDS Group, Ltd., in July of 2012, including Jungo, CastUP, and SiVenture. NDS was a provider of video software and content security solutions that enabled service providers to deliver and monetize new video entertainment experiences.

The cloud and network components power new, personalized video services and enable multiple screens to be synchronized to create a single unified experience for the subscriber, so things look and feel the same no matter what device they use.

Client components use the Cisco Snowflake interface design model and NDS Media Highway multiplatform clients. This approach enables network operators to design exciting user experiences, engineer them into clients for connected devices and set-top boxes, and quickly deploy them across multiple screens and throughout large service footprints.

Deployment

Cisco offers a number of ways in which Videoscape Unity can be deployed for optimal usability. Deployment options include

- Videoscape can be deployed in one of many preconfigured, end-to-end configurations, which can be tailored to each operator's service plan.

- Operators can also opt to select individual components and tailor them into their operations via open interfaces.

- Cisco offers Videoscape "as a service," allowing operators to have Cisco build, monitor, operate, and even host their video infrastructures in the cloud.

Advantages

Beyond simply being Cisco's answer to video content delivery, Videoscape Unity offers a number of other beneficial features, including:

- Multiscreen experiences delivered from Cisco's video experience platform and continuously refreshed by Cisco's 7,500+ video engineers.

- A modular open platform, which operators can enhance with third-party components using open interfaces built into the Videoscape Unity platform.

- Operators who deploy Videoscape Unity for one service can easily enhance and add to the modules they initially deploy to bring other services to market quickly.

- Reduced operations costs via the elimination of single-service "siloed" platforms, and the need for constant in-house engineering to keep platforms current.

Video Collaboration

We've touched on collaboration already in this book, but for the sake of completeness, let's talk about it a bit more. Collaboration—which is one of Cisco's five business priorities that we discussed at the start of this chapter—is achieved largely through TelePresence.

TelePresence

We have talked about TelePresence in a couple other places in this book. It is the *Star Trek*-like tool that places a screen on your desktop or converts a room into a huge meeting venue so that collaborations across great distances can be accomplished with relative speed and cost effectiveness. TelePresence serves a broad range of audiences, which—quite frankly—is limited only by how industries choose to use this tool. Some of the primary audiences served by TelePresence include

- **Meetings**   This is the primary function of TelePresence and is used for communication and collaboration with clients, partners, and team members. Meeting participants can participate at their desks with single endpoints, in large conference rooms with big screen displays and multiple cameras, or while traveling via their laptops.

- **Events**   The simple meeting can be transformed into an event, by providing an interactive experience. Event attendees can participate whether they are within the company's intranet, in a public forum, at home, or on the road.

- **Organizational communications**   TelePresence can be used within an organization to reach one person, a team, or the entire organization.

- **Safety and security**   Surveillance video can be streamed to any device or can be shared across devices to respond quickly to security issues.

- **Advertising**   Video can be used within an advertisement to create more interesting, attention-grabbing content. It can be used via in-store signage, at home, or virtually.

- **Customer interaction**   This allows for interpersonal interaction with customers to create a more personalized customer service experience.

Video Intelligence

But with video being such an important part of networks, it isn't enough simply to be able to watch the video—your organization must be able to analyze and organize the video. Cisco's Video Intelligence makes it possible to extract relevant information from video surveillance and analyze that data.

Video is everywhere, and organizations are relying on it more and more—whether it be in the form of mission-critical data to surveillance video from the parking lot, a lot of video information is being generated, and there needs to be an effective, efficient way to catalog, search within, and access it.

Video Intelligence extracts that information from video in two ways:

- **Automated video indexing and keyword recognition**   This system analyzes the embedded audio so that relevant video data is located.

- **Translating audio information into video**   This method recognizes specific objects within the video.

MXE 3500

The mechanism behind Cisco's Video Intelligence is a technology called Cisco Pulse Video Analytics, which is a feature on the MXE-3500 (Media Experience Engine). It allows organizations to find and view video quickly. Users can search for specific content or individual speakers within a video. Pulse Video Analytics allows users to:

- Specify index requirements to search for individual spoken phrases or words

- Create a list of customized vocabulary tags so that specific words or phrases are identified

- Identify speakers so that content can be sorted by who is saying it

The MXE-3500 facilitates video everywhere in the organization and is used to extend the reach of video for collaboration and communications through media tools, along with the integration into media workflows as video streams traverse the network.

Playback   A major feature of the MXE-3500 is its any-to-any capabilities. That is, any video—be it live or recorded—is adapted to a number of media formats, resolutions, and speeds, whether it is standard definition or high definition. This allows them to be played on a range of playback devices—from dedicated displays to PCs, smartphones, and tablets.

Editing The MXE-3500 also provides a host of professional-quality post-production features that can be used on source video files. For instance, lead-in video can be added to the video file, as well as titling and graphic overlays.

Features The MXE-3500 includes the following features:

- High-quality media transcoding for file-based and live multimedia for any-to-any capture and playback on the network and end devices.

- Professional video and audio enhancement options including studio-quality editing, graphic overlays, and watermarking.

- Pulse video analytics makes videos easy to find and utilize, based on what's being said and who's saying it.

- A browser-based interface simplifies content management, making it easy for end users to transform videos.

- Live streaming formats, including Windows Media and live MPEG-2 Transport Stream (MPEG-2 TS), allow users to deliver live streams of content to Cisco Digital Signs for communications, training, events, or other applications.

Data

Cisco touts that using its video intelligence features makes culling intelligence from video can make the video as easy to search as a text document. Such capabilities as speaker recognition on automated keyword tagging allow viewers to identify and move immediately to the portions of a video that are most relevant to them.

NOTE Cisco offers automated advertisement detection and insertion, allowing service providers the opportunity to turn their video into moneymakers. This is good news for advertisers but bad new for those who hate the pervasiveness of advertising.

Relevance

While video intelligence is a helpful tool for searching and cataloging video, it is an especially important capability in the world of surveillance and security. Video analytics can be used to identify and detect objects and find video information related to specific incidents. These capabilities allow response to real-time video, as well as pulling historical information from existing video.

CDNs in general and IP video in particular provide rich features for a network. Whether you are interested in caching data so that it is faster and more easily transmitted to clients or you want to develop a video or videoconferencing solution, the core of any effort will be a CDN.

PART IV | Designing Cisco Networks

CHAPTER 15 | Routing Protocols

Over the preceding few chapters, we've covered the gamut of network devices. Switches sit in a data closet, taking twisted-pair cables from host devices and forming the LAN, and they also pack the power to support VLANs. Another inhabitant of the data closet is the security and access servers, used to link remote users into internetworks through Internet VPNs or dial-in telephone lines. If a packet moves beyond its source LAN segment, it flows onto a backbone LAN, where it encounters a router and (if it's a secured internetwork) a firewall. After that point is the Great Beyond. Once the packet goes past the local network, it enters a realm of seemingly infinite complexity.

Internetworks are complex because they're big and subject to endless fluctuation. An internetwork's topology is altered whenever a new switch is added or when a router is inserted to help direct growing internetwork loads. As usage patterns evolve, traffic congestion seems to pop up in different spots every day. If network devices crash, they take their connected LAN segments down with them, and traffic must be immediately redirected—and then redirected back once the downed device is brought back online. More frequently, the network device is up but one of its network interfaces has gone down, or the interface is okay but a cable was accidentally knocked from its port. To top it all off, sometimes all the physical network equipment is running fine, but things *still* go awry because a bad configuration file was somehow introduced into the mix!

The point here is that large internetworks are simply too complicated to be managed by people alone. Imagine a roomful of network administrators trying to manually control each and every network event in a Fortune 500 company, and you'd see a portrait of creeping disorganization. Now imagine that same room—or even a building—filled with people attempting to corral the Internet itself, and you see unmitigated chaos. There's just too much complexity and change to handle without a constant source of reliable help—automated help.

So how does it all work? How do packets find their way across internetworks with the reliability we've come to take for granted? The answer is routing protocols.

Overview of Routing Protocols

As you've learned, a *protocol* is a formalized system for exchanging a specific type of information in a certain way, and an *algorithm* is a system of rules carefully crafted to control a process that must contend with varying factors.

In our context, a *routing protocol* formalizes the ongoing exchange of route information between routers. Messages called *routing updates* pass information used by routing algorithms to calculate paths to destinations. A *routing algorithm* is a system of rules that controls an internetwork's behavior in such a way that it adapts to changing circumstances within the internetwork's topology. Ongoing changes include such things as which links are up and running, which are fastest, whether any new equipment has appeared, and so on. Each router uses its own copy of the algorithm to recalculate a map of the internetwork to account for all the latest changes from its particular perspective.

The routing algorithm coordinates updates.	The shared topology view exerts collective influence.				
Each router recalculates its own routing table.	New table	New table	New table	New table	New table

Routing protocols use a peer arrangement in which each router plays an equal role. Those new to internetworking often think that routers are somehow coordinated by a centralized management server. They are not. There is no routing protocol server to centrally manage routing processes. Ongoing routing table maintenance is handled in real time through an arrangement in which each router makes its own route selection decisions. To configure a routing protocol for an internetwork, the routing protocol process must be configured in each router that will be involved in the arrangement. In practical terms, the IOS config file for every router must have parameters set to send and receive routing updates, run the algorithm, and so forth. Properly configured, the routing protocol is able to collectively influence all these machine-made decisions so that they work in harmony. The area within which routing information is exchanged is called a *routing domain*, sometimes also referred to as an *autonomous system*.

NOTE   The terms "path" and "route" are synonymous. "Path" is widely used for no other reason than it's hard to discuss routing protocols that use routing algorithms to calculate new optimal routes for distribution in routing updates sent to all routers for use in recalculating their respective routing tables. You get the point.

Routing Protocol Basics

Of the many routing protocols, some are standards-based and others are proprietary. Several are old and fading from use, a few are used only within narrowly defined market niches, and others are in such wide use that they are de facto standards. Routing protocols also differ in the types of internetworks they're designed to manage and in the size of internetworks they can handle. Naturally, these differences are manifested in each routing protocol's algorithm. Yet all their algorithms share these two basic processes:

- Routers send one another update messages, advising of changes in internetwork topology and conditions.

- Each router recalculates its own routing table based on the updated information.

Updating one another helps each individual router know what's going on. More importantly, it helps orchestrate an internetwork's routers by maintaining a common set of information with which to operate.

The Routing Table's Central Role

A *routing table* is a list of routes available to forward traffic to various destinations. Every router in an internetwork maintains its own routing table, the contents of which differ from those maintained by other routers. Each router maintains a single routing table (not one per interface). The majority of routers run just one routing protocol, although specialized border routers run two in order to pass routes between areas using different protocols (more on that later).

NOTE Routing tables often refer to multiple tables for a given routing protocol. For instance, Open Shortest Path First (OSPF) maintains multiple tables of information that are all part of the routing table.

A routing table constitutes the router's self-centered view of the internetwork's topology—sort of its personal formula for conducting business. Every time an update is received, the routing protocol takes the information and mashes it through its algorithm to recalculate optimal paths to all destinations deemed reachable from that router. Figure 15-1 illustrates the routing table update process.

Each router must have its own routing table to account for conditions specific to its location in the internetwork. In a routing domain, the routers collectively share the same news about any change, but then each puts that information to use individually.

The Routing Protocol Is an Internetwork's Intelligence

The goal of routing protocols is to let an internetwork respond to change. They do this by providing routers with a common framework for decision-making about how to respond to topology changes within the internetwork. The routing protocol coordinates the passing of updates between routers, and then each router recalculates optimal routes in its own table. If, after recalculation, all the routing tables have arrived at a common view of the topology—albeit each from its self-centered perspective—the internetwork is said to have reached *convergence* (so called because the router community has converged on a singular view of the topology). A converged topology view means all the routers agree on which links are up, down, running fastest, and so on.

Routing protocols are the quintessence of high-tech internetworking. They represent the ability of individual devices, and even whole networks, to help manage themselves. One could say that internetworks have become organic in the sense that routing protocols make them self-aware and self-correcting. As topologies grow from day to day or circumstances change from moment to moment, internetworks can respond, because routing protocols enable the router community to converse intelligently about what to do.

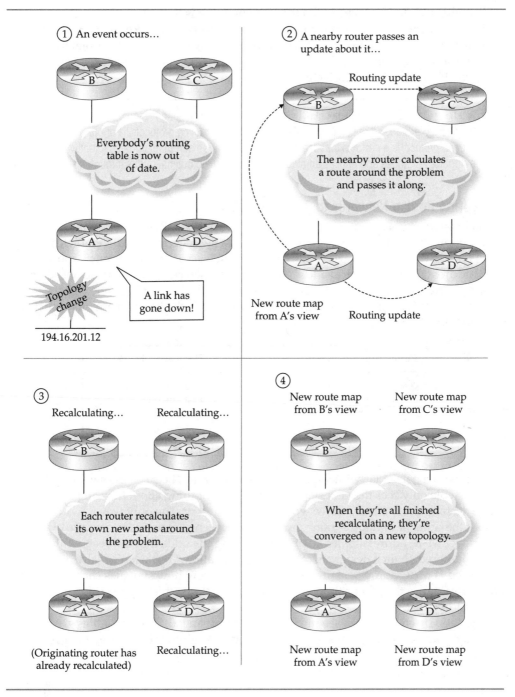

Figure 15-1. Routing update messages coordinate routing tables.

A trendy marketing cliché holds that "the network is the system." If that's true, then routing protocols serve as the network's operating system. Routing protocols raise the limit on what is practical in terms of internetwork size and complexity. It's no exaggeration to state that the development of sophisticated routing protocols is what has made the Internet's explosive growth possible.

NOTE Cisco Discovery Protocol (CDP), the Hot Standby Routing Protocol (HSRP), and other specialized protocols are sometimes also referred to as "routing protocols." For our purposes, a *routing protocol* is a protocol that coordinates the exchange of routing updates to notify other routers of topology changes and applies an algorithm to recalculate optimal routes through an internetwork.

Comparing Routed Networks to Switched Networks

A good way to explain routing protocols is by comparison. Remember switching tables from Chapter 7? To refresh: Switches keep track of switched network topologies by brute force. Every time a message arrives, the switch associates the frame's source MAC address (layer-2 physical address) with the switch port it came in on and then makes an entry into its MAC address table. In this way, the switch builds a list of destination MAC addresses for each switch port. Here's the basic layout of a switch's address table:

Destination MAC Address	Destination Switch Port
0060.2fa3.fabc	Fast Ethernet0/8
0050.0465.395c	Fast Ethernet0/4
0010.5a9b.b5e6	Fast Ethernet0/12
⋮	⋮

This isn't a particularly intelligent way to map routes, because the switch's MAC address table only sees the next step. The table says nothing about the complete route to the destination; it merely shows you out the next door. The only way a switch can reduce the number of hops a frame must take between switches is to compile bigger and bigger MAC address tables, thereby increasing the odds that the best path will be encountered. Switch designers call this "optimization," but what's really being optimized is MAC addresses. (In case you're wondering how switches choose among alternative paths, they favor those most frequently used, which appear higher in the MAC address list.)

Routers, by contrast, *can* see more than one step ahead. Routing tables give routers the ability to see farther into an internetwork without expanding their lists.

Whereas switches substitute quantity for quality, routers apply intelligence. Here's the basic layout of a simple type of routing table:

Destination	Next Hop	Hop Count
209.98.134.126	209.126.4.38	3
	127.197.83.128	5
	202.8.79.250	9
⋮	⋮	⋮

This example may not look like much, but it's "smarter" than the switch table in a fundamental way. The switch plays the odds, but the router plays it smart, because the Hop Count column gives the router additional information about the entire route. Knowing how many routers a packet must hop through to reach its destination helps the sending router choose the best path to take. This kind of measurement is called a *routing metric* (or *metric* for short). Metrics such as hop count are what separate routing from the switch's abrupt "out this door, please" approach. Metrics supply the intelligence needed by routing algorithms to calculate best paths through internetworks.

Routing Updates Are Control Messages

Routed networks carry an undercurrent of specialized traffic that exchanges routing update messages. Switched networks do no such thing; they guess at what's going on by looking only at the source MAC address and incoming port of payload packets. A *payload message,* by the way, is one that carries content useful for an application instead of for the internetwork's internal operations. Figure 15-2 outlines the difference.

Routing updates aren't payload messages, they're *control messages*. The content they deliver is used by the internetwork for internal operations. This second type of traffic-carrying routing updates is the lifeblood of internetworking, delivering the intelligence an internetwork must have to act in a unitary fashion and survive in the face of change. Given their importance, to reach a basic understanding of routing protocols, you need to know what routing updates contain, how and where they're sent, and how they're processed.

Dynamic vs. Static Routing

Before we go further, a little background is in order. There are two basic types of routing:

- **Static routing**   A static route is a fixed path preprogrammed by a network administrator. Static routes cannot make use of routing protocols and don't self-update after receipt of routing update messages; they must be updated manually.

- **Dynamic routing**   This is the type of routing made possible by routing protocols, which automatically calculate routes based on routing update messages. The majority of all internetwork routes are dynamic.

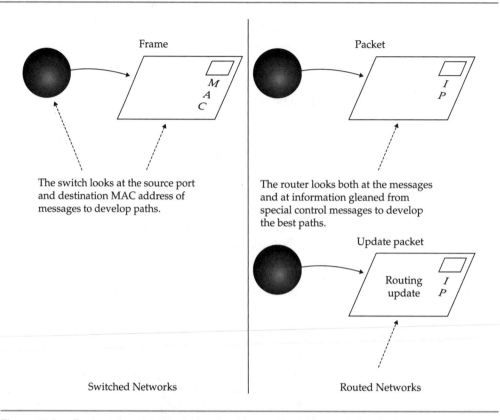

Figure 15-2.   Routers use control messages to update routing tables; switches don't.

This distinction is made here to drive home a key point. Not all routes are automatically (dynamically) calculated by routing protocols—and for good reason. In most situations, network administrators will opt to retain direct control over a minority of routes.

The best example of how static routes are used is the default gateway. A router can't possibly know all routes to all destinations, so it's configured with a *default gateway* path to which packets with unknown destinations are sent. Default gateways are entered as static routes to make sure undeliverable traffic is steered to a router that has routing table entries leading outside the internetwork. Figure 15-3 shows a default gateway in action in two places: first at the PC, which has been told its default gateway is on an interface of a particular router, and then at the router, where its default gateway is out of its Internet interface.

The ability of routing protocols to automate routing table selection is a good thing, but only in measured doses. The use of static routes as default gateways to handle unanticipated messages exemplifies this.

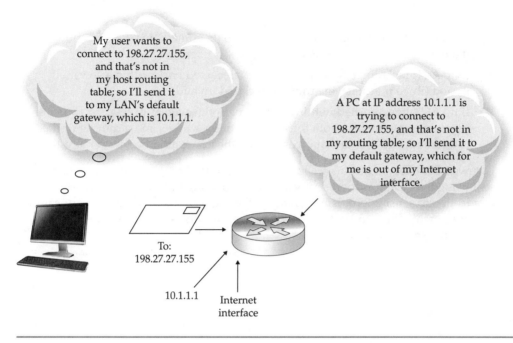

Figure 15-3. The classic example of a static route is a network's default gateway.

Routers Collaborate to Attain Convergence

Convergence is when all routers in an internetwork have agreed on a common topology. For example, if a particular network link has gone down, the internetwork will have converged when all the routers settle on new routes that no longer include that link. Yet each router must have its own routes to account for its unique position in the network topology. Thus, the routers act collectively by sharing updates, yet take independent action by calculating their own routes. When the process is complete, they have converged, in the sense that all the routes were calculated based on a common set of assumptions about the network's current topology.

This collaboration is orchestrated by the internetwork's routing protocol. Having routers work collectively gives internetworks their strength, because it may take more than one router to isolate a network problem. And, until a problem is isolated, no router has the information needed to calculate new routes around the problem.

How Routers Sense Topology Change

Routers use gateway discovery protocols to keep track of one another. A *gateway discovery protocol* is a system that coordinates the exchange of small "Are you still there?"

messages between routers in an internetwork, mainly as a way of sensing downed links:

■ Each router broadcasts "hello" messages to its immediate neighbor routers at a fixed interval (say, once every 90 seconds).

■ If no ACK (acknowledgment message) is received back within a specified period (three minutes), the route is declared invalid.

■ If no ACK has returned within a longer period (seven minutes), the router and its routes are removed from the sending router's table, and a routing update is issued about all routes that incorporated the nonresponding router as a link.

Gateway discovery protocols are low-overhead control protocols that in IP networks are sent using the UDP transport protocol. Figure 15-4 illustrates how they work.

In addition to sensing problems, gateway discovery protocols detect the appearance of new equipment. The four types of gateway discovery messages in Figure 15-4 are collectively referred to as *timers*.

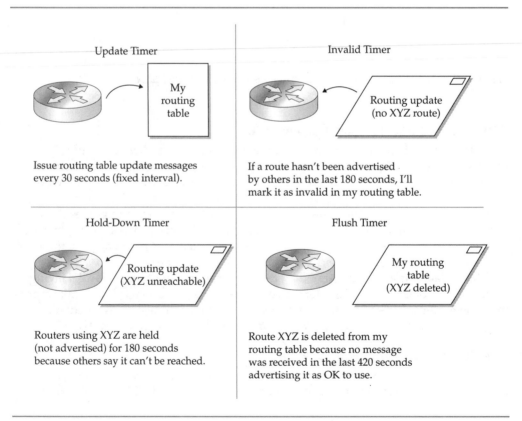

Figure 15-4. Gateway discovery protocols use timers to detect topology changes.

How Routing Updates Converge

Sensing a topology change is only the first step. From the point of discovery, routing updates must be passed until all routers can converge on a new topology by incorporating the change.

Let's take an example. Figure 15-5 shows a relatively simple four-router topology with route redundancy, in that messages have alternative paths to destinations. A message sent from Manufacturing to Accounting could travel through either the R&D or Marketing router. If packets sent from Manufacturing through the R&D router to the Expense Report server suddenly become undeliverable, the Accounting router can't be relied upon to diagnose the problem on its own. This is because there are so many

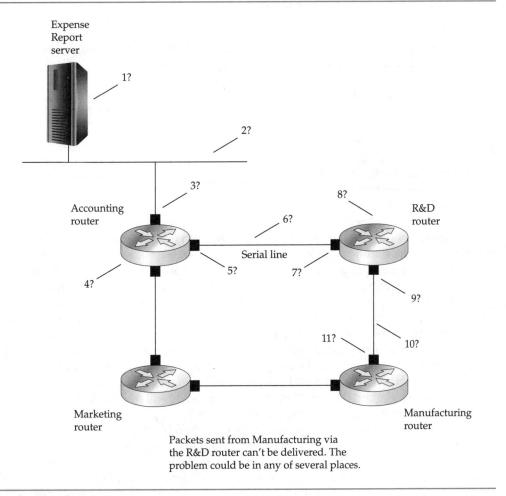

Packets sent from Manufacturing via the R&D router can't be delivered. The problem could be in any of several places.

Figure 15-5.   Routers must collaborate to locate network problems.

potential sources for the problems, as depicted by the question marks in Figure 15-5. Here's a roundup of the most likely suspects of what caused the problem:

1. The Expense Report server has crashed.

2. The LAN connection to the Expense Report server has failed.

3. The Accounting router's interface to the Expense Report server's LAN segment has failed.

4. The Accounting router has totally failed.

5. The Accounting router's serial interface to the R&D router has failed.

6. The serial transmission line connecting Accounting with R&D is down.

7. R&D's serial interface to the Accounting router has failed.

8. The R&D router has totally failed.

9. R&D's serial interface to the Manufacturing router has failed.

10. The serial transmission line connecting R&D with Manufacturing is down.

11. Manufacturing's serial interface to the R&D router has failed.

The Accounting router can't have definitive knowledge as to problems 1, 7, or 8 because it's not directly responsible for these network devices, and the Accounting router would be of no use at all in the event of problem 4.

Packets can't be routed to detour around the failure until the problem has been located. Also, the problem must be located in order for the routers to converge on a new (post-failure) network topology.

If, in our sample topology, the serial line between Accounting and R&D has failed, both routers would sense this at about the same time and issue updates. Figure 15-6 tracks the routing update as it flows from the Accounting and R&D routers. Once the router has sensed the problem, it deletes the failed path from its routing table. This, in turn, causes the routing algorithm to calculate a new best route to all destinations that had incorporated the failed link. When these new routes are calculated, the router issues them in a routing update message sent out to other routers in the internetwork.

Updated routing information is sent from the Accounting and R&D routers to announce that they are no longer using the serial line in their routes. These are routing update messages. The Manufacturing and Marketing routers, in turn, replace any routes they have using the serial link. In the example in Figure 15-6, it took two routing updates for the internetwork to converge on a new topology that's minus the serial line. When the serial line is brought back online, the connected routers will also sense the topology change, and the whole route update process will repeat itself in reverse.

Short convergence time is a primary design goal when laying out an internetwork's topology. In big networks, it can take several updates to converge. The length of convergence time depends on the routing protocol used, the size of the internetwork, and where in the topology a change takes place. For example, if the problem in Figure 15-5 had occurred behind the Accounting router's gateway, only the Accounting router would have originated a routing update, which would have resulted in a convergence time of three updates.

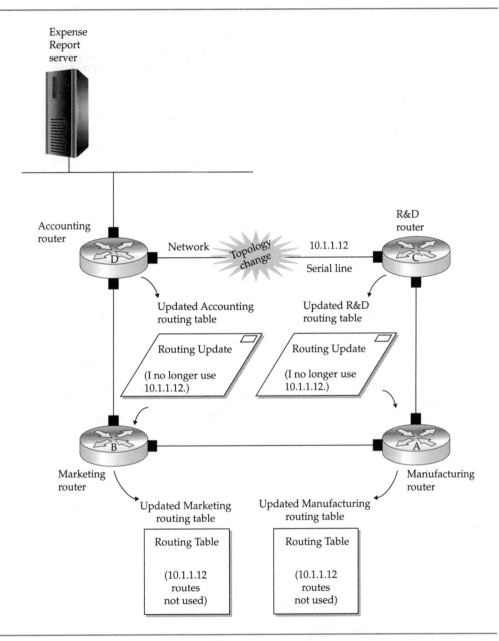

Figure 15-6.   Only two routing updates are necessary to converge.

Long convergence time is a symptom of a poorly functioning internetwork. Many factors can slow convergence, but the major factor in convergence times is propagation delay.

Propagation Delay

A network phenomenon called *propagation delay* is the delay between the time a packet is sent and when it arrives at its destination. Propagation delay isn't a simple matter of geographical distance or hop count; other factors can also have an influence. Figure 15-7 shows various propagation delay factors.

Obviously, something as basic as the time required for data to travel over a network is important to all areas of internetworking. But propagation delay is a factor for routing protocols, because not all routers receive a routing update at the same moment. No matter how fast the network medium, convergence takes time, as a routing update is passed from router to router until it arrives at the farthest router.

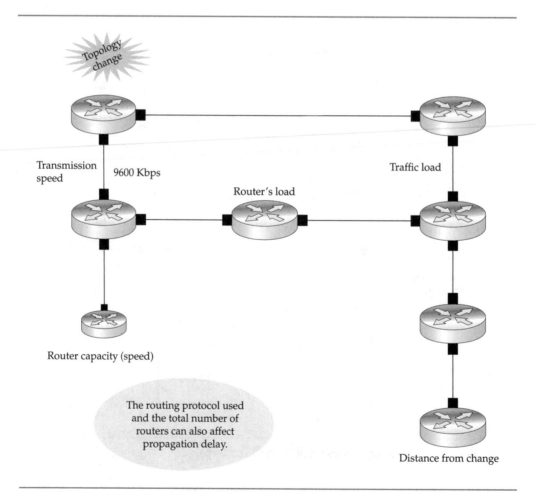

Figure 15-7.   Several factors can influence the length of propagation delay.

The importance of propagation delay grows with an internetwork's size. Big internetworks have dozens of routers and hundreds of connected LAN segments—each a potential source of topology change. All other things being equal, the bigger the network, the greater its propagation delay; and the more redundant paths are used, the greater the potential for confusion.

Routing Loops

Propagation delay wouldn't pose a problem to routing protocols if routers always converged before any new changes emerged. But they don't. The longer propagation delay is in an internetwork, the more susceptible it is to something called a routing loop. A *routing loop* is when payload packets can't reach their destinations because of conflicting routing table information. This happens in large or change-intensive internetworks when a second topology change emerges before the network is able to converge on the first change.

Taking the example shown in Figure 15-8, the R&D router senses that network 10.1.1.12 has gone down and issues a routing update. But before the Manufacturing router receives the update, it issues a routing update indicating that network 10.1.1.12

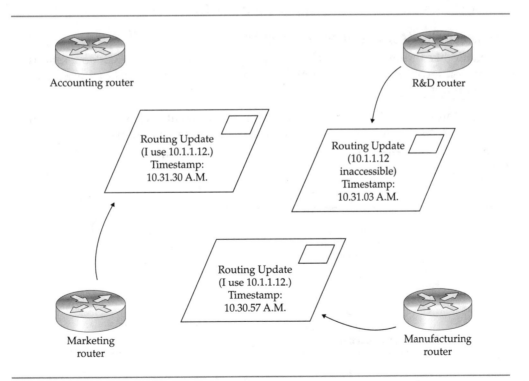

Figure 15-8.   A routing loop can start when routing updates overlap.

is still good (because the update has paths that incorporate this network). The updates from R&D and Manufacturing conflict and, depending on how the timing works out, can confuse the other routers and even each other, throwing the internetwork into a routing loop.

Routing loops can be self-perpetuating. If the conflicting routing updates are persistent enough, each repeatedly nullifies the other in route decisions made by the affected routers. If the router's primary route vacillates each time it receives an update, the internetwork has become unstable. If things go too far out of balance (for example, there are too many loops in progress and primary route selections are flapping), the protocol's collective topology can begin to disintegrate altogether. The downward spiral goes like this:

- Two or more conflicting routing updates cause messages to be routed via downed routes, and therefore they are not delivered.

- As the loop persists, more bandwidth is consumed by inefficiently routed payload packets and routing updates trying to fix the problem.

- The diminishing bandwidth triggers still more routing updates in response to the worsening throughput.

The vicious circle of a routing loop is depicted in Figure 15-9.

Mechanisms to Keep Internetworks Loop-Free

A scenario like the one just described is unacceptable to effective network operations. Routing protocols incorporate a number of sophisticated mechanisms to thwart the onset of routing loops:

- **Hold-downs**   Suppression of advertisements about a route that's in question long enough for all the routers to find out about its true status.

- **Split horizons**   The practice of not advertising a route back in the direction of the route itself.

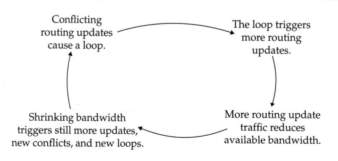

Figure 15-9.   If network events outpace convergence, infinite loops can occur.

- **Poison reverse updates**   A routing update message that explicitly states a network or subnet is unreachable (instead of a nearby router merely dropping it from its routing table for lack of use).

- **Maximum hop count**   Packets traverse a maximum number of hops between source and destination. Once they have exceeded their limit, they are dropped, thus avoiding a loop.

Hold-Downs   A *hold-down* is a way to help prevent bad routes from being reinstated by mistake. When a route is placed in a hold-down state, routers will neither advertise the route nor accept advertisements about it for a specific interval called the hold-down period. Hold-downs have the effect of flushing information about a bad route from the internetwork. It's a forcible way to take a bad apple from the barrel to help reduce the chances of it starting a routing loop. At the extreme, a hold-down period would be an interval slightly longer than it normally takes for the entire network to learn of a routing change—its average convergence time.

But holding back the release of routing updates obviously slows convergence, so there's a harsh trade-off between the loop-prevention benefit of hold-downs and the quality of network service. This is because delaying the release of an update leaves a bad route in play for a longer period. In internetworks of any size, setting hold-down intervals to match average convergence time results in frequent timeout messages to end users. In the real world, hold-down times are often set to an interval far less than the network's average convergence time to partially ameliorate loop risk, but at the same time avoid most network timeouts for users. This trade-off is depicted in Figure 15-10.

Split Horizons   A split horizon is a routing configuration that stops a route from being advertised back in the direction from which it came. The theory is that it's basically useless to send information back toward its source. An example of this is outlined in Figure 15-11. Router B, in the middle, received a route to network 10.1.99.0 from Router A on the left. The split-horizon rule instructs Router B not to include that route in updates

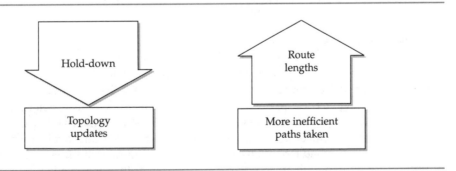

Figure 15-10.   Hold-downs prevent routing loops, but can slow down network performance.

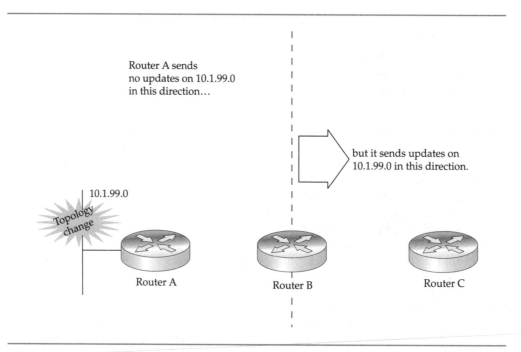

Router A sends
no updates on 10.1.99.0
in this direction...

but it sends updates on
10.1.99.0 in this direction.

10.1.99.0

Topology change

Router A

Router B

Router C

Figure 15-11. A split horizon stops a routing update from echoing back to its source.

it sends back toward Router A. The assumption is that Router A was probably the source of the route (given that it is in the direction of network 10.1.99.0); therefore, it doesn't need to be informed of the route. If Router A's interface to network 10.1.99.0 went down and it didn't have enough built-in intelligence, it might take its own routing update back from Router B and try to use it as a way around the downed interface.

Hold-downs can normally prevent routing loops on their own, but split horizons are generally configured as a backup measure because there's no particular trade-off in using them.

Poison Reverse Updates   By now, you've probably noticed that routing protocols work implicitly. In other words, they steer traffic around a bad link by not including routes involving that link in routing updates. Poison reverse updates, by contrast, explicitly state that a link is bad. Poison reverse works by having a router check for overlarge increases in metrics. Routing metrics are designed such that an increase reflects deterioration. For example, an increase in the number of hops a route must take makes it less desirable. A router compares an incoming routing update's metric for a route against what it was when the router itself had issued an earlier update including that same route. The routing protocol is configured with an acceptable increase factor that, if exceeded, causes the router to assume the route is a "reversing" message. Figure 15-12 depicts the process.

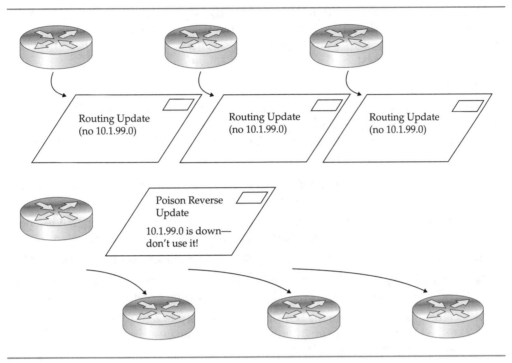

Figure 15-12. Most routing updates are implicit corrections; poison reverse updates are explicit.

In Cisco routing protocols, the default increase for a routing metric is a factor of 1.1 or greater. In other words, if a route returns in an update with a metric that is 110 percent or more of what it was on the way out, it's assumed that a loop is in progress. For example, if a router sends out an update with a route with a hop count metric of 1, and it returns in someone else's update with a hop count of 2, the assumption is that a loop is under way. When this happens, the router is placed into a hold-down state in which it neither sends nor receives updates on that route. The hold-down state stays on for a period deemed sufficiently long to flush the problem from the update system—thus the name *poison reverse.* The loop is a bad metric "reversing" onto the router; the hold-down is a way of "poisoning" (or killing) updates that could contain the bad metric.

Split horizons are a good way to prevent routing loops among adjacent routers. But in large internetworks in which routing updates are passed between routers far removed from one another, poison reverse updates help prevent bad routes from starting to loop before update convergence can take place.

Maximum Hop Count   This refers to the number of routers a packet can move through. Every time a packet moves through a router, another hop is added to the count. Once it reaches the given number of hops, the packet is discarded.

Hop counts are used to avoid problems caused by loops. For example, if the maximum hop count is 15, then if the packet moves through 14 routers, if the next hop does not take it to its destination, it will be dropped. This prevents packets from eternally hopping from one router to the next.

Routing Metrics

A routing metric is a value used by a routing protocol to influence routing decisions. Metric information is stored in routing tables and is used by routing algorithms to determine optimal routes to destinations. The terminology takes some getting used to, but here are the most widely used metrics:

- **Cost**   Not financial cost, but a theoretical "cost" number used to represent the time, difficulty, risk, and other factors involved in a route.

- **Distance**   Not physical distance in miles or cable feet, but a theoretical "distance" number. Most distance metrics are based on the number of hops in a route.

- **Bandwidth**   The bandwidth rating of a network link (100 Mbps, for example).

- **Traffic load**   A number representing the amount of traffic (such as the number and size of packets) that traveled over a link during a specified period of time.

- **Delay**   In this context, the time between the start of a routing update cycle and when all routers in an internetwork converge on a single topology view (also called *propagation delay* or *latency).*

- **Reliability**   A relative number used to indicate reliability of a link.

- **MTU**   The maximum packet size (maximum transmission units) that a particular network interface can handle, usually expressed in bytes.

NOTE   Sometimes, "cost" is used as a general term for the result calculated by an equation inside the routing protocol algorithm. For example, someone might state that the overall cost of one route was more than another's, when actually the routing algorithm used metrics for distance, bandwidth, traffic load, and delay.

Some simple routing protocols use just one metric. However, usually more than one routing metric goes into determining optimal routes. For example, a two-hop route traversing a 9,600 Kbps serial line is going to be much slower than a three-hop route going over T3 circuits at 44 Mbps. You don't have to be Euclid to figure out that moving bits 4,000 times faster more than compensates for an extra hop.

Sophisticated routing protocols not only support multiple metrics, they also let you decide which to use. In addition, you can assign relative weights to metrics and more precisely influence route selection. If the network administrator sets the metrics properly, the overall behavior of the internetwork can be tuned to best fit the enterprise's objectives. Figure 15-13 shows some routing metrics in action.

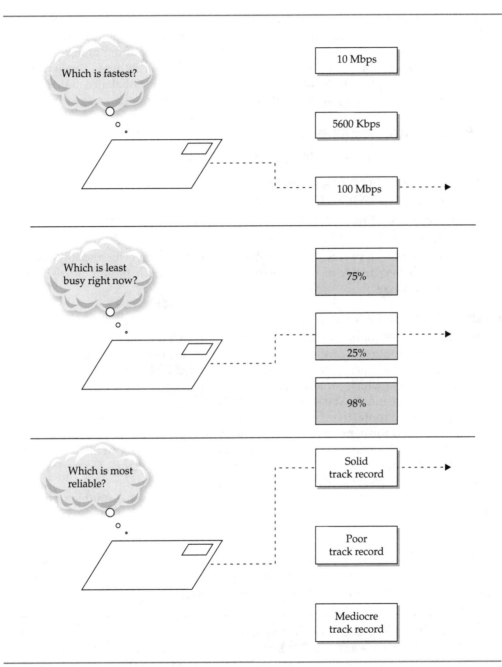

Figure 15-13. Routing metrics are used to influence decisions that routing algorithms make.

All Cisco routing protocols come with default settings for metrics. These default settings are based on design calculations made in Cisco's labs and on real-world experience gained in the field. If you ever get your hands on a routing protocol, think long and hard before you start changing routing metric default settings. The domino effect of a bad routing metric decision can be devastating. Out-of-balance metric settings can be manifested in the form of poor network performance and routing loops.

Routing Protocol Architectures

There are three basic types of routing protocol architectures:

- **Distance-vector routing protocols**   Simple algorithms that calculate a cumulative distance value between routers based on hop count

- **Link-state routing protocols**   Sophisticated algorithms that maintain a complex database of internetwork topology

- **Hybrid routing protocols**   A combination of distance-vector and link-state methods that tries to incorporate the advantages of both and minimize their disadvantages

Distance-Vector Routing

Early distance-vector routing protocols used only a so-called distance metric to calculate the best route to a destination. The distance is the number of router hops to the destination. Distance-vector algorithms (also called Bellman-Ford algorithms) operate a protocol in which routers pass routing table updates to their immediate neighbors in all directions. At each exchange, the router increments the distance value received for a route, thereby applying its own distance value to it. The updated table is then passed further outward, where receiving routers repeat the process. The fundamental theory is that each router doesn't need to know all about other links, just whether they are there and what the approximate distance is to them. Figure 15-14 depicts the distance-vector routing update process.

Distance-vector routing can be slow to converge. This is because routing updates are triggered by timers to take place at predetermined intervals, not in response to a network event that causes a topology change. This makes it harder for distance-vector protocols to respond quickly to the state of a link's current operating condition. If a network link goes down, the distance-vector system must wait until the next timed update cycle sweeps past the downed link to pick it up and pass an updated routing table—minus the downed link—through the internetwork.

NOTE   The name "distance-vector" can be confusing, because some advanced distance-vector protocols use routing metrics other than theoretical distance. In fact, some newer so-called "distance-vector installations" only partially rely on the hop count metric. The best way to think of distance-vector protocols is that they update routing topologies at fixed intervals.

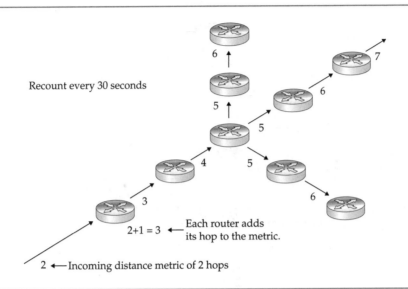

Figure 15-14. Distance-vector routing propagates routing updates at fixed intervals.

Relying on fixed-interval updates renders distance-vector protocols slow to converge on topology changes and, therefore, more susceptible to routing loops. Also, most distance-vector protocols are limited to 16 hops and are generally used in internetworks with fewer than 50 routers.

Despite their unsophisticated ways, distance-vector protocols are by far the most widely used. Although the distance-vector method is simple and easy to configure, it doesn't scale well. On the other hand, because it doesn't do a lot of calculating, it consumes little router CPU or memory resources. Generally, distance-vector algorithms are good enough to adapt to topology changes encountered in smaller internetworks. The most widely installed distance-vector routing protocols are RIP and the now depreciated IGRP.

Link-State Routing

Link-state routing is event driven. Also known as *shortest path first (SPF)*, link-state routing protocols focus on the state of the internetwork links that form routes. Whenever a link's state changes, a routing update called a *link-state advertisement (LSA)* is exchanged between routers. When a router receives an LSA routing update, the link-state algorithm is used to recalculate the shortest path to affected destinations. Link-state routing attempts to always maintain full knowledge of the internetwork's topology by updating itself incrementally whenever a change occurs. Figure 15-15 depicts the link-state process.

The link-state algorithm does much more than just have a router add its local distance value to a cumulative distance. After an LSA update is received, each router

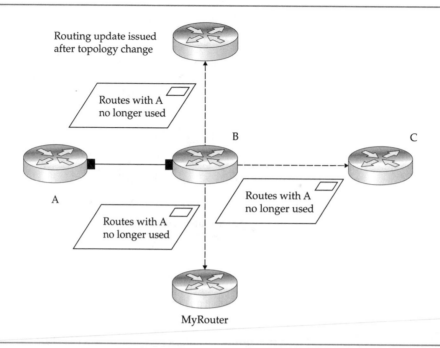

Figure 15-15. Link-state routing is event driven.

uses the algorithm to calculate a *shortest path tree* to all destinations. Link-state calculations are based on the Dijkstra algorithm. This process yields entirely new routes instead of merely applying new distance values to preexisting routes. Think of it this way: Distance-vector routing places a new value on the same old route; link-state routing's SPF algorithm builds whole new routes piece by piece, from the link up. SPF is able to do this because the link-state database contains complete information on the internetwork's components and its topology.

New routes calculated by SPF are entered into the updated routing table. These entries include recalculated values for all metrics configured for use in the link-state implementation. Possible metrics include cost, delay, bandwidth, reliability, and others, with their values updated to reflect the new route. This is done by rolling up metric information for each link incorporated into the newly calculated route. Figure 15-16 shows how the SPF algorithm picks the best route.

There are two other advantages to link-state routing, and both have to do with bandwidth conservation. First, because LSA updates contain only information about affected paths, routing updates travel faster and consume less bandwidth. Second, in distance-vector routing, most update cycles are wasted because they take place even though there was no topology change. Unnecessary update cycles not only increase bandwidth overhead, but also boost the odds that conflicting routing updates will be

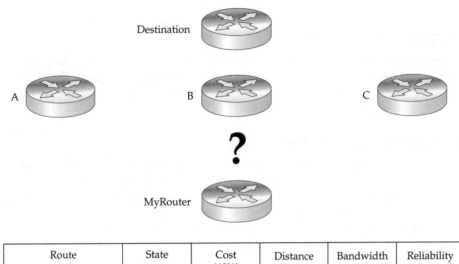

Destination

A   B   C

?

MyRouter

Route	State	Cost (40%)	Distance (10%)	Bandwidth (20%)	Reliability (30%)
Via Router A	Down	100	5	100	75
Via Router B	Up	50	5	100	75
Via Router C	Up	100	4	1,000	100

Figure 15-16. Link-state routing's SPF algorithm builds the shortest paths from the link up.

converging simultaneously. By issuing LSA updates when required—in addition to their regular update intervals—link-state protocols diminish the opportunity for the self-perpetuating conflicts of routing loops.

Because link-state protocols are event driven, adaptation to topology change need not wait for a series of preset timers to go off before the convergence process can begin. This not only makes link-state protocols less prone to loops, but also makes them more powerful in that there is no limit on the number of hops in the routes they calculate.

The drawbacks to link-state routing protocols mainly have to do with logistics and expense. During the initial stages of implementation, LSA traffic tends to flood an internetwork with database building control messages, making implementation expensive. Because it does so much more calculating, link-state routing also can consume considerable router CPU and memory resources when recalculation is necessary. This means that those considering an upgrade to a link-state routing protocol must face the prospect of spending money on equipment upgrades. Yet perhaps the biggest hurdle to link-state protocols is that they're complicated. These are sophisticated routing protocols that can be intimidating to network administrators, especially those set in their ways. The best-known link-state protocols are OSPF and IS-IS.

Hybrid Routing

Hybrid routing protocols use more accurate distance-vector metrics in a protocol designed to converge more rapidly. Although open standards have been developed for so-called "hybridized routing," the only Cisco product based on the concept is the Enhanced Interior Gateway Routing Protocol (EIGRP).

How Routing Protocols Are Implemented

Much like firewalls, routing protocols take their own particular view of the internetwork landscape. To a firewall, networks are either *inside* or *outside*, and connections are controlled accordingly. Routing protocols have as their overriding concern the gathering and dissemination of updated topologies, not connections. Thus, routing protocols define the networking landscape in terms of *interior* and *exterior*, where one routing domain ends and another begins. This is because a router needs to know which other routers are part of its own routing domain (are in the interior) and, therefore, should share routing updates.

Autonomous Systems

Administrative control is defined as who controls the configuration of equipment in a network. Because the Internet interconnects so many organizational entities, it has developed the concept of an autonomous system. An *autonomous system* is defined as a collection of networks that are under the administrative control of a single organization and that share a common routing strategy. Most autonomous systems are internetworks operated by corporations, Internet service providers (ISPs), government agencies, and universities.

Looking at the three autonomous systems in Figure 15-17, you can see that each regards the other two as exterior (or external) autonomous systems. This is because the other two are under the administrative control of someone else, and they are running a separate *routing strategy* (a term used to describe the fact that routing updates are being exchanged under a common routing protocol configuration). Thus, a routing strategy implies running a single routing process to exchange updates and sharing other configuration parameters, such as the relative settings of each path's metrics.

The three autonomous systems in Figure 15-17 could be running the same routing protocol software—even the same *version* of the same routing protocol—but because the autonomous systems aren't within the same routing process of update messages and relative metrics settings, they don't share a common routing strategy.

The Difference Between Interior and Exterior Gateway Protocols

So what we have, then, is a nice, neat little package where routing domains and administrative domains overlay one another, right? Well, as always seems to be the case in internetworking, things aren't quite so tidy. If routing strategy were as simple

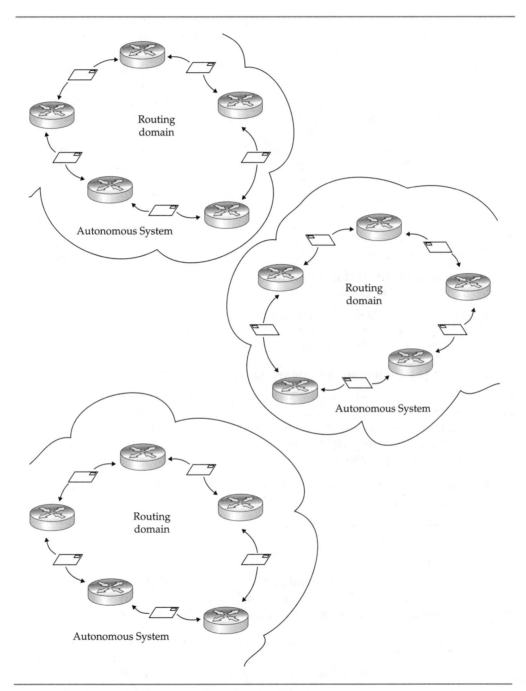

Figure 15-17. Routing protocols draw maps largely based on administrative control.

as configuring one routing protocol for every administrative domain, there could be no Internet. After all, if everything were internal, who or what would coordinate routing updates between the millions of autonomous systems making up the Internet?

The answer is exterior gateway protocols. An *exterior gateway protocol* runs on routers sitting at the edge of an autonomous system and exchanges routes with other autonomous systems. These edge routers are also called *border routers, boundary routers,* or *gateway routers.* A routing protocol that operates within an autonomous system is an *interior gateway protocol.* Figure 15-18 shows the two side by side.

In practical terms, the most obvious difference between the two is where the routers running the protocol sit in the topology. Exterior routers sit at the edge of autonomous systems; interior gateway routers sit toward the middle. A closer inspection of how the exterior protocols are implemented brings out more fundamental differences:

- An exterior protocol lets an autonomous system designate certain other routers as peers. The border router exchanges updates with its peer routers and ignores other routers (in interior protocols, all routers participate in router updates).

- Routing tables maintained by exterior protocols are lists of autonomous systems (interior protocols keep lists of LAN segments).

- Exterior protocols simply insert a new route received for a destination into the routing table; no recalculation of new best paths is computed after an update is received (interior protocols recalculate new routes based on weighted metrics).

Methods That Let Autonomous Systems Interconnect

Reaching beyond an autonomous system invites potential trouble. For a firewall, the potential trouble is a security breach. For an exterior gateway protocol, the trouble can be either bad information about routes to other autonomous systems or just too much information to handle. The problems inherent in connecting to the outside also hold for exterior and interior protocols alike:

- Without some way to filter route exchanges, exterior protocols would be overwhelmed by a torrent of traffic flowing in from the Internet.

- Interior protocols could be confused about the best connections to take to the outside without being able to identify and select from various sources providing new routes.

Interior and exterior gateway routing protocols use a set of techniques to handle these problems. As a group, these techniques are intended to cut down on the volume of routing information and to boost the reliability of new route information that is received:

- **Route summarization**   A technique that divides an internetwork into logical areas, with the area's border router advertising only a single summary route to other areas, thereby cutting down on the size of routing tables.

- **Route filtering**   Also called *administrative distance,* an add-on metric that rates the relative trustworthiness of individual networks as a source from which to learn optimal routes.

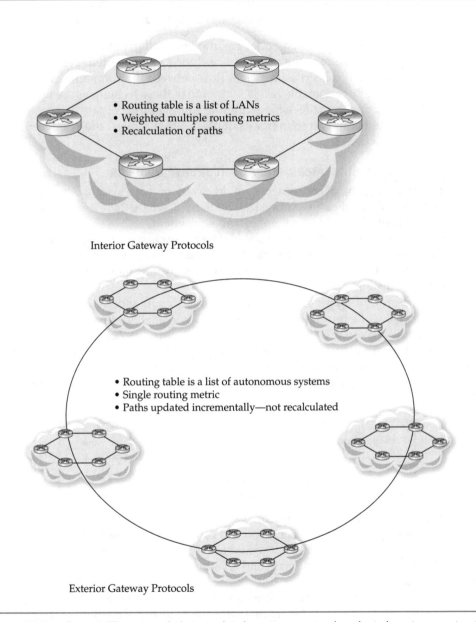

Interior Gateway Protocols

- Routing table is a list of LANs
- Weighted multiple routing metrics
- Recalculation of paths

- Routing table is a list of autonomous systems
- Single routing metric
- Paths updated incrementally—not recalculated

Exterior Gateway Protocols

Figure 15-18. Several differences exist between interior gateway protocols and exterior gateway protocols.

■ **Route tagging** A technique that tags a route in a number of ways to identify the source from which it was learned. Tags can include router ID, autonomous system number, exterior protocol ID, and exterior protocol metric.

■ **Router authentication**   In effect, this requires a communicating router to present a password before the receiving router will accept routing updates from it.

It's notable that some of the techniques are implemented in both internal and external systems, not just one or the other. This is done to enable interior and exterior routing domains to act in concert as messages flow between the autonomous system and outside world. Another notable fact is that some of these techniques are applied between interior routing domains where differing routing protocols are being run within the same autonomous system (for example, route summarization between OSPF and RIP routing processes).

Routing Domains, Routing Areas, and Administrative Domains

A *routing domain* is a group of end systems within an autonomous system. An autonomous system, in turn, is defined as an administrative domain, where there exists singular administrative control over network policy and equipment.

Most routing protocol architectures coordinate the exchange of *complete* route information between all routers in the routing domain. However, this practice can become inefficient as internetworks grow, because that means more updated traffic traveling longer distances.

State-of-the-art routing protocols use the concept of routing domain areas. A *routing area* is a subdivision of a routing domain into logically related groups, with each area uniquely identified by an area name or number. The primary benefit of areas is that route information can be summarized when exchanged between areas, cutting down on network overhead and enhancing control over traffic flow. Routing domain areas are also used to unify several smaller routing domains into a single, larger routing process.

Routing area	Routing area	Routing area
Routing domain		

The typical global enterprise implements a single routing domain worldwide. This is done so that employees on one continent can connect to company colleagues and resources anywhere in the world. So it would follow, then, that there is always a one-to-one relation between a routing domain and an administrative domain. Until recently, this was the case.

A new phenomenon called external corporate networks extends routing domains across administrative domains. An *external corporate network* is a configuration in which two or more enterprises build a unified routing domain to share routes between their respective organizations. The shared routing domain is the subset of each enterprise's overall autonomous system, and contains the resources and users that are to participate in the shared business process. Figure 15-19 illustrates how such a configuration is set up.

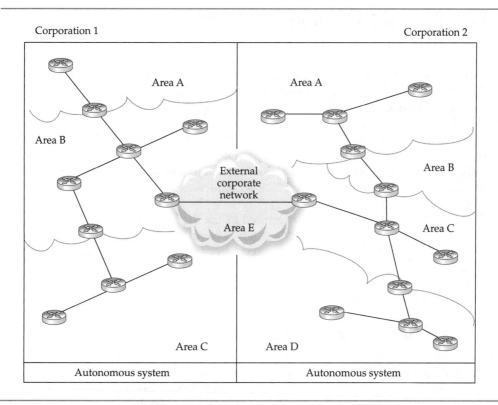

Corporation 1

Corporation 2

Area A

Area A

Area B

Area B

External
corporate
network

Area C

Area E

Area C

Area D

Autonomous system

Autonomous system

Figure 15-19. An external corporate network is a routing domain across autonomous systems.

The thing to focus on with external corporate networks is that routes are being freely exchanged between enterprises—at least within the shared routing domain area in the middle. The external corporate network configuration enables routers within two or more enterprises to keep up an ongoing dialogue on how to route cross-border connections. This is a relatively new internetworking practice. Not that long ago, the idea of directly trading route information between autonomous systems was unthinkable, not only out of concern for system security, but also for competitive reasons.

This is the most advanced form of extranet, in that one *system* is allowed behind another's firewall. Think of it this way: Most extranets involve a person logging on through a firewall by entering a username and password. In the example in Figure 15-19, the system of one enterprise is able to freely conduct business behind the firewall of another, system to system (not person to system). Harking back to the coverage of firewalls in Chapter 10, in an external corporate network, the extranet is *route based,* not *connection based.* Put another way, routes are shared between enterprises for long-term use. In the traditional extranet relationship, a user is allowed to connect to a resource on a per-session basis.

Overview of Cisco Routing Protocols

When internetworking started to take off during the mid-1980s, internetworks were smaller and simpler. The interior gateway protocol of choice back then was Routing Information Protocol (RIP). At that time, the two predominant proprietary networks were IBM SNA and Digital Equipment's DECnet implementation of Ethernet, each with its own routing scheme. But at the time, the "open" networking market was booming, with Unix servers connecting to Novell's NetWare IPX LANs. RIP shipped with most Unix server systems and emerged as the de facto standard. Thus, RIP is an open standard, not a Cisco proprietary technology.

RIP is simple to understand, easy to configure, and works well enough for small, homogeneous networks. To this day, RIP is still the most widely installed routing protocol in the world.

But the early versions of RIP were limited to just the hop-count metric. This didn't provide the routing flexibility needed to manage complex environments. Also, RIP was slow to converge, and thus limited to a maximum hop count of 16. Configure a longer route and the user will encounter a "destination unreachable" message. As a distance-vector protocol, RIP issues routing updates at a fixed interval. (The default update interval for most RIP products is every 90 seconds.)

Cisco's Interior Gateway Routing Protocol

It gradually became apparent that RIP was a roadblock to continued internetwork expansion. The 16-hop-limit, single-metric scheme constrained network size and capacity, partly due to RIP being a classful routing protocol. Cisco seized the opportunity by devising a replacement routing technology that did away with most of RIP's disadvantages: a more robust distance-vector protocol named IGRP (Interior Gateway Routing Protocol).

IGRP, a company-proprietary extension of the open RIP standard, was first released by Cisco in 1986 for IP only. In the succeeding years, IGRP implemented support for other network-layer protocols (IPX, AppleTalk, and so on), and it became the standard in customer shops using only Cisco equipment. By around 1990, RIP's limitations had become apparent, and IGRP was positioned as its general replacement for client/server networks.

Many observers regard IGRP as the single most important factor behind Cisco's explosive growth. The competition had devised OSPF as their primary replacement to RIP—but it was (and still is) limited to IP-only networks. Cisco was able to couple IGRP's superior functionality with the 1990s' Unix/Internet juggernaut to attain the market dominance it enjoys today.

IGRP was a major departure in that it used multiple metrics: distance, delay, bandwidth, reliability, and load. This advance was a big deal, because it enabled network administrators to get a handle on increasing network complexity and provide better service. Figure 15-20 compares IGRP's features with RIP's.

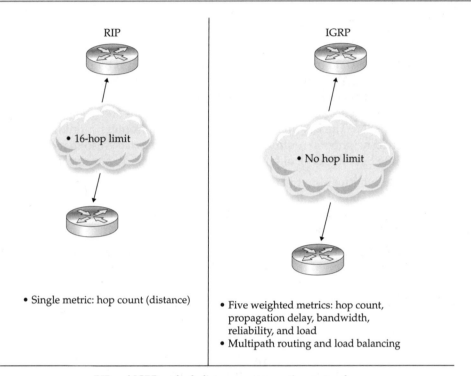

RIP

IGRP

- 16-hop limit

- No hop limit

- Single metric: hop count (distance)

- Five weighted metrics: hop count, propagation delay, bandwidth, reliability, and load
- Multipath routing and load balancing

RIP and IGRP are both distance-vector routing protocols in that fixed-interval routing update cycles are used.

Figure 15-20. Cisco's IGRP eclipsed RIP and helped vault the company to its dominant market position.

A big virtue of IGRP is the granularity of its metrics. For example, being able to set parameters for reliability or load to any value between 1 and 255 gives administrators the granularity needed to finely tune IGRP route selection. IGRP's ability to specify alternate routes boosts reliability and performance. This provides redundancy, so if a link goes down, the IGRP routing algorithm dynamically begins to steer traffic to the secondary route. Multipath routing also introduced *load balancing*—the ability to dynamically shift traffic between alternate routes, depending on how busy each is. These were important benefits during a period when most internetworks were in their infancy and prone to slowing to a crawl or going out altogether.

In 1994, Cisco augmented IGRP with a product called Enhanced Interior Gateway Routing Protocol (EIGRP). EIGRP is a substantial advance over its predecessor—so much so that Cisco touts it as a hybrid routing protocol instead of a mere distance-vector protocol. In fact, Cisco has completely depreciated IGRP as of IOS 12.3.

EIGRP combines the advantages of link-state protocols with those of distance-vector protocols. It provides superior convergence properties and operating efficiency. Here are the key EIGRP features:

- **DUAL finite state machine**   The software engine used by the EIGRP algorithm. DUAL (Diffusing Update Algorithm) is used to provide loop-free operation at every instant throughout a route computation. DUAL allows routers to synchronize route changes and does not involve routers unaffected by the change. The key architectural feature is that routers running DUAL store all of their neighbors' routing tables (called *neighbor tables)* so that they can more intelligently recalculate alternate paths in order to speed convergence.

- **Variable-length subnet masks (VLSMs)**   The ability to automatically summarize subnet routes at the edge of a subnet. Before VLSM, routing protocols such as RIP could not build routes with subnet addresses included. All subnets had to be the same.

- **Partial updates**   Also called *event-triggered updates,* this means routing updates are issued only when the topology has changed. This saves control message overhead.

- **Bounded updates**   The method whereby routing update messages are sent only to those routers affected by the topology change. This saves overhead and helps speed convergence.

- **Reliable Transport Protocol (RTP)**   A protocol guaranteeing the orderly delivery of priority update packets to neighbor routers. RTP works by classifying control message traffic into four priority groups: Hello/ACKs, updates, queries and replies, and requests. Only updates and queries/replies are sent *reliably.* By not sending Hellos/ACKs or requests reliably, resources are freed to guarantee the delivery of message types more critical to EIGRP's internal operations.

It is commonplace for enterprises using Cisco hardware to migrate their internetworks from IGRP to EIGRP over time. EIGRP routers can be operated as compatible with IGRP routers. The metrics between the two are directly translatable. EIGRP does this by treating IGRP routes as external networks, which allows the network administrator to customize routes to them. EIGRP advertises three types of routes:

- **Internal routes**   Routes between subnets in a network attached to a router's interface. If the network is not subnetted, no interior routes are advertised for that network.

- **System routes**   Routes to networks within the autonomous system. System routes are compiled from routing updates passed within the internetwork. Subnets are not included in system routing updates.

- **External routes**   Routes learned from another routing domain or those entered into the routing table as static routes. These routes are tagged individually to track their origin.

Figure 15-21 shows the interplay between these three types of EIGRP routes. Breaking down routes into these three categories facilitates advanced functions within the EIGRP algorithm. The internal routes designation enables EIGRP to support variable-length subnet masks; external routes make it possible for EIGRP to exchange routes that are discovered outside the autonomous system.

NOTE Although EIGRP has been proprietary for years, at 2013's Cisco Live! in London, the company announced its intent to release EIGRP to the IETF as an Informational RFC. This means that EIGRP will be available as an open standard, usable by any vendor. That said, Cisco will retain control of EIGRP to protect customer investments and maintain the level of customer experience that we all expect, hence the "Informational" framing of the RFC. There will be some advanced features, such as EIGRP stub, that Cisco will not be releasing, and thus will only be available on Cisco products.

General Configuration Steps of a Cisco Routing Protocol

Configuring any Cisco routing protocol is largely a matter of setting its options. The number of steps is a function of how many options the routing protocol has for you to set. The more options a routing protocol has to set, the more commands there are for you to use. Because all Cisco routing protocols are implemented within IOS software, the initial configuration steps are the same. Table 15-1 explains the standard IOS routing protocol configuration steps.

Routing domains are built router by router. In other words, because routing protocols are peer arrangements, the routing process must be configured in each router that

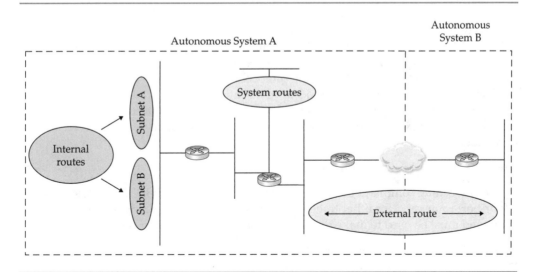

Figure 15-21. EIGRP defines three types of routes: internal, system, and external.

Configuration Step	Description
Initialize and number the routing process.	The routing protocol must be running on a router so it can begin exchanging routing updates with other routers. This is done using the **router** command and giving the new routing domain an autonomous system number.
Configure LANs into the routing domain.	The **network** command is used to configure networks into the routing domain.
Set other routing protocol parameters.	Once the routing domain is constructed, its behavior is specified by using the routing protocol's various commands from the **(config-router)#** prompt.

Table 15-1.   Initial Steps to Configure Cisco's Routing Protocols

will be included in the routing domain. This is done by working with each router's configuration file individually. Once all the routing processes are configured on all the routers in the internetwork, the routing domain is complete.

Configuring EIGRP

The **router** command initializes the routing process on a router. In this example, an EIGRP for autonomous system 999 is turned on in a router called MyRouter:

```
MyRouter(config)#router eigrp 999
MyRouter(config-router)#
```

An autonomous system number must be given in order to start a routing process. IOS uses the autonomous system number to distinguish one routing process from others. Notice that the IOS prompt changed to **MyRouter(config-router)#** when the **eigrp 999** routing process was invoked. All routing protocol parameters are set from this prompt.

The **network** command is used to start the routing protocol running over specific networks. The network must be connected to a corresponding interface on the router. Sticking with our example, the following command would make network 10.1.13.0 part of the routing process:

```
MyRouter(config-router)#network 10.1.13.0
```

The preceding command initializes EIGRP across network 10.1.13.0. If MyRouter is a four-port router and the other three LAN segments are also to run EIGRP, the **network** command must be used to make them part of the **eigrp 999** routing process also:

```
MyRouter(config)#router eigrp 999
MyRouter(config)# network 10.1.14.0

MyRouter(config)# network 10.1.15.0

MyRouter(config)# network 209.168.98.32
```

Now the EIGRP routing process is running across all four of MyRouter's LAN segments, subnets 10.1.13.0–10.1.15.0, and network 209.168.98.32.

 NOTE   When you're establishing a routing configuration on NX-OS, the setup is the inverse of IOS. Routing protocols are enabled globally, and EIGRP settings regarding interfaces are set directly on those affected interfaces. This is a departure from IOS. You'll notice many "gotchas" like this when learning NX-OS.

Each routing protocol has its own command set. These commands reflect the protocol's particular capabilities. Once a routing protocol is initialized, its commands are used to set various parameters in the configuration file to tune the behavior of the routing process as it operates in that router. EIGRP's command set is listed in Table 15-2.

Given that this is an introductory guide, we won't go into the commands for EIGRP or the other Cisco protocols—each one has its own complete command reference manual. But looking at the commands in Table 15-2 gives you a notion of how the concepts introduced in this chapter are implemented. Let's take one example of an advanced command to give you an idea of how things work:

```
MyRouter(config-router)#metric maximum-hops 25
```

EIGRP Command	Description
auto-summary	Enables automatic network number summarization
default	Sets a command to its defaults
default-information	Controls distribution of default information
default-metric	Sets the metric of redistributed routes
distance	Defines an administrative distance
distribute-listeigrp	Filters networks in routing updates (used with commands that are specific to EIGRP)
maximum-paths	Forwards packets over multiple paths
metric	Modifies IGRP routing metrics and parameters
neighbor	Specifies a neighbor router
network	Enables routing on an IP network
offset-list	Adds or subtracts offset from IGRP or RIP metrics
passive-interface	Suppresses routing updates on an interface
redistribute	Redistributes information from another routing protocol
timers	Adjusts routing timers
traffic-share	Computes traffic share for alternate routes
variance	Controls the load-balancing variance

Table 15-2.   EIGRP's Command Set

What the preceding command does is set a maximum network diameter for the routing domain. *Network diameter* is a limit on how many hops a route may have before the routing protocol stops advertising it. The setting in this use of the **maximum-hops** command will enforce a limit of 25 hops. Should the router receive a routing update with 26 or more hops indicated in its distance metric, the router will decline to enter it into its routing table. The **maximum-hops** command is an easy way to limit the kind of traffic a router will carry.

Configuring RIP 2

Although the severe limitations of early RIP versions opened the door for EIGRP, the competition fought back. The Internet Engineering Task Force (IETF) oversaw the release of the RIP 2 open standard in 1998. RIP 2 has most of the advanced functionality of other state-of-the-art interior gateway protocols such as EIGRP and OSPF. None of the improvements are unique to RIP 2, but they go a long way toward catching up RIP's functionality with other routing protocols. The IETF felt this was a good thing because RIP has such a huge installed base and is still quite useful for small internetworks.

But even with its advances, the use of RIP 2 is still limited to smaller internetworks by its 16-hop limit. Also, RIP 2 still issues routing updates on a fixed-interval cycle, causing it to converge more slowly than EIGRP or OSPF.

Configuring RIP 2 involves the same generic commands as other Cisco routing protocols, where the commands must be used to initialize the routing process on the router and its networks:

```
MyRouter(config)#router rip
MyRouter(config-router)#version 2
MyRouter(config-router)#network 209.11.244.9
```

You'll notice that no autonomous system number was entered (as in **router rip 999**) because neither RIP nor RIP 2 supports this. Also, the command to initialize RIP 2 is **router rip**. The version of RIP is defined by running the version command from the router configuration mode, as previously shown, when in router config mode. If the version command is omitted, then the router defaults to sending RIPv1, but can receive both RIPv1 and RIPv2.

```
MyRouter(config-router)#version ?
  <1-2>  version
```

Once the RIP 2 process is launched, configuring it is a matter of setting its other parameters. In RIP 2, these include router authentication using the **rip authentication** command, route summarization using the **auto-summary** command, and validation of the IP addresses of routers sending routing updates using the **validate-update-source** command.

Let's take a look at a sample RIP 2 command that's more generic in nature. The **timers basic** command is used to set the routing update intervals within an RIP routing domain. The default is 30-second intervals. If you wanted to change the routing update frequency to every 25 seconds, you'd enter the following command:

```
MyRouter(config-router)#timers basic 25
```

However, changing basic metrics such as this is discouraged. Making updates five seconds more frequently will help speed convergence, but will increase network overhead by causing more routing messages.

Configuring Open Shortest Path First

In 1991, the industry moved to establish what could best be called an open standard replacement for RIP. The result was OSPF (Open Shortest Path First), which, as the name implies, is an open standard used to seek out shortest-path routes just like RIP. But that's where the similarities end. OSPF is a link-state (not distance-vector) routing protocol. OSPF converges faster than RIP and operates under the link-state concept, in which each router keeps a database of all links in a network and information on any delays it might be experiencing. In addition, OSPF saves control message overhead by issuing routing updates only on an event-driven basis.

OSPF Routing Areas

Most OSPF features are designed to help cope with internetwork size. The central concept behind OSPF is internetwork areas. As stated earlier in the chapter, an *area* is a zone within an autonomous system that is composed of a logical set of network segments and their attached devices. The areas are used by the routing system as a strategy to control traffic flow and sift out unwanted routing table details. Every OSPF domain must have a backbone area with number 0, and all inter-area routing must pass through area 0, as displayed next. Areas are created by using the keyword **area** as an argument with the **network** command, as shown next:

```
MyRouter(config-router)#network 10.0.0.0  0.255.255.255 area 0
```

This command puts the subnet 10.0.0.0 into OSPF area 0. It's possible to run a one-area OSPF network, having only an area 0. Figure 15-22 shows a three-area OSPF network.

A key functionality of OSPF is that it can redirect routing updates between areas. *Redirect* is a routing update that passes through one or more areas of a routing domain, usually through a number of filters designed to cut down routing update traffic.

OSPF networks are frequently used to tie together preexisting routing domains, such as RIP internetworks. This is done by creating an OSPF area for each RIP domain and passing routing updates between them through the OSPF backbone (area 0). The routers at the edges of the areas are called *autonomous system boundary routers* (or *ASBRs,* for short). The ASBRs sit between the OSPF autonomous system and the RIP networks, and run both OSPF and RIP protocols.

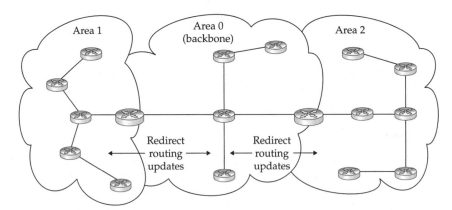

Area boundary Routers A and B selectively redirect
routing updates between OSPF routing domain areas.

Figure 15-22.   OSPF implements routing areas and redirects routes between them.

Variable-Length Subnet Masks

Whereas Variable-Length Subnet Mask (VLSM) support is available in EIGRP and
RIPv2, it is a critical feature for OSPF due to the size of the routing tables used on the
Internet. Respective areas often have their own subnet schemes that fit their particular
needs. In Figure 15-23, all the serial-line-based networks in area 0 use the .252 subnet
mask, typical for long-distance connections. This is because the .252 mask allows up to
64 subnets, but only two hosts per subnet. Although the subnet mask could vary, based
on a given set of requirements, this is ideal for networks composed of a serial-line
connection because only two hosts are needed: one at each end of the line.

Each of the other end-system areas uses its own scheme. Area 1 uses the .248 mask
(yielding a maximum of 32 subnets and six hosts each), area 2 uses the .192 mask (up
to four subnets with 62 hosts each), and area 3 uses the .224 mask (up to eight subnets
with 30 hosts each).

VLSM support means that the routes exchanged in updates passed among the OSPF
areas can include the subnet addresses (instead of just the network address). This is an
important feature, because it allows complete routes to be shared across areas using
differing subnet schemes, which means each area can use only the amount of address
space required for its needs. For example, in area 0 in Figure 15-23, there are only a few
hosts connected to the serial lines, and being able to use the .248 masks lets area 0 use
up only a few addresses (a .248 mask has only six hosts per subnet).

Even with all of OSPF's power, it would be hard to scale internetwork size very
much without VLSM. This is because most LANs use subnetted addressing schemes
in order to conserve precious IP address space. OSPF areas make possible large-scale
expansion of routing domains and, therefore, internetwork size. VLSM enables routers to

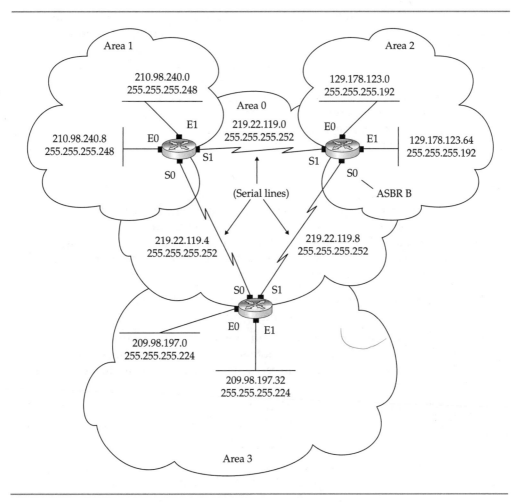

Figure 15-23. The Variable-Length Subnet Mask feature makes areas possible.

have full address visibility between areas, and thus route traffic within internetworks with much greater efficiency.

Border Gateway Protocol

The Border Gateway Protocol (BGP) is the high-level routing protocol that makes the Internet possible. Optimized to coordinate internetworking between autonomous systems, BGP is, at this point, virtually the only exterior gateway protocol in use today.

There are several versions of BGP, and Cisco IOS supports all of them. BGP version 2 is defined in RFC 1163, version 3 in RFC 1267, and version 4 in RFC 1771. It's a worthwhile read for those interested in digging deeper into BGP. But for now, let's keep it above ground.

EIGRP and OSPF let network operators scale their internetworks to large capacities, but it is BGP that ties them all together along so-called Internet trunks or peer networks. Most networking types will never work with BGP; its use is mainly left to ISP administrators concerned with discovering routes across high-speed backbones. However, it's helpful to briefly review how BGP fits in.

The predominance of a single exterior routing protocol is unsurprising in light of the fact that the world's network operators need a single standard to integrate the millions of autonomous systems operating in the world. If the industry hadn't settled on BGP as the common platform, some other exterior gateway protocol would be the de facto standard instead.

BGP Routing

Like interior gateway protocols, BGP uses routing update messages and metrics to maintain routing tables. BGP is a modified link-state architecture routing protocol, but obviously is radically different in architecture to be able to scale to Internet growth. BGP's architecture is characterized by the use of route aggregation and the ability to work with interior gateway protocols. BGP supports three types of routing:

- **Inter-autonomous system** Inter-autonomous system routing is the basic function of BGP in the Internet routing operations.

- **Intra-autonomous system** Intra-autonomous system routing is performed by BGP when two or more BGP routers operate inside the same autonomous system. This is generally seen in cases in which it's necessary to cross a large internetwork from one edge to the other.

- **Pass-through autonomous system** Pass-through autonomous system routing occurs when it is necessary for BGP traffic to traverse a non-BGP autonomous system in order to connect to another BGP autonomous system.

As an exterior gateway routing protocol optimized to scale to Internet size, BGP differs sharply from interior protocols in some fundamental ways:

- **Peer routers** The network administrator specifies a list of BGP routers representing other autonomous systems (usually other ISPs or large internetwork portals). This is done because it isn't feasible to pass routing updates through a worldwide routing domain.

- **Routing table contents** A table entry in BGP is an autonomous system (not a LAN, as it is in an interior gateway protocol). Each route consists of a network number and a list of autonomous systems that must be passed through, called an AS path.

- **Static routing metrics** BGP uses several static metrics to determine the best path to a given network. These metrics consist of arbitrary numbers to weigh the degree of preference to a particular link. It's not dynamic; it must be input and updated by a network administrator. The most important metrics are WEIGHT, LOCAL_PREF, and whether the route is local or learned (aggregated). Did we mention that it's statically configured?

■ **Incremental route updates**   When a routing update is received, BGP simply replaces the old route with the new one. No best path recalculation is done because maintaining a link-state database on the Internet's topology is not feasible.

Cisco's implementation of BGP supports each router establishing a set of neighbors, or peers, with which to exchange reachability information. A variety of techniques is used to aggregate routes to help simplify route processing and to reduce the size of routing tables. One is the use of *route maps*—a practice that restricts the dissemination of routing updates to certain routers. Another is the use of a simplified form of administrative distance, where, instead of having the choice among 255 relative weightings, a route can take on any of three trustworthiness ratings, depending on the topology position of the router.

BGP's key facet is its ability to filter, reduce, and simplify the routing information it gathers from the Internet.

Multiprotocol Label Switching

Another way to route packets through an internetwork is with a protocol that streamlines the whole process. Multiprotocol Label Switching (MPLS) is a way to forward packets through an internetwork. Routers situated on the edge of a network apply simple labels to packets. Then routers, switches, or other network devices within the network can switch packets based on the labels. This process is ideal, because it requires minimal lookup overhead.

How It Works

Conventional layer-3 IP routing is based on the exchange of network availability information. As a packet winds its way through a network, each router makes decisions about where the packet will be sent next. This information is based on information in layer 3 of the header, and is used as an index for a routing table lookup to determine the packet's next hop. This process is repeated at each router in the network. At each hop, the router has to resolve the next destination for the packet.

The downside of this process is that the information within the IP packets—information about precedence or VPN data, for example—is not considered when forwarding packets. For best performance, only the destination address is considered, but, because other fields within the packet could be relevant, an in-depth header analysis must take place at each router along the packet's path.

MPLS streamlines this process by placing a *label* on each packet. Think of conventional IP routing like addressing a letter. It tells the post office where to send the letter. MPLS takes addressing to another level by adding extra instructions—like writing "Perishable" or "Do Not Bend" on the envelope.

The label includes important information about the packet, including:

■ Destination

■ Precedence

■ A specific route for the packet, if one is needed

■ Virtual private network membership

■ Quality of Service (QoS) information

MPLS causes the layer-3 header analysis to be performed only twice—at the edge label switch router (LSR) as it enters and exits an internetwork. At the LSR, the layer-3 header is mapped into a fixed-length label and applied to the packet. Figure 15-24 shows how a label is applied to a packet.

The 32-bit MPLS header contains the following fields, as numbered in Figure 15-24:

■ The label field (20 bits) carries the actual value of the MPLS label.

■ The Class of Service (CoS) field (3 bits) can affect the queuing and discard algorithms applied to the packet as it is transmitted through the network.

■ The Stack (S) field (1 bit) supports a hierarchical label stack.

■ The TTL (time-to-live) field (8 bits) provides conventional IP TTL functionality.

Next, as the packet crosses the routers in an internetwork, only the label needs to be read. Once it reaches the other end of the network, another edge LSR removes the label, replacing it with the appropriate header data linked to that label.

A key result of this arrangement is that forwarding decisions based on some or all of these different sources of information can be achieved by means of a single table lookup from a fixed-length label. Label switching is the merger of switching and routing functions—it combines the availability information of routers with the traffic engineering benefits of switches.

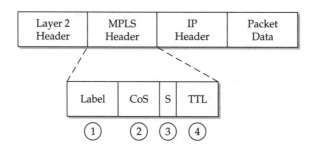

Figure 15-24. MPLS packets contain seven fields.

Benefits

MPLS offers many advantages over traditional IP and ATM routing protocols. Label switching and hardware switching work together to deliver high degrees of performance. For multiservice networks, MPLS allows a switch to provide ATM, Frame Relay, and IP services on a single platform. This is ideal, because supporting all these services on a single platform is not only cost effective, but it also simplifies provisioning for multiservice providers.

The following benefits highlight some of the usefulness of MPLS:

- **Integration** MPLS combines IP and ATM functionality, making the ATM infrastructure visible to IP routing and eliminating the need for mappings between IP and ATM features.

- **VPN performance** With an MPLS backbone, VPN information need only be processed where packets enter and exit the network. In addition, BGP is used to deal with VPN information. The use of both MPLS and BGP makes MPLS-based VPN services easier to manage and much more scalable.

- **Reduction of burden on core services** Because MPLS examines packets when they enter and exit a network, internal transit routers and switches need only process the connectivity with the provider's edge routers. This prevents the core devices from becoming overwhelmed with the routing volume exchanged over the Internet.

- **Traffic engineering capabilities** MPLS's traffic-engineering capabilities enable network administrators to shift the traffic load from overburdened sections to underused sections of the network, based on traffic destination, type, load, and time of day.

The MPLS Network Structure

An MPLS network has three basic components:

- **Edge label switch routers** Edge LSRs are situated at the physical and logical boundaries of a network. These devices are usually routers (like the Cisco 12000), but can also be multilayer LAN switches (like the Cisco Catalyst 6500) or a proxy device.

- **Label switches** These devices switch packets based on the labels. In addition, label switches may also support layer-3 routing or layer-2 switching. An example of a label switch is the Cisco 6500.

- **Label Distribution Protocol** The Label Distribution Protocol (LDP) is used alongside network layer routing protocols and distributes label information between MPLS network devices.

MPLS provides internetworks with an unprecedented level of control over traffic, resulting in a network that is more efficient, supports more predictable service, and can offer the flexibility required to meet constantly changing networking situations.

Cisco's Routing Protocol Strategy

The move around 1990 to replace RIP with a more robust interior gateway protocol was a key moment in the history of the internetworking industry. (Keep in mind that 1990 is ancient history in Internet time.) The ability to scale beyond 16 hops or a network diameter of 50 routers was sorely needed. Faster convergence was also on the critical list, because loops were becoming a pressing problem.

Cisco exploited the moment by promoting IGRP as a RIP replacement. This was a risk, because IGRP was (and is) a proprietary standard. But the strategy was wildly successful because it solved customers' needs to continue internetwork expansion and, at the same time, persuaded network managers to standardize on Cisco equipment. Most of those that did have since migrated to EIGRP.

OSPF is an IP-only routing protocol. The technology planners on the OSPF Working Group were right to promote a RIP replacement. The reality is that most enterprises still have a mix of network-level protocols and need to support them using an interior gateway technology like EIGRP. This was the marketing window Cisco exploited.

Cisco supports an OSPF product as a complement to its EIGRP strategy. OSPF is a powerhouse in its own right. Most ISPs (and an increasing number of enterprises) are running large IP-only routing domains, and given the standards-setting clout of the Internet, many think that one day everybody will be IP only. OSPF has built the mission-critical infrastructure surrounding and sustaining the BGP peer networks. Without OSPF, BGP peer networks probably wouldn't be possible. Both are enabling technologies that made the explosive growth of internetworks and the Internet possible. Also, EIGRP and IGRP are only used in complete Cisco environments. When other vendor's equipment is added to the network, OSPF becomes important.

Furthermore, Cisco support of MPLS streamlines routing through internetworks. As we've seen, by affixing a header on a packet when it enters your network, then stripping it as it leaves, MPLS improves network functionality and eases the burden on core network devices. The use of MPLS is certainly beneficial when issues of network performance and capacity are involved.

Comparing the functionality of current routing protocols can be confusing. Although RIP is the lowliest of the interior gateway protocols, it has been so heavily enhanced that it now shares much of the advanced functionality available with EIGRP and OSPF. Further confusing the routing protocol landscape is that RIP and other protocols are being subsumed into OSPF domains as routing domain areas. Things get more clouded because OSPF is so scalable that it has a lot of the size-scaling functionality associated with BGP.

Suffice it to say that today's routing protocols overlap so much that they're hard to keep straight. Just keep in mind that the essential distinctions are distance-vector versus link-state architectures and interior gateway protocols versus exterior gateway protocols.

CHAPTER 16 | Network Management

We've now covered the major pieces of technology that compose internetworks. Routers, switches, firewalls, and access servers are cabled together to form network topologies. Most configurations run over twisted-pair copper feeding into fiber-optic backbones that move data at speeds from 1 Gbps up to a mind-boggling 100 Gbps. Although network devices vary in type and size, most look like PCs or servers in that they have memory, CPUs, and interface cards. They are, however, diskless, seldom have monitors, and use their interfaces to connect networks instead of peripherals.

Cisco's software infrastructure to make it all go is its various operating systems, such as the Internetwork Operating System (IOS). Compared to Microsoft Windows, IOS is a lean package of commands, protocol software, and the all-important config file. IOS software images differ greatly, depending on the type of device. The switch has a modest version of IOS, whereas the behemoth Cisco 12000 Series Gigabit Router is loaded with protocols and specialized management software packages. Regardless of device type or IOS functionality, network behavior is controlled by setting parameters in the config file.

As you saw in the previous chapter, perhaps the most sophisticated internetworking technology of all is the routing protocol. Routing protocols give internetworks a level of self-awareness and self-adaptation without which large-scale configurations wouldn't be practical. They do this by constructing a hierarchy of LANs and autonomous systems to find optimal paths to get across the office campus—or to the other side of the world.

It takes more than optimal routes to run an internetwork, though. The ability to self-operate is only part of the network management equation. Routing protocols may be able to handle most minute-to-minute issues, but internetworks still require constant management effort from people. Without persistent review and intervention from administrators, an internetwork's ability to self-operate will be overwhelmed by a progressive deterioration in operating conditions. Internetworks must be constantly updated and even upgraded to accommodate problems, growth, and change. Network teams need tools for managing change and anticipating problems (and, hopefully, avoiding them).

If left alone, even a perfectly configured internetwork will degrade under the strain of added users, increased loads, shifting traffic, new hardware and software versions, and new technology. Network administrators must monitor, reconfigure, and troubleshoot without end. The recent boom in users—and the increase in the amount of traffic generated per user—has left network teams scrambling to keep up. Routing protocols and other automated features only make effective internetwork management feasible—they don't make it easy. Network management tools are needed also. The industry's response has been a stream of standards, technologies, and products focused on the configuration and operation of internetworks.

Overview of Network Management

Network management can be confusing to newcomers. By its nature, the field involves a daunting list of tasks. Figure 16-1 outlines the range of chores performed by the typical network management team.

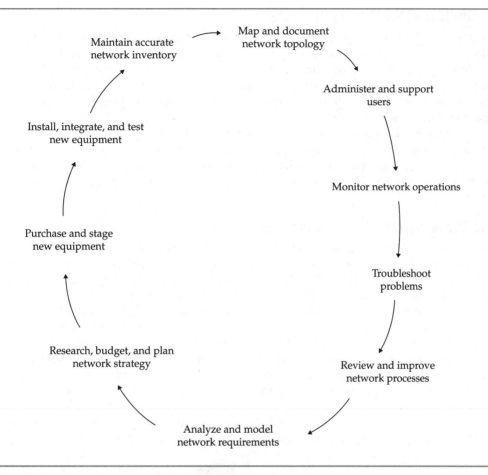

Figure 16-1. Network management tasks follow an intensive cycle.

Internetworks must be planned, modeled, budgeted, designed, configured, purchased, installed, tested, mapped, documented, operated, monitored, analyzed, optimized, adjusted, expanded, updated, and fixed. That's a lot. No single tool can do all these tasks—at least not yet. Suffice it to say that network management products and services are an industry unto themselves, composed of a complex array of technologies, products, and vendors providing everything from simple protocol analyzers that measure a single link to worldwide network command centers.

NOTE You may have noticed that the term "network management" is used in connection with internetworks. (Almost nobody manages just one LAN anymore.) The term has held on since the rise of internetworking and is still in universal use. There is no real difference between network management and internetwork management.

The Evolution of Management Tools

Historically, the problem with computer management tools has been delivering true multivendor support. In other words, it's hard to find a single tool that can handle equipment from different manufacturers equally well. Multivendor configurations—the norm in virtually all enterprise IT (information technology) infrastructures today—are tough to manage using a single tool because of subtle differences in each manufacturer's equipment.

Computer management tools have evolved from opposite poles of the computing industry: systems and networks. The goal is to bring all computing assets under the management control of a single tool, and the prevalence of placing host systems on networks is driving existing system and network management tools into one another's arms.

Traditional System Management Consoles

Sophisticated computing management systems called *system consoles* have been around for decades. These consoles were generally hooked up to mainframes sitting in a data center and used to schedule jobs, perform backups, and fix problems. Over time, they developed more and more capabilities, such as managing remote computers.

The best-known product from the data center mold is Unicenter from Computer Associates (CA). Unicenter is actually an amalgamation of products that CA has woven into a single management solution. Unicenter evolved from a sophisticated console for managing IBM mainframes and disk farms to an integrated management system with support for all the important hardware and software platforms. Most Unicenter product growth has been achieved by acquisition, which is understandable given the product scope.

The key to Unicenter and other system consoles is the ability to handle the various computer architectures that enterprises are likely to put into a configuration.

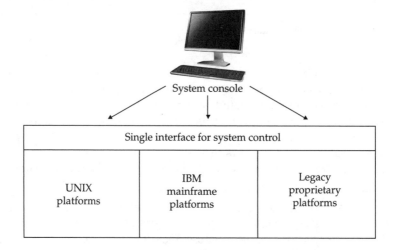

Network Management Systems

Over the past two decades, a second breed of management tool emerged in the form of network management systems. These tools focus on network infrastructure instead of the data center. They use the networks they manage as the platform for monitoring events and are controlled from a console referred to as the *network management station (NMS).*

For years, the leading NMS was OpenView from Hewlett-Packard (HP). There's a bit of history as to how HP ended up in this enviable position. HP had committed to Unix as its strategic operating system in the mid-1980s—years earlier than other enterprise platform vendors. (Don't give HP too much credit; they did so out of desperation because their proprietary 16-bit operating system had run out of gas.) By that time, Unix and IP had become closely linked in the market, mostly because IBM and other big system vendors were still pushing their proprietary networking schemes. Around 1990, HP seized the moment, and OpenView rode the Unix bandwagon to become the predominant network management tool. There are now over 100,000 OpenView installations.

As with Unicenter, the key to OpenView's success is its ability to work with devices from various manufacturers, but HP had a built-in design advantage in the form of a then-new IP network management standard called SNMP (Simple Network Management Protocol). Instead of having to design dozens of proprietary interfaces, HP was able to let the network equipment vendors design products to the SNMP standard. OpenView was the first major management product to implement SNMP.

Network management station (e.g., HP OpenView or IBM NetView)					
Device inventory	Configuration	Topology mapping	Device monitoring	Troubleshooting	Analysis
SNMP/RMON					
Routers	Switches	Hubs	Access servers	Servers	
CiscoWorks		Nortel Optivity	Others (e.g., Castle Rock, NetScout, etc.)		
Resource mgr. essentials	CWSI				

But the field is very crowded these days. A lot of times the management tool you need is dependent on what sort of system you're using. For instance, if you run a Unix shop, you'll be best served with a Unix NMS. If you run Microsoft, Active Directory would be a good call. A generic NMS—such as Splunk or ManageEngine NetFlow— offers good results, but for vendor-specific environments, tools such as OpenView and Cisco Prime Infrastructure are generally the best.

The defining difference between system and network consoles is the level at which they operate. System management tools focus on operating systems, transactions, data files, and databases as they exist across servers, storage controllers, and disks. Network management tools focus on packets and connections as they exist over network devices, interfaces, and transmission links.

System and network consoles are now converging into a single technology class some call Enterprise System Management (ESM) tools. Convergence into ESM is inevitable as the line between network and computer blurs and enterprises complete the shift to client-server architectures that move resources from the data center out into their internetwork topologies.

The focus of this book is internetworking, so we'll cover only the networking components of ESM.

Network Management Tools Today

Historically, it has proven to be quite difficult to manage an internetwork using a single tool. The major issue has been the inability to collect consistent data from the variety of devices that exist in most enterprise IT infrastructures. This problem isn't so much old versus new equipment, although that's part of it. The major hang-up is that most network management systems were shallow in their implementations; in other words, most could manage only a few aspects of device operation and would leave some devices unmanaged altogether. Consider routers, switches, application servers, access points, controllers, and so on. Generally speaking, until quite recently, Network Management Systems (NMSs) handled classes of devices individually, and integration and visibility of all that data was difficult to manage.

This is so despite the fact that all major network equipment makers bundle SNMP into their device operating systems. The base SNMP infrastructure is there, but device manufacturers (sans Cisco) historically have seldom implemented it fully within their products. There are a variety of reasons for this:

- **Consumption of resources by network management** Every CPU cycle spent gathering a measurement or sending an SNMP message is a cycle not used for payload traffic. Network management extracts a cost either in slower performance or extra hardware. SNMPv3 is worse in this regard because it adds differing levels of encryption depending on how it's configured.

- **Spotty standards support by manufacturers** It was expensive for device makers to build complete compliance into their products. Device hardware would need to be beefed up to handle the additional SNMP work, pushing up prices in the process. In addition, some manufacturers decided to add a dash of SNMP incompatibility to steer customers toward standardizing on their product line, because implementing SNMP from one manufacturer is easier than bringing devices of different manufacturers under the same management regime.

- **Labor** A lot of time and attention is required for enterprises to implement and operate a network management system. Management teams are hard-pressed just to keep up with network growth. Few have the manpower to make greater use of SNMP-based systems.

- **Price-conscious customers** Customers have always been fixated on low price points. You wouldn't believe the number of demos and proof-of-concept projects where a company's network engineers make a decision on the best technology for their environment and the finances force a different conclusion. The network half of IT shops is regarded as infrastructure, and managers demand commodity pricing. The relentless focus on driving down the cost per port looks good on paper, but incurs hidden costs in the form of poorly utilized assets.

For these reasons, many SNMP implementations gather only high-level information on generic SNMP data, such as which interfaces are up/down as well as I/O versus vendor-specific data—buffer information, power use per port, and so on. Fewer processes (called *objects)* are monitored, samples are smaller, polling cycles are less frequent, and so on.

Often, even when an enterprise *does* want more network management controls, blind spots are still created by noncompliant devices. Blind spots occur when a policy cannot be enforced in part of a network because a device doesn't support it. Blind spots often occur at backbone entryways, especially to switched backbones where disparate IT departments within a company utilize distinct vendors. Take the scenario depicted in Figure 16-2. The part of the topology on the bottom has implemented a policy to manage traffic usage between a pair of communicating hosts. But the switch in the middle is not configured to monitor that, leaving that SNMP policy unenforced beyond the switch.

The IETF (Internet Engineering Task Force) is responsible for the SNMP standard, and it has a tough job. The implementation of any standard requires coordinated acceptance from both manufacturers and users. This is difficult to pull off, because manufacturers are wary of market acceptance and the potential loss of competitive advantage. Understandably, then, standards setting is always a tricky process. Yet the goal of an integrated NMS console has proved to be particularly elusive for these reasons:

- **Hardware dependencies** Any computer standard must contend with various architectures used for CPUs, buses, device interfaces, drivers, and the like. This both complicates the standards-setting process and makes it more expensive for manufacturers to comply with. The problem is exacerbated by the internetworking industry's habit of using so many different parts in their product lines. Remember all the different CPU architectures that go into Cisco's router line?

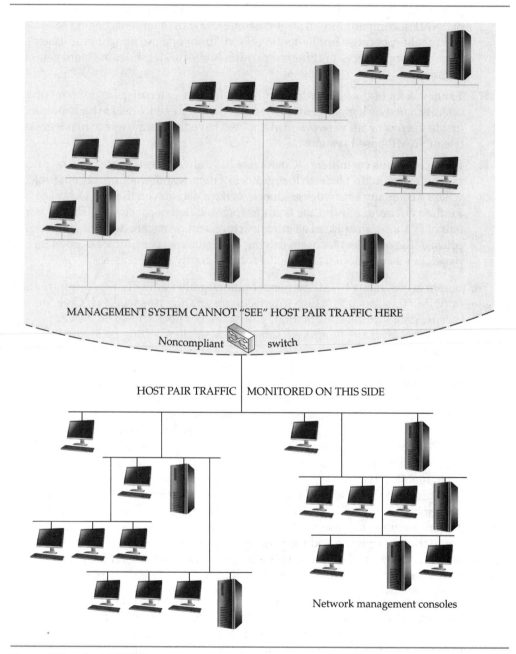

MANAGEMENT SYSTEM CANNOT "SEE" HOST PAIR TRAFFIC HERE

Noncompliant switch

HOST PAIR TRAFFIC | MONITORED ON THIS SIDE

Network management consoles

Figure 16-2. Partial SNMP management causes network management blind spots.

■ **Converging technology**   Until recently, telecommunications, data networking, and computing were viewed as separate and distinct industries. Each had its own industry bodies, standards, and so on. But nowadays, all this equipment has fallen under the purview of network managers. This has increased the scope of the standards and brought together different engineering fields, which creates increasingly more complex work environments for network managers.

■ **Technology onslaught**   Relentless technology advances in all quarters of computing (telecommunications, operating systems, CPUs, cabling, and so on) have presented the IETF with a constantly moving target, and a manufacturer that has won a hard-earned advantage is often reluctant to fall into line with standards and make life easier for competitors.

Progress was slow, but the IETF was able to create a uniform set of standards that has been implemented by almost every network vendor imaginable. Even SOHO appliances purchasable at big-box stores have some form of SNMP built in these days. The lack of integrated management hasn't impeded the explosive growth in the size and use of networks. To accommodate this conflict, management teams use several products to track different parts of their internetworks. Most big enterprises have an ESM, but they augment it with dedicated tools to manage critical parts of internetworks. Figure 16-3 illustrates a typical scenario, with OpenView used to watch the overall network and manufacturer-specific tools to manage critical assets.

The most significant manufacturer-specific tool is Cisco Prime Infrastructure—a collection of network management tools (previously known as CiscoWorks), with broad enough functionality to be considered an ESM unto itself, but only as long as

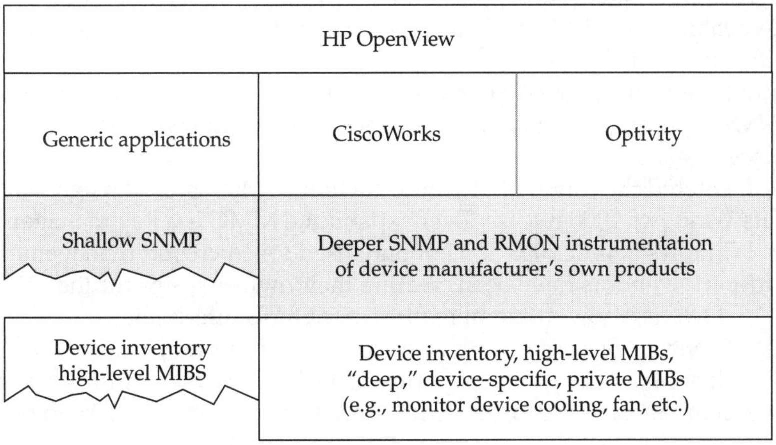

Figure 16-3.   Most network teams use several tools to manage their networks.

you're strictly running Cisco gear. For that reason, CiscoWorks was usually snapped into an ESM suite like OpenView or NetView. That all is beginning to change with Prime.

NOTE Management standards aren't just a problem in internetworking. An industry group called the Distributed Management Task Force (DMTF) has been trying for years to get a standard called the Desktop Management Interface (DMI) implemented. The purpose of DMI, aimed at distributed PCs and small servers, is to let consoles monitor inventory—disks, drivers, BIOS versions, memory configurations, and so on—and to perform remote upgrades. DMI 2.0 products include IBM's Universal Management Agent, Intel's LANDesk Manager, HP's TopTools, and others. Trouble is, these products pretty much work only with platforms of their own manufacture. Microsoft has weighed in with an open standard called WBEM (Web-Based Enterprise Management), now under the auspices of the DMTF. Intel is working on a complementary standard at the hardware level called WfM (Wired for Management). For now, you either restrict the number of vendor product lines you use or use individual tools to manage each of them. Sound familiar?

Trends in Enterprise System Management

ESM tools have been criticized as being difficult to implement, labor intensive, expensive, slow, and ineffective. They're priced at up to $250,000 and cost at least that much again to implement. Often networks, especially those in medium- and small-sized organizations, rely on the monitoring tools specific to the major equipment manufacturers used in their configuration. A second result is that fewer things are monitored, thus diminishing proactive network management.

The market for tools is robust anyway because the potential for savings from NMS tools is enormous. Some estimate that during a typical IT infrastructure's lifecycle, 75 percent or more of all costs are spent on operations. There is a double benefit of enabling network administration personnel to be more productive and getting better results in available bandwidth. NMS tools help enterprises reduce costs and boost service at the same time.

There are now many major NMS tools. In addition to OpenView, other notables are Solarwinds Orion, ManageEngine, IBM's Tivoli NetView, CA Spectrum, Infoblox, and Evidian's OpenMaster.

Microsoft entered the fray with the introduction of Microsoft Management Console (MMC) in its Windows 2000 release. Ever expanding, MMC is a key management interface in Windows Server 2003. It's not only used for Microsoft management tools, either. Third-party vendors have been creating their own snap-ins for the MMC as well. See Figure 16-4 to chart how different management tools interrelate.

The cast of contenders comes from three sources: computer platform makers, such as HP and IBM; network device manufacturers, such as Cisco and Juniper Networks; and software companies in the form of Microsoft, Oracle, and others. Who prevails will

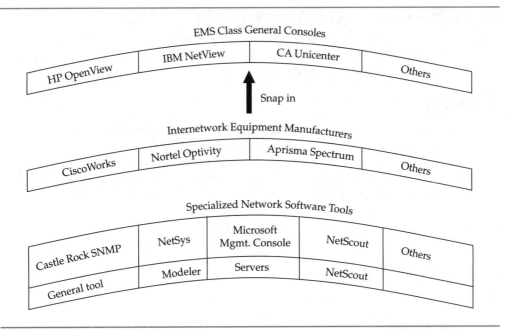

Figure 16-4.   There are a number of network management tools and applications at the network administrator's disposal.

tell which is most important: the wire, the desktop, or the mainframe. Regardless of vendor, NMS technology is headed toward these goals:

■   **More coverage**   As greater management control is placed on devices and network processes, faster device hardware will be required and more data will be available.

■   **Simplicity**   As internetworking has exploded in popularity among small- and medium-sized enterprises, more networks are being operated by non-experts.

■   **Automation**   As underlying network management technologies improve, more management tasks are being automated to improve Quality of Service (QoS).

■   **Proactive management**   A new breed of tools helps isolate emerging problems and avert major network problems by taking early corrective action.

Nearly all progress in computing results directly or indirectly from industry standards. Internetworking ushered in the era of open computing with the help of several standards: the seven-layer OSI reference model, IP, Ethernet, Unix, HTTP, SQL, and others. Now it's time to bring everything all under control with integrated management technology driven by SNMP and NetFlow.

SNMP Is IP's Common Management Platform

Almost all modern internetwork management suites are built atop the Simple Network Management Protocol. Therefore, before discussing the Cisco management applications, a look at their underlying network management technology is in order.

What Is SNMP?

SNMP is a TCP/IP protocol purpose-built to serve as a communications channel for internetwork management operating at the application layer of the IP stack. Although SNMP can be directly operated through the command line, it's almost always used through a management application that employs the SNMP communications channel to monitor and control networks. As Figure 16-5 shows, SNMP has two basic components: a network management station and agents.

Agents are small software modules, residing on managed devices, that can be configured to collect specific pieces of information on device operations. Most of

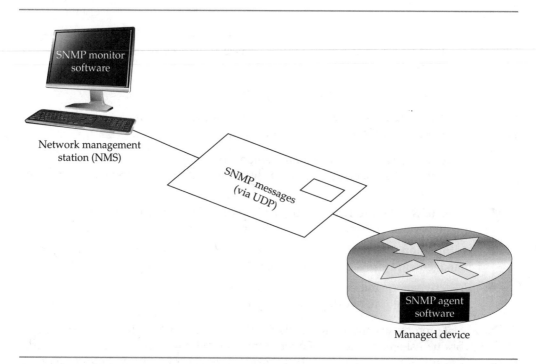

Figure 16-5.   SNMP is a communications channel for network management.

the information consists of totals, such as total bytes, total packets, total errors, and the like. Agents can be deployed on the panoply of devices, such as:

- Routers
- Switches
- Access servers
- Firewalls
- Servers (Windows, Unix, Linux, MVS, VMS, and so on)
- Workstations (Windows PCs, Macs, Unix, and Linux desktops)
- Printers
- UPS power backup systems

The idea is to place agents on all network devices and manage things according to the status information sent back. A piece of equipment with an SNMP agent loaded onto it is referred to as a *managed device* (also called a *network element*).

The NMS is the internetwork's control center. Usually, there's just one NMS for an autonomous system, although many large internetworks use more than one NMS—usually arranged in a hierarchy. Most NMSs today run on either a dedicated Linux/Windows server or virtual machine. For large NMS deployments, it's not unusual to see several collectors reporting to one primary management server or cluster.

SNMP Polling and Managed Objects

SNMP is a fairly simple request/response protocol. It is usually deployed by having the NMS periodically poll managed devices for fresh information, but sometimes devices are configured to send alerts (called traps) too. It's usually more efficient and less complicated to allow the polling station to send the alert. The polling frequency is a matter of configuration choice, but it usually takes place once every few minutes or so. There are three types of polling:

- **Monitor polling**   To check that devices are available and to trigger an alarm when one is not

- **Threshold polling**   To detect when conditions deviate from a baseline number by a percentage greater than allowed (usually plus or minus 10 percent to 20 percent) and to notify the NMS for review

- **Performance polling**   To measure ongoing network performance over longer periods and to analyze the data for long-term trends and patterns

The agent responds to the poll by returning a message to the NMS. It's able to do this by capturing and storing information on subjects that it has been configured to monitor. These subjects are usually processes associated with the flow of packets.

A process about which the agent collects data is called a *managed object,* which is a variable characteristic of the device being managed. The total number of UDP connections open on a managed device, for example, could be a managed object. One open UDP session on a specific interface is an *object instance,* but the total number of simultaneously open UDP sessions on the device (say, a router) is a managed object. Figure 16-6 shows our sample UDP connections as managed objects and instances.

Managed objects are usually operating characteristics of managed devices. The managed devices can be anywhere in the topology—backbone devices, servers, or end systems. Most objects are physical pieces, such as a network interface, but a managed object isn't necessarily a physical entity. An object could also be a software application, a database, or some other logical entity.

The MIB

The agent stores the information about objects in specialized data records called *MIBs (management information bases).* An MIB is the storage part of the SNMP agent software. Information stored in MIBs is referred to as *variables* (also called *attributes*). MIBs usually collect information in the form of totals for a variable during a time interval, such as total packets over five minutes. Figure 16-7's example shows variables being

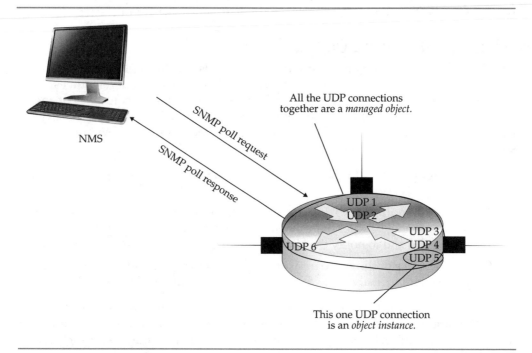

Figure 16-6.   SNMP gathers information on managed devices.

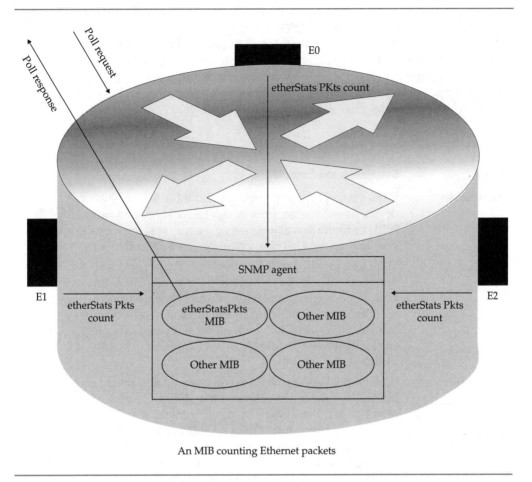

An MIB counting Ethernet packets

Figure 16-7. MIBs are the basic building blocks of an SNMP management system.

extracted from instances and processed through managed MIBs and the managed object—in this example, a count of total Ethernet packets going through a router's interface. Again, the packet count from each interface is a managed object instance; the count for all three interfaces is the managed object.

By collating data from multiple objects, the MIB lets the agent send the NMS information concerning everything on the device that is being monitored.

Types of MIBs

MIBs are prefabricated to perform specific jobs. Basic MIBs usually come packaged inside the network device operating system. For example, IOS comes packaged with MIBs for most network management jobs.

Generally, MIBs are named using a convention that indicates the relevant category. This is known as the MIB Object ID (OID).

For example, a Cisco MIB object that deals with a specific network interface will have "if" in its name (from the letters *i* and *f* in "interface"). The ifInErrors MIB object monitors incoming packet errors on an interface; the ifOutErrors object monitors the outgoing errors, sysLocation reports a device's network location, and so on. Table 16-1 shows six basic MIB categories used in most SNMP systems.

Category	Description and Examples
Configuration	MIBs that report basic management information, such as device name, contact person, device location, and uptime. MIB configuration objects are sysName, sysDescr, sysContact, sysLocation, sysUpTime, ifNumber, romID, and others.
Interface error rates	MIBs that monitor specific interfaces. Packet errors are a normal condition, but watching their trends indicates device health and helps isolate faults. For Ethernet interfaces, use ifInErrors, ifOutErrors, locifCollisions, locIfInRunts, locIfInGiants, locIfCRC, and others. For serial interfaces, use locIfInFrame, locIfInAbort, locIfInIgnored, locIfResets, locIfRestarts, and others.
Bandwidth	ICMP is a layer-3 protocol that reports on IP packet processing. It's best known for its **echo** command, used to verify the presence of other devices by pinging them. Timed pings are used to determine how far away a device is (much like in the submarine movies). SNMP sends ping input and output messages to measure available bandwidth. Cisco's MIB objects for this are icmpInEchos and icmpInEchoReps as well as icmpOutEchos and icmpOutEchoReps. Generally speaking, these are the only SNMP messages not sent as UDP messages.
Traffic flow	Performance management is largely a matter of measuring traffic flow. There are Cisco MIBs to measure traffic rates, both as bits per second and packets per second: locIfInBitsSec, locIfOutBitsSec, locIfInPktsSec, and locIfOutPktsSec.
Unreachable address	The object to measure how often a router is asked to send messages to an unreachable address is icmpOutDesUnreachs.
SNMP data	There are even objects to measure how much time the router spends handling SNMP messages. The objects include snmpInGetRequests and snmpOutGetRequests, snmpInGetResponses and snmpOutGetResponses, and others.

Table 16-1.   Basic Cisco MIB Objects Commonly Used in SNMP Implementations

It is possible to gather information on a single object instance only, called a *scalar* object. Most managed objects, however, are composed of several related instances. This practice, called *tabular* objects, is the rule in most MIBs, because it's more efficient to manage as much as possible from a single data collection point. As the name implies, a tabular MIB keeps the information straight by storing it in rows and tables.

 NOTE   MIB lingo can be confusing. You'll hear references to the MIB as if it were a single MIB object. But that's not the case. For example, the Cisco MIB is not an MIB as such; it's actually the root of about 1,000 private Cisco MIB objects.

 NOTE   See http://tools.cisco.com/ITDIT/MIBS/MainServlet for a cool MIB search tool and ftp://ftp .cisco.com/pub/mibs/ for a direct link to the files themselves.

What Makes SNMP Machine Independent

We don't want to get too technical in this book, but you should understand how the SNMP standard makes itself machine independent. In other words, how is it able to run on different brands of equipment, each with its own proprietary operating system?

The SNMP standard requires that every MIB object have an object ID and a syntax. An object ID identifies the object to the system and tells what kind of MIB to use and what kind of data the object collects. *Syntax* means a precise specification a machine can understand in binary form.

To understand a field's contents, IOS must know whether the field contains a number, text, a counter, or other type of data. These are called data types. *Data types* specify the syntax to be used for a data field. A *field* is any logical piece of data, such as a model number or temperature reading. In the same way that a field has its own box on an input screen, it has its own position in a computer file. A file represents data in binary (0's and 1's), and a set of binary positions are reserved for each field within the file. All fields must be declared as some data type or another, or else the machine cannot process the data held there.

Computer hardware architectures, operating systems, programming languages, and other environmentals specify the data types they're willing to use. A data type represents the layer where software meets hardware. It tells the machine what syntax to use to interpret a field's contents. A different syntax is used for floating-point numbers, integer numbers, dates, text strings, and other data types.

SNMP makes itself independent by declaring its own data types. It does so in the form of the Structure of Management Information (SMI) standard. SMI is a standard dedicated to specifying a machine-independent syntax for every data type. These data types are independent of the data structures and representation techniques unique to particular computer architectures. SMI specifies the syntax for data types such as object IDs, counters, rows, tables, octet strings, network addresses, and other SNMP elements.

MIBs are programmed by vendors using an arcane programming language called ASN.1, created just for programming SMI data types. ASN.1 (Abstract Systems Notation One) is an OSI standard, from the same people that brought us the seven-layer reference model. Figure 16-8 shows how SMI data types universalize MIB information.

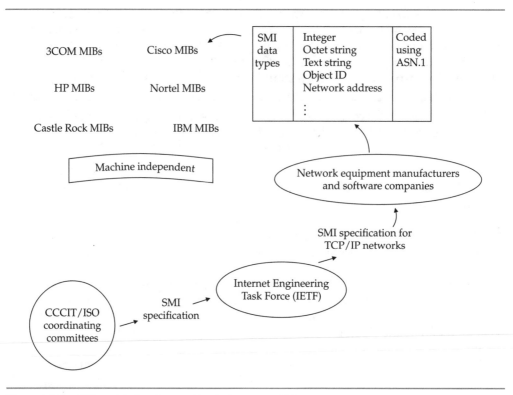

Figure 16-8.   MIBs are built using machine-independent SMI data types.

SMI tries to let vendors code "write-once, run-anywhere" MIB objects. In other words, someone should be able to write a single piece of MIB software—a packet counter, for example—and the counter MIB should be able to run on any device that supports the SMI syntax definition for a counter.

SMI data types are SNMP's building blocks at the lowest level. They are used to construct MIB object formats in a syntax any machine can understand. From there, object instances are measured and rolled up into managed objects, which in turn are reported by the SNMP agent to the NMS. This is how NMSs can operate across disparate device architectures.

Standard MIBs and Private MIBs

The current MIB standard is MIB-II, which has nearly 200 standard MIB objects. The standard is implemented as a hierarchy that starts from a root and continues to branch down from the source MIB to the root Internet MIB. Looking at Figure 16-9, you can see that each branch is marked both by a name and a number (the numbers are used to build object IDs).

Figure 16-9 also shows the players in the history of the Internet. ISO is the International Standards Organization, and DoD is the U.S. Department of Defense (which started it all with ARPANET). CCITT is the Consultative Committee for International Telegraph and Telephone. The CCITT is only a distant cousin of the Internet, handling telephony and other communications standards. The CCITT is now known as the ITU-T (for Telecommunication Standardization Sector of the International Telecommunications Union), but you'll still see the CCITT acronym attached to dozens of standards.

Because they're more user friendly, text strings are usually used to describe MIB objects in directories. Object IDs are mainly used by software to create compact, encoded representations of the names.

Working from the tree structure in Figure 16-9, the Internet root's object ID is 1.3.6.1, named iso.org.dod.internet. The two main branches beyond the Internet root are the management and private MIBs. Industry-standard MIBs go through the management branch to become iso.org.dod.internet.mgmt.mib with the object ID 1.3.6.1.2.1. Private MIBs become iso.org.dod.internet.private and 1.3.6.1.4. Cisco's private MIB is represented as iso.org.dod.internet.private.enterprise.cisco, or object ID 1.3.6.1.4.1.9.

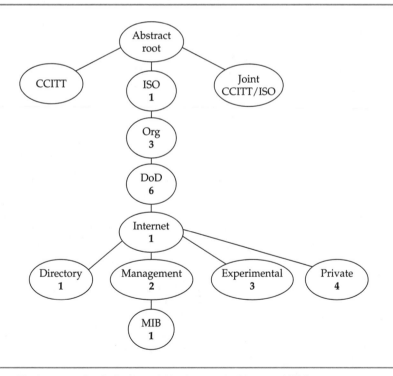

Figure 16-9. The Internet's family lineage yields the standard Internet MIB lineage.

Vendors can build private MIBs by extending standard MIB branches. In this way, they can customize MIBs to better fit their particular needs. Figure 16-10 shows Cisco's private MIB hierarchy and how private MIBs extend from the standard Internet MIB.

Many of the object groups within the Cisco Management, Temporary Variables, and Local Variables subgroups measure Cisco proprietary technology. For example, the Cisco Environmental Monitor group in the Cisco Management subgroup (object ID 1.3.6.1.4.1.9.9) looks after such things as the operating temperature inside the device. This type of information is the "deep" stuff we were talking about that management applications from other manufacturers have trouble getting at.

Another important thing to see in Figure 16-10 is support for legacy desktop protocols. Novell NetWare IPX, VINES, AppleTalk, DECnet, and even Xerox XNS networks can be managed using Cisco MIBs. These are "legacy" in that the IP LAN specification has steamrolled the market, but the others are still out there and therefore worthy of mention.

Polling Groups and Data Aggregation

MIBs are frequently placed into polling groups to facilitate SNMP data collection. A *polling group* is a set of logically related managed objects that are reported and analyzed as a cohesive entity. For example, Figure 16-11 shows polling groups for three

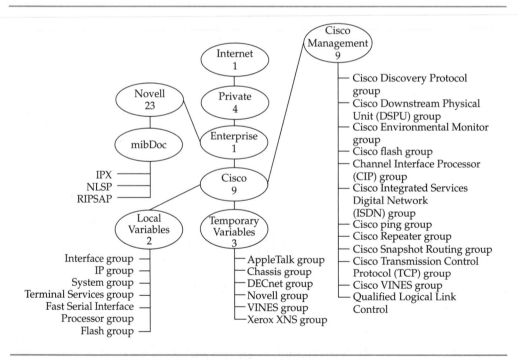

Figure 16-10.   Cisco's private hierarchy branches into four subgroups.

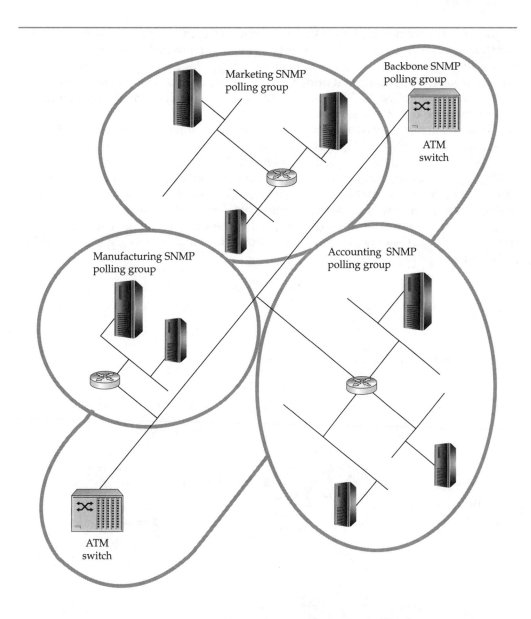

Figure 16-11. Polling groups are used to help make SNMP data more manageable.

different classes of equipment in an internetwork: the backbone switches, routers, and application servers. Different MIB variables are likely to be collected for each type, so each gets its own polling group. In this way, logically related management information is compiled and stored into the SNMP database under group names.

Grouping simplifies the network administrator's job. In the example in Figure 16-11, thresholds can be set to fit tolerances appropriate for each group. For example, a network team is likely to set alarm variables to be more sensitive for the backbone switches because trouble with them could bring the entire internetwork down. Polling similar MIBs en masse simplifies SNMP operations and helps ensure data that's consistent, trustworthy, and easier to assimilate.

Groups also make it easier to limit the amount of information stored in the NMS database. SNMP could build mountains of data on every device in a network, but doing so would be neither practical nor worthwhile. Storing information on related MIB groups facilitates the movement of raw data through a cycle of aggregation and purging. Figure 16-12 shows a typical scenario, in which MIB variables in a group are polled and stored in the NMS database every five minutes. Each midnight, the data is aggregated into minimums, maximums, and averages for each hour and stored in another database. The data points are purged from the database weekly, leaving behind only the aggregated data.

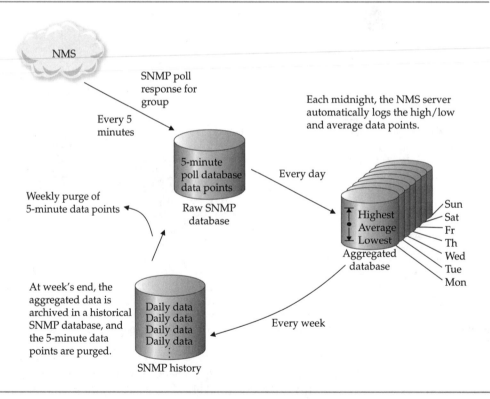

Figure 16-12. Data aggregation summarizes data while preserving its integrity.

The collect-aggregate-purge cycle has several benefits. It keeps disk space open on the NMS server for storing new MIBs and maintains statistical integrity of the data record. At the same time, it also keeps a consistently fresh picture of network operations.

SNMP Commands

The *simple* in Simple Network Management Protocol comes from the fact that the protocol has just six root commands. They're used to set SNMP parameters within the device's config file. Here are the root SNMP commands:

- **Get**   Used by the NMS to retrieve object instances from an agent.
- **GetNext**   Used to retrieve subsequent object instances after the first instance.
- **GetBulk**   This operation retrieves all instances in a managed object (replacing the need for iterative **GetNext** operations).
- **Set**   Used to set values for object instances within an agent (such as a threshold).
- **Trap**   Used to instruct an agent to unilaterally notify the NMS of an event (without being polled).
- **Inform**   This command instructs one NMS to forward trap information to one or more other NMSs.

 NOTE   Most of the time, SNMP commands are used by computer programs rather than by people directly. For example, if an administrator enters the location of a router in an inventory screen in the Essentials console, a process is launched from Essentials that changes the **set snmp location** in IOS inside that router, and the MIB value is updated accordingly.

SNMP's two basic commands are **get** and **set.** The **set** command is used to set managed parameters in managed objects. When you issue an SNMP **set** command, it configures the network device with the corresponding value (as defined by the MIB). So, for example, if an administrator enters the location of a router in an inventory screen of an SNMP management station, this, in turn, uses SNMP **set** commands to set this location value on the router.

Conversely, the **get** command is used to fetch stored variables from agents and bring them back to the NMS.

SNMP needs to be simple in order to make itself supportable by disparate architectures. Doing so is a practical requirement for SNMP interoperability.

Thresholds

A *threshold* defines an acceptable value or value range for a particular SNMP variable. When a variable exceeds a policy, an *event* is said to have taken place. An event isn't necessarily an either/or situation, such as a switch going down. Events are usually operational irregularities that the network team would want to know about before service is affected. For example, a network administrator may set a policy for the number of packet errors occurring on router interfaces in order to steer traffic around emerging traffic bottlenecks. Thresholds can be set either as a ceiling or as a range with upper and lower bounds. The two types of thresholds are depicted in Figure 16-13.

The shaded portions of the graph in Figure 16-13 are called *threshold events*. In other words, an event is when something has taken place in violation of the set policy. A *sampling* interval is the period of time during which a statistic is compiled. For example, an MIB object can store the total number of packet errors taking place during each five-minute period. Intervals must be long enough to gather a representative sample, yet short enough to capture events before they can substantially affect network performance.

Events and Traps

When an event occurs, the network administrator can specify how the SNMP agent should respond. The event can either be logged or an alarm message can be sent to the NMS. An SNMP alert message is called a *trap*, so named because it catches (or traps) the event at the device. For the sake of clarification, an alarm is a type of alert message.

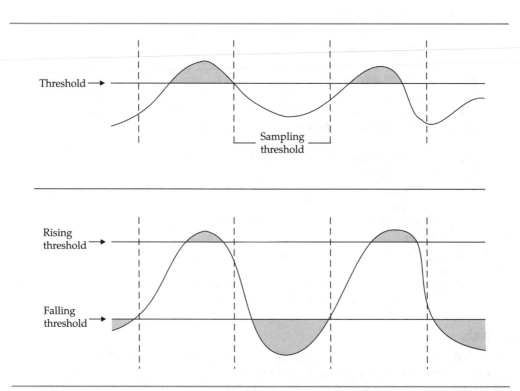

Figure 16-13.   Thresholds set a normal operating range for a managed object.

A trap contains information about the event. Figure 16-14 shows the course of events leading up to an alarm.

Alarms can take many forms. They're often configured to show themselves as a blinking icon on the NMS console, but you could have a noise generated. Networks that don't have administrators present at the NMS all the time have the trap dial a phone number or send an SMS message and a priority e-mail to alert the person on response duty at the time.

Traps aren't used just to send alarms. As an internetwork grows in size, SNMP overhead traffic will increase along with it. Network managers can reduce SNMP overhead by stretching the polling frequency, but doing that makes the NMS less responsive to emerging network problems. A better way to limit SNMP overhead is to use traps. Given that they're unsolicited messages instead of SNMP poll responses, traps consume a negligible amount of bandwidth.

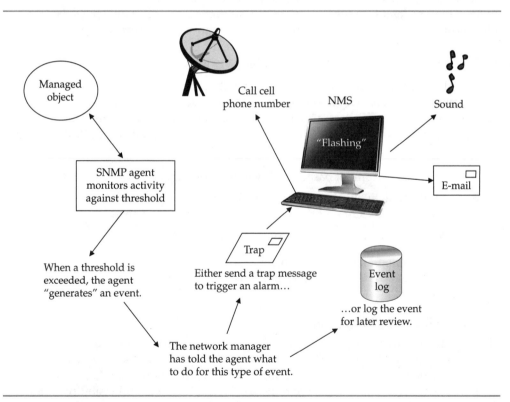

Figure 16-14. An SNMP trap proactively reports an event to the NMS.

The following code snippet is from a Cisco router's config file. It shows the SNMP settings made for the device. RO and RW mean that these are the read-only and read-write (respectively) community strings that make the device a member of a particular management group.

```
MyRouter(config)#snmp-server community yellow RO
MyRouter(config)#snmp-server community blue RW
MyRouter(config)#snmp-server enable traps snmp
MyRouter(config)#snmp-server enable traps isdn call-information
MyRouter(config)#snmp-server enable traps config
MyRouter(config)#snmp-server enable traps bgp
MyRouter(config)#snmp-server enable traps frame-relay
MyRouter(config)#snmp-server enable traps rtr
MyRouter(config)#snmp-server host 10.1.1.13 traps vpi
```

A number of SNMP traps are enabled in this config file. This tells the SNMP agent on the device to send trap messages if anything changes. The last line gives the IP address of the NMS so that the agent knows where to send the trap messages.

RMON: Hardware Probes for Switched Networks

RMON (short for *remote monitoring*) is a separate but related management standard that complements SNMP. RMON is similar to SNMP in several ways: It is an open standard administered by the IETF; it uses SMI data types and the root MIB format; and it collects device data and reports it to an NMS. But RMON differs from normal SNMP in these fundamental ways:

- RMON is instrument based, in that it uses specialized hardware to operate.
- RMON proactively sends data instead of waiting to be polled, making it bandwidth efficient and more responsive to network events.
- RMON allows much more detailed data to be collected.

RMON instrumentation is more powerful, but more expensive. Consequently, RMON probes tend to be placed on critical links, such as network backbones and important servers.

RMON and Switched Networking

The movement toward RMON-based network management is closely linked to the rise of switched networking. Although LAN switching is on the rise as the way to improve network performance, it poses special problems for conventional SNMP management methods. In a network formed using hubs, a LAN analyzer has full visibility because the medium is shared by all nodes. But a switched LAN isn't a shared medium, so to maintain the same level of visibility, the analyzer would have to be placed on each switched port. The solution is to incorporate the analyzer (or at least the sensor part of it) directly into the switch's hardware. That's what an RMON probe is. Figure 16-15 shows a switched network managed with and without RMON.

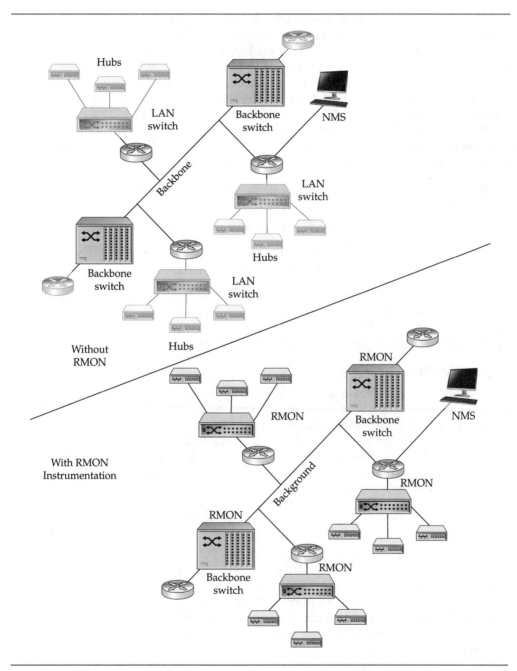

Without RMON

With RMON Instrumentation

Figure 16-15. RMON probes provide management visibility across switched networks.

RMON became a standard in 1992 with the release of RMON-1 for Ethernet. The RMON-2 standard, the current version, was completed in early 1997. Whereas RMON-1 operated only at the physical and data-link layers (layers 1 and 2) of the seven-layer OSI reference model, RMON-2 adds the capability to collect data at higher layers, giving it more reporting capability. The ability to monitor upper-layer events has been a boon to the popularity of RMON. For example, RMON-2 can report what's happening with IPX traffic as opposed to IP on a multiprotocol LAN segment.

RMONs replace expensive network analyzer devices that must be physically attached to the approximate area of a network problem. RMON probes come in different forms, depending on the size and type of device to be monitored:

- An RMON MIB that uses the monitored device's hardware (called an *embedded agent*)
- A specialized card module inserted into a slot within the monitored device
- A purpose-built probe externally attached to one or more monitored devices
- A dedicated PC attached to one or more monitored devices

Having specialized hardware remotely located with a monitored device brings advantages. RMON probes can yield a much richer set of measurement data than that of an SNMP agent. The dedicated hardware is used as a real-time sensor that can gather and analyze data for possible upload to the NMS.

The Nine RMON MIB Groups

Another advantage RMON enjoys is its freedom as a separate standard. The root RMON MIB defines nine specialized MIB groups (and a Token Ring group). The nine groups let RMON collect more detailed and granular management information than can be collected using SNMP. Figure 16-16 charts the RMON MIBs.

RMONs, at a minimum, come with the Events and Alarms groups. Most come with four groups needed for basic management: Events, Alarms, Statistics, and History. Because of hardware expense and response time concerns, resource-intensive groups, such as the Traffic Matrix group, are infrequently deployed.

The Alarm RMON MIB is a more powerful mechanism for event management than SNMP. For example, because there's a separate MIB just to keep track of events, RMON can adjust itself to avoid sending too many alarms. In addition, the Matrix MIB can monitor traffic on a "conversation" basis. In other words, it can be set up to monitor connections between pairs of MAC addresses and report on what's happening with each connection. For example, if a Matrix MIB was set up to watch an expensive link, say, between New York and London, and someone was using it to play a transatlantic game of *Portal 2*, the MIB could see that and alert the NMS that valuable bandwidth was being wasted.

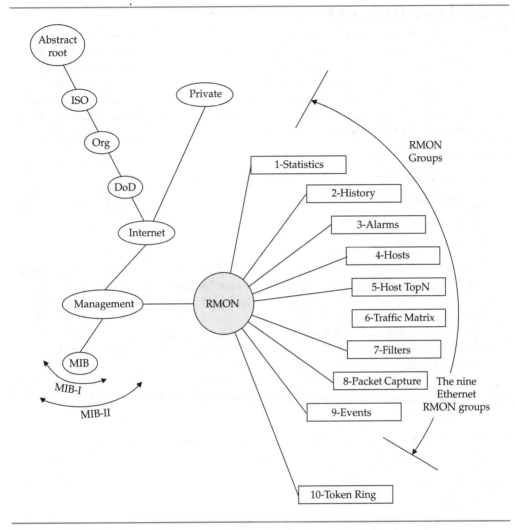

Figure 16-16. RMON stores Ethernet management data in nine specialized groups.

The problem with RMON is that it's expensive. It takes extra hardware to store and analyze packets in real time, and that costs money. Although Cisco has Network Analysis Module (NAM) cards that may be inserted directly into some models of routers rather than requiring separate sniffing devices entirely, it's still an upcharge. Consequently, RMON is being put to use to manage just links that are mission critical or expensive. This is likely why the industry has moved towards NetFlow.

NetFlow: Software Traffic Flow-Recording

NetFlow is the newest kid on the monitoring block. Unlike RMON, NetFlow does not require special hardware to capture traffic. NetFlow is also built into many vendors' network devices. NetFlow is an open but proprietary network protocol developed by Cisco Systems to run on Cisco IOS-enabled equipment for collecting IP traffic information. Cisco has defined network flows with the following common five-tuple (five-data-point) definition, where a flow is defined as a unidirectional sequence of packets that all share the following five attributes:

1. Source IP address
2. Destination IP address
3. Source TCP port
4. Destination TCP port
5. IP protocol

A flow-providing device will output a specific flow record when it has determined that the flow is completed. It accomplishes this task by paying attention to a flow's age: When the router sees new traffic for an existing flow, it resets the aging counter. Also, TCP session termination in a TCP flow may also cause the router to expire that specific flow. Devices delivering flow data can also be configured to release a flow record at a fixed interval—even if the flow is continual. Utilizing Flexible NetFlow (FNF), a network admin may actually define flow properties on the source device.

NetFlow can be configured on individual interfaces, thereby providing information on traffic that passes through those interfaces and collecting the following types of information:

- Source and destination interfaces and IP addresses
- Input and output interface numbers
- TCP/UDP source port and destination ports
- Number of bytes and packets in the flow
- Source and destination AS numbers (BGP)
- Time of day
- IP ToS

The most recent version of NetFlow (version 9) introduced a dictionary, making its data captures even more granular. One can configure a sending device to use a dictionary record stating the following, for example:

Router Blue I will send you record type number 97 and it will contain the following fields, x, y and x.

When record type 97 arrives from router Blue, you will know from the dictionary the first n byes is the IP number, the second m bytes is when the router booted, and so on.

Creating and maintaining the tables required to continually pass on NetFlow data can be very computationally costly for the sending device and burden the network device's CPU to the point where it simply runs out of juice and starts dropping actual traffic. To avoid problems caused by router CPU exhaustion, Cisco provides Sampled NetFlow. Rather than looking at every packet to maintain NetFlow records, the router looks at every nth packet, where n can be configured or can be a randomly selecting interval (as used in Random Sampled NetFlow, which is used on some other Cisco platforms). When Sampled NetFlow is used, the NetFlow records must be adjusted for the effect of sampling—traffic volumes, in particular, are now an estimate rather than the actual measured flow volume.

NetFlow-enabled network gear can collect and then send data to a collector, where the data is collated. Real-time alerts may be generated based on preset thresholds, and reports based on historical data may be generated, much like RMON. The difference is RMON requires additional sensors at every point collected and, due to cost, perhaps only data from the primary firewall is collected. Figure 16-17 depicts a generic network configured with NetFlow.

Trends in Network Management Technology

SNMP compliance issues have left new versions of the standard mired in political infighting. In addition, the fast development of powerful RMON-based tools is pushing the approach to network management in a new direction. The technology underpinnings of network management applications exhibit these trends:

- More powerful data collection (more information reported faster)
- More proactive management
- Improved built-in hardware support for management
- Better security for protecting management tools themselves

The trend toward more intensive management of internetworks is coming up against the same old problem: Every management message is overhead that consumes precious bandwidth. This dilemma is what's pushing the industry toward RMON, because that technology captures better information and works locally (instead of through NMS polling).

The other trends have to do with making management systems more efficient and providing SNMP itself with better security.

Advanced SNMP Commands

The evolution of SNMP can be seen in the **GetBulk** and **Inform** commands. **GetBulk** makes it easier for the agent to fetch MIB information from multiple object instances. **Inform** makes it easier to use a hierarchy of NMSs to manage complex internetworks, as shown in Figure 16-18.

SNMP's added support for protocols beyond IP was a substantial change. Doing this extended the reach of SNMP into non-IP topologies. This was an important advance

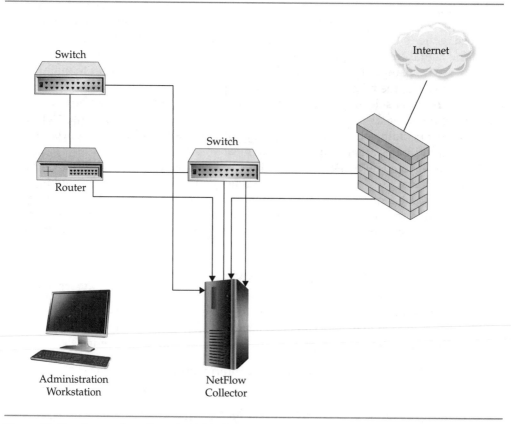

Figure 16-17.   A network configured with NetFlow

for network managers overseeing multiprotocol internetworks. Although they will not continue to do so (since TCP/IP clearly won the protocol wars), extended SNMP protocol support helped bring these topologies under the control of centralized NMSs.

SNMP Version 1 Versus SNMP Version 2

Keeping track of standards can be confusing because they overlap. For example, right now, the majority of all SNMP implementations are of version 2 (SNMPv2). Whatever the version, here are the components of the basic SNMP message format:

- **Version**   The SNMP version being used.
- **Community string**   The equivalent of a group password used by all devices in the same administrative domain. The SNMP message is ignored without the proper community string.

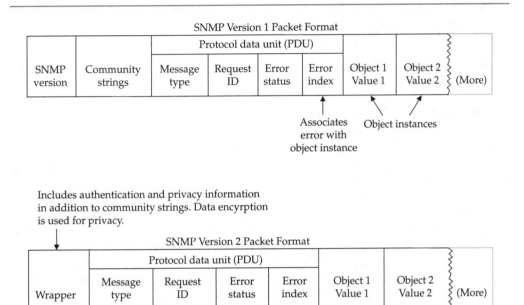

SNMP Version 1 Packet Format

SNMP version	Community strings	Protocol data unit (PDU)				Object 1 Value 1	Object 2 Value 2	(More)
		Message type	Request ID	Error status	Error index			

Associates error with object instance

Object instances

Includes authentication and privacy information in addition to community strings. Data encyrption is used for privacy.

SNMP Version 2 Packet Format

Wrapper	Protocol data unit (PDU)				Object 1 Value 1	Object 2 Value 2	(More)
	Message type	Request ID	Error status	Error index			

Also includes *context*, specifying which managed objects the BNMP request can view.

Figure 16-18.   SNMP version 2 emphasizes flexibility and security.

- **Protocol Data Unit (PDU) type**   The instructions about what to do. The PDU specifies the operation to be performed (**GetBulk, Trap**, and so on) and the object instances on which to perform the operation. The PDU is composed of the following fields:
  - **Error status**   This field defines an error and error type.
  - **Error index**   This field associates the error with a particular object instance.
  - **Variable bindings**   Don't be intimidated by the fancy name; a variable binding is the data collected on the object instance—it's the SNMP packet's payload.

SNMPv2 enhances the message format with these changes:

- **Wrapper**   This includes destination and source party identifiers for SNMP message authentication and privacy, and also identifies context in the form of the managed objects on which the PDU is to perform its operation.
- **Enhanced PDU**   The **GetBulk** and **Inform** operations.

- **Multiple transport protocols**   Originally, all SNMP packets were transmitted through UDP (User Datagram Protocol). SNMPv2 supports Novell NetWare IPX, AppleTalk DDP, and OSI CLNS.

The enhancements in SNMPv2 reflect the demand for more powerful controls and better security.

Better Security for SNMP Messages

Support for SNMP has been hindered by security concerns. A smart hacker armed with a protocol analyzer would like nothing more than to intercept SNMP messages. Instead of just getting some user's file download, hacking an SNMP system could yield a virtual blueprint of the internetwork topology.

Today, most networks rely on a combination of access lists and SNMP community strings to secure their management systems. If a hacker somehow obtains the community string for an SNMP system, he might navigate around the access list controls and retrieve data on all network devices. Worse, knowing the Read-Write community strings would allow a hacker to alter config file settings on the community's network devices. This would be a devastating security breach, especially if community strings on **set** operations were stolen, because that would hand over control of all devices configured for remote management.

Both customers and manufacturers called for more stringent SNMP security. Keep in mind that a *user* here doesn't necessarily have to be a person; it could just as easily be an automated process (such as a **get** request) as part of an SNMP poll. In SNMPv2 format, the wrapper contains authentication information that identifies approved destination and source parties to the SNMP transaction. The authentication protocol is designed to identify the originating party reliably. Beyond authentication, SNMPv2 makes it possible to specify which managed objects can be included in a message. Figure 16-19 outlines measures taken to secure SNMPv2 messages.

SNMPv3

SNMPv1 and SNMPv2 are the big dogs on the management block. However, they are not perfect. As noted earlier, neither version offers tight enough security features. To be more precise, neither version is able to authenticate the source of a management message or provide encryption. Without authentication, it is possible for outsiders to use SNMP functions. Without encryption, it is possible for your network's management commands to be monitored.

Because of this shortcoming, many SNMPv1 and v2 implementations allow just read-only capability. This reduces their usability to serve only as a network monitor. SNMPv3 looks to correct this deficiency.

The SNMPv3 functionality has been described in its IETF drafts as "SNMPv2 plus administration and security." SNMPv3 adds three services:

- **Authentication**   This ensures that SNMP commands are being issued by the appropriate person or application.

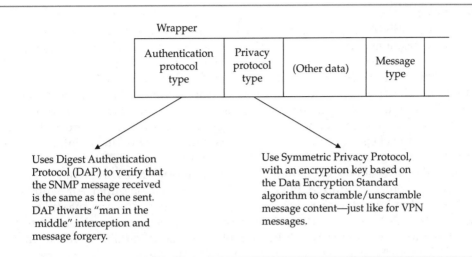

Wrapper

Uses Digest Authentication Protocol (DAP) to verify that the SNMP message received is the same as the one sent. DAP thwarts "man in the middle" interception and message forgery.

Use Symmetric Privacy Protocol, with an encryption key based on the Data Encryption Standard algorithm to scramble/unscramble message content—just like for VPN messages.

Figure 16-19.   SNMPv2 messages are secured by authenticating parties and control measures.

■   **Privacy**   Encryption enables network administrators to ensure that their SNMP commands are not being eavesdropped upon.

■   **Access control**   Different levels of access to the agent's MIB can be established for different managers. Agents can restrict access to its MIBs by either allowing read-only access or by limiting the actions that can be taken upon the MIB.

These services are delivered through a concept called a *principal.* This is the entity on whose behalf services are provided or processing takes place. A principal can be an individual acting in a certain role; a group of individuals, each acting in a certain role; an application or group of applications; or any combination of these.

A principal operates from a management station and issues SNMP commands to the agents. The identity of the principal and the target agent, together, determine which security features will be used. Because a principal is used, security policies can be tailored to the specific principal, agent, and information exchange, allowing flexibility to the network administrator.

Cisco ships full SNMPv3 support starting in IOS version 12.0(3)T. It is implemented for all IOS platforms that have 12.0(3)T-based images.

Cisco's SNMP and RMON Implementations

Cisco claims unparalleled SNMP and RMON capability. Virtually all the company's devices ship with SNMP agents, and most switches ship with RMON and NetFlow support. As the internetworking industry's powerhouse, Cisco sits on the major standards-setting committees and is among the first to release products supporting new standards.

Cisco and SNMP

Cisco includes SNMP support in the form of agent software on every router and communications server it makes. According to the company, its SNMP agents can communicate successfully with OpenView and NetView. Cisco supports over 1,000 MIB objects. Their private MIB objects feature support for all the major LAN protocols.

Cisco uses its private MIB to enhance system monitoring and management of Cisco devices. For example, Cisco routers can be queried both by interface and by protocol. You can query for the number of runt packets on a network interface or query for the number of IPX packets sent or received from that interface. This kind of information is invaluable to baselining the traffic profile of a network. Average CPU usage statistics are sampled by five-second, one-minute, and five-minute intervals to ascertain whether a router is being properly utilized. Physical variables are also measured. Air temperature entering and leaving a device as well as voltage fluctuations can be monitored to ensure continued device operation. Cisco's private MIB includes chassis objects to report the number of installed modules, module types, serial numbers, and so on. Figure 16-20 depicts some of Cisco's advanced SNMP features.

To help secure SNMP messages, IOS provides the ability to prohibit them from traversing certain interfaces. SNMP is further secured by the option to designate certain community strings as read-only or read/write, thus restricting the ability to configure certain devices remotely. Also, a device can be assigned more than one community string, enabling key routers or switches to fall under multiple SNMP regimes (sometimes used in large internetworks).

Cisco has committed to making their routers "bilingual" in their simultaneous support of both SNMPv1 and SNMPv2. The coexistence strategy uses two techniques—a proxy agent that translates messages between versions, and the support of both versions in a single NMS platform.

Cisco and RMON

Cisco integrates RMON into all its platforms. The greatest RMON capabilities are packaged into the high-end Catalyst 6500 and Nexus line.

The Catalyst simultaneously acts as a LAN switch and a network probe because of its multiprocessor design. One CPU does the switching, and the other handles management data collection and forwarding duties. The Catalyst can be configured to collect traffic data in either of two modes:

- **Standard RMON mode** The RMON agent collects data for up to all nine RMON groups across all attached switch ports.

- **Roving RMON mode** A focused mode that collects more detailed data for just one or two RMON groups across all eight ports, and then focuses on a single LAN when an event takes place there.

In either mode, the RMON follows a structured course of action to enforce thresholds, generate events, and send alarms. Figure 16-21 depicts the structure.

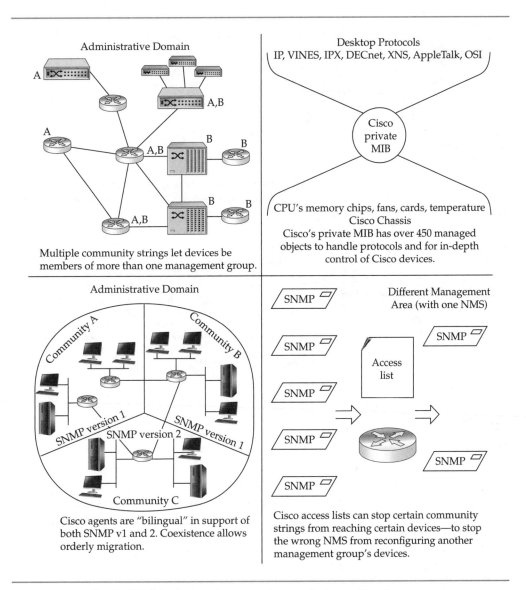

Figure 16-20. Cisco's SNMP implementation supports several advanced functions.

The concurrent RMON configuration is the normal mode. Its ability to see across all connected LANs is particularly valuable for troubleshooting, especially client-server applications in which the communicating hosts are on different LANs.

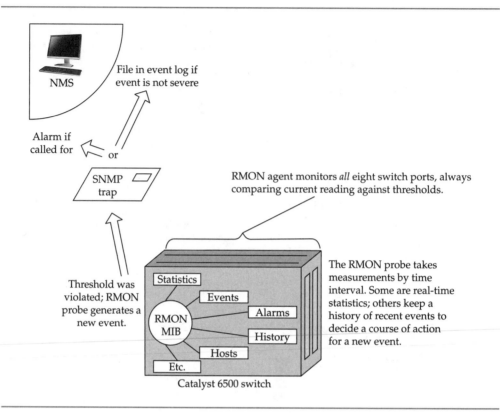

Figure 16-21.   This is how a standard Catalyst switch RMON works.

Catalyst's roving RMON is as advanced as it gets. Normally, it works at collecting detailed historical information on a per-port and even per-host level. But when a trap is sent, the stripped-down, two-group RMON spawns a fully configured nine-group RMON probe that automatically begins collecting troubleshooting data just from the offending connected LAN. Figure 16-22 depicts how a roving RMON changes to handle an event.

By the time the administrator responds to the alert, the roving RMON has already reconfigured itself and started intensive monitoring of the LAN segment in which the problem emerged.

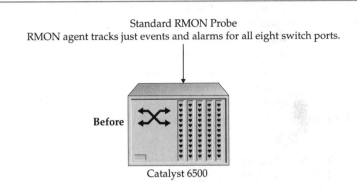

Standard RMON Probe
RMON agent tracks just events and alarms for all eight switch ports.

Before

Catalyst 6500

Roving RMON Probe
When an event occurs on a switched LAN, RMON probe automatically
reconfigures itself to monitor all specified groups (e.g., Statistics, Hosts,
Host TopN Packet Capture and Traffic Matrix, in addition to events and
alarms) but *only* for the switch port where the event took place.

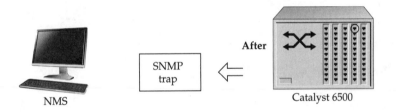

After

SNMP
trap

NMS

Catalyst 6500

Figure 16-22. Roving RMON marshals instrumentation to focus on an emerging problem.

Cisco Prime Infrastructure

Cisco's network management flagship is Cisco Prime Infrastructure. The application is
really the culmination of integrating the many sundry management applications that
fell within the CiscoWorks moniker over the past decade—which is certainly useful
and worthwhile. However, it also comes with a beefy price tag: upwards of US$20,000.

Cisco Prime Infrastructure does what CiscoWorks could not: It integrates wireless
and wired networks. We previously spoke about Cisco Wireless Control System (WCS)
as well as mentioned CiscoWorks LAN Management System (LMS) and Assurance.
These three tools have now been merged under the oversight of Prime Infrastructure—

and more tools are coming. Many other GUI client-based management tools will soon find themselves under this umbrella.

The primary dashboard shown in Figure 16-23 for Prime Infrastructure provides a customizable overview of your entire infrastructure—wireless and wired. All the menus are gotten to easily from the drop-down lists in the top-middle of the frame.

Cisco Prime Infrastructure is available as a virtual appliance ready for use within VMWare or as a physical appliance. Four sizes of appliances are available for scaling purposes, and licensing is modular. After purchasing the base license, you may add the following features:

- **Device lifecycle**   Available in quantities of 25, 50, 100, 500, 1,000, 2,500, 5,000 or 10,000 devices. Devices that count against the license pool are routers, switches, access points, and so on. Quantities are additive, so if you start with 25, you can grow further. Lifecycle management consists of device configuration, software image management, basic health and performance monitoring, fault management, troubleshooting, and network client visibility.

- **Automated deployment gateway**   A license that allows the use of the Automated Deployment feature on a separate server from the primary manager. New devices can check in with the gateway to receive their configuration and software image.

Figure 16-23.   Cisco Prime Infrastructure's dashboard allows you to see your entire network.

- **Assurance**   Based on the number of managed NetFlow-enabled interfaces and available in quantities of 15, 50, 100, 500, 1,000 and 5,000 NetFlow-enabled devices. Assurance grants end-to-end network visibility of application and service performance to help validate a very high end-user experience. The Assurance feature set also provides the ability to manage data and views across multiple Cisco Prime Network Analysis Modules (NAMs).

- **Compliance**   Allows access to regulatory compliance reports based on common government and industry regulatory standards. The following standards are supported today: PCI, HIPAA, CIS, DHS, DISA, NSA, SANS, SOX, ISO-17799, and Cisco SAFE. Compliance is licensed similarly to lifecycle, and the licensed device quantities should match.

Table 16-2 shows the available configuration options for Cisco Prime Infrastructure. Cisco has learned from the mistakes of the past. CiscoWorks LMS was available for Solaris and Windows platforms, and Cisco WCS was available for Windows or Linux. That's a lot of variety to program around, and a lot of variables to deal with at customer sites, performance-wise. With Prime Infrastructure, Cisco took those lessons to heart. The operating system is now included with Prime so that the underlying drivers, not just the application and database, are no longer variables. CiscoWorks LMS had a terrible reputation for usability and performance. Within the Prime Infrastructure platform, Cisco has rectified the situation—the new Prime Infrastructure NMS is easy to install and operate and is generally easier to understand.

Size	Hardware Requirements for Virtual Appliances
Small	Minimum 8GB RAM, minimum 200GB hard disk, and four virtual CPUs (vCPUs).
Medium	Minimum 12GB RAM, minimum 300GB hard disk, and four vCPUs.
Large	(VMware ESX/ESXi 5.0 only.) Minimum 16GB RAM, minimum 400GB hard disk, and 16 vCPUs.
Extra Large	(VMware ESX/ESXi 5.0 only.) Minimum 24GB RAM, minimum 1,200GB hard disk, and 16 vCPUs.
Cisco Physical	Appliance correlates with a large virtual appliance.

Table 16-2.   Cisco Prime Configuration Options

Prime Infrastructure supports many standards, such as SSH, Telnet, HTTP, HTTPS, and SNMPv1, v2c, and v3 for communicating with devices and other NMS. It supports TACACS+ within all aspects of the system and, in fact, has very deep integration with the Cisco Identity Control System. PNG, JPEG, and AutoCAD (DXF and DWG) import file types supported for the mapping functions. Some of the goodies inside include further integration with the Cisco knowledge base (which ensures optimal service and support), product updates, best practices, and reports to improve network availability. It's possible to open service requests and upload logs without leaving the system using Smart Interactions, as shown in Figure 16-24.

Just about every feature that had an issue in CiscoWorks LMS has been reinvented. The Device Work Center centralizes the simplified management of network inventory. Discovery, bulk and manual import, and software image management all live here. Customizable, predefined Cisco best practices and validated design configuration templates are included for speedy and straightforward device and service deployment. A new template called a *composite* allows greater tractability and packaging of individual templates into larger, reusable, purpose-built configurations for more consistent network designs. Figure 16-25 shows the out-of-the-box (OOTB) device management templates and the ease of generating your own templates.

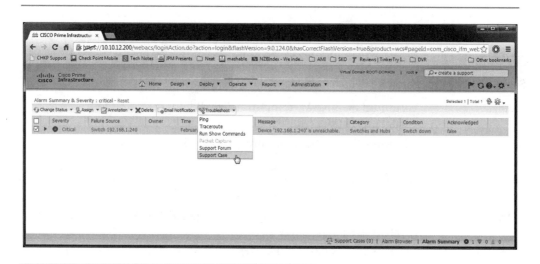

Figure 16-24.   Opening a service request within Prime Infrastructure

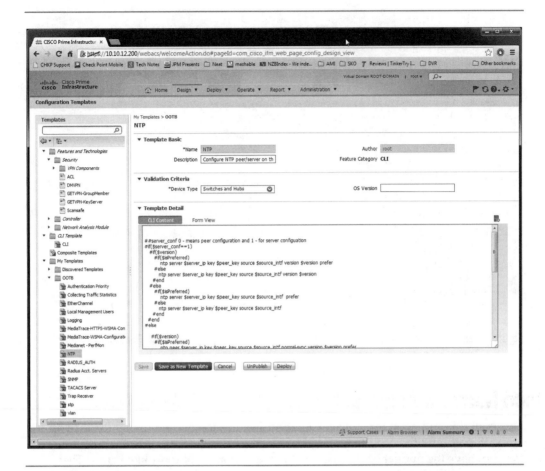

Figure 16-25. Cisco Prime Infrastructure features OOTB device management templates.

We've established that Prime Infrastructure is a vast improvement over CiscoWorks LMS, but the *coup de grâce* is the reporting. We had reporting before and—sorry to sound repetitive—this new version is so much easier to work with. *Dozens* of report templates are included with Prime Infrastructure, as shown in Figure 16-26.

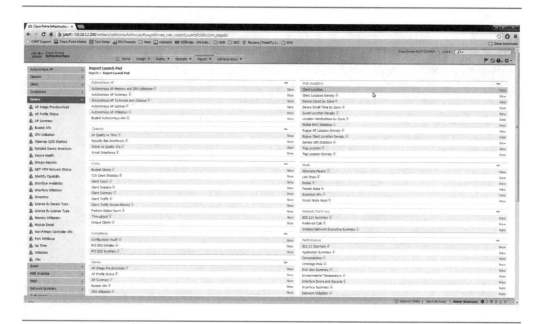

Figure 16-26.   Network admins will be happy to see all the reporting features in Prime Infrastructure.

Cisco Network Assistant

This is all fine and good for a big corporation that has the budget to pay for such an array of tools (and the need to manage many dozens of devices). Smaller companies may not have the budget or the need for such a robust set of tools like Prime. That doesn't leave them out in the cold when it comes to network management applications, however. Cisco Network Assistant (CNA) is a tool that can help.

CNA 5.8(5) is a PC-based network management application for small- and medium-sized organizations with networks of up to 250 users. The tool features network management and device configuration capabilities from a centralized location.

How much does this application cost? That's the best part. It's free.

Features

CNA utilizes a graphical user interface (GUI), so Cisco switches, routers, and access points can be easily configured and managed. CNA's features include

- Configuration management
- Troubleshooting information
- Inventory

- Event logging
- Network security
- Password synchronization
- IOS upgrades

CNA manages *communities* of devices. Communities are groupings of up to 80 networked devices (not including access points). The devices use the Cisco Discovery Protocol (CDP) to identify *qualified* network devices ("qualified" means that they are Cisco devices). Once a device has been added to the community, it becomes a *member device*.

Because each member device is individually managed, monitored, and configured, it must have its own IP address.

Communities might sound a lot like clusters. However, there are some important distinctions between the two. First, clusters can only support up to 16 devices, whereas communities can support 80 devices. Second, only switches are clusterable. Communities allow the inclusion of APs, routers, switches, and other network devices.

In addition, CNA can communicate securely with each device in a community. In a cluster, secure communications are only possible between CNA and the command device—the primary switch in the cluster.

Communities offer more failover support than clusters. If a command device fails, CNA won't be able to manage any other devices in the cluster. However, using communities, CNA is able to manage any other device in the community in the event another device fails.

Installation

Installing CNA is simple and free of charge. All you need is an account at www.cisco.com. Don't worry, this account is also free; you just need to fill out some online forms and you'll be able to download CNA in no time.

System Requirements

Before you download CNA, you must ensure that the computer you'll be running it on is up to speed. Table 16-3 outlines the system requirements.

How To

To install CNA, follow these steps:

1. Go to www.cisco.com/go/can.

2. Locate and download the CNA installer: cna-windows-k9-installer-5-8-5-en.exe.

3. Double-click the installer on your computer and follow the onscreen instructions to complete installation and setup.

4. Once installation is complete, double-click the Cisco Network Assistant icon on your desktop or locate it on your Start menu.

Feature	Requirement
Processor	1 GHz
Memory	1 Gb recommended
Hard drive space	50 MB minimum, 200 MB recommended
Colors	65,536
Screen resolution	1,024 x 768
Supported operating systems	Windows 7, 2008, 2003, Vista, XP/wSP3 Apple OS X

Table 16-3.   System Requirements for Cisco Network Assistant 5.8

Views

There are two ways you can look at your community and devices. CNA offers the Front Panel view and the Topology view.

Front Panel View

The Front Panel view is used to manage the port settings and configuration details for one or more devices. The Front Panel view of a Cisco Catalyst 2960 switch is shown in Figure 16-27.

To access the Front Panel view, click Front Panel on the toolbar, or click Monitor | View Front Panel.

This displays the front panel of the device. If the device belongs to a community, all the devices that were selected the last time the Front Panel view was displayed appear for that community. If the device is a command device of a cluster, cluster members that were selected the last time the view was selected are displayed.

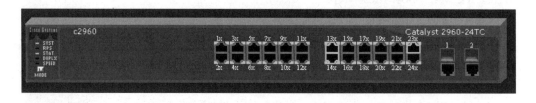

Figure 16-27.   Cisco Network Assistant's Front Panel view gives an overview of your device's status.

The Front Panel view allows you to do the following:

- Rearrange devices
- Select and configure devices
- Configure individual ports
- Configure multiple ports on multiple devices simultaneously

Topology View

Whereas the Front Panel view allows you to examine a specific device or devices, the Topology view shows the entire membership of your community or cluster. The Topology view is the default view. If you need to switch back to the view once in Front Panel view, click Topology view on the toolbar or click Monitor | View | Topology.

The Topology view allows you to view VLAN links and add or remove devices from the community. Figure 16-28 shows the Topology view of a small network with a router and an AP.

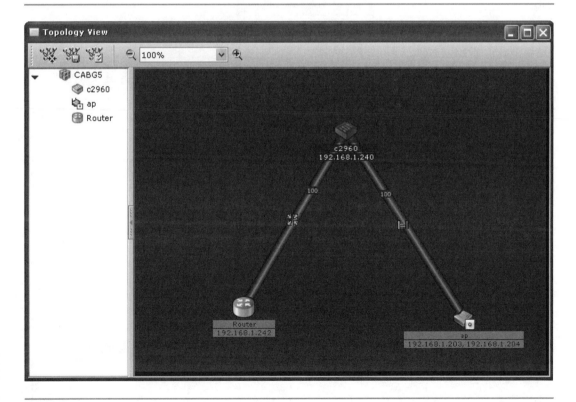

Figure 16-28. Cisco Network Assistant's Topology view shows a diagram of your network's managed devices.

Interaction

CNA allows you to configure and manage devices in several ways. This section explains the various ways you can interact with CNA.

Guide and Expert Mode

The two fundamental ways to interact with CNA are through Guide mode or Expert mode. Guide mode is oriented more to beginners because it walks you through configuration and management steps one at a time. Expert mode presents all the configuration options at once.

By default, CNA is in Expert mode. Clicking a feature on the Feature bar that shows a signpost icon, as shown in Figure 16-29, takes you to Guide mode.

If you select a feature without this icon, you will be in Expert mode.

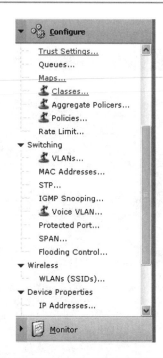

Figure 16-29.   Signpost icons on the Feature bar show items that can be managed in Guide mode.

Wizards

CNA also offers a number of wizards to help with configuration and management. Wizards are like Guide mode in that they are meant to simplify the configuration process. However, they are unlike Guide mode in that they do not prompt you for every bit of information. Rather, they prompt you for minimal information and fill in the blanks with default settings.

Smartports Advisor

Smartports Advisor uses predefined settings, or *roles,* for devices. When CNA starts, it checks to see if Smartports have already been applied to the devices. If they have not been applied, CNA will ask you if you want those roles applied to your devices.

Smartports can help you configure your devices with optimal security, availability, Quality of Service, and manageability.

Smartports Advisor shows you the devices to which you are connected, and then the ports to which Smartports roles have been applied are shown. Smartports Advisor also shows the ports to which Smartports roles could be applied.

Communities

Once you've installed and started CNA, you can connect to an existing community or device. You can also create a new community.

Connecting

When you start CNA, use the Connect window, as shown in Figure 16-30, to connect to a specific device or an existing community.

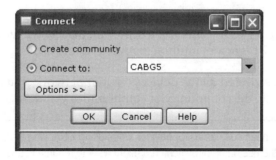

Figure 16-30. The Connect window allows you to select which community you'll connect to.

To connect to a specific community, click the Connect to a New Community option. To connect to a specific community, click the Connect To option and then select the community from the drop-down menu. To connect to an existing cluster, select the command device's IP address from the drop-down menu.

Clicking the Options button allows you to do the following:

- Communicate with a stand-alone device or cluster command device using HTTPS rather than unsecure HTTP
- Use an HTTP port other than 80
- Connect with read-only access

Once you've selected the community that you want to access, you'll be prompted for a username and password.

If you are connecting to a cluster, CNA asks you if you'd like to convert the cluster to a community. You simply enter the cluster command device's IP address, and CNA will convert it. Don't worry if you want to retain the cluster's properties. CNA will not delete that information, and you can still use it as part of a cluster.

Planning

Although CNA is rather user friendly, it is not without its limitations and rules for developing your own communities.

As noted earlier, a community cannot exceed 80 devices (access points do not count against this limit). When you exceed the number of maximum allowable devices, a window will open and tell you how many of each type of device you have. You will not be able to manage the community until you get to the appropriate number of devices.

But what if you have too many devices? Easy: Just create a new community. There is no limit on the number of communities you can manage with CNA.

Discovery

When CNA starts, you enter the IP address of one of your devices, as shown in Figure 16-31. Then, using CDP, CNA will discover all the Cisco devices in your network. CNA can discover devices across multiple networks and VLANs, assuming they have valid IP addresses.

Once CNA has discovered all the devices on your network, you can sort through them to place them into the community or communities you desire.

 NOTE   You won't need hostnames for devices when using CNA. However, IOS automatically assigns switches the hostname of Switch. You might want to rename your switches before running CNA, simply to make it easier to know which switch is which.

You will be prompted for passwords only when an already entered password does not work on a given device. For example, if you have 20 devices and they all have the

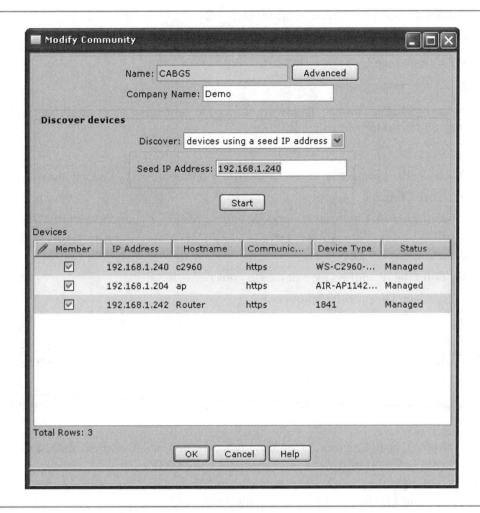

Figure 16-31.   Enter the IP address of one of your devices to start the discovery process.

same password, you will only have to enter the password once. However, if they all
have different passwords, you'll have to enter 20 different passwords. The most current
version will allow you to tie your device credentials to an encrypted local file that is
opened by logging in to the application with your CCO account. Handy, huh?

Creation

The aforementioned sections were useful when connecting to an existing community,
but you'll likely need to create your own community before you start.

Communities can be created in one of three ways:

- Discovering and adding devices
- Adding members manually
- Converting a cluster

Discovering and Adding Devices   Follow these steps to generate a list of candidate devices and then add them to your community:

1. Start CNA.
2. Select the **Connect to a New Community** option in the Connect window.
3. Click **Connect.**
4. In the Create Community window, enter a name for your community.
5. If you want to select an HTTP port other than 80, click the **Advanced** button and then click **OK.**
6. Enter the IP address for a device in your network.
7. Click on **Discover Neighbors.**
8. In the Devices Found list, select devices you wish to remove.
9. Click the **Remove button.**
10. To add the remaining devices to your new community, click on **Add All to Community.**

Adding Members Manually   You can manually add member devices to a community in two ways:

- In the Create Community window, enter the device's IP address and then click **Add to Community.**
- In the Topology view, right-click a candidate device's icon and select **Add to Community** from the resulting context menu.

 NOTE   Members of a community are labeled green, whereas candidate devices are cyan.

Converting a Cluster   If you want to convert a cluster to a community from the application, you can do so by clicking Configure | Cluster | Cluster Conversion Wizard.

Using CNA

Once you're connected to your community, using CNA is simply a matter of navigating the GUI. In this section, the configuration and management of a Catalyst 2960 switch is examined.

There are many ways to get to the different settings and windows described in this section. We'll turn our attention to the leftmost pane (also called the Feature bar) in CNA. This contains the various settings we can manage, but many can also be set via an icon at the top of the screen or from within a context menu somewhere within the application. For the sake of consistency, we'll talk about the attributes as they are accessed from the Feature bar.

Configure

The Configure portion of the CNA tool allows you to manage such features as ports, security, QoS, switching, and device properties.

Ports This window allows you to manage port settings and EtherChannels. Figure 16-32 shows the Configuration Settings tab of Port Settings. Making a change is as easy as right-clicking an attribute and selecting the new setting from the drop-down menu.

The Runtime Status tab shows the current status of the device. Selecting EtherChannels beneath the Configure\Ports heading allows you to manage EtherChannel settings for your device.

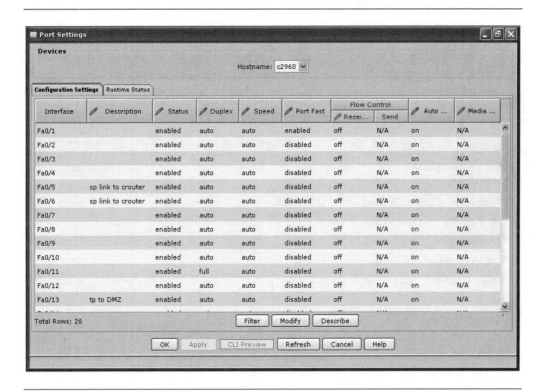

Figure 16-32. Port Settings is where you can manage attributes of your device's ports.

Security Port security is managed with this setting. This window has two tabs:

- **Security Configuration** This is used for checking port security settings and configuring a secure port. Secure ports are ports where a user-specified action initiates whenever an address-security violation occurs.

- **Secure Address** This is used for adding, removing, or managing secure addresses. Secure addresses are MAC addresses that are forwarded to only one port per VLAN.

To manage this setting, select a device from the Hostname list whose security settings you want to manage. You can filter the results of the list by clicking Filter and using the Filter Editor window.

Quality of Service The device's Quality of Service (QoS) settings are managed with this attribute. Incoming packets contain a Class of Service (CoS) value (0 to 7) or a Differentiated Services Code Point (DSCP) value (0 to 63).

You decide which marker you want to trust and what default CoS value to assign a packet if it contains no marker. This is done by selecting Trust Settings under the Quality of Service setting. The resulting window is shown in Figure 16-33.

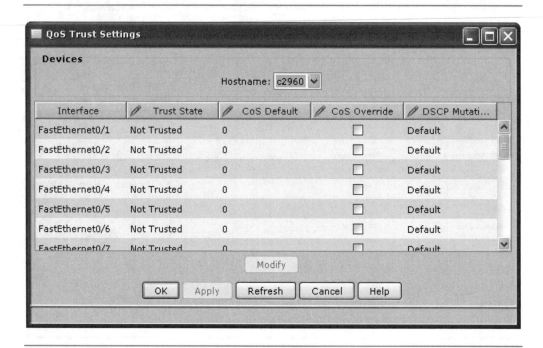

Figure 16-33. Quality of Service management in Cisco Network Assistant helps control network traffic flow.

Switching   This attribute allows you to configure various features of your switch. The features here are similar to the configuration capabilities of Cluster Management Suite (CMS), which was covered in Chapter 5. CNA simply provides another way to configure these settings. It also provides an environment in which you can apply consistent configuration settings across all or select devices in a community.

For more information on configuring a switch, flip back to Chapter 5.

Device Properties   The Device Properties setting allows you to manage such device basics as IP address, gateway information, and usernames and passwords.

Monitor

The Monitor section of the Feature bar allows you to review various bits of information and statistics about your device. The two portions of the Monitor attribute are Reports and Views.

Reports   The Reports setting lets you review statistics for your device, including the following:

- **Inventory**   Gives a listing of devices in your community, along with device type, serial number, MAC address, IP address, and IOS version.
- **Port statistics**   Gives information about port transmit and receive rates.
- **Bandwidth graphs**   Provides line and bar charts depicting bandwidth usage, like the one shown in Figure 16-34.
- **Link graphs**   Provides line and bar charts depicting link statistics.
- **ARP**   Provides a table linking the device and its MAC address to its IP address. The table also shows the age of the entry in the table, its encapsulation method, and the device interface.

Views   Views allows you to review system events and messages. For example, the Event Notification setting will alert you to events that CNA deems important, such as the following:

- A device with a high temperature
- A device with a broken fan
- A port with a duplex mismatch
- An unknown device on the network

System messages can be configured to send you an e-mail when a message is generated.

Troubleshoot

If you're having trouble with a device, the Troubleshoot attribute offers a Ping and Trace feature.

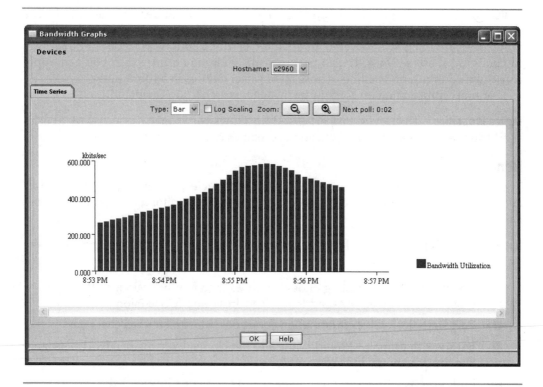

Figure 16-34.   The Bandwidth graphs show line and bar charts showing bandwidth usage.

You can trace on a layer-2 or layer-3 route. A layer-2 route determines the source-to-destination network path of a layer-2 device. A layer-3 trace determines the path that a packet travels in a layer-3 network, but does not include information about layer-2 devices.

The Ping and Trace window is shown in Figure 16-35.

Maintenance

The final attribute is Maintenance, where you can manage the functionality of CNA. One of its best features is the ability to upgrade software for devices in your community. Click on Software Upgrade, and the window shown in Figure 16-36 opens.

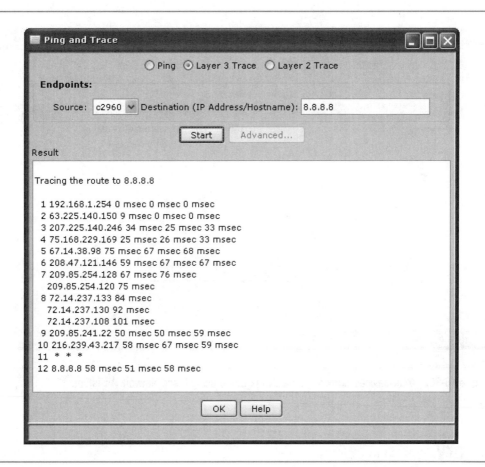

Figure 16-35.   Cisco Network Assistant provides Ping and Trace services to help with troubleshooting.

This allows you to select specific devices in your community that you wish CNA to upgrade. When you select Upgrade Settings, you specify where on your computer or in the network the updated file is located. Your devices' upgrade files can be found on www.cisco.com.

Configuration Archive stores old community and device configurations, and System Reload saves the current device configuration and restarts the device.

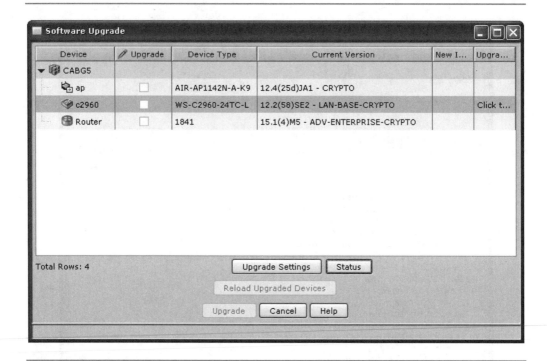

Figure 16-36.   Your devices' firmware is easily upgraded using Cisco Network Assistant.

Summary

Network management is an incredibly important task to keep up on. The work on a network doesn't stop once it has been built and configured. Networks are dynamic environments, and it is necessary to constantly monitor your network's performance and make the requisite tweaks. Happily, Cisco offers a number of applications to keep on top of your network's behavior.

CHAPTER 17 | Network Design Process

W e've now covered the components that make up an internetwork. In this chapter, we'll put this knowledge to work by examining the network design process and configuring networks to fit various design scenarios.

As you've seen, there is no shortage of technologies and products to choose from—even in Cisco's product line alone. You've also seen how there is no free lunch in networking: every design move brings a trade-off of one kind or another. Trade-offs can come in the form of reduced bandwidth to carry payload traffic, increased complexity, additional expense, or other disadvantages. When designing a network, you need to know not only what the options are, but also how to juggle them to strike the best possible balance.

Each year brings so many new products and advances in technology that just keeping the acronyms straight is difficult. In this chapter, we'll sort things out a bit by applying Cisco's array of products to real-world problems. Looking at internetwork configuration problems will help put things into perspective and bring those critical trade-offs into sharper focus.

Internetwork Design Basics

Internetworking is geographical by nature, so most design practices have to do with matching topology to needs. (Recall from Chapter 7 that a *topology* is a map of an internetwork's physical layout.) The layout of an internetwork largely dictates how it will perform and how well it can scale. In networking, *scale* (or *scalability)* means how much an internetwork can grow without having to change the basic shape of its topology (that is, without having to replace or excessively reconfigure an existing infrastructure).

Internetworking Basics Reviewed

One last run-through of what you've learned thus far is in order. Doing so is especially important here, because in this chapter we'll be looking at a variety of design factors and options. Therefore, we need to be clear on the various components that make up an internetwork.

LAN Segments

Switches form LAN segments, the basic building block of every internetwork. Each switch port is a segment brought through a process called "microsegmentation." A LAN segment could be a departmental LAN or a high-speed LAN backbone servicing dozens of other LAN segments within an enterprise.

NOTE To review, a LAN segment is a physical medium shared among a group of devices. Most LAN segments are formed by hubs or VLANs within switches. Strictly speaking, a LAN segment is a LAN. Usually, though, the term LAN is used to refer to a local network consisting of many LAN segments.

Collision and Broadcast Domains

A *collision domain* is a shared network medium in which Ethernet packets are allowed to collide; a broadcast domain is the area within which messages may be sent to all stations using a so-called broadcast address. Collision domains should be kept small because collisions limit the use of bandwidth. The more hosts that are connected to a LAN segment, the slower the traffic moves.

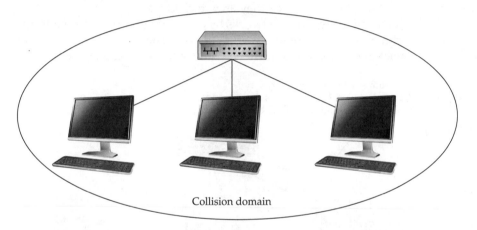

Collision domain

Most collision domains are formed by hubs that connect host devices to the internetwork. Hubs are the functional equivalent of the Ethernet cable segments used in the early days of local area networking. Switches segment collision domains on each switch port.

NOTE Collision domains exist in environments in which hubs are used. This being the twenty-first century and all, not many networks are going to install new hubs as part of their topology. That said, you may encounter some networks with legacy hubs; therefore, understanding how collision domains work is useful.

Some broadcasts are useful, but too many can bog down a network in useless overhead traffic—an unwelcome phenomenon called a "broadcast storm." Broadcast domains are, by default, the same as a network's collision domain for shared media (in other words, hubs), but the scope of broadcast addresses can be made smaller than a collision domain using switches. Routers normally limit broadcasts, but a broadcast domain can be extended by configuring a router to let broadcast messages pass.

Shared Bandwidth vs. Switched Bandwidth

Switches also connect hosts to networks, but in a fundamentally different way. A switch "time slices" network access among its attached hosts in such a way that each switch port forms a channel with a collision domain of one. This is called *switched bandwidth*, as opposed to the *shared bandwidth* of hubs. Switched networks are estimated to be ten times faster than shared networks over the same medium.

Moreover, switched networks support virtual LANs (VLANs), enabling administrators to group users rationally instead of being forced to group them according to the host devices to which they are attached.

In addition to forming switched networks by connecting hosts, larger switches connect LAN segments to form internetworks. To avoid confusion, the two types of switches are sometimes called access switches and LAN (or backbone) switches.

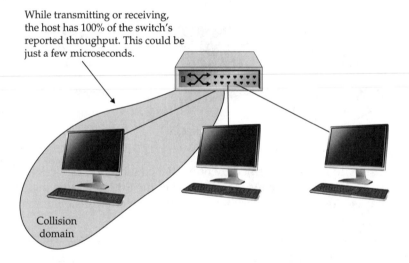

While transmitting or receiving, the host has 100% of the switch's reported throughput. This could be just a few microseconds.

Collision domain

Routers Control Internetworks

The third basic device in internetworking is the router. Routers connect LAN segments instead of connecting hosts, as do hubs and access switches. Routers are used to isolate intramural traffic and to provide internal security. In addition, they can extend broadcast and multicast domains to specified LAN segments to help bind those networks into a functional unit.

Routers are deployed both inside internetworks and at the edge of autonomous systems. Inside routers are sometimes called internal routers or access routers. Routers that concentrate on communicating with the outside are called edge or gateway routers. For example, an Internet service provider (ISP) will use gateway routers to connect to the Internet. By contrast, a big company will place at least one internal router at each of its major sites to help manage in-house traffic.

Routers are more intelligent than hubs and switches because they are able to interpret network addresses. They read network addresses in order to filter traffic, control access to networks or services, and choose the best path to reach a destination. Routers bring internetworks to life. It's no coincidence that the three most basic devices in internetworking operate at different levels of the seven-layer OSI reference model, as illustrated here:

Level 3 Network layer		209.98.123.74 IP address

Level 2 Data-link layer	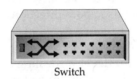 Switch	4254.1d83.ec07 MAC address

Routers operate at the network layer (layer 3). Today, most internetworks use IP network addresses—all Internet routers do. But many internal routers must still use a legacy desktop protocol such as IPX, AppleTalk, or DECnet. For that reason, Cisco and its competitors have invested heavily in engineering multiprotocol products to allow legacy LANs to interoperate with IP. Cisco's IOS feature sets exist mostly to give network designers options in purchasing system software that fits their network protocol needs.

Routers Use Layer-3 Network Addresses

Whether IP or a legacy layer-3 protocol, network addresses are inherently hierarchical. One way to look at it is that as a router works its way rightward through an IP address, it zeros in on the LAN segment to which the destination host is attached. Over long-haul routes, moves through the address are manifested in hops between routers. A one-hop route would require only finding the LAN segment on which the destination resides.

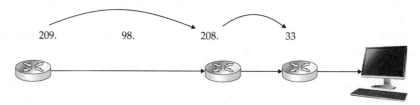

Routes are often summarized before being shared with other routers. This improves performance by greatly reducing the number of address entries carried inside a router's route table. Route summarization, called *route aggregation,* works by relying on a gateway router to know the target LAN segment's full address and allowing interim routers to carry fewer, summarized entries in their respective routing tables, thereby improving performance. Address translation is also frequently used, where internal addresses are either altered or grouped into a global address in packets sent outside an internetwork. Mechanisms such as Port Address Translation (PAT) and Network Address Translation (NAT) are used at edge routers or firewalls to make these translations in the packet address fields in both directions.

Switches Use Layer-2 MAC Addresses

Switches operate at the data-link layer (layer 2), dealing in MAC addresses instead of network addresses. A MAC address is a long number that uniquely identifies physical hardware devices. MACs combine a manufacturer code with a serial number. Even routers use MAC addresses for a message's last step—resolving an IP address to the physical MAC address to locate the destination host within the LAN segment.

MAC addresses are topologically flat. The logical profile of a MAC address appears as if all hosts are connected to the same cable; it offers no clue as to where hosts are located because it's basically a serial number. Switched networks, therefore, must operate by brute force, flooding broadcasts of MAC addresses to all ports when a destination MAC is unknown.

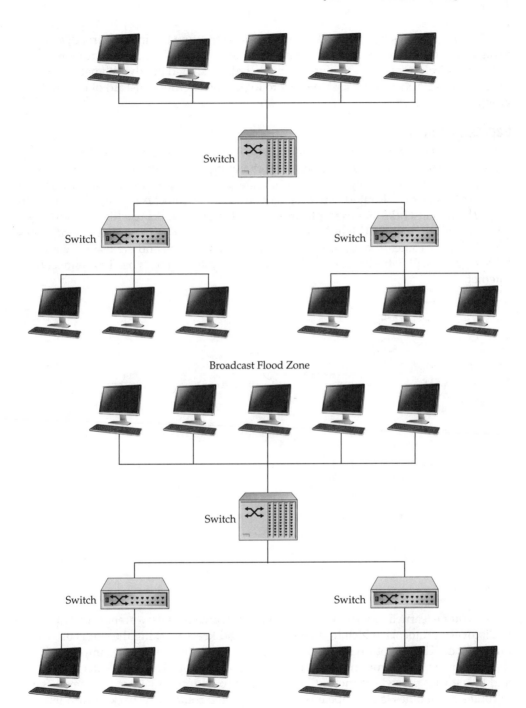

Broadcast Flood Zone

VLAN Broadcast Flood Zone

VLANs give switched networks a hierarchical structure by limiting broadcasts to discrete groups of users. This combines the speed of switched bandwidth with the hierarchical topology heretofore available only in shared bandwidth networks. In addition, VLANs flexibly assign users to logical workgroups instead of having to group users by device.

Path Optimization

Internetworks use control protocols to route messages. There is so much dynamic change in internetworks—through growth, changing traffic patterns, a device going down, and the like—that they must self-operate to some degree by constantly updating device routing tables. Routed networks rely on routing protocols to keep track of paths through internetworks. For example, many small internetworks use RIP 2; most large ones use EIGRP or OSPF (EIGRP is Cisco proprietary; OSPF is an open standard). These trade in lists of routes, mostly within an autonomous system, and are used to connect LAN segments. BGP trades in lists of autonomous systems and is used to connect the Internet.

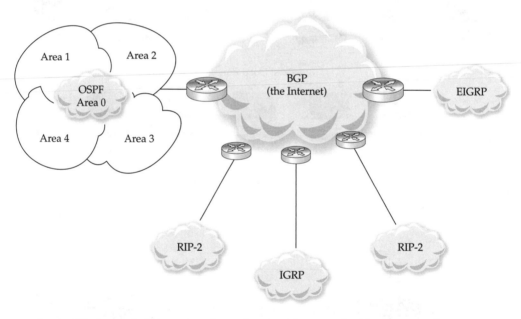

As you've learned, internetworks maintain a degree of self-awareness by way of discovery protocols, which find new devices and keep checking the status of known ones. These protocols—Cisco Discovery Protocol (CDP) is an example—are the supporting cast to routing protocols. When an event takes place, it's discovered and the news is passed around until the device population converges on a new list of routes. Sometimes loops appear where a suggested route turns back toward its source device, creating nonsensical routes that can slow or even crash an internetwork.

Routing protocols use metrics to tune internetworks. RIP uses only hop count, but the more sophisticated protocols use several metrics that can be combined into a weighted matrix to steer traffic along desired links.

Switched networks aren't so sophisticated. Switches only maintain lists of MAC addresses, with the most recently used MACs appearing toward the top, the highest one being the first choice. Switched networks use the Spanning Tree Protocol (STP) to prevent loops.

Internetwork Architectures and Applications

In just the past few years, the design requirements of the typical enterprise have changed radically. These changes have occurred at opposite ends of the topology. At the bottom, segmentation using hubs with access switches has greatly increased the number of LAN segments and, therefore, the amount of traffic to go over the backbone between segments. At the top, whole new computing architectures are becoming standard, with web-based intranets replacing traditional client-server management systems, extranets transforming traditional electronic data interchange (EDI) systems, and virtual private networks (VPNs) replacing leased-line wide area networks (WANs).

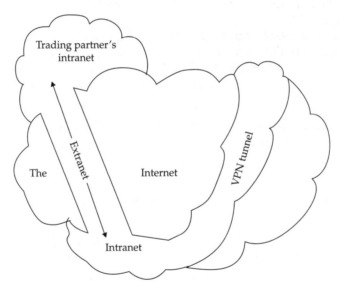

Driving even more change is the fact that new network applications have changed traffic characteristics. For example, videoconferencing is becoming popular, increasing the need for configurations optimized to handle multicasts—where a single copy of a message is forwarded to a subset of destination hosts.

The Three-Layer Hierarchical Design Model

Hierarchical topologies are inherently better than flat ones for a number of reasons, the main one being that hierarchy contains traffic to its local area. The rule of thumb designers use is that broadcast traffic should not exceed 20 percent of the packets going over each link—the implication being that segmentation will naturally boost throughput by isolating traffic to its most likely users. This rule of thumb applies only to the amount of broadcast packets in the traffic mix, and is not to be confused with the 80/20 rule. The 80/20 rule states that 80 percent of all traffic stays home and only 20 percent goes beyond the local area.

A flat topology—one in which each device does more or less the same job—increases the number of neighbors with which an individual device must communicate. This increases somewhat the amount of payload traffic the device is likely to carry and greatly increases overhead traffic. For example, each time a router receives a broadcast message, its CPU is interrupted. For many small internetworks, a flat topology is sufficient, and the added expense and complexity that hierarchy requires isn't warranted. But it doesn't take many LAN segments to hurt an internetwork's performance and reliability, with devices and hosts bogged down in unnecessary traffic.

This is why the industry adheres to a classical hierarchical design model. The model has three layers: the access, distribution, and core layers. This separates local traffic from high-volume traffic passing between LAN segments and areas, and lets network devices at each layer concentrate on doing their specific job. The hierarchical model is depicted in Figure 17-1.

Hierarchy is made possible by segmentation—the practice of dividing hosts into smaller LAN segments. Fifteen years ago, most LAN segments were actual cable spans running through walls and ceiling plenums. Today, most are formed by "cable-in-a-box" using VLANs within access switches. Segmentation and hierarchical topology yield several benefits:

- **Performance**   Traffic is isolated to source areas, thereby narrowing Ethernet packet collision domains and speeding throughput.

- **Reliability**   Most faults are isolated to the segment from which the problem originated.

- **Simplicity**   By separating dissimilar areas, network elements can be replicated as needed throughout the internetwork.

- **Scalability**   Modular design elements can be added as the internetwork grows over time, with minimal disruption of existing networks.

- **Security**   Access can be controlled at well-defined junctures between the layers.

Internetworks naturally tend toward a two-level hierarchy. Hubs and switches connect host devices into LAN segments, and the backbone connects the segments into a local network, whether within a floor, building, office campus, or even a metropolitan area. This is a relatively flat topology in the sense that, even though collision domains are limited, excessive broadcast traffic still chews into available bandwidth. This makes the distribution layer the key. By isolating traffic, the distribution layer also isolates problems and complexity.

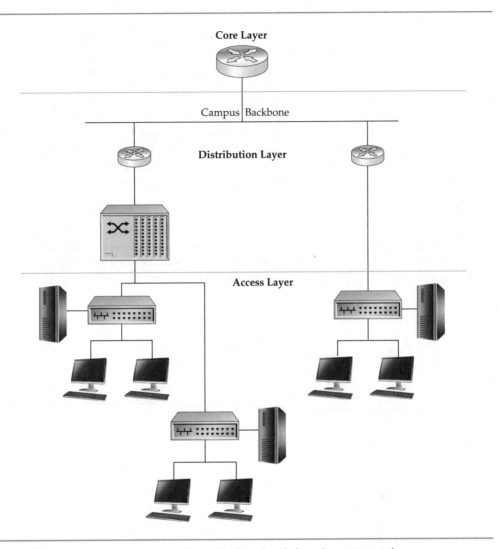

Figure 17-1. The classical three-layer hierarchical topology is based on segmentation.

Hierarchy also helps reduce costs. By dividing hosts and traffic, variations are limited to fewer LAN segments, or even to a single segment. Variations include such things as desktop protocols (mostly variations of IP), traffic volumes (workgroup versus backbone), and traffic type (big graphical files, e-mail, and HTTP). Hierarchy allows the network designer to tune the configuration for the particular job at hand. Adjustments are made in the model of network device purchased and in how it is configured in terms of memory, modules, software, and config file parameter settings.

The Access Layer

The access layer is made up mostly of hubs and switches, which serve to segment host devices, such as PCs and servers, into many LAN segments made up of either shared or switched bandwidth. This is where MAC-layer filtering can take place.

If an internetwork has remote sites, such as branch offices or home offices, the access layer would also include access servers and access routers. WANs must use some type of long-distance transmission medium. There is a wide selection of media now, such as leased digital T1 or T3 lines and Frame Relay public digital networks. Dial-in remote users employ analog modem lines and, in populated areas, higher-bandwidth technologies, such as Digital Subscriber Line (DSL), DOCIS cable, and Integrated Services Digital Network (ISDN). Figure 17-2 shows access-layer functionality.

In large internetworks, the access layer can include routers. These internal routers serve mostly to isolate overhead, control traffic, and enhance internal security. The access layer encompasses a mix of technologies in most internetworks. Dial-on-demand routing (DDR) has become popular for remote connections, because it keeps a link inactive except when traffic needs to be sent, thereby reducing telecommunication costs.

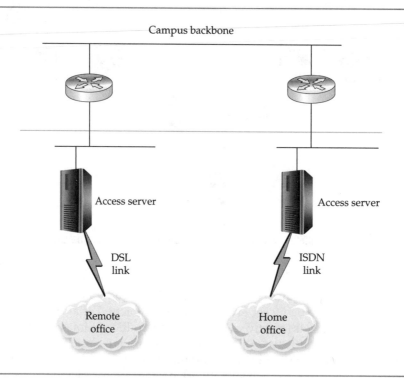

Figure 17-2. The access layer provides both local and remote connectivity to hosts.

Most enterprises have legacy technologies that are being gradually phased out as new ones are implemented. For example, many big companies still use their leased-line T1 WANs alongside growing VPNs, substituting shared network usage for dedicated leased lines. From a practical standpoint, this is necessary because the routers must be upgraded along each VPN link.

The Distribution Layer

The distribution layer is made up mostly of routers and layer-3 switches. They're used to separate slow-speed local traffic from the high-speed backbone. Traffic at the access layer tends to be bandwidth intensive because that's where most LAN and host addresses reside. Network overhead protocol traffic for discovery protocols, SNMP, routing protocols, and other network control systems is heavier at the access layer.

Because routers are intelligent enough to read network addresses and examine packets, they also improve performance by sending traffic as directly as possible to its destination. For example, distribution-layer routers define broadcast and multicast domains across LAN segments. Domains are, by default, limited to LAN segments; routers can extend domains across segments as the hierarchy design dictates. Figure 17-3 depicts distribution-layer functionality.

In configurations using multilayer switches, distribution-layer devices route messages between VLANs. *Multilayer switching* is a technology in which packets are filtered and forwarded based on both MAC and network addresses. The Catalyst 6500 is perhaps the best example of a multilayer switch, incorporating various Multilayer Switch Feature Cards (those currently being the MSFC 3, 4 and 5) in addition to those with typical switch electronics.

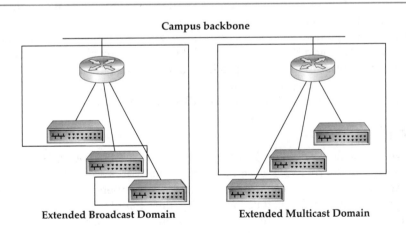

Figure 17-3. The distribution layer is the key to providing a functional hierarchy.

Most value-added services are provided by devices at the distribution layer. Address translation takes place at this layer, usually on a gateway router or a firewall (itself a type of router). Address aggregation also takes place here, as well as area aggregation if the internetwork is running OSPF routing domains. Other services are also performed on distribution-layer routers: translation between protocols such as IPX and IP, encryption for VPN tunneling, traffic-based security using access lists and context-based firewall algorithms, and user-based security using RADIUS, TACACS+, or Kerberos.

The Core Layer

The core layer is the backbone layer. In large internetworks, the core incorporates multiple backbones, from campus backbone LANs up through regional ones. Sometimes, special backbone LANs are configured to handle a specific protocol or particularly sensitive traffic. Most backbones exist to connect LAN segments, usually those within a particular building or office campus. Figure 17-4 depicts how the core layer might look in a typical large-enterprise internetwork.

To run fast, a backbone LAN should be configured to experience a minimum of interruptions. The goal is to have as many backbone device CPU cycles as possible spent transferring packets among segments. The distribution layer makes this possible by connecting workgroup LAN segments and providing value-added routing services. A minimum of packet manipulation should occur at this level. This is why most new backbones are switched LANs. The need for address interpretation at the core is minimized by the processing already performed by distribution-layer routers, so why not use switching technology to move data over the backbone much faster?

ATM (Asynchronous Transfer Mode) and Gigabit Ethernet battled to become the switched backbone technology of choice. ATM had an edge for multimedia applications because it uses fixed-sized cells instead of Ethernet's variable-length packets. The obvious advantage of Gigabit Ethernet switched backbones is easier compatibility with the millions of Ethernet LANs already installed throughout the world. In the end, however, Gigabit Ethernet won the war.

ATM is an international cell relay standard for service types such as video, voice, and data. The fixed-length 53-byte cells speed data transfer by allowing processing to occur in hardware. Although ATM products exist to take data all the way to the desktop, the technology is optimized to work with high-speed transmission media such as OC-48 (2.5 Gbps), T3 (45 Mbps), and T3's European counterpart, E3 (34 Mbps).

Design Methods

Over the years, the networking industry has developed a set of concepts and best practices for use in internetwork design. Most internetworks are works in progress; very few are designed from a clean sheet of paper. As internetwork topologies evolve through time and circumstance, it becomes difficult to maintain a rigorous hierarchical network design—especially in large enterprises with distributed management structures or in shops that have high personnel turnover in their network teams. This is where reference designs come into play. A *reference design* is one that can be templated and replicated repeatedly. Cisco has been very good about plentiful documentation and drawings on their reference designs in years past, and will continue to do so.

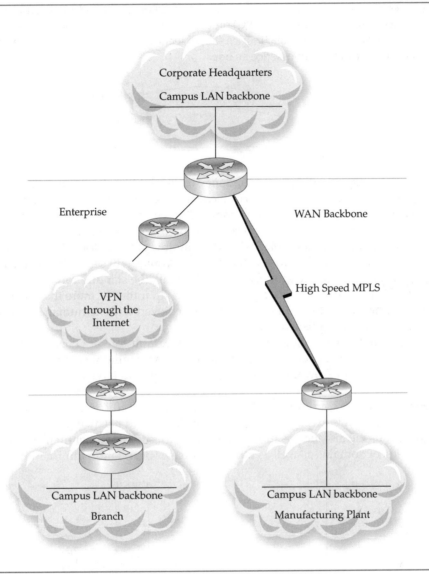

Figure 17-4. The core layer includes campus LAN backbones and WAN backbones.

Redundancy and Load Balancing

Redundancy is the practice of configuring backup equipment. This is done to provide fault tolerance, where traffic will shift to the backup device if the primary unit fails, which is a process called *failover*. For example, most high-speed backbones have dual-configured switches at each end in case the primary switch goes down. A common safeguard is to have redundant power supplies within a device, so that if one fails, the device keeps running. Cisco also has other technologies that address redundancy issues such as Virtual PortChannel (VPC) on the Nexus platform and the Virtual Switching System (VSS) on the 6500 series. These technologies allow pairs of chassis-based switches to function in essence as one.

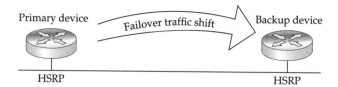

Cisco's technology to support redundancy is the Hot Standby Router Protocol (HSRP), a suite of commands in IOS. *Hot standby* is a computer industry term meaning that the backup unit is always up and running, thereby allowing automatic in the event of a failure. HSRP works by creating a group of routers, where one is elected as the active router and another is elected as the standby, or "phantom," router. They all share a virtual IP and MAC address that the active router will serve. The active router is monitored by others in the group, and should it fail, the standby router will take over the traffic-processing duties, and another backup router (if more than two) will be elected as the new standby router. Failovers are achieved with no human intervention and are generally accomplished in a few seconds.

Because redundant configurations are expensive, fault-tolerant configurations are usually limited to critical devices. Redundancy is most commonly configured into backbone devices and firewalls, where device failure would have the broadest effect on the overall network.

Load balancing is a configuration technique that shifts traffic to an alternative link if a certain threshold is exceeded on the primary link. Load balancing can be achieved through various means, such as tuning routing metrics in router config files within routing protocol domains as well as traffic's source or destination information.

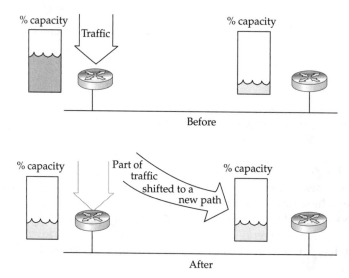

Load balancing is similar to redundancy in that an event causes traffic to shift directions, and alternative equipment must be present in the configuration. But in load balancing, the alternative equipment isn't necessarily *redundant* equipment that only operates in the event of failure.

Topology Meshing

A good design will incorporate a meshed topology to achieve redundancy and load balancing. A *mesh* is where two network devices—usually routers or switches—are directly connected. In a fully meshed topology, all network nodes have either physical or virtual circuits connecting them to every other node in the internetwork. You can also have a partially meshed topology, in which some parts of the topology are fully meshed but some nodes are connected only to one or two other nodes. Figure 17-5 depicts the two.

At first blush, all meshing seems to be an inherently good thing. Looking at the example in Figure 17-5, you can readily see the benefits in the full-mesh topology:

- **Performance**   It's only a single hop to any network attached to one of the other routers, and the fewer the hops, the faster the speed.

- **Availability**   Having redundant paths means that if any one router goes down, one or more alternate routes are always available.

- **Load balancing**   Alternative paths can also be used for normal operations, where routing parameters can be configured to use alternate paths if a preset traffic load is exceeded on the primary router.

The partially meshed internetwork on the bottom of Figure 17-5 doesn't have these advantages. For example, to go from router A to C takes two router hops, not one. If routers on both sides of router F go down, it will be unable to communicate with the rest of the internetwork. Also, fewer mesh connections reduce opportunities for load balancing. However, although meshing can bring benefits, it must be used carefully, because it comes at the following costs:

- **Expense**   Every router (or switch) interface dedicated to meshing is one that can't be used to connect a LAN segment. Meshing consumes hardware capacity.

- **Overhead traffic**   Devices constantly advertise their services to one another. The more mesh links a device has, the more advertisement packets it broadcasts, thereby eating into payload bandwidth.

- **Vulnerability**   Meshing makes it more difficult to contain problems within a local area. If a misconfigured device begins propagating indiscriminate broadcast messages, for example, each element in a mesh will cause the broadcast storm to radiate farther from the source.

- **Complexity**   Additional connections make it more difficult to isolate problems. For example, it would be harder to track down the device causing the broadcast storm in a fully or heavily meshed internetwork, because there would be so many trails to follow.

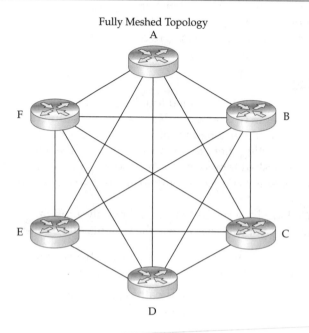

Fully Meshed Topology

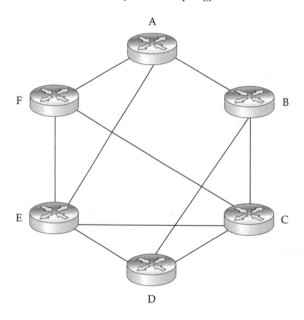

Partially Meshed Topology

Figure 17-5.   Fully meshed and partially meshed topologies each offer their pros and cons.

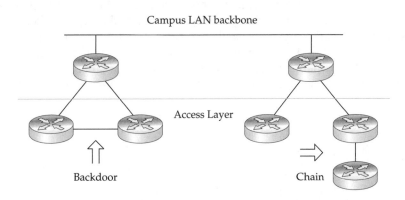

Figure 17-6.   Backdoors and chains violate the ideal three-layer hierarchical topology.

For these reasons, few internetworks are fully meshed. The general practice is to fully mesh the backbone portion of topologies to provide fault tolerance and load balancing along these critical links, but only partially mesh the access and distribution layer topologies.

Backdoor and Chain Configurations

Circumstance sometimes dictates deviating from the strict hierarchical model. The two most common topology deviations are so-called backdoors and chains. A *backdoor* is any direct connection between devices at the same layer, usually the access layer. A *chain* is the addition of one or more layers below the access layer. Figure 17-6 depicts the two.

Sometimes, it makes sense to configure a backdoor. For example, you might want to directly link two remote sites if the links to the distribution-layer routers are costly or slow. Backdoors also provide a degree of redundancy: If the backdoor link goes down, the two remote sites can fail over to the distribution-layer router and keep communicating. More often than not, however, backdoors and chains emerge because of poor network planning or a renegade manager who installs networking equipment or links without involving the network or security team.

Designing to Fit Needs

You'd be surprised how many internetworks—even big sophisticated ones—have grown haphazardly. Unmanaged network growth occurs for any number of reasons. The most common one is that things simply happened too fast. Keep in mind the realities we now take for granted—client-server computing, intranets, the Web, extranets—were mere concepts until the millennium. This left many IT managers unprepared to formulate well-researched, reasoned strategic network plans for their enterprises.

In many cases, a plan wouldn't have done much good. Management fads come and go, but one fad that stuck is the credo "If I pay, then I have the say." The management trend has been toward flat organizational structures, with minimum layers between the CEO and worker. Most IT departments are now "budgeted" by individual divisions, groups, or even departments. In other words, IT decisions are increasingly being made from the bottom up by the entity that owns the budget, not the central IT department.

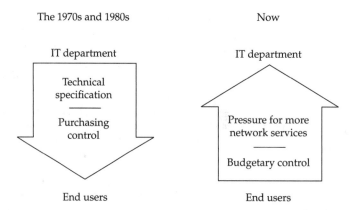

This kind of distributed decision-making has been magnified by the slowness of many IT departments to respond to emerging customer demands driven by such things as business process reengineering, mergers, acquisitions, and trading partner cooperatives. So it got to the point where many end-user managers simply threw out the corporate technical architecture, picked up the phone, and ordered new networks on their own.

The trend over the last several years has been for IT departments to break off networking into a separate group called "infrastructure"—separate the chip heads from the wire heads, so to speak. This is being done because internetworking has simply become too big and too complicated to be left to a manager who, say, has a background in COBOL and mainframe software project management. Networking is its own game now. It quickly became its own discipline with its own set of best practices—some of which we'll review in the remainder of this chapter.

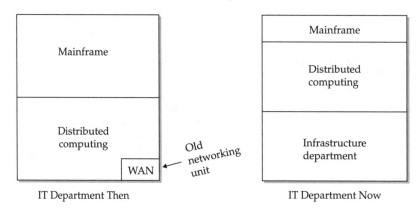

Methodologies have been developed to help bring network planning under control. Not surprisingly, these bear a strong resemblance to data-processing methodologies. First and foremost, of course, is to fit the solution to the business needs through some form of needs assessment—both present and future.

Understanding Existing Internetworks

As mentioned earlier, few network designs start from scratch. Although it would be nice to work from a blank sheet of paper, most designs must accommodate a preexisting network. Most are incremental redesigns to serve more users or to upgrade bandwidth capacity, or both. A common upgrade, for example, is to insert a layer of routers between the LAN backbone and the layer at which hosts access the network. This is being done in many enterprises to improve performance and accommodate projected growth. Whatever the change, the preexisting infrastructure must be thoroughly analyzed before a purchase is even considered.

The next section describes methods for network planning and design. They focus on establishing a baseline of how the network will look upon implementation. To refresh your memory on the subject, a *baseline* is a network's starting point, as expressed in traffic volumes, flows, and characteristics. Allowances are made for margins of error and projected growth over and above the baseline.

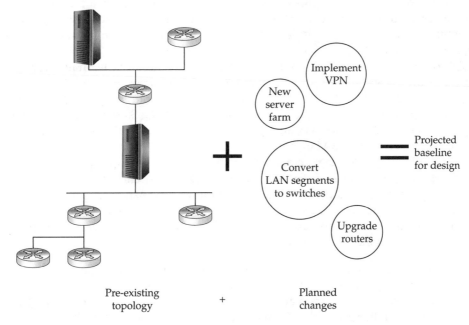

When designing an entirely new network area, you must arrive at a design baseline based on well-researched assumptions, often derived from paperwork or other non-networked data traffic already in place. If an existing network topology is being upgraded, the baseline is taken by measuring its characteristics. If the design scenario encompasses non-networked and networked elements, then the two must be compiled together. Whatever the case, the principles and methods of good network design remain the same.

Characterizing Networks

There are several methods for understanding an internetwork well enough to formulate a proper design. These methods apply whether it's an existing internetwork or a topology to be built from scratch. As you might expect, the methods focus on geography and traffic—in other words, where network nodes are and what travels between them. A network node is any device in the topology—including network devices, such as routers, and payload hosts, such as servers. For our purposes, when you're designing a network from scratch, a node could be a noncomputer entity such as a desk or a file cabinet. The point is to identify where the users are and what they're using.

Quality of Service

Characterizing networks is good for managing as well as designing. The industry is pushing the concept of Quality of Service (QoS)—an approach largely based on characterizing traffic. QoS is the technique of ensuring throughput for traffic through an internetwork. It is more sophisticated than just guaranteeing that a certain link will run at a certain throughput level. Most QoS guarantees are associated with a particular type of traffic (say, prioritizing video multicasting for distance learning over e-mail and other less critical traffic).

As you might imagine, QoS policy implementation relies heavily on information gathered through SNMP, RMON, and NetFlow, and presented through NMS consoles, such as Prime Infrastructure LAN Management Solution (LMS) and Prime Infrastructure Assurance. Like those console applications, QoS uses the client-server model by storing a QoS database, and it implements policies through purpose-built applets, such as QoS Policy Manager.

Cisco's QoS Policy Manager creates abstract commands that group individual IOS commands to perform a task from the Cisco Policy Manager GUI. As with other NMS console applets, when you push a button, one or more commands are put to use on the client network device being configured. Some QoS subcommands are generic IOS commands (the **interface** command, for example); others are QoS specific. The major QoS abstract commands are as follows:

- ■ **WFQ**   Stands for *Weighted Fair Queuing*. Combines the **interface** and **fair-queue** commands to let network managers prioritize how a mix of traffic types will flow through certain areas of the topology. For example, e-mail might be given a higher priority on Lotus Notes servers, but not elsewhere.

- ■ **WRED**   Stands for *Weighted Random Early Detection*. Combines the **interface** and **random-detect** commands. (The **random-detect** command accepts a weighted value to represent the relative importance of a traffic type.) WRED tries to control traffic congestion as it begins to emerge.

■ **CAR**   Stands for *Committed Access Rate*. CAR is the fundamental QoS bandwidth control technology. It uses a sophisticated RMON MIB to recognize traffic types, set priorities, and limit packet rates as needed.

QoS techniques are mostly applied at the network interface level, and make heavy use of access control lists to filter packets. The idea is to differentiate traffic types within topology areas and influence network behavior—a technique dubbed "traffic shaping." The goal of traffic shaping is to guarantee minimum levels of end-to-end service for various types of traffic.

Understanding Traffic Flow

Understanding and documenting traffic flow is the first step in network design. Drawing an analogy to highway design might seem too obvious, but the two are remarkably similar. A road designer must know where the roads should be, how wide, what type of surface to use, and what traffic control rules are to be applied. All these things are largely a function of traffic flow.

Traffic characteristics are largely a matter of directionality, symmetry, packet sizes, and volumes. A unidirectional flow does most communicating in one direction; a bidirectional flow communicates with roughly the same frequency in both directions of a connection. An asymmetrical flow sends more data in one direction than the other; a symmetrical flow sends roughly equal amounts of data back and forth. For example, an HTTP session's flow is bidirectional and asymmetric because a lot of messages are sent both ways, but data is mostly downloaded from the web server to the browser client.

Identifying Traffic Sources   To understand traffic flow, you must know its sources. This is done by identifying groups of users, not individual persons. In the parlance of computer methodology, a group of users is often called a *community* (probably because the obvious term, *user group*, is already used by customer associations—for example, the Cisco User Group).

An inventory of high-level characteristics, such as location and applications used, should be gathered. This isn't to say that one would go around with a clipboard gathering the information. Most network designers would pull this information off a database from such tools as Prime LAN Management Solution (LMS). The following example shows a form that might be used to gather user information:

Community	# Persons	Locations	Applications	Host Type
Accounting	27	St. Louis	AR, AP, GL	AS/400
Customer Service	200	Minneapolis	Call Center	Windows NT 4.0

You can gather whatever information you want. For example, you might not want to document the type of host the group uses if everybody has a PC with an i5 processor. On the other hand, if there's a mix of dumb terminals, thin clients, PCs, and souped-up Unix/Linux workstations, you might want to know who has what. This information can help you more accurately calculate traffic loads.

If you're analyzing an existing network, this information can be gathered by turning on the record-route option in IOS. This information can also be gathered using Prime LAN Management Solution.

Identifying Data Sources and Data Sinks   Every enterprise has major users of information. The experts identify these heavy data users as "data sinks" because it's useful to trace back to the data sources they use to help identify traffic patterns. The most common sources are database servers, disk farms, tape or CD libraries, inventory systems, and online catalogs. Data sinks are usually end users, but sometimes servers can be data sinks. The following illustration shows information to gather on data sinks.

Data Sink	Locations	Applications	User Communities
Server farm 3	St. Louis	AR, AP, GL	Accounting
CCSRV	Denver	Call Center	Customer Service

Documenting which communities use each data sink enables you to correlate traffic. You can now begin connecting user desktop hosts to data sink servers. Combining the information in the preceding two illustrations lets you begin drawing lines between client and server. Correlate every user community to every data sink, and an accurate profile of the network's ideal topology begins to emerge.

Identifying Application Loads and Traffic Types   Most network applications generate traffic with specific characteristics. For example, FTP generates unidirectional and asymmetric traffic involving large files. Table 17-1 is a sampling of typical message types and their approximate sizes. Obviously, sizes can vary widely, but these are industry rules of thumb useful for estimating traffic loads.

Message Type	Approximate Size
Web page	50KB
Graphical computer screen (such as a Microsoft Windows screen)	500KB
E-mail	10KB
Word processing document	100KB
Spreadsheet	200KB
Terminal screen	5KB
Multimedia object (such as videoconferencing)	100KB
Database backup	1MB and up

Table 17-1.   Typical Message Sizes and Types

Beyond traffic loads, it's also useful to know the traffic type. Traffic types characterize the kinds of devices connected and how traffic flows between them:

- **Client-server**   Usually a PC talking to a Unix/Linux or Windows server, this is the standard configuration today. In client-server types, traffic is usually bidirectional and asymmetrical.

- **Server-to-server**   Examples include data mirroring to a redundant server backing up another server, name directory services, and so on. This type of traffic is bidirectional, but the symmetry depends on the application.

- **Terminal-host**   Many terminal-based applications run over IP, even IBM terminal connections to mainframes. Another example is Telnet. Terminal traffic is bidirectional, but symmetry depends on the application.

- **Peer-to-peer**   Examples include videoconferencing and PCs set up to access resources on other PCs, such as printers and data. This type of traffic is bidirectional and symmetric.

Understanding what types of traffic pass through various links gives a picture of how to configure it. The following illustration shows information used to identify and characterize traffic types.

Application	Traffic Type	User Community	Data Sinks	Bandwidth Required	QoS Policy
Web browser	Client-server	Sales	Sales server	350 Kbps	CAR
TN3270	Terminal	Purchasing	AS/400	200 Kbps	WRED

Frequently, a link is dominated by one or two traffic types. The Bandwidth Required column in the preceding illustration is usually expressed as a bit-per-second estimate and could be Mbps or even Gbps. Once all the applications in an internetwork are identified and characterized, the designer has a baseline from which to make volume-dependent configuration decisions. Traffic typing is especially useful for knowing where and how to set QoS policies. In other words, you must identify which applications go through a router before you can properly set QoS parameters in its config file.

Understanding Traffic Load

After the user communities, data sinks and sources, and traffic flows have been documented and characterized, individual links can be more accurately sized.

The traffic flow information in the following illustration ties down the paths taken between sources and destinations.

	Destination 1	
	Link	**Mbps**
Source 1: Accounting	Frame Relay	0.056
Source 2: Call Center	Point-to-Point	1.54

	Destination 2	
	Link	**Mbps**
Source 1: Accounting	Frame Relay	0.256
Source 2: Call Center	Frame Relay	1.54

	Destination 3	
	Link	**Mbps**
Source 1: Accounting	Frame Relay	0.256
Source 2: Call Center	Frame Relay	0.512

Designing internetworks to fit needs is more art than science, however. For example, even after having totaled the estimated bandwidth for a link, you must go back and pad it for soft factors, such as QoS priorities, anticipated near-term growth, and so on.

Cisco Network Designs

Designing networks is largely a matter of making choices. Most of the choices have to do with selecting the right technologies and products for the job. Even design elements over which you have no control may still leave choices to make. For example, if the company's art department uses AppleTalk to communicate with their ancient large-scale printers and has no intention of changing, you must decide whether to run it over multiprotocol links or break it off into one or more AppleTalk-only LAN segments.

Once the present and future needs of the enterprise have been researched and documented, the next step is to choose technologies for various functional areas:

- **Backbone technology selection**   A variety of backbone LAN technologies exist, chosen mostly based on the size of the internetwork and its traffic characteristics.

- **Protocol selection**   It's assumed here that IP is the network protocol, but choices remain as to which routing and other network control protocols to use.

- **Access technology selection**   A mix of switches and VLANs is usually configured to best fit the needs of a workgroup or even a particular host.

After the underlying technologies are chosen, specific products must be configured to run them. After that step, more design work must be done to implement the configuration. For example, an IP addressing model must be configured, a name services subsystem must be set up, routing metrics must be tuned, security parameters must be set, and so on.

Internetwork design takes place at two levels: the campus and the enterprise. Campus designs cover the enterprise's main local network, from the desktop up to the high-speed backbone to the outside. The enterprise level encompasses multiple campus networks and focuses on WAN configurations—whether a private leased-line WAN or an Internet-based system tunneled through the Internet.

Logical Network Design

An internetwork design is defined by both a physical and a logical configuration. The physical part deals with topology layout, hardware devices, networking software, transmission media, and other pieces. Logical configuration must closely match the physical design in three areas:

- **IP addressing**   A plan to allocate addresses in a rational way that can conserve address space and accommodate growth

- **Name services**   A plan to allow hosts and domains to be addressed by symbolic names instead of dotted-decimal IP addresses

- **Protocol selection**   Choosing which protocols to use, especially routing protocols

Internetwork design should always start with the access layer, because higher-level needs cannot be addressed until the device and user population are known. For example, estimating capacity is virtually impossible until all hosts, applications, and LAN segments have been identified and quantified, and most of these elements reside in the access layer.

From a practical standpoint, the three logical design elements of addressing, naming, and routing are good first steps in nailing down how the physical hardware should be laid out. Each of the three requires forethought and planning.

IP Addressing Strategies

The number of available addresses is called *address space.* Enterprises use various addressing schemes to maximize address space within the block of IP addresses they had assigned to them by their ISPs. Various addressing strategies have been devised, not only to maximize address space, but also to enhance security and manageability.

Private IP Address Blocks An enterprise receives its public IP address from the Internet Assigned Numbers Authority (IANA). The IANA usually only assigns public addresses to ISPs and large enterprises, and then as a range of numbers, not as a single IP address. In actual practice, the majority of enterprises receive their public IP addresses from their ISP. When designing IP, the IETF reserved three IP address ranges for use as private addresses:

- 10.0.0.0 through 10.255.255.255
- 172.16.0.0 through 172.31.255.255
- 192.168.0.0 through 192.168.255.255

These three IP address blocks were reserved to avoid confusion. You may use addresses within any of these reserved blocks without fear of one of your routers being confused when it encounters the same address from the outside, because these are private addresses that never appear on the Internet.

Private IP addresses are assigned by the network team to internal devices. Because they'll never be used outside the autonomous system, private addresses can be assigned at will as long as they stay within the assigned range. No clearance from the IETF or any other coordinating body is required to use private addresses, which are used for these reasons:

- **Address space conservation** Few enterprises are assigned a sufficient number of public IP addresses to accommodate all nodes (hosts and devices) within their internetwork.

- **Security** Private addresses are translated through PAT or NAT to the outside. Not knowing the private address makes it tougher for hackers to crack into an autonomous system by pretending to be an internal node.

- **Flexibility** An enterprise can change ISPs without having to change any of the private addresses. Usually, only the addresses of the routers or firewalls performing address translation need to be changed.

- **Smaller routing tables** Having most enterprises advertise just one or perhaps a few IP addresses helps minimize the size of routing tables in Internet routers, thereby enhancing performance.

This last item perhaps explains why the IETF settled on a 32-bit IP address instead of a 64-bit design. Doling out infinitely greater address space would discourage the use of private addresses. The use of global IP addresses would be rampant, engorging routing tables in the process. This would create the need for routers to have faster CPUs and lots more memory. Back when IP was designed, during the 1970s, network devices were in their infancy and were quite slow and underconfigured by today's standards.

Obtaining Public IP Addresses Registered IP addresses must be purchased from the nonprofit IANA, which is responsible for ensuring that no two enterprises are assigned duplicate IP addresses. But few enterprises obtain their IP addresses directly from the IANA; most get them indirectly through their ISP.

Available IP
address pool

InterNIC

⇓

Tier-1 ISPs

Large
enterprises
Tier-2 ISPs

⇓

Smaller enterprises

For example, Tier 1 ISPs, such as Verizon Business and CenturyLink, secure large blocks of IP addresses from the IANA. They, in turn, dole them out to Tier 2 ISPs (there are probably dozens in your town alone), who, in turn, assign them to end-user enterprises. Most large companies deal directly with Tier 1 ISPs. IP addresses are doled out in blocks. The bigger your enterprise, the larger the range of IP addresses you should obtain.

Dynamic Addressing   Dynamic addressing is a technique whereby end-system hosts are assigned IP addresses at login. Novell NetWare and AppleTalk had built-in dynamic addressing capabilities from the beginning. That's not the case with IP, however. Remember, desktop protocols such as NetWare IPX were designed with the client-server model in mind, whereas IP was originally designed to connect a worldwide system: the Internet. IP dynamic addressing came to the fore only in the mid-1980s to accommodate diskless workstations that had nowhere to store permanent IP addresses.

A couple of earlier dynamic IP address assignment protocols led to the development of the Dynamic Host Configuration Protocol (DHCP). DHCP, now the de facto standard, uses a client-server model in which a server keeps a running list of available addresses and assigns them as requested. DHCP can also be used as a configuration tool. It supports automatic permanent allocation of IP addresses to a new host and is even used for manual address assignments as a way to communicate the new address to the client host. Figure 17-7 depicts DHCP's processes.

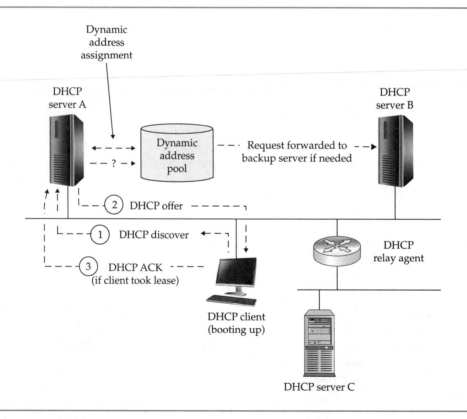

Figure 17-7.   DHCP can dynamically assign IP addresses to end-system hosts.

Dynamic allocation is popular because it's easy to configure and conserves address space. DHCP works by allocating addresses for a period of time called a "lease," guaranteeing not to allocate the IP address to another host as long as it's out on lease. When the host logs off the network, the DHCP server is notified and restores the address to its available pool.

To ensure service, multiple DHCP servers are often configured. When the host logs in, it sends a DHCP discover message across the network to the server specified by the DHCP identifier field of the message. The DHCP server responds with a DHCP offer message or passes the discover request to a backup server. The client accepts the offer by sending the server a DHCP ACK message as acknowledgment.

If the offer is accepted, the server locks the lease in the available address pool by holding the assignment in persistent memory until the lease is terminated. Lease termination occurs when the client logs off the network (accomplished usually by the user turning off his or her PC at day's end). If the identified DHCP server is down or refuses the request, after a preset timeout period, the client can be configured to send a discover request to a backup DHCP server. If the server isn't on the same subnet, a router can be configured as a DHCP relay agent to steer the request message to the LAN segment on which the server resides.

Domain Name System

As discussed in our review of internetworking fundamentals in Chapter 2, people almost always reach network nodes by name, not by address. Think about it—how many times have you typed a dotted-decimal IP address into the address field in your browser? In most cases, you type a URL instead or simply click one sitting beneath a hypertext link on a web page.

The service used to map names on the Internet is called the Domain Name System (DNS). A DNS name has two parts: host name and domain name. Taking toby.velte.com as an example, *toby* is the host (in this case, a person's PC), and *velte.com* is the domain. Up until 2000, domain names had to be registered with InterNIC (which stands for Internet Network Information Center), a U.S. Government agency. However, that responsibility was transferred to several private companies, taking the government out of the URL business.

The IETF has specified that domain name suffixes be assigned based on the type of organization the autonomous system is, as listed in Table 17-2.

There are also geographical top-level domains defined by country—for example, .fr for France, .ca for Canada, .de for Germany (as in Deutschland), and so on. For domain names to work, they must, at some point, be mapped to IP addresses so that routers can recognize them. This mapping is called *name resolution*—a task performed by name servers. Domain Name Systems distribute databases across many servers in order to satisfy resolution requests. A large enterprise would distribute its DNS database throughout its internetwork topology. People can click their way around the Internet because their DNS databases are distributed worldwide. Figure 17-8 depicts the name services process.

Domain	Autonomous System Type
.com	Commercial company
.edu	Educational institution
.gov	Governmental agency
.org	Nonprofit organization
.net	Network provider
.biz	Restricted to businesses

Table 17-2.   IETF Domain Name Suffixes

When a client needs to send a packet, it must map the destination's symbolic name to its IP address. The client must have what's called *resolver software* configured in order to do this. The client's resolver software sends a query to a local DNS server, receives the resolution back, writes the IP address into the packet's header, and transmits. The name-to-IP mapping is then cached in the client for a preset period of time. As long as the client has the mapping for a name in cache, it bypasses the query process altogether.

Name Server Configuration   Many internetworks have multiple DNS servers for speed and redundancy, especially larger autonomous systems on which hosts frequently come and go. Usually, name services are handled from the central server within the internetwork. For example, Windows networks have so-called domain controller (DC) servers, which are responsible for various housekeeping duties, including logon requests.

Besides DNS, the other two major naming services are the Windows Internet Name Service (WINS) and Sun Microsystems' Network Information Service (NIS). Whereas DNS is optimized for Internet mappings, WINS and NIS were designed to manage name services at the internetwork level. WINS servers use DHCP to field requests, because DNS doesn't lend itself to handling dynamic names. (It wants them stored permanently.) NIS performs a similar duty among Unix hosts. WINS is not deployed on new networks any longer, with Microsoft implementing a hybrid LDAP/DNS system within Active Directory.

DNS is an important standard. You're able to click between hosts throughout the world because there are hundreds of thousands of DNS servers across the globe, exchanging and caching name mappings across routing domains so that it takes you a minimum of time to connect to a new website.

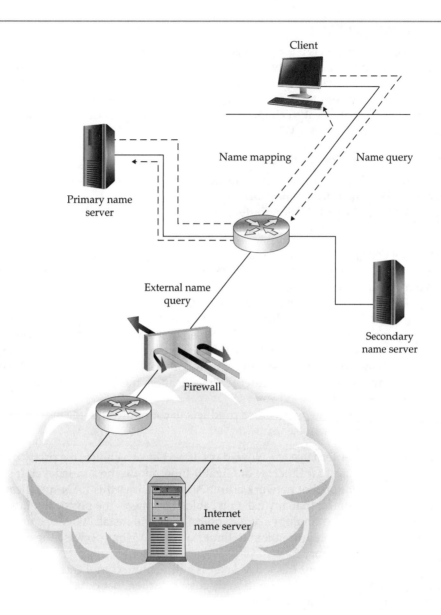

Figure 17-8.   Domain names must be resolved by a name server.

Campus Network Designs

The term *campus network* is a bit of a misnomer. What's meant is any local internetwork with a high-speed backbone. For example, the local network of a company's headquarters located entirely in a skyscraper is an example of a campus network. The term has had such heavy use in computer marketing that it's stuck as the term for medium-to-large local networks. Whatever it's called, several models have been developed for how to configure campus networks. We'll review them here.

The Switch-Router Configuration

The so-called switch-router configuration covers the access and distribution layers of the three-layer hierarchical network design model. The two layers are considered together because the distribution routers are generally located in the same building as host devices being given network access.

Access-Layer Configuration   The access layer of the three-layer hierarchical model is largely a function of the so-called switch-router configuration. The major exception to this is remote access, covered later in this chapter (see the section titled "Connecting Remote Sites"). Configuring the access layer is largely a matter of wiring together hosts in a department or floor of a building. As far as physical media, we'll assume that Category 6 unshielded twisted-pair (UTP) cable is used to wire hosts into access devices.

An important consideration, when configuring the access and distribution layers, is what type of network you'll be deploying. Most access-layer LAN segments being designed today run over Gigabit Ethernet specification, the 1,000 Mbps variant of the Ethernet standard.

These decisions dictate what Cisco products to configure and, to some extent, how to lay out your topology.

Selecting Access-Layer Technology   Nowadays, if you have a choice, it's pretty much a given that you'll use Fast Ethernet or Gigabit Ethernet for the access layer. It's fast, cheap, and the talent pool of network administrators knows this LAN specification best. You must be careful that any existing cable plant meets the physical requirements specified by the LAN technology—you wouldn't want to install 100 Mbps or 1 Gbps switches and have to configure them to limit ports to 10 Mbps because the cabling at the facility is only Category 3.

Exactly how you lay out the access layer is a little more complicated. If you've gathered the needs-analysis information discussed earlier, that data will go a long way toward telling you two important things:

- **Workgroup hierarchy**   Large homogenous workgroups lend themselves to flat switched networks. For example, large customer service departments or help desks tend to connect to a fairly consistent set of hosts to run a limited set of applications. These shops are great candidates for flat (non-VLAN) switched networks.

■ **Traffic loads**   If traffic volumes will be heavy and QoS policies stringent, you might want to look at a VLAN switched network, or at least high-bandwidth routed network configurations.

As you answer these two questions for various areas across the topology, the configuration begins to take shape. Quite often, this process is iterated floor by floor and building by building. This shouldn't surprise you. After all, networking isn't the only field of endeavor that is geographical in nature—so is operations management. It usually makes sense for managers to group certain types of workers and/or certain types of work tasks into one physical location.

Physical Layout   The classical access-layer topology is the data closet-MDF layout. A *data closet* (also called a *wiring closet* or *phone closet)* is a small room housing patch panels connecting hosts to hubs or access switch ports. The patch panel is where networks start. A *patch panel* is a passive device with rows of RJ-45 jacks similar to the RJ-11 jacks for telephones. The host device's unshielded twisted-pair (UTP) cable plugs into one jack, and a cable from another jack plugs into the switch port. This modular arrangement gives flexibility in moving devices between ports.

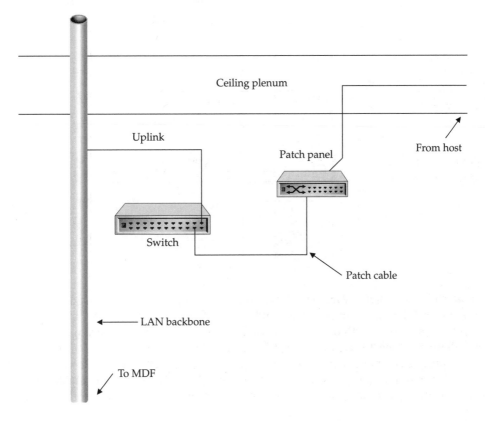

Signals go through the switch by going out its uplink port to connect to the building's riser. *Riser* refers to the bundle of individual cables running from each floor down to a termination point. An *uplink* connects the switch "up" in the logical sense, in that the riser is headed toward a larger piece of equipment—usually a router or a LAN switch.

MDF stands for *main distribution facility*—usually a room in a secure location on the building's first floor. The MDF serves as the termination point for the wiring emanating from the data closets, often equipment for both voice and data. The trend has been to locate the MDF in the enterprise's computer room, if there's one in the building. Depending on the building's setup, the backbone travels either through holes punched through the floors or through the elevator shaft.

A riser's medium is almost always fiber-optic cable in larger buildings. The main reason for using fiber is that it can carry data more than 100 meters and is unaffected by electrical noise in buildings.

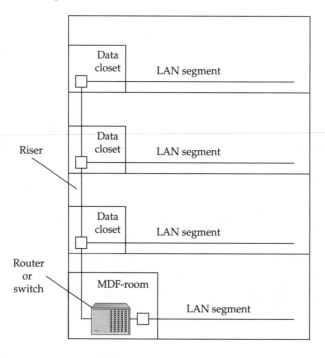

The Switch Configuration   Various rules of thumb are applied when configuring the access layer. UTP cable can span up to 100 meters from the data closet. This is almost always more than enough on the horizontal plane. (Few work areas are wider than a football field is long.) If the data closet is located at the center of a floor, the effective span would be 200 meters. As shown in Figure 17-9, not all buildings are vertical. Many are large horizontal structures of one or two floors, such as manufacturing plants and warehouses. For very large floors, the practice is to place data closets on either side.

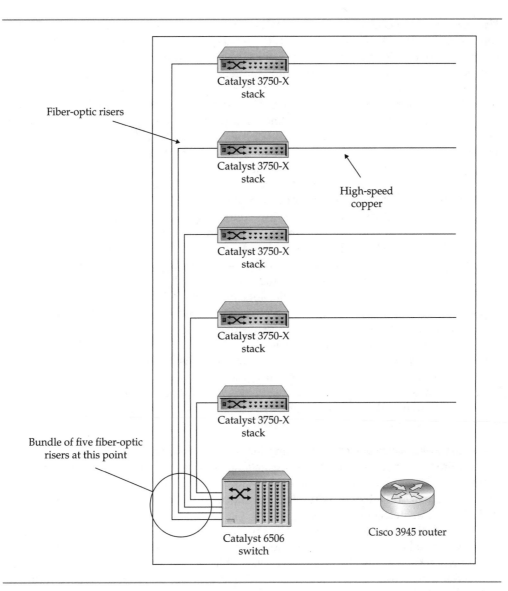

Fiber-optic risers

Catalyst 3750-X
stack

Catalyst 3750-X
stack

High-speed
copper

Catalyst 3750-X
stack

Catalyst 3750-X
stack

Catalyst 3750-X
stack

Bundle of five fiber-optic
risers at this point

Catalyst 6506
switch

Cisco 3945 router

Figure 17-9.   The classical router-switch configuration employs smaller switches connected to a large switch, which is then connected to a router.

From a logical standpoint, it doesn't make sense to place a router on every floor. Doing so would be prohibitively expensive. The strategy, then, is to minimize the number of router interfaces servicing a given number of hosts. Switches fulfill this. Figure 17-9 shows a configuration for a medium-sized company holding a few hundred employees in a building. To connect users on each floor, at least one Cisco Catalyst

3750-X is placed in each data closet. Catalyst 3750-X models connect 12, 24, or 48 hosts per unit and are stackable up to nine units per stack. The size of the stack depends on the number of employees on the floor. Which particular Catalyst 3750-X model you use depends on the population density: Some models support 12 ports for a stack density of 108 ports, and others support 48 ports for a density of 432 ports. If the population goes beyond 432, simply put another stack in the data closet to increase the number of ports.

The bottom-left area of Figure 17-9 shows how a riser is not a backbone in the proper sense of the term. The uplink running out of the Catalyst 3750 on the ground floor expands the riser bundle to a total of five fiber cables, which are essentially long wires used to avoid having to put a terminating device on each floor. The backbone is defined logically, so you can think of riser cables as "feeder wires" instead of as a backbone.

The LAN technology throughout the sample building is Gigabit Ethernet, which runs at 1000 Mbps. That speed is plenty for connecting most individual host devices. In practical terms, this means our riser is heading into MDF with 5,000 Mbps raw bandwidth, so a fast device is needed to handle the connections. We've configured a Cisco Catalyst 6506-E switch for the job. With a 480 Gbps backplane, the Catalyst 6506-E has plenty of horsepower to maintain satisfactory throughput for traffic from the five LAN segments. This box has six module slots, but a single 12-port 1000SX card will handle all five LAN segments, leaving plenty of room for growth. A second slot is used to connect to the outside, leaving three open slots.

Figure 17-9 draws out the inherent advantages of LAN switching. You'll remember from Chapter 7 that a switch is roughly ten times quicker when it has a MAC address in its switching table. Our sample company has 300 employees, and the Catalyst 6506 has more than adequate memory and backplane speed to handle a switching table of that size. (It can handle many thousands.) Because the switch is talking to all 300 hosts, it has their MAC addresses readily available.

The Access Switch Configuration   We've mentioned that hubs have given way to switches. What we're talking about here is *access switching,* as opposed to the LAN switching example in Figure 17-9. An access switch connects hosts to a LAN segment. This extends switched bandwidth all the way out to the desktop or server. Figure 17-10 shows a typical access switch configuration.

It wouldn't be practical to run a fiber-optic cable all the way down to the MDF for every switched host. As Figure 17-10 shows, an interim step can be configured using an access switch such as the Cisco Catalyst 2960, which is able to connect up to 24 devices. A lower-end switch isn't used here because it doesn't have an FX port for connecting to a fiber-optic riser.

It should be pointed out that in high-density environments, users are faced with either configuring high-end Catalyst switches in the data closet or running riser cables to the MDF.

The Switch-Router Configuration   To be able to internetwork, users need to be routed at some point. The standard practice is to configure a local router in the MDF room.

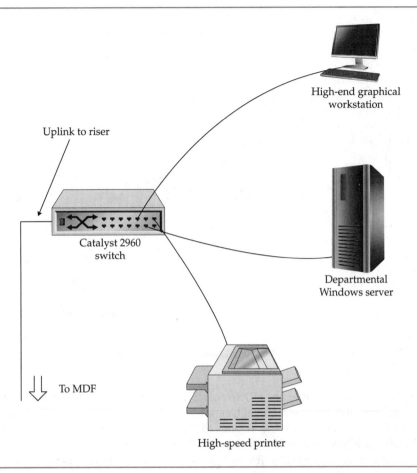

Figure 17-10.   Access switches replace hub ports to connect bandwidth-hungry hosts.

That way, users inside the enterprise are connected to the enterprise internetwork for intramural communications, as well as to the firewall to access the Internet.

Figure 17-11 zooms in on our sample company's MDF room. A Cisco 3945 router is configured in this situation because it has eight module slots that can accommodate LAN or WAN modules. One slot is filled with a one-port 100BaseTX LAN module to connect the Catalyst 6500 switch; the other houses a one-port T1 WAN module connecting the building to the outside world.

If you're thinking that with all the bandwidth floating around the building, a mere 1.544 Mbps pipe to the outside might not provide sufficient capacity, you're catching on. A T1 link indeed might not be enough, depending on how much of the local traffic load flows to the outside.

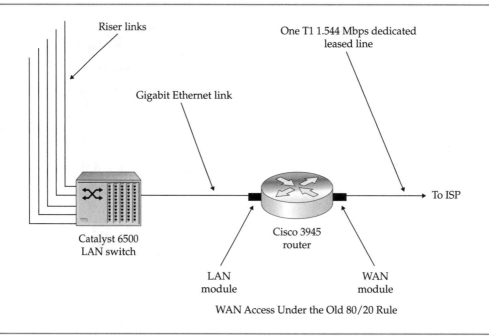

Riser links

One T1 1.544 Mbps dedicated
leased line

Gigabit Ethernet link

To ISP

Catalyst 6500
LAN switch

Cisco 3945
router

LAN
module

WAN
module

WAN Access Under the Old 80/20 Rule

Figure 17-11.   Switched networks need routers to talk to the outside world.

The New 80/20 Rule   Remember the 80/20 rule discussed earlier in the chapter (see the section "The Three-Layer Hierarchical Design Model")? The traditional dictum has been that only 20 percent of the traffic goes to the outside. But things have changed. Now the gurus are talking about the "new 80/20 rule," also known as the 20/80 rule, where as much as 80 percent of traffic can go to the outside as users reach into the Internet to download files, talk to other parts of the enterprise intranet, or even deal with trading partners through an extranet.

The single biggest driver turning the 80/20 rule on its head is e-commerce, where networked computers are taking over traditionally human-based sales transactions. Websites such as Amazon.com and E*Trade are famous for cutting out the middleman, but electronic business-to-business trading—called electronic data interchange (EDI)— is generating more IP traffic with each passing day.

Assuming the new 80/20 rule holds for our sample enterprise, the MDF room might be configured along the lines of Figure 17-12, where a much fatter pipe is extended to the outside in the form of a T3 line—a 43 Mbps, leased-line, digital WAN link medium.

Now the router is bigger and the switch is smaller. If the users are talking to the outside 80 percent of the time, there's less need to switch traffic within the building. We've configured a Cisco Catalyst 2960 switch instead of the Catalyst 6500-E because there's less LAN switching work to do. The high-end ASR 1001 router is configured for greater throughput capacity, with a faster processor and a three-slot chassis.

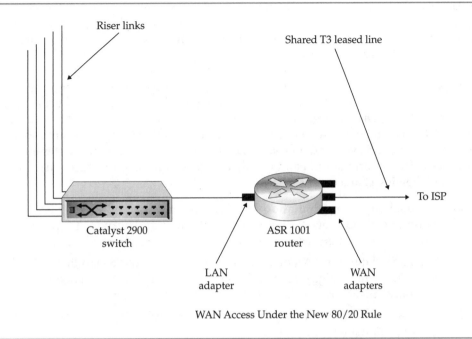

Riser links

Shared T3 leased line

To ISP

Catalyst 2900
switch

ASR 1001
router

LAN
adapter

WAN
adapters

WAN Access Under the New 80/20 Rule

Figure 17-12.   Heavy Internet use is driving enterprises to install bigger edge routers.

At 45 Mbps, T3 runs nearly 30 times faster than a T1 line. More and more enterprises are turning to T3 to make the point-to-point connection to their ISPs. Few, however, need all that capacity, so most ISPs resell a portion of the bandwidth to individual customers according to their needs, a practice called "fractionalizing," in which the customer signs up for only a fraction of the link's capacity. Even more popular than the T3 is a Metro Optical Ethernet (MOE) link. Enterprises may connect to the ISP with a 1 Gbps fiber link, and the ISP provisions (throttles) the bandwidth based on what service level the customer is paying for, commonly in 50 Mbps increments.

Choosing a High-Speed Backbone

Backbones are used to connect major peer network nodes. A backbone link connects two particular nodes, but the term *backbone* often is used to refer to a series of backbone links. For example, a campus backbone might extend over several links.

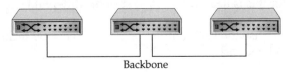

Backbone

Backbone links move data between backbone devices only. They don't handle traffic between LAN segments within a site. That's done at the distribution layer of the three-layer hierarchical model by LAN switches and routers. Backbones concentrate on moving traffic at very high speeds over land.

Campus backbones obviously cover a short distance, usually through underground fiber-optic cabling. WAN backbones—used by big enterprises and ISPs—move traffic between cities. Most WAN backbone links are operated by so-called Internet backbone providers, although many large enterprises operate their own high-speed long-distance links. WAN links run over high-speed fiber-optic cable links strung underground, on electrical pylons, and even under oceans. Satellite links are also becoming common. Regardless of transport medium and whether it's a campus or WAN backbone, they share the following characteristics:

- **Minimal packet manipulation** Such processing as access control list enforcement and firewall filtering are kept out of the backbone to speed throughput. For this reason, most backbone links are switched, not routed.

- **High-speed devices** A slower device such as a Cisco 2960 would not be configured onto a high-speed backbone. The two ends of a backbone link generally operate over a Catalyst 4500, 6500 link, or faster.

- **Fast transport** Most high-speed backbones are built atop transport technology of 1 Gbps or higher.

The main backbone technology is now Gigabit Ethernet. FDDI was once widely installed, but with a total capacity of only 100 Mbps, it was quickly displaced.

ATM Backbones Asynchronous Transfer Mode (ATM) uses a fixed-length format instead of the variable-length packets Ethernet uses. The fixed-length format lends itself to high-speed throughput, because the hardware always knows exactly where each cell begins. For this reason, ATM has a positive ratio between payload and network control overhead traffic. This architecture also lends itself to QoS—a big plus for operating critical backbone links.

Figure 17-13 shows a campus backbone built over ATM. The configuration uses Catalyst 4500 LAN switches for the outlying building and a high-end Catalyst 6500 Multiservice switch router to handle traffic hitting the enterprise's central server farm.

A *blade* is an industry term for a large printed circuit board that is basically an entire networking device on a single module. Blades plug into chassis slots. For a Catalyst switch to talk in ATM, the appropriate adapter blade must be configured into the chassis. Cisco Catalyst 6500 OC-12 ATM LANE Module is used here because it was designed for short-haul traffic—there are other "edge" ATM blades for WAN traffic. One reason for this is to allow Cisco to support different technologies in a single product.

Cisco ATM devices use the LAN emulation (LANE) adapter technology to integrate with campus Ethernet networks.

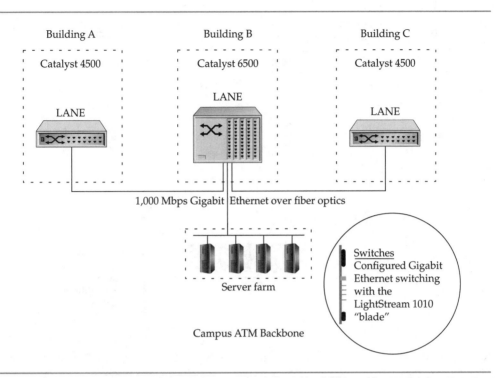

Figure 17-13.   An ATM campus backbone can connect central resources.

Switched WAN backbones run over very high-speed fiber-optic trunks running the SONET specification. Most new trunks being pulled are OC-48, which run at about 2.5 Gbps. OC stands for Optical Carrier, and SONET stands for Synchronous Optical Network. This is a standard developed by Bell Communications Research for very high-speed networks over fiber-optic cable. The slowest SONET specification, OC-1, runs at 52 Mbps—about the same speed as T3. OC SONET is an important technology because it represents the higher-speed infrastructure "pipe" the Internet needs to continue expanding. We mention this here, because ATM and Gigabit Ethernet R&D efforts are carried out with the SONET specification in mind, and it's the presumed WAN link transport.

Gigabit Ethernet Backbone   Although Gigabit Ethernet is a much newer technology than ATM, many, many network managers have turned to it for their backbone needs instead of ATM. Figure 17-14 shows that a Gigabit Ethernet backbone can be configured using the same Catalyst platforms as for ATM. This is done by configuring Gigabit Ethernet blades instead of ATM blades. Note, also, that the same fiber-optic cabling can be used for Gigabit Ethernet, but the adapters must be changed to those designed to support Gigabit Ethernet instead of ATM.

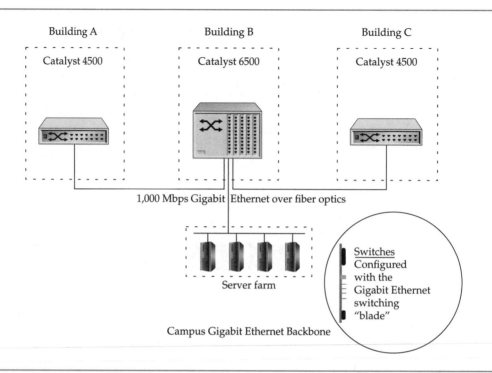

Figure 17-14.   Gigabit Ethernet can also be run in high-end Catalyst switches.

As you might imagine, the technology-specific blades and adapters represent the different electronics needed to process either variable-length Ethernet packets or fixed-length ATM cells. Ethernet has won over FDDI and ATM, and the most commonly deployed backbone today is 10 Gbps Ethernet.

Connecting Remote Sites

There are two kinds of remote locations: the branch office and the small office/home office (SOHO). The defining difference between the two is the type of connection. Because they have only one or two users online at any given moment, SOHO sites use dial-in or VPN connections, whereas branch sites use some form of a dedicated circuit or a site-to-site VPN. Three major remote connection technologies are configured here. You might want to flip back to Chapter 2 to review how these respective technologies work.

Frame Relay   Frame Relay is ideal for "bursty" WAN traffic. In other words, dedicated leased lines such as T1 or T3 only make economic sense if they're continually used. Frame Relay solves that problem by letting users share WAN infrastructure with other enterprises. Frame Relay can do this because it's a packet-switched data network (PSDN) in which end-to-end connections are virtual. You only need to buy a local phone circuit between your remote site and a nearby Frame Relay drop point. After that point, your packets intermix with those from hundreds of other enterprises.

Normally, a device called a FRAD is needed to talk to a Frame Relay network. FRAD stands for Frame Relay Assembler/Disassembler, which parses data streams into the proper Frame Relay packet format. But using a mere FRAD only gets you connected and offers little in the way of remote management, security, and QoS. Cisco has built Frame Relay capability into almost all of its routers to provide more intelligence over Frame Relay connections. Figure 17-15 shows a typical Frame Relay configuration using Cisco gear.

Because Frame Relay uses normal serial line connections, no special interfaces need be installed in a router to make it "Frame Relay compatible." The Cisco 2900 router is a cost-effective solution for the stores in the example in Figure 17-15, because they have sufficient throughput capacity to handle the traffic loads these remote locations are likely to generate.

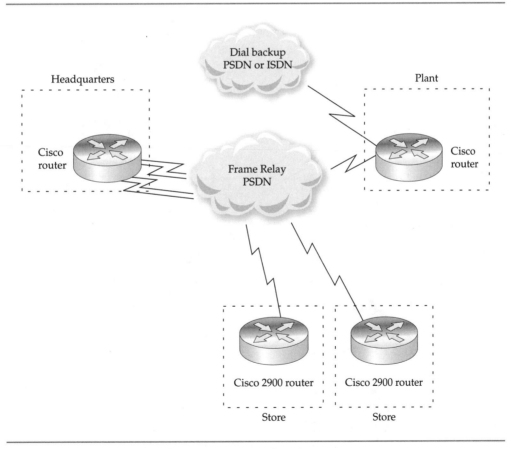

Figure 17-15. Frame Relay–capable routers are superior to FRADs for managing links.

Integrated Services Digital Network   Integrated Services Digital Network (ISDN) can be used for either dial-in or dedicated remote connections. It provides much more bandwidth than normal analog modem telephone connections, but must be available from a local carrier to be used on your premises. ISDN has channel options called BRI and PRI. BRI has two so-called B-channels to deliver 128 Kbps bandwidth, and is generally used for dial-in connections from home or small offices, or for backup in case the main connection fails. PRI packages 23 B-channels, for about 1.48 Mbps bandwidth, and is generally used for full-time multiuser connections. This is commonly referred to as a T1.

Figure 17-16 shows a typical Cisco ISDN configuration. The Cisco 800 Series routers are targeted to connect ISDN users. The 881 has four ports and is able to handle VPN needs, allowing it to be deployed as the router in the lower-right area of Figure 17-16. In this case, the router is able to form a secure tunnel through the Internet.

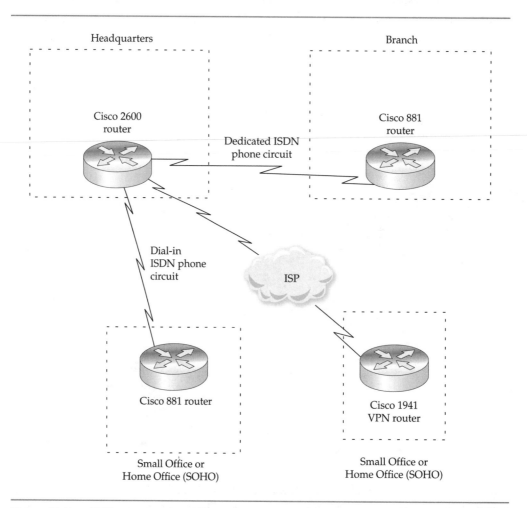

Figure 17-16.   ISDN supports both dial-in and dedicated circuit connections.

Digital Subscriber Line Digital Subscriber Line (DSL) is competing with ISDN for the small office/home office market. To use DSL, you must be serviced by a local telephone switch office that supports DSL and be within a certain distance of it—usually a few miles.

There are different types of DSL, including:

- **ADSL** Characterized by asymmetrical data rates, where more data comes down from the phone company than the user can send back up. This means that ADSL should be selectively used where traffic characteristics match this constraint—in other words, where the user does a lot of downloading but not a lot of uploading. This is the case with most Internet users, though, and ADSL has become quite popular where the phone companies offer it.

- **SDSL** Characterized by symmetrical data rates, where the same amount of data goes either way. This is usually a more expensive solution than ADSL.

- **IDSL** A slower symmetrical solution for locations that are not close enough to the local telephone switch office, **IDSL** offers a maximum throughput of 144 Kbps in both directions.

The configuration in Figure 17-17 shows a Cisco 881 ISR router—it can handle all flavors of DSL. The Cisco 881 looks like a cable TV decoder, but has an Ethernet interface on the back to connect local users.

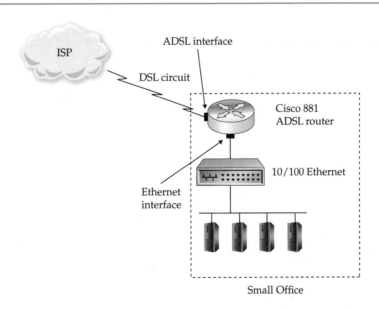

Figure 17-17. The Cisco 881 ISR router is ideal for DSL or cable connections.

CHAPTER 18 | Troubleshooting Cisco Networks

Keeping an internetwork going is a full-time job. As you saw earlier, problems emerge with such frequency that the industry invented routing protocols to deal with them automatically, not even waiting for a network administrator to intervene. They do a pretty good job, at least with problems that can be ameliorated by detouring to a new route. But changing routes is only a temporary solution. In order for a network to run effectively, all its components must be running properly and constantly. After all, delivering available bandwidth to users under normal circumstances is hard enough without having a LAN segment out of commission or a router functioning at partial capacity.

For this reason, a big part of a network team's time is spent troubleshooting. Problems range from a single user unable to access a service to an entire LAN segment crashing. Troubleshooting isn't just a matter of finding and fixing broken parts; much of it is dedicated to fixing performance bottlenecks. When a problem emerges, the network administrator often has no idea which device is causing the trouble. And once the problem device is identified, the cause of the problem must be diagnosed. Then decisions must be made on how to fix the situation.

A methodical approach should be taken to troubleshooting; otherwise, a lot of time can be wasted trying to figure out what's causing the problem. Like a doctor, the troubleshooter must recognize the symptoms, associate them with a set of probable causes, and then progressively narrow down the list until the culprit is finally identified. From there, a proper action plan must be devised and implemented. That's troubleshooting.

In this chapter, we'll review how to troubleshoot problems in a variety of Cisco configurations by running through some troubleshooting scenarios. For simplicity's sake, we'll assume IP as the network protocol and the Microsoft Windows platform as the host. Although the terminology can vary, networking problems are largely the same, regardless of the protocol or host environment. We'll also restrict the examples to troubleshooting routers, which is where most of the action is.

The Mechanics of Network Troubleshooting

In internetworks, trouble is often caused either by failing device hardware or a configuration problem. The location of most problems can be identified remotely, and to some extent, the problems can also be diagnosed and even fixed remotely (but the hardware must still be running for that). By "fixing remotely," we mean without walking over and actually inspecting and touching the device; we don't necessarily mean being geographically removed. If, say, an enterprise's campus internetwork is experiencing a problem, network administrators usually do most troubleshooting tasks without even leaving their desks.

In Cisco environments, remote work can be done through a network management console or by logging directly in to a device's IOS command-line environment through Telnet or Secure Shell (SSH). As you learned, the Cisco NMS consoles—Cisco Prime Infrastructure LAN Management Solution (LMS), Prime Infrastructure Network Control System, and Prime Infrastructure Assurance Manager—use graphical interfaces to indirectly manipulate IOS commands inside the remote device. Thus, most of the real troubleshooting work takes place inside the device's IOS environment. Here are the major IOS commands used to perform most troubleshooting tasks:

- **ping**   Indicates whether "echo" packets are reaching a destination and returning. For example, if you enter **ping 10.1.1.1**, IOS will return the percentage of packets that echoed back from the 10.1.1.1 interface.

- **traceroute**   Reports the actual path taken to a destination. For example, if you enter **traceroute ip 10.1.1.1**, IOS will list every hop the message takes to reach the destination 10.1.1.1 interface.

- **show**   Reports configuration and status information on devices and networks. For example, the **show memory** command displays how much memory is assigned to each network address and how much is free.

The source of problems must be in either device or network media (cabling, connectors, and so on). Even if the trouble is in a cable, the way to it is through IOS. The **ping** and **trace** commands are used to locate problems. If the device is still running, the **show** and **debug** commands are employed to diagnose them. Actual fixes are done by changing either the hardware or its configuration. The **debug** command is similar to **show**, except it generates far more detailed information on device operations—so much so that running **debug** may greatly slow down device performance.

Network Troubleshooting Methods

Problems are usually brought to a network administrator's attention by users. They want to know why they can't access a service within the enterprise's internetwork, or they complain that performance is slow. The location and nature of the complaint are themselves strong clues as to what's causing the problem. Many times, the administrator immediately knows what's wrong and how to fix it, but oftentimes an investigation must be launched to figure out which device is the source of the trouble, what's causing it, and what the best way to fix it is. The network administrator must find answers by methodical troubleshooting. As you might imagine, troubleshooting largely works by a process of elimination, as in the following:

- **What are the symptoms?** Usually, this boils down to users not being able to reach a destination. Knowing both endpoints of a network problem—the source and destination addresses—is the base information in most troubleshooting situations.

- **Where do I start looking?** Does the scenario fit a known pattern that suggests probable causes? For example, if a server isn't responding to service requests from a client, there could be a problem with the server or the client itself. If the server is working okay for other clients, then it might be the client device. If not that, then the problem must reside somewhere between the two.

■ **Where do I start?** There are rules of thumb that short-list what's most likely causing a certain type of symptom. The administrator should diagnose "best-candidate" causes first. For example, if a server accessed over a WAN link seems slow to remote dial-in users, the link could be going bad, usage could be up, there could be a shortage of buffer memory in the router interface servicing the link, or the hosts could be misconfigured. One of these probable causes will explain the problem 95 percent of the time.

■ **What's the action plan?** Finding the exact cause of a problem in a malfunctioning device means dealing with one variable at a time. For example, it wouldn't make sense to replace all network interface modules in a router before rebooting. Doing so might fix the problem, but it wouldn't define the exact source or even what fixed it. In science, this is called changing one variable at a time. The best practice is to zero in on the source by cutting variables down one by one. That way, the problem can be replicated, the fix validated as a good one, and the exact cause recorded for future reference. An action plan also allows you to undo changes that don't fix the problem (or may even make it worse).

NOTE   Before you get too bogged down in trying to isolate the problem with checking IP addresses or other configuration information, check the cables. You might save yourself hours of trouble and effort by reconnecting a loose cable or a power cord that has come undone.

Most internetwork problems manifest themselves as either seriously degraded performance or as "destination unreachable" timeout messages. Sometimes, the problem is widespread; other times, it's limited to a LAN segment or even to a specific host. Let's take a look at some typical problems mapped to their probable causes. Table 18-1 outlines problems with host connectivity. (Hosts are usually single-user PCs, but not always.)

Symptoms	Probable Causes
Host can't access networks beyond local LAN segment.	Misconfigured settings in host device, such as bad default gateway IP address or bad subnet mask. The gateway router is malfunctioning.
Host can't access certain services beyond local LAN segment.	Misconfigured extended access list on a router between the host and the server. Misconfigured firewall, if the server is beyond the autonomous system. The application itself may be down.

Table 18-1.   Typical Host Access Problems and Causes

Symptoms	Probable Causes
Most users can't access a server.	Misconfigured default gateway specification in the remote server. Misconfigured access list in the remote server. Hosts unable to obtain IP addresses through DHCP.
Connections to an area can't be made when one path is down.	Routing protocol not converging within the routing domain. All interfaces on router handling alternative path not configured with secondary IP addresses (discontinuous addressing). Static routes incorrectly configured.

Table 18-2.   Typical Router Problems and Causes

Unfortunately, most internetwork problems aren't limited to a single host. If a problem exists in a router or is spread throughout an area, many users and servers are affected. Table 18-2 outlines a couple of typical network problems that are more widespread.

Many times, networks and services are reachable, but performance is unacceptably slow. Table 18-3 outlines factors that can affect performance within a local network. It doesn't address WAN links, however. They're covered separately later in this chapter because serial lines involve a slightly different set of technologies and problems.

Symptoms	Probable Causes
Poor server response; hard to make and keep connections.	Bad network link, usually caused by a malfunctioning network interface module or LAN segment medium. Mismatched access lists (in meshed internetwork with multiple paths). Congested link, overwhelmed by too much traffic. Poorly configured load balancing (routing protocol metrics). Misconfigured speed or duplex settings.

Table 18-3.   Campus LAN Performance Problems and Causes

Troubleshooting Host IP Configuration

If a user is having trouble accessing services and the overall network seems to be okay, a good place to start looking for the cause of the problem is inside that person's computer. Here are a few things that could be misconfigured in the user's host computer:

■ **Incorrect IP information**   The IP address or subnet mask information could be missing or incorrect.

■ **Incorrect default gateway**   The default gateway router could be misconfigured.

■ **Nonfunctioning name resolution**   DNS or WINS could be misconfigured.

To refresh your memory on the subject, every host has a default gateway specified in the host's network settings. A *default gateway* is an interface on a local router that is used for passing messages sent by the host to addresses beyond the LAN. A default gateway or route is configured because it makes sense for one router to handle most of a host's outbound traffic in order to keep an updated cache on destination IP addresses and routes to them. A host must have at least one gateway, and a second one is sometimes configured for redundancy in case the primary gateway goes down.

Checking the Host IP Address Information

Misconfigured network parameters in desktop hosts are usually attributable to a mistake by the end user. Keep in mind that—on Windows computers, at least—administrators and power users can easily access and modify network settings. To check the host's IP address information in Windows 7, for example, click the **Start** button on the menu bar, type **cmd**, and then press ENTER. This will open the Windows command prompt window. At the command prompt type **ipconfig/all** and then press ENTER. This will display the host's IP address, gateway, DNS configuration, and a few more interesting bits.

If you need to configure the host's IP address settings, this is done through the Network Properties screen. To access the network properties in Windows 7, for example, click the **Start** button on the menu bar and then type **network** into the search bar. Right-click on network from the resulting list of items with "network" in their names and then select Properties.

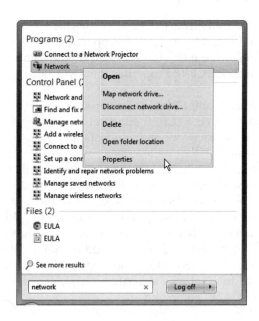

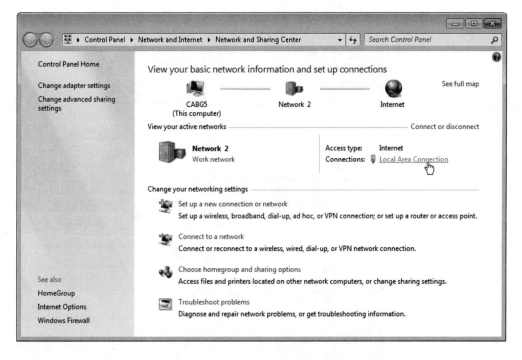

Click the **General** tab. In the This Connection Uses the Following Items box, click **Internet Protocol (TCP/IP)** and then click the **Properties** button. In Windows NT/2000/XP, click the **Start** button on the menu bar and then choose **Control Panel | Network |** Configuration and then click **TCP/IP Properties.** This will allow you to set the IP address and default gateway.

The protocol will usually point to a network interface card (NIC) connecting the host to the LAN, as is the case with the TCP/IP Ethernet PC card highlighted in Figure 18-1. (If the host dials into the internetwork, the protocol that points to the dial-up adapter should be selected instead.)

Once you're pointed at the right NIC, start by making sure that the host is identifying itself correctly to the network. The example in Figure 18-2 shows a statically defined IP address and subnet. These must match what's on file for the host in the config file of the router serving as the default gateway. If the Obtain An IP Address Automatically check box is selected, the host's IP address is dynamically assigned by a server—a Dynamic Host Control Protocol (DHCP) server. Although DHCP can make address assignment much easier and somewhat foolproof, rogue DHCP servers can be problematic, so be sure to check IP address settings to verify which DHCP server is assigning the IP address using the **ipconfig /all** command.

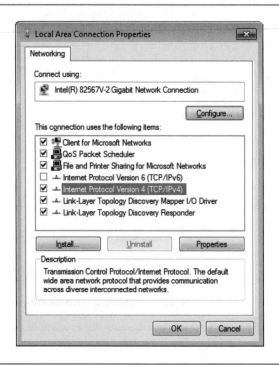

Figure 18-1.   To troubleshoot a host, the place to start is the network interface card.

Note in Figure 18-2 that IPV6 is unbound from the NIC, effectively disabling it. Disabling unused protocols is a good security practice.

Next, make sure the host's declared IP address is the right one by logging in to its gateway router and entering the **show arp** command. You'll remember that ARP stands for Address Resolution Protocol, a utility that maps the physical device's media access control (layer-2) address to its assigned IP (layer-3) address in order to handle the final stage of delivery between the gateway router and the host. Figure 18-3 shows the ARP table in the config file of our sample gateway router. The shaded line shows that the Ethernet interface indeed has the address 10.1.13.12 on file, as was declared in the host's IP Address tab. The MAC address can also be verified using the **ipconfig /all** command.

Another potential host problem is the config settings for the default gateway itself. In other words, you have to make sure the host has the correct IP address configured as its default gateway router, as shown in Figure 18-4.

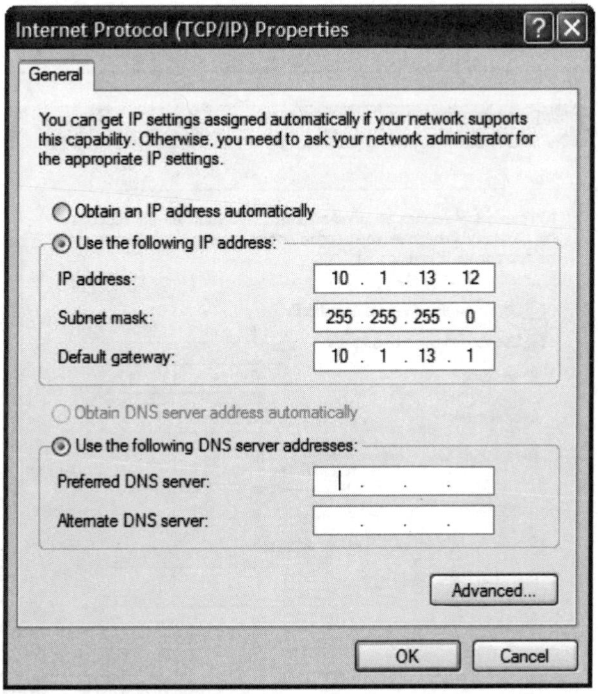

Figure 18-2.   The host's IP address settings and those in the default gateway must match.

```
vsigate#show arp
Protocol  address     Age (min)   Hardware Addr   Type    Interface

Internet  10.1.13.11      0        0050.0465.395c  ARPA    Ethernet1
Internet  10.1.11.1      12        0060.3eba.a6a0  SNAP    TokenRing0
Internet  10.1.13.12      9        00a0.c92a.4823  ARPA    Ethernet1
Internet  10.1.11.2      -         0006.f4c5.5f1d  SNAP    TokenRing0
Internet  10.1.11.3     190        0006.c1de.4ab9  SNAP    TokenRing0
Internet  10.1.12.3      -         0006.f4c5.5fdd  SNAP    TokenRing1
Internet  10.1.13.12     15        0050.04d7.1fa4  ARPA    Ethernet1
```

Figure 18-3. The host's IP address must match the one for the gateway router in the ARP file.

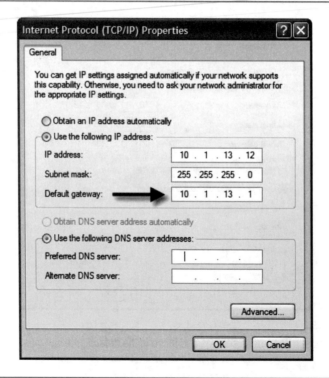

Figure 18-4. Check to make sure the correct default gateway IP address is configured.

The host's default gateway IP address must match the one set for the network interface module on the gateway router. To check that this is the case, go to the gateway router and enter the **show interfaces** command, as shown here:

```
MyRouter#show interfaces
.
.
.
Ethernet1 is up, line protocol is up
  internet address is 10.1.13.1/28
  ip accounting output-packets
  ip nat inside
  ip ospf priority 255
  media-type 10BaseT
.
.
.
```

As you can see, our sample interface, Ethernet1, is indeed addressed 10.1.13.1, as declared in the host's Gateway tab.

This is also where you can check to make sure the host's declared subnet mask matches the one on file in the gateway router. Mask/28 is also correct, because it matches the one (255.255.255.240) declared in the host's IP Address tab.

Obviously, if any of the host's network settings are incorrect, the administrator should adjust them to match the gateway router's settings, reboot the PC, and try to make a network connection. On the other hand, if the PC's settings are okay, the troubleshooter must work outward from the operable host to identify the source of the problem.

Isolating Connectivity Problems

Most network problems have to do with the inability to connect to a desired host or service. Connectivity problems—also called "reachability problems"—come in many forms, such as attempted HTTP connections timing out, attempted terminal connections getting no response from the host, and so on. As just outlined, the troubleshooter should first make sure the host reporting the problem is itself properly configured, and then work outward. To draw an analogy, the troubleshooter must work the neighborhood door to door, much like a cop searching for clues.

Checking Between the Host and Its Gateway Router

If the host's network settings are configured properly, the next step is to work outward from the host to the gateway router. This should be done even if the host's problem is failing to connect to a remote server. Before working far afield, the best practice is to first check the link between the host and its gateway router.

Using the ping Command   The easiest way to check a link is to use the **ping** command. This command sends ping packets to a specific network device to see if it's reachable. In technical terms, **ping** sends its packets through the ICMP transport protocol instead of through UDP or TCP. It actually sends several packets, as shown here:

```
MyRouter#ping 10.1.1.100

Type escape sequence to abort.
Sending 5, 100-byte ICMP Echos to 10.1.1.100, timeout is 2 seconds:
!!!!!
Success rate is 100 percent (5/5), round-trip min/avg/max = 1/1/1 ms
MyRouter#
```

Host computers and network devices both have **ping** commands. The preceding example was taken from a Cisco router, and the ping successfully reached the destination. But one could just as well use the **ping** command available in the command line of the host. We're using a Windows host for our examples, but other platforms—such as Macs, the various Unix platforms, IBM's OS/400, and other proprietary server architectures—all have **ping** and other basic network commands built into their operating systems.

Usually, the first ping test from a host is the link to its gateway router. On a computer running Windows 7, check this by clicking the **Start** button in the menu bar and choosing **All Programs | Accessories | Command Prompt** to open a command prompt window. Then check to see if the gateway router is responding by entering the **ping** command, as shown in the following code snippet:

```
Microsoft Windows [Version 6.1.7601]

Copyright (c) 2009 Microsoft Corporation.  All rights reserved.

C:\users\dalek1>ping 10.1.13.1

Pinging 10.1.13.1 with 32 bytes of data:

Request timed out.
Request timed out.
Request timed out.
Request timed out.

Ping statistics for 10.1.13.1:
    Packets: Sent = 4, Received = 0, Lost = 4 (100% loss),

C:\Documents and Settings\dalek1
```

The preceding example shows that four ping packets were sent to the gateway router, which failed to respond. This tells the troubleshooter a few things:

- The host PC's NIC is good; otherwise, the operating system would have generated an error message when the card failed to respond to the **ping** command.

- The Ethernet LAN segment might be down—a condition often referred to as a "media problem." (The shared medium is apparently not working.)

- The network interface module on the gateway router might be faulty.

If the host checks out okay, the troubleshooter must move outward. As mentioned, the investigation should start with the link to the gateway router.

Extended Ping   As useful and utilitarian as the **ping** command is for troubleshooting, it does have its limits. When you're using the **ping** command, the source address of the **ping** is the IP address of the interface that the packet uses as it exits the router. If you need more precision out of your **ping**, you can upgrade to the *extended* **ping** command, performs a more advanced check of your system's ability to reach a particular host. This command works only at the privileged EXEC command line, whereas a regular **ping** command works in both user EXEC and privileged EXEC modes.

Usage of an extended ping on Cisco routers is fairly straightforward. Simply enter **ping** at the command prompt and then press ENTER. You will be prompted with a number of conditions and variables. The default setting is enclosed in brackets. If you like the default, simply press ENTER; otherwise, enter your preferred setting.

The following shows an example of an extended **ping** at work:

```
Router<>ping
Protocol [ip]:
Target IP address: 64.66.150.248
Repeat count [5]: 100
Datagram size [100]:
Timeout in seconds [2]:
Extended commands [n]:
Sending 100, 100-byte ICMP Echos to 64.66.150.248, timeout is 2
seconds:
!!!!!!!!!!!!!!!!!!!!!!!!!!!!!!!!!!!!!!!!!!!!!!!!!!!!!!!!!!!!!!!!!!!!!!!!!!!
!!!!!!!!!!!!!!!!!!!!!!!!!!!!!!!!!!!!
Success rate is 100 percent (100/100), round-trip min/avg/max =
12/19/280 ms
```

NOTE   The **ping** command also exists in its own form in Windows and Unix/Linux environments. Simply add the switch –s (Unix/Linux) or –t (Windows) after the **ping** command.

Using the show interfaces Command   To check whether the problem is the gateway router's interface or the LAN segment's medium, log in to the gateway router and enter the **show interfaces** command to obtain the following report:

```
MyRouter#show interfaces
Ethernet1 is up, line protocol is down
  Hardware is MyRouter, address is 0060.2fa3.fabd (bia 0060.2fa3.fabd)
  Internet address is 10.1.13.1/28
  .
  .
  .
```

In the preceding example, the router reports both that the Ethernet1 network interface module is up and the line protocol is down. The term *line protocol* denotes both the cable into the router and the LAN protocol running over it. A line protocol reported as down probably indicates that the LAN segment's shared medium—a hub, an access switch, or a cable—is faulty. From there, you would physically check the medium to identify the hardware problem. (How to do that is covered later in this chapter in the section "Troubleshooting Cisco Hardware.")

Another potential condition could be that a network administrator has turned off the interface or the line, or both. This is routinely done while a piece of equipment is being repaired, upgraded, or replaced. Notifying IOS that a piece of equipment is down for maintenance avoids having needless error messages generated by the router. The following example shows the report when a network interface module is administratively down:

```
MyRouter#show interfaces
Ethernet1 is administratively down, line protocol is down
  Hardware is MyRouter, address is 0060.2fa3.fabd (bia 0060.2fa3.fabd)
  Internet address is 10.1.13.1/28
  .
  .
  .
```

Whether a piece of equipment is down by design or because of a malfunction, it still stops traffic. So it's important to know when a piece of equipment is being worked on in order to make sure an alternative path is available to handle traffic.

If both the gateway router interface and line protocol are up and running fine, the cause of the connectivity problem probably resides in a link to another network.

Troubleshooting Problems Connecting to Other Networks

Things get a little more complicated beyond the home LAN segment. If the host can't connect beyond the gateway router, there are at once both more potential sources and more types of trouble to check out. What's meant by potential problem *sources* here is that many more hardware devices must be considered as potential causes of the reachability problem. What's meant by potential problem *types* is that such things as access lists, routing protocols, and other factors beyond hardware must now also be considered.

Using the trace Command to Pinpoint Trouble Spots   Instead of pinging outward from the host one link at a time, the route between the host and the unreachable server can be analyzed all at once using the **trace route** command. In our sample Windows host, do this by choosing Start | Run and then typing **cmd** to access the command prompt. Once there, enter the **tracert** command, Microsoft's version of the **trace route** command. The example in Figure 18-5 shows the route being traced from the host PC to www .PayrollServer.AcmeEnterprises.com, which is a fictional internal server several hops away. It's optional to use either the domain name or the IP address. Each line in the **tracert** command represents a hop along the path to the destination.

In TCP/IP internetworks, **trace route** commands work by sending three "trace" packets to each router three times and recording the echo response times. As with the **ping** command, the packets use the ICMP transport protocol. However, these packets differ from ping packets in that they have a time-to-live (TTL) field used to increment outward from the host one step at a time. The TTL field causes the packet to die when

```
Microsoft(R) Windows NT(TM)
(C) Copyright 1985-1996 Microsoft Corp.


C:\>tracert www.PayrollServer.AcmeEnterprises.com


Tracing route to www.PayrollServer.AcmeEnterprises.com [10.1.22.19]
over a maximum of 30 hops:


  1    <10 ms    <10 ms    <10 ms   10.1.13.12  ◄──────── Host's gateway router
  2    <10 ms     12 ms    <10 ms   10.1.5.3
  3     17 ms     20 ms     19 ms   10.1.17.22
  4     22 ms     19 ms     23 ms   10.1.31.2                Slow response indicates
  5    768 ms    831 ms    790 ms   10.1.49.12  ◄──────── that this router is probably
  6     31 ms     40 ms     42 ms   10.1.22.19                the culprit.


Trace complete.


C:\>
```

Figure 18-5.   The **trace route (tracert)** command is a great way to pinpoint the source of a problem.

the counter hits zero. The **trace route** command uses the TTL field by sending the first trace packet sent to the nearest router with a TTL of 1 to the next router with a TTL of 2, and so on. This process is repeated until the destination host is reached—if it's reachable. The network administrator can put a limit on how many hops the trace may take to automatically stop the process if the destination proves unreachable.

The "ms" readings are milliseconds, and you can see that nearby routers naturally tend to echo back faster. Under 10 ms is fast; anything over 100 ms or so is getting slow—but one must always adjust the timings according to how many hops removed the router is. As you can see, the router in the shaded line in Figure 18-5 is the likely suspect for the slow service because of its slow response times. The probable explanation is that the router's interface or the LAN segment attached to it is either congested or experiencing hardware faults. The next step would be to Telnet into router 10.1.49.12 (if possible) and diagnose the system, the involved network interface, and so on. If making a Telnet connection isn't possible, the troubleshooter must go in through the Console or AUX port, which, of course, requires that somebody be physically present at the device, unless a dial-in maintenance solution has been configured beforehand.

Sometimes, a trace route will locate a node that's stopping traffic altogether. An example of this is shown in Figure 18-6, where 10.1.49.12 now is dropping trace packets instead of merely returning them slowly. The asterisks indicate a null timing result because nothing came back, and the message "request timed out" is inserted. Take note that this does not necessarily mean the entire router is down. It could be that only the network interface or LAN segment that connects the suspect router may be down or configured not to respond to pings.

If possible, first try to Telnet into the router through one of its other interfaces. If this doesn't work, the next move depends on the router's proximity. If it's nearby, go to it and log in through the Console or AUX port. If it's remote, you should contact the person responsible for dealing with it and walk that person through the diagnostic steps.

NOTE   Troubleshooting almost always takes place within the enterprise's internetwork. This is because the network team can control events only within its autonomous system. The **trace route** command is a good example of this. If you traced a route through the Internet—say, to troubleshoot a VPN connection—many lines between your gateway router and the destination node will return asterisks instead of timings and "request timed out" messages instead of IP addresses. This is because almost all edge routers are configured by their network teams not to respond to trace routes. This is done as a security precaution. The point here is to highlight the trade-off a VPN must incur: Loss of control is exchanged for very low-cost WAN links; you generally can't troubleshoot somebody else's network.

Using the show interfaces Command   Once the suspect network interface module has been identified, the troubleshooter must diagnose what's causing the problem. The best way to do that is to run the **show interfaces** command and review the latest statistics on the interface's operations. Remember, this information not only reflects on the interface module itself, but also gives a rich set of clues as to what's happening out on the network.

```
Microsoft(R) Windows NT(TM)
(C) Copyright 1985-1996 Microsoft Corp.

C:\>tracert www.PayrollServer.AcmeEnterprises.com

Tracing route to www.PayrollServer.AcmeEnterprises.com [10.1.22.19]
over a maximum of 15 hops:

  1    <10 ms    <10 ms    <10 ms   10.1.13.12
  2    <10 ms     12 ms    <10 ms   10.1.5.3
  3     17 ms     20 ms     19 ms   10.1.17.22
  4     22 ms     19 ms     23 ms   10.1.31.2
  5      *          *         *      request timed out
  6      *          *         *      request timed out
  7      *          *         *      request timed out
  8      *          *         *      request timed out
  9      *          *         *      request timed out
 10      *          *         *      request timed out
 11      *          *         *      request timed out
 12      *          *         *      request timed out
 13      *          *         *      request timed out
 14      *          *         *      request timed out
 15      *          *         *      request timed out

Trace complete.

C:\>
```

Host's trace route command is set to stop after 15 hops in this example.

This time, the host could not reach 10.1.49.12.

Each failed trace to 10.1.49.12 is counted against the 15-hop limit.

Figure 18-6.   Here's what happens if a traced route finds a router stopping traffic.

A sample **show interfaces** report is given in Figure 18-7. Don't let its size and cryptic terminology intimidate you. There is indeed a lot of information in it, but nothing that takes a rocket scientist to understand.

This report is a snapshot of the interface at a particular instant in time. To check for trends, the troubleshooter must run the **show interfaces** command intermittently to look for changes. The interface is identified by private IP address 10.1.49.12/28. Remember, usually only routers on the edge of an autonomous system—firewalls, web servers, FTP servers, and the like—use public Internet addresses. The /28 notation lets other routers know that LAN segments attached to RemoteRouter are subnetted using

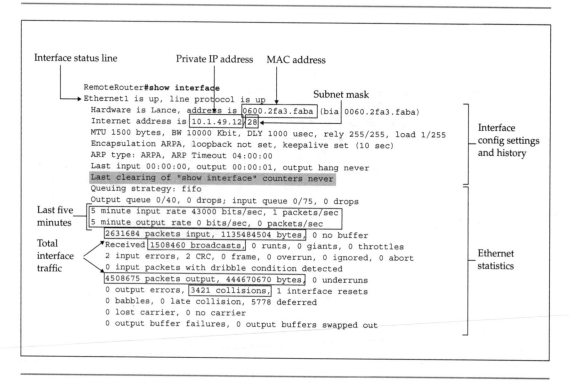

Figure 18-7.   The **show interfaces** command is one of the troubleshooter's best tools.

the 255.255.255.240 subnet mask. The notation uses 28 because the 255.255.255.240 mask has 28 bits available for network addressing (as opposed to hosts). As mentioned earlier, mismatched subnets often cause problems.

The first thing to look at is the seventh line of the **show interfaces** report that reads "Last clearing of show interfaces counters never" (highlighted in Figure 18-7). The example states that nobody has reset the report's counters to zero since the last time the router was rebooted. The length of time since the statistics were last cleared is important because most of the statistics are absolute numbers, not relative values, such as percentages. In other words, the longer IOS has been compiling the totals, the less weight the statistics should be given. For example, ten lost carriers in a day is a lot, but the same total over six months is not. To see when the last reboot was, use the **show version** command, as shown here:

```
RemoteRouter#show version
Cisco Internetwork Operating System Software
IOS (tm) 4500 Software (C4500-IS-M), Version 11.2(17),
RELEASE SOFTWARE (fc1)
Copyright (c) 1986-1999 by Cisco Systems, Inc.
```

```
Compiled Mon 04-Jan-99 18:18 by etlevynot
Image text-base: 0x600088A0, data-base: 0x60604000

ROM: System Bootstrap, Version 5.3(10) [tamb 10],
RELEASE SOFTWARE (fc1)
BOOTFLASH: 4500 Bootstrap Software (C4500-BOOT-M), Version 10.3(10),
RELEASE SOFTWARE (fc1)

RemoteRouter uptime is 2 weeks, 3 days, 13 hours, 32 minutes
System restarted by power-on
```

.

.

.

The second-to-last line in the preceding example shows that the router has been up for about two and a half weeks. Knowing this lets the troubleshooter more accurately judge whether certain error types are normal or excessive.

NOTE   Historically, a wide range of interoperability issues has been identified between different versions of IOS. When troubleshooting, one should make note of the IOS versions running in the environment and assess the impact of running different versions.

The exception to this sampling window can be found in the two lines sitting in the middle of Figure 18-7. These report input and output to the interface over the five minutes prior to the report having been run. A troubleshooter trying to discern a trend in traffic patterns would periodically generate the **show interfaces** report and look at these numbers.

Statistics differ on what constitutes excessive. For example, Ethernet arbitrates media access control by collisions, so it's normal for them to occur to some degree in a shared media environment—one with a hub, for example. The count of 3,421 collisions in Figure 18-7 is okay for a period of two weeks or so, but a figure of 50,000 would indicate congested bandwidth. Broadcast packets are also normal, because they perform positive functions, such as alerting routers of topology changes and providing other useful updates—again, within limits. There are over one and a half million in Figure 18-7, which might be excessive. However, what's considered excessive is subject to so many variables that it must be left to the judgment of the troubleshooter. That's where experience comes into play. For a properly configured switched environment, there should be almost no collisions on a single port. If you are seeing collisions, it's quite possible that you have a speed or duplex mismatch.

Many statistics should ideally be low, or even at zero (depending on the time period reported). For example, *runts* and *giants* are malformed packets sometimes caused by a poorly functioning network interface card or an improperly configured VLAN. In a WAN link, lost carrier events probably indicate a dirty line or a failing telecommunications component.

Table 18-4 defines many of the items reported using the **show interfaces** command. Knowing the items will help you understand how they can be used to diagnose problems.

Statistic	Explanation
Five-minute rates (input or output)	The average number of bits and packets passing through the interface each second, as sampled over the last five-minute interval.
Aborts	Sudden termination of a message transmission's packets.
Buffer failures	Packets discarded for lack of available router buffer memory.
BW	Bandwidth of the interface in kilobits per second (Kbps). This can be used as a routing protocol metric.
Bytes	Total number of bytes transmitted through the interface.
Carrier transitions	A *carrier* is the electromagnetic signal modulated by data transmissions over serial lines (like the sound your modem makes). Carrier transitions are events where the signal is interrupted, often caused when the remote NIC resets.
Collisions	The number of messages retransmitted due to an Ethernet collision.
CRC	Cyclic redundancy check, a common technique for detecting transmission errors. CRC works by dividing the size of a frame's contents by a prime number and comparing the remainder with that stored in the frame by the sending node.
DLY	Delay of the interface's response time, measured in microseconds (μs), *not* milliseconds (ms).
Dribble conditions	Frames that are slightly too long, but are still processed by the interface.
Drops	The number of packets discarded for lack of space in the queue.
Encapsulation	The encapsulation method assigned to an interface (if any). Works by wrapping data in the header of a protocol to "tunnel" otherwise incompatible data through a foreign network. For example, Cisco's Inter-Switch Link (ISL) encapsulates frames from many protocols.
Errors (input or output)	A condition in which it is discovered that a transmission does not match what's expected, usually having to do with the size of a frame or packet. Errors are detected using various techniques, such as CRC.
Frame	The number of packets having a CRC error and a partial frame size. Usually indicates a malfunctioning Ethernet device.

Table 18-4.   Definitions of Useful Ethernet Statistics *(continued)*

Statistic	Explanation
Giants	Packets larger than the LAN technology's maximum packet size—1,518 bytes or more in Ethernet networks. All giant packets are discarded.
Ignored	Number of packets discarded by the interface for lack of available interface buffer memory (as opposed to router buffer memory).
Interface resets	When the interface clears itself of all packets and starts anew. Resets usually occur when it takes too long for expected packets to be transmitted by the sending node.
Keepalives	Messages sent by one network device to another to notify it that the virtual circuit between them is still active.
Last input or output	Hours, minutes, and seconds since the last packet was successfully transmitted or received by the interface. A good tool for determining when the trouble started.
Load	The load on the interface as a fraction of the number 255. For example, 64/255 is a 25-percent load. This counter can be used as a routing protocol metric.
Loopback	Whether loopback is set to on. *Loopback* is where signals are sent from the interface and then directed back toward it from some point along the communications path; used to test the link's usability.
MTU	The maximum transmission unit for packets passing through the interface, expressed in bytes.
Output hang	How long since the interface was last reset. Takes its name from the fact that the interface "hangs" because a transmission takes too long.
Overruns	The number of times the router interface overwhelmed the receiving node by sending more packets than the node's buffers could handle. It takes its name from the fact that the router interface "overran" the sender.
Queues (input and output)	Number of packets in the queue. The number behind the slash is the queue's maximum size.
Queuing strategy	FIFO stands for "first in, first out," which means the router handles packets in that order. LIFO stands for "last in, first out." FIFO is the default.

Table 18-4.   Definitions of Useful Ethernet Statistics *(continued)*

Statistic	Explanation
Rely	The reliability of the interface as a fraction of the number 255. For example, 255/255 is 100-percent reliability. This counter can be used as a routing protocol metric.
Runts	Packets smaller than the LAN technology's minimum packet size—64 bytes or less in Ethernet networks. All runt packets are discarded.
Throttles	The number of times the interface advised a sending NIC that it was being overwhelmed by packets being sent and to slow the pace of delivery. It takes its name from the fact that the interface asks the NIC to "throttle" back.
Underruns	The number of times the sending node overwhelmed the interface by sending more packets than the buffers could handle. Takes its name from the fact that the router interface "underran" the sender.

Table 18-4.   Definitions of Useful Ethernet Statistics

Now that you're introduced to the various statistics compiled in the **show interfaces** report, let's review how to read it. Figure 18-8 shows the Ethernet statistics portion of the report—this time, with some of the more important variables highlighted. These are the variables an experienced network administrator would scan first for clues.

More often than not, connectivity problems are caused by some type of configuration problem, not by a piece of failing equipment. Depending on the Ethernet statistic that is high, the interface may be overwhelmed by incoming traffic, have insufficient queue size configured, have insufficient buffer memory, or be mismatched with the speed of a network sending input.

Checking Access Lists for Proper Configuration   The classic example of a device malfunctioning even though its hardware is running fine is the misconfigured access list. You'll recall that access lists are used to restrict what traffic may pass through a router's interface, thereby cutting off access to the LAN segment attached to it. The access list does this by inspecting for source and destination IP addresses—a way of controlling who may go where. The extended access list also uses port numbers to further restrict which applications may be run once you're admitted. Indeed, access lists are the most rudimentary form of internetwork security, used as a kind of internal firewall. Not all use of access lists has to do with security; sometimes they're used to steer traffic along certain routes in order to "shape" traffic to best fit the internetwork's resources.

The first step in checking for access list problems is to determine whether a suspect router—or a suspect interface on a router—is even configured with an access list.

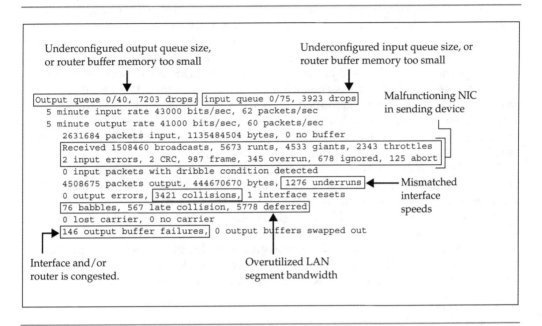

Figure 18-8.   Each interface item likely has reasons for its statistic being high.

To find this out, log in to the router and enter the **show access-lists** command to see if all the access lists are configured:

```
RemoteRouter#show access-lists
Extended IP access list 100
    deny    ip any host 206.107.120.17
    permit ip any any (5308829 matches)
Extended IP access list 101
    permit tcp any host 209.98.208.33 established
    permit udp host 209.98.98.98 host 209.98.208.59
    permit icmp any host 209.98.208.59 echo-reply
    permit tcp any host 209.98.208.59 eq smtp
    permit tcp any host 209.98.208.59 eq pop3
    permit tcp any host 209.98.208.59 eq 65
    permit tcp any host 209.98.208.59 eq telnet
    permit tcp host 209.98.208.34 host 209.98.208.59
    permit tcp any 209.98.208.32 0.0.0.15 established
    permit icmp any 209.98.208.32 0.0.0.15 echo-reply
    .
    .
    .
```

Looking at the preceding example, access list 100 explicitly denies traffic to a certain IP address. This is frequently done to stop outbound traffic to a known undesirable IP address or some other type of router that could allow hackers a crack at the enterprise's edge router. Access list 101 is more sophisticated, with a series of permit rules to control which applications may be used between hosts. The application's IP port is defined behind each **eq** modifier, such as **eq smtp** for e-mail or **eq 65** for TACACS+ database service. (Certain ports can be identified by an acronym; others must be identified by a number.) Also note that access list 101 has only permit rules. This is possible because if a packet's request for service isn't explicitly permitted, it will be denied by the "implicit deny" rule when it reaches the bottom of the access list.

It could be that the inadvertent deny rule, lack of a permit rule, or simple typo is causing the problem. The troubleshooter would scan the access lists for any rules that might be causing the problem at hand. For example, if a person can't connect to the mail server, the troubleshooter would look for statements containing **eq smtp** or the mail server's IP address. The next step would be to go to the interface connecting the network experiencing the problem to see if the **access-group** command was used to apply the questionable access list to it. To do this, you must enter privileged EXEC mode and go into configure interface mode pointed to the interface in question, as shown here:

```
MyRouter#enable
Password:
MyRouter#show running-config
 .
 .
 .
interface Ethernet1
  ip address 10.1.13.1 255.255.255.240
  ip access-group 100 in
  ip access-group 101 out
 .
 .
 .
```

If the questionable access list is in force, double-check that the access list is being applied in the correct direction for the interface. If that checks out, temporarily disable it to see if traffic can pass the router without it. There are two access lists in our example, so we would disable them both to see if the problem is being caused by access lists. Disable access lists on the interface as follows:

```
MyRouter#config terminal
MyRouter(config)#interface ethernet1
MyRouter(config-if)#no ip access-group 100 in
MyRouter(config-if)#no ip access-group 101 out
```

In case you forgot, the **in** modifier at the end of each access-group statement configures the access lists to be applied to inbound packets only. An **out** modifier would do the opposite; the absence of a modifier applies the list to both inbound and outbound traffic.

Once the access lists are disabled, attempt to make the connection between the host and the server reported as nonresponding. If the traffic goes through with the access lists disabled, then a statement somewhere in one of the access lists is probably the cause. The next step is to see which list contains the problem by reenabling one of the two. Access list 101, with all its rules, is the most likely culprit. To find out if this is the case, put it back into force with the following command:

```
MyRouter(config-if)#ip access-group 101 out
```

Now try to connect to the server again. If the problem has returned, you've established that the problem resides somewhere inside access list 101.

To debug the access list, carefully review it to find the offending rule. It could be a misplaced deny rule, but a missing TCP or UDP port in a permit rule could also be the problem. Don't forget to check for any typos in your ACL. A simple mistyped IP address can easily be the source of your problem.

Remember, each access list rule must declare to which IP transport protocol it applies: TCP, UDP, or ICMP. Most often, however, offending application ports are the source of the problem, simply because there are so many of them and the network applications being used change frequently. For example, if users are having a problem making a connection to a web server, look to make sure that HTTP port number 80 is permitted between the host and server addresses.

It's also possible that the traffic is being denied before getting to the permit rule designed to let it through. Remember that access control lists read from the top down until a match is found. If this is the case, the sequence in which rules are listed should be adjusted accordingly by putting the priority rules nearer the top.

Redirecting Traffic from Congested Areas   Sometimes traffic becomes congested in a particular router. This could be the result of new hosts having been added in the area, new network applications coming online, or other causes. When this happens, log in to the congested router and enter the **show ip traffic** command to generate the following report:

```
MyRouter#show ip traffic
IP statistics:
  Rcvd:  7596385 total, 477543 local destination
         0 format errors, 0 checksum errors, 96 bad hop count
         0 unknown protocol, 1 not a gateway
         0 security failures, 0 bad options, 0 with options
  Opts:  0 end, 0 nop, 0 basic security, 0 loose source route
         0 timestamp, 0 extended security, 0 record route
         0 stream ID, 0 strict source route, 0 alert, 0 cipso
         0 other
```

```
Frags: 0 reassembled, 0 timeouts, 0 couldn't reassemble
       0 fragmented, 0 couldn't fragment
Bcast: 53238 received, 280 sent
Mcast: 205899 received, 521886 sent
Sent:  738759 generated, 6113405 forwarded
       13355 encapsulation failed, 374852 no route
```

.

.

.

In addition to reporting IP traffic, the **show ip traffic** command reports traffic generated by transport protocols, routing protocols, ARP translation requests, and even packet errors. The report also breaks out broadcast and multicast messages. It's a quick way to understand the loads being put on a router and what options you might have to lighten the load.

For example, if broadcast traffic seems excessive, you might look into tightening restrictions in the access lists governing the surrounding routers. But, if it appears that all or most of the heavy traffic is legitimate, traffic affecting neighboring routers should also be analyzed. If there is an inequity in loads between routers of similar power, perhaps load balancing is in order. In most cases, this makes more sense than buying more powerful hardware.

One way to balance traffic loads between routers is to log in to the congested router and enter config-router mode by calling up the routing protocols; then set individual distance metrics for each router to steer traffic away from the congested router to its less congested neighbor.

Troubleshooting WAN Links

Troubleshooting WAN problems entails using a slightly different set of tools. This is because most connections into WAN links must go through a serial line. To refresh your mind on the subject, a serial line connects a CSU/DSU unit to a router. Telephone networks don't transmit signals using a data-link layer (layer-2) network technology such as Ethernet. Routers aren't telephone switches, so the transitions between the two technologies must somehow be made. The CSU/DSU-to-serial-line interface gives the router signals it can understand.

 NOTE A CSU/DSU is like a modem, but it works with digital lines instead of analog ones. CSU stands for *channel service unit*, an interface connecting to a local digital telephone line, such as a T1 (instead of a modem connecting to an analog phone line). DSU stands for *data service unit*, a device that adapts to the customer end of the connection, usually into a router or LAN switch.

Serial links have an obvious importance because they extend internetworks beyond the office campus to remote locations. A remote link of any size requires using a digital telephone circuit of some kind, ranging from a fractional T1 up to a full T3 (DS3) line.

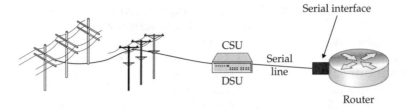

A serial line provides a window through which its entire WAN link can be diagnosed. In other words, not only can you analyze the serial line and its interfaces, but by looking at the traffic it carries, you can also diagnose the digital phone loop and, to some extent, what's happening at the remote end of the link.

Differences in the show interfaces serial Report

Cisco provides a special tool for troubleshooting serial links in the **show interfaces serial** command. It's largely the same as the normal **show interfaces** command, but with some important differences, as highlighted in Figure 18-9. Specifically, it shows information for the serial port.

```
RemoteRouter>show interface serial0
Serial0 is up, line protocol is up
  Hardware is HD64570
  Internet address is 10.1.14.1/30
  MTU 1500 bytes, BW 1544 Kbit, DLY 20000 usec, rely 255/255, load 217/255
  Encapsulation HDLC, loopback not set, keepalive set (10 sec)
  Last input 00:00:00, output 00:00:00, output hang never
  Last clearing of "show interface" counters never
  Input queue: 0/75/390 (size/max/drops); Total output drops: 54920
  Queueing strategy: weighted fair
  Output queue: 0/1000/64/12921 (size/max total/threshold/drops)
     Conversations  0/1/256 (active/max active/max total)
     Reserved Conversations 0/0 (allocated/max allocated)
  5 minute input rate 39000 bits/sec, 52 packets/sec
  5 minute output rate 36000 bits/sec, 48 packets/sec
     26405 packets input, 1977458 bytes, 0 no buffer
     Received 12385 broadcasts, 0 runts, 0 giants, 0 throttles
     1294 input errors, 0 CRC, 0 frame, 0 overrun, 0 ignored, 397 abort
     4783008 packets output, 2510565558 bytes, 0 underruns
     0 output errors, 0 collisions, 9172 interface resets
     0 output buffer failures, 0 output buffers swapped out
     12 carrier transitions
     DCD=up  DSR=up  DTR=up  RTS=up  CTS=up
```

Figure 18-9. Many WAN links still use serial lines to connect routers to phone loops.

One way serial links differ is the type of encapsulation used over digital telephone loops. The High-Level Data-Link Control (HDLC) encapsulation protocol is indicated in the top shaded box in Figure 18-9. Encapsulation is necessary to maintain Ethernet packets over the digital telephone link. Sometimes, encapsulation may have been inadvertently turned off, so the Encapsulation field should be selected.

Another difference is that conversations (sessions) are reported in the **show interfaces serial** *interface_number* report. WAN links have less bandwidth than local shared media. To wit, a T1 (DS1) circuit has a data rate of 1.544 Mbps, and a T3 (DS3) has a rate of 45 Mbps. Most enterprises use fractional T1 or T3 by purchasing channels within them (T1 has 24 channels; T3 has 672). WAN bandwidth, therefore, is limited compared to, say, a 100 Mbps LAN segment, and sometimes a particular user session takes more than its share. Therefore, when you're troubleshooting a WAN link, it helps to know how many conversations are going on. In case you're wondering, the Reserved Conversation field has to do with the Resource Reservation Protocol (dubbed RSVP). RSVP is an industry standard designed for use in QoS (Quality of Service) tools to help guarantee service levels.

The box at the bottom of the figure shows a third difference in the **show interfaces serial** *interface_number* report. These five fields are the same as the blinking lights you may have noticed on external modems. For example, DTR stands for Data Terminal Ready, an EIA/TIA-232 (née RS-232) circuit that is activated to notify the data communications equipment at the other end that the host is ready to send and receive data. DCD stands for Data Carrier Detect, which is important because it senses the actual carrier signal (the modem noise you hear when making a modem connection). The five modem circuits are included in the **show interfaces serial** *interface_number* report for troubleshooting serial links that run over analog/modem lines instead of digital lines.

Key Diagnostic Fields in the show interfaces serial Report

Serial links differ by nature from LAN segments, so diagnosing them takes a different focus. Certain things that are, to some extent, taken for granted in LAN segment links are often the cause of performance problems or even failures in serial links. Figure 18-10 highlights the items that troubleshooters look at first in a serial interface.

As you can see, troubleshooting serial links emphasizes looking at errors and line activity. This is natural, given that the middle part of a WAN link—the telephone circuit—is basically invisible to networking equipment.

Looking at Figure 18-10, we see a case in which input traffic seems to be going okay, but a lot of output packets are being dropped. Given that the serial line is being pushed hard, running at about 80 percent of available bandwidth, we can conclude that the drops are being caused by overuse, not by faulty hardware in the link.

The first line of output in Figure 18-10 can also help your troubleshooting efforts. In the **show interfaces serial** display, the first line will give one of five status indications.

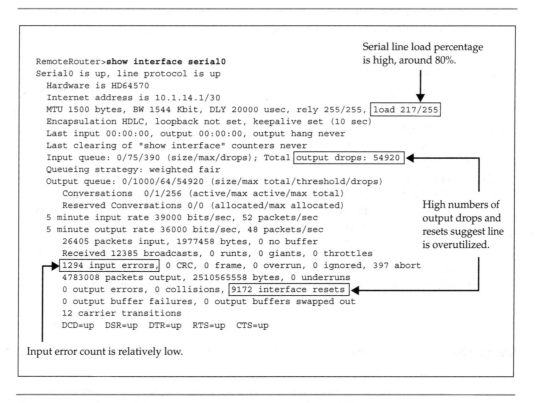

```
RemoteRouter>show interface serial0
Serial0 is up, line protocol is up
  Hardware is HD64570
  Internet address is 10.1.14.1/30
  MTU 1500 bytes, BW 1544 Kbit, DLY 20000 usec, rely 255/255, load 217/255
  Encapsulation HDLC, loopback not set, keepalive set (10 sec)
  Last input 00:00:00, output 00:00:00, output hang never
  Last clearing of "show interface" counters never
  Input queue: 0/75/390 (size/max/drops); Total output drops: 54920
  Queueing strategy: weighted fair
  Output queue: 0/1000/64/54920 (size/max total/threshold/drops)
     Conversations  0/1/256 (active/max active/max total)
     Reserved Conversations 0/0 (allocated/max allocated)
  5 minute input rate 39000 bits/sec, 52 packets/sec
  5 minute output rate 36000 bits/sec, 48 packets/sec
     26405 packets input, 1977458 bytes, 0 no buffer
     Received 12385 broadcasts, 0 runts, 0 giants, 0 throttles
     1294 input errors, 0 CRC, 0 frame, 0 overrun, 0 ignored, 397 abort
     4783008 packets output, 2510565558 bytes, 0 underruns
     0 output errors, 0 collisions, 9172 interface resets
     0 output buffer failures, 0 output buffers swapped out
     12 carrier transitions
     DCD=up  DSR=up  DTR=up  RTS=up  CTS=up
```

Serial line load percentage is high, around 80%.

High numbers of output drops and resets suggest line is overutilized.

Input error count is relatively low.

Figure 18-10.   Certain fields are usually the focus when troubleshooting a serial link.

Ideally, as Figure 18-10 shows, you want this line to read "Serial x is up, line protocol is up." However, if there is a problem, that status might be one of the following:

- **Serial x is down, line protocol is down.** This is an indication that the router is not sensing a signal from the WAN connection, there is a problem with the cabling, or even a problem at the telephone company.

- **Serial x is up, line protocol is down.** This is an indication that a local or remote router has been misconfigured, keepalives are not being transmitted by the remote router, or local or remote channel service unit or digital service units have failed.

- **Serial x is up, line protocol is up (looped).** This is an indication that there is a loop in the circuit.

- **Serial x is up, line protocol is down (disabled).** This is an indication that there is a high error rate because of a problem with the telephone carrier, the channel service unit or digital service units are experiencing a problem, or the router interface is faulty.

■   **Serial *x* is administratively down, line protocol is down.** This is an indication that the router configuration includes the **shutdown** command or that a duplicate IP address exists.

Troubleshooting Serial-Line Input Errors   One of the most common causes of serial-line problems is input errors—in other words, data inbound from the remote site. Probable causes of serial-line input errors, with suggested actions, are outlined in Table 18-5.

Troubleshooting Serial-Line Input and Output Errors   Another clue to serial-line problems is an increase in dropped packets at the interface. A *drop* occurs when too many packets are being processed in the system and insufficient buffer memory is available to handle the packet. This applies to both input and output drops, as outlined in Table 18-6.

Drops taking place in one direction but not the other (input versus output) can point the troubleshooter toward the problem's source. If they're happening both ways, the router or its serial interface is probably the culprit.

Troubleshooting Serial Links   Most of us have used modems long enough to know that sometimes an established connection can falter, or even be broken. This goes for serial lines, too, usually because of interface resets or carrier transitions, as outlined in Table 18-7.

Input Error Symptoms	Probable Causes and Suggested Actions
Input errors along with CRC or frame errors	A dirty line, where electrical noise interferes with the data signal. Serial cable exceeds maximum length specified for the type of phone circuit. Serial cable is unshielded. The phone circuit itself may be malfunctioning.
	Actions: Reduce cable length. Install shielded cable. Check phone loop with a line analyzer.
	Clocking jitter in line where data signal varies from reference timing positions, or clocking skew where device clocks are set differently.
	Actions: Make sure all devices are configured to use a common-line clock.
Input errors along with aborts	The transfer of a packet terminated in midtransmission. Usually caused by an interface reset on the router being analyzed. Can also be caused by a reset on the remote router, a bad phone circuit, or a bad CSU/DSU.
	Action: Check local hardware, then remote hardware. Replace faulty equipment.

Table 18-5.   Input Errors Causes and Actions

Packet Drop Symptoms	Probable Causes and Suggested Actions
Increase in dropped input packets	Input drops usually occur when traffic is being routed from a local interface (Ethernet, Token Ring, FDDI) that is faster than the serial interface. The problem usually emerges during periods of high traffic. **Actions:** Increase the interface's input hold queue size in the router's config file.
Increase in dropped output packets	Output drops happen when no system buffer is available at the time the router is attempting to hand the packet off to the transmit buffer during high traffic. **Actions:** Increase the interface's output hold queue size. Turn off fast switching. Implement priority queuing.

Table 18-6. Dropped Packet Causes and Actions

Line Error Symptoms	Probable Causes and Suggested Actions
Increasing carrier transitions	Interruption in the carrier signal. Usually due to interface resets at the remote end of the link. Resets can be caused by external sources such as electrical storms, T1 or T3 overuse alerts, or faulty hardware. **Actions:** Use breakout box or serial analyzer to check hardware at both ends. Then check router hardware. Replace faulty hardware as necessary. No action required if problem was due to external cause.
Increasing interface resets	Interface resets result from missed keepalive messages. They usually result from carrier transitions, lack of buffer, or a problem with CSU/DSU hardware. Coincidence with increased carrier transitions or input errors indicates a bad link or bad CSU/DSU hardware. **Actions:** Use breakout box or serial analyzer to check hardware at both ends. Contact leased-line vendor if hardware is okay.

Table 18-7. Serial Line Error Causes and Actions

Although they're not LAN segments per se, serial links are integral to geographically distributed internetworks. Don't forget to consider them, even when a serial-line problem is not initially apparent. For example, when you're evaluating performance problems, it could be that a faulty serial link is shifting traffic loads elsewhere within the internetwork.

Client-Server VPNs

As we've discussed already, VPNs are a cost-effective way to use the Internet as your own private WAN. If you're having trouble getting a VPN to work, there are four areas in which VPN problems generally fall:

■ Blocked VPN traffic

■ Bad Internet connections

■ Configuration errors

■ Network Address Translation (NAT) tunneling problems

At the risk of insulting anyone's intelligence, when problems arise (not only VPN issues), the first thing to do is to check for loose cables. Wiggle the cables on the client's modem, the router, and the firewall to ensure they are seated properly. It's also a good idea to make sure you're using straight-through Cat 6 or 7 cabling and didn't pick up a length of crossover cable.

Blocked Traffic

The next step is to ensure your Internet service provider (ISP) allows IPSec VPN traffic. If your provider does not, it will not matter if your VPN is properly configured, because the packets won't be going anywhere. If your ISP does not allow IPSec VPN traffic, you might have to consider changing ISPs.

Check your firewall to ensure that it isn't blocking IPSec or PPTP traffic. To make a VPN connection, it is necessary to configure outbound IPSec traffic on the firewall. To do this, you must configure your firewall to enable IPSec, and then create a rule allowing the passage of traffic between the LAN and WAN. If that's not possible, it might be necessary to locate the client in the DMZ or consider investing in a different router or firewall.

Hardware firewalls block traffic, but so can software firewalls. This is another easy place to check, especially for clients who are traveling or trying to connect from locations that aren't equipped with hardware firewalls, but are set up with software firewalls. Just disable the software firewall and see if that works. Some software firewalls will ask you if they should allow VPN traffic to be passed, and you can add the desired destination IP address to the trusted-zone setting.

NAT

Make sure your NAT is tunneling correctly. A good place to start is by making certain you have the most current firmware updates and software. When IPSec tries to verify the packets' integrity, NAT changes the source IP address to the firewall's WAN address to properly navigate the Internet. Unfortunately, this causes problems with IPSec because the packets fail an integrity check.

You can get a listing of your NAT translations and an overview of your NAT statistics by using two simple EXEC commands:

- **show ip nat translations verbose** This displays the active NAT translations with additional information for each translation table, including how long the entry has been used.

- **show ip nat statistics** This displays a variety of NAT statistics, including the number of active translations, interfaces, and total translations.

Configuration

Configuration can also be the culprit when trying to track down VPN problems. Ensure that the correct IP addresses are being used. For client VPNs, checking and renewing the IP address in Windows is accomplished by opening a command prompt and then entering **ipconfig /all.**

If the IP address issued by the network administrator to connect to the VPN does not fall within the range shown, then the IP address is not valid. To correct this, renew the lease. This is accomplished by opening a command prompt window and typing **ipconfig/renew** and the IP address of the adapter.

NOTE If the client is using PPPoE to connect to the ISP—which will be the case if a static IP address has not been assigned—make sure the client is connecting to the Internet using whatever connection application is needed.

Send a **ping** command to your VPN server's IP address. If you get a response, you know the client is connected to the Internet and able to see the VPN server. Next, you should rule out any DNS configuration problems. This time, conduct a ping test, but use the domain name (for example, www.velte.com). If you get a response, the Internet connection is working fine. If not, it means DNS is misconfigured either at the client or on the DNS server itself.

The client and the VPN server must be able to speak the same language to get the job done. As such, it's important to make sure the encryption settings on both the client and VPN server are the same. Authentication algorithms must be configured properly on both the client and VPN server. Both devices will need the shared secret. Alternatively, if certificates are being used, the correct public key is necessary.

Bad Connections

Next, check whether the client is trying to connect over a slow connection. Latency can cause VPN connections to fail, because they like consistent traffic; otherwise, they tend to drop off. You're most likely to see this as an issue with satellite connections where latency can run from half a second to several seconds.

Connection speed can be checked with the **ping** tool. Using the **-t** switch, you can get a continuous test of connection speeds between the client and the VPN server. Here's an example:

```
ping 68.93.44.123 -t
```

This produces a list of the test's efforts to send packets to the address. The test is ended by pressing CTRL-C. Take a look at the results. If you see any stray "Request timed out" error messages, try increasing the timeout value so that you can accurately gauge how much latency your connection suffers. This value can be changed by using the **-w** switch, as follows:

```
ping 68.93.44.123 -t -w 7000
```

This increases the timeout value to 7,000 ms. This should be enough to indicate how much latency is present on your link. Connection times at 1,500 ms and above will cause the VPN link to fail.

NOTE It might not sound important at first blush, but if the VPN server and client are not in the correct time zones and have the correct time settings, they might not be able to hook up. This is because correct time settings are necessary for key expiration.

Troubleshooting Cisco Hardware

When the likely location of the problem has been identified, the first step is to physically examine and test the suspect device. This will identify the problem's cause in a surprising number of troubleshooting situations. Sometimes, the problem is caused by something as simple as a loose component; other times, something is damaged.

Inspecting Devices

Once a suspect device is identified, it should be physically inspected. This is routine procedure. (Even when a suspect or troubled device is in a remote location, a contact person is sent to make an inspection.) Earlier, we stated that most troubleshooting tasks are done from the administrator's desk, and that's true. Most tasks are done from the administrator's PC or an NMS console. However, there's no substitute for actually looking at a device to see what's going on. The two parts of inspecting a device are reading its LEDs and inspecting the device's components.

Reading Device LEDs

If the device is still online, the first thing to do is to read the LEDs (light-emitting diodes). You probably recognize LEDs as those blinking lights on the front of many electronic devices. Virtually all network devices have LEDs to assist in troubleshooting. The LED bank arrangement follows the device layout:

- **Access devices with a bank of ports on the front, with a twisted-pair cable plugged into each port using an RJ-45 phone-style jack.** Products from the Cisco Catalyst 2960 to the Catalyst 4500 Switch fit this description. There is usually one LED per port.

- **Motherboard-based routers with LAN segments plugged into the back, usually through twisted-pair cable, but also fiber-optic cables for uplinks.** The Cisco 7400 Router fits this description. LEDs on these devices appear on the front of these boxes.

- **High-end routers and switches of the bus-and-blade configuration, again with networks plugged into the back, both fiber-optic and twisted-pair cable.** The Cisco ASR 1000 Router and Catalyst 6500 Switch fit this description. LEDs on these devices appear both behind smoked-plastic panels on the front and on the blades (card modules) themselves on the back (remember, a *blade* is basically an entire router or switch on a board).

LEDs are also called *"activity lights."* Each LED on an access device represents a host. Router and LAN switch LEDs represent entire LAN segments.

LEDs blink and change colors according to the port's status. Green means okay, and orange means the port is coming up. If the port is down, its LED goes dark. The port's LED blinks when packets are passing through it. A common practice is to press RESET to see what happens. LEDs temporarily go orange or even red if they encounter trouble during the power cycle. They will eventually go green, but the temporary error condition may indicate a nonfatal configuration error.

The rule is that if an activity light is green, the line is good and the problem must stem from some type of configuration problem. If the light is orange, the line is operating but malfunctioning. If the activity light is off, the line is down.

Physically Inspecting Devices

The next step is to physically inspect the device itself. Start by making sure the device is offline and then remove the cover from the top of the device chassis and inspect the interior, looking for the following:

- **Loose connections** Look for any loosely attached card (module) or cable. Reseat any that are found.

- **New cards** If you know any card to be new, reseat it into its connection several times. New cards are more prone to oxidation or carbon film buildup on their backplane connections.

- **Burned or damaged parts** Look for any burned wires, ribbon cables, or cards. Also look at the backplane to see if it's okay. Closely inspect the wires leading to the device's power supply. Also look for any crimped wires.

■ **Dirty device interior**   If the device has dust and lint in the interior, turn off the device and clean it. Devices can accumulate a lot of foreign substances from the air in dusty or dirty environments, which sometimes can affect performance.

After completing the inspection, try rebooting the device to see if power-cycling it will fix the problem. One important caution: Don't change anything in the configuration. Doing so before rebooting can make it difficult to determine the problem's source afterward; it only adds more variables to the mix.

The Reboot Test

If no severe problem was found inspecting the device, the next step is to try a power-cycle test to see how it responds. *Power-cycle* means to turn a device off and then turn it on again, which you probably know as the cure-all for Microsoft Windows. As you saw in Chapter 4, rebooting devices can tell you a lot about their status; in some cases, it even makes the problem go away.

When you reboot, if the configuration in memory is mismatched with the hardware, a variety of problems can ensue. Ports might hang, bus timeout errors may occur, and so on. If the device reboots and prompts for a password, the circuitry and memory are working properly. Some major symptoms and probable causes are outlined in Table 18-8.

When hardware problems this extreme are encountered, it's time to call in support from Cisco or a third-party maintenance organization with which your enterprise has contracted. Typically, devices are shipped into the maintenance center for bench repair. Only end-user enterprises with spare parts, Cisco-trained personnel, and proper instruments attempt to repair networking hardware devices in-house.

Reboot Symptom	Probable Causes
No response	Bad power supply; blown fuse; bad breaker; bad power switch; bad backplane
Won't reboot	Bad or miswired power supply; bad (or poorly seated) processor card; bad memory board; bad IOS image in NVRAM; shorted wires
Partial or constant reboot	Bad processor, controller, or interface card; bad backplane; bad power supply; bad microcode
No cards show up in boot display	Bad processor, controller, or interface card; bad backplane; cards not seated in backplane; bad power supply

Table 18-8.   Typical Reboot Problems and Probable Causes

Troubleshooting Network Configurations

As your network grows and evolves, you'll likely encounter some LAN segments that have wireless capabilities—and their own set of problems. In addition, you'll more than likely want to track down issues related to your network's overall performance. In this section, let's take a closer look at how to track down and resolve problems with a wireless network, as well as some good methods for locating and fixing problems stemming from performance issues.

Wireless Networks

Wireless networks provide a whole new level of convenience to the world of networking. The ability to connect computers without having to worry about wiring—not to mention the ability to take your laptop anywhere in the office—and still maintain network connectivity is a huge plus.

Many wireless deployments fire up as soon as you connect your access point and wireless card. For example, if you're using a Plug-and-Play–capable version of Windows (Windows 7, for example), most times, the wireless card will be instantly recognized and, security issues aside, you'll have access to the network with no problems. Regrettably, it doesn't always work that smoothly.

Address Filtering

Like so many facets in networking, what is meant to keep the bad people out can also keep the good guys out. One of Wi-Fi's methods of security is MAC and IP address filtering. That is, your APs (access points) can be configured to allow or reject traffic from specific IP or MAC addresses. If clients are having trouble connecting, make sure their IP or MAC addresses are not being blocked by the AP. When properly configured, however, this feature is a nice way to add a layer of security.

Channel Interference

In a single-band 2.4 GHz 802.11b/g/n network, only three channels are really usable: channels 1, 6, and 11. If you're having trouble with your autonomous AP network, you might check to see if there aren't other networks already existing on one of those channels. You may be experiencing interference from another device on your own network, or you might be experiencing complications from a neighbor's wireless network. The solution to your problem might be as simple as changing the AP and clients' channel.

 NOTE Automated channel tuning is one of the strengths of a controller-based lightweight access point system.

Encryption

The ideal means of security for your wireless network is to employ 802.1x authentication along with encryption. However, if you aren't using authentication, you should at least use encryption. An easily overlooked component of wireless networking is enabling encryption on your access points and clients. As mentioned in Chapter 11, this is extremely important for the sake of protecting your data.

If encryption is not enabled, it is relatively easy for someone to sniff the wireless network traffic and glean all sorts of information—from user ID and password information to the contents of e-mails being sent and received.

Even though it has been found to be quite insecure, Wireless Equivalent Privacy (WEP) is still in use in the field today. It uses a key that you establish on the access point and then enter into your wireless-enabled devices. This key is used to encrypt the data being transmitted and decrypt incoming data. Without the key, no one else can "see" the data as it is transmitted. WEP is easily hackable with free tools. Do not deploy WEP if you have a choice—we recommend WPA2.

The next level of wireless security is Wi-Fi Protected Access (WPA). It's like WEP, but provides a much higher level of encryption and authentication security. It's not available on very old access points, and it may take an OS or Wi-Fi NIC upgrade on the client side to enable it there, but if you are still running Windows XP SP2 and haven't upgraded to SP3, you should to upgrade ASAP, regardless.

NOTE   It is wise to become familiar with the encryption and overall security features available on your hardware and software—the standards and technology are advancing quickly in the wireless arena, and sometimes, a more secure environment is only a firmware or software update away.

WEP/WPA   With encryption, however, comes its share of problems. If your encryption scheme is incorrectly set on either the access point or the clients, then expect problems. If you're having problems getting your wireless clients to connect, the first place to start is by checking encryption settings. Follow these steps to ensure your encryption settings are correct:

1. **Turn off encryption.** Even though we just said it was important to have encryption enabled, if you turn off encryption and are still having problems, you know encryption isn't to blame. If it turns out that everything is running fine, move on to step 2.

2. **Count characters.** Check your access point and Wi-Fi card instructions to make sure you're entering the correct number of characters for the encryption key. For instance, when using a 256-bit WPA key, Cisco Aironets require 8–63 ASCII or 64 hexadecimal characters for its encryption key (this is shown in Figure 18-11). Also, check to see if you must specify whether you are using an ASCII string or hexadecimal string for the key. Table 18-9 shows how many characters are needed for various bit-lengths of keys.

WEP Bit Levels	ASCII	Hexadecimal
40/64	5 characters	10 characters
128	13 characters	26 characters
WPA Bit Level	ASCII	Hexadecimal
256	8–63	64

Table 18-9.   The Number of Characters Needed in Various Key Lengths

3. **Configure authentication methods.** When Wi-Fi is being used, two types of authentication are employed: *open system* and *shared key*. Reconfigure the access point and client to allow open system, thus disabling WEP. When you enable WEP, change over to the shared-key authentication.

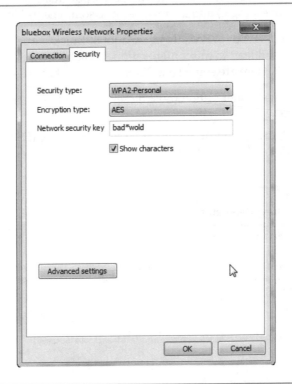

Figure 18-11.   Mistyping a character in the WPA key can cause Wi-Fi networks to fail.

4. **Match your WEP levels.** Although it's possible to mix environments in which 40/64-bit and 128-bit devices are operating (we'll talk about that more in a moment), it's best to make sure everyone is using the same level. That said, if it turns out you need to work in a mixed environment, 128-bit devices can talk to 40/64-bit WEP devices only if they are set to use 40-bit keys.

5. **Check your passphrases.** Some Wi-Fi vendors (including Cisco) allow you to enter *passphrases* for key generation on SOHO access points. That is, you don't have to come up with a string of hexadecimal characters. If you like, you can come up with a simple phrase. (For instance, Figure 18-12 shows the passphrase "bad*wolf" turned into a hexadecimal WPA key.) This is a convenient tool, because when setting up the key, you don't need to remember a series of meaningless letters and numbers—"bad*wolf" is easier to remember than "e92...661." (We omitted the whole string, but you get the idea.) When you use passphrases, there are a couple things you should keep in mind. First, keep the passphrase string short. You don't need to come up with phrases such as "supercalifragilisticexpialidocious"—it won't result in a key that is any more secure than one generated with a shorter passphrase. Second, use letters and numbers only if possible—don't throw spaces, punctuation, or other symbols (like an umlaut, for example) into the mix, because some clients have issues with them.

WPA   If you're using WPA or WPA2, there are a lot of finicky little steps in the configuration that could lead to misconfiguration. Look back on the WPA configuration outlined in Chapter 8. Here are some sources of problems that might be possibilities:

- With WPA, the Cipher option must be selected and TKIP chosen from the drop-down menu.

- With WPA2, the Cipher option must be selected and "AES-CCMP or higher" chosen from the drop-down menu.

WPA PSK (Raw Key) Generator

The Wireshark WPA Pre-shared Key Generator provides an easy way to convert a WPA passphrase and SSID to the 256-bit pre-shared ("raw") key used for key derivation.

Directions:

Type or paste in your WPA passphrase and SSID below. **Wait a while.** The PSK will be calculated by your browser. Javascript isn't known for its blistering crypto speed. **None** of this information will be sent over the network. Run a trace with Wireshark if you don't believe us.

Passphrase	bad*wolf
SSID	bluebox
PSK	e922f416d5343213e0f258f09c6da8ff0bd65a40a7e1b1eaa29500a1594aa661

Generate PSK

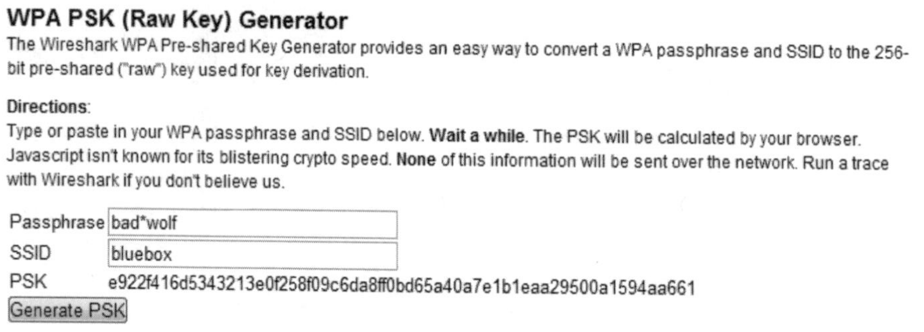

Figure 18-12.   Tools can be utilized to generate WPA keys.

- Either WPA requires that the encryption key be entered in key number 2, not key number 1. Ensure that this has been properly set.

- The correct SSID must also be selected. This setting is made using the SSID Manager and then selecting the correct SSID from the Current SSID List.

- You might also be experiencing problems depending on the authentication method you've chosen (or need to choose). The authentication method, which is also set from the SSID Manager screen, should be set based on which type of clients your Wi-Fi network is using. If you only have Cisco clients, select Network-EAP. If you're using third-party clients, select Open Authentication with EAP. If you're in a mixed environment with both Cisco and third-party clients, select both Network-EAP and Open Authentication with EAP.

Also, take a look back on the suggestions for key problems. Because WEP, WPA, and WPA2 utilize keys, check such things as key lengths and ensure that the keys have been properly entered on both the AP and the clients.

Antenna Placement and Interference

With a wired network, you don't need to worry too much about interference from other devices. For instance, running the photocopier probably won't cause any trouble with your wired workstations, but curiously, it may cause your wireless connection to drop out. And even though your wireless-enabled laptop affords you the freedom to go anywhere in your office, you can only be from 100 to about 300 feet from your access point. After that, interference from walls, floors, and other obstructions will cause connections to slow appreciably or drop out altogether. Of course, this still beats the pants off a wired connection, which only lets you roam as far as the Cat 6 tether allows, which might be no further than one corner of your desk. Wireless networking can be worth doing, just remember to keep in mind where your wireless devices will be in relation to an access point. In most cases, try and locate your access point as centrally as possible to the clients.

No matter where you place your access points, always be aware of sources of interference. It was mentioned earlier that photocopiers have been known to reduce connectivity in Wi-Fi networks, but be mindful of other devices that can wreak havoc on your system. A main culprit comes in the guise of the 2.4 GHz cordless telephone. Because this operates on the same frequency as single-band 802.11b/g/n, it can cause some headaches. If you suspect a cordless phone or other 2.4 GHz device, try using other Wi-Fi channels to see if things improve.

 NOTE Even worse than cordless phones are microwave ovens. Some of these things can kill just about any radio signal near them. If you are having Wi-Fi connectivity issues, check to see if there is a cafeteria above or below your problem site.

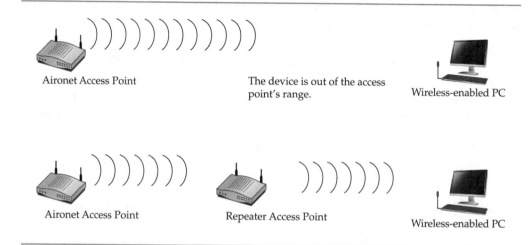

Aironet Access Point

The device is out of the access point's range.

Wireless-enabled PC

Aironet Access Point

Repeater Access Point

Wireless-enabled PC

Figure 18-13.   It's possible to extend your wireless network's range with additional access points configured as repeaters.

Extending Your Wireless Network's Range   What if you just can't get a good signal in some areas of your space and you really want wireless there? After ruling out interference from another device, repositioning your antenna(s), and perhaps relocating your access point, you may just want to buy an additional access point. This extra access point can be used to extend the range of your wireless network, as Figure 18-13 shows.

When using an access point to extend range, you can do so without needing a wired connection by configuring the access point as a bridge from an existing access point. Just make sure you are monitoring performance and capacity as your user count grows, because the wired access point could become saturated with network traffic and become a network bottleneck.

Checking Your Levels   A simple way to check your connectivity levels is to start the client in the same room or location as the access point. When you've got the two devices communicating, it's easy enough to start moving the client away from the access point and check the levels, as in Figure 18-14. This will give you a quick and dirty idea of the range between the two.

You can, however, plot your devices' connectivity with a little more finesse by using any number of free or purchased Wi-Fi site survey tools. A site survey tool shows the quality and strength of your wireless signal—it will help you plan before and test after deployment. Several of these packages are open sourced (free) and will use your existing Wi-Fi card, with the majority being Linux based. The reason for that is most Windows drivers are closed source and in order to run true spectrum analysis you'll need your card to run in promiscuous mode (a.k.a. sniffer mode). To use Windows for this purpose, you'll need a special Wi-Fi card and its appropriate drivers, which are written to allow promiscuous mode.

Currently connected to:

Network 6
Internet access

Unidentified network
No Internet access

Wireless Network Connection   ^

Snowman

Blume6426

SSID-2

Open Network and Sharing Center

Figure 18-14.   The Windows Wireless Connection tool shows your signal strength.

NOTE   Cisco controllers have this feature built in. You can temporarily install one LWAP in "sniffer" mode, enabling the system to create radio heat maps prior to actually deploying any permanent LWAP.

Figure 18-15 depicts a Cisco WCS heat map. Notice the LWAP are all operating on different channels because the controller knows where each is located on the map and has assigned them different channels automatically.

Point-to-Point Troubleshooting   If your wireless bridge link stops working, it is possible that there is a problem with your system's antennas, cabling, or connectors. Check your antennas and ensure they have not come out of alignment.

Also, antennas and connections can be damaged by moisture. If the antennas are not sealed properly when they're installed, moisture can condense inside the antenna feedhorns, ultimately filling them with water. Moisture that makes its way into coaxial cabling can be even more problematic. Coax cables have a foam internal dielectric. This can act like a sponge, sending moisture along the length of the cable.

NOTE   If you determine that coax cabling has been compromised and is sucking up moisture, replace the entire length, rather than snipping off a few feet and replacing the connector.

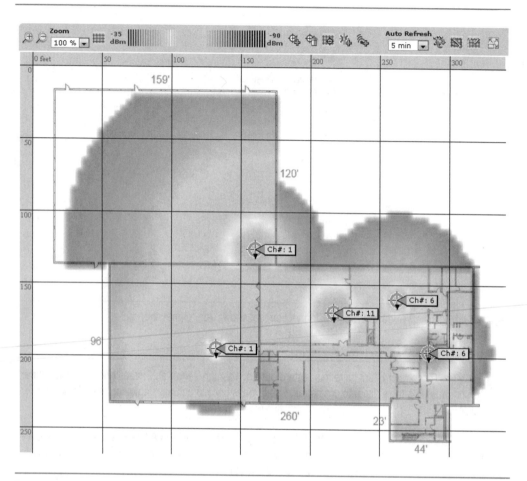

Figure 18-15. A Cisco WCS heat map shows controller operating values.

When problems manifest themselves in outdoor systems, the effect will appear on both ends of the link to the same degree. This is relevant to know, because if you see a degraded signal on one end of your link, don't automatically think you've found the location of the problem. It might very well be on the other side of the link. Check both ends.

On the other hand, if the receive-signal is low on one end but not the other, generally, this is a problem caused by misconfiguration of the radio units or by interference. As such, don't make a bad situation worse by realigning antennas. If you determine that the setup is correct and the equipment is working properly, check for anything that might cause interference before adjusting the antennas.

If you suspect interference as the culprit, examine your system and its behavior. Is the problem continuous, or is it intermittent? Most often, interference occurs intermittently, when the source of interference becomes active.

For point-to-point wireless networks, determining the source of interference can be a horrendous chore. First, look around the antennas at each end of your link. Is another antenna present? If so, do a little sleuthing to determine who owns it, who operates it, at which frequency it operates, how much power it is transmitting, and what type of antenna polarization is being used.

Once you've tracked down this data (it could be just as simple as asking around in the building on which the antenna is mounted), the next step is to ask the owner if he or she would be willing to help you determine if their system is the source of your system's interference.

When you have all the pertinent information about the interfering source, you can much more easily resolve the problem. First, consider your own antennas. Are any of them pointed at the other system's antennas? Is it possible to reposition your antennas so they are out of the other system's broadcast path?

Often, changing the polarization of your antennas to the opposite polarization of the interfering system will fix the problem. This is an easy and inexpensive solution to try first, as it doesn't require the repositioning of any equipment.

If that doesn't work, try changing the frequency of your system. Systems on different frequencies tend not to interfere with each other. One simple way to change your frequencies is to simply swap the transmit and receive frequencies on your system.

Troubleshooting Network Performance

If you're trying to pinpoint and troubleshoot problems in network performance, the first, best advice is to laboriously test and document your system, its configuration, maintenance, and anything else that you do to it. That way, should the network start operating in a sub-par fashion, you have a history with which to compare it.

Change Management and Your Network

There are two ways you can approach troubleshooting a network with performance problems. The first is to go in, oblivious to any changes and modifications that have been made to the system. That is, you go in to fix the problem, but have no clue what has already been done. When this happens, the best you can do is start making changes here and there, based on your educated guesses and experience, not on fact. The second, and obviously better, solution is to gather basic performance trend information and refer to your network's change management log so that you have a functional baseline from which to begin the troubleshooting process.

A change management log is a document where you record each and every change and bit of maintenance that is performed on your system, no matter how big, no matter how small. If you installed a new router, that should be in the document, but so should someone going into the server room to reset a device.

> **NOTE** There's a story about a network technician performing the simple task of blowing dust out of a router's fan. Ultimately, the dust was worked deeper into the fan, causing it to intermittently stop and cause the router to overheat. Because the technician didn't record this "simple" task in a change management document, it was never thought to be checked, until it was too late and the router burned up.

It is also helpful, when making changes to your network's configuration, to make as few changes at once as possible. That way, if your network either takes a performance hit or goes down altogether, it's easier to undo than if you've performed a dozen different things.

If you have a change management document and know when the system started having problems, you can start analyzing changes that were made to the network and its devices. You might discover that a new routing protocol was introduced or a new Quality of Service policy was implemented. If you were to shoot blindly in the dark, it could take you weeks to find these issues. If you have a change management document, however, it's much easier to pin down the problem.

An effective, well-implemented change management plan has a number of useful attributes that will help your overall network management and also aid in troubleshooting. Benefits include the following:

- A checkpoint that allows you to measure performance, both before and after changes are made to the network

- A journal of network updates, maintenance, and reconfigurations, allowing you to compare your network and its changes to previous configurations in your network's history

- A rollback tool, which makes it easier to restore your system to an optimal configuration if the performance of a new configuration does not live up to your expectations

For best results, you'll have the proper software and hardware devices that will help you gather and analyze your performance metrics. For some suggestions, flip back to Chapter 13.

Router Performance Problems

If you suspect there are performance problems with your router, consult your change management document. Have you changed anything recently? Once a networking device has been set up and is working, problems generally stem from a person trying to improve the device's performance. Assuming there isn't some hardware problem (an unplugged cable or network card improperly seated), then the next place to look is if there were any changes made to the device's configuration.

NOTE   Don't dismiss hardware problems too quickly. It is always possible that someone went to perform a seemingly unrelated task and accidentally pulled a power cord a bit too hard or pinched a network cable with a floor tile or the rack door. Always inspect your hardware before you commit hours of your time to sorting through configuration files. One of the biggest sources of network snafus is cabling plugged into the wrong ports. Don't be sheepish about preparing a map showing which cables go where between your devices and making sure that all your cables are labeled properly on both ends so that you can instantly find where the cable is plugged in. It beats the tedious alternative: pulling on cables to see where they go.

Hopefully, you backed up your router's configuration file. Taking the few seconds to back up the file when it is working optimally will save you untold hours trying to restore the system. The time to back up the configuration file is when everything is working well. Backups should also be made before and after every single change is committed to the device. This allows you to see exactly what is different between the pre- and post-change configuration.

If you don't have a backup of the configuration file, the next step is to study your change management documentation. This documentation should describe all the changes that have been made to the router. Examine the document and see which changes might be responsible for your router's problems. You might have to go back to the router's configuration file and undo those changes, one by one, until the problem has been resolved.

NOTE   Better yet, if you don't have a backup of your router's configuration file, put this book down right now and go make one. Don't worry; we'll wait for you.

The culprit might also be changes in the device's operating system. If you've recently upgraded your operating system or applied a patch, that's a good place to check. Before adding new operating systems or applying patches, you should understand just how you can roll back the operating system to the previous, operational operating system if something goes wrong. Remember, however you attack a troubleshooting problem, the goal is to "follow the wire" and track the source of the problem down to the end.

Keep in mind that the most important thing to do when troubleshooting is to proceed carefully and logically. Don't change several variables at the same time. Make a change, observe (be patient), document if necessary, and then proceed to the next step. Fixing problems in complex systems is more about process than luck. That said, we wish you the best of luck in troubleshooting and in life.

Index

A

O

P

S

W

Z